WITHDRAWN

HISTORY OF
PALESTINE AND SYRIA

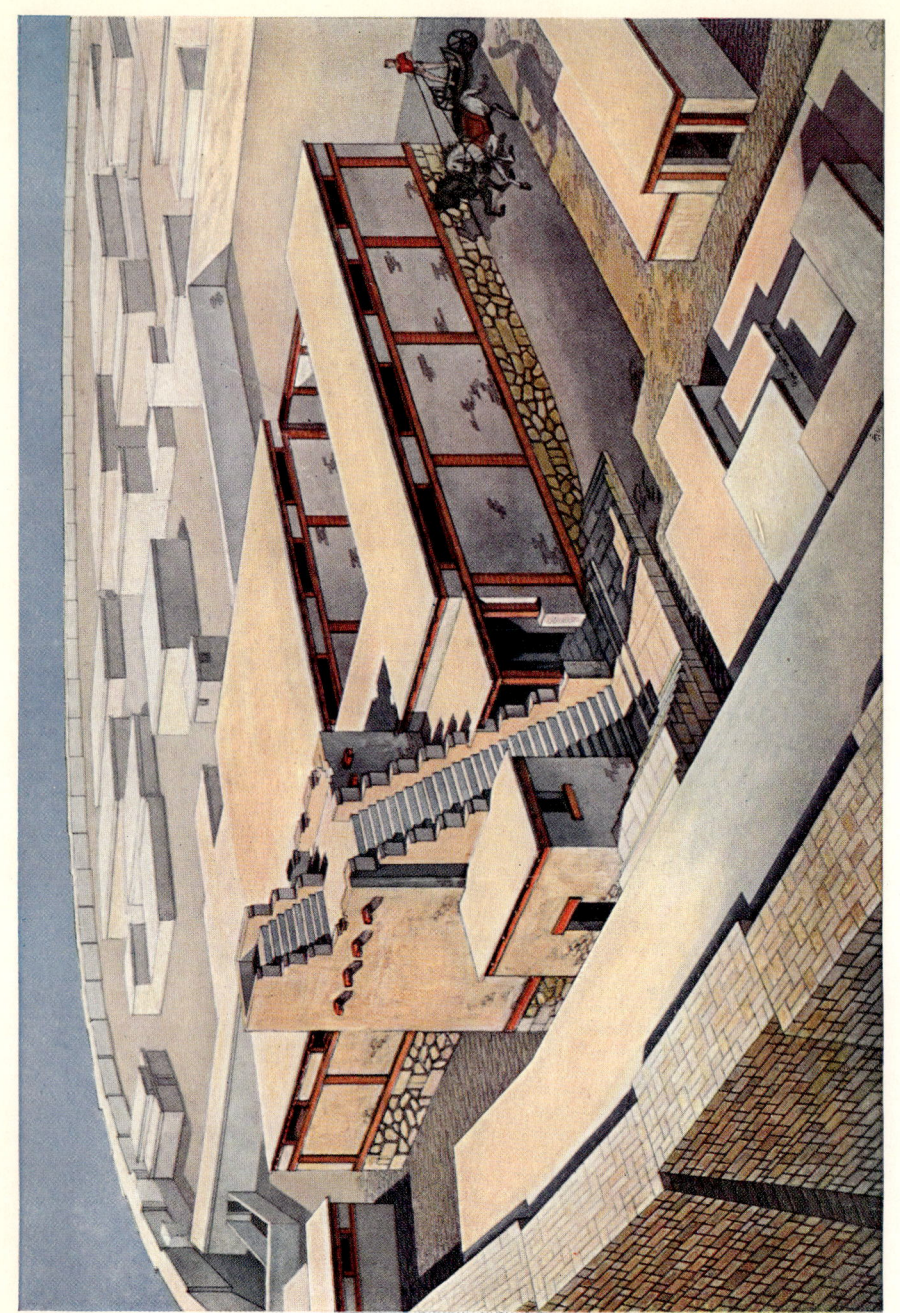

MEGIDDO: CITY WALLS, GOVERNOR'S PALACE, AND SOLOMON'S STABLES.

History of Palestine and Syria

TO THE MACEDONIAN CONQUEST

By
A. T. OLMSTEAD

PROFESSOR OF ORIENTAL HISTORY
UNIVERSITY OF CHICAGO

CHARLES SCRIBNER'S SONS
NEW YORK · LONDON
1931

COPYRIGHT, 1931, BY
CHARLES SCRIBNER'S SONS

Printed in the United States of America

*All rights reserved. No part of this book
may be reproduced in any form without
the permission of Charles Scribner's Sons*

TO
JAMES HENRY BREASTED
FOR A QUARTER-CENTURY MY FRIEND
AND NOW MY CHIEF

PREFACE

HISTORIES of the Hebrews have been written in the past and will doubtless be written in the future. Unified treatment of Hebrew development from barbarous nomads to the world's great religious teachers affords certain obvious advantages, but it inevitably ignores equally important aspects whose full significance we are only beginning to realise.

In by-gone days Biblical history was a thing apart. The Bible presented the one detailed picture of an ancient oriental people, and ancient oriental history must centre about its narrative. Now the Biblical writings are, numerically considered, but a tiny fragment of the huge amount of source material available for writing the history of the Ancient Near East. We have come to realise that the Hebrew kingdoms were minor states, helpless before the advance of the great empires. This political insignificance only heightens the miracle of Hebrew religious supremacy, but it warns us that we cannot hope to understand Hebrew religion unless we project its development against the background of contemporary history.

Contemporary background alone is not enough. We must venture far back into geological time to discover how the land was prepared for man. We must note how man himself made his first appearance in our land, how by the use of tools he slowly conquered a hostile nature, how he learned to till the soil and worship Mother Earth. We must study too this land, a world in miniature, whose broken contour prohibits the formation of a single great state yet enforces a certain unity of culture, whose position makes it the great Bridge between sea and desert.

Since geography has made of Syria a Bridge, Syrian history is only a part of the wider history of the Near East. We must visit the Semites in their first Arabian home, for repeatedly waves of Semites have swept in from the desert, destroyed the older cultures, and then built new cultures on the ruins of the old. From the sea came Egyptian and Philistine attack, but more frequently Egyptian and Minoan traders, the sea afforded opportunity for Phœnician merchandising.

The Bridge led from Egypt to Asia Minor, Assyria, Babylonia, and Persia. Egyptian armies invaded Syria throughout all history, Babylonian armies touched its northern border. Later came the Hittites, then the Assyrians and Chaldæans, finally the Persians and Macedonians. Over long centuries the empires held Syria in whole or in part. Wide-reaching as was the effect of this foreign rule, yet more significant were the influences which passed over the Bridge with the traders. Syrian culture, Syrian religion above all, cannot be fully understood until we have evaluated all these foreign influences.

Excavations at home and records from abroad picture Syria from the dawn of history. They show us that all the races which were to enter into the composition of the Hebrew people were in Syria a millennium or more before the conquest of the Promised Land. The very language in which our Old Testament is written was spoken by Canaanites and Phœnicians from these same early days. Already Syria possessed a high culture, mixed to be sure with foreign elements, but made its own; before the Hebrew conquest, its civilisation might be compared without disparagement to that of the great empires.

Thus the broad outlines of Hebrew culture were firmly fixed long centuries before the entrance of the Hebrews into Canaan. At their entrance, the Hebrews were simple nomads, blessed no doubt with high potentialities, but still at an extremely low cultural stage. Their conquest of the land was slow, and during its progress they intermarried with the earlier inhabitants and accepted much of the earlier civilisation.

Assimilation is particularly evident in the realm of religion. Nomad religion was extremely simple and primitive; when the Hebrews at last settled down to agriculture, they perforce adoped the ancient fertility cults. The religion pictured in the earlier portions of our Bible is essentially Canaanite, and Hebrew cult practices may be illustrated from the excavation of sites occupied long before the Hebrew invasion. Despite this wholesale adoption of Canaanite cults, the old nomad simplicity was never completely forgotten, and from time to time great religious leaders preached return to the purer desert ways.

Contemporary records have remade Hebrew history. We may never solve to our complete satisfaction the problem of Hebrew origins, but at least we now possess an amazingly full picture of the world into which the Hebrews came, and this picture must form the background into which we fit our hypothesis of Hebrew origins. Letters from Egyptian Amarna show us the Habiru or Hebrews in the very act of conquest, and we meet the historical Joshua east of the Jordan, while excavation proves that Jericho, Ai, and Bethel fell in this very period. The Egyptian Merneptah mentions an Israel in Canaan, Shishak lists conquered Hebrew cities. Assyrian monarch after monarch boasts of victories in Syria; Shalmaneser III adds a new page to Hebrew history, Sennacherib parallels the Biblical account. Through the Assyrian royal annals, the Hebrew prophets for the first time find their proper place in international history. Only with the aid of the contemporary accounts do we understand why Samaria and Jerusalem fell, why the first Zionists were permitted to return. These are but illustrations of the manner in which the Biblical narrative is confirmed, explained, or supplemented by the evidence from foreign sources.

Biblical history will always remain our chief interest, yet the general history of Syria is well worth study for its own sake. The Bible itself introduces us to many a neighbour whose historical importance we are only beginning to appreciate. Edomites, Moabites, and Ammonites were in some respects more truly "Hebrew" than those to whom we give that name; Edomite elements were incorporated in the later Judah, the Moabitess Ruth was great-grandmother of Judah's greatest hero, Rehoboam's mother was an Ammonitess, yet these tribes were ultimately pushed beyond the Jewish pale. While the Hebrews abandoned their native Aramaic for the "lip of Canaan," other tribesmen retained their Aramæan consciousness and founded such states as Geshur, Maacah, and Damascus.

We are coming to know the history and to realise the culture of these Aramæan states and we can trace the steps by which the Aramaic became the international language of the Near East until it forced its way into our Old Testament and to the lips of the infant Jesus.

Philistines gave their name to Palestine and more than their name. No longer may we call a self-satisfied ignoramus a "philistine"; through excavation of their cities we discover that the Philistines brought to Palestine the last fading relics of the glorious Minoan civilisation.

Phœnician seafarers have long intrigued our imagination. Two generations ago, all that was strange in Mediterranean culture was attributed to the Phœnicians. In natural reaction, the last generation virtually denied all Phœnician influence. Now we can trace the Phœnicians to the very beginnings of written history. From the tombs of their kings we learn their great wealth and their high civilisation; their temples and their religious records parallel those of the Hebrews. Through archæology, we can trace Phœnician advance westward through the Mediterranean and can date with close accuracy the impinging of their culture on that of the native Europeans. No longer do we believe that the Phœnicians invented that alphabet whose use they did so much to spread; centuries before its first appearance in Phœnicia some Canaanite genius in Sinai had invented the first pure alphabet in imitation of that used sporadically by the Egyptians.

Not many years ago, the pre-classical history of Central and North Syria was a virtual blank. To-day, we are able to present a consecutive narrative from Egyptian, Hittite, and Assyrian records. North Syria itself speaks to us in a strange new alphabet adapted from the cuneiform and written on clay tablets or in later inscriptions in the Phœnician character and in language strangely reminiscent of our Bible. Cities whose names were utterly unknown or known only to the specialist have suddenly come alive; their temples and palaces lie open before us, their superb new art has contributed some of the finest illustrations to our book.

PREFACE

Great as is the interest of these new sources of information, the chief source of any history of Palestine and Syria must be the Sacred Book. To utilise that collection of literature for historical purposes, much preliminary spade work is required. Our current English translations are based on Hebrew manuscripts the earliest of which are a thousand years later than the latest parts of our Old Testament and a good two thousand years later than the earliest. This long interval has allowed ample opportunity for errors of transcription, and the scribes have taken full advantage of their opportunity. Our first task must be the reconstruction of the text.

A single page of our Hebrew Bible, written on papyrus about the beginning of the second Christian century, agrees so well with the Greek translations whose earliest manuscripts are a century or so later that we may use these translations to correct our present Hebrew text. Proper use of these Greek translations demands highly technical procedure whose discussion would be here out of place;[1] it need only be said that we are on fairly safe ground when we are sure of the original Hebrew text read or too often misread by the Greek translator. Now and then, the other versions contribute something for the text, but for many of the most desperate text problems we are reduced to pure conjecture, unsatisfactory as this must always be. After the text, we have interpretation, and here the cognate languages often give the clue, especially in the use of technical terms.

As in the companion volume, the *History of Assyria*, attempt is made to give atmosphere by the employment of the very words of the ancient writers, sometimes in direct quotation, sometimes in a running paraphrase. Biblical quotations are derived from the author's own translations of the various books, made with reference to the versions and to the vocabulary of the cognate languages, and employed in mimeograph form as source material for classes in Hebrew history at the University of Illinois.

Much of the Biblical literature is in poetical form. This has

[1] Cf. *AJSL.*, XXX, 1913, 1 ff.; XXXI, 1915, 169 ff.; XXXIV, 1918, 145 ff.

long been recognised for the so-called "Poetical Books," but only to the extent of admitting deliberate parallelism. More recent studies have proved a somewhat complicated system of rhythm and verse structure, which is not confined to the "Poetical Books." The earlier prophets without exception and not a few of the later employ rhythm, while snatches of poetry, often of extremely early date, are scattered throughout the narrative books. Some of these poems are here presented in English form; they make no pretense of contributing to English poetical literature, they seek merely to illustrate Hebrew metrics. Hebrew rhythm is remarkably like that native to English, and the rhythm of many a Hebrew line is exactly repeated in our Authorised Version; this unconsciously rhythmical prose, the result of literal translation from the Hebrew original, is in no small degree responsible for the majestic swing of that great monument of English style.

The last step to be taken before the composition of the actual history is the investigation of the sources, their dates, authors, and character. This is the most complicated of all Biblical problems and has been the most bitterly contested. The principles underlying these preliminary investigations and the results thus secured are given more detailed exposition in a study, "Hebrew History and Historical Method," which is to appear this year in a volume dedicated to Professor George Lincoln Burr, who long years ago taught the writer the "Science and Art of History."[1] Here it need only be said that the principles are exactly the same as those employed by fellow historians in other fields of history. For many, the results may appear too radical, some Biblical scholars will doubtless consider them too conservative; questions of language, vocabulary, style, and thought have been given due weight, but the final test for the historian must be the check of the assumed fact by other known facts and by its ultimate incorporation into the unified picture. Stated facts in the Bible may often be checked by facts from non-Biblical sources, no hypothesis, however attractive, can be safely accepted unless it fits with-

[1] *Persecution and Liberty: Essays in Honor of Professor George L. Burr*, 1931.

out contradiction the recorded history of the whole ancient Near East.

Millions of books and articles have been written about the Bible. For our present purpose, we may ignore works of pure devotion, compilations at second or third hand, the all too numerous freak publications, and there still remains an appalling number of worth-while studies. To master the non-Biblical literature on the ancient Near East is in itself a life task. It is now thirty-one years since the writer first began the study of Hebrew, still longer since he received his first introduction to oriental bibliography. During that time, the leading works have been read, the periodicals and serials digested, but it is too much to hope that nothing of importance has been missed.

It is obviously impossible to present in one book the bibliography of the subject. The way was paved for the *History of Assyria* by a series of detailed studies with full bibliography and discussion of problems; the articles were generally ignored, while reviewers of the book demanded full discussion of problems long since discussed in full by the articles. In view of this experience, few preliminary studies for the present book have been printed.

The book has, however, been composed directly from the sources, written or archæological. Care has been taken to furnish exact reference to each source of importance; since practically all sources are available in translation in one of the modern languages, the reader is in the position to check the author's conclusions by the sources themselves. Care has also been taken to indicate the author of recent conclusions not yet generally accepted and a few general works are cited in addition. To have given references to those whose interpretations disagree would have filled the volume, to have discussed these disagreements in detail would have resulted in a series of tomes which would have deservedly remained in dusty manuscript. Reviewers are especially begged not to assume ignorance of works not specifically cited. This book has been written, not for the professional scholar, but for that wider public which desires to know how the old Sacred Book has become a new Sacred Book in the light of the ancient Near Eastern history.

Excavations during the last quarter century have completely revolutionised our knowledge of Syrian art and archæology. A selection of this new material is presented in the illustrations, the best examples of art, typical categories of archæological objects, the evolution of writing and of the alphabet, together with a few sites of historical importance. Each is chosen to illustrate the text into which it has been carefully tied. Thus it is hoped that the illustrative material will form an inexpensive atlas which will assist in making Bible times live.

Appropriate thanks must be given to those who have so kindly loaned original photographs or have allowed their illustrations to be reproduced. Photographs from Tell Beit Mirsim have been utilised through the courtesy of Professor W. F. Albright of Johns Hopkins University, Professor O. R. Sellers of the Presbyterian Theological Seminary, Chicago, and the American Colony, Jerusalem, for Figs. 60, 61; Professor Albright and the American Schools of Oriental Research have allowed the use of Fig. 126 and Plan 11 from the Gibeah excavations. Professor W. F. Badè of the Pacific School of Religion has given the original photograph of Fig. 127 and permission for Fig. 57 and Plans 9, 10 of Mizpah. Mr. Horace H. F. Jayne of the University of Pennsylvania Museum has placed at the author's disposal the whole series of original photographs used for the publication of the splendid Beth Shan finds; selections appear in Figs. 59, 70–77, 84, 90, 92–97, Plan 6. Photographs of the "Man of Galilee" and of its place of discovery have been furnished for Figs. 3, 5 by Professor G. G. MacCurdy of Yale University. Professor C. C. Torrey of Yale has given photographs of the Ammonite seal and the Sidon sarcophagus, Figs. 176, 186. The Marash reliefs, Figs. 168, 169, now in the Metropolitan Museum of New York, have been photographed by that Museum; the Lion of Marash, Fig. 170, is from a photograph by Doctor H. H. von der Osten,

PREFACE

Director of the Hittite Expedition of the Oriental Institute of the University of Chicago. Permission has been granted by the Carnegie Institution of Washington for Fig. 67, by the Oxford University Press of New York for Fig. 29, and by Professor D. G. Lyon for Figs. 154–156 from the Harvard excavations at Samaria.

To the Palestine Exploration Fund is due permission for Figs. 13, 120, 121, 134, 136, 137, and Plans 1–3, 7, 12, 18 and for photographs of Figs. 10, 11, 22, 129, 135, 143; to the Deutsche Palästina-Verein and Messrs. J. C. Hinrichs of Leipzig for Figs. 49, 124, 125, 173–175, and to Messrs. Hinrichs for Figs. 157, 181–183; to the Deutsches evangelisches Institut and E. S. Mittler und Sohn, Berlin, for the Yahweh seal, Fig. 177; the *Revue Biblique* for Figs. 65, 66; to Professor E. Sellin, Berlin, for Fig. 47; to Messrs. John Murray of London for Figs. 8, 16–18, 21, 33, from Sinai; to Sir William M. F. Flinders Petrie for Figs. 118, 119, from Gerar; to Professor J. L. Myres and the British School of Archæology in Jerusalem for Fig. 6; to Mr. S. R. K. Glanville, Honorary Secretary of the Egypt Exploration Society, for Figs. 35, 158.

Especially illuminating are the finds from Phœnicia and Central and North Syria. The earlier German excavations are represented by courtesy of the Deutsche Staatliche Museum in Figs. 81, 113, 115, 164, 165, and Plan 16. Professor T. E. Peet, editor of the Liverpool *Annals of Archæology,* and Professor John Garstang have allowed the use of the Sake Geuzi and Carchemish finds in Figs. 12, 30–32, 107–110, 160–163, as well as Plans 5 and 17. The British Museum has authorized the reproduction of its Carchemish reliefs in Figs. 147–153, 166, 167, 178, as well as the Joshua tablet in Fig. 78. By permission of M. Paul Geuthner, examples of the Byblos finds may be seen in Figs. 25, 26, 37–44, 53, 102, 103, 145. Professor René Dussaud, editor of *Syria,* has made possible the large selection of illustrations from that journal, Figs. 3, 34, 45, 46, 50–52, 54, 58, 79, 91, 98, 99, 144, 146, 179, 187, and also Fig. 85. Fig. 69 is used by permission of the *Revue Archéologique,* Fig. 7 of *L'Anthropologie.*

The Oriental Institute of the University of Chicago, through its Director, Professor James Henry Breasted, and its editorial secretary, Doctor T. George Allen, has given original photographs and plans for the frontispiece, Figs. 36, 55, 56, 62–64, 104, 112, 114, 116, 117, 139–142, 171, and Plans 13, 14. Mr. Richard Martin, Assistant Director of its Hittite Expedition, has redrawn Plans 8, 9 and 15. Figs. 100, 101 have been redrawn from the publications of Professor W. R. Taylor of Toronto University and of Professor Albright. The other illustrations are from photographs made by Doctor B. B. Charles of Salamanca, N. Y., Professor J. E. Wrench of the University of Missouri, and the author, while students at the American School in Jerusalem; Figs. 1, 2, 19, 20, 86–89, 105, 106 have already been published by the annual director, Professor Nathaniel Schmidt of Cornell University.

If the book is relatively complete or relatively free from error, a large part of the credit must be given to the friends who have so generously offered aid. It is now twenty-five years since oriental history and oriental languages were studied at Cornell University under Professor Nathaniel Schmidt, yet doubtless he will find many an echo of his teaching in these pages. Although few of these pages have been hitherto printed, all the major problems have been discussed at meetings of the American Oriental Society and its Middle West Branch, the American Historical Association, the Society of Biblical Research, the Society of Biblical Literature, and the Central Branch of the American Anthropological Association, and the ensuing discussion has done much for their solution. Among those whose conversations have been even more suggestive than their printed studies, I may especially note Professor T. J. Meek of the University of Toronto, Professor J. A. Montgomery of the University of Pennsylvania, President Julian Morgenstern of Hebrew Union College, Professor C. C. Torrey of Yale University, and Professor Leroy Waterman of the University of Michigan.

For twenty years the results have been presented to classes in Hebrew History at the Universities of Missouri and Illinois, to classes in Oriental History there and at the University of Chicago. Each period has been studied in turn by the Seminar in Oriental History. To my graduate students I owe much. During all these long years the problems of Hebrew history have been discussed with my wife, to whose insight I owe many a promising suggestion.

It has been a special stroke of good fortune that the work has been brought to completion within the walls of the Oriental Institute and with the most generous aid from my fellow members. My Old Testament colleagues, Professor J. M. P. Smith, Professor Ira M. Price, Professor W. C. Graham, and Professor W. A. Irwin, have naturally borne the heaviest burden; Professor Price and Professor Graham have read the entire manuscript with meticulous care, Professor Irwin a large part. Professor Martin Sprengling has checked my knowledge of the Arabs and Aramæans and of Aramaic literature. In matters Assyriological, I have gone to Professor Edward Chiera, Professor Arno Poebel, and Doctor F. W. Geers; Doctor Geers has aided with puzzling passages in the Amarna letters, Professor Poebel has also revised the majority of the North Semitic inscriptions. For problems of Egyptian interpretation and archæology, I have enjoyed the assistance of Professor W. F. Edgerton and Doctor T. George Allen, who as editorial secretary has also given me access to valued material as it was passing through our press. It need scarcely be said that they are not responsible for any failure to heed their words.

For a quarter of a century the Director of the Oriental Institute has been my friend, a constant source of encouragement and inspiration. His *History of Egypt* was the model for my *History of Assyria*, as it is now for the *History of Palestine and Syria*. It is therefore but right that this book, first fruits of the new Professor of Oriental History, should be dedicated to the first Professor of Oriental History, Professor James Henry Breasted.

A. T. OLMSTEAD.

THE ORIENTAL INSTITUTE,
 THE UNIVERSITY OF CHICAGO,
 August, 1931.

CONTENTS

		PAGE
Preface		vii
Illustrations		xxi
Maps and Plans		xxxi
Abbreviations		xxxiii

CHAPTER		
I.	In the Beginning	1
II.	Cave Men, Farmers, and Giants	16
III.	Arab Tribesmen	35
IV.	The Bridge of Assembly	43
V.	Egyptian Warriors and Canaanite Peasants	52
VI.	Ships of Gebal	66
VII.	Waves from Euphrates and Nile	79
VIII.	The Manner of Canaan	104
IX.	Northern Invaders	115
X.	Egyptian Overlords	129
XI.	Egyptianised Syria	140
XII.	Letters from Syria	155
XIII.	Monotheism and its Results	171
XIV.	Habiru Inroads	185
XV.	Hebrew Origins	194
XVI.	Hittite and Egyptian Masters	216
XVII.	Moses and the Southland	245
XVIII.	Palestine of the Philistines	257
XIX.	Yahweh's Wars	270
XX.	Saul, First King of Israel	294

xix

CONTENTS

CHAPTER		PAGE
XXI.	David's Empire	311
XXII.	Solomon in All His Glory	334
XXIII.	Jeroboam and Israel's Revolt	351
XXIV.	Repulse of Ashur and of Baal	362
XXV.	Reforms of Blood	388
XXVI.	Interlude	404
XXVII.	High Lights and Shadows	417
XXVIII.	Assyria's Return	433
XXIX.	Israel's Fall	441
XXX.	Isaiah and Hezekiah	455
XXXI.	The Rod of Yahweh's Anger	471
XXXII.	Reaction	482
XXXIII.	Josiah's Reform	494
XXXIV.	Jeremiah the Pessimist	505
XXXV.	The Fall of Jerusalem	517
XXXVI.	By Babylon's Rivers	531
XXXVII.	Prophets of Hope and of Hate	541
XXXVIII.	The First Zionists	553
XXXIX.	The Yoke of the Law	576
XL.	Building the Walls	588
XLI.	These from the Land of Sinim	598
XLII.	Last Days	611
XLIII.	Coming Judaism	625
	Index of Proper Names	641
	Index of Subjects	657

ILLUSTRATIONS

Megiddo: City Walls, Governor's Palace, and Solomon's
Stables . . . . *Frontispiece*
(From P. L. O. Guy, *New Light from Armageddon*, fig. 22.)

FIG.		FACING PAGE
1.	On the Shores of the Dead Sea	6
	(From N. Schmidt, *Jour. Biblical Literature*, XXV, 1906, fig. 1.)	
2.	The Hills about the Dead Sea	6
	(From Schmidt, *op. cit.*, fig. 2.)	
3.	Within the Cave of el Zuttiyeh	8
	(From G. G. MacCurdy, *Bull. Amer. School of Prehistoric Research*, III, 1927, 21.)	
4.	Prechellean Artifacts	8
	(From E. Passemard, *Syria*, VIII, 1927, pl. XCV.)	
5.	The "Man of Galilee"	8
	(From MacCurdy, *op. cit.*, 20.)	
6.	Mousterian Fist Hatchet . . . . *Page*	11
	(From F. Turville-Petre, *Researches in Prehistoric Galilee*, pl. X ff.)	
7.	Early Neolithic Implements	16
	(From G. Zumoffen, *L'Anthropologie*, VIII, 1897, pl. IV.)	
8.	Flint Implements from Sinai	16
	(From W. M. F. Petrie, *Researches in Sinai*, fig. 170.)	
9.	Gilgal	18
10.	Megalithic Fort with Round Tower	18
	(From D. Mackenzie, Palestine Exploration Fund, *Annual*, I, 22.)	
11.	Sacred "Place" at Gezer	18
	(From R. A. S. Macalister, *Excavations at Gezer*, II, 379.)	
12.	Black Ware from Sakje Geuzi . . . . . . *Page*	20
	(From J. L. Myres, *Liverpool Annals of Archæology*, I, 1908, pl. XLV, 4.)	
13.	Development of the Dolmen . . . . . . *Page*	25
	(From C. R. Conder, *Survey of Eastern Palestine*, 128, 130, 166, 230.)	
14.	The "Bridge of Assembly" over the Jordan	44

xxi

FIG.		FACING PAGE
15.	On the Road to Egypt—the "Well of Hagar"	44
	(From Schmidt, *Jour. Biblical Literature*, XXIX, 1910, fig. 9.)	
16.	A Nawami or "Mosquito House"	54
	(From Petrie, *Researches*, fig. 176.)	
17.	Huts of the Miners	54
	(From Petrie, *op. cit.*, fig. 42.)	
18.	Semerkhet Smites the Chief of the Nomads	54
	(From Petrie, *op. cit.*, fig. 47.)	
19.	The Dead Sea Peninsula of the "Tongue"	60
	(From Schmidt, *Jour. Biblical Literature*, XXV, 1906.)	
20.	Tent Village on the "Tongue"	60
	(From Schmidt, *op. cit.*, fig. 7.)	
21.	Objects from the Nawamis	62
	(From Petrie, *op. cit.*, fig. 179.)	
22.	Early Canaanite Tunnel at Gezer	62
	(From Macalister, *op. cit.*, I, 258.)	
23.	Sacred Standing Stones at Gezer	64
24.	Monastery with Sacred Fish in Pool	64
25.	Gebal and Its Port	68
	(From P. Montet, *Byblos et l'Égypt*, pl. III.)	
26.	Hills Back of Gebal	68
	(From Montet, *op. cit.*, pl. III.)	
27.	Aphek, Home of Adonis and Ashtart	70
28.	Harbor of Beirut, Mount Sanin in the Distance . .	70
29.	Pot Grave (Carchemish)	80
	(From D. G. Hogarth, *Kings of the Hittites*, 24.)	
30.	Bronze Implements and Silver Pin (Carchemish) . .	80
	(From C. L. Woolley, *Liverpool Annals of Archæology*, VI, 1913, pl. XIX.)	
31.	Champagne-Glass Jars (Carchemish)	80
	(From Woolley, *l. c.*)	
32.	Bull's Head Rhyton (Carchemish)	80
	(From Woolley, *op. cit.*, pl. XX.)	
33.	Sacred Circle and Bethel at Wadi Serabit, Sinai . .	88
	(From Petrie, *op. cit.*, fig. 79.)	

ILLUSTRATIONS   xxiii

FIG.		FACING PAGE
34.	Temple at Gebal	88
	(From M. Dunand, *Syria*, VIII, 1927, pl. XXIX.)	
35.	The Desert Chief Abishai Brings Eye Paint to Sesostris III	
	(From P. E. Newberry, *Benihasan*, I, pl. XXXI.) *Page*	89
36.	Sinaitic Inscription . . . . *Page*	92
	(From Martin Sprengling, *The Alphabet*, 33.)	
37.	Sarcophagus of Abi-shemu, King of Gebal	94
	(From Montet, *Byblos*, pl. XI.)	
38.	Obsidian Ointment Jar and Coffer Sent by Amenemhet III and Amenemhet IV to Kings of Gebal	94
	(From Montet, *op. cit.*, pl. LXXXVIII.)	
39.	Scepter of Iapa-shemu-abi, King of Gebal	94
	(From Montet, *op. cit.*, pl. XCIX.)	
40.	Silver Vessels from Gebal	94
	(From Montet, *op. cit.*, pl. CXI.)	
41.	Mirror from Gebal	96
	(From Montet, *op. cit.*, pl. XCII.)	
42.	Pectoral and Necklace of Iapa-shemu-abi	96
	(From Montet, *op. cit.*, pl. XCIV.)	
43.	Ornament from Gebal	96
	(From Montet, *op. cit.*, pl. XCVII.)	
44.	Hawk Collar from Gebal	96
	(From Montet, *op. cit.*, pl. XCV.)	
45.	A Native Prince of Gebal	98
	(From M. Dunand, *Syria*, X, 1929, pl. XXXVII.)	
46.	Bronze Torques, Diadems, and Awls from Gebal but of Northern Origin	98
	(From H. Hubert, *Syria*, VI, 1925, pl. II.)	
47.	Seal of Atanah-ili of Taanach . . . . *Page*	100
	(From E. Sellin, *Tell Taannek*, 28.)	
48.	Plain of Shechem from Jacob's Well	106
49.	Temple, Altar, and Sacred Standing Stone at Shechem .	106
	(From E. Sellin, *Zeitschrift des Deutschen Palästina-Vereins*, LI, 1928, pl. 12.)	
50.	Head from Gabbula	118
	(From R. Dussaud, *Syria*, VII, 1926, pl. LXXI.)	

ILLUSTRATIONS

FIG.		FACING PAGE
51.	Bronze Figure of a God from Qatna . . . . (From Dussaud, *op. cit.*, pl. LXX.)	118
52.	Great Rampart of Qatna . . . . (From Comte du Mesnil du Buisson, *Syria*, VII, 1926, pl. L.)	118
53.	Hand-made Jars from Early Gebal . . . . (From Montet, *Byblos*, pl. CXLIV.)	122
54.	Bronze Age Jars from Qatna . . . . (From Comte du Mesnil du Buisson, *Syria*, XI, 1930, pl. XXXV.)	122
55.	Scarabs of the Hyksos Period . . . . (From C. S. Fisher, *Excavation of Armageddon*, 46.)	124
56.	Pottery of the Hyksos Period . . . . (From P. L. O. Guy, *New Light from Armageddon*, fig. 8.)	124
57.	The South Wall of Mizpah . . . . (From W. F. Badè, *Excavations at Tell en-Nasbeh*, 24.)	126
58.	Temples and Palace at Qatna . . . . (From Comte du Mesnil du Buisson, *op. cit.*, pl. XXIX.)	126
59.	Lapis Lazuli Seal of Manum the Diviner from Beth Shan (From Alan Rowe, *Topography and History of Beth-Shan*, pl. 34, 3.)	132
60.	Canaanite Offering Table . . . . (From W. F. Albright, *Bulletin Amer. Schools of Oriental Research*, 39, 1930, 7.)	132
61.	Backgammon Set from Kiriath Sepher . . . . . . (From Albright, *op. cit.*, 9.)	132
62.	Mound of Megiddo from the Plain . . . . (From Fisher, *op. cit.*, 2.)	134
63.	The Pass of Megiddo . . . . (From Fisher, *op. cit.*, 5.)	134
64.	View from Megiddo . . . . (From Fisher, *op. cit.*, fig. 5.)	138
65.	Jetty Between the Two Ports of Arvad . . . . . . (From R. Savignac, *Revue Biblique*, XXV, 1916, op. p. 569.)	142
66.	Great Wall at Arvad . . . . (From Savignac, *l. c.*)	142
67.	The Prince of Tunip . . . . (From W. M. Müller, *Egyptological Researches*, II, pl. 8.)	144
68.	Syrian Brickmakers and Egyptian Taskmasters . . . (From P. E. Newberry, *Life of Rekhmara*, pl. XXI.)	144

ILLUSTRATIONS

FIG.		FACING PAGE
69.	Phœnician Ships at the Quay of Thebes . . . . (From G. Daressy, *Revue Archéologique*, III Sér., XXVII, 1895, pl. XIV.)	146
70.	Sacred Standing Stone in Mekal Temple, Beth Shan . . (From Alan Rowe, *op. cit.*, pl. 21.)	150
71.	Temple of Mekal at Beth Shan . . . . (From Rowe, *op. cit.*, pl. 17.)	150
72.	Relief from Mekal Temple, Beth Shan . . . . . (From Rowe, *op. cit.*, frontispiece.)	152
73.	Ashtart with the Egyptian Waz Scepter . . . . (From Rowe, *Museum Journal*, 1929, 40.)	154
74.	Pottery Stands . . . . (From Rowe, *op. cit.*, 1926, 297, 299.)	154
75.	Ring Flower Vase . . . . (From Rowe, *op. cit.*, 1926, 300.)	154
76.	Model of Shrine . . . . (From Rowe, *op. cit.*, 1926, 294.)	154
77.	Temple Built by Amenhotep III for Mekal at Beth Shan (From Alan Rowe and L. H. Vincent, *Quarterly Statement*, Palestine Exploration Fund, 1931, pl. II.)	Page 157
78.	Letter of Mut-baal Mentioning Job, Benjamin and Joshua (From C. Bezold and E. A. W. Budge, *The Tell el-Amarna Tablets in the British Museum*, pl. 5.)	196
79.	Tablets with a Cuneiform Alphabet . . . . . (From C. Virolleaud, *Syria*, X, 1929, pl. LXXVIII.)	196
80.	Jericho before Excavation	200
81.	Jericho's Walls . . . . (From E. Sellin and C. Watzinger, *Jericho*, pl. 5.)	200
82.	The Lake of Galilee from Tiberias	208
83.	Bay and City of Accho	208
84.	Stele Dedicated to Ashtart of the Two Horns . . . (From Rowe, *Beth-Shan*, pl. 48, 2.)	212
85.	Stele of a Moabite God or King . . . . . . (From R. Dussaud, *Monuments palestiniennes*, 2.)	212
86.	Entrance to the Arnon Gorge . . . . (From N. Schmidt, *Jour. Biblical Literature*, XXIV, 1905, fig. 1.)	214

ILLUSTRATIONS

FIG.		FACING PAGE
87.	The Arnon Crossing . . . . (From Schmidt, *op. cit.*, fig. 7.)	214
88.	In the Arnon Gorge . . . . (From Schmidt, *op. cit.*, fig. 4.)	216
89.	Waterfall in the Arnon Gorge . . . . (From Schmidt, *op. cit.*, fig. 5.)	216
90.	Temple of Seti I at Beth Shan . . . . . *Page* (From Rowe and Vincent, *op. cit.*, pl. II.)	218
91.	Seti I at Kadesh . . . . *Page* (From M. Pézard, *Syria*, III, 1922, 108.)	220
92.	Stele of Mekal, Lord of Beth Shan . . . . . . (From Rowe, *Beth-Shan*, pl. 33.)	222
93.	Hittite Axehead from Beth Shan . . . . . . (From Rowe, *op. cit.*, pl. 35, 2.)	222
94.	Mediterranean Spear Butt from Beth Shan . . . . (From Rowe, *op. cit.*, pl. 39, 3.)	222
95.	Cylinder Seal of Ramses II Found at Beth Shan . . (From Rowe, *op. cit.*, pl. 34, 4.)	222
96.	Temple of Anath Built by Ramses II at Beth Shan *Page* (From Rowe and Vincent, *op. cit.*, pl. III.)	223
97.	Temple of Reshuph Built by Ramses II at Beth Shan *Page* (From Rowe and Vincent, *l. c.*)	223
98.	The Mycenæan Mother Goddess at Sapuna . . . . (From F. A. Schaeffer, *Syria*, X, 1929, pl. LVI.)	234
99.	Bronze Tripod from Sapuna . . . . (From Schaeffer, *op. cit.*, pl. LX.)	234
100.	Potsherd from Gezer with Earliest Known Canaanite Inscription. . . . . *Page* (From W. R. Taylor, *Jour. Palestine Oriental Society*, X, 1930, pl. 1.)	239
101.	Potsherd from Lachish with Name of Bela . . *Page* (From W. F. Albright, *Archiv f. Orientforschung*, V, 1929, 150.)	239
102.	Sarcophagus of Ahirom, King of Gebal . . . . . (From Montet, *Byblos*, pl. CXXVIII.)	240
103.	Inscription of Ahirom, King of Gebal . . . . *Page* (From Montet, *op. cit.*, 216, 236 f.)	241
104.	Evolution of the Alphabet . . . . *Page* (From M. Sprengling, *The Alphabet*, 55.)	243

ILLUSTRATIONS   xxvii

FIG.   FACING PAGE
105. Kadesh Barnea 246
    (From N. Schmidt, *Jour. Biblical Literature*, XXIX, 1910, fig. 1.)

106. The "Gorge of the Fount" 246
    (From Schmidt, *op. cit.*, fig. 11.)

107. Bronze Fibula or Safety Pin (Carchemish) . . . 258
    (From C. L. Woolley, *Liverpool Annals of Archæology*, VI, 1913, pl. XXVI.)

108. Cinerary Urn (Carchemish) 258
    (From Woolley, *l. c.*)

109. Cinerary Urn (Carchemish) 258
    (From Woolley, *l. c.*)

110. Figurines (Carchemish) 258
    (From Woolley, *l. c.*)

111. Warriors from Carchemish 260
    (From D. G. Hogarth, *Carchemish*, I, pl. B. 2b.)

112. Philistine Captives 260
    (From Oriental Institute, University of Chicago, *Medinet Habu*, I, pl. 52, C.)

113. Sculptures from the South Gate of Samal . . . 262
    (From F. von Luschan, *Ausgrabungen in Sendschirli*, III, pl. 34.)

114. Philistine Prisoners . . . . *Page* 264
    (From Oriental Institute, *Medinet Habu*, pl. 44.)

115. Sculptures from the Citadel Gate at Samal . . . 264
    (From von Luschan, *op. cit.*, pl. 37.)

116. Land Battle with the Philistines 268
    (From Oriental Institute, *Medinet Habu*, pl. 34.)

117. Naval Battle with the Philistines 270
    (From Oriental Institute, *Medinet Habu*, pl. 39.)

118. Gold Frontlet and Gold Earrings from Gerar . . 272
    (From W. M. F. Petrie, *Gerar*, pl. I.)

119. Iron Implements from Gerar 272
    (From Petrie, *op. cit.*, pl. LXVI.)

120. Middle and Late Bronze Pottery 274
    (From W. J. Phythian-Adams, *Quarterly Statement*, Palestine Exploration Fund, 1923, op. p. 66.)

121. Philistine Pottery 274
    (From Phythian-Adams, *op. cit.*, op. p. 68.)

122. Source of the Jordan at Dan 276

ILLUSTRATIONS

FIG.		FACING PAGE
123.	Source of the Jordan at Banias	276
124.	Altar and Standing Stone at Shechem	288
	(From E. Sellin, *Zeitschrift des Deutschen Palästina-Vereins*, LI, 1928, pl. 11.)	
125.	East Gate of Shechem and Israelite Houses	288
	(From Sellin, *op. cit.*, XLIX, 1926, pl. 43.)	
126.	Gibeah	300
	(From W. F. Albright, *Annual*, Amer. Schools of Oriental Research, IV, 60.)	
127.	Israelite Sanctuary at Mizpah	300
	(From W. F. Badè, *Excavations at Tell en-Nasbeh*, 33.)	
128.	Rock Altar at Zorah	300
	(From R. Kittel, *Hilprecht Anniversary Volume*, op. p. 244.)	
129.	West Gate of Jebusite Jerusalem	300
	(From J. W. Crowfoot and G. M. Fitzgerald, *Excavations in the Tyropoeon Valley, Jerusalem*, frontispiece.)	
130.	In the Wilderness of Judah	308
131.	The Fountain of Goliath under Mount Gilboa	308
132.	Bethlehem from the Church of the Nativity	312
133.	Hebron, the Mosque over the Cave of Machpelah	312
134.	Jebusite Wall of Jerusalem	318
	(From R. A. S. Macalister and J. G. Duncan, *Excavations on the Hill of Ophel*, 62.)	
135.	The Breach in the Jebusite Wall	318
	(From Macalister and Duncan, *op. cit.*, 45.)	
136.	North Bastion and Tower in Ophel Wall	318
	(From Macalister and Duncan, *op. cit.*, op. p. 127.)	
137.	David's Wall	318
	(From Macalister and Duncan, *Quarterly Statement*, Palestine Exploration Fund, 1924, op. p. 63.)	
138.	Joppa, Port of Jerusalem	342
139.	The Excavation of Megiddo	342
	(From P. L. O. Guy, *New Light from Armageddon*, fig. 13.)	
140.	Solomon's Stables (Restored)	344
	(From Guy, *op. cit.*, fig. 29.)	
141.	Solomon's Stables (Present Condition)	344
	(From Guy, *op. cit.*, 18.)	

ILLUSTRATIONS   xxix

FIG.
142. Fragment of Shishak Stele at Megiddo . . . Page 355
    (From C. S. Fisher, *Excavation of Armageddon*, 13.)

                                                                                                        FACING PAGE

143. The Gezer Calendar 356
    (From Macalister, *Gezer*, III, pl. 127.)

144. Inscription of Shishak and of Abibaal, King of Gebal . 356
    (From R. Dussaud, *Syria*, V, 1924, pl. XLII.)

145. Bust of Osorkon I with Inscription of Elibaal, King of Gebal 358
    (From Montet, *Byblos*, pl. XXXVI.)

146. A King of Damascus 358
    (From G. Contenau, *Syria*, V, 1925, pl. LIII.)

147. South Gate at Carchemish . . . . Page 363
    (From C. L. Woolley, *Carchemish*, II, 85.)

148. The King of Carchemish Presents the Crown Prince . 364
    (From D. G. Hogarth, *Carchemish*, I, pl. B. 7a.)

149. The Royal Children at Carchemish 364
    (From Hogarth, *op. cit.*, I, pl. B. 7b.)

150. Officials of Carchemish 366
    (From Hogarth, *op. cit.*, I, pl. B. 5b.)

151. Ladies of Carchemish 366
    (From Woolley, *op. cit.*, II, pl. B. 21a.)

152. Teshup and His Companion Kill the Lion 368
    (From Hogarth, *op. cit.*, I, pl. B. 11a.)

153. Heraldic Figures 368
    (From Hogarth, *op. cit.*, I, pl. B. 14b.)

154. Samaria 370
    (From G. A. Reisner, C. S. Fisher, and D. G. Lyon, *Harvard Excavations at Samaria*, II, pl. 1a.)

155. Ahab's Palace at Samaria 370
    (From Reisner, Fisher, and Lyon, *op. cit.*, II, pl. 27a.)

156. Inscribed Potsherds from Samaria . . . . Page 373
    (From Reisner, Fisher, and Lyon, *op. cit.*, I, 239.)

157. The Moabite Stone . . . . Page 391
    (From M. Lidzbarski, *Handbuch der nordsemitischen Epigraphik*, pl. 1.)

158. Phœnician Shell Engraving from Nineveh 406
    (From L. W. King, *Jour. Egyptian Archæology*, I, 1914, pl. XXXVI.)

xxx ILLUSTRATIONS

FIG.		FACING PAGE
159.	Bronze Vase from Præneste	406
	(From *Corpus Inscriptionum Semiticarum*, I, pl. XXXVI.)	
160.	Lions, Male Sphinx, and Prince	410
	(From J. Garstang, *Liverpool Annals of Archæology*, I, 1908, pl. XL.)	
161.	Servants with Fly Flapper and Falcon	410
	(From Garstang, *l. c.*)	
162.	Lion, Winged Demon, and Good Genii	412
	(From Garstang, *op. cit.*, pl. XLI.)	
163.	Pillar Base Supported by Female Sphinxes . . .	412
	(From Garstang, *op. cit.*, pl. XLII.)	
164.	Early Hadad Statue and Base	434
	(From von Luschan, *op. cit.*, IV, 365.)	
165.	Hadad Statue with Inscription of Panammu I . . .	434
	(From von Luschan, *op. cit.*, I, pl. 6.)	
166.	God Throned on Lions	458
	(From Woolley, *Carchemish*, II, pl. B. 25.)	
167.	A King of Carchemish	458
	(From Woolley, *op. cit.*, II, pl. B. 27a.)	
168.	Woman with Child	460
	(From H. H. von der Osten, *Metropolitan Museum Studies*, II, 1929, 113.)	
169.	Scene of Worship	460
	(From von der Osten, *op. cit.*, 115.)	
170.	Lion with Pictographic Inscription	460
	(From von der Osten, *op. cit.*, 112.)	
171.	Hebrew Pottery, 800–600 . . . . *Page*	465
	(From Fisher, *Excavation of Armageddon*, 67.)	
172.	Royal Jar Stamps . . . . *Page*	466
	(From E. J. Pilcher, *Proceedings of the Society of Biblical Archæology*, XX, 1898, pl. I.)	
173.	The Siloam Inscription . . . . *Page*	477
	(From A. Socin, *Zeitschrift des Deutschen Palästina-Vereins*, XXII, 1899, op. p. 104.)	
174.	Seal of Asaph (Megiddo)	488
	(From C. Watzinger, *Tell el-Mutesellim*, II, 65.)	
175.	Seal of Shema, Servant of Jeroboam (Megiddo) . .	488
	(From Watzinger, *l. c.*)	

ILLUSTRATIONS   xxxi

FIG		FACING PAGE
176.	Seal of Adonipelet, Servant of Amminadab, King of Ammon	488
	(From C. C. Torrey, *Annual*, Amer. Schools of Oriental Research, II–III, op. p. 104.)	
177.	Seal of Elishama, Son of Gedaliah, with Figure of Yahweh	488
	(G. Dalman, *Palästinajahrbuch*, II, 1906, pl. I.)	
178.	Cylinders, Seals, and Jeweler's Mould (Carchemish) . .	488
	(From Woolley, *Carchemish*, II, pl. 25.)	
179.	Bronze Vase of Amasis from Sidon	536
	(From M. Dunand, *Syria*, VII, 1926, pl. XXXII.)	
180.	Grave Monument of an Aramæan in Egypt	536
	(From *Corpus Inscriptionum Semiticarum*, II, pl. XIII.)	
181.	Lion on the Processional Street of Babylon	550
	(From R. Koldewey, *Excavations at Babylon*, op. p. 28.)	
182.	Dragon of the Ishtar Gate at Babylon	550
	(From Koldewey, *op. cit.*, op. p. 47.)	
183.	Aramaic Papyrus from Elephantine	608
	(From E. Sachau, *Aramäische Papyrus und Ostraka*, pl. I.)	
184.	Phœnician Shrine in Artificial Lake (Marathus) . . .	618
185.	Tripolis	618
186.	Anthropoid Sarcophagus from Sidon	622
	(From C. C. Torrey, *Annual*, American Schools of Oriental Research, I, 9.)	
187.	Hadad in the Persian Period	622
	(From R. Dussaud, *Syria*, I, 1920, 12.)	

MAPS AND PLANS

PLAN		PAGE
1.	Megalithic Residence and Dolmen Tomb (Rabbath Ammon)	26
2.	Megalithic Fort and Tower (Rabbath Ammon) . . .	27
3.	Fortified Residence (Rabbath Ammon)	29
	(From D. Mackenzie, Palestine Exploration Fund, *Annual*, I, pl. II, IV, VI.)	
4.	The Site of Gebal	68
	(From P. Montet, *Byblos et l'Égypte*, pl. I.)	

MAPS AND PLANS

PLAN		PAGE
5.	Hyksos Camp at Hazor	121
	(From J. Garstang, *Liverpool Annals*, XIV, 1927, 40.)	
6.	Beth Shan in the Time of Thutmose III	150
	(From Alan Rowe, *Topography and History of Beth-Shan*, 12.)	
7.	The Walls of Jericho	199
	(From J. Garstang, *Quarterly Statement*, Palestine Exploration Fund, 1930, op. p. 132.)	
8.	Shechem	286
	(Redrawn by Richard Martin from E. Sellin, *Zeitschrift der Palästinaverein*, XLIX, 1926, pl. 32.)	
9.	Mizpah	297
	(Redrawn by Richard Martin from W. F. Badè, *Excavations at Tell en-Nasbeh*, pl. I.)	
10.	Prehistoric Rock Altar and Israelite Temple at Mizpah	298
	(From Badè, *op. cit.*, 31.)	
11.	Saul's Palace at Gibeah	305
	(From W. F. Albright, *Annual*, American Schools of Oriental Research, IV, 77.)	
12.	Jebusite Jerusalem and the City of David	317
	(From R. A. S. Macalister and J. G. Duncan, *Excavations on the Hill of Ophel*, plan.)	
13.	Megiddo	344
	(Redrawn from P. L. O. Guy, *New Light from Armageddon*, Fig. 14.)	
14.	Megiddo, Solomon's City . . . . . *Facing page*	344
	(From P. L. O. Guy, *op. cit.*, Fig. 17.)	
15.	Samaria, Palaces of Omri, Ahab, and Jeroboam II	370
	(Redrawn by Richard Martin from G. A. Reisner, C. S. Fisher, and D. G. Lyon, *Harvard Excavations at Samaria*, II, pl. 5.)	
16.	Samal . . . . *Facing page*	408
	(From F. von Luschan, *Ausgrabungen in Sendschirli*, II, pl. 29.)	
17.	Palace Enclosure at Sakje Geuzi	413
	(From J. Garstang, *Liverpool Annals*, V, 1912, pl. III.)	
18.	Fort of Azariah in the Negeb	418
	(From C. L. Woolley and T. E. Lawrence, *Wilderness of Zin*, 65.)	
	Syria and Palestine . . . . *At end of volume*	

ABBREVIATIONS

AJSL.	*American Journal of Semitic Languages.*
AJT.	*American Journal of Theology.*
Ann.	*Annual of the American Schools of Oriental Research.*
BB.	C. Bezold and E. A. W. Budge, *The Tell el-Amarna Tablets in the British Museum*, 1892.
BoTU.	E. Forrer, *Die Boghazköi-Texte in Umschrift.*
Bull.	*Bulletin of the American Schools of Oriental Research.*
CH.	*Code of Hammurabi.*
Cowley.	A. Cowley, *Aramaic Papyri of the Fifth Century B. C.*, 1923.
JAOS.	*Journal of the American Oriental Society.*
JBL.	*Journal of Biblical Literature.*
JEA.	*Journal of Egyptian Archæology.*
JPOS.	*Journal of the Palestine Oriental Society.*
K.	J. A. Knudtzon, *Die el-Amarna-Tafeln*, 1915.
KBo.	*Keilschrifttexte aus Boghazköi.*
KUB.	*Keilschrifturkunden aus Boghazköi.*
OLZ.	*Orientalistische Literaturzeitung.*
QS.	*Quarterly Statement*, Palestine Exploration Fund.
RB.	*Revue Biblique.*
S.	O. Schroeder, *Die Tontafeln von el-Amarna*, 1915.
Sachau.	E. Sachau, *Aramäische Papyrus und Ostraka aus Elephantine*, 1911.
Sayce-Cowley.	A. H. Sayce and A. Cowley, *Aramaic Papyri discovered at Assuan*, 1906.
Sprengling.	M. Sprengling, "The Aramaic Papyri of Elephantine," *AJT.*, XXI, 1917, 411 ff.; XXII, 1918, 349 ff.
Ungnad.	A. Ungnad, *Aramäische Papyrus*, 1911.
ZAW.	*Zeitschrift für die alttestamentliche Wissenschaft.*
ZDPV.	*Zeitschrift der deutschen Palästinaverein.*

ABBREVIATIONS

AJSL.	American Journal of Semitic Languages.
AJT.	American Journal of Theology.
Ann.	Annual of the American School of Oriental Research.
BE.	C. Harold and E. A. W. Budge, The Tell el-Amarna Tablets in the British Museum, 1892.
BoTU.	E. Forrer, Die Boghazköi-Texte in Umschrift.
Bull.	Bulletin of the American Schools of Oriental Research.
CH.	Code of Hammurabi.
Cowley.	A. Cowley, Aramaic Papyri of the Vth Century B. C., 1923.
JAOS.	Journal of the American Oriental Society.
JBL.	Journal of Biblical Literature.
JEA.	Journal of Egyptian Archæology.
JPOS.	Journal of the Palestine Oriental Society.
K.	L. A. Knudtzon, Die el-Amarna-Tafeln, 1915.
Mits.	Mitteilungen aus Boghazköi.
KUB.	Keilschrifturkunden aus Boghazköi.
OLZ.	Orientalistische Literaturzeitung.
QS.	Quarterly Statement, Palestine Exploration Fund.
RB.	Revue Biblique.
S.	O. Schroeder, Die Tontafeln von el-Amarna, 1915.
Sachau.	E. Sachau, Aramäische Papyrus und Ostraka aus Elephantine, 1911.
Sayce-Cowley.	A. H. Sayce and A. Cowley, Aramaic Papyri discovered at Assuan, 1906.
Spurrelling.	M. Spurrelling, "The Aramaic Papyri of Elephantine," AJT, XXI, 1917, 411 ff.; XXII, 1918, 240 ff.
Ungnad.	A. Ungnad, Aramäische Papyrus, 1911.
ZA.	Zeitschrift für die alttestamentliche Wissenschaft.
ZDPV.	Zeitschrift des deutschen Palästinavereins.

HISTORY OF
PALESTINE AND SYRIA

HISTORY OF PALESTINE AND SYRIA

CHAPTER I

IN THE BEGINNING

At the dawn of earth history there was no Holy Land. From the waste of primæval waters projected areas of granite, gneiss, and similar crystalline rocks; their deep-lying remnants may yet be detected east and southeast of the Dead Sea and in Sinai. Over these in Precambrian times were deposited regular water-laid strata, torn and shot through by porphyries and like igneous products of the subterranean forces which have left their trace in ash and volcanic bombs.

Life made its appearance in the Cambrian seas with brachiopods and trilobites. Equally portentous for the future was the building up of the strata which one day were to be exploited for their copper. During the remainder of the Palæozoic Period and well into the Mesozoic, our territory was an outlier of a huge continent which stretched in a solid block from Australia to South America. Only its northern and southern borders were washed by the waters. Sandstones deposited in the southern seas during Carboniferous times were to give the effect of watered silk to the rock-cut Edomite capital of Sela; the contemporary red sandstones of Sinai were to furnish copper for Egyptian technology and turquoise for Egyptian ladies.

Then the land began to sink. A sea of unknown extent touched the East Jordan country in Triassic times. The Jurassic sea intruded into what was to be Central Syria, laid the foundations of Lebanon, and formed the rocks whose mines were to provide a scant supply of easily worked iron; it likewise touched the East Jordan region and covered the southern margin.

For a brief age all Syria was dry land, but subsidence quickly recommenced and on a greater scale. The Central Syrian gulf again appeared towards the end of Lower Cretaceous or Chalk times, and in it were deposited the Nubian sandstones whose varied colours, red, ochre, brown, violet, black, lend such picturesqueness to the landscape. Strange cycad-like trees were washed down into the shallow waters, where their trunks and leaves were preserved in lignite or in pyrites while their resin was transformed into a poor variety of amber. Water seeped through the crumbling sandstone to pour forth in springs where it met the more massive underlying limestone, the easily disintegrated rock permits to-day the growth of that band of pines which declares the sandstone level to the distant sea. Other sandstones appear in Galilee and Samaria, east of the Dead Sea, and so into Edom. Here and there basaltic rocks broke through.

The waves of a far-extending east to west sea covered the whole land in Upper Chalk times, and in it were formed the rocks which constitute the backbone of the country. Among them were the limestones, whose greyish colour dominates the landscape and whose wealth of fossil shells and fish permits such exact delimitation of the various horizons. In these limestones were carved the caves and shelters which man was to take as his first abode; from their included flint nodules he manufactured his first implements; their erosion produced the soils for his still later agriculture; at the margin between their softer and their harder strata gushed forth springs of sparkling water. When free-standing buildings were erected, it was from these same limestones that man quarried his blocks, the *meleki* or "royal," rose white or bright rose, easily worked and beloved of early architects, or the more refractory *mizzi*, the "excellent," green, green red, or delicately streaked with prismatic colours, preferred by their present-day successors. Marls, clays, gypsum and asphalt deposits—all were to be turned to man's use.

For a short age, at the very close of Chalk times, the land rose above the seas, only to be covered again at the beginning of the third and last great geological division, the Cenozoic. The waters of the Eocene, the "Dawn of the New," covered less territory than did the Chalk sea, for Lebanon, Upper Galilee, and perhaps Judah, were islands with something of their present contour. Serpentines were intruded through the crust in North Syria, basalts were scattered farther south.

With the Oligocene, a "Little of the New," dry land was everywhere in our region. Denudation began to wear down the uplifted strata, tilting and faulting changed the contour, perhaps already the strain on the earth's crust was producing north and south faulting to eventuate later in the great Jordan-Dead Sea depression. A rich and varied vertebrate life had made its appearance in Egypt by the Upper Eocene, and soon after the land was covered with extensive forests of tall trees; we may be sure that much the same wealth of animal and vegetable life was to be found in our territory.

Meanwhile, the once-great ocean was slowly contracting towards the limits of the historical Mediterranean. But the shore line sank some fifteen hundred feet below its present level along the Central Syrian coast during the Miocene, the "Middle of the New," and in these waters were built up the cliffs at the Dog River, to become the greatest outdoor museum of history. Already earth stresses had produced a notable fault between Amanus and Casius, the last outlier of the mountain systems of Asia Minor and Armenia, and had thus prepared the great highway from the sea to North Syria; now the waters entered the break and extended as far as the future site of Aleppo. An inland Mesopotamian sea washed the coast of a narrower North and Central Syria, and laid down clays, marls, and gypsums bearing salt and oil, the result of a dry desert climate. The Mediterranean likewise broke through into the sunken area between the hills of Galilee and Samaria, and filled the prototype of the Megiddo plain; as yet there was no connection with the Jordan-Dead Sea depression, which was evolving through the same earth stresses that were forming the Red Sea to the south.

Still nearer to the present was the contour of the Pliocene,

"More of the New." At first our entire area was above the sea. As the land was being elevated the terrific strain proved too much for the tortured crust. Portions of the surface were raised still higher, other sections cracked under the strain and dropped down into great fissures running east and west or southeast and northwest. Breaks between Casius and Bargylus and between Bargylus and Lebanon were added to the already-formed break between Casius and Amanus, and all three were to afford coming man entrances from the coast to the interior. The great sinks in the Megiddo and Jordan-Dead Sea regions became more pronounced, the south sank from three to six hundred feet. Through the fissures produced by the earth stresses igneous rocks flowed forth and great sheets of basalt covered whole sections. Contours were increasingly irregular and the surface waters collected into streams which cut down through the rocks and deposited alluvium along their banks in their effort to reach the Mediterranean.

By the middle of the Pliocene the sea rose to about its last level. The three passages into North Syria were partially filled, a parallel line of shallow fresh-water lakes cut through what are now Lebanon and Anti-Lebanon, the level of the Jordan-Dead Sea waters rose with the heavy rains. For a time the Mediterranean gulf of Megiddo forced its way into the Jordan, but before the end of the Pliocene the watershed between the Jordan and the Kishon had been established. Sheets of basalt closed in part the gap between Lebanon and Bargylus and extended far east, volcanoes were upreared in the Megiddo plain and the Hauran. Living species of shell-forming animals are found in blue clay beds along the southern coast.

Was man already in our territory at the beginning of the Pleistocene, the "Most of the New"? No evidence compels an affirmative answer, yet there are indications which make us hesitate to reply with a direct negative. Primates had appeared on earth in the Eocene. An exceedingly primitive ape lived in Egypt during the Oligocene and his cousins may have roamed our area. By the Miocene apes were well distributed over the world, and in the Pliocene there were species which were not far distant from man.[1]

Primitive man undertook his long upward climb towards civilisation with nothing but his bare hands and his partially developed brain. Under the pressure of a bitterly hostile environment he advanced to the use of tools. His earliest, the branch of a tree, a bit of wood, have naturally left no traces. The next step was the use of rocks, at first in their natural state, then with a slight chipping of the edges to better fit his hand. Such eoliths or "dawn stones" can with difficulty be distinguished from the sports of nature; alleged eoliths have been picked up in Moab and Ammon, but their human manufacture remains doubtful.

With the transition from the Pliocene to the Pleistocene our area had assumed essentially its present character, yet the work of nature was still incomplete. A new Red Sea sent forth its arms east and west of the Sinaitic peninsula, and through the more westerly its waters for a time united with those of the Mediterranean; the waves reached a hundred feet or more above their present level and laid down sandstones and conglomerates over the Negeb and the Shephelah, and along the Syrian coast. Long, narrow, north-and-south lakes occupied the interior and deposited their sands, gravels, clays, and conglomerates.

Already in the later Pliocene there had been heavy rains; during the ages of transition they culminated in the First Pluvial Period. In the northern portions of Europe and America the cold and moisture produced glaciation, and so the period is there called the First Glacial; in our area the cold and moisture resulted only in a lowered temperature and in greater precipitation. The streams were filled to overflowing, great banks were piled up at their deltas and along their courses; cut down by the lessened flow of a succeeding period of aridity, they tower seven hundred feet above the shore line of the present Dead Sea.[2]

There followed a yet more pronounced faulting of the earth's

[1]Cf. G. G. MacCurdy, *Human Origins*, 1924, I, 294 ff.   [2]Fig. 1 f.

surface. The Jordan-Dead Sea depression assumed approximately its present character, Anti-Lebanon and Hermon were raised to new heights, between them and Lebanon was a place for Hollow Syria, the territory beyond the southeastern border sank. While the depression of Hollow Syria was to give man a soil and a location well suited for future development, far different results followed the other changes. Dead Sea and Jordan shut off definitely what lay east from what lay west. The great sink to the eastward once for all made impossible ordered settlement in the whole region, for its level was now just too low to catch the moisture-laden winds from the Mediterranean. Thus began the desert which through all history was so to influence the settled country. The terrific faulting gave opportunity for still more terrific outpourings of igneous rock, which covered the Golan and Hauran with basalt and extended north to the Taurus.

This First Pluvial Period was followed by the First Interpluvial Period, relatively short to the geologists, but enormously long in actual number of years. A desert climate dried up the brackish interior lakes and left behind great deposits of gypsum and rock salt, such as Mount Sodom at the southwest corner of the Dead Sea. Man was now certainly at home in our region, and he had made long steps forward.

The world into which man had adventured was on the whole not unlike that which he inhabits to-day. There were still to be slight changes in contour, due to deeper erosion of the valleys or to the capture of one river by the backward cutting of another, bottom lands were yet to be created, sand banks were to form along the coast from the drifting sediment borne across the sea from the northward moving mouths of the Nile, climate was to be both warmer and colder, the landscape was to be remade by the advance of culture, but the land itself was to remain in all essentials henceforth the same.

A glance at the map and we realise that our land is the centre of the Near East as the Near East is the centre of the Old World. Primitive man knew no map, he was at best conscious that there were regions beyond his own, yet even then

FIG. 1. ON THE SHORES OF THE DEAD SEA.
(Cape Tafileh from the North.)

FIG. 2. THE HILLS ABOUT THE DEAD SEA.
(Wadi esh-Sheqiq and Mount Jerrah.)

position meant much, and its significance was to increase with the ages. The Near East, the geographical centre of the Old World, was its cultural centre as well, and from it cultural waves repeatedly passed to the periphery. Our land, the centre of the Near East, might have played a similar part, but this it has not done. Always its culture has been largely formed of elements borrowed from its neighbours; that this habit dates back to prehistoric times is proved by the unity of the oldest palæolithic culture.

Man had somehow discovered that flint can be broken to any desired shape and he used this knowledge to make tools. The earliest implement certainly manufactured by man was the fist-hatchet, a core of flint from which fragments had been flaked off to produce a rude pear-shaped object, easily grasped in the hand and available for either cutting or pounding. Such artifacts, in their crudest form, have been found on the promontory of Beirut, on the hills back of Sidon, and in the Bargylus.[3]

After centuries of unconscious experimentation, how many we cannot even conjecture, a more developed fist-hatchet was evolved, and this we call Chellean. In Upper Egypt similar Chellean artifacts have been found embedded in a great terrace a hundred feet above the present Nile, and over three other terraces which have preserved Palæolithic implements of later date. Chellean man was therefore in Egypt before the pluvial period whose rains raised the river to a height sufficient to deposit these enormous masses of gravel. To which pluvial period must we assign this terrace? If it was laid down only in the Second Pluvial Period, Chellean man was in Egypt by the First Interpluvial; if the terrace is rather to be dated to the First Pluvial, the first appearance of the already developed Chellean culture must be pushed back to the very dawn of the Pleistocene, while we are left with a vista of still longer and yet earlier ages during which man was taking his first timid steps towards civilisation. Any estimate in actual years of the age of this early culture is obviously absurd, but

[3]Fig. 4; E. Passemard, *Syria*, VIII, 1927, 342 ff.

it is equally obvious that such an estimate must be in hundreds of thousands of years.[4]

Implements of essentially this same type have been found in a long semicircle, extending from Western Europe through North Africa to Arabia and Persia. This likeness in type presumes a common culture, amazing as it may appear at so primitive a stage. Our land cannot have been far from the original centre of dispersion, and Chellean man must have been there about the same time that he appeared in Egypt.

We can learn something of his life from the implements he left, we may conjecture a trifle more from primitive races of the present. He owned no home or at best a mere wind break. His tools lie in the open, on the plateaus east and west of the Jordan, or are buried in stratified deposits along the Phœnician coast. The fist-hatchet remained his chief implement, but it was more carefully flaked, while to it were added other flint tools, a hammer to flake the stone, a scraper to prepare the skins for clothing, a borer to punch holes for the sinews which took the place of thread. Workshops have been found with the cores from which the fist-hatchets were flaked; the flakes themselves were then chipped to produce smaller artifacts.

Chellean man was not even a hunter, for he has left no hunting weapons. The land was roamed by savage animals, the elephant, the woolly rhinoceros, the early bison, the wild ox, the Syrian bear, the wild boar. They brought sudden danger and great fear, but now and then they might be trapped, as might the red, fallow, or Mesopotamian deer or the early goat. Otherwise, his food was what might be caught with his hands or what grew by itself. He had presumably discovered fire to warm him and to roast his food. Doubtless he possessed a single mate, but there could have been little family life, and beyond the family there would be no social organization. There was small need of language, since there were few with whom to converse. His fear of a hostile nature may have led him to suspect some power beyond himself.[5]

[4]K. S. Sandford and W. J. Arkell, *First Report of the Prehistoric Survey Expedition*, 1928; *Paleolithic Man and the Nile-Faiyum Divide*, 1929, and especially the remarks of J. H. Breasted, p. ix.

[5]For general sketches of early Near Eastern prehistory, cf. J. H. Breasted,

Fig. 3. WITHIN THE CAVE OF EL ZUTTIYEH, THE FINDING PLACE OF THE SKULL.

Fig. 4. PRECHELLEAN ARTIFACTS FROM THE CAPE AT BEIRUT.

Fig. 5. THE "MAN OF GALILEE."

So brief, geologically speaking, was the First Interpluvial Period, that the Second Pluvial Period may be considered as in a sense the continuation of the First. In Egypt, the second artifact bearing terrace shows that man had advanced to another culture stage, the Acheulean. Acheulean implements have not been so clearly differentiated in our region, but there are sufficient examples of smaller and more finely flaked fist hatchets and parallel types of lesser artifacts found at higher levels to assure us that the Acheulean innovations had reached its inhabitants.

What race of man inhabited the Near East during earlier Palæolithic times we cannot say; it is only with the cultural period we now enter, the Mousterian, that we can speak with certainty. Late Mousterian strata in a cave on the northwest shore of the Lake of Galilee have given us a skull which shows the closest affinity to the remains of that Neanderthal race which occupied Western Europe in Mousterian days. The characteristics of this "Man of Galilee," in reality, it would appear, a young woman, may be described in terms of the better preserved skeletons from the west.[6]

Neanderthal man was short in stature, the tallest male reaching but five feet five inches. He was stocky in build and was heavily muscled. His spine was almost straight and he could not stand quite erect. As might be expected from his build, he possessed a huge chest with massive ribs. Although his upper arm was long, his forearm was short. Hands and feet were large and did not much differ, for while the fingers were short and stubby and the thumb was close in, his great toe was almost a thumb and could be used for picking up food or for climbing. He was flat-footed and intoed, and his short curved lower leg forced him to shamble along. When at rest he assumed a squatting position.

His head was huge and set forward on his stooping shoulders, his lower jaw was outjutting and with practically no

Scientific Monthly, 1919, 289 ff.; M. Blanckenhorn, *Die Steinzeit Palästina-Syriens und Nordafricas*, 1921; J. L. Myres, in *Cambridge Ancient History*, I, 1923, 1 ff.; V. G. Childe, *The Most Ancient East*, 1928.

[6]Fig. 3 f.; F. Turville-Petre, *Researches in Prehistoric Galilee*, 1927.

chin, his teeth were large, his nose was flat. Heavy brow ridges projected over his large eye sockets, his head and face were long, his cheeks were flat, and flat also was the top of his skull, which projected far back. This huge head and thick skull held a brain which was decidedly large but with extremely simple convolutions. Neanderthal man was in every sense of the word a "low brow," for the frontal portion of the brain, where the higher mental activities are controlled, was little developed. In body and brain alike he was greatly inferior to any living race.

From the high plateaus, then more wooded than now, he descended into the valleys and to the sea coast. He was not, however, the only being that found the land good, and he must contest its possession with the whole list of savage animals. Like them, he hunted the various species of goat and deer, the stag and the antelope. His home was now more frequently a cave, cut by the waves of the sea or etched out by the waters seeping through the limestone hills. Hearths, ashes, and charcoal testify to the more frequent eating of cooked meats.

Mousterian tools, though still of flint, were more numerous and more varied. The fist-hatchet had become an axe, triangular or ovoid, and delicately retouched. Smaller flakes were formed into points; some, long, narrow, and sharp, may have been bound on a wooden staff to serve as spear heads. True borers appeared and bone needles were manufactured for the sinews used as thread.

Man had passed the age of pure utility and was thinking of the beautiful. Beauty he found in sea shells or in the teeth of the bear which he pierced and strung for his neck. In Europe, Neanderthal man buried his dead with their most prized possessions and thus indicated his belief in a future existence; no doubt it is mere accident that similar interments have not been found in our area.

A Third Pluvial Period brought renewed rains and cold of still greater intensity. Along the Mediterranean coast the land sank some two hundred and fifty feet. Glaciers or near glaciers appeared on the summits of Lebanon and Amanus, Anti-Leb-

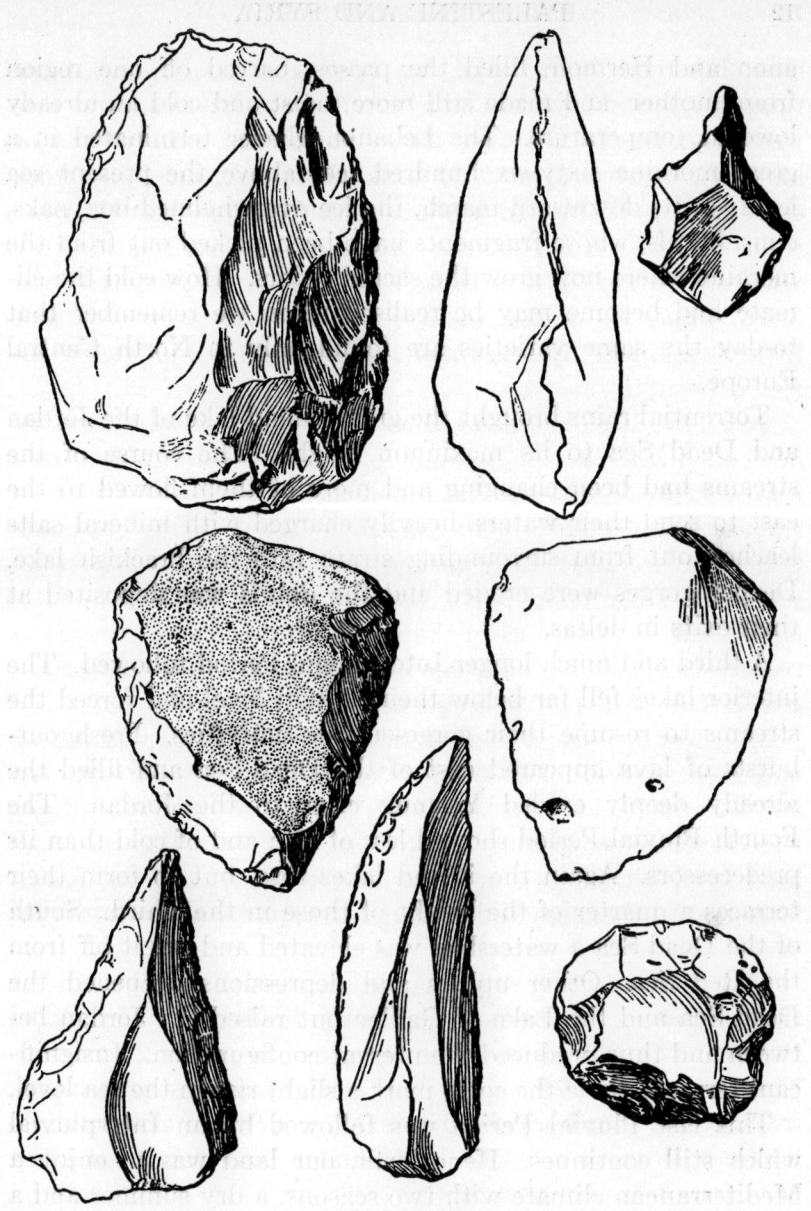

FIG. 6. MOUSTERIAN FIST HATCHET, BORER, SIDE SCRAPER, POINT, BLADE, AND DISK.
(Implements associated with the "Man of Galilee.")

anon and Hermon, filled the passes, barred off one region from another, and made still more moist and cold an already lowered temperature. The Lebanon glacier terminated in a great moraine sixty-six hundred feet above the present sea level; in its downward march, the ice overwhelmed box, oaks, elms, hazels, whose fragments have been picked out from the moraine where now grow the sacred cedars. How cold the climate had become may be realised when we remember that to-day the same varieties are found only in North Central Europe.

Torrential rains brought the great inland lake of the Jordan and Dead Sea to its maximum height. The course of the streams had been changing and more of them flowed to the east to send their waters, heavily charged with mineral salts leached out from surrounding strata into the brackish lake. Deeper gorges were eroded and the debris was deposited at their exits in deltas.

A third and much longer Interpluvial Period followed. The interior lakes fell far below their present level and forced the streams to resume their gorge-cutting activities. Fresh outbursts of lava appeared east of the Dead Sea and filled the already deeply eroded Yarmuk clear to the Jordan. The Fourth Pluvial Period showed less of rain and of cold than its predecessors. Again the inland lakes rose, but to form their terraces a quarter of the height of those in the Third. South of the Dead Sea a watershed was elevated and cut it off from the Red Sea. Other uplifts and depressions deepened the Dead Sea and the Lake of Galilee but raised the Jordan between and thus produced the present configuration. Insignificant terraces along the coast mark a slight rise in the sea level.

This last Pluvial Period was followed by an Interpluvial which still continues. Henceforth, our land was to enjoy a Mediterranean climate with two seasons, a dry summer and a rainy winter. Man might use the same products of wild nature as to-day.[7]

---

[7] This sketch of geological history is based on M. Blanckenhorn, *Syrien, Arabien, und Mesopotamien* (*Handbuch der Regionalen Geologie*, V, 4), 1914,

Mousterian remains are found in Egypt in both the third and fourth artifact-bearing terraces. Furthermore, the native Mousterian culture is directly continued through three phases of the Sebilian to the close of the Palæolithic. Much the same phenomena are to be observed in Palestine. The late Mousterian implements associated with the "Man of Galilee" show the industry still in its prime and even employing numerous fist-hatchets, yet some of the artifacts would be called Aurignacian in Europe, where they are associated with men of our own human species. The cave of Shukbah, northwest of Jerusalem, was occupied before the last Pluvial Period, but here again we find a varied series of finely worked artifacts, some of which, like the scrapers, also have an Aurignacian appearance. Could we be certain that the skeletal remains of present-day type belong to this stratum, we should prove that the two species actually lived side by side and borrowed cultural elements from each other.[8]

The three phases of the Egyptian Sebilian seem to be paralleled by the three Upper Palæolithic strata found in Mugharet el-Wad near Shukbah.[9] Throughout Syria and Palestine we have numerous sites where the remains have been ascribed to the Upper Palæolithic, but the exact determination is uncertain. Flint was flaked into many shapes, such as points, knives, scrapers, and saws; hammers were of basalt, awls of bone, polishing implements of stag horn. As compared with the earlier artifacts, the flint industry shows definite decline; the average implement was roughly shaped and retouching was rare.

For food these men of the Upper Palæolithic preferred the Mesopotamian deer, the stag, the chamois, the wild goat, and the gazelle. More rarely they dined on the wild bison, the boar, the horse, the bear, the lynx, the panther, the fox, the

checked by such later studies as P. Range, *Die Isthmuswüste und Palästina*, 1926; G. Zumoffen, *Géologie du Liban*, 1926; L. Picard, *ZDPV.*, LI, 1928, 5 ff.; LII, 1929, 24 ff.; F. M. Abel, *RB.*, NS., XXXVIII, 1929, 513 ff.; and especially by the already mentioned works of Sandford and Arkell.

[8]Fig. 6; Turville-Petre, *op. cit.*; Dorothy A. E. Garrod, *QS.*, 1928, 183 ff.; 1929, 220 ff.

[9]Garrod, *QS.*, 1929, 221.

marten, or the hare. The bones were split for the extraction of the much loved marrow; split bones from human skeletons prove them at least occasional cannibals.

In the last phase of the Egyptian Sebilian and at the very close of the European Palæolithic, the typical implement is the microlith or tiny artifact. The same date is now established for the microlithic industry of Syria and Palestine. Small triangular points with blunted edges and squared ends may have been fitted into a holder of wood or bone, which was then used as a harpoon to catch fish or as a spiked club to strike down game. Other microliths are crescent knives, borers, scrapers, or pygmy cores. Bone is in general use for points and for needles. Art appears in bone beads, a bone plaque with parallel lines incised in groups here and there on its edge, a bull calf carved in bone, a pebble shaped to represent a human head. Like their contemporaries to south and west, the men of the microlithic period found their chief food supply in snails and shell fish. Burial was by family, in one case six children and four young people, and the dead took with them to the after world their most prized possessions.[10]

During the enormously long ages of the Palæolithic, man was slowly advancing, though the whole evolution did not take place in our area. By its close, something like ten thousand years ago, certain ground had been won. The family had been consolidated, perhaps the germs of a higher social organisation were already in evidence. If war was yet to be born, struggle was constant, and with fellow men as well as with beasts. Man's food supply had enormously increased in variety and in certainty, and he could roast the food which his better weapons secured. The cold had taught him to use clothing and he was becoming vaguely conscious of modesty. The cold had also forced him to take refuge in a cave, and henceforth he possessed something which he might call a home.

Above all, and of special importance to the student of Pales-

[10]Garrod, *QS.*, 1928, 182 ff.; 1929, 220 ff.; G. Zumoffen, *L'Anthropologie*, VIII, 1897, 272 ff.; H. Vincent, *Canaan*, 1907, 361 ff.; P. Karge, *Rephaim*, 1917; M. Blanckenhorn, *Die Steinzeit;* H. Obermaier, in M. Ebert, *Reallexikon der Vorgeschichte*, X, 1927, 7 ff.

tinian history, man had begun to sense a something outside himself. No longer was he helpless in the face of a hostile nature. He might be surrounded by powers which killed or maimed or caused his all too frequent illness or deprived him of sorely needed food; by practices handed down from the fathers the evil could be warded off and the good secured. The most efficacious charms were in possession of the medicine man, whose mystic knowledge might bring him leadership in times of crisis.

Death itself was no longer supreme. By magic, death could be warded off; by magic, one could avert the now malignant spirit of the dead companion. By magic again, aided by the tools and ornaments placed in the grave, the dead might hope for a happy life in the after world. To us of to-day this is magic of the lowest sort, but it was the beginning of religion. From it were to come the highest forms of religious thought, for in these first sensings of a power beyond the individual was a something which was to end in the conception of a God.

CHAPTER II

CAVE MEN, FARMERS, AND GIANTS

LATE Palæolithic culture, after a relatively brief dominance, was succeeded by a newer manner of living, the so-called Neolithic. One of the earliest elements of this culture was the polishing of stone implements, which has given to this period the name of the "Polished Stone Age." A transitional stage in this evolution has been found at the promontory of the Dog River, at its source near the Honey and Milk Springs, and near Harajel and Jaita, under the foot of Mount Sanin. The majority of the flint implements, scrapers, knives, awls, chisels, continue the Palæolithic technique, which reaches its climax in the beautifully pointed lance heads. A new culture is predicated by the saws, the triangular arrow heads, carefully retouched at the edges, and the numerous triangular axes. Half-polished axes, chisels, and daggers mark the initial stages of the polishing technique which culminates in other fully smoothed implements.[1]

Pottery was a more important element in this new culture. The whole early evolution of the art can be traced on these sites. At first the jars were baked in the sun. Next the jars were placed in an open hearth which fired only the outer surface. The third step was an arrangement of the fire which permitted both outer and inner faces to receive the direct heat. By the end of our period the fourth step had just been taken, the application of semicircular or triangular handles which left only tiny orifices.

No attempt was made to cleanse the clay. The jars were rudely shaped by hand. Their only colour was the natural black or brown produced by the firing, with perhaps a slip of finer clay dissolved in water and washed on the surface. For

[1]Fig. 7.

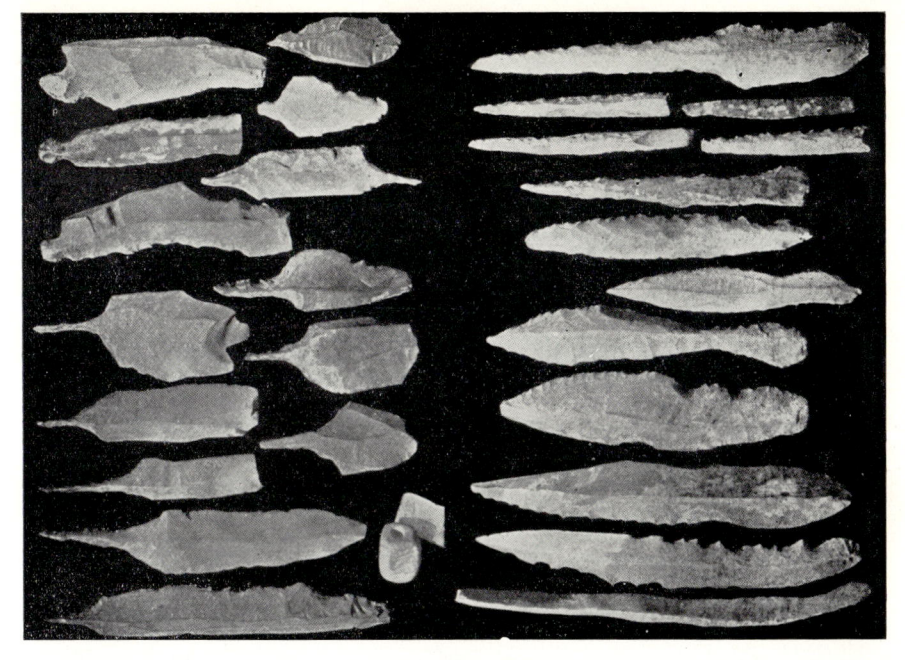

Fig. 8. FLINT IMPLEMENTS FROM SINAI.

Fig. 7. EARLY NEOLITHIC IMPLEMENTS.
(From Jaita and the Beirut Cape.)

ornament there was the crisscross or line impressed by the finger or the finger-print itself.

This invention marked an epoch. For contemporary man it made possible the transport and preservation of liquids; boiling of food was added to roasting. To the historian of modern times it affords a reliable chronology. Fashions in pottery change slowly but quite as surely as fashions of dress or of thought. More violent changes may indicate the advent of new cultural influences or even of new races.

Wild beasts contested with man the possession of the caves and furnished the major portion of the food supply; birds and shell fish varied the diet. For ornament these men wore pierced shells, especially of the petunculus, which was considered particularly efficacious as an amulet.[2]

For the racial character of the men who inhabited the Lebanon caves we have little evidence, only the fact that they were short. In this they agree with the denizens of the caves at Gezer and it is possible that they belonged to the same race. Gezer man averaged about five feet and a half in height. His arms were slender and his legs straight, though he often squatted, his skull was thick and long, with strong muscular ridges, rather flat-sided but well arched longitudinally. Brow ridges were moderately marked, the forehead was low and deeply notched. The jaw projected somewhat, the chin was low and small, the molar teeth were large. As might be expected from his debased appearance, his brain was of small capacity. Similar types are to-day scattered thinly over South Persia, Babylonia, and Arabia; from these modern representatives of the Gezer race we may add the further characteristics of a dark skin and fuzzy hair.[3]

Gezer's rocky hill, on the margin of a fertile coastal plain and at an exit from the plateau, was full of natural caves where the first inhabitants took refuge. These caves were then enlarged or were imitated in new grottoes. Entrance through the low roof was by a rock-cut staircase, a ramp, or a mere

[2]G. Zumoffen, *L'Anthropologie*, VIII, 1897, 426 ff.
[3]R. A. S. Macalister, *The Excavation of Gezer*, 1912, I, 59.

hole. Fat-burning lamps lighted the dark interior and were set in rock-cut niches.

Flint was still the material employed for common implements and so it was to remain far into historical times. The most usual forms were flakes roughly struck from the core or long ribbon knives, generally with blunt edges. Occasionally a sharp cutting knife was produced by fine secondary flaking along the edges.

Pottery was in general use. The clay was uncleansed and the pots were moulded by hand, though larger vessels might be built up in sections. Some were baked only in the sun, others in an open fire. Jars, jugs, amphoræ, cups, bowls, and saucers made up the forms. Ledge and loop handles had become common, bases were round or flat, the bodies tended to be globular. The commonest ornament was a moulding or incision in imitation of the cords which held the vessel together while being baked, or there were rows of punched holes or raised knobs. In all these characteristics the pottery showed close affiliation to the wares which dominated the Mediterranean in the latest prehistoric period.[3a]

To the earlier culture elements had now been added the cultivation of plants. Barley and wheat still grow in their natural wild state in our region and lend some credence to the theory that Syria was their original home. Millet was another early cereal. Flax was available for clothing and the print of textiles is to be seen on potsherds from Mizpah. Agriculture began as primitive hoe culture. In all probability the only domesticated animal was the forest beast, the pig.

Gezer's religious life centred around the sacred "Place," a roughly levelled surface covered with eighty-three cup holes, which range from eight feet in diameter and nine inches deep down to six inches across. Large cup holes are circular, small ones are generally oval or rectangular with the long side vertical and the short sides curving.[4] They are regularly found on such sites as the "Well of Souls" under the Sacred Rock at

---

[3a] *Ibid.*, I, 100 ff.; J. G. Duncan, *Corpus of Palestinian Pottery*, 1930, 10 ff.
[4] Fig. 11.

Fig. 9. GILGAL.

Fig. 10. MEGALITHIC FORT WITH ROUND TOWER NEAR RABBATH AMMON.

Fig. 11. SACRED "PLACE" AT GEZER.

CAVE MEN, FARMERS, AND GIANTS

Jerusalem, the cave of Machpelah at Hebron, and the cave at Sinai, or at Bethel, and on Mount Nebo, all of which retained their sanctity to Hebrew days.

Beneath Gezer's sacred "Place" were three caves. At the north end of the second largest was an apse with raised floor and above it an opening for the sacrificial blood, conducted by a channel from the cup holes on the upper surface where the animal was slaughtered. The heap of bones under the opening indicates that the pig was the preferred animal for sacrifice by the prehistoric peoples; this very fact made the pig an object of abhorrence to their enemies and successors, the Semites.[5] In these caverns, the first abodes of man, we learn the worship of underground powers whose dim memory was to be perpetuated in many a Biblical cave.

Another large cave was reached by a stairway and a long narrow passage ending in a chimney. On the sill of this passage the dead man was laid; the draft soon reduced his body to that peculiar white ash which fills the cave and makes its traverse so unpleasant to the modern visitor. With the corpse was placed pottery filled with food and drink, or a prized bone amulet.[6] Thus the soul was prepared for its future existence; by the burning the ghost was safely laid and no harm could touch the survivors. Under the difficult conditions of cave life it is not remarkable that few of the occupants reached an advanced age.

Armenia is to-day inhabited by a peculiar race. In height the Armenoid is medium, his body, legs, and neck are all short and stocky, his shoulders and hips, hands and feet are broad, his ankles and wrists are thick. His skin is sallow and coarse, his body is well covered with hair, the abundant hair of his head and beard is brown and wavy. But his head shape especially intrigues us, for it is the so-called "Jewish type" in its most exaggerated form. We note at once the generous nose, strongly curved and ending in a hook; it is the nose of the beauty of Canticles, "like the Tower of Lebanon that looks towards Damascus." The brown eyes, "pools of Heshbon," are

[5] Macalister, op. cit., II, 378 ff. [6] Ibid., I, 74 ff.; 285 ff.

somewhat large and are set in wide round orbits with heavy drooping upper and folded lower lids. Cheek bones are broad, the mouth is small, but the jaw is wide and square with rounded chin. In profile the forehead slopes rapidly upward, to be continued without marked break to a peak at the back of the skull, whence it drops suddenly in an almost straight

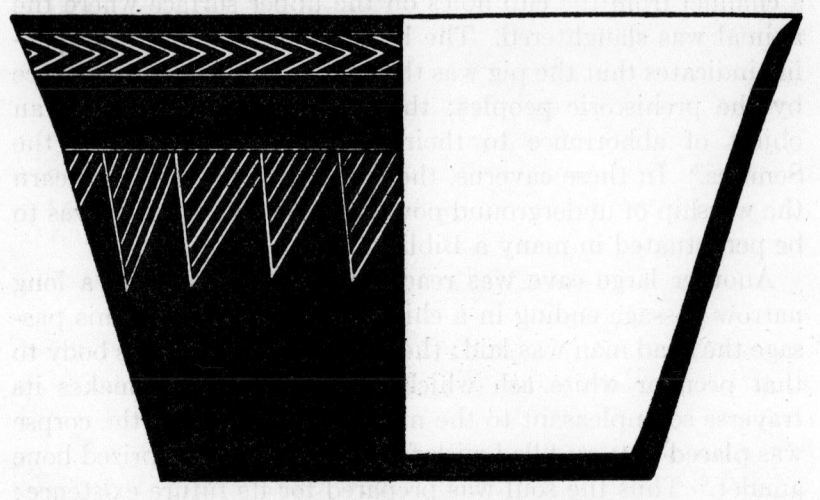

FIG. 12. BLACK WARE FROM SAKJE GEUZI.

line to the neck; now we understand why the lover of Canticles adds: "Your head is like Carmel," for there is in the headland the same sudden drop to the shore.[7]

Sakje Geuzi, in the far north of Syria, has three early levels. The first inhabitants possessed rude implements of flint, obsidian, ivory, and bone, while spindle whorls imply spinning and weaving. Sometimes the jars imitate gourds, sometimes skin vessels. Their most characteristic feature is the intense black of the surface, obtained by smoking the jar in a smothered fire, and then burnishing by hand. Ornament is secured by incision of bands, triangles, lozenges, with now and then dots, all filled with white paste.[8] In a second period the clay is

[7] Figs. 114, 169; Cant. 7:4; F. von Luschan, *Jour. Roy. Anthrop. Inst.*, XLI, 1911, 221 ff.; C. G. Seligman, *ibid.*, XLVII, 1917, 214 ff.; R. N. Salaman, *QS.*, 1925, 39; R. B. Dixon, *Racial History of Man*, 1923, 318 ff.
[8] Fig. 12.

grey with polished black slip, the jars have thinner walls, handles are rare, the bowl is the most common form. Analogies thus far are with the common early Mediterranean wares.

Painted pottery makes its appearance in the third period with dull red on yellow red, black on greenish-yellow, and black on yellow. Closely similar painted wares are found at an extremely early date and already in an advanced state of evolution on sites farther east, for example, a crisscross within lozenge pattern recalls the earliest pottery from Susa in Elam; perhaps we should look in this direction for the earliest home of the painting technique, it is not impossible that it was brought in by Armenoid invaders. The high temperature demanded for the better wares, approximately the same as for the smelting of copper, makes it reasonable to suppose this settlement was already in the Chalcolithic age, when to the flint implements were added a few copper tools.[9]

Carchemish, on a conglomerate hill thirty feet above the Euphrates and at the north end of a long fertile plain, was occupied by men with the same culture. Their pottery, found in the rectangular stone houses or in circular kilns outside the village, differs little from that of Sakje Geuzi, while geometric designs in brown, black, and red once more point the way to Susa. Placed within jars in the contracted position, the dead were buried under the beaten earth floors of their homes.[10]

Whatever the time when the Armenoids entered North Syria, they dominated the region in the historical period. Place names of unsemitic etymology may mark their advance into Central Syria.[11] They formed an important element in Canaan, they became an integral part of the Hebrew people, and to-day Armenoid features are supposed to indicate the "Jewish type" par excellence. That Armenoids were already in Canaan by late prehistoric times is proved by the discovery of their skeletons in the earliest dynastic cemeteries of Egypt.[12]

[9] J. L. Myres, *Liverpool Annals of Archæology*, I, 1908, 112 ff.
[10] C. L. Woolley, *ibid.*, VI, 1913, 87 ff.; *Carchemish*, II, 1921, 38.
[11] W. F. Albright, *AJSL*, XLI, 1925, 74.
[12] D. E. Derry, in H. Junker, *Bericht über die Grabungen in Turah*, 1912, 86 ff.

Not long before the close of the prehistoric period Gezer was encircled by a rude wall. The main structure, two feet thick and six and a half in height, was constructed of small rocks, held together by mud mortar; against this the earth was packed in rounded form with a thin surfacing of smaller stones. Flint implements remained much the same, but occasionally there was a new form, such as the knife, with larger teeth, which just at the end of the period was to evolve into the true saw.

Painted wares came down from the north, beginning with a dark brick red around the rim of the jug or saucer; later the potter imitated the drip from this line and still later the crisscross was introduced. All these were applied through the slip with which the vase was coated before firing; in the last prehistoric period, and probably under Egyptian influence, a wash of white lime was applied after the firing, and as it adhered only where the jar had no slip, the red appeared on the white. Stone palettes were employed in mixing the paint.[13]

Occasional scenes were scratched on the cave walls of Gezer. In artistic merit they barely excel the uncorrelated lines, rows of dots, and checker-board patterns by whose side they appear, but they do add to the knowledge of their culture. An ownerless bow and arrow pointing to a stag shows that the hunting habits of their ancestors had not been completely forgotten. Another scene proves that agriculture was no longer primitive hoe culture; the hoe had been reversed, perhaps first in Egypt, had been given two tiny handles, and had been hitched to the ox, tamed by castration. The horns of bulls were knobbed to prevent goring.

Domestication of the pig had been thus followed by domestication of other animals, borrowed perhaps from nomads or mountaineers, such as the bull, the buffalo, the sheep, and the goat. Beef and pork furnished the greater part of the meat diet, though mutton and goat's flesh were also eaten, but the staple food was barley or wheat cakes from meal ground by

---

[13] Macalister, *Gezer*, II, 132 ff.

rubbing stones. Grapes and olives were grown and trodden out in pits with a lower cup for the dregs.[14]

Hebrew tradition believed that the earliest inhabitants of Canaan were giants. Their race was traced back to the days before the universal flood when the sons of the gods married with the daughters of men and their progeny were mighty heroes of renown.[15] Bashan was the home of the giants, its King Og was of the remnant of the giants, for his iron bed was nearly fourteen feet long. Edrei, with its caves, and Ashtaroth Karnaim, the city of Ashtart with the two horns, were their centres. Farther south, in Moab, were the Emim, likewise counted to the giants.[16]

West of the Jordan, giants were listed among the earliest races of Canaan,[17] there was a Land of the Giants in the territory of the Joseph tribes,[18] a Valley of the Giants was near Jerusalem.[19] Around the Cave of Machpelah at Hebron lived the Sons of Anak, in whose sight the Hebrews felt themselves grasshoppers.[20] Their remnant was thought to exist in Gaza, Gath, and Ashdod, from which came such giants as Goliath to fight with David and his followers.[21] To this day the chief town of the region is called Beit Jibrin, the "House of the Giants." We can understand why the name has persisted when we enter the huge cave tombs, one four hundred feet long and eighty feet high, another containing sixty separate chambers, with their cisterns and oil presses. From the marks of metal implements on their walls we know that they cannot be earlier than Chalcolithic times.

Traditions of prehistoric giants are widely distributed over the face of the earth. Frequently they are connected with those structures of large unworked stones to which we give the name of megalithic. Such monuments, "Homes of the Giants" and the like in popular nomenclature, are also widely dis-

[14]*Ibid.*, II, 49.   [15]Gen. 6:4.
[16]Deut. 3:11 ff.; Josh. 12:4; 13:12; Gen. 14:5; Deut. 2:10 f.
[17]Gen. 15:20.   [18]Josh. 17:15.
[19]Josh. 15:8; 18:16; II Sam. 5:18; 23:13; I Chron. 11:15; 14:9; Is. 17:5.
[20]Num. 13:33; Deut. 1:28; 9:2.
[21]Josh. 11:22; II Sam. 21:16 ff.; I Chron. 20:4 ff.

tributed, through eastern and southern Asia, in South Russia, and in a long arc from North Africa and Malta, through Portugal and France to Britain and Scandinavia. They belong to a common culture which flourished during the early Chalcolithic period and they may have originated in Canaan where the megalithic monuments are found in their most primitive forms.

One of the largest and most ancient of the dolmen fields extends west from Heshbon and down the valley towards the Jordan. Along the western slopes are dolmens of the earliest type, a slab pried off the native rock and raised on one side by a smaller stone. In a second form the rocks are piled one above the other in sloping rows. At times the big cover slab is slid down hill into position over two smaller blocks. Still later types have larger covers, up to six feet in breadth, and reach higher, some enough to permit a man to stand upright within the burial chamber. A few of the finer dolmens show traces of dressing, doubtless with flint flakes. Occasionally a stone floored the chamber; more often the body was laid on the bare rock. Nearby is a five foot high standing stone with pointed top. At the west end of the spur is a heap of small stones, fifteen feet in diameter, around which is a forty foot stone circle, while rock cut cup holes are not far away. Another double circle with eight feet between the lines has a diameter of six hundred feet. Two miles farther west, at the site of Sibmah, are small tomb chambers hewn in isolated boulders; in the whole region are fifty dolmens and twenty chambers.[22]

At the head of the Zerqa is another field, a mile and a half long by a half mile wide, and containing a hundred and fifty dolmens. On a flat plateau is the "Erected Stone," eight feet high, with pointed top and a squared vertical groove in one side. West of this are two little hills, a thousand feet above a spring, with seventy dolmens. Still farther west is a smaller hill with a forty foot circle of standing stones, five to six feet high, while the hill itself is surrounded by another circle of

[22] Fig. 13; C. R. Conder, *Survey of Eastern Palestine*, 1889, 125 ff.; 159 ff.; 225 ff.

smaller stones nine hundred feet in diameter. Outside is a properly oriented square fifteen hundred feet on the side. East of the group on the hill are three parallel alignments running north and south.[23]

Other sites in Moab and Ammon show the same dolmen tombs, the same ritual standing stones, circles, and alignments.

FIG. 13. DEVELOPMENT OF THE DOLMEN.

One offers a figure eight circle with triple walls and a central standing stone in the upper half. Another shows an oval of undressed stones two hundred and fifty feet in diameter, with walls five feet high, from forty-one to twenty-seven feet thick, and divided into two unequal portions by a line somewhat north of east. Half a mile southeast on a hilltop is a disk stone six feet in diameter. North of sacred Mount Nebo with a cairn on its summit lie dolmens and a two hundred and fifty foot circle. Another disk stone of limestone is over eleven feet in diameter and is three and a half feet high, with a two foot hole in the centre; it must have been brought from a great distance, yet it weighs nineteen tons.[24]

A somewhat later type of dolmen is found to the north in Bashan and Golan. Here the dolmen is placed on a round stone foundation, five feet in height; sometimes there is a single row of stones, sometimes there are two stepped rows,

[23]*Ibid.*, 184 ff. [24]*Ibid.*, 10 ff.; 98 ff.; 158; 202 f.; 193.

sometimes three without steps. The dolmen is not placed in the middle of the platform, but towards the northeast wall; its main axis is east and west, though the two main sides are not perfectly parallel but are always closer at the east. The body,

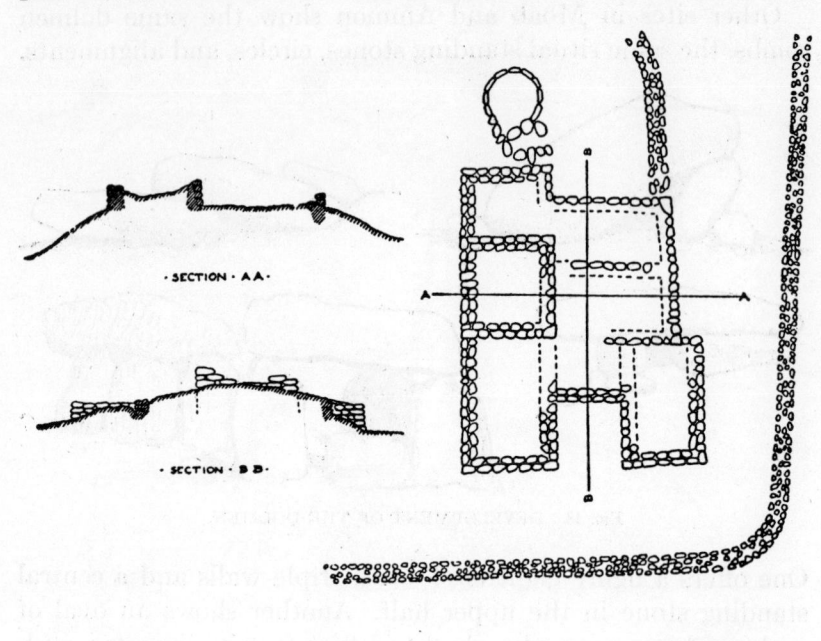

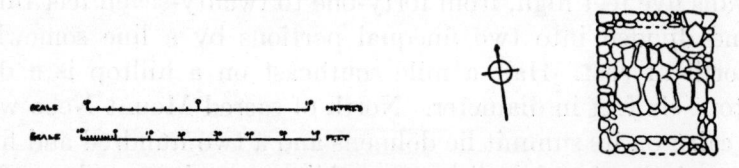

PLAN 1. MEGALITHIC RESIDENCE AND DOLMEN TOMB.
(Rabbath Ammon.)

placed on a stone, was cremated. In a single field there are close to a thousand dolmens; they are accompanied by a circle of huge blocks, forty-three feet in diameter. A few copper rings unearthed in some of the graves prove their Chalcolithic date.[25]

[25] G. Schumacher, *Northern Ajlun*, 1890, 169 ff.; 131 ff.

Still later is the tomb where the single stone is replaced by a row of massive slabs along the sides and on the top, though the single stone at the end is retained. In one of the sides is a round hole, plausibly explained as an exit for the spirit. The

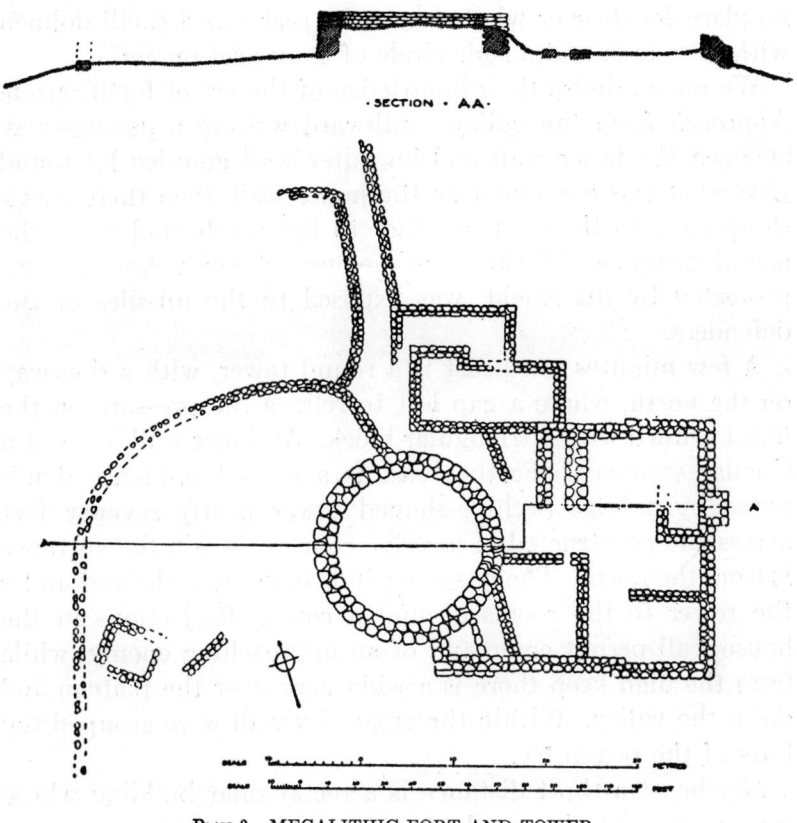

PLAN 2. MEGALITHIC FORT AND TOWER.
(Rabbath Ammon.)

latest dolmen form is the rectangular structure of several chambers, built of huge stones and roofed with yet greater slabs resting on a false vault; the chambers are oriented east and west and the opening is always to the sunrise.

Such a tomb was the last resting place of a princely family which ruled the plateau over the valley where later stood

Rabbath Ammon. A few feet away is the rounded corner of their palace enclosure wall. Two quadrangular rooms project outward and so protect the entrance to the court behind which are other chambers. Living quarters were presumably on an upper floor, since the massive courses of unhewn chert allow no place for door or window. At the rear was a small dolmen with false arch and a rude circle of stones set on end.

We must admire their knowledge of the art of fortification. Approach from the valley southward was up a passage-way between the inner wall and an outer wall guarded by round towers; it was continued by the house wall, then there was a sharp turn to the west, another to the north, and so to the actual entrance. All this time the enemy's right shoulder, unprotected by his shield, was exposed to the missiles of the defenders.

A few minutes southeast is a round tower, with a doorway on the north, where a gap left to relieve the pressure on the lintel is filled with a triangular block. An inner wall hints at a circular stairway. Farther east is a second residence dominated by a huge beehive-shaped tower nearly seventy feet across and constructed in massive courses. Again the entrance is from the north. The passage winds between walls and under the tower to the rooms around a court. Projections in the house wall permit command of an approaching enemy, while from the high keep there is a wide view over the plateau and down the valley. Within the great city wall were grouped the huts of the peasantry.

Northeast a short distance is a rectangular building whose rooms are grouped around a huge central court. Square towers jut out to east and west. A small guardroom gives entrance through the east tower to a large hall and a smaller bedroom. Use of the square tower and the balanced proportions indicate a date for this building at the end of the prehistoric period or even beyond.[26]

All the megalithic monuments hitherto described have been

---

[26] Fig. 10; plans 1-3; D. Mackenzie, *Annual of Palestine Exploration Fund*, I, 1911, 1 ff.

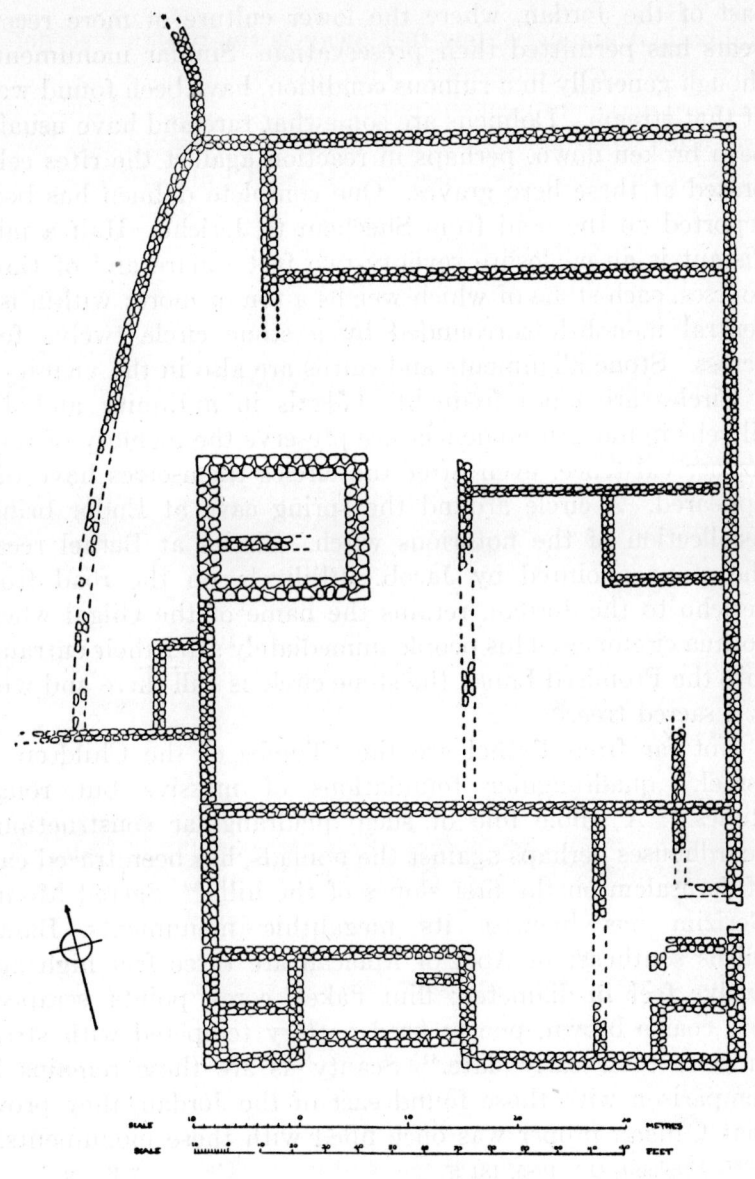

PLAN 3. FORTIFIED RESIDENCE.
(Rabbath Ammon.)

east of the Jordan, where the lower culture of more recent years has permitted their preservation. Similar monuments, though generally in a ruinous condition, have been found west of that stream. Dolmens are somewhat rare and have usually been broken down, perhaps in reaction against the rites celebrated at these hero graves. One complete dolmen has been reported on the road from Shechem to Jericho. Half a mile distant is an enclosure seventy-two feet square and of three courses, each stone of which weighs a ton or more; within is a central monolith surrounded by a stone circle twelve feet across. Stone alignments and cairns are also in the vicinity.[27]

Circles are more frequent. Gilgals in antiquity and Jiljiliyehs in modern nomenclature preserve the memory of their former existence, even after the circles themselves have disappeared. A circle around the spring cave at Endor brings recollection of the notorious witch. Circles at Bethel recall the stone anointed by Jacob. Jiljiliyeh, on the road from Jericho to the Jordan, retains the name of the Gilgal where Joshua circumcised his people immediately after their entrance into the Promised Land; the stone circle is still there and with it a sacred tree.[28]

Not far from Bethel are the "Tombs of the Children of Israel," quadrangular foundations of massive but rough stones.[29] A whole line of such quadrangular constructions, guardhouses perhaps against the nomads, has been traced east of Jerusalem on the first slopes of the hills.[30] Sacred Mount Gerizim has likewise its megalithic monuments. Basalt cairns southeast of Abel of Maacah are three feet high and twelve feet in diameter; flint flakes, cores, points, scrapers, and coarse brown, poorly fired pottery tempered with straw indicate their early date.[31] Scanty as are these remains in comparison with those found east of the Jordan, they prove that Canaan proper was once filled with these monuments.[32]

[27]L. Oliphant, *QS.*, 1885, 181 ff.   [28]Fig. 9.
[29]H. Vincent, *Canaan*, 257; R. A. S. Macalister, *QS.*, 1912, 82.
[30]H. Vincent, *RB.*, X, 1901, 278 ff.
[31]P. L. O. Guy, *Bull. British School Jerusalem*, VI, 75.
[32]H. Vincent, *Canaan*, 408 ff.; R. Kittel, *Gesch. des Volkes Israel*, 5 ed., 1923, 33 ff.; P. Karge, *Rephaim*.

These monuments carry us down to, perhaps beyond, historical times. They mark many a site which retained its sanctity into Biblical days; they contributed the standing stone, the circle, and the cairn to historical religions. Despite undoubted connections with similar remains in Asia, Africa, and Europe, their builders are to-day almost as mysterious as when the Hebrews gave the explanation "There were giants in the earth in those days."

All these peoples had reached the agricultural stage. Agriculture brought about a series of political, social, and religious changes which were nothing less than revolutionary. There was a rise in the standard of living. A much wider range of more attractive foods might be enjoyed. Population increased in numbers and was improved in quality. Men settled down and became attached to the soil. Permanent homes with village life were now the rule. Walls surrounded the village as at Gezer and afforded protection against enemies. A leader chosen for an emergency remained a permanent chief and erected such a palace as we have visited east of the Jordan. Henceforth there was a sharp dividing line between ruler and ruled. Behind the protecting village wall there was the give and take of daily life, individualism was subordinated to the common good. Specialisation of function increased, there were peasants to farm the field, merchants to trade at a distance, elders to sit in council at the village gate, and priests to invoke the will of the gods.

With the new opportunities went new dangers which must be faced. Attacks from savage beasts or from nomads who envied the new wealth were not the only dangers. Man was now dependent on the earth, which must bring forth her fruits in their seasons, and the earth was dependent on the rain that falls from the heavens. To assure himself of these blessings man must invoke new powers.

Already in Palæolithic times it was recognised that woman was the source of all life, that a mother deity was demanded to explain and to govern the phenomena of life. This belief was embodied in statuettes of the divine female, with the feminine attributes so rudely exaggerated, the first indication of a deity more clearly defined than the old vaguely recognised powers. Now it was realised that life was not confined to man or beast, it was likewise a property of the plants by which man was more and more nourished. As the child is born of the mother, so the plant is born of Mother Earth, and the Earth Mother must be propitiated and aided that she continue fruitful.

To this concept was added another equally powerful. In Palæolithic days it was the man who provided the food for the household by his hunting of the wild animals. Agriculture could be carried on by woman, for its exercise did not take her far from home or child. For these reasons religion assumed a distinctly feminine cast. By what name or names this earth goddess was invoked is unknown, but that she was in truth worshipped is indicated by the nude figurines and by the symbols of fertility which may be found wherever the agricultural stage has been reached. Such figurines have indeed been unearthed from the earliest sites in Asia Minor and North Syria, but they were slow in reaching Canaan. More rarely, a figurine represents the male companion who completes the divine family.

Nature was thus considered primarily from the view point of fertility. Plants and animals were the product of the two forces, male and female, but the forces themselves were of the earth. Even the life-giving waters sprang from Mother Earth. Such a water deity was the "Lady of the Well," Baalath Beer, whose title was preserved in a Hebrew place name.[33] Gifts were presented at her watery home, one came to the waters for purification, an oracle was located at the "Spring of Judgement," En Mishpat, the truth of a statement was sworn at the "Well of the Oath," Beer Sheba. By the sacred spring stood the sacred tree, an oak, a terebinth, a palm, or an acacia. Offerings were made to this tree, perhaps the worshipper tied to its branches a bit of his garment, as he does to this day. Oracles might be secured from the rustling

[33] Josh. 19:8.

of its leaves or by sleeping in its shade. Shrines were often set on the high places, under an isolated tree, which was a landmark for the whole country.

While the worshipper might visit the local shrine at any time, a man to ask for the success of his crops, a woman to pray for children, worship of the powers of fertility centred in the agricultural feasts. From these feasts a sacred calendar evolved.

First came New Year's Day, at the spring equinox, when the sun crossed the line and began his northward progress. At the close of the old year the old food was destroyed, all but what was needed for the sacred cakes. Fasting made certain that none of the old food was left in the body. All leaven was destroyed and for seven days the celebrants ate only the sacred unleavened bread. On the seventh day there was a sacred dance followed by sacred marriages, for now there was assurance of abundant offspring. The eighth day the villagers marched forth in solemn procession to the fields where the ripe barley was standing. A sickle of flint teeth set in wood cut the first sheaf for presentation to the deity who abode in the local sanctuary. Then only were the villagers permitted to eat the new crop, redeemed by payment of first fruits to the god whose bounty it was.

Seven weeks later, at the close of the barley and wheat harvest, two loaves baked from the new wheat were presented to the local divinity. Towards the end of summer came the turn of the vineyards. Fasting and lamentation bewailed the god of vegetation, dead from the summer heat; dancing on the floors around the vineyards, sacred marriages, and feasts witnessed the joy of his resurrection. "Profaned" by the first fruits offered the deity the grapes might now be safely eaten or pressed into the wine "that cheers both gods and men."[34] At this same time also the wood was brought in from the surrounding forests.

At the turn of the year, the fall equinox, when the sun returns south for the winter, was the feast of ingathering, the

[34]Judges 9:13.

close of the agricultural year. Pilgrims flocked to the sanctuary where they lived in booths. Again there was mourning and affliction followed by joy and the sacred dance. Water was drawn and poured out to bring by sympathetic magic the autumn rains which should revive the earth, parched by six months of drought. The sacred fire was purified. As a further rite of purification, a scapegoat was driven to the desert, so hostile to the cultivator.[35]

There were other and less innocent customs. With the sacred marriage was associated religious prostitution. In times of emergency the sacrifice of the first fruits or of animals might be supplemented by that of a human being, perhaps already the first fruits included the first-born of man. There was a sacrifice for the dead, that of the red heifer, for red was the color of death. The heifer must be slaughtered outside the sanctuary, the blood must be poured out on the ground, the flesh must be completely burned.[36] Man has always wished to know the future. Soothsayers and diviners provided this information; there was augury by birds, fire, and rain, by barley, or crumbs of bread.[37]

Such was the religion of these earliest cultivators of the soil. Parallel customs are to be traced throughout the whole Mediterranean world, and they all without question go back to the first peoples who practised agriculture. They were taken over with little change by the invading Semites, who "knew not the law of the gods of the land," and therefore worshipped the local divinities of the soil when they at last settled down. Later they were borrowed by the Hebrews, and though in time the rites were purged of their less pleasant features, there remained much that the religious leaders did not dare reject. To-day, under the thin veneer of Muslim theology, they dominate the religious life of the modern "people of the land."

[35]Cf. J. Morgenstern, *AJT.*, XXI, 1917, 275 ff.; *Jewish Quarterly Rev., N. S.*, VIII, 1917, 31 ff.; *Hebrew Union College Annual*, I, 1924, 13 ff.

[36]Num. 19; cf. J. Bewer, *JBL.*, XXIV, 1905, 41 ff.; H. P. Smith, *AJT.*, XIII, 1909, 225 ff.

[37]Cf. Ezek. 13:17 ff.

CHAPTER III

ARAB TRIBESMEN

FROM the primitive hunting stage of Palæolithic man, two parallel lines of development emerge. One, through the cultivation of plants, leads to agriculture and to a settled civilisation. In the more fertile lands around the Mediterranean this is represented by the communities we have already discussed. The other, by the domestication of animals, leads to nomadism. Through the hostility, interrelation, and ultimate fusion of these two elements a major portion of Near Eastern history has been produced.

"Arabia is the home of the Semites" is an almost universally accepted truism. It is indeed true, but with certain qualifications. "Semite" is an acceptable term for a race only if we confine its use to the natives of the North Arabian Desert. Under this definition the Semites form a subdivision of the Mediterranean race.

Egyptian monuments of nearly five thousand years ago picture the same Bedawi as can be met in the desert to-day.[1] While the Arabs belong to the Mediterranean race, they have certain peculiarities of their own. Despite his hard life the Arab is moderately tall; the males range somewhat over five feet six with now and then a man of considerably greater stature; the females are rarely over five feet five. Legs are somewhat long and with poorly developed calves, the body is slender, the muscular development is moderate. The head and face are decidedly long and narrow. In profile the head is round with no pronounced projection at the back, and with the upper portion of the skull merging roundly into the somewhat low and narrow brow. The nose is almost aquiline, large at the lower end and with moderately good-sized openings. The brows are heavy. Eye openings are rather broad and

[1]Fig. 18; cf. Fig. 2, *History of Assyria*.

square, with oblique axis; the eyes are large and prominent; in colour they range from a yellowish-brown to a brown which is almost, and in some of the women is, quite black. The mouth is generous but straight, the coarse lips are sometimes turned out, the teeth are large. Jaws are heavy, almost, but not quite, to the point of projecting; the down-dropping chin is heavy but not strong. Hair on the face is scanty, the curly beard is short by nature and is cut to a point by art, it is in colour usually dark brown.[2]

Arab nomads were the first to speak a Semitic language; we must still listen to the Arab if we would learn the essential character of this linguistic group. Like our own Indo-European languages, the Semitic is elaborately inflected, but along quite different lines. Inflection of nouns is simple, there are no compound words; this lack is partially compensated by the "construct," in which the first word of a genitival group is modified to produce a temporary compound. Suffixes and prefixes are employed as with us, especially to indicate pronominal modifications. Masculine and feminine genders are recognised but there is no neuter, for nothing is lifeless to the Semite. The complicated inflection of the verb is quite alien to our thinking. Time is little considered, and the normal tenses are but two, for continuing and completed action. Moods are numerous, as many as eight in the Arabic; they represent reflexive or causative or exaggerated action with their passives. Syntax is simple, clauses are regularly strung together with only a connecting "and."

Pronunciation of Semitic languages is difficult for the foreigner. The most characteristic sounds are the five laryngeals, the so-called "gutturals," which the stranger rarely learns. Slurred or lost when spoken by alien races, one must go to the men of the desert to hear them in their true quality. Only then do we recognise the majesty these deep singing tones give to this more than masculine language. Semitic words are

---

[2] C. G. Seligman, *Jour. Roy. Anthrop. Inst.*, XLVII, 1917, 214 ff.; R. N. Salaman, *QS.*, 1925, 39 ff.; R. B. Dixon, *Racial History of Man*, 246 ff.; Macalister, *Gezer*, I, 59 ff.

generally based on three root sounds, all consonantal; vowels are employed, in certain cases with added consonants, to modify these roots. Thus is produced that wealth of vocabulary which distinguishes the Semitic, and which permits the most subtle modification of the original concept. Nevertheless, these concepts remain concrete. Words expressing abstractions are rare, for Semitic thought clings close to the earth. It is therefore little inclined to abstract speculation, and to us appears deficient in logic, but it is full of striking images taken from nature.[3]

From times immemorial the Arabs have rejoiced in poets. To the early mind the poet was inspired by the deity, and proud indeed was the tribe which could transmit to posterity by his word of mouth the exploits of its heroes. The rhythm was accentual and its verse structure simple, but by its play of fancy and by its frequent similes it raised the hearts of all.[4]

Whence the Semites came and at what time they entered Arabia may be conjectured, but the conjectures are hopelessly varied. In prehistoric times the climate of the peninsula was more favourable than it is to-day. Water-worn Upper Chellean implements have been found nearly twelve feet deep in the gravels by the wells of Bair east of Sela or Petra. Mousterian artifacts closely similar to those found with the "Man of Galilee" are scattered over the desert between Palestine and Babylonia. Later artifacts of "neolithic type" are even more common.[5] Whether they were manufactured by Semites may be left an open question. At any rate the Semites were in North Arabia by the dawn of history.

Only North Arabia need concern us, for the inhabitants of South Arabia belonged to the Armenoid race.[5a] Central Arabia, with its east to west line of oases, whose streams permit irri-

---

[3] A. Socin, *Arabic Grammar*, 1895; K. Brockelmann, *Grundriss der vergleichenden Grammatik der semitischen Sprachen*, 1908.

[4] For modern example, all the more interesting because it was taken down by phonograph at Kadesh Barnea, where once the Moses cycle developed, cf. B. B. Charles, "A Song from the Negeb," *AJSL.*, XXXVII, 1921, 300 ff.

[5] Henry Field, *Natural History*, XXIX, 1929, 33 ff.

[5a] Seligman, l. c.

gation and the growth of towns, has little more significance. To understand the early Semites we must turn our attention to the nomads who wander the North Arabian or Syrian desert, for they alone have preserved almost without change the customs of a more primitive day.

North of the Nefud, the lesser sand waste of the peninsula, the Syrian Desert is a great wedge thrust into the Fertile Crescent which surrounds it on three sides. A few oases, in which a stream flows a short distance before it is exhausted by irrigation or is lost in the sands, or where water is found not far beneath the surface, were before the end of our story to support a few towns. At the opposite extreme are the barren deserts of drifting sands or the still more inhospitable regions covered by igneous rocks. These are all exceptions; as a whole the territory is a steppe, fit only for grazing.[6]

Rainfall is always scanty and a slight decrease in precipitation means starvation for man and beast. Even in the best years the nomad lives on short rations. Often he must content himself with milk or its products, clabber and cheese. He may buy or steal a little wheat or barley from the peasants along the desert edge, he may even demean himself enough to plant a small patch. From the oases he may secure dried dates, which furnish so much energy in so small a bulk. For the rest he is dependent on the rare life of the steppe itself, the truffles which spring up after the infrequent rains, the animals he may hunt. He may prefer the flesh of the gazelle, the antelope, or the ibex, the hare, the porcupine, and hedgehog, the bustard, ostrich, or sand grouse, but he will eat any available bird or animal, the vulture, the lizard, the hyena, while he shows no aversion to the wild boar.

Nomad life was simple. It centred around the flocks of sheep and goats domesticated in the peninsula from remotest antiquity. In them was all the nomads' scanty wealth. From their hair was made the rough clothing or the black goat's-

---

[6] C. M. Doughty, *Arabia Deserta*, 1888; D. G. Hogarth, *Penetration of Arabia*, 1904; H. Philby, *Heart of Arabia*, 1922; B. Moritz, *Arabien*, 1923; A. Musil, *Northern Hegaz*, 1926; *Arabia Deserta*, 1927; *Northern Negd*, 1928.

hair tent.[7] By their milk or more rarely by their flesh the nomads were fed. Forage for their flocks and protection against other nomad enemies was their chief occupation. When all was well there was plenty of leisure while watching the flocks or lying about the tent pole. To fill this leisure there was little but talk or sleep. Repose alternated with sudden action, the repulse of the enemy, the long journey to find fresh pastures, the welcome call to raiding or to more formal war.

Society was patriarchal in character. In marriage the husband was the *baal* or lord of his wife. Girls might watch the flocks in time of peace, but men were needed to lead the march to distant pasturage or to fight off the foe. Then a chief was demanded, and to him grudging obedience was accorded, but the crisis over, the incurable individualism of the nomad reasserted itself. The chief was now little more than the first among equals, marked out only by his superior wealth or hospitality.

Nomad individualism was little checked by the chief or even by the tribe, for the various subdivisions hung loosely enough together. The true unit and the true check was the enlarged family. Membership in a tribe and in a family was imperative, for the stranger was always in danger of his life. He was only safe when he had claimed the protection or had been offered the hospitality of an individual; then indeed the honour of the whole group was at stake. Were he killed, the blood revenge came into effect as it did in the case of one's own kinsmen, and its avenging lay on all who were closely related until the murderer was punished or the blood price was paid.[8]

In the desert there was small regard for law and no adequate means for enforcement, but there was custom, solidified public opinion. Justice might mean self help, as in the case of the blood revenge, or friends might arbitrate the difference,

---

[7] Fig. 1, *History of Assyria*.
[8] II Sam. 2:14 ff.; 3:27 ff.; 21:4; I Kings 2:5 ff.; Deut. 21:1 ff.; Num. 35:33; cf. M. Buttenwieser, *JAOS.*, XXXIX, 1919, 303 ff.

but it was always within the narrow limits of custom and of an elaborate code of honour. The man who sins against custom is an outlaw. He must leave the tribe and become a wanderer upon the face of the earth. No longer under the protection of his kinsmen, all who meet him may slay him.

Nomad religion is simple and intensely practical. As the nomad is an individualist, so are his clear-cut gods. They are primarily gods of the atmosphere, the sun who burns by day, the moon who guides by night, the storm with its thunder and lightning. All are rather terrible deities; the sun destroys the forage of the flocks, the moon drives men mad, the storm devastates while granting the longed-for rain. Yet their terror is especially directed against the enemies of the tribe, of which, after all, they are fellow members. They may punish their fellow tribesmen for sin, and the sin is more likely ritual than ethical, but they meet with them at rare feasts and they protect their own against the foe. Warfare thus partakes the character of a holy war. The gods are also exclusive, they recognise no friends outside their worshippers' range of pasturage.

Sacrifice was relatively unimportant. The Arab *Kahin*, the ancestor of our many Cohens, was no priest but rather a diviner. Animals in the desert were too precious to be often slain, and so animal sacrifice was rare.[9] When sacrificed, the bones must not be broken, lest the animal not live again, nor must the blood be eaten, for in it was the life.[10] At the spring equinox, when the evil spirits who haunt the desert endangered the lives of the nomads, the passover was sacrificed, a lamb whose blood was sprinkled on the tent posts. To the gods belonged the firstlings, including those of man himself, though these might be redeemed by substitution. These sacrifices could not be eaten by the worshipper; in other sacred meals the nomad partook of the covenant sacrifice in company with his fellow tribesmen, the gods.[11]

Beneath and upon the earth, in trees or animals, and in the

---

[9] Cf. Amos 5:25; Jer. 7:22.　　[10] Ex. 12:46; Num. 9:12; Ezek. 37.
[11] Cf. J. Morgenstern, *JAOS.*, XXXVI, 1916, 146 ff.; XXXVIII, 1918, 133.

heavens were other spirits, often malignant, whose dangers must be avoided. The moon set times and seasons which were lucky or the reverse. The will of the gods might be observed from omens or the god might make his appearance in a dream. Soothsayers and seers predicted the future, witches brought harm by their magic. Circumcision was a rite of importance.

Life in the desert is hard and there is nothing to hope in the next. Death is virtually the end. Great heaps are piled over the wicked and each passer-by adds his stone accompanied by a curse. Ordinary men are at once wrapped in their robes and are placed under the earth. Sheep may be sacrificed and the blood allowed to run down into the grave as a "blessing on account of the sheep." Rude headstones will be set on the grave, blood from the sacrifice will be smeared upon it, the hands of the mourners will be washed, and the jars broken.

Nevertheless, the dead, if good or strong, may help the living. Pilgrimage is therefore made to the grave. Sacrifice of a lamb insures recovery of sickly flocks, a similar sacrifice when a child has died will save the remainder of the family, promise of a lamb will bring return from a dangerous journey.

In the North Arabian Desert the Semite wandered for long centuries. The hard life and the severe climate trained him to the limit of endurance. Then continued years of drought or perhaps overpopulation drove him out to fall upon the settled country whose comforts he had long envied from afar. This process was repeated time and again, frequently on a small scale, at almost regular intervals in a mightier wave of migration.

All his nomad qualities persist long after he has left the desert. As he wandered in the desert, so he wanders still, whether at the head of an army or as a merchant. He is the middleman, rather than the originator or the man who brings matters to completion. When he settles down to agriculture he takes over the religion of the land. Sometimes he yields to its seductions and gives himself up to sensual indulgence. Yet ever there is reaction and reform. Sensuality is replaced by asceticism, the severe custom of the desert. "Back to the desert ways" is the cry of prophet and reformer, and their call is heard by many. Neolithic religion gave much to the Hebrew, but it was the desert influence which raised it to the heights.[12]

[12]Cf. *History of Assyria*, 1 ff.

CHAPTER IV

THE BRIDGE OF ASSEMBLY

Three miles south of the Lake of Galilee the Jordan is crossed by two bridges. One is a modern railway bridge. At rare intervals a locomotive puffs over on the last lap of its easy path across the series of small plains from the sea before it begins its sharp climb to the plateau east of the river and so on to Damascus. The other bridge is older. Its pointed arch is Saracenic, but its lower courses are of Roman construction. The natives call it Jisr el Mujamia, the "Bridge of Assembly"; the name comes from the same Arabic root as *jami,* "mosque," and a more free translation might be the "Bridge of Assembled Peoples."[1]

The line followed by the railroad has always been one of the great world routes. Before the railroad it was traversed by the Arabs, still earlier by the Romans, but long before the day when they built and rebuilt the bridge many peoples had forded the river at this spot. It was on the line of the greatest of all roads of oriental antiquity, the "Great Trade Route" of the Ancient Orient.

"Bridge of Assembly"—the very name is a parable. Canaan and Syria do form a bridge. Passage is possible only in a north and south direction, since on the west is the sea and the desert is on the east.

A large part in the history of the Bridge was played by the desert, but not as an element of culture. Wave after wave of barbarism came from its wastes and destroyed the older civilisations; only after long and painful struggles was the new blood civilised in its turn and started on an upward career. Once civilised, the new peoples lost their ability to face their ancestral desert. Never was it crossed by a civilised road, never did the great powers secure political control of its huge

[1] Fig. 14.

but sparsely populated stretches; the most they could accomplish was a hasty raid in retaliation for nomad incursions, and at that the desert proper was never penetrated.

Because of the desert and the sea, the higher cultures, whether operating in the guise of invading armies or in the more frequent but less spectacular march of the caravan, must follow the roundabout but relatively safe road by the Bridge. In its long, straight, almost due north and south lines of mountains, the Bridge forced a north and south march, and all its chief routes ran in this direction.

The Great Road took its faint beginnings far up the Nile. Dropping down the river it turned east in the Delta and passed the guardhouse erected to check nomad incursions. Shortly after a track branched off southeast along the shore of the Gulf and ran to the copper and turquoise mines of Sinai.

Narrow footpaths, now parallel, now converging, form an intricate pattern as the Great Road monotonously winds through the desert. In January there is a thin film of grass brought to life by the few winter showers, but by another month the birds will have migrated north, the flowers will have disappeared, only the bare sand will remain. Four days of utter desert bring the traveller to a half-way settlement on the "Dry River Bed of Egypt" which comes down from the right. Now it is simply a broad basin of sand and gravel, but a few days ago, after a sudden thunder shower, it was for an hour or so a raging torrent. Throughout the year water may be found by digging pits a few feet deep in its bed. Thus a little cultivation is made possible, a few sickly fig trees, a few stunted palms whose fruit is already covered with a thick coating of sand.[2]

The desert becomes a little less forbidding. Here and there are the black tents of the nomads with smoke rising from their camp fires. Flocks of sheep are seen; the boys and girls who guard them scamper away at our approach. Glimpses are caught of a distant escarpment, steep and level topped, which rises sharply from the rolling country that extends from our

[2] Fig. 141, *History of Assyria*.

FIG. 14. THE "BRIDGE OF ASSEMBLY" OVER THE JORDAN.

FIG. 15. ON THE ROAD TO EGYPT—THE "WELL OF HAGAR."

road to its base. Beyond lie open plains between low hills, the Negeb.

Two days more bring us to the edge of the settled country. We cross a broad stream bed, with high dirt banks and pools of stagnant water, which sweeps down from Beersheba, and are on an extensive and fertile plain which has not yet won the name of Philistia. We reach Gaza near, but not directly on, the sea. As we swing inland the plain rises gently to the east, until it is closed by a line of low, often isolated hills which frequently hide from our sight the high deeply seamed plateau beyond. Huge gashes indicate the stream exits from the hills, but it is often difficult to trace their courses in the plain. Water in abundance comes from the wells, ever growing deeper as we approach the hills, there are frequent showers in the rainy half of the year, the soil is fertile, though sometimes near the shore the sands blown by strong southwesterly winds from the Nile Delta encroach upon the gardens and orchards. Along this route are strung the only important towns which date from so early a period.

As we march on north the plain becomes narrower. We turn in towards the hills, now more rounded and with fertile valleys between. We avoid the long mass of Carmel with its abrupt descent to the shore, for that is the road to Phœnicia. Phœnician towns lie in tiny pockets of soil surrounded by hills with terraced slopes; they are separated by jutting promontories which will soon force the Phœnicians to the sea and will make them the one thoroughgoing exception to the general statement that the ancient oriental states were land powers. Already Kupna or Gebal is a flourishing seaport, in close relation to Egypt.

Instead, we turn east by a low pass between Carmel and the main ridge and see below us the fertile Plain of Megiddo, surrounded by high and picturesque hills. Thanks to its fertility and to its position on the Great Road, the plain is already enjoying that prosperity which never left it in ancient times. The exit of the road into the plain is commanded by Megiddo, which has already passed through two building periods. Following the southern slopes to avoid the entangling mud, we pass Taanach and reach Beth Shan at the junction of the plain with the Jordan valley.

The Jordan valley has reached its most flourishing stage. Swamps have been drained, Egyptian or Babylonian irrigation methods have been introduced. At the southern end, near the Dead Sea, is Jericho. Along the upper course are other good sized towns, Abel, Laish, Yanoam, Rehob, Hamath, Pella.

Beth Yerah, the "Moon's House," was the most important settlement, for it commanded the exit of the Jordan from the Lake of Galilee and the Jordan ford where later was to cross the "Bridge of Assembly." Three quarters of a mile it stretched along the lake shore and covered an area of almost sixty acres. A high degree of culture is indicated by its fine pottery. There was a large repertory of forms, jugs and juglets, pots, bowls, and plates, flasks and œnochoes. The most characteristic feature was the ledge handle, which was perhaps borrowed from later predynastic Egypt. Bases were flat or rounded, handles might be looped as well as made with short smooth ledge, bowl rims were turned in, handles were rare. Often the red hæmatite slip was completely burnished. A peculiar type showed the red inside while the outside was burnished in black with a red rim; a wavy fluting imitated silver vases. Comb facing was in horizontal bands and patterned hatching. The commonest ornament was the band slip, parallel vertical bands of brown, red, or orange, applied now and then upon a slip of contrasting colour. Wavy ledge handles, net decoration, vase forms, all point to close relationship with Egypt, now fairly well Semitised; the disappearance of the earlier connections with North Syria and Babylonia show how the invading Semites have broken the earlier cultural relations.[3]

From Beth Yerah we climb by the pass of Aphek to the fertile plateau above, pass Hermon, its summit covered with snow, and reach Damascus in its luxuriant oasis between

[3] W. F. Albright, *JPOS.*, II, 1922, 133 ff.; *Ann.*, VI, 13 ff.; 49 f.; *Sellin Festschrift*, 1927, 1 ff.

THE BRIDGE OF ASSEMBLY

mountain and desert. Toiling over barren Anti-Lebanon we find ourselves in Hollow Syria with its wonderfully productive soil. On either side is a line of mountains, to the east Anti-Lebanon, to the west cedar-clad Lebanon, its sky line rising higher and higher until the topmost crest just misses reaching two miles above sea level.

Meanwhile the valley has grown rougher and more infertile, the mountains sink down into hills and fade away to leave a broad rolling plain around the site of "Holy" Kadesh, destined to become the capital of North Central Syria. An easy route turns west to the sea and to the north Phœnician cities. Then the hills begin to rise again, though never so high as the Lebanon, and we follow the Orontes river whose chief source is not far from Kadesh. Another two days' journey brings us to Hamath in the deep sunk river valley. At last we open out into the broad plains of North Syria whose fertility, combined with its position at the crossing of the ways, has brought into being such famous cities as Aleppo.

To the west, a sharp but not over long pass, the Syrian Gates,[4] brings an abrupt descent to the sea at its northwest corner. As alternative, we may traverse the Amanus Gates a little to the north, advance through the fertile but unhealthy Cilician plain, climb up the difficult Cilician Gates of Taurus, and reach the silver mines from which the whole world secures the precious metal. From here the whole Anatolian plateau lies open before us. Due north of Syria a steep track from Marqasi penetrates the huge block of Anti-Taurus within whose recesses important towns already flourish.

On all these roads nature has placed definite barriers; to the east alone there is no obstacle. Custom has indeed set a frontier at the Euphrates, but it is no true boundary. At numerous points the river may be forded with ease, and beyond the North Syrian plain merges into the yet wider plains of Mesopotamia. Assyria and Babylonia may be reached without traversing country rough enough to cause serious inconvenience.

[4]Fig. 78, *History of Assyria*.

Such is the course of the Great Road which crosses the Bridge and connects Egypt at one bridgehead with Asia Minor, Assyria, and Babylonia at the other. The country described is that which has played the greater part in world history because it does lie on the Great Road. All this time the reader has been conscious of a growing uneasiness. He is interested in our region because of its relation to the Bible, yet thus far he has heard only a few names and those rarely mentioned in the Sacred Book. The chief sites of Biblical history have been conspicuously missing.

Strange as it may appear, there has been emerging the most significant factor which modern archæology has taught; our region does indeed form the "Bridge of Assembly," but the term may be applied only in modified form to the portions of Canaan occupied by the later Hebrews.

Upper Galilee is a fertile and picturesque but isolated plateau. Lower Galilee consists of equally fertile little pockets of soil among low hills. A shunt line of the Great Road crossed one of its corners and small but open valleys permitted easy branches. From a hill only a mile from Nazareth one could look down on the Great Road itself as it crossed the Plain of Megiddo, covered then by long lines of donkeys or by a marching army, as now one sees the lines of rails which may soon connect Paris with Cape Town.

Samaria was likewise somewhat open to outside influences, for the Great Road traversed the extreme northwest border. It too consisted of open plains between rounded mountains over whose shoulders one might pass without too much difficulty. Civilisation was therefore more advanced than in other parts of the hill country. As we travel southward the country becomes rougher and rougher, arable fields are fewer. The level rises, and the waters descend to the Mediterranean through tremendous gorges or to the Dead Sea by even more magnificent outlets, for the great sink is now far below the level of the ocean.

The Wilderness of Judah is indeed a desert, not of drifting sand, but a high bare rocky plateau, fit in most portions only for grazing, and seamed to east and west by huge clefts whose crossing means a day's hard labor. Here there is but one main road, again due north and south, along the crest of the plateau, while descent to east or west is made forbidding by dangerous canyons. Yet more to the south is the Negeb, another series of little plains between low lying, smoothly rounded hills; the soil is fertile enough in the valleys, but there is little rain and no running water, only a few water holes in the stream bottoms to furnish the precious fluid to the scanty flocks of goats and sheep, the poor wealth of the nomads.

If the highlands west of the Jordan are not properly part of the Bridge, still more is this true of the trans-Jordanic country, completely isolated from civilisation by the Jordan-Dead Sea depression. The great sink takes its start in North Syria, becomes more pronounced as Hollow Syria between Lebanon and Anti-Lebanon, captures the infant Jordan, passes under Hermon, and then begins to drop below the level of the ocean. Already at the Lake of Galilee it is almost seven hundred feet lower than the sea, and the additional atmospheric pressure is distinctly noticeable. The Jordan now deserves its name of "Descender," for it twists and turns and leaps down rapids until it reaches the Dead Sea, nearly thirteen hundred feet below the level of the ocean, and the deepest spot open to the sun on our globe.[5] Great masses of overturned and splintered rocks line the cliffs along the Jordan and the Dead Sea and explain the stories of Sodom and Gomorrah. The great depression is continued south through the Arabah, with more splintered rocks fringing the broad but desolate valley, dips into the Gulf of Aqaba, and completes its career as the Red Sea with its shores shimmering in an intolerable heat.

The influence of this great rift has always been divisive. East of the rift are rich soils, and in times of security their tillers have attained high culture, but they were far from the Great Road, and their fields lay wide open to the desert, from which they are separated only by an invisible line of down-

[5] Figs. 122 f., 82, 1 f., 14, 19 f., 86.

ward slope which allows the rain-bearing clouds to pass without dropping and be consumed.

War is the destined lot of the Bridge. Its broken topography permits the growth of numerous independent states, chronically at war with one another, but never allows the formation of a single powerful kingdom. A thin line of fertility beyond the desert, the Bridge is a standing invitation to the nomad to invade and to settle.

Throughout all history wave after wave of Semites has swept out from the desert. The movement had already begun in prehistoric times. A first wave brought Semitic invaders into predynastic Egypt and Shumerian Babylonia; since early Egyptian and early Akkadian have much in common, the ancestors of the men who spoke these languages must have been closely allied while still in the desert.[6]

At much the same time a somewhat different group entered Syria. They intermarried with the older population, and the intermixture of races is shown by a lowered height, a more projecting chin, a broader nose, as compared with the original nomad characteristics. The women, more conservative racially it would seem, retained the very dark hair and eyes, the regularly depressed nose, the flatter foreheads.[7]

If we may judge by the proper names reported for the earlier periods and by the later inscriptions, the men of this group already spoke a language essentially the same as the Biblical Hebrew.[8] To late Bible times this language was known as the "lip of Canaan."[9] We follow Old Testament usage when we identify Canaan with the modern Palestine; strictly speaking, Canaan, the "Low Country," applies only to the coastal plain and includes the whole of Phœnicia.

War came also to the Bridge from Egypt to the south and from Asia Minor, Assyria, and Babylonia to the north. Invaders of the Armenoid race were already in North Syria; they

---

[6] Cf. D. D. Luckenbill, *AJSL.*, XL, 1923, 1 ff.
[7] Macalister, *Gezer*, I, 59 ff.
[8] W. F. Albright, *JPOS.*, II, 1922, 124; cf. H. Bauer and P. Leander, *Historische Grammatik der hebräischen Sprache*, 1922.
[9] Is. 19:18.

reached Canaan proper about the commencement of historical times. Although they were not yet numerous enough to affect the general appearance and although they produced no change in the language, now and then their broad heads are noted. As time goes on there is a slight but unmistakable swing to a broader form of the head.

Lying on the narrow path between sea and desert Canaan was on the direct route which led out from Egypt, and Canaan must be conquered before an Asiatic power could invade the Nile valley. With monotonous but terrifying regularity Egyptian armies trampled her soil. Egyptians made acquaintance with Syria, Syrians were carried captive to Egypt. To these Egyptian raids we owe such knowledge of early Canaan as may be secured from written records.

Where an army appeared once in a score of years caravans could be seen toiling along at any season. Canaan was a Bridge no less for traders than for monarchs. Over it passed, even before Egypt was united and written history began, many an object of value on its way from the Tigris or the Euphrates to the Nile. Rarities such as the deep blue lapis lazuli, whose ultimate home was the Iranian plateau, the precious metals in manufactured form, many a piece of more ordinary merchandise, were transported along this route. A certain proportion remained in Canaan as pay for the protection of some petty kinglet, for the daily support of the merchant, or through simple theft. Soon imitations, just as good in the eye of the uninitiate, were being manufactured by native artisans.

We can prove easily the passage of material objects, for specimens have been recovered through the excavations. They were accompanied by less tangible gifts. Art motifs can be traced from Babylonia to Egypt and in the reverse direction; they naturally left their traces also in Canaan. Borrowing of art motifs implies still less tangible loans, forms of government, commercial practices, religious beliefs, myths and stories, manners and customs. Before the early historical period was ended Syria enjoyed a complex civilisation.

CHAPTER V

EGYPTIAN WARRIORS AND CANAANITE PEASANTS

SINAI is the most utterly desolate portion of our region; strangely enough it is in Sinai that are found our earliest written records. Neither peaceful agriculture nor industry led men to the triangular peninsula; copper for implements and turquoise for adornment induced them to visit the waste country ruled by the "Lady of Turquoise."

Long before history the peninsula supported a few nomads. Scattered through its deep cut gorges and over its gravelly upraised beaches are chipped flints. Some are so rude and their patina is so thick that they may well have been exposed to the atmosphere since Palæolithic days. Others, less primitive, are buried under pluvial gravels, and these are followed by types which find parallels in the predynastic of Egypt.[1]

Prehistoric man has also left his buildings. Earliest are the stone circles. Some may be mere wind breaks or walls to protect the sheep and goats, others may be foundations for huts of brush or wood or skin, for they have doorways with door posts. The greater number mark burials. A few of these sepulchral circles reach a hundred feet in diameter and are composed of boulders five feet long. In the centre, under a heap of huge rocks, is the cist, the bodies laid on the left side and in the contracted position, the knees elevated to the chin. Beside the dead are laid shells and flints. A burial ceremony is indicated by charred spots in the circle and by bits of burned wood.

A later stage is represented by the nawamis or "Mosquito Houses," traditionally erected by the Israelites to escape a plague of these insects. Generally they are of a curious beehive shape, the outer wall of rough stones horizontally coursed and drawn in an accurate circle and built up by a false arch to a capstone. Bones and charred wood in a central hearth prove

[1] Fig. 8.

that a few were habitations but the majority were tombs. These nawamis were filled with earth and the tiny door was faced to the west; perhaps, like the soldiers in the Great War, their makers believed that the dead "went west."[2]

Something of their life is revealed by the objects deposited in the tombs. Arrow heads of flint, chisel shaped and quite unlike those of Egypt, prove that their owners were hunters. Adornment was normally of shells. One large shell had been cut into a bracelet, smaller shells were strung for the same purpose. Copper began to be smelted in a double-walled furnace with two blast holes and was manufactured into long thin tools. The predynastic tombs of Egypt show already a large use of malachite for painting the body, a turquoise bead is rarely found, copper makes its appearance in the yet earlier Badarian culture. Long before the dawn of written history the nomads of Sinai were exporting their valued products to the Nile.[3]

Meanwhile the predynastic states of Egypt had been united into two kingdoms and these again into the Egypt of the first dynasty. Turquoise from Sinai was highly prized, copper was affording a basis for a new technology. It was inevitable that Egypt should attempt to make safe her possession of commodities so necessary for her future development.

Zer, successor of that Menes who had united Egypt, began the visits to the "Terraces of Turquoise," and likewise began the "slaughter of the Setet."[4] The fourth king of the dynasty, Semti-Den, records the "first occurrence of the smiting of the Easterners" as if it were quite to be expected in the natural course of events. His ivory plaque represents the crowned monarch with uplifted mace and about to brain the bearded Semite in short skirt who kneels before him; the motif was to be repeated again and again on the rocks of Sinai. The next

[2] Fig. 16.
[3] Fig. 21; C. Wilson, *Ordnance Survey of the Peninsula of Sinai*, I, 1871, 194 ff.; E. H. Palmer, *Desert of the Exodus*, 1872, 120 ff.; R. Savignac, *RB.*, XVI, 1907, 398 ff.; W. M. F. Petrie, *Researches in Sinai*, 1906, 15 ff., 50, 242 ff.; T. E. Peet, *Man*, 1915, 151 ff.
[4] L. Borchardt, *Mitth. Vorderas. Gesell.*, XXII, 1918, 342 ff.

king, Merpeba, claims that he smote the Troglodytes of the peninsula.[5]

Semerkhet, the sixth king of the dynasty, was to our knowledge the first to reach the mines. Semti-Den's ivory plaque was imitated in a relief, high up and far from the paths, lest it be mutilated by the natives after the return of his expedition. The nomad might well be the Bedawi of to-day. His body is thin to the point of emaciation, his nose is that of the pure Semite, his only dress is a loin cloth. His hair is elaborately puffed out in the rear, behind his ear falls the lovelock, his beard is small and pointed. He crouches before his captor and raises his right hand to his forehead in abject submission, while he tears from his hair the ostrich feather which marks his rank as chief. Semerkhet has seized the long quivering spear with its tassel and is about to brain him with his mace.[6]

Semerkhet was followed by Qa who has left in his tomb an ivory in the form of a reed. It is carved to represent a bound captive with the typical pointed beard and plaited lock of the nomad and wearing the typical nomad waist cloth; he is labelled Seti, the "Asiatic."[7] There is no indication of renewed contact with Sinai until the third dynasty whose second king, Zoser, is depicted in the smiting of the Asiatic which had become conventional. His successor, Senekht, placed his inscription above the mines.

The great age of exploitation begins with Snefru. Sinai furnished no small part of the wealth that erected the pyramids and is mentioned by the builder of the greatest, Khufu.[8] Egypt never enjoyed effective military control of Sinai and every mining party assumed the character of a regular expedition. In charge would be a prince, a general, or a "seal-bearer of the god"; there would also be a commander of recruits, a chief of the storehouse, a chief of the "elders" or foremen, inspectors, and scribes.

The motley crowd passed the frontier where one day was

[5]J. H. Breasted, *History of Egypt*, 2 ed., 1912, fig. 26; *Rec.*, I, 59.
[6]Fig. 18.
[7]W. M. F. Petrie, *Royal Tombs*, 1900, pl. XII, 12 f.; XVII, 30.
[8]Breasted, *Rec.*, I, 83.

FIG. 16. A NAWAMI OR "MOSQUITO HOUSE."

FIG. 17. HUTS OF THE MINERS.
(Wadi Maghareh.)

FIG. 18. SEMERKHET SMITES THE CHIEF OF THE NOMADS.

to be the southern entrance to the Suez Canal. At first the way was easy along the shore, the limestone hills that bound the great barren plain in the background. Here and there the travellers came upon water, often brackish and sometimes warm; at these spots they found a little vegetation, the tamarisk, the thorny ghurkud with its juicy red berries, the beautiful flowered but parasitic broom rape, the sweet-scented bitter-tasting broom itself, perhaps even a few stunted palms. A rare acacia towered in the open with its gum arabic of commerce. More frequent were the desert herbs, myrrh, thyme, mallow, and Jericho rose, but for the most part nothing was seen but desert thorns which only the camel's extraordinary digestion could assimilate. A nomad hurried off his flocks before the invaders or the cerastes, the hooded snake, challenged their progress. Herds of timid gazelles were sighted in the distance, mountain goats watched from the nearby heights.

Now the way became more rugged and there was a mixture of marls and limestones. A small plain was entered, contact was made with those who had brought the heavier supplies by sea. Native guides were obtained and the Amu were recruited, the seal-bearer, through an interpreter, made with them individual contracts; a special overseer was appointed to house them.

Climbing up the gorge to its end and over the red sandstone by the "Pass of the Sword's Point," the expedition entered the wilderness of red granite and descended into the Wadi Maghareh, the "Gorge of Caves." Around the main sandstone mass, reaching to thirty-five hundred feet, tower granite mountains, their basalt or sandstone caps giving a weird appearance to the landscape. Below a band of sandstone which at times becomes almost pure hæmatite is the turquoise bearing stratum, a hydrous phosphate of alumina, blue with iron phosphate, or green with copper; the turquoise is hidden in hard nodules which must be broken to extract the precious gem.

Arrived at the mines, the "deviser of minerals" at once began the search for new veins. Although no permanent settlement was to be made, so large a body of men demanded shelter of a sort, for even in summer the intense heat of the day is followed by cool nights and in winter snow sometimes falls and ice is formed before morning. Houses for the higher officials were well built of stone and roofed, but the workmen were protected by mere windbreaks, set in regular rows. Protection was not alone needed against the wind, for each night lions roared and hyenas yelled around the encampment. Bread from flour ground on the spot by rubbing stones was the ordinary food of the workmen, but shellfish and echini were added delicacies. Before their return to Egypt the thrifty miners buried their rubbing stones and pottery neatly in pits under their huts.[9]

The oldest mine at Maghareh, opened by order of Senekht, was a long gallery five feet high. Marks of the copper chisels yet scar its walls. The blocks were crushed by huge pointed stone mauls, by picks grooved and bound to a handle, or by large rounded crushers, and thus the nodules in which the turquoises hid were discovered. After the Egyptians disappeared the nomads resumed their mining; as they possessed only rude flint implements their task was difficult and their success indifferent.

Copper was mined high up the narrow valleys. No fuel could be secured at this elevation, and the ore must be packed down to the encampment or to the tiny plain near the shore, where a growth of desert shrubs might be utilised. Here is a furnace of granite blocks, fifteen feet across, while on the adjacent hillside is a huge mass of black slag; imperfect smelting has left much of the copper unextracted. Farther up one of the valleys, near other furnaces, is a slag heap which has been estimated to weigh a hundred thousand tons. Smelting was also carried on in the settlement itself where tools were manufactured, in particular the tips of the copper chisels. Charcoal, crucibles, and moulds are common; one crucible was found still filled with crushed ore, which a sudden departure, hastened perhaps by nomad attack, had not allowed time to reduce.[10]

[9]Fig. 17.   [10]Petrie, *Researches in Sinai*, 18, 27.

Snefru was the first to turn his attention to the Wadi Serabit, farther inland in a contorted mass of valleys. He found there a cave which the nomads had dedicated to the "Lady of Turquoise," for in it they were accustomed to sleep that in dreams they might locate the mineral-bearing veins. Snefru dedicated his hawk in the sacred cave and later centuries regarded him as the patron saint of the place. By the side of the Lady of Turquoise was her consort; him the Egyptians identified with Soped, god of the zodiacal light, who was worshipped in the Arabian nome on the edge of the desert and was more Semitic than Egyptian, while the Lady of Turquoise became Hathor.

Jars bearing the Horus banner and dating from the early dynasties cover the site of a guardhouse on the Isthmus of Suez. When the living Horus, the Egyptian king, undertook the conquest of Canaan from this base, it came to be known as the "Ways of Horus."[11] The name hints at earlier land expeditions, but the first recorded was by Sahure, second king of the fifth dynasty, and his forces went by sea. Reliefs in Sahure's mortuary temple picture the return of his twelve ships, laden with spoil of sheep and goats, cattle and asses, Syrian bears as a curiosity, olive wood and olive oil in Canaanite jars. The captives wear only short trunks and headbands, their hands are bound uncomfortably behind their backs or over their heads.[12] Asiatic captives are also portrayed by Nuserre, the sixth monarch of the dynasty.[13] Under one of the kings of this dynasty, a certain Inti took part in an expedition against Canaan. He proudly displays in his tomb the capture of Netia, perhaps Lydda,[14] and Ain Ka . . ., compounded with the well-known Semitic word for "spring," and so proving that the inhabitants already spoke Canaanite. Outside the town a great slaughter is taking place. The roped captives are being hauled away and one struggling girl has been thrown over her

[11] J. Clédat, *Annales du Service*, XIII, 1914, 115 ff.
[12] L. Borchardt, *Das Grabdenkmal des Königs Sahu-re*, II, 1913, 16 ff.
[13] L. Borchardt, *Das Grabdenkmal des Königs Ne-user-re*, 1907, 46 ff.
[14] W. F. Albright, *Ann.*, VI, 34, n. 70.

captor's shoulder. The towered brick walls, a means of defense learned from Babylonia, are being attacked by scaling ladders or are being breached with poles. Within the citizens listen anxiously to the ominous sounds. Their women are nursing the wounded, the men have abandoned hope, and are breaking their bows. The chief sits on a stool and tears his hair; before him stand old men and children who beg him to surrender.[15]

Sahure, Nuserre, Menkuhor, and Isesi all record mining expeditions to Sinai, and so does Pepi I, third king of the sixth dynasty. Uni, Pepi's general, requires a poem to do justice to his leadership when he conducted an army of many ten thousands against the sand-dwellers. He destroyed their land, overturned their strongholds, cut down their vines and fig trees, threw fire on all their troops, killed many ten thousands, and carried off many captives alive. Thus did he five times, every time they revolted. When it was reported that there was revolt among the barbarians in the land of the Gazelle Nose, Uni hurried across the sea in ships and went to the back of the ridge on the north of the land of the sand-dwellers, that is, Mount Carmel; meanwhile the army had marched by the road and had taken and killed every rebel.[16] How the "Barbarians" themselves took it does not appear from the poem, but the repeated inroads may have united the Canaanites against the invader; at any rate after Pepi I there is a lull in the exploitation of the Sinai mines and there are no more Asiatic victories recorded.

While Egyptian armies were tramping through Canaan the country entered a second phase of culture which may be dated roughly to the middle of the third pre-Christian millennium. The most flourishing cities were still along the Great Road or in the Jordan valley. Hitherto the highlands, little adapted to the dominant irrigation practices and covered with forests, had remained sparsely inhabited, but their occupation began in this period. Great heaps of wood ashes prove the wide-spread use of timber dwellings at Kiriath Sepher in the hill country

[15] W. M. F. Petrie, *Deshasheh*, 1898, pl. IV.
[16] Breasted, *Rec.*, I, 142 ff.; cf. W. F. Albright, *JPOS.*, II, 1922, 119.

between Gaza and Hebron, for the slopes were then well wooded.[17] Under the oldest Jebusite city on the Ophel hill are traces of a similar settlement. At the north entrance is a rock altar with three holes in its side and beyond is a field of cup holes. Basins comparable to a bath are connected with a channel and nearby is a group of eight oval cups surrounding a circular ninth. Burial caves are numerous, while a huge heap of ashes filled with human bones and coarse potsherds shows that here the dead were cremated. Despite the evident analogies to the prehistoric settlement at Gezer, the pottery proves the later date.[18]

Mizpah, the "Watch Tower," which from its hill dominated the north and south road along the central ridge, was protected by a narrow wall; the enormous quantity of potsherds indicates a surprisingly large population.[19] Potsherds of like character mark the beginnings of settlement on other sites in the hill country.

Sodom and Gomorrah, with their sister towns of Admah, Zeboim, and Zoar, then occupied the well-watered Circuit of Jordan, like the garden of Yahweh, like the land of Egypt;[20] to-day their ruins may be covered by the shallow waters at the southern end of the Dead Sea. On festal occasions the citizens climbed the five hundred feet to the plain of ed-Dra on the Lisan, the great "Tongue" which projects from the eastern shore.[21] On the cliff above the plain was an open area a thousand feet long by three hundred wide, surrounded by a wall of rough stones ten to fifteen feet thick, which was stepped up the slope and was protected by a sixteen foot high revetment. Within the enclosure were only a few buildings of unworked stones, for it served merely as protection against sudden raids of the wild tribes from the eastern plateau.

Outside the enclosure were great numbers of square or round foundations; hearths and household wares show that here the

[17]W. F. Albright, *ZAW.*, NF., VI, 1929, 3 f.
[18]R. A. S. Macalister and J. G. Duncan, *Excavations on the Hill of Ophel*, 1926, 12 ff.; 35 f.
[19]W. F. Badè, *Excavations at Tell en-Nasbeh*, 1928, 23; *QS.*, 1930, 13.
[20]Gen. 13:10.   [21]Fig. 19 f.

peasants camped while on festival. Seven limestone standing stones, brought from a great distance, mark the sanctity of the place and hint of orgies which have made the name of Sodom infamous.[22] A rare bit of bronze proves that the artificial metal was already known, but flint was still in common use. Knives with one or two blades killed the sacrifice and cut up the meat, scrapers cleansed the hide, and awls pierced the holes for the thread. Agriculture is witnessed by the sickle blades, textile manufactures by loom weights and spindle whorls. Flour was ground by rubbing stones of basalt.

Pottery is for the most part handmade. Large bowls and platters in red with turned-in rims were irregularly burnished. Jugs and amphoræ bore plastic rings, cord marked by the fingers. Projecting or wavy narrow ledge handles were affixed to some of the jars. Small water decanters had narrow necks and vertical loop handles. A globular teapot form was given a horizontal projecting spout under the brim. Bowls and wider mouthed jugs were decorated with one or more rills under the rim. To complete the picture the dead made their last journey to the shrine which they surrounded with their stone heaps or circle graves.[23]

Chinnereth on the Lake of Galilee regained the importance of Palæolithic times.[24] Jericho possessed a mud-brick wall fifteen feet thick.[25] Lachish began its career in the same period on a hill sixty feet above a stream to the west, dry in summer but supplemented by fine springs close by. A ten foot wall of thin bricks, laid with alternate headers and stretchers, and with corner tower, was joined by rubble to a second wall three feet out and enclosed an area almost a quarter of a mile square. Houses were small and rude. Tools were of hardened copper; there were local types of battle-axes, adzes, and knives; mace heads resembled those from Egypt and Babylo-

[22]Gen. 19.
[23]W. F. Albright, *Bull.*, 14, 2 ff.; *Ann.*, VI, 56 ff.; M. G. Kyle and W. F. Albright, *Bibliotheca Sacra*, LXXXI, 1924, 276 ff.; P. Mallon, *Biblica*, V, 1924, 413 ff.
[24]W. F. Albright, *Ann.*, VI, 24 ff.
[25]E. Sellin and C. Watzinger, *Jericho*, 1913, 17 f.; J. Garstang, *QS.*, 1930, 130.

FIG. 19. THE DEAD SEA PENINSULA OF THE "TONGUE."

FIG. 20. TENT VILLAGE ON THE "TONGUE."

nia. Polished points of bone occur. The pottery is comb faced with ledge handles, thick brimmed bowls have a peculiar spout, a red faced ware has patterned burnishing. A wooden seal with the figure of a deer, potter's marks on the vases hint that writing was not unknown.[26]

Our best picture of contemporary culture is secured from the excavation at Gezer. When the Canaanites first entered the city they found the old Neolithic wall in fair condition, though here and there were breaches; in one they erected a standing stone. As the population increased a new wall was demanded. Fair sized blocks were quarried, roughly dressed with the hammer, and set with mud mortar in irregular courses; the wide joints were filled with smaller stones. Every ninety feet were rectangular towers, forty by twenty-five feet, with interior chambers. The north gate, guarded by two towers, was the main entrance. As in the modern gates of Jerusalem, the passage was so arranged as to force a right turn, while in time of danger it could be filled by a wooden barrier. The southern gate was also flanked by two towers, but the passage was straight.[27]

In time of siege the water of the private cisterns or even the six hundred gallons of the public reservoir might not suffice. To avoid this danger the citizens dug with their rude flint tools a passageway through the rock to a subterranean spring nearly a hundred feet below the surface. This great tunnel, thirteen feet wide and twenty-three feet from its steps to its vaulted roof, is impressive testimony to the engineering skill of these early Canaanites.[28]

Close by the south gate, with the tunnel entrance in its courtyard, was the palace of the local ruler. No particular plan was followed, but a large hall, supported by pillars which rested on massive stone bases, was doubtless the audience chamber.[29] His subjects contented themselves at first with

[26] W. M. F. Petrie, *Tell el-Hesy*, 1891; F. J. Bliss, *Mound of Many Cities*, 1894; cf. W. F. Albright, *JPOS.*, II, 1922, 130 f.
[27] Macalister, *Gezer*, I, 238 ff.
[28] Fig. 22; Macalister, *Gezer*, I, 256 ff.   [29] *Ibid.*, I, 205.

tents or huts, but ultimately all settled down. House foundations and walls were of stone, roughly hammer dressed, joints were poor, mud was the only mortar, the superstructure was of sun-dried brick. Doorways were small and without jambs but with a stone or wooden lintel; the doors were of wood and turned on a stone socket. In the homes of the better class the walls were plastered. Rarely was there more than one story. The flat roof was covered with mud and supported by wooden beams; if the room was too wide to be spanned by a single beam, wooden pillars were set on a stone base to prevent them from sinking through the smoothed mud floor. Hearths of up-ended stones cooked the meals. Plans were irregular, but the court was a common element. Streets were narrow and crooked.[30]

Agriculture was the chief industry. Domesticated animals were much the same as those favoured by their predecessors, notably the cow with long smooth curved horns. The humped cattle of Babylonia and the buffalo were somewhat rare, but sheep and goats were numerous. The donkey was the common carrier, the dog was the only garbage collector. Wild animals added to the food supply, the stag, gazelle, ibex, porcupine, badger, hare, jerboa, or the more repulsive jackal, wolf, or hyena. Special delicacies were the crane, the dove, the oyster, or the various sea and shellfish.

The modern summer crops were absent, but the winter crops were much the same as to-day. Cereals were represented by barley, wheat, and oats; vegetables by beans, bamieh, and three species of vetch; fruits by the fig, pomegranate, olive, and grape, pistachio nuts, terebinth seeds; and acorns completed the menu. Chopped straw was fodder for the beasts.

A simple form of the plow had been borrowed from Egypt. Sowing was by hand. The harvest was reaped with a sickle, a handle of wood or bone in which were set teeth of flint. Grain was threshed by a sledge whose bottom was filled with sharp flints and was winnowed with a wooden fork.

Flour was ground by pestle and mortar. Bread was baked

[30]*Ibid.*, I, 167 ff.

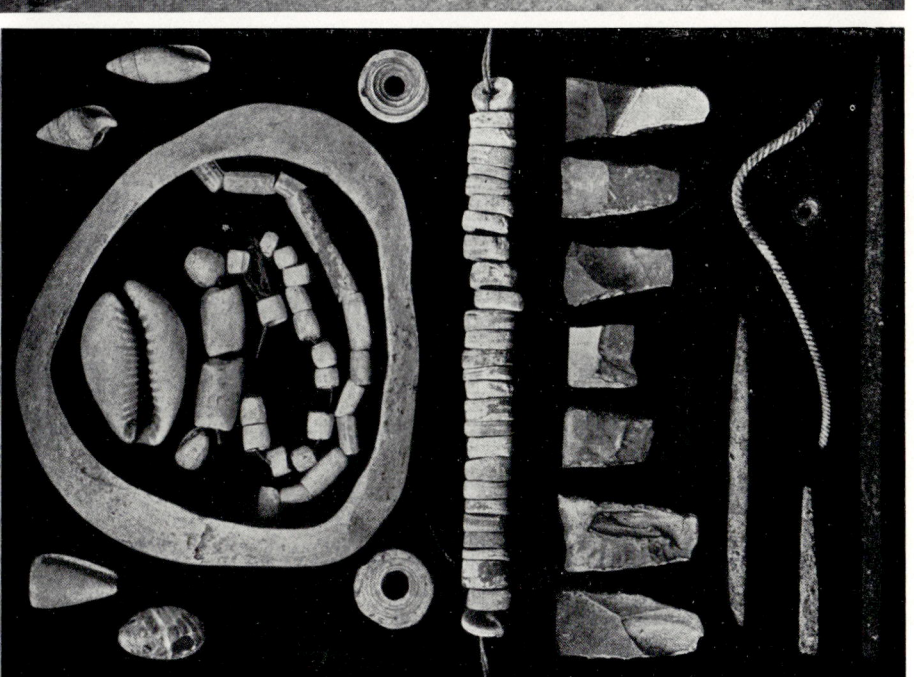

Fig. 21. OBJECTS FROM THE NAWAMIS.
Bracelets and Beads of Shell, Flint Arrowheads, and Copper Tools.

Fig. 22. EARLY CANAANITE TUNNEL AT GEZER.

in a cylindrical covered mud brick oven; the round cakes were laid on small stones over which was built the charcoal or manure fire, kindled by the drill. Meats and cereals were boiled in a large wide-mouthed pot; the food was served in dishes with the aid of shell spoons riveted to a handle. Water for household use was dipped from the cistern by jugs and poured into water jars or skins, which were carried by the women on their heads or backs, or one jar was fixed on either side of a donkey. Oil and wine were trodden out in a simple press, not much advanced over the form used by their Chalcolithic predecessors.

Bone borers suggest that skin dresses had not entirely gone out of fashion, though the regular employment of textiles is witnessed by the numerous heavy loom weights and the enormous quantity of spindle whorls, circles of stone or clay or disks cut from an old jar. Needles and pins were in daily use and were preserved in bone needle-cases. Buttons were round and pierced by two holes; ivory or bone was the material for the better classes, a bit of old jar was formed into buttons by the poor. Rings, earrings, bracelets, and anklets were as yet rare; the common adornment was the necklace of limestone, crystal, quartzite, or carnelian beads. Towards the end of the period beads enamelled in green or yellow came in as imports from Egypt.[31]

The potter's wheel, driven by the left hand, had been introduced and the wares were now generally wheel-made. Jars, jugs, bowls, saucers, fire trays, cups, and ointment jars make up the list of forms. Bases were usually flat, handles were of the loop or ledge variety, spouts appeared, occasionally there were stoppers. Combing was employed, burnishing often covered the entire vase. For ornamentation, there was the red drip line, the moulded rope, the incised herring-bone, or the new banding in alternate red, greyish black, and opaque white. Rude potter's marks appear.[32]

Cakes of paint, iron oxide for the red, limonite for the yellow, more rarely blue and green, were spread on a stone

[31]Macalister, *Gezer*, II, 1 ff.   [32]*Ibid.*, II, 136 ff.

palette and laid on with a brush. Ivory or bone was employed as inlay for boxes; one box, probably an Egyptian import, was in deep blue enamel. Stone bowls imitated pottery originals.

Celts of the chalcolithic types continued in use, though copper was well known and bronze was coming in. The precious metals were yet too rare to be made into anything but beads. The blast furnace was employed for smelting, the bronze alloy was melted in pottery vessels and run into stone moulds to produce spears, swords, daggers, axes, arrow heads, or pins. Timber was cut by the axe, smaller axes trimmed the beams, saws and chisels were of bronze, hammers were of stone with a hole for the handle. Wood was fitted by the mortice and tenon joint, nails were utilised.[33]

The prehistoric inhabitants had sacrificed their sacred animal, the pig, over the whole site and had thus profaned it for cult purposes in the eyes of the Canaanites. A ritually clean spot was found in a depression with a rise on either side. Beneath were two caves, once abodes of their predecessors. One was turned into a place of worship whose centre was a rough limestone block, an altar profaned by no tool;[34] the last sacrifice, a tiny infant, rested there still when it was uncovered by the excavators. The second cave was connected with the first by a narrow winding passage while the original entrance was blocked. Through the passage the priest crawled into the inner cave and from there gave oracles to the mystified inquirer. Two pillars, male and female, stood close by; the top of the female pillar is much worn by the kisses of the faithful.[35]

Around the sacred standing stones was a wide open space, paved in part, in part covered with limestone chips. South and again north of the standing stones was a circular structure; a bronze model of a cobra found nearby suggests that they were pits for the sacred serpents.[36] To the east of the cave was a bell-shaped cistern, cut sixteen feet into the rock and surrounded by cup marks, for the disposal of the sacrificial refuse. Bones of cows, sheep, goats, and deer are here found mixed

[33]*Ibid.*, II, 241 ff. [34]Cf. Exod. 20:25. [35]Fig. 23.
[36]Cf. II Kings 18:4.

FIG. 23. SACRED STANDING STONES AT GEZER.

FIG. 24. MONASTERY WITH SACRED FISH IN POOL.

with those of ritually sacrificed human beings. The entire free area is filled with the bodies of new-born infants, the sacrifice of the first born. The tiny bodies were pushed head first into a large two-handled jar with pointed base; a bowl and a jug were then placed over the body in the jar or over the jar itself. Similar burials of infants were also made as foundation deposits at the corners of the houses.[37] More rarely, an old man or woman, no longer of value to the community, was thus sacrificed.[38]

Images of the deity are rare, a rude clay figurine of the goddess or a limestone figure of the god. Amulets were universal. A boar's tusk averted the evil eye; disks of black slate or basalt with rectangular or triangular perforations, club-shaped pendants of slate, bone, or ivory, all were employed as charms.[39]

Citizens of Gezer who were fortunate enough to escape the human sacrifice were given somewhat informal burial. The corpse was laid on the floor of the cave, accompanied by food and water in two or three little jars. A few beads or simple trinkets were quite enough to assure the wealthier of happiness in the after life.[40]

Not only does Gezer afford our best picture of early Canaanite religion, it illustrates the manner in which the older agricultural religion was taken over and modified by the former nomads. The power of the mother goddess, Ashtart or Anath, was fully recognised, but the emphasis was now on the masculine deities. It was to a Baal, a "Lord," that one prayed for the success of the crops. The feasts continued to be held at their appropriate seasons, and with their dances and fertility rites, but they were celebrated in honour of a god. Nevertheless Canaanite religion was far already from the simple nomad worship.

[37]Cf. I Kings 16:34.
[38]Macalister, *Gezer,* II, 381 ff.; 426 ff.
[39]*Ibid.,* II, 449 ff.   [40]*Ibid.,* II, 449 ff.

CHAPTER VI

SHIPS OF GEBAL

PHŒNICIANS already occupied the greater portion of the Syrian littoral at the beginning of history. They had formed a part of that same wave of Semitic migration which had introduced the Canaanites. Their language was pure Semitic and differed only in minor respects from Canaanite and from the later Hebrew.[1] Whether in earlier times a native term was applied to the land as a whole is uncertain; later, Canaan was occasionally so employed. The Egyptians called them Fenkhu, perhaps to be interpreted as "shipbuilders;"[2] following the example of the Greeks we name them Phœnicians. A derivation of Phœnician from Fenkhu remains doubtful, and the most plausible explanation is that the Greeks so named them as makers of the famous purple.[3]

Phœnicia consists of fertile little pockets of soil, sufficient to permit a start towards a high civilisation, entirely inadequate to meet the needs of a rapidly expanding population. Behind these tiny plains stretch high mountains, once covered with forests, while the plains themselves are shut off from one another by sharp promontories. The Phœnicians were therefore early driven to a nomadism of the sea which was a congenial renewal of the desert nomadism. In winter, when storms from west and northwest compel shipping to abandon the open harbours, the boats were drawn up on the sandy shore. Storms are virtually unknown in the warmer half of the year and the tideless Mediterranean offers easy passage for the tiniest of ships. Port by port, the Phœnicians ventured southwest and

[1]Grammar, P. Schroeder, *Phönizische Sprache,* 1869; inscriptions, *CIS.,* I; the Phœnician in the Pœnulus of Plautus, L. H. Gray, *AJSL.,* XXXIX, 1923, 73 ff.

[2]K. Sethe, *Mitth. Vorderas. Gesell.,* XXI, 1917, 305 ff.

[3]F. C. Movers, *Die Phönizier,* 1841 ff.; J. Kenrick, *Phœnicia,* 1855; G. Rawlinson, *History of Phœnicia,* 1889; R. Pietschmann, *Geschichte der Phönizier,* 1889; G. Contenau, *La civilisation phénicienne,* 1926.

northwest until they were famed as the great traders of the ancient world.

The central position on this long stretch of coast was occupied by Kupna, a spot of green on a low level plateau backed by an amphitheatre of mountains. The fertility of the soil, the rocky headlands to either side, the tiny inset harbour, guarded by bare rocks, the sandy reaches, fit for the beaching of ships, all contributed to its unique position.[4] Kupna's name is non-Semitic, and its foundation must date back to the prehistoric population whose slab-covered graves contain rude hand-made pottery and whose flint knives and scrapers persist into the historical period, while their cave sanctuary was transformed into a Phœnician temple.[5]

While the older Kupna was retained in Egyptian usage the Phœnicians changed the name to Gebal, the "Mountain."[6] The memory of its antiquity was lasting, for Philo, a citizen of Roman Byblus, insisted that his native town was the earliest in all Phœnicia. According to Philo it came into being when El, the "God" par excellence, encircled his own abode with a wall. This El was represented with four eyes, in front and behind, two of them closed; he likewise possessed four wings, two folded and two open, while two more grew on his head. When war came upon him, he placed the trappings of royalty on Ieud, his "only son" by the nymph Anobret, and inaugurated the custom of human sacrifice; in actual fact a human sacrifice joined the prehistoric cave to the new Phœnician temple. On the same occasion El circumcised himself and thus became the patron of this rite. He then granted the rule to his daughter Baalath Gebal, the "Lady of Gebal," and henceforth she was Gebal's chief goddess. After his death El was identified with the planet Saturn.[7]

From its rudest origins Gebal was a trading city. Objects of

[4] Fig. 25 f.
[5] Fig. 53; W. F. Albright, *Sellin Festschrift*, 4; M. Dunand, *Syria*, X., 1929, 206 ff.; P. Montet, *Byblos et l'Égypte*, 1928, 239 ff.
[6] Ezek. 27:9; I Kings 5:18.
[7] Philo Byblius, in Eusebius, *Evangelicæ Præparatio*, ed. E. H. Gifford, 1903, i, 10, 37 ff.; Steph. Byz., *s. v. Byblos*; Damascius, in Phot., *Bibl.*, 1049.

the first Egyptian dynasty found in its ruins prove that it was already in contact with the Nile. Throughout their whole history the Phœnicians willingly accepted a nominal foreign rule, provided it was not too expensive and provided it opened to

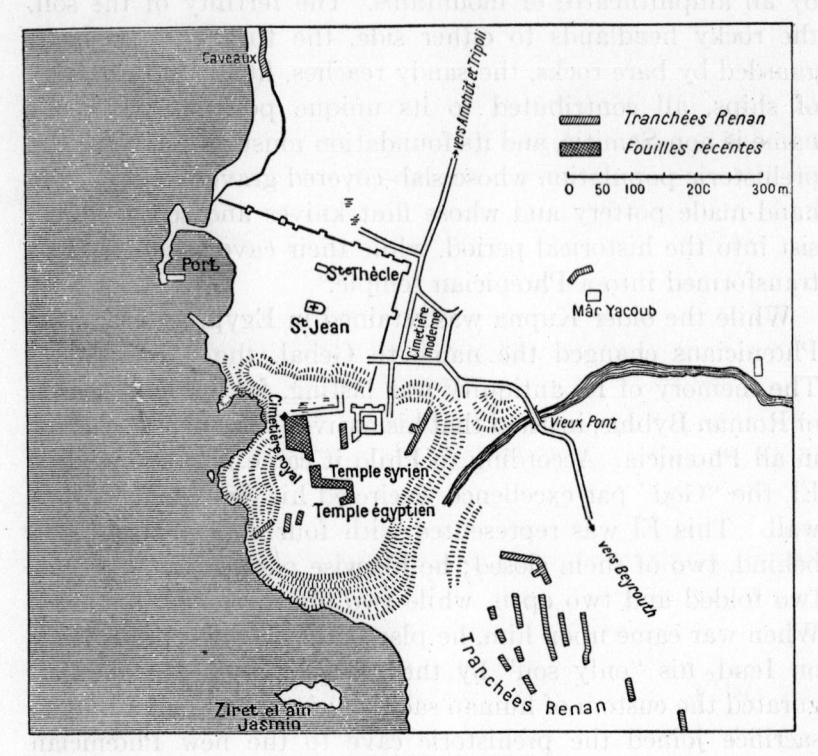

PLAN 4. THE SITE OF GEBAL.

them wider fields of trade. We are therefore not surprised to find in Gebal an inscription of Khasekhemui, last king of the second dynasty; from the same period comes a dedication by the scribe of the royal carpenters, for Gebal was the port from which the coveted cedar of Lebanon was forwarded to Egypt. By the fourth dynasty "ships of Gebal" were well known in Egypt, only four days distant with favouring southerly winds. Khufu, builder of the great pyramid, and his wife, Menkure, builder of the third pyramid, all incised their names on lime-

FIG. 25. GEBAL AND ITS PORT.

FIG. 26. HILLS BACK OF GEBAL.

stone or alabaster vases to be sent as gifts to the Lady of Gebal.

Unis, last king of the fifth dynasty, held the city by his fleet, and identified the local El with his own Re, calling him "Re who is by the Lake of Pharaoh," "Re of the Mountain," or "Re of the Mountain Land." A contemporary ruler of Gebal possessed an Egyptian cylinder seal; in rude Egyptian hieroglyphics he calls himself the beloved of the goddess, the son of the lion and the son of the sun god Re, but the god is localised as Re of the Mountain Country and he gives health in Gebal; in other words he is El in Egyptian dress and the goddess is the Lady of Gebal. Teti, first king of the sixth dynasty, refers to the local god Khai-tau or is identified with Khai-tau who is in the midst of Nega.

Alabaster offering disks come from the first Pepi, the second Pepi dedicated vases showing the mother ape holding an infant to her breast. A stele represents an Egyptian monarch, perhaps one of the Pepis, kneeling before the god and then the goddess, as he presents two Egyptian vases; both are seated on square block-like thrones with low back and three flowers on the side, each wears the disk and horns, each holds the sceptre in the right hand and places the left on the knee, each is accompanied by the inscription "Beloved of Hathor, lord of Gebal." Another stele shows the goddess as a full Egyptian Hathor, embracing the Egyptian king. Egyptian victories are celebrated by ivory figures of Asiatic captives, kneeling and with elbows thrown back.

Everywhere is Egyptian influence. Isis is symbolised by her sistrum or her rattle, the jackal-headed Anubis has his statuettes, there are copies of the Nile lotus, the sacred bark, the dog-headed baboons, the sign of life, the stepped pyramidion of the sun worship. Figurines of ivory or of bronze gilt sometimes imitate Egyptian modes, at other times they are nude in Syrian fashion. Cylindrical stone vessels, pierced and polished palettes, barrel-shaped alabaster beads, find their prototypes in early dynastic Egypt, clay birds' heads or an ox hoof in painted pottery resemble Egyptian wood engravings. Gold is plentiful, some of it cloisonné, there is a golden horn for a statue of the Lady of Gebal. Miniature pots, one-handled jugs, offering tumblers are the chief pottery types. A cubical vase shows a Phœnician house with low gates at the corners, adorned with lozenges on the jambs, and above a frieze of vertical markings. Statuettes imply that already the camel was a beast of burden.[8]

Five miles south of Gebal is a river. In ancient times it was called the Adonis, to-day Adonis has been supplanted by Abraham. The traveller at once begins his ascent along the side of a deep gorge, with houses here and there by its dashing stream. Soon the moist heat of the coast gives place to a refreshing coolness. Half way up and close to the gorge are ruins of a temple, still called in local tradition the "House of King Adonis," where in antiquity the pious pilgrim was shown the "Tombs of Adonis,"[9] or saw in relief Adonis struggling with the boar. Finally a great amphitheatre is reached directly under the towering crest of Lebanon, the "White Mountain." Beneath a low natural bridge and a cave a great spring bursts forth in the stream bed. The road winds south through pines along a terrace and comes to a second cave and a second spring with beautiful waterfalls. Facing them on a bluff, from which a third spring gushes forth through a tunnel, are the ruins of Aphek.[10] Above are fine groves of walnuts, below is a view of a fertile though narrow valley.

In this charming spot on the rocky slopes of Lebanon, far from the travelled roads, the ancients localised the story of the Lady of Gebal and her lover, the "Lord" Adonis, son of Cinyras, king of Gebal. Under these trees they loved, at these springs Adonis hunted the wild boar, here he was tusked by the beast, and was borne dying to his sorrowing mistress. Each spring the river ran red with his blood; rationalist moderns ruin the story by pointing to the purple soil washed down by the spring floods.

[8]Montet, *Byblos*, 29 ff.; *Syria*, II, 1921, 333 f.; *Kemi*, I, 1928, 84; K. Sethe, *Ztf. f. ägyptische Sprache*, XLV, 1908, 7 ff.
[9]Lucian, *Dea Syria* 9.
[10]Fig. 27; Josh. 13:4; classical Aphaca, modern Afqa.

FIG. 27. APHEK, HOME OF ADONIS AND ASHTART.

FIG. 28. HARBOR OF BEIRUT, MOUNT SANIN IN THE DISTANCE.

Here, therefore, as in the temple founded by his father Cinyras at Gebal, were celebrated the rites which mourned his death. Beating their breasts, his worshippers lamented loudly. Offerings proper to a corpse, including the so-called gardens of Adonis, were made to the dead god. In one form of the myth Adonis was changed into an anemone, and to this day the anemone is called the flower of Noman, an alternate name of the god.

Next day Adonis was once more alive. Wild with joy his devotees carried his image in procession. Under the divine ecstasy women shaved their heads or sacrificed their honour and men their virility; dressed in female garb these self-made eunuchs henceforth served in the sanctuary.[11]

When certain rites were completed on a given day, fire dropped from the summit of Lebanon like a star and fell into the river below. Fire came also from a pool into which sank gifts accepted by the goddess while those rejected remained floating on the surface.[12] To this day the spring is inhabited by a "Lady," whose aid the sick implore by hanging rags on the sacred fig tree by the water.

Marked as was the influence of Egypt on Phœnicia, there are yet more striking indications of the reverse movement. We find traces of contact in the most conservative part of Egyptian religion, the cult of the Dead. When the monarch would safeguard his journey in the after world by magical texts on the walls of his pyramid, he asserts control of the Haunebu, the men of the Mediterranean coast, or claims that it is for his own royal self that Re "hacks up the strongholds of Asia." More amazing still, we observe Syrian influence in that most sacred of Egyptian stories, the passion play of Isis and Osiris. For when the malignant Set had at last succeeded in destroying his rival, the mutilated corpse of Osiris was carried by the waves across the sea to the shore of Nedyt near Gebal.[13] After

[11]Ezek. 8:14; Is. 17:10; Lucian, *Dea Syr.*, 6 ff.; Theocritus, 15; Bion, 1; Ovid, *Metamorph.*, x, 503 ff.; Apollodor., iii, 14, 4; Euseb., *Vit. Const.*, iii, 55.

[12]Sozomen, *Hist. Eccl.*, ii, 5; Socr., *Hist. Eccl.*, i, 18; Theoph., *Chron.*, 24; Zosimus, i, 58.

[13]J. H. Breasted, *Development of Religion and Thought in Ancient Egypt*, 1912, 14, 20, 26.

all, this is not so surprising when we remember that the story of Isis and Osiris belongs to the same cycle of fertility myths as that immortalised by Shakespeare in his "Venus and Adonis."

A day's hard journey from this hallowed spot brings the traveller to the Cedars, preserved by their sanctity from the fate of their brethren. A mere dot in an immense amphitheatre, they look straight down the Qadisha, the "Sacred River," with its frowning cliffs and scattered villages, to its death in the Sacred Bay. We climb to the crest at their back, almost two miles above sea level and the most elevated in all Syria, and enjoy a marvellous view. From the near glacier under our feet the eye sweeps down slopes whose barrenness is broken only by the Sacred Cedars to the middle distance with its gorges and its villages half hidden amid terraced gardens, and comes to rest on the sea far below, the plain of Tripolis and the outjutting "Face of God." To the east the view is if possible more extensive, from the Lake of Kadesh and the Orontes in its deep-cut valley, through all Hollow Syria with its fertile length stretched out like a map of green, across to the long brown lines of barren Anti-Lebanon, and to Hermon, hazy in the far distance.

The whole long almost level spine of Lebanon is bare of vegetation. Its colour is greyish blue, save where its limestone is covered with dazzling snow or glows with all the colours of the setting sun. Lower down a stratum of sandstone adds its palette of tints, browns, purples, reds, and yellows; from the far off sea it can be traced by a line of green, the stone pines which favour its easily disintegrated soil.

On the middle terraces are the villages, which owe their existence to the waters that everywhere spring from the mountainside through the loose limestone strata. Persuaded by these crystal-clear, ice-cold fountains, the inhabitants have constructed terraces, often higher than they are wide, so that every vestige of soil is green with their gardens or their groves of walnuts, figs, olives, plums, or mulberries. Summer travel in the Lebanon is a continued delight, but it is bitter cold in winter and huge drifts bar off each village from its neighbour.

In antiquity the Lebanon was visited for its cedar. Millennia of exploitation have completed the work of deforestation, and now it is difficult to envisage the days when these bare mountain slopes were covered to their summits with the sweet-smelling cedar forests. The Sacred Cedars, with their few aged trunks, afford some slight aid in reconstructing the scene,[14] but it is better imagined a few miles southwest, where acres of younger trees fairly hide the bare rock.

From Gebal the ships followed the coast north. Soon they rounded a short east and west ridge of bare rock, easily crumbling into white dust, which the sailors called the "Face of God."[15] Passing Calamus, with the reeds from which it took its name, there followed a dreary stretch and then in contrast a little plain whose gardens revelled in many waters. Behind some islets of rock was sheltered the harbour of one of the three tiny villages which divided the plain. A second lay near the coast, where splendid fountains gave refuge to sacred fish; so tame were these fish that they rushed in solid masses to the pilgrims, who might acquire merit by their feeding.[16] Coasting around the deep but open bay the voyager remarked the sudden descent of Lebanon, to leave an easy pass through a fertile central plain and over basalt and gravel wastes to Central Syria.

Once more the hills, now called Bargylus, begin to rise, but less imposingly and at a greater distance from the shore. Orthosia, with its cult of El and Ashtart, lies on the south bank of the "Cold River," like the other streams of this region with a course of not over twenty-five miles. Seven miles back on a terrace which overlooks to the south the deep gorge of a river with the same name, lies Arka, a small village despite its temple of Ashtart, but with a fine view towards Lebanon and over the plain to the sea.[17] The coastal plain is now most

[14] Fig. 124, *History of Assyria.*

[15] Theuprosopon, Polyb. v, 68; Strabo, xvi, 2, 15,; Scylax, *Peripl.*, 104; native name perhaps Penuel, cf. Gen. 32:30.

[16] Fig. 24; modern Qubbet el-Bedawi.

[17] Gen. 10:17; I Chron. 1:15; Pliny, *Hist. Nat.*, v. 74; Joseph., *Ant.*, i, 138; ix, 285; *Bell.*, vii, 97; Macrob., *Sat.*, i, 21.

desolate and is used only for grazing. Stagnant pools lie at the mouths of the ravines, for the water reaches the sea only at the flood season. Even the "Great River" is but six feet wide and carries a few inches of water in summer.[18] Zemer or Simyra is perhaps to be sought in this region.[19]

We now reach the second great city of earlier times, Amor or Marath. Amor is connected with the Amorites, so often mentioned in the Bible; from it was derived Martu and Amurru, the names employed by the Babylonians for Syria, and the "Great Sea of Amurru," as they called the Mediterranean. In later days the place was celebrated for its fennel, which took its name from the city and was held in the left hand of its bearded god, now known as Marathus. A small stream, the classical Marathias, has preserved the ancient name as Amrit. Close to the sea on the north is the earlier site, a circle in the dunes is all that is left of its port. South of the stream is a mass of rough rock covered with later ruins.[20]

If we return to Gebal and sail south we pass the yet to be celebrated Dog River and reach Beruth, though in these early days there was small promise of the famous law school of Roman Berytus or of the commerce of present Beirut, but prehistoric flint saws and laurel-shaped lance heads afford unsuspected evidence to its claim that it was founded by El and that it was the oldest of Phœnician cities. There was little appeal to the early Phœnicians in its wide but open harbour, sheltered by a headland only to the south, in its reddish sands populated by the scarabæus beetle, symbol of immortality in Egypt, in its background of the purplish-grey peaks of Lebanon, in its view of the coast from "God's Face" to Sidon. Perhaps its sweltering humidity with never a change in summer, perhaps the poison wind from the north that prohibits sleep and sets the nerves on edge was the cause of its relative neglect.[21]

[18]Classical Eleutherus, Strabo, xvi, 2, 12; Pliny, *Hist. Nat.*, v, 78; I Macc. 12:30.
[19]Gen. 10:18; Strabo, l. c.; Pliny, *Hist. Nat.*, v, 77.
[20]References, *AJT.*, XXIII, 525 ff.; cf. fig. 51, *History of Assyria.*
[21]Fig. 28; Philo Bybl., 38; Steph. Byz., *s. v. Berytos;* Nonnus, *Dionys.*, xli, 68.

Beruth's patron god was Eshmun, the "Eighth," the son of Suduk, "Righteousness." Eshmun was another aspect of the hunter god; like Adonis, he was beloved of the mother goddess, called locally Astronoe. To escape her unwelcome attentions he deprived himself of his manhood and so died. The sorrowing goddess brought about his resurrection and set him among the gods, where he became the patron of the Galli, the eunuch attendants of the sanctuaries. Eshmun was "Eighth" by the side of his seven brothers, the Kabirim or "Great Ones," dwarfs with hammer in hand as patrons of the metal workers. As gods of navigation they invented ships and their gear, and sailors placed their figures at stem and stern of boats. Early identified with the Egyptian Ptah they borrowed his form for their statuettes, and in this guise they were carried over seas to be reverenced by the Greeks as Cabeiroi.[22] If we climb the terraced hillsides east of the city, famous in antiquity for their raisins and wines,[23] we may visit the high isolated knoll where was worshipped Baal Markod, the "Lord of the Dance."

We follow the coast south, where the huge sultan crab dashes from his sandhole into the water to ride back with the inrushing waves. Inland the mountains are still high, with two and even three terraces on their slopes. Bare as the land appears villages are numerous. Rock masses reach down to the shore and retreat, leaving a path for the Bostrenus River as it descends from its cave under the mountain crest. Near its mouth is a temple to Eshmun. From the hills by this temple we look over the long sandy shore on which the ancient galleys were beached, and upon gardens abounding with every fruit, oranges and lemons, apricots and almonds, figs and pomegranates, plums, peaches, and cherries, even a few date palms.[24]

In the midst of the plain is a low hill, now crowned by a

[22]Herod., iii, 37; Damascius, in Phot., 1074; Strabo, x, 3, 7; Philo Bybl., 36, 39; Hesych., *s. v. Kabeiroi*; Suidas, *s. v. pataikos*.
[23]Fig. 125, *History of Assyria*; Pliny, *Hist. Nat.*, xiv, 74; xv, 66.
[24]Fig. 37 f., *History of Assyria*.

mediæval castle, under which is hidden the earliest Sidon. The later city, on the shore, possessed two ports. The more important was the north harbour, protected by an island to the west, by reefs to the north, and by a wall along the east to a tiny islet. On the south side of the city was a smaller basin oval in shape and open only to the west. South of the two rises a huge heap of murex shells, debris from the famed purple industry.

Sidon was called by the Hebrews the first born of Canaan, while its own citizens boasted that it and not Gebal or Beruth was the oldest city in Phœnicia. Its name was derived from the hunter-god Sid, though in later times Sidon was connected with the Phœnician word for fish. To this day the natives reverence Nebi Seidun, the "Prophet Sidon," whose place of pilgrimage, southeast of the city, probably marks the site of his former temple. According to tradition the Sidonians first discovered the pole star and were the first to sail by night.[25]

Back from the gardens the hills slope gently upward to an even skyline broken only by the Twins of Niha. From the crest our view is different. Rivers curve sharply down narrow gorges thinly fringed with trees, clumps of verdure distinguish the squares of the fields. Progress on the road which clings to the upper terrace is slow, so numerous are the detours around the heads of the gorges. Fountains are abundant and each village street hears the music of running waters. Snows lie deep in winter; in summer the carefully stored snow is carried on donkey back to Sidon to cool the parched throat.

The Zaherani deserves its name of "Flowery," but to the south Lebanon declines lower and lower to a broad, open, and rather barren plateau. Villages are few and none is large. Cutting straight through this plateau and with banks of so nearly equal height that its presence is not suspected until the traveller is on the very brim is the deep gorge of the Litani, the true southern boundary of Phœnicia. In a cleft a thousand

[25]Gen. 10:15; Justin, xviii, 3, 2; Manil., i, 304 ff.; Strabo, xvi, 2, 24; cf. F. C. Eiselen, *Sidon*, 1907.

feet in depth, the home of the eagle and the coney, and so narrow that at one point it is crossed by a natural bridge, the Litani flows south along the eastern ridge of Lebanon until it suddenly turns at right angles due west and pours its deep green waters into the sea. The outer post of early Phœnicia is Tyre, as yet a tiny village; from the water it seems to be nestling at the very foot of Hermon whose peaks shine with old rose above drifting clouds in the sunset glow.

Although not the highest mountain in Syria, Hermon is the most impressive. In elevation it is little more than nine thousand feet, but its isolation forces a five thousand foot climb at almost any point in its circuit. On its outjutting foothills and looking up its valleys is a ring of temples which testify to its sacred character. If we compare the Muslim Harams at Mecca and at Jerusalem, we may conclude that its name impiies a holy "Place," set off from profane touch.[26]

As the sun declines we begin our ascent from the west. First we traverse sandstone, then the rock changes to limestone, and there are many springs. A long climb through a gorge and we hear dogs barking at a sheepfold. The trail is rougher, the wind strengthens, patches of snow appear. Each summit must be the last, but when we have topped it, there is another beyond. Just as the rosy light appears in the east we reach the true summit and watch the huge pyramidal shadow of the mountain creeping over the landscape below.

Three peaks compose this summit, to the north, the south, and the west. In the saddle between the northern and the southern is a small cave, rough hewn, its roof supported by a rude column of native rock. The flat space above was once the floor of the temple which crowned the sacred cave. An oval ring, sixty-five feet in diameter, encircles with rough cut stones a rock fifteen feet high, in whose centre is a cup eight feet deep. We have found the abode of Hermon's Baal, to whom all the temples below were dedicated.[27]

[26]Cf. Enoch, 6:5 ff.; J. A. Montgomery, *Aramaic Incantation Texts*, 1913, 126.
[27]Judges 3:3; I Chron. 5:23; Jerome, Onom., *s.v. Aermon*.

The view from Hermon is the widest and most instructive in all Syria. To the west the sea in appearance lies at our feet, from the distant projection of Carmel to Tyre near the exit of the Litani gorge, whose inmost recess is exposed to our gaze. Upper Galilee is spread before us and Tabor rises beyond. Now we realize how sharply Galilee is cut off by the Litani from Lebanon. Lebanon's increasing height prevents a view of the northern coast, but the southern group of cedars is in plain sight and the highest crest of the Cedar Mountain towers almost due north.

Next we look down into Hollow Syria, from this elevation as level as a floor, and across to Anti-Lebanon, whose sky line is less even than that of its mightier rival. All but a corner of the Damascus gardens and an oasis of green to our northeast is cut off by Hermon's lower slopes. Never again shall we enjoy such opportunity to study the desert edge. The long level swell of Iturea, the line of hills south of Damascus, the sharp break to their south, the more distant mass of the Leja, a strange wilderness of igneous rocks, all stand clear cut in the rays of the mounting sun, while only a glance at the cloudless sky convinces us that the dim something far beyond is the rough but fertile Hauran. To the southeast a continuous row of volcanic cones, aping exactly the mounds of ruined towns, cast their long shadows over the level Golan. From the southern slopes the view may be extended over the plateau of Bashan, famous for its bulls, or down into the Waters of Merom and the Lake of Galilee. The vague suggestion of land far to the south is the home of another "Lord," the Baal of Hazor, almost at the gates of Judah; from this spot, on a later journey, we shall again observe the magnificent blue-white summit of snow-clad Hermon.

CHAPTER VII

WAVES FROM EUPHRATES AND NILE

CENTRAL and Northern Syria have hitherto played little part in our story. Northern Syria comes into closest contact with Mesopotamia where the Euphrates, attempting in vain to reach the Mediterranean, is pushed southeast to Babylonia and the Persian Gulf. Through this gateway Babylonian influences swept westward and southward to rival those from the mighty power on the Nile.

Shumerian influence can be traced in Egyptian art back to predynastic times, and they did not cross Syria without leaving an impression. Nor was this influence merely in culture. As early as the twenty-seventh century, a king of Uruk, Lugal-zaggisi, boasted of conquests to the Upper Sea, the Mediterranean. His immediate successor, Sargon of Agade, is more specific, for he mentions the "Upper Land, that is, Mari, Iarmuti, and Ibla, as far as the cedar forest and the silver mountain." The silver mountain is in Asia Minor, just north of the Cilician Gates, the cedar forest is on Amanus or Lebanon, Mari is probably Amor or Amurru; the other places may be located in North Syria. These expeditions appear to have led to no conquest, but they did open the land to Babylonian contacts; for example, Gudea, the governor of Lagash under Gimil Sin (2221–2213), secured building material from Tidanum or Syria.[1]

Carchemish was at this time the most important gateway. A new people took advantage of the gateway position to create a new prosperity, but the older race continued to exist as a subject population and still buried their dead in pots under their house floors. Entirely new customs and a new technol-

[1] A. Poebel, *Historical and Grammatical Texts*, 1914, no. 34; Ira M. Price, *Great Cylinder Inscriptions of Gudea*, 1927, 62; cf. *AJSL*, XXXIII, 1917, 308 ff.

ogy came in with the invaders. Carchemish was fortified by ring walls, on the land side of heaped-up earth, on the river a brick-lined water-gate was flanked by adobe walls over stone foundations. Blocks intended to be seen were hammer-dressed, now and then the edges were drafted by hammer or chisel.

Bronze was in full use. Spears of poker shape, sometimes with a tang, and bent toggle pins with eyelets were the most characteristic metal objects. The potter's wheel was known, though the execution was rather rough; the champagne-glass form was almost exclusively employed. Paint was rarely applied and then only an inferior reddish-brown; decoration was equally simple, a mere zigzag or wave. The dead were buried under or close to the houses in large cists of rough blocks; the body was laid contracted on its side and with a north-south orientation.

The newcomers reached Carchemish towards the end of the third millennium, probably from Asia Minor. For a thousand years their culture remained unchanged in essentials, though in details there was active development. A second bronze age shows the disappearance of the characteristic poker spears and champagne vases, the dead are no longer buried under the houses but in regular cemeteries, the cists are smaller and are constructed of better-made slabs; there is no longer orientation, and the bodies are laid full length.

Many European analogies may be cited for the bronze implements. A socketed bronze axe is parallelled from Hungary. The rivetted dagger blade has an Ægean appearance, the leaf-like spear head is more slender and shows the beginning of a central rib, the long narrow celt is pierced for a rivet. Pins, often with round head, are numerous, and some of the shanks are pierced. Earrings of twisted bronze and torques with curled ends serve as ornament. Light pinkish jars are burnished in a spiral, starting from the base, or are banded with red hæmatite paint. Spindle whorls of steatite attest the textile arts. Beads are of paste, rock crystal, carnelian, lapis lazuli, or shell; there are shell pendants and

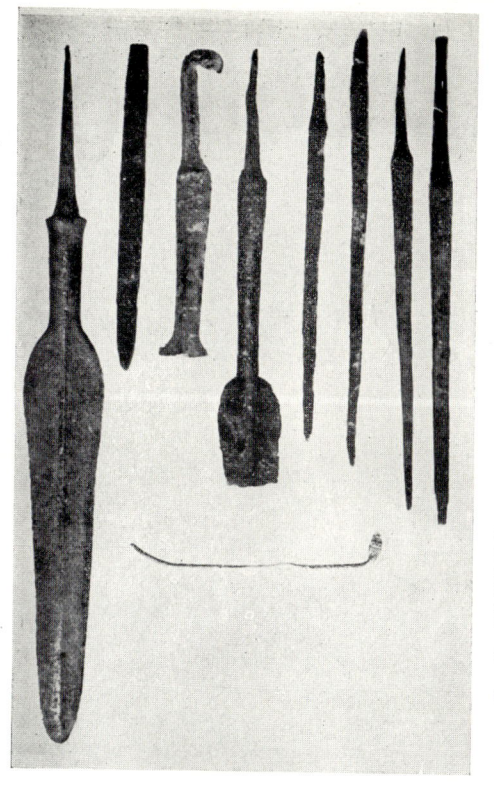

FIG. 30. BRONZE IMPLEMENTS AND SILVER PIN. (Carchemish.)

FIG. 32. BULL'S HEAD RHYTON. (Carchemish.)

FIG. 29. POT GRAVE. (Carchemish.)

FIG. 31. CHAMPAGNE-GLASS JARS. (Carchemish.)

mother-of-pearl disks. Trade down the river is indicated by steatite cylinders bearing Shumerian designs and an isolated cuneiform inscription, as well as by references to Carchemish in business documents dated under the first dynasty of Babylon.[2]

Amorites were in Central Syria by the commencement of the second millennium. Heated discussions have raged over Amurru and the Amorites; they have been credited with the major part of Babylonian culture, but this has been as emphatically denied. They first appear at Mari, on the middle Euphrates, to which an early Babylonian dynasty is assigned. Amurru was attacked by Shar-gali-sharri, a late king of the Agade dynasty, and Amorite workmen appeared at the same time. They had risen from workmen to mercenaries by the close of the third dynasty of Ur, and this dynasty was supplanted by an Amorite dynasty at Isin. The more important first dynasty of Babylon was likewise Amorite.

From their names, regularly a sentence, we learn that the Amorite language belonged to the West Semitic group. It was thus akin to Phœnician, Canaanite, the later Hebrew, and the still later Aramaic, as contrasted with the East Semitic Akkadian of Babylonia, the Semitic element of Egyptian, the South Arabian, and the Ethiopic. Yet its vowels were typically Akkadian and it shared certain peculiarities, especially its shift of the sibilants, with the South Arabian. Often the proper names are identical with those of the South Arabian inscriptions, and in both there are frequent compounds with Abi or Ammi, the divine Father or Uncle. As they spoke a Semitic language the Amorites must have contained an Arab element, but in Syria they were well mixed with Armenoids.

The Amorites took their name from their chief god, Amurru or Amor, a mountaineer, a hunter, and a warrior. His consort was the goddess of the waste places, Ashirat, connected in some manner with Ashur, eponym of the Assyrians, with Asher, god of the Hebrew tribe, and with the Asherah, the

---

[2]Fig. 29–32; C. L. Woolley, *Carchemish*, 38 ff.; *Liverpool Annals of Archæology*, VI, 1913, 88 ff.; IX, 1922, 47 ff.; D. C. Hogarth, *Kings of the Hittites*, 1926, 26 f.

sacred pole. Another much worshipped deity was the rain god, Hadad, Adad, or Addu, or again Rimmon or Ramman. Grain was personified in Dagan.[3]

Best known of the sites in Central Syria is Qatna, on an affluent of the Orontes, a short distance northeast of Homs, its modern successor. Palace and temple formed one great centre and occupied an elevated platform over four hundred feet from east to west and some two hundred and thirty from north to south. The platform was of beaten clay laid on reed mats and was faced by thick brick walls on stone foundations; the site was consecrated by foundation deposits of jars in which were buried children from two months to three years in age. A round tower and projecting wall guarded the main entrance on the south, which gave access to a court sixty-six by thirty-three feet, with thirteen feet thick brick walls bordered by polished orthostate slabs. In its centre were two small lustration jars set deep in the ground and surrounded by square wooden balustrades, in the middle of the north wall was a platform set on three supports, nearby was a relief of goats. On the east side of the court two good sized doors with bronze hinges and bolts led to the private apartments of the king and beyond; in the northeast corner of the complex was the harem, the women's quarter. On the north side were the service court and the storeroom with jars three feet tall. To the west the court permitted entrance to a long narrow room, broken by half walls into three sections, from which the visitor was conducted to the throne room at the north. Floors were of beaten earth, the walls were plastered and painted in simple colours. Roof beams were of cedar, fifteen feet long and a foot wide.

From the middle section of the ante-chamber to the throne room the royal gate led to the temple court; at its west end was a circular basin whose roof was supported by four wooden columns resting on basalt bases no less than six and two-

---

[3]A. T. Clay, *Empire of the Amorites*, 1919; D. D. Luckenbill, *AJSL.*, XL, 1923, 1 ff.; W. F. Albright, *JPOS.*, II, 1922, 125; cf. *AJSL.*, XXXIII, 1917, 319; XXXV, 1919, 87 ff.; *AJT.*, XXIII, 1919, 525 ff.

thirds feet across, and on either side of the basin was a room. At the northeast corner of the court was the holy place, its walls faced by orthostates, from which a curtained door permitted access to the tiny holy of holies hidden in the eastern wall and lighted only by a lamp. Here was the tiny golden statue of the goddess Nin-egal, the Lady of Qatna, and here were stored the treasures enumerated by a contemporary inventory. Nin-egal bears a Shumerian name, the shaven head of a priest or king follows the canons of Shumerian art, the inventory is written in Akkadian on a clay tablet but Shumerian influence cannot conceal the Syrian nature of her worship. Among the complex of rooms to the northwest is a typical open high place.[4]

While North and Central Syria were thus falling under the spell of Babylonia, Egypt was declining. As the sixth dynasty faded out and was succeeded by petty rulers too unimportant for remembrance, Asiatics in their turn invaded the Nile valley. Long centuries after, Hebrews told how their ancestor Abraham descended into Egypt. Now Abraham, it would appear, was not originally Hebrew but Amorite, in fact, an Amorite of this name actually lived in the Babylonian Dilbat under Ammi-zaduga about this time; there may well be some connection between the Hebrew story and the Asiatic invasion of Egypt.[5]

An Egyptian sage, Ipuwer, paints a dark picture. Men of the desert are in the land and lay it waste, the foreign bowmen have come to Egypt. Asiatics are in the marshlands of the Delta. Men no longer sail north to Gebal, how shall Egypt secure cedarwood for her coffins?[6] Gebal too suffered attack and its temple was burned.[7]

There was no improvement under the ninth and tenth dy-

[4]Fig. 58; Comte du Mesnil du Buisson, *Syria*, VII, 1926, 289 ff.; VIII, 1927, 13 ff.; 277 ff.; IX, 1928, 6 ff.; XI, 1930, 146 ff.
[5]Gen. 12:10 ff.; A. Ungnad, *Vorderasiatische Schriftdenkmäler*, VII, 1909, 92, 97, 101 f., 198; *Urkunden aus Dilbat*, 1909, 82.
[6]A. H. Gardiner, *Admonitions of an Egyptian Sage*, 1909; Breasted, *Religion*, 203 ff.; A. Erman, *Literature of the Ancient Egyptians*, 1927, 92 ff.
[7]M. Dunand, *Syria*, X, 1929, 207.

nasties. An unknown king of the period gives admonitions to his son Merikere. He has recovered the Delta from the invaders, the Horus Way on the Isthmus of Suez has been equipped to repel their attacks; he has caused the Delta to smite them, he carried captive their inhabitants. "Behold the wretched Asiatic, evil is the land in which he is, a land troubled with water, made inaccessible by many trees, its paths made toilsome by reason of the mountains. He dwells not in a single place, but his legs are ever driven wandering. He is fighting from the days of Horus. He conquers not nor is he conquered. He announces not a day in fighting." Let not Merikere trouble himself about the Asiatic, he plunders a lonely settlement but will not attack a populous city.[8]

Egypt was still overrun with Asiatics when the eleventh dynasty began the reconquest of the Nile valley. One of the Mentuhoteps pictures alike the defeat of Egyptian rebels and of Asiatic Setetiu. Another warred with the Amu and Mentiu, who are shown on his temple walls, the men pierced by arrows or smitten by battle-axes, the women bearing their infants in baskets.[9]

Under one of these Mentuhoteps, the sea-captain Akhthoi was treasurer of the god king in making impotent the foreign lands. He inspected the Mineral Country, Sinai, and traversed the lands of Thenhet. When he was in the houses of the Northerners he sealed up the treasuries in that mountain of the House of Horus of the Turquoise Terraces, after having taken turquoise from the gallery of Per Shema. A second time he made trial with another gallery which had been made for Horus himself. He punished the Asiatics in their countries and returned in peace to the palace, bringing his master the best of the foreign lands, new, shining, and hard metals, lapis lazuli, and other unknown commodities.[10] His expedi-

[8] W. Golénischeff, *Les papyrus hiératiques de l'Ermitage*, 1913; Gardiner, *JEA.*, I, 1914, 20 ff.; Erman, *Literature*, 75 ff.
[9] Breasted, *Rec.*, I, 204 f.; F. W. von Bissing, *Denkmäler ägyptischer Sculptur*, 1914, pl. 33 a; E. Naville and H. R. Hall, *Deir el-Bahari, XIth Dynasty Temple*, I, 1907, pl. XIV f.
[10] A. H. Gardiner, *JEA.*, IV, 1917, 28 ff.

tion was apparently the first attempt to work the mines at the Wadi Serabit since the days of Snefru.

A remarkable illustration of the renewed interest in Syria may be found in certain platters and bowls. On them were written in ink the names of "all Amu of Gebal," and a long list of lands and princes, "their mighty men, swift runners, allies, and associates, who shall rebel, intrigue, fight, or talk of fighting or intriguing in any part of this land." The pots were then deliberately broken that through sympathetic magic the enemy might likewise be destroyed. The list provides a regular onomasticon of states and rulers at the end of the third millennium, but unfortunately identification is not always sure. Among the states or peoples may be found the Amu, Gebal without a king, Ullaza, Arka, Ushu or Old Tyre, Iarimuta, Ashkelon, possibly Jerusalem, the Jordan Hamath, Aijalon. Nearly all the rulers have good Semitic names, some familiar from the Bible. They reverence Shemesh and Sin, the sun and moon gods, Hadad the weather god, the divine king Milk, the Amorite Amurru and Amm, Anu and Damu who may be Babylonian, or simply El, the "God."[11]

Definite information as to the final expulsion of the Asiatics is given in a prophecy attributed to Neferrohu and said to have been delivered before Snefru. Quite in Biblical fashion, Neferrohu predicts the time when Egypt shall be utterly destroyed, when the sun shall be veiled, the Nile be dry, the crops a failure, and beasts occupy the land, with none to affright them. The Asiatics shall approach in their might, their hearts shall rage against the harvesters, they shall take away the cattle from the plowing. Then shall a king named Ameni come from the south, and the Asiatics shall fall by his sword. He shall build the "Wall of the Prince" to bar the Asiatics from descending into Egypt, thenceforth they must beg water for their cattle as aforetime.[12]

[11] K. Sethe, *Die Ächtung feindlicher Fürsten, Abh. Berl. Akad.*, 1926, 5; R. Dussaud, *Syria*, VIII, 1927, 216 ff.; F. L. Griffith, *JEA.*, XIII, 1927, 274 f.; W. F. Albright, *JPOS.*, VIII, 1928, 223 ff.

[12] Golénischeff, *l. c.*; A. H. Gardiner, *JEA.*, I, 1914, 100 ff.; Erman, *Literature*, 110 ff.

This is prophecy after the event. Ameni and his son Sesostris had been cursed by the broken pots; soon after he was to ascend the throne as Amenemhet I (2000–1970) and to found the twelfth dynasty. He did not stop with the expulsion of the Asiatics, but carried the war into Canaan. His lieutenant, Nessumontu, defeated the Asiatic Troglodytes, the Intiu-Mentiu-Setet, the sand-dwellers, overthrew the strongholds of the nomads, and coursed through the fields, going forth in the presence of those who were behind the defenses (1977).[13] Amenemhet ordered his statue placed in the temple of the Lady of Turquoise, and Sinai enjoyed a new prosperity.

Gebal again recognised Egyptian suzerainty. The seal of its local dynast well illustrates the mixed Phœnician culture at the beginning of the second millennium. In form it is a Babylonian cylinder. Its material is lapis lazuli, brought from the far mountains of the Iranian plateau. On it are inscriptions in two languages. That in Egyptian hieroglyphics reads "King of Upper and Lower Egypt, Amenemhet, beloved of Hathor," and we are doubtless to add "of Gebal"; having thus honoured his master by the use of the royal language, he adds his own name in the more familiar cuneiform, "Iakin-ilu, servant of" Amenemhet.[14]

At the death of Amenemhet, while it was still a state secret, a courtier named Sinuhe heard the startling news. In mortal fear he fled to the "Wall of the Prince," built to repel the Setetiu, where he hid behind a bush out of sight of the watcher on the tower until darkness permitted him to slip across the frontier. By daybreak he had reached the land of Peten and the island of Kemwer in the isthmus lakes. He was ready to die of thirst when he heard the lowing of cattle and the Setetiu appeared. The chief had visited Egypt and recognised Sinuhe; he gave water to the fugitive, cooked him milk, and allowed him to remain with his tribe.

Sinuhe was then passed on from country to country until he

---

[13]Breasted, *Rec.*, I, 227 f.
[14]T. G. Pinches and P. E. Newberry, *JEA.*, VII, 1921, 196 ff.; W. F. Albright, *JPOS.*, II, 1922, 120.

reached Gebal. Gebal was Egyptian and no safe refuge, so he fled to Qedem, the region about Kadesh, where he abode a year and a half. At last he found a home with the chief of Upper Tenenu, Ammi-enshi, whose name shows the Amorites already in Central Syria. Other Egyptians were with Ammi-enshi, whether as exiles or as traders, and Sinuhe once more heard the speech of his native country. He claims that he urged submission to the new Egyptian monarch, Sesostris I; Ammi-enshi was quite willing to admit that Egypt was fortunate, but manifested no desire to surrender his independence.

Sinuhe was given the chief's daughter to wife and was assigned to the best lands in the frontier region of Yaa. A goodly land it was, with figs and grapevines, honey and olive oil, and every fruit on the trees. Wine was more abundant than water, there was barley and wheat also, and every kind of herd. Sinuhe was made a tribal chief, with daily rations of bread and wine, cooked meats and roast fowl, and every sort of cooked milk, game brought in by the hunters, and what he took with his own coursing dogs.

Many years he passed in this delightful land, while his sons grew up to be chiefs of their tribes. True to desert custom, Sinuhe urged each guest to remain as long as he desired; he gave water to him who was athirst, he set the lost on the road, he rescued those who had been plundered. When the nomads warred with the chiefs of the lands he showed another side of his character. Made general of his army by Ammi-enshi, Sinuhe drove the nomads from their pastures and wells, slaughtered their defenders, and carried off herds and captives as spoil. A mighty man of Tenenu challenged him to single combat, the women shrieked, the men shouted encouragement; Sinuhe avoided the arrows, javelins, and axe of his opponent, ran him through the neck, and despatched him with his own weapon.

Homesickness came upon Sinuhe in his old age. Thought of burial in a strange land by strange Amu and with only a goat skin for wrapping was abhorrent. Sesostris heard of this longing and sent word that the exile might return. His eldest son received his possessions and Sinuhe took his homeward journey. His beard was shaved, his nomad garb was removed, once more he could indulge the luxury of a bath and a real bed. Let the sand be restored to its inhabitants and the tree oil to those who knew no better ointment; Sinuhe would in due time be buried with full Egyptian rites.[15]

Meanwhile, Sesostris I (1980–1935) had been busy in Sinai. Around the hillside temple of the Lady of Turquoise the natives had piled up cairns or laid stones in circles with the pointed end upright or had erected standing stones as Bethels. A stele carved on all four sides with an inscription from the reign of Sesostris is an Egyptian imitation of such a Bethel.[16] A rude figure of the same king is dedicated by four Egyptians and a native Amu named Lua, which in Hebrew would be Levi. The finding of his amethyst scarab at Beth Shan suggests relations with Canaan, while a sphinx with the name of Ita, daughter of his successor Amenemhet II, reached more distant Qatna.[17]

Not long after, a certain Shamshi Adad set up his memorial stele in Laban, or Lebanon, on the shore of the Great Sea. Shamshi Adad was the first of that name to rule at Ashur, but he was not an Assyrian; his capital was Tirqa, in Mari on the middle Euphrates, and North Syria was included in his empire. His relation to contemporary powers is a tantalising mystery.[18]

Sesostris II (1906–1887) sailed north in twenty ships of cedarwood and slew the Setetiu. So we learn from his nomarch Khnumhotep, who has also depicted in his tomb the arrival of thirty-seven Amu led by the desert chief Abishai. All are pure Semites. Their thick black hair falls to the neck, the beard is pointed but without mustache. Their garments, kilts or long cloaks, are close fitted and fringed with elaborate decoration; the men wear sandals, the women high shoes.

[15]Erman, *Literature*, 14 ff.   [16]Fig. 33.
[17]Alan Rowe, *Topography and History of Beth-Shan*, 1930, 9; Comte du Mesnil du Buisson, *Syria*, IX, 1928, 10 f.
[18]*History of Assyria*, 28.

FIG. 33. SACRED CIRCLE AND BETHEL AT WADI SERABIT, SINAI.

FIG. 34. TEMPLE AT GEBAL, WITH REMAINS OF THE THREE COLOSSAL IMAGES IN THE EGYPTIAN STYLE.

Spears, clubs, and bows are their weapons; an ass carries a pannier and a lyre of Asiatic form. They are bringing eye paint as a gift.[19]

Canaan was again disturbed by an Egyptian invasion when Sesostris III (1887–1849) overthrew the Mentiu Setet. His

FIG. 35. THE DESERT CHIEF ABISHAI BRINGS EYE PAINT TO SESOSTRIS III.

advance carried him to Sekmem, plausibly identified with Shechem; the expedition enjoyed a doubtful success, for on the return journey the men of Sekmem united with the vile Retenu and were only held off by the rear guard under Sebek-khu.[20]

On his pectoral, Amenemhet III (1849–1801) strikes down the Mentiu and Setetiu, two bearded Semites armed with daggers.[21] Of all his dynasty Amenemhet III laboured most on the shrine of the Lady of Turquoise. His men were guided on three separate occasions by Khebdet, brother of the Retenu chief; reliefs show Khebdet on the back of a donkey, led by

[19] Fig. 35; P. E. Newberry, *Benihasan*, I, 1893, pl. XXXI.
[20] Breasted, *Rec.*, I, 302 ff.
[21] J. de Morgan, *Fouilles à Dahchour*, I, 1895, pl. XXI.

one of the Retenu, while another trudges behind with the water-skin.

Along the approach to the temple was a circle with standing stone and altar, dedicated in the forty-fourth year of Amenemhet (1805) as a royal offering to Hathor, Lady of Turquoise, for the *kas* of the chief chamberlain and of the deputy chief of the seal-bearers. The sacred cave was hewn into a rectangle, the walls and the rock pillar in the centre were smoothed. Prayers for the officials covered the walls, representations of the king the pillars. A niche at the far end of the room sheltered the sistrum of Hathor, two altars of sacrifice complete the inventory of the sacred furniture. Before the cave was a portico, faced with Amenemhet's stelæ, but completed by his son Amenemhet IV (1801–1792), on its front the seated goddess received offerings from the king. Outside was a court, along the approach were a dozen stelæ in rock-cut sockets.

More than a thousand years before Shumerians and Egyptians had invented the art of writing; whether the invention was made independently and if not which people can claim priority we cannot tell. In any case each followed the same principle. The writing was at first purely pictographic, mere representations of concrete objects. Later, the sound already connected with the sign was indicated without any reference to the object originally depicted. Early in their history the Egyptians made a further advance by specialising certain signs to represent the various consonants by the acrophonic principle; that is, they took as the phonetic value of the character the initial sound of the word it represented. Thus they formed a true alphabet of twenty-four signs, but the scribes refused to abandon completely the complicated hieroglyphics whose knowledge made their profession a learned mystery; normally the alphabetic characters were used merely to supplement the pictographs, and it was only in the transliteration of foreign names and words that the pictographs were abandoned.

Despite all the hieroglyphic inscriptions in Sinai to commemorate Egyptian mining expeditions, the natives retained their own Canaanite language and interpreters were always needed. During this period of intensive Egyptian exploitation, perhaps in the reign of Amenemhet himself, a native of Sinai learned from some Egyptian scribe the principle on which the Egyptian alphabet had been formed. He imitated the Egyptian hieroglyphs, upright in this period alone and not horizontal, which he saw on the monuments about him, but he gave to these signs Canaanite values and Canaanite names. The ox head was *aleph,* the house *beth,* the calyx *gabi,* the thornbush *dardar,* the figure with uplifted hands shouted *hallel,* familiar to us as "Hallelujah," the peg was *waw,* two twigs were *zain,* the pack was *hetel,* the hand *yad,* the frame *kaphis,* the ox goad *lamed,* waters *maim,* the snake *nahash,* the fish *samak,* the eye *ayin,* the corner *peah,* the pouch *serur,* the looped wavy line *qaw,* the head *rosh,* the tooth *shin,* the mark *taw.* Some of the names and all the sounds are preserved in the later scripts.

Unlike the cuneiform syllabary the Egyptian hieroglyphics did not represent the vowels; it was unfortunate that our inventor followed in this respect Egyptian rather than Babylonian practice. This failure to indicate the vowels was a serious defect, which was not even partially corrected until long after our story ends; in consequence we can rarely be sure that Semitic names and words are correctly vocalised.

Our unknown miner also borrowed the Egyptian order of writing, in vertical columns from right to left. Once the columns run from left to right, once the new Egyptian fashion of horizontal lines from right to left is imitated, once the lines run from left to right. At times the characters sprawl over the surface and defy arrangement. Now and then the inscriptions are incised within round-topped rectangles.

At first our inventor appears to have employed his alphabet for writing on scraps of papyrus and the forms of the letters became more rounded as he wrote them in ink with the Egyptian reed-brush pen. Soon he attempted brief inscriptions. Eighteen of these inscriptions have been thus far reported. The soft crumbling local red sandstone in which they are carved, the fact that some and perhaps the greater number are rejects, the primitive nature of the writing, the few signs in each inscription with a total known vocabulary of about thirty-seven words, all add to the difficulty of decipherment.

The clue is given by a small sphinx beneath whose paws and under whose shoulder is an inscription in Egyptian hieroglyph-

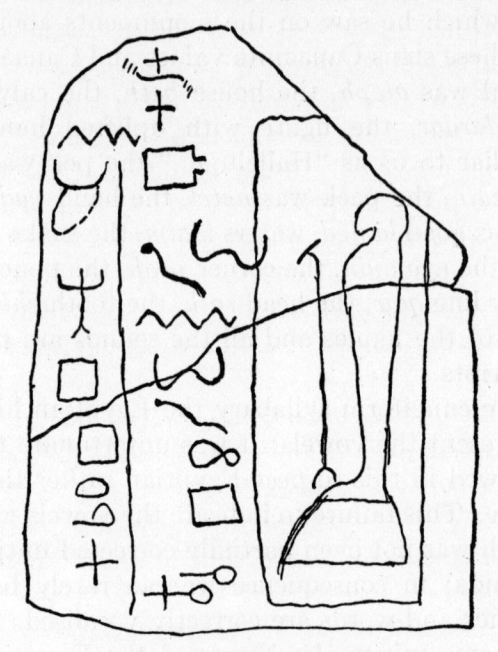

FIG. 36. SINAITIC INSCRIPTION.

ics: "Beloved of Hathor, Lady of Turquoises"; the accompanying Sinaitic inscription is deciphered: "Devoted to Baalat." Baalat, the local "Lady," is identified as usual with the Egyptian Hathor and is represented as a sphinx. Two similar sphinxes are a "Gift to Baalat." A seated statuette is "For fulfilment of my prayer, for favour, a votive offering to Baalat, for the favour of the chief of the stele makers."

A stele with a figure of the Egyptian god Ptah in his shrine and with his staff is presumably intended for the Lady's consort; the text is translated: "Gift of Ben Shemesh, the stele maker of Wepwawet, beloved of Baalat."[22] Another stele is

[22]Fig. 36.

"Gift of Ben Shemesh, beloved of Baalat"; the figure of the Egyptian jackal god Wepwawet has been erased, but there follows his proper title, "leader of the ways." A third commemorates "Sindan of Seir, chiseller of stelæ, beloved of Baalat." In the name of one dedicator we find Shemesh, the sun god, in that of the other moon god Sin; the appearance of a devotee of Sin at Sinai makes more probable the old hypothesis that Sinai does receive its name from this same moon god.

Three inscriptions are more boastful: "I am . . ., maker of stelæ, beloved of Baalat"; "I am . . ., chief of the stele makers from Seir of the Sea," "to Baalat"; "I am Hur, son of . . ., beloved of Baalat." We are reminded of Hur, one of the kings of Midian, next door to Seir, who was killed by Moses.[23] An inscription within a mine says: "I am badger," that is burrower or miner, "Sahmilat, chief of mine shaft number four"; the name of the miner is Arabic and commemorates the ancient Arab goddess Ilat. All these inscriptions come from the Wadi Serabit; a single inscription from the Wadi Maghareh is a "Gift of the beloved of Baalat."

The chief value of these short and difficult inscriptions is the evidence of the first invention of the alphabet. In due time the alphabet was carried to South Arabia, which developed its own peculiar forms among the Minæans and Sabæans, pushed north in late days into the Syrian desert as Thamudæan, Lihyanian, and Safaitic, and won a final victory in Ethiopia. The alphabet was likewise carried to Canaan at an early date, as is proved by a single sherd of Middle Bronze Age pottery (2000–1600 B. C.) from Gezer on which is incised the proper name "Ben Y. . . ."[24] Here it was met by the cuneiform and for centuries its progress was checked; at last it was adopted by the Phœnician merchant princes and its success was henceforth assured.[25]

[23] Num. 31:8, Josh. 13:21.
[24] Fig. 100; W. R. Taylor, *JPOS.*, X, 1930, 17, 79 ff.
[25] The original account has been completely revised in the light of the brilliant decipherment by my colleague Martin Sprengling, *The Alphabet: its Rise and Development from the Sinai Inscriptions,* 1931; cf. also W. M. F. Petrie, *Researches in Sinai,* 129 ff.; A. H. Gardiner and T. E. Peet, *Inscriptions*

Gebal flourished under renewed vassalage to Egypt. The city wall, fourteen feet thick at the northwest corner, followed the rock in scarped steps. Alterations were made to the sacred cave and a second human sacrifice renewed its connection with the temple of the Lady of Gebal, which rose again from its ashes. A long approach, later flanked by columns, led to the north gate with lintel of uræi serpents in the great quadrangular enclosure wall of the sacred "place." Within the enclosure was a great open court paved with stone slabs where stood the bronze altar on a stone foundation, but the most sacred spot was in the centre where within an open balustrade was the four-foot pyramid on whose northern side was rudely depicted the death of Adonis and the sorrow of his Lady. Opposite the north gate was the royal gate which led between two columns to a vestibule; during the eighteenth dynasty the entrance was flanked to the west by a squarely posed standing colossus, the fists held tight against the sides, to the east by three colossi on square thrones with feet firmly planted on footstools. West of the vestibule was a small room for a large well-built lustral basin, east of the vestibule and behind the three seated colossi was a small shrine with an altar of incense.[26]

A large jar under the pavement held a foundation deposit, whose contents well indicate the mixed character of Phœnician culture. An elaborate medallion of two gold disks soldered together and adorned with inset six petalled flowers, crescents and disks of stone, follows Egyptian technique, but is of native manufacture. Scarabs of gold, silver, crystal, carnelian, or bone, often set as bezels in rings, are copied from the Egyptian, but the designs show a certain originality. Bronze figures of the sacred ibis or baboon or of the infant Harpocrates with

of Sinai, 1917; A. H. Gardiner, *JEA.*, II, 1915, 61 ff.; H. Grimme. *Althebräische Inschriften vom Sinai*, 1923; *Die altsinaitischen Buchstabeninschriften*, 1929; K. Lake, R. P. Blake, R. F. Butin, *Harvard Theol. Rev.*, XXI, 1928, 1 ff.; A. E. Cowley, *JEA.*, XV, 1929, 200 ff.; J. Leibovitch, *Ztf. deutsch. Morgenländischen Gesell.*, NF., IX, 1930, 1 ff.

[26]Fig. 34; Plut., *de Isid.*, 13, 16; Luc., *Dea Syr.*, 6 f.; Montet, *Byblos*, 32 ff.; M. Dunand, *Syria*, VIII, 1927, 93 ff.; IX, 1928, 173 ff.; X, 1929, 206 ff.; M. Pillet, *ibid.*, VIII, 1927, 105 ff.; R. Dussaud, *ibid.*, VIII, 1927, 113 ff.

FIG. 39. SCEPTER OF IAPA-SHEMU-ABI, KING OF GEBAL.

FIG. 40. SILVER VESSELS FROM GEBAL.

FIG. 37. SARCOPHAGUS OF ABI-SHEMU, KING OF GEBAL.

FIG. 38. OBSIDIAN OINTMENT JAR AND COFFER SENT BY AMENEMHET III AND AMENEMHET IV TO KINGS OF GEBAL.

finger in mouth came straight from the Nile as did the necklace of faience beads. Seal cylinders with hunting scene or the bull with cone on back facing the seated goddess are as evidently North Syrian. Diadems, torques, spirals, and elaborately headed pins can only be parallelled from South Russia.[27]

Gebal's wealth and the foreign trade which made this wealth possible are even better illustrated in the tombs of its local kings. Under an upper structure, now destroyed, a walled shaft descended through the rock and led to a small room containing a massive sarcophagus of polished white limestone, whose only ornament was the curious knobs on its lid. Around it were placed jars and saucers of clay or bronze or of Egyptian alabaster, once filled with offerings of food and drink. In the sarcophagus, oriented due north and south, lay the dead Abi-shemu, extended on his back and with his head to the south. For his soul's refreshment he took with him mutton, beef, partridge, and fish. His dress was sewn with gold and ivory. Around his neck were a gold hawk collar and a necklace of a hundred and two amethyst beads with a heart-shaped pendant of limonite. His Egyptian sandals were silver. On his arm was a gold bracelet, on his fingers a scarab set in gold and a gold ring with a fine amethyst for bezel. By his right side lay his bronze sceptre, of the Babylonian sickle shape but adorned with the gold-headed uræus snake of Egypt, the wooden handle ornamented with golden rosettes. A small vase of Nubian obsidian, banded with gold and with the hieroglyphic indication of "first quality of incense" in golden characters, bore on its cover the cartouche of Amenemhet III; it contained the ointment sent for the coronation, and so much did Abi-shemu prize it that he carried it, still half full of the precious substance, with him to the after world.[28]

Iapa-shumu-abi connected his tomb with that of his father Abi-shemu by a winding passage, for like contemporary Egyptians he hoped thus to see his father daily. Unlike his father, he was buried in a simple coffin of wood, but his grave furniture was equally rich. We learn his name from his sceptre, a

[27]Montet, *Byblos*, 111 ff.   [28]Fig. 37 f., 40.

wooden handle with gold rosettes, the curved upper half of bronze; on it is inlaid on either side a bronze serpent, its head and scales of gold, with the inset hieroglyphic inscription: "Count of Kupna, Iapa-shumu-abi, renewed of life, born of the count Abi-shemu, deceased." Although he thus admits himself an Egyptian vassal by his use of the Egyptian administrative title "count," he nevertheless imitates the full royal pomp of Egypt. On his brow is a golden diadem ornamented with repeated Egyptian hieroglyphics above which rises the royal Egyptian uræus serpent of bronze with silver inlay. His gold repoussé collar is tipped by royal hawks' heads, around its lower edge are tear-shaped drops, in the centre a hawk spreads his wings and holds in his claws rings from which stretch ropes to other rings. His pectoral imitates that of an Egyptian monarch, the shrine with winged disk and two uræus serpents as cornice, the two supporting lotus columns, the hawk with extended wings and rings in claws above the sign for gold, the royal figure on either side, seated on a lion-footed throne and wearing the royal collar and the white Egyptian crown; inset in the gold is carnellian for the disk, wing tips, and thrones, emerald and lapis lazuli for the garments and the field. A cloisonné pendant is in the form of a gold shell. Around its border runs a row of four petalled flowers, each petal an emerald set in gold, with lapis lazuli between. A scarabæus beetle is flanked by uræus serpents, one with the crown of Upper Egypt, the other of Lower; that these crowns are not for his Egyptian master is shown by the royal cartouche with Iapa-shumu-abi's name within. Below is the golden-headed hawk, his body of multi-colored stones. Despite this independence he took to his grave the obsidian coffer inlaid with gold and the vase of grey granite which bore the name of Amenemhet IV. A gold bracelet was set with a magnificent amethyst, a silver mirror had a wooden handle of papyrus form covered in part with gold foil. Knives, spoons, and forks of gold, silver, and bronze could be used for the funeral feast.[29]

One of these princes may have dedicated a nine foot statue

[29] Figs. 39, 41–43.

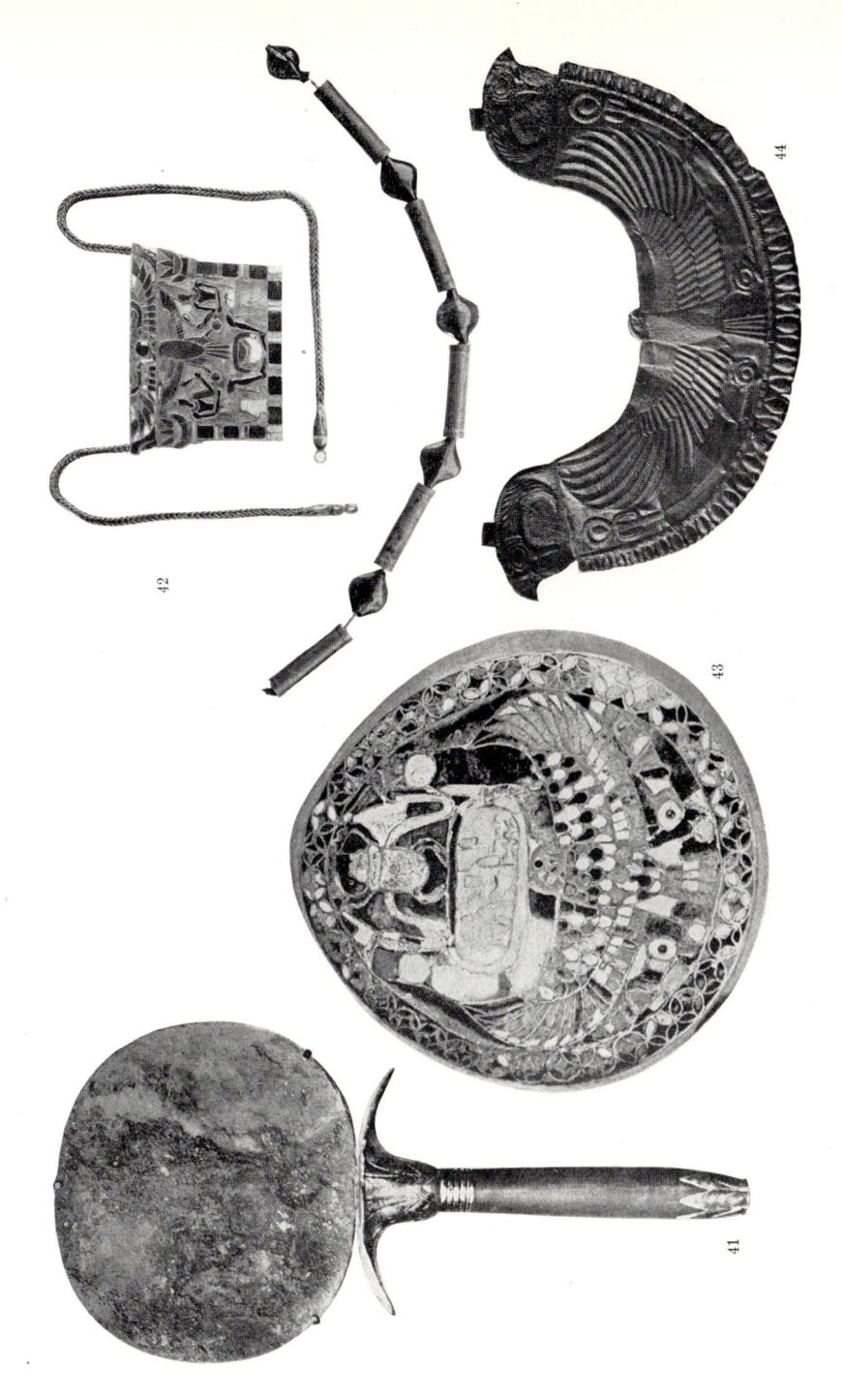

Fig. 41. MIRROR FROM GEBAL. Fig. 42. PECTORAL AND NECKLACE OF IAPA-SHEMU-ABI. Fig. 43. ORNAMENT FROM GEBAL.
Fig. 44. HAWK COLLAR FROM GEBAL.

of poor local limestone. The smiling face is Semitic enough, but the pose, hands at side, left foot front, the short girdled robe, and royal headdress, all are copied from some statue of the Pharaoh.[30]

Another royal tomb contained much the same equipment. Specially to be noted is the gold bracelet with beautifully polished amethyst and a gold hawk collar, whose face has been so carefully retouched as to produce one of the most superb objects of ancient art.[31] A fourth tomb belonged to a prince whose name cannot be read with certainty, though he bears the Egyptian titles hereditary prince, count, chief of chiefs, count of Kupna, and the vase is inscribed for his *ka*. The appearance of a "mayor of Kupna" seems to indicate the abolition of the royal office, but if so Gebal won back her autonomy under the weak thirteenth dynasty. A grave stele depicts the "count of Kupna, Yinnaten, renewed of life, born of the count Riyin, deceased," clad in a long robe and seated in a chair with lion's feet, his right hand extended to the cartouche of Neferhotep I, his nominal lord. Still later would seem to be a group of four royal tombs more roughly constructed and without Egyptian imports; vases bear within cartouches the names "Count of Kupna Abi" and "Abi-shemu, renewed of life," or the Hyksos title "chief of chiefs."[32]

Egyptian influence is as obvious in religion as in art. An ivory statuette represents the Lady of Gebal as nude but the technique is Egyptian. Ptah, the artificer god of Memphis, and Bast, the cat goddess, crossed the seas. Amon, the ram-headed god of Thebes, had become divine king of Egypt through the accession of a family from that district; in Egypt he was identified with the sun god Re, in Phœnicia with the solar Baal. Osiris, the dead god who ruled the underworld, shared the universe with Amon; he too was taken over by the Phœnicians and identified with his close relative Adonis, so

[30] Fig. 45. [31] Fig. 44.
[32] Montet, *Byblos*, 143 ff.; *Syria*, VIII, 1927, 85 ff.; X, 1929, 12 ff.; *Kemi*, I, 1928, 90 ff.; P. E. Newberry, *JEA.*, XIV, 1928, 109; C. Virolleaud, *Syria*, III, 1922, 273 ff.; H. Vincent, *RB.*, XXXII, 1923, 552 ff.

that his tomb could be shown in Gebal.[33] If the Lady of Gebal lost many of her native characteristics through absorption into the Egyptian Hathor, she was rewarded by honour in Egypt. Egyptian Coffin Texts assign to Hathor, Lady of Gebal, the task of marking the rudder for the sea bark of Osiris, and native Egyptian ladies bore her name.[34]

Egypt was crowded with Asiatic slaves. The Amu were employed as herdsmen and are frequently mentioned in contemporary records or are depicted in the tombs; the name Amu is followed by the sign for captive even when an embassy is described. We see captive Asiatics roughly pushed into the presence of a noble. Asiatic cattle, the fat long-horned "bulls of Amu," are congratulated by their herdsmen on the betterment of their condition. Once they trod the sand, now they walk on herbage; evil has been the voyage but disembarking is pleasant; now their master Thuthotep comes to them in peace.[35]

While Syrians were being carried into Egypt as captives or were entering as traders Egyptian influence swept over Canaan, carried at times by Egyptians themselves. Such an Egyptian occupied a house at Gezer. He has left us his figure in sandstone, knees to chin in the normal posture, but he has neglected to tell us his name. Perhaps he came to Gezer to practice his art, for a diorite palette with green paint still adhering, together with green enamel, ivory, and alabaster, was found in his home. The Egyptians Heqab and Dudu Amen died at Gezer and were buried without the longed-for embalming, but at least they could voice a prayer to Osiris and be commemorated by a funerary statue.

Scarabs entered Canaan in great numbers, as that of the "scribe of the vizier, Senbef," found in Jericho.[36] Those in enamel may have been Egyptian imports, but local craftsmen

[33] Steph. Byz., *s. v. Amathous;* Luc., *Dea Syr.*, 7; Plut., *Isis et Osir.*, 15 f.
[34] Breasted, *Religion,* 279; A. Erman, *Ztf. f. ägypt. Sprache,* XLII, 1905, 109 f.
[35] F. L. Griffith, *Hieratic Papyri from Kahun and Gurob.* II, 1898, 32, 35, 60, 73; P. E. Newberry, *el-Bersheh,* 1893, I, 29; A. M. Blackman, *Rock Tombs of Meir,* III, 1915, 11 ff.; *JEA.,* II, 1915, 13 f.
[36] Sellin-Watzinger, *Jericho,* 156.

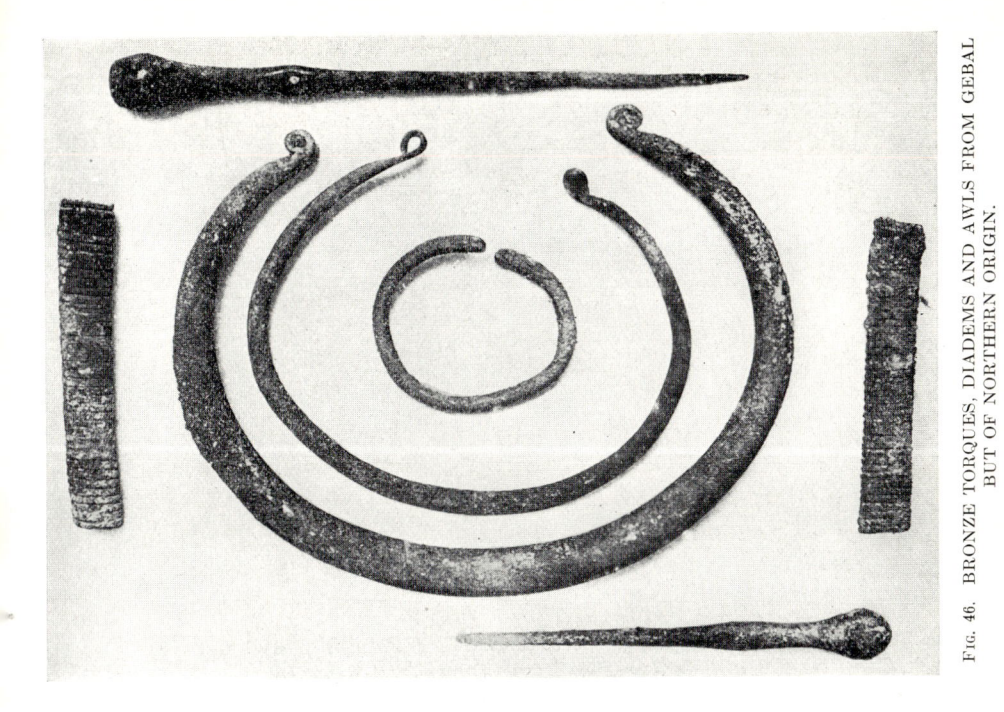

FIG. 46. BRONZE TORQUES, DIADEMS AND AWLS FROM GEBAL BUT OF NORTHERN ORIGIN.

FIG. 45. A NATIVE PRINCE OF GEBAL.

produced imitations in steatite, limestone, diorite, and basalt. Few could read the hieroglyphics they imitated, but they must often have inquired the meaning of the symbols, the sign of life, the lotus, the sphinx, the scarab itself, the scarabæus beetle with its promise of immortality. Other Egyptian symbols, the eye of Horus, the image of Khnum or of Hathor, testify to Egyptian ideas in religion.

Egypt likewise exported vases, in alabaster or in green enamel. Native potters now and then imitated their forms, but followed their own technique. A new potter's wheel, worked by the foot, had been introduced, and with it came a great improvement in the cleansing of the clay and in the execution. The walls were thinner and the clay baked much harder. These changes justify our forming a new group of pottery, the so-called Second or Middle Bronze which lasted some four centuries after the beginning of the second millennium. Combing soon disappears, moulding and incision are common, burnishing reaches its climax in red or yellow ware, ledge handles become debased and disappear. Flat-bottomed cooking pots, with punch holes below the rim and then an encircling raised rope band, are numerous. Bottoms are rounded to secure greater ease in handling. Lamps, mere saucers with one side slightly pinched out, make their first appearance. Cream slip is more common and paint more frequent. Colours are flat, there is red or brown and black polychromy. Designs are geometric, the so-called metope and triglyph encloses a bird and a fish or goats attack a tree. The new designs may have drifted in from far-away Elam.[37]

While Egyptian scarabs were employed as a rule for sealing, the Babylonian cylinder was known and copied. Atanah-ili of Taanach owned such a cylinder; Egyptian symbols were in the field, but the design was Babylonian and in Akkadian cuneiform Atanah-ili announced himself the servant of the Babylonian pest god Nergal.[38] Local copies of Babylonian scenes, the

[37]Macalister, *Gezer*, II, 155 ff.; H. Vincent, *Syria*, V, 1924, 82 ff.; W. F. Albright, *Ann.*, VI, 52 ff.; *ZAW.*, NF., VI, 1929, 4; Duncan, *Corpus*, 16 ff.
[38]Fig. 47; E. Sellin, *Tell Taannek*, 1904, 28.

100 PALESTINE AND SYRIA

prehistoric hero capturing the gazelle, the deer attacked by the divine eagle, the man on either side the altar, the priest introducing two worshippers to the god, so favoured by lapidaries of the last Ur dynasty, all are found at Gezer.[39] As with the

FIG. 47. SEAL OF ATANAH-ILI OF TAANACH.

Egyptian symbols, questions must have been asked as to the meaning of these scenes.

Philo of Byblus, who lived early in the second century of our era, has recorded the Phœnician cosmology and theogony. He claims to have translated the account from the Phœnician history of a certain Sanchuniathon, who dedicated his work to Abi-baal, king of Berytus in the eleventh or twelfth century before Christ. Sanchuniathon, Sakkon-yaton, "the god Sakkon has given," in Phœnician, in turn derived his information from official city or temple records, from a narrative by Hierombalus or Jerubbaal, priest of Ieuo, the Hebrew deity, and from the history of the Egyptian god Thoth. The pedigree is somewhat suspicious and Philo has doubtless added his own contribution; when all deduction is made we possess a valuable source for early Phœnician thought.

Air dark with cloud and wind and dark turbid chaos existed for countless ages. At last the wind, enamoured of its own parents, produced Desire, the beginning of creation. From

[39]Macalister, *Gezer*, II, 307 ff.

Desire came Mot, the primæval slime, and from Mot every germ of creation. From these senseless beings grew egg-shaped Zophe Shamim, "Observers of the Heavens," who possessed intelligence. Mot itself burst forth into light, the sun, moon, stars, and constellations.

With the light, sea and dry land appeared and were heated; winds and clouds arose and great floods from the waters of heaven. Divided and removed by the sun's heat, they met again in the air, and, dashing against each other, produced thunder and lightning. Startled by the noise, the animals awakened and began to move on land and sea, male and female.

From the wind Kol-piah, "Voice of a Breath," and his consort Bahau, "Void," were born Life Time and First Born, an Eve and an Adam, and Life Time discovered that food could be secured from the trees. Their offspring were Mankind, in Hebrew Enosh, and Womankind; in time of drought they stretched forth their hands to the sun, Baal-shamim, the sole "Lord of Heaven," and thus inaugurated divine worship. In the third generation were born Light, Fire, and Flame, the Reshuphs, who discovered how to make fire by rubbing sticks together. Their sons were mighty giants who gave their names to the mountains they occupied, Casius, Lebanon, Anti-Lebanon, and Brathy. Next were born Shamim-rum, "Heaven High," and Ousous or Esau, the "Maker."

Shamim-rum lived at Tyre and invented reed huts; as the first city builder, he naturally quarrelled with his hunter-brother Esau. Esau prepared garments of skin from captured beasts and poured libations of their blood on two pillars consecrated to Fire and Wind. After their death both Shamim-rum and Esau were worshipped by poles, pillars, and festivals.

Many years thereafter from the race of "Heaven High" were born Sid, the "Hunter," and Dayyog, the "Fisher," and from these came two brothers who invented metal working. Harosh, the "Smith" or "Magician," practised oratory, incantations and divination, invented hook, bait, line, and raft, and first made voyages. Walls of brick were the invention of his brothers. Of their race were Workman and First Earth Born, perhaps a Cain and another Adam, who mixed clay with straw for bricks, baked them in the sun, and invented roofs. From them came Shad, the greatest god of Gebal, whose shrine was drawn by yoked oxen; courtyards, sheep enclosures, and caves were his discovery. Hammon, the "Sacred Pillar," and Maon established villages and sheepfolds; from them came Misor and Suduk, "Righteousness and Justice." Suduk was the father of the Kabirim, the "Great Ones," who first constructed a ship; their descendants discovered herbs and the healing of venomous bites and charms.

In their time was born Eliun, the "Most High," and his consort Beruth. Eliun met his death fighting wild beasts—he is thus another form of Adonis—and his place was taken by Shamim, "Heaven." By his sister, Eres or "Earth," Shamim begat El, the "God," Bethel, the "House of God," the holy stone, Dagon, "Grain," the inventor of the plow, and a fourth son whose native name is unknown. Angered by his frequent infidelities, "Earth" broke with "Heaven," who attempted to slay her children but was driven off. Grown to manhood, El made alliance with the Elim, or gods, and dethroned his father. Then El founded Gebal, the first city in Phœnicia. At the same time the descendants of the Kabirim put together rafts and ships and made voyages; cast ashore near Mount Casius they consecrated there a temple. Suspicious of his youngest brother, El buried him alive in a great pit. This was followed by the murder of his own son Sadid and the beheading of his daughter. The gods now became alarmed. "Heaven" in exile dispatched his daughters, Ashtart, Tanit, and the "Lady of Gebal," to slay their brother by craft, but El detected their plan and married them by force. Another expedition led by Meni, "Fate," and Ate, was no more successful.

In the thirty-second year of his reign El set an ambush for his father "Heaven" and castrated him; the blood of the dying god dripped down into the fountains and rivers, which henceforth were sacred. El begat many sons and daughters, "Desire" and "Love" by Ashtart, Muth or "Death" by Tanit,

Anath, and others. He saw also grandsons, Eshmun, son of Suduk, a great-grandson, Yam, the "Sea," whose daughter Sidon invented song, perhaps Baal Tamar, whose son was Melkart. Finally El handed over Gebal to its "Lady," Beruth to Yam and the Kabirim, and the remainder of Phœnicia to Baal Tamar and Hadad, king of the gods.[40]

Such is the account of Philo, interpreted in the light of our present knowledge. The account is obviously composite, for it has incorporated the myths of more than one Phœnician city. Strata of different periods may be suspected, but the portions we have excerpted must date back at least to the earlier half of the second millennium. Echoes of Shumerian myths are recognisable; they are re-echoed in Hesiod's Theogony and in Genesis. Babylonian cosmology is on its way to the Hebrews.

[40]Philo Bybl., 32 ff.; cf. L. B. Paton, in J. Hastings, *Encyclopædia of Religion and Ethics*, XI, 1921, 177 ff.

CHAPTER VIII

THE MANNER OF CANAAN

SHECHEM is well called the natural capital of Canaan. Seen from the Mediterranean, its site marks the one break in the hills; closer inspection shows it the natural pass through the range to the Jordan and to the East Jordan country, the "Road of the Setting Sun."[1] Curiously enough, it is actually situated on the watershed, a part of its many waters flowing to the Mediterranean and a part to the Jordan on their way to the Dead Sea. Its name, the "Shoulder," is due to its location on a saddle between two imposing mountains, Ebal and Gerizim.

Ebal is the higher, a little over three thousand feet. A climb to its flat summit is rewarded, not by one view but by many. The greater part of middle Canaan lies map=like below, its hill top villages almost level from this height. To the north the view is especially fine; Carmel and Megiddo's plain appear but a few miles distant. Eastward, at our very feet, is the level expanse to which Shechem owes its wealth. Wet by the winter rains, its mud is amazingly tenacious, but spring presents a picture of beauty; the intense green of the growing grain, the more delicate green of the olive orchards, the dark blood red of the plowed fields, all contrast sharply with the greyish white of the barren hills which enclose it on all sides and with the lighter greys and yellows of the hamlets which follow its rocky border.[2] Beyond the plain and the break where the Jordan sinks down, stretches a far vista, from the line of the Moabite plateau, dimly seen through the haze, over the levels of Gilead and Bashan, broken by the deep gorges of the Jabbok and Yarmuk, to the dimmer Hauran, on the eastern desert border.

Descending through the great natural amphitheatre, we ascend again through a less marked amphitheatre to Gerizim,

[1] Deut. 11:30.
[2] Fig. 48.

THE MANNER OF CANAAN

white chalk below and dark blue limestone above, more than two hundred feet lower than its companion, but far more holy in the eyes of Shechem's inhabitants. Our direct view north and south is obstructed, but in compensation there is another picturesque survey of the plain a thousand feet below, of Mount Osha in Gilead and ice-crowned Hermon, of Mount Carmel, the plain of Sharon, and the sea.

Shechem is a veritable paradise, for in the narrow vale which opens out from the plain may be counted no less than eighty springs. Fruit trees or noble walnuts and sycamores crowd its limits. A little poem, attributed to Jotham but doubtless far older, tells its wealth:

> Once the trees went forth
>   To anoint over them a king,
>   And they said to the olive "Rule us."
> The olive replied to them:
> "Shall I leave the fatness in me
>   Which is honored by gods and men,
>   And go to wave o'er the trees?"
>
> Then said the trees to the fig:
>   "Come thou and reign over us."
>   But the fig replied to them:
> "Shall I leave my sweet and my fruit,
>   And go to wave o'er the trees?"
>
> Then said the trees to the vine:
>   "Come thou and reign over us."
>   But the vine replied to them:
> "Shall I leave my excellent wine
>   That cheers both gods and men,
>   And go to wave o'er the trees?"
>
> Then said the trees to the thorn:
>   "Come thou and reign over us."
>   And the thorn said to the trees:
> "If in truth you anoint me king,
>   Then come, be safe in my shade;
>   But if not, from the thorn will come fire,
>   And Lebanon's cedars shall eat."[3]

[3]Judges 9:8 ff.

On the edge of the plain lie two sites of unique importance. One is Jacob's well, dear to the Christian, for there Jesus once talked with the Samaritan woman. Cut to the depth of a hundred feet through earth and the soft rock of a spur from Gerizim, its abundant water is clear and cold. Hebrew tradition asserted it had been dug by their ancestor Jacob, but Jacob lived here long before the Hebrews entered Canaan. Two Hyksos rulers bore the names of Jacob-el and Jacob-baal, "Jacob is god" and "Jacob is lord," full evidence that Jacob was once a true deity. Jacob-el is also found as a place name in Egyptian lists. Under the sacred oak at Shechem Jacob buried the images of his family gods.[4]

Joseph's tomb was shown in the parcel of ground which his father Jacob bought from the sons of Hamor, the father of Shechem, the eponymous founder of the city, and so it is shown to this day, in the open plain just beyond Jacob's well. Joseph too was originally a divinity, for the Egyptians list a place name Joseph-el, "Joseph is god."[5]

From early times, Shechem was a centre of Canaanite religious life. Its patron deity was Baal Berith, "Lord of the Covenant," also called El Berith, the "God of the Covenant." Here was a holy "Place," a sacred stone, an altar, and an oak, variously called the "Oak of the Sacred Stone," the "Oak of the Soothsayer," or the "Oak of the Lawgiver," to which the men of Shechem assembled to crown a king; the site is still named Balata, the "Oak." Below the later temple recent excavation has uncovered traces of a shrine which dates back to our period. Under the altar of the second temple was an altar base of regular mud bricks, twenty-three by seventeen feet and ten inches high; under the pedestal of the god's statue was a beehive pit plastered with clay, a foundation deposit filled with animal bones and potsherds. The temple floor and the entrance sill, of large and small stones closely packed,

---

[4]John 4:6; Gen. 35:4; cf. 33:18; Thutmose III, no. 102; Ramses II, no. 9; Ramses III, no. 104; W. M. Müller, *Mitth. Deutsch. Vorderas. Gesell.* XII, 1, 1907, 27.

[5]Josh. 24:32; Gen. 33:19; Thutmose III, no. 78.

FIG. 48. PLAIN OF SHECHEM FROM JACOB'S WELL.
The traditional Tomb of Joseph at extreme left.

FIG. 49. TEMPLE, ALTAR, AND SACRED STANDING STONE OF THE LORD OF THE COVENANT AT SHECHEM.

was also laid bare. A narrow wall of thin crude bricks surrounded the little settlement.[6]

Under the auspices of this "Lord of the Covenant" and at this very "Oak of the Lawgiver" was probably issued the first Canaanite Code of Law, preserved through incorporation in the Hebrew Covenant Code. The Near East had early learned the rule of law. While Babylonia was still Shumerian, a code had been promulgated which was amazingly humane for so distant a time.[7] This code was translated into Akkadian by order of Hammurabi (1955–1913), but its provisions were thoroughly revised, and we can often trace the stratification, the basal principles, and their later development.[8]

Hammurabi's code shows us the Babylonian trader at work in foreign countries, his ventures closely restricted by legal rules. His business agreements were recorded on clay tablets, he may have carried a copy of Hammurabi's law or he may only have told of the code which bound him. Thanks to his influence, the Canaanites determined to prepare a code of their own. Tradition said it was written on two "tablets," the word used in Babylonia for tablets of clay, though later writers changed these "Tablets of the Covenant" to stone; the code we are about to study would indeed fill two such tablets as were used for copies of Hammurabi's Code.[9]

At first the code must have been oral, for its fifty provisions are divided into five "decalogues," and each of these into two "pentads," the more easily to memorize its contents. In each pentad, the first law is based on a provision of Hammurabi's code, but adjustment to a more purely agricultural society with lower cultural standards has resulted in significant changes. The purely secular character of the code is its most surprising feature.

[6]Fig. 49; Gen. 12:6 f.; Josh. 24:26; Judges 8:33; 9:4 ff.; 37, 46; E. Sellin, *ZDPV.*, XLIX, 1926, 313; L, 1927, 207; G. Welter, *Forschungen und Fortschritte*, IV, 1928, 317 f.

[7]A. T. Clay, *Miscellaneous Inscriptions*, 1915, no. 28.

[8]V. Scheil, *Mémoires de la Délégation en Perse*, IV, 1902; R. F. Harper, *Code of Hammurabi*, 1904; G. A. Barton, *Archæology and the Bible*, 5 ed., 1927, 340 ff.; stratification, M. Jastrow, *JAOS.*, XXXVI, 1916, 1 ff.

[9]Ex. 24:12; 31:18; Deut. 9:9; D. D. Luckenbill, *AJT.*, XXII, 1918, 46.

The first decalogue deals with enslavement for debt. Its basis was a law of Hammurabi: "If a man falls into debt and sells his wife, his son, or his daughter for silver, or hands him over for bond service, three years shall they labor in the house of their purchaser or their employer, in the fourth year their liberty shall be established."[10] From this, ten Canaanite laws, five dealing with males and five with females, were built up in the same precedent fashion: (1) "If you purchase a slave, six years shall he serve you, but in the seventh he shall go free without ransom." We at once recognise a difference between the two codes, the Canaanite slave must serve six years instead of three. There was definite realisation that in this respect the code was on a lower level than the Babylonian; when Hebrew masters attempted to evade even the six-year rule the humanitarian authors of Deuteronomy reminded them: "It shall not seem hard to you when you let him go free from you, for to double the hire of a hireling has he served you six years."[11]

Following provisions are mere expansions of the first: (2) "If by himself he came in, by himself shall he go out." (3) "If he were the husband of a wife, then his wife shall go out with him." (4) "But if his master has given him a wife and she has borne him sons or daughters, the wife and her children belong to his master, and the man shall go out by himself." (5) "But if the slave say: 'I love my master, my wife, and my children, I will not go out free,' his master shall bring him before the gods," the same phrase occurs in the Babylonian code, "and take him to the door or the door post, and his master shall bore his ear with an awl, and the slave shall serve him forever."

Woman was the equal of man in Babylonia, and there was no need for special legislation; such equality was specifically denied by the Canaanite code: (1) "If a man sells his daughter for a slave, she shall not go out as do the male slaves." Worse was to come. In Babylonia, a woman enslaved for debt was a servant, she owed service to her master but her honour was protected; in Canaan, her body was at the disposal of the

[10]CH. 117. [11]Deut. 15:18.

man who bought her and at best there was only an attempt to protect her rights as concubine. (2) "If she is unpleasing in the eyes of her master, so that he does not espouse her, then he shall permit her to be redeemed; to a foreign people he cannot sell her, for he has treated her treacherously." (3) "But if he espouses her to his son, by the custom of daughters shall he treat her." (4) "And if he takes to himself another wife, he shall not diminish her food, her raiment, or her marital rights." (5) "But if he does not do for her these three things, then shall she go out free for nothing without money."

For assault, Hammurabi's code provided: "If a man strikes a man in a quarrel and wounds him, he shall swear: 'I struck him without malice prepense,' and he shall be responsible for the physician. If he dies of the blow, he shall take oath, and if he is the son of a noble, he shall pay half a mana of silver."[12] This is the basis for three laws of the second decalogue: (1) "If a man smites a man, so that he dies, he shall be put to death." (2) "But if a man lies not in wait, but the gods deliver him into his hand, there shall be a place to which he may flee." (3) "But if a man comes upon his neighbour with intent to slay him by guile, though he flees to the altar, from the altar shall you take him that he may die." According to the Babylonian code, "If a son strikes his father, they shall cut off his fingers";[13] the Canaanite code is more severe, (4) "He who strikes his father or his mother shall be put to death." "If a man steals the minor son of a man," says the code of Hammurabi, "he shall be put to death";[14] the later code paraphrases: (5) "He who steals a man or sells him or he is found in his hand shall be put to death."

(1) "If two men contend and one smites his companion with a stone or with his fist, and he does not die but must keep his bed, if he rises again, even though he must walk with a staff, he who smote him is without guilt, only he must pay for his loss of time and must see that he is healed completely." (2) "If a man strikes his male slave or his female slave with a staff, and he dies under his hand, he shall be punished." This

[12]CH. 206 f.   [13]CH. 195.   [14]CH. 14.

on its face is an advance beyond the legislation of Hammurabi, but since no specific provision was made for the punishment, it must have remained a pious hope, ignored in practice, especially as it is largely nullified by the next section: (3) "Nevertheless, if he survives a day or two, he shall not be punished, for he is his own property." (4) "If a man smites the eye of his male slave or the eye of his female slave, and destroys it, he shall send him out free on account of his eye." (5) "If he knocks out the tooth of his male slave or the tooth of his female slave, he shall send him out free on account of his tooth."

Babylonia, the land of settled agriculturalists, needed careful rules for the misdeeds of animals: "If a bull gores a man as he is passing through the street and kills him, that case has no penalty. If an ox belonging to a man was wont to gore, and that he was wont to gore was made known to his owner, and he had not tipped his horns and had not kept him in, then if that ox gores the son of a noble and kills him, he shall pay half a mana of silver. If he is the slave of a noble, he shall pay a third of a mana of silver."[15]

The Canaanite lawgiver follows these provisions closely, at times literally, but he has not freed himself from the primitive concept of blood guilt, incurred even by beasts: (1) "If an ox gore a man or a woman and he dies, the ox shall be stoned and his flesh shall not be eaten, but the owner is without guilt." (2) "But if the ox was wont to gore in times past, and it was made known to his owner, and yet he had not kept him in, then, if he kills a man or a woman, the ox shall be stoned and its owner shall also be put to death." Nevertheless, provision is made for the weregeld, should this be acceptable to the surviving relatives: (3) "If the blood money is enforced against him, he shall ransom his life by the payment of all that is laid upon him." (4) "Whether he has gored a son or has gored a daughter, according to this decision shall it be done unto him." (5) "If the ox gore a male slave or a female slave, thirty shekels of silver shall be given to their owner and the ox shall be stoned."

[15]CH. 250–252.

THE MANNER OF CANAAN 111

In cases of negligence, the Babylonian code ordered: "If a man hire an ox, and through neglect or blows kills him, ox for ox to the owner of the ox shall he render."[16] This was diluted into three sections: (1) "If a man open a pit or digs a pit and does not cover it, and an ox or an ass falls into it, the owner of the pit shall make it good, he shall give its value to the owner, and the carcass shall be his." (2) "If the ox of a man injures the ox of his neighbour, so that it dies, they shall sell the living ox and divide its price, and the carcass they shall likewise divide." (3) "Or, if it was known that the ox was wont to gore in times past, and it was made known to its owner, and its owner had not kept it in, he shall pay ox for ox, but the carcass shall be his."

Regarding theft the code of Hammurabi decrees: "If a man steals an ox or a sheep or a pig or a goat, whether it belonged to a god or to the palace, thirtyfold shall he restore; if it belonged to a peasant, tenfold shall he restore; if he has not the money to pay the fine, he shall be killed."[17] This is turned into: (4) "If a man steals an ox or a sheep and slaughters it or sells it, five oxen for an ox and four sheep for a sheep shall he pay; if he has nothing, he shall be sold for the theft." (5) "If the stolen goods are found in his hand alive, whether it be ox or ass or sheep, he shall pay double."

Loss of property, either through trespass or through negligence, is the subject of the fourth decalogue. For trespass, the Hammurabi code decrees: "If a shepherd pastures his flocks on the grass without having made an agreement with the owner of the field, and has pastured his flock in the field without the consent of the owner of the field, the owner of the field shall harvest his field and the shepherd who has pastured his flock in the field without the consent of the owner of the field shall give twenty gur of grain per gan to the owner."[18] The simpler code of Canaan merely says: (1) "If a man causes a field or vineyard to be pastured, and lets loose his beast, and it pastures in another man's field, he shall make restitution from his own field, according to its yield, but if all the field

[16]CH. 245.　　　　　[17]CH. 8.　　　　　[18]CH. 57.

has been pastured, from the best of his own field and the best of his vineyard shall he make restitution." The addition of the vineyard shows different crops in cooler Canaan, while the assumption that the trespasser will have his own field and vineyard proves that there was not the sharp contrast between shepherd and farmer as existed in Babylonia.

In the Babylonian alluvium, negligence was best illustrated by irrigation: "If it is the duty of a man to strengthen his part of the dyke in his field, and he has not strengthened his dyke, and a break appears in his dyke, and the water injures the cultivated field, the man in whose dyke the break appeared shall restore the grain which he destroyed."[19] In Canaan, where there was little need of irrigation, the great danger to be apprehended was fire: (2) "If fire breaks out and catches in thorns, so that the shocks or the grain or the standing grain is consumed, he who kindled the fire shall make restitution."

There is a specific law of bailments in the Babylonian code: "If a man gives anything of his on deposit, and at the place of deposit, whether by burglary or by theft, something of his has been lost, together with something belonging to the owner of the house, the owner of the house who has been negligent and who has lost what was given him on deposit shall make restitution, and to the owner of the goods shall he restore it. The owner of the house shall search out whatever of his was lost and shall take it from the thief."[20] This is broken up into three laws: (3) "If a man deposits with his neighbour silver or implements to guard, and it is stolen from the house of the man, if the thief is found, he shall restore double." (4) "But if the thief is not found, then the owner of the house shall draw near to the gods and shall take oath that he has not put forth his hand to any of his neighbour's goods." (5) "For every case of breach of trust, for ox, for ass, for sheep, for clothing, for every lost object, of which it may be said 'This is it,' the case of both of them shall come before the gods; the one whom the gods condemn shall make double restitution to his neighbour."

[19]CH. 53.   [20]CH. 125.

Grazing was an important industry in the Babylonian alluvium, and its code applies a special rule to shepherds: "If in a sheepfold a stroke of god has befallen or a lion has killed, the shepherd shall declare himself innocent before the god and the owner of the fold shall suffer the damage to the fold."[21] This is changed to: (1) "If a man gives to his neighbour an ox or an ass or a sheep or any beast to guard, and it is injured or is driven off, and no man sees it, the oath of the gods shall be imposed between them that he has not put forth his hand to any of the goods of his neighbour, and its owner shall accept it, and he shall not make restitution." (2) "But if it is stolen from him, he shall make restitution to its owner." (3) "And if it is torn to pieces, let him bring it as witness; for the torn beast he shall not make restitution." (4) "If a man borrows from his neighbour a beast, and it is injured or dies or is driven off, and its owner was not with him, he shall make restitution." (5) "But if its owner was with him, he shall not make restitution."

The fifth and last decalogue deals with crimes against the family.[22] Hammurabi's code declared: "If the wife of a man be taken lying with another man, they shall bind them and throw them into the water." But it adds a proviso: "If the husband of the woman wishes to save alive his wife or the king his servant, it is permitted." The Canaanite code is simpler: (1) "If a man is found lying with a woman married to a husband, then they shall both die." Betrothal in the orient is the virtual equivalent of marriage; the Babylonian code therefore enacts: "If a man assaults the betrothed wife of a man, who has not yet known a man, and is dwelling in the house of her father, and has lain in her bosom, and they take him, that man shall be killed, but that woman shall go free."[23] This is broken into two laws: (2) "If there is a girl, a virgin, but betrothed to a husband, and a man find her in the city and lie with her, then shall you bring them both out to the

[21] CH. 266.
[22] Its first pentad restored from Deut. 22:13-19, L. B. Paton, *JBL.*, XII, 1893, 79 ff.
[23] CH. 129 f.

gate of that city, and you shall stone them to death with stones." (3) "If the man find the girl that is betrothed in the field," where obviously she cannot call for aid, "and the man forces her and lies with her, the man who lay with her shall die alone, to the girl you shall do nothing." (4) "If a man seduces a virgin who is not betrothed, he shall pay a dowry for her to be his wife." (5) "If her father refuses to give the woman to him, he shall weigh out to her father the money according to the dowry of virgins."

The last pentad is miscellaneous. Two provisions deal with the newly married wife, accused by her husband as not a virgin. Should the charge prove false, the husband is to be chastised by the city elders, is to pay a fine of a hundred silver shekels to the bride's father, and is to lose the right of divorce; should it be found true, the culprit is to be stoned. Unnatural lust is punished by the death penalty. "You shall not suffer a sorceress to live" follows Babylonian precedent.[24] The fiftieth and last provision is lost.[25]

[24] CH. 2.
[25] The Canaanite code is preserved, with certain later additions which break the numerical arrangement, in Exod. 21:2–22:19; its extent and the parallels with the code of Hammurabi are cleverly worked out by Leroy Waterman, *AJSL.*, XXXVIII, 1921, 36 ff.

CHAPTER IX

NORTHERN INVADERS

UNDER the twelfth dynasty pavement at Gebal was found a great jar. Mixed with Egyptian objects were others of appearance hitherto unknown in Syria. A hundred bronze torques or collars with rolled ends, three similar torques of silver, a hundred large bronze awls, a few circles, some girdles of thin silver or bronze, rolled at the tips and decorated with repousse dots along the edge, all are types well known from contemporary South Russia.[1] In Gebal, they were rarities worthy a foundation deposit; to us they afford the first indication of a southward movement of northern peoples.

Nordics dwelt early in the great plains of Central Asia and Europe. One group settled in South Russia. We know their culture, not alone from their tombs, but from their common language, for these men were the original Aryans. They had barely progressed beyond the nomad life, and their peculiar animal, the horse, bore them with a rapidity unknown in the south on many a daring raid. When whole tribes moved to a new home their families and possessions were carried in an ancestor of the "Covered Wagon." At need, they cultivated a little grain, but their chief wealth was in their cattle and their flocks. In strange contrast was their highly developed metallurgy, devoted to the production of weapons, for these Aryans were great warriors. Each tribe was ruled by a king, a descendant of the gods, but his power was closely limited by a council of elders and by the whole assembly of the people in arms. Village life was little favoured; the tribe preferred to throw up earth ramparts in the form of a quadrangular camp. Aryan gods were divinities of the open air, the sky father, the sun god, and the more important were masculine. Relationship was likewise counted on the father's side. At death the chief was buried under a huge mound, his body covered with

[1] Fig. 46; H. Hubert, *Syria*, VI, 1925, 16 ff.

red ochre, the sign of life, and accompanied to the after world by his wealth and his retainers.

From this original "Home of the Aryans," about the middle of the third millennium, hordes of half-nomad Aryans poured out. Along nearly every segment of a huge circle whose centre is South Russia their progress can be traced through archæology, but it is only in the Near East that they appear in written records. Everywhere they conquered the older inhabitants and established themselves as a small but powerful aristocracy. Normally they imposed their own Aryan language on their subjects, whose unaccustomed tongues soon produced extraordinary sound shifts. In course of time the Aryan nobles intermarried with their dependents and the peculiar Nordic racial characteristics tended to disappear.

Somewhere about the beginning of the second millennium Aryan tribes appeared in Asia Minor. Nordic racial types are seen now and then in their sculptures, and their language was Indo-European. Racial purity was soon lost and it is significant that not one of their monarchs has a name of Indo-European etymology.

Asia Minor and North Syria had already much in common in prehistoric times. Towards the end of the third millennium, there were foreign trading centres at Ganesh and at Alishar in Cappadocia, and from them the natives learned the use of the clay tablet, the cuneiform writing, and the Akkadian language; later they adapted the cuneiform signs to their own Hittite language, akin to the Hurrian tongues current in northern Mesopotamia and Armenia and preserved in the present-day Caucasus. In their turn the Aryan invaders adopted the cuneiform writing, and thus preserved for us the earliest known examples of our own Indo-European group of languages.

The term Hittite continued to be applied to the new people, though not to the new language. Hittite culture was high. There was an art, crude but vigorous, and with a distinct individuality. A father god had been introduced by the Aryan nobles, but the mother goddess of the original inhabitants continued to hold her own. Elaborate rituals filled numerous clay tablets, others recited myths. Local wars gradually united the scattered tribes and Hattushash became the capital. Conquered subjects were treated as allies, quite in the Roman fashion, and treaties with historical introduction defined in elaborate detail the rights and duties of the contracting parties.

Not long after the unification of the Hittites by Labarna, attention was directed to Sura or Syria. In former days, we are told by a Hittite scribe, the kings of the land of the city Halap or Aleppo possessed a mighty kingdom. This kingdom was brought to an end by Hattushilish I, the successor of Labarna, and his grandson Murshilish I destroyed the kingdom and the land of Aleppo about 1750. Then there is a blank in our knowledge.[2]

Carchemish flourished at its Euphrates crossing, and left traces of a rich culture showing obvious relations to the west. A small marble figure from an adjacent Euphrates site is much like the well-known idols of the Cyclades. Straight-sided double-edged daggers with three slight ribs have rivets at the base and another in the short tang that fits into the handle. Pins are straight or curved, with heads flattened and curled, or grooved around the shank with rectangular head and four small knobs. Vases are generally rounded, though there may be a slight base ring or the bottom may be flat. Paint is rarely employed; instead there is on the black ware a fine ring burnishing. Cylinder seals with geometric patterns keep up the connection with Mesopotamia.[3]

Not long after the twelfth dynasty had come to a lingering death in 1788, Egypt became the prey of foreigners. Egyptians called them the Hyksos, using the same term, "desert chief," which was applied to Abishai by Khnumhotep and by which Sinuhe calls the enemies of his Amorite host; possibly it is a translation of the Babylonian "King of Lands." Con-

[2] *KBo.*, I, 6; D. D. Luckenbill, *AJSL.*, XXXVII, 1921, 188 ff.; *KBo.*, III, 57; *BoTU.*, 20; *KBo.*, III, 60; *BoTU.*, 21; *KBo.*, I, 11; *KBo.*, III, 1; *KUB.*, XI, 1; *BoTU.*, 23.
[3] C. L. Woolley, *Liverpool Annals*, VI, 1914, 90 ff.

temporaries labelled them Amu or Asiatics, and a later writer could even identify them with the Hebrews. A considerable proportion of their names have good West Semitic etymologies; others defy such an explanation. Their use of the horse, hitherto unknown in Western Asia, and of the chariot, unknown at least in Egypt, their archers and their rectangular earthwork camps, all seem to indicate that a considerable element came from the great plains of Asia or Europe, and some of them may even have been Aryans.[4]

Half way between Gebal and Amor, the coastal range breaks down and there is an easy road between Lebanon and the lower hills of Bargylus to the north. This in turn opens into a broad plain, stretching without break to the desert. The plain is nearly treeless and is swept by violent winds, but its soil is extremely fertile, especially where formed by the decomposition of igneous rocks. It is watered by the Orontes, whose chief springs are well to the south, at Ain, the "Fountain," at Libo, the so-called "Entrance of Hamath,"[5] and at the "City of the Sun," famous to-day as Baalbek. Over Baalbek's oracle presided a youthful sun god, a Baal, who is represented nude and beardless, with well-marked Adam's apple, prominent nose, high eyebrows, and pierced ears. He wears a small conical cap with uræus serpent and ostrich feathers and the horns of the ram and bull. He is symbolised especially by the young bull whose horns are just sprouting, but he also honours the eagle. With him is associated a mother goddess.[6]

From its rise at the extreme upper end of Hollow Syria, the Orontes passes through rough, waterless country and sinks into a gorge four hundred feet deep. Near Riblah it reaches a broad plain once covered with flourishing cities and villages. On a tongue of land between the Orontes and an affluent, and protected on the third side by a ditch, lay the Hyksos capital. They called it Kinza, but to surrounding peoples it was still

[4] W. F. Albright, *JPOS.*, II, 1922, 122 ff.
[5] Num. 34:11; *Sargon*, 52 n. 21.
[6] Lucian, *Dea Syr.*, 5; Macrob., *Sat.*, i, 23, 14 ff.; Euseb., *Vit. Const.*, iii, 58; Theod., *Hist. Eccl.*, III, 7, 3; iv, 22, 22; Malalas, 280; Anthol. Palat., xiv, 75; T. Wiegand, *Baalbek*, 1921 ff.; R. Dussaud, *Syria*, I, 1920, 3 ff.

Fig. 50. HEAD FROM GABBULA.
(North Syria.)

Fig. 51. BRONZE FIGURE OF A GOD. From Qatna.

Fig. 52. GREAT RAMPART OF QATNA.
(Air view.)

Kadesh, the "Holy," perhaps so called from the goddess of that name who stands nude, flowers and snakes in her hand, on a lion.[7] Kadesh was guarded by a great camp to the east, some four hundred yards square, with its corners oriented to the compass points; the ramparts were nearly fifty feet high and were constructed with the earth taken from the surrounding ditch, fifteen feet deep and sixty-five broad. Towers protected the corners.

A day's journey northeast, half way between Aleppo and Damascus, and on a small stream flowing into the Orontes, the main camp was established round Qatna. Its size was huge, over a thousand yards square; its orientation was northern, for its sides faced the cardinal points. Chalky earth was excavated from the ditch, at times more than three hundred feet wide, from whose level the rampart rose sheer to the height of sixty-five feet; this height was probably increased by a more narrow wall above. Outside the corners were rounded, inside they were sharp, but the rampart itself sloped more gently down into the interior. Each side was cut by a main gate and in addition there were five secondary entrances. The chief gateway was on the west of the camp, two hundred and thirty-three feet wide and probably guarded on the north by a tower. Its structure was of course limestone blocks, often polygonal and generally with a high boss; at the entrance were upended orthostate blocks on a foundation of smaller stones. The plan is typically North Syrian, with three separate halls; the traveller must turn to the left to pass out the gate, to the right to enter the city. A similar plan was followed at the south gate, where the ditch was interrupted to permit passage, and the entrance was therefore guarded by projecting segments of the wall, as well as by a flanking tower. The north and east gates were straight. In the light of our present knowledge it is not possible to decide whether these gates belonged to the original Hyksos camp, or whether the structures within date earlier or later.[8]

[7] Excavation, M. Pézard, *Syria*, III, 1922. 89 ff.
[8] Figs. 52, 58, 51, 54; Comte du Mesnil du Buisson, *Syria*, VII, 1926, 289 ff.

The southward march of the Hyksos can be traced by other camps and by the ruins of the cities they destroyed. Beth Yerah, the great city at the Jordan exit from the Lake of Galilee, never rose from its ashes.[9] Its place was taken by a camp a short distance north of the lake and commanding the northern shunt line of the Great Road as Beth Yerah had the south. Like the camp at Qatna, its length was over a thousand yards, but its width was only four hundred. The rounded corners were oriented to the compass points and were revetted with rock walls. Where the lines were not protected by the natural slope there was a ditch. At one point there was a sloping ramp for entrance. Here again we cannot be sure how much of the inner construction of Hazor can be dated to the Hyksos.[10]

An earth rampart by the sea at Ashkelon marks another step towards Egypt.[11] Not far from 1700 the Hyksos were in the Delta, and at once established a great fortified camp at Avaris, east of the Pelusiac branch of the Nile. In the Wadi Tumilat, the Goshen where the nomad Hebrews were permitted to dwell, another great camp was established, on a desert spur which projected into the cultivated land and allowed a wide view. The rough square was about four hundred yards on the side, the same dimensions as the Kadesh camp. Its walls, forty-five to sixty-five yards thick, were of brick, covered with a sloping mantle of sand faced with stucco, and its only entrance was a gently rising causeway two hundred feet long. Egyptian weapons, battle-axe and dagger, were adapted to close fighting; should the camp be attacked by natives, they could be swept away by archers who themselves were well out of range. Even if they survived the hail of arrows, the Egyptians found themselves at a disadvantage when met by the curved Hyksos swords. In time the Hyksos learned from their subjects the use of the flanking wall and at last they surrounded the whole camp with a wall of the finest white limestone.

[9] W. F. Albright, *Ann.*, VI, 31.
[10] Plan 5; J. Garstang, *Liverpool Annals*, XIV, 1927, 35 ff.
[11] J. Garstang, *QS.*, 1922, 112.

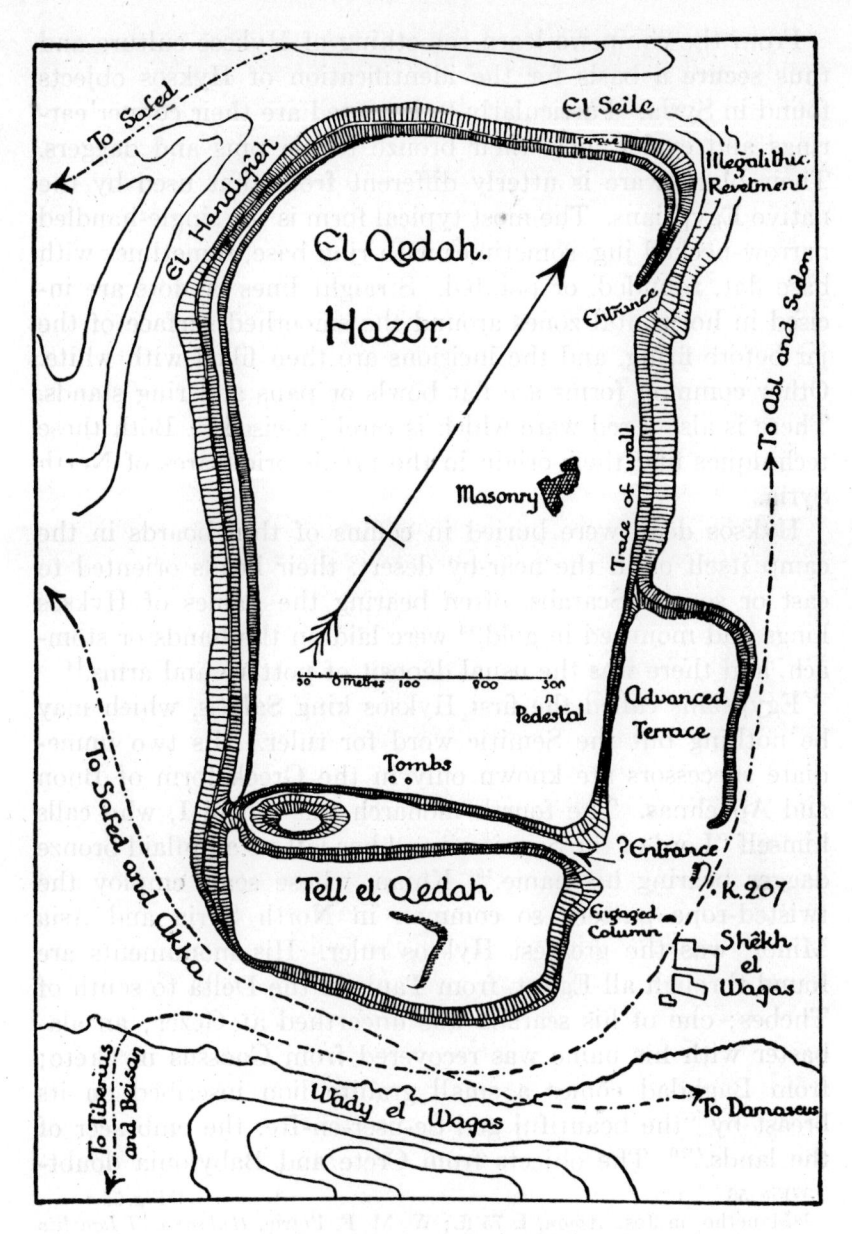

PLAN 5. HYKSOS CAMP AT HAZOR.

From the camp we learn something of Hyksos culture and thus secure a basis for the identification of Hyksos objects found in Syria. Particularly to be noted are their copper earrings and eyelet pins, their bronze toggle pins and daggers. Their black ware is utterly different from that used by the native Egyptians. The most typical form is the single-handled narrow-necked jug, sometimes with ring base, sometimes with base flat, rounded, or pointed. Straight lines or dots are incised in horizontal zones around the smoothed surface of the jar before firing, and the incisions are then filled with white. Other common forms are flat bowls or pans and ring stands. There is also a red ware which is rarely incised.[12] Both these techniques find their origin in the prehistoric wares of North Syria.

Hyksos dead were buried in coffins of thin boards in the camp itself or in the near-by desert, their heads oriented to east or south. Scarabs, often bearing the names of Hyksos kings and mounted in gold,[13] were laid on the hands or stomach, and there was the usual deposit of pottery and arms.[14]

Egyptians called the first Hyksos king Salatis, which may be nothing but the Semitic word for ruler. His two immediate successors are known only in the Greek form of Bnon and Apachnas. The fourth monarch was Apepi I, who calls himself "Lord of the Scimitar" and has left us an inlaid bronze dagger bearing his name.[15] Khian, whose seals employ the twisted-rope pattern so common in North Syria and Asia Minor, was the greatest Hyksos ruler. His monuments are found through all Egypt, from Tanis in the Delta to south of Thebes; one of his scarabs was unearthed at Gezer; an alabaster with his name was recovered from Cnossus in Crete; from Baghdad comes a small granite lion inscribed on its breast by "the beautiful god Se-user-en-Re, the embracer of the lands."[16] The objects from Crete and Babylonia doubt-

[12]Fig. 56. [13]Fig. 55.
[14]Manetho, in Jos., *Apion*, I, 75 ff.; W. M. F. Petrie, *Hyksos and Israelite Cities*, 1906; T. E. Peet, *Cemeteries of Abydos*, 1914, II, 68.
[15]G. Daressy, *Ann. de Service*, VII, 1906, 115 ff.; W. R. Dawson, *JEA.*, XI, 1925, 216 f.
[16]W. M. F. Petrie, *History of Egypt*, I, 10 ed., 1923, 252 ff.; Macalister,

Fig. 53. HAND-MADE JARS FROM EARLY GEBAL.

Fig. 54. BRONZE AGE JARS FROM QATNA.

less imply diplomatic or trade relations rather than conquest.

Khian was followed by a king named Assis, and then our fragment from Manetho breaks off. Scarabs of Hyksos[17] type furnish other names within cartouches which we may consider royal. Jacob-el and Jacob-baal proclaim that Jacob is god or lord; Anath-el perhaps invokes the Anath, the consort of the god. Other kings worthy of mention are Khenzer, Osehre, who erected an obelisk at Thebes, and Apepi II, who dedicated an obelisk to "his father Sutekh, lord of Avaris, when he set all lands under his feet."[18]

We know the history of the Hyksos but vaguely and our literary evidence is only Egyptian. Egypt, however, was but an outlier of the Hyksos empire, which included all Syria and may have extended yet farther. The Hyksos conquerors brought much that was new into Egypt, notably the horse and the chariot; that both were received through Semitic intermediaries is shown by the fact that one Egyptian word for each is identical with the common Semitic form.

It is still more difficult to evaluate the effect on Syria itself of this conquest of the ancient culture land. Did they desire, the Syrian princes might become "learned in all the wisdom of the Egyptians." That such learning is not entirely conjectural is indicated by the copying of a famous mathematical papyrus in the reign of the second Apepi.[19] Egyptian influence, already strong, must have tremendously increased; when seen through the eyes of Egyptian artists and scribes of the next generations, Syria has become itself a culture land, whose civilisation is in many respects comparable to that on the Nile.

Once the Hyksos fury had been sated, Syria rose to a new prosperity. There were great walled cities on many a Biblical

Gezer, II, 316; A. Evans, *Palace of Minos,* I, 419; G. Devéria, *Rev. Arch.,* NS., IV, 1861, 256 ff.; *Mémoires et Fragments,* 1896, I, 217 f.

[17]Cf. fig. 55.

[18]Breasted, *Hist. Egypt,* 217 f.; P. E. Newberry, *Scarabs,* 1908, 150 ff.; H. Gauthier, *Le Livre des Rois d'Égypte,* II, 1910, 133 ff.; Petrie, *Hist. Egypt,* I, 247 ff.

[19]T. E. Peet, *Rhind Mathematical Papyrus,* 1923, 3.

site, Lachish, Gaza, Joppa, Gezer, Beth Shemesh, Schechem, Megiddo, Taanach; that the list is not longer is due entirely to the fact that other sites have not been excavated. The burned Kiriath Sepher revived and to the strong unevenly built wall of polygonal stones, three to four yards thick, was added a massive sloping revetment of beaten earth. Two great gates, to east and west, each with a turn through a single chamber and with chambers to either side, were supplemented by a stepped approach over the wall on the north, where the slope was steep and where it could be protected by a buttress. The village "king" possessed an unusually well-built house, storerooms around a courtyard and above living-rooms. One of these upper rooms was a sort of chapel, for in it was found a limestone stele of the serpent goddess, clad in a long dress reaching the ankles, but barefoot, with a serpent coiling around her legs, its head to her thigh. A limestone tablet imitates one in clay, but has only a maze pattern.[20]

Mizpah has become famous for its great wall, which still rises twenty feet above its base; the upward slope of one of its revetted towers leads the excavators to estimate a total height of at least forty feet and to quote the complaint of the Hebrew spies that the Canaanite cities were fortified up to heaven.[21] Huge limestone blocks, three feet or more in depth, with openings between for drainage, were laid as foundation. On it, set back a foot or two, rose the wall proper, of limestone bound with clay, the larger stones on the face. The joints were hidden to a height of fifteen feet by a hard yellow plaster of pulverised limestone, whose slippery surface prohibited the enemy's climb. Four towers projected a foot or two feet from the wall into which they were tied, but three others, thirty feet long and seven feet deep, a sloping revetment of smaller stones covering the first twenty feet, were free of such connection; thus, if destroyed by the enemy, the main wall was still untouched. The total width of the wall plus tower and revet-

[20] W. F. Albright, *ZAW.*, NF., VI, 1929, 5 ff.; M. Kyle, Bibliotheca *Sacra*, LXXXIII, 1926, 390.
[21] Deut. 1:28.

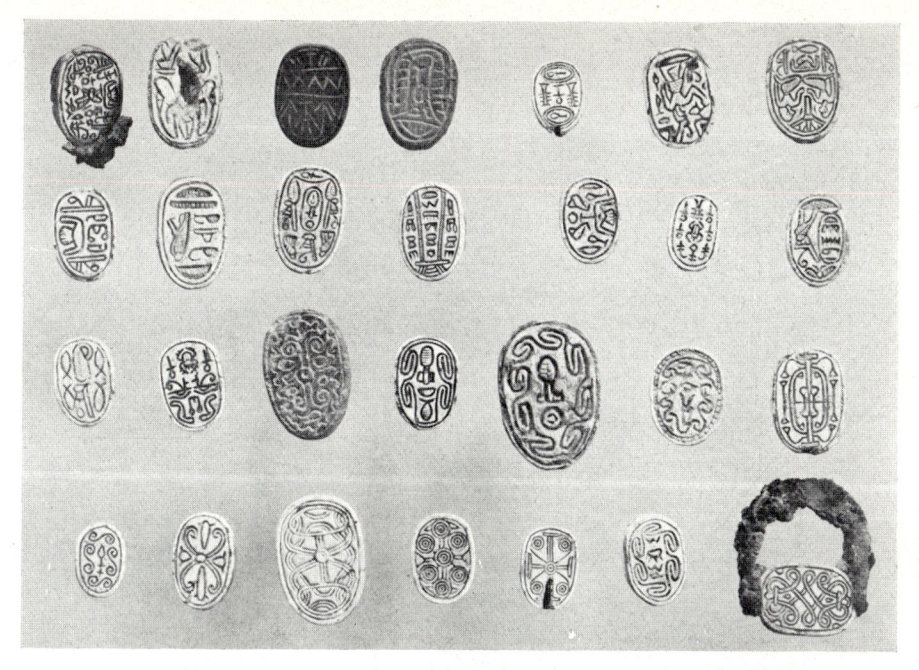

FIG. 55. SCARABS OF THE HYKSOS PERIOD. (Megiddo.)

FIG. 56. POTTERY OF THE HYKSOS PERIOD. (Megiddo.)

ment was then thirty-five feet at the base and twenty-nine at the summit; the wall proper approached twenty feet and allowed passage of soldiers along its whole surface. Their passage was further facilitated by a broad open space between the new fortifications and the earlier and narrower wall. Close to this inner wall was a paved walk, edged by storage-bins, where in peace the merchants congregated. In the southeast corner of the city was the small water-gate, with short stub walls for barricades; a steep embankment held in place by a retaining wall permitted access to the path which led to a fine spring in the hillside to the southeast.[22]

Similar fortifications protected the Jebusite settlement at Jerusalem. A road along a shelf some twelve feet wide led to the twelve-foot entrance of a gate; massive towers sixty-two feet long and twenty-seven feet deep, still standing to a height of twenty feet, formed its protection. The rubble core was set on the rock and faced by regularly coursed blocks, some of which were over four feet long and two feet high. Should the gates be forced, the invaders found themselves trapped on a second shelf barely thirteen feet wide and facing an unscalable cliff a dozen feet high from which the defenders could pick them off at their leisure.[23]

Jericho's oval walls, nearly nine hundred yards in circuit, enlarged the protected area by a third to enclose some twelve acres. The inhabitants could never be cut off from water, for the wall included the magnificent fountain at the foot of the hill. Behind a deep moat, the foundations were laid on the rock, over which was stamped four feet of well-cleansed clay. On this rose the stone substructure, two courses of medium-sized stones, one course of large rocks three by four to three by seven feet, another course of medium-sized blocks, and a cover course of thin flat stones. Over this was a battered wall, the stones becoming smaller towards the top. The blocks were roughly hammer-dressed with here and there traces of the pick, and every crevice was artfully filled with splinters to

[22] Fig. 57; W. F. Badè, *Excavations at Tell en-Nasbeh*, 1928.
[23] Fig. 129; J. W. Crowfoot, and G. M. Fitzgerald, *Excavations in the Tyropœon Valley, Jerusalem*, 1929.

protect the wall against mining. This stone wall was fifteen to eighteen feet high, though in part covered by the soil, but above it and set back a trifle was a rampart of straw-tempered mud brick six feet wide and preserved even yet to the height of eight feet.[24]

The massive fortifications are not the only indications of the rich culture of the period. Everywhere we find the polished black Hyksos ware, the punctuations filled with white. Again we have the pear-shaped juglets with button base and double-loop handle, attached to the neck below the mouth. Handleless amphoræ covered with a white slip show trumpet foot and carinated body. A slender pitcher has pointed base and elongated loop handle. Thin-necked bottles with button base and divided handles curving high above the rim are in bright yellow clay with polished red slip. A great bowl with red cross in centre, a deeper color applied to rim and cross, is then hand-burnished; smaller bowls, the upper half red-painted, imitate metal shoulders. A teapot shape has a tubular spout below the rim. Staring whites and blues make an early appearance. A geometric band and zigzag is in black and red or brown. Animals are in red or black silhouette; outlined objects may be filled in by spots or lines of vermilion or black. Although generally handmade, a superior technique and a better slip are everywhere evident. Natural motifs, trees, plants, fish, birds, animals, are common, but human figures are rare, and all are stylised. Colours are still flat, burnishing in net designs is frequent. A coarse porridge ware is tempered with limestone and mica.

Just at the end of the period, Cypriote imports begin to be found, open bowls with wishbone handles the most common form. Their yellow clay is unusually well cleansed and worked; their ornament consists of bands of lustrous or semi-lustrous orange-red paint; a black slip on which are painted close parallel brush strokes of red also occurs.[25]

[24] Fig. 81; plan 7; E. Sellin and C. Watzinger, *Jericho*, 1913; J. Garstang, *QS.*, 1930, 123 ff.

[25] W. J. Phythian-Adams, *QS.*, 1923, 60 ff.; H. Vincent, *Syria*, V, 1924, 83 ff.; 194 ff.; W. F. Albright, *Ann.*, IV, 146 ff.; VI, 52 ff.; *ZAW.*, NF., VI, 1929, 5 ff.

Fig. 57. THE SOUTH WALL OF MIZPAH. (Restoration.)

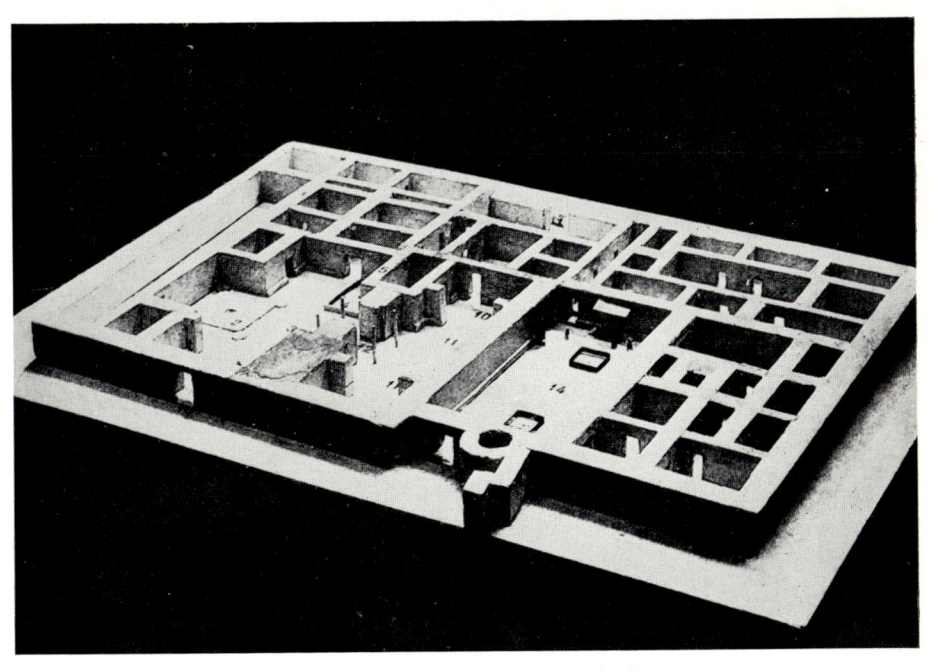

Fig. 58. TEMPLES AND PALACE AT QATNA. (Restoration.)

Hyksos seals and scarabs afford our best evidence for dating. Egyptian scarabs likewise were imported. The Babylonian diviner Manum, servant of the god Enki, left his beautiful lapis-lazuli cylinder seal. In view of the present-day craze for backgammon, it is interesting to discover that this game, still the favourite pastime of the Syrians, was played in the palace of Hyksos date at Kiriath Sepher; the pieces consisted of five tiny three-cornered pyramids and five tiny cones of faience and an ivory die in the form of a truncated pyramid. Graves of the period may be illustrated from Beth Shan, where a young woman was laid on her side in the half-contracted position, a necklace of glazed quartzite around her neck, within a stone ellipse backed by large jars and smaller jars behind her. In a more pretentious burial at Megiddo, a shaft led to a small round door which gave access to a circular chamber with two or three side alcoves; nearly a hundred jars, polished red or white filled black jugs, a duck-shaped cosmetic box, bronze hairpins, Hyksos scarabs comprised the grave furniture.[26]

While the Hyksos had been conquering the coast lands, the Amorites had pushed down from Central Syria into interior Canaan. East of the Jordan they had, by the close of the period, built up two kingdoms, in Bashan as far north as Hermon and between the Jabbok and the Arnon. Their culture may be learned from potsherds on the site of the later Rabbath Ammon.[27] They occupied much of the West Jordan hill country, and Shechem, Mount Heres, Aijalon, Shaalbim, and Gibeon are all considered Amorite.[28] Amorite kings ruled in Jerusalem, whose father, according to Ezekiel, was of this race; in Hebron, whose celebrated oak belonged to the Amorite Mamre; in Jarmuth, Lachish, and Eglon. They settled the oasis of Hazezon Tamar on the west shore of the Dead Sea and even reached as far south as the hill country due north of the Negeb.[29]

[26]Figs. 55 f., 59, 61; Alan Rowe, *Topography and History of Beth-Shan*, 1930, 23; W. F. Albright, *Bull.*, 39, 6; C. S. Fisher, *Museum Journal*, XIII, 1922, 34 ff.; *Excavation of Armageddon*, 47.
[27]Num. 21; Deut. 2; 3:8; 4:48; W. F. Albright, *Ann.*, VI, 19, n. 20.
[28]Num. 13:29; Deut. 1:7, 19; Gen. 48:22; Judges 1:34 ff.; II Sam. 21:2.
[29]Josh. 10:3 ff.; Ezek. 16:3; Gen. 14:7, 13; Deut. 1:44.

One question remains to be answered: "What was the relation of the Hyksos to the Hebrews?" Manetho, the Ptolemaic historian of Egypt, we know, identified the two peoples and considered the Hebrew stories of the Exodus to be mere variants of the expulsion of the Hyksos. He is undoubtedly mistaken in his second assumption, but there is much to be said for his first. We cannot ignore the cryptic statement that Hebron was founded seven years before Zoan in Egypt,[30] for Zoan is Tanis in the Delta, the Hyksos stronghold. Joseph was carried as a slave into Egypt, but died there as its virtual ruler; his father, Jacob, descended after him to Egypt and there ended his life in honour. It is little less than startling when we remember that two of the Hyksos kings reigning in Egypt bore names compounded with Jacob; perhaps the Hebrew stories retain faint recollections of the Hyksos empire.

[30]Num. 13:22.

CHAPTER X

EGYPTIAN OVERLORDS

APEPI III ruled in Avaris, and the south under Thebes paid him tribute. Sutekh he made his lord and served no other god in the whole land; to him Apepi built a beautiful temple, everlasting work. Then Apepi and his wise men took counsel together, how they might get the upper hand of Sekenenre, vassal at Thebes. At last this message was sent him: "Let the hippopotamus pool in the well spring of the city be abandoned, for they permit not sleep to come to me by day or by night." Sekenenre lamented long and could find no answer; he must therefore send back the messengers laden with gifts and he promised his lord to do all that was demanded.[1]

At this point the folk tale which is our only authority for these events breaks off; the war which followed is more grimly witnessed by the five gaping head wounds in the mummy of Sekenenre. His son Kemose advanced in his third year to the Hyksos boundary at Cumæ and defeated Apepi's son Teti in Nefrusi.[2] Ahmose (1580–1557), another son of Sekenenre, at last succeeded in expelling the hated barbarians. A namesake of the king, Ahmose of el Kab, followed on foot the royal chariot and showed his valour before his majesty when Avaris was besieged. Next he fought in a naval battle on the canal which surrounded Avaris. In his various engagements he twice cut off a hand, took a prisoner, and was granted the gold of valour. At the capture of the city this Ahmose made spoil of one man and three women, who were assigned him as slaves by the king.[3] Scant as are the details, he is describing the end

[1] B. Gunn and A. H. Gardiner, *JEA.*, V, 1918, 40 ff.; Erman, *Literature*, 165 ff.
[2] A. H. Gardiner, *JEA.*, III, 1916, 95 ff.; B. Gunn and A. H. Gardiner, *JEA.*, V, 1918, 45 ff.; Erman, *Literature*, 52 ff.
[3] Breasted, *Rec.*, II, 6 ff.; B. Gunn and A. H. Gardiner, *op. cit.*, 48 ff.; Ptolemy Mendes, in Tatian, *Oratio ad Græcos*, 38.

of an era. The mutilated hand carried off as trophy, the captive women condemned to slavery, were symbols of what Syria might now expect from Egyptian revenge.

Avaris had been captured and the Hyksos expelled from Egypt; so long as their armies held the border there could be no safety for the Nile valley. A sound strategy, justified in every succeeding century to our own,[4] demanded that the Egyptians should hold a bridgehead across the desert on Canaanite soil. Just within the fertile well-tilled coastal plain lay Sharuhen, now occupied by a Hyksos garrison; it was taken after a three years siege and the countries of the Amu came humbly bowing down to stand before Ahmose's gates. His shouting was heard in the land of the Fenkhu, the Phœnicians, from the choicest of the Lebanon terraces he brought new cedar sufficient to build a ship, the stones from his quarries were drawn by oxen captured from the Fenkhu.[5]

Amenhotep I (1557–1537) raided all Syria, at least his successor Thutmose I (1537–1529) claimed at his accession a boundary at the Euphrates, "that inverted water which goes down stream in going up stream." Thutmose himself journeyed to Retenu to "wash his heart in the foreign countries." The foe whom Thutmose found plotting destruction in Naharina was probably the Hittites, for they were now once more in a position to take advantage of the decay of the Hyksos empire. Naharina, the "land of the rivers," was the Semitic name of the country within the Euphrates bend; the native name was Mitanni or Maiteni or the alternative Hani Galbat. Its inhabitants spoke a Hurrian tongue, connected with the modern languages of the Caucasus. The ruling class, however, bore Indo-Iranian names of such a character as to suggest that Indians and Iranians had not yet separated. This is further supported by a few words of their own language and by their gods, Varuna, Indra, Mithra, and the Nisatya twins, all good Indo-Iranian divinities. Egyptian tomb paintings show their white robes edged with red and blue and with red dots, and their weapons the bow and the long-pointed sword. Their lips

[4]Cf. *Sargon*, 61 ff. [5]Breasted, *Rec.*, II, 8 ff.

are thick and the lower projects, the nose is beaked near the top and is slightly tilted, the forehead is sloping but high, and the rise is continued in the skull which is well rounded to the back, the ear is long and narrow, and before it hangs the half lock. That they are truly Nordic is proved by their pinkish complexions and reddish eyebrows.[6] Their descendants have been sought in the Kurds of the nearby mountains, where the greater proportion is still long-headed and blond;[7] so like is their intonation to English that the traveller instinctively turns to discover who is speaking his language, only to find a gaudily dressed Kurd.

Thutmose claims a great slaughter of the enemy at Nia. He then crossed the Euphrates and set up a boundary tablet on the east bank, while his north border was at the marshes of Qebeh. Tribute was received from the sand-dwellers, flag staffs of new cedar came from the best of the terraces and Asiatic copper.[8]

Thutmose II, ruling for a time with the great queen Hatshepsut (1529–1483), made but a single expedition against the Shasu, a good Canaanite name for bandit.[9] Hatshepsut herself manifested no interest in foreign conquests, though she does claim that the sword-bearing chiefs of Retenu saw their children fill her city as captives, that the Asiatics brought malachite in their country of Reshet, with cedar and juniper wood, and that her boundary was the marshes of Asia.[10]

Thutmose III (1483–1451) disposed of Hatshepsut just in time. All Syria had thrown off the Egyptian yoke. To clear the road in southern Canaan an advance guard was sent under the general Thutiy. According to a well-known folk tale, Thutiy induced the prince of Joppa to attend a conference on the pretext that he had gone over to the rebels. The drunken prince desired to look upon the great club of king Thutmose, the general's emblem of command; the club was brought and

[6] W. M. Müller, *Egyptological Researches*, II, 32 ff.; pl. 17 ff.
[7] F. von Luschan, *Jour. Roy. Anthrop. Inst.*, XLI, 1911, 229.
[8] Breasted, *Rec.*, II, 31 ff.
[9] Breasted, *Rec.*, II, 51; I Sam. 14:48.
[10] Breasted, *Rec.*, II, 67, 91 f., 134 f., 160.

with it Thutiy smote the prince on the temple. Like Ali Baba and the Forty Thieves, Thutiy filled five hundred baskets with two hundred soldiers who were to be carried by five hundred picked warriors. The groom of the prince was to inform the princess that Sutekh had delivered up Thutiy with his wife and children; in proof was the loot in the baskets. The gates were opened, the soldiers were released, and the inhabitants of Joppa were placed in fetters. That night Thutiy wrote his master to send men as convoy to the captives who were to fill the temple of Amon at Thebes with male and female slaves.[11]

On April 19, 1483, Thutmose himself left the frontier post of Sillu with twenty thousand men, for the most part bowmen or spearmen, though with some chariots. The desert was crossed at the rate of fifteen miles per day, and on the 28th he was at Gaza. Lachish and Gezer were burned and the invaders reached Yehem, at the northern end of the plain, where Carmel blocked further advance.

At the first news of an awakened Egypt, the king of Kadesh, last relic of the Hyksos power, had collected his subject chiefs from Kharu, Qode, and Naharina, and had taken up his position at Megiddo. Progress into the Megiddo plain was barred by a row of fortresses. Thutmose could not flank Carmel, traverse the plain of Accho, and thus regain the Great Road, for the passage of the Kishon was blocked by a small fort and east of this lay the fortified city of Jokneam. At the other end of the Megiddo plain was Beth Shan, shutting off any advance up the Jordan valley. If he attempted the road to En Gannim, out in the open plain, he must first capture Ibleam, on a hill cut off entirely on three sides and connected on the fourth with other hills to the west only by a narrow saddle, while a rock-cut tunnel to the east permitted access to a spring. Next west lay walled Taanach, while the main line of the Great Road was guarded by Megiddo itself.[12]

Three days after the Pharaoh encamped at Yehem his spies brought news of the allied disposition. A council of war was

[11]T. E. Peet, *JEA.*, XI, 1925, 226 ff.; Erman, *Literature,* 167 ff.
[12]Cf. W. J. Phythian-Adams, *QS.*, 1922, 142 ff.

Fig. 59. LAPIS LAZULI SEAL OF MANUM THE DIVINER, SERVANT OF THE BABYLONIAN GOD ENKI. (Beth Shan.)

Fig. 60. CANAANITE OFFERING TABLE. (Kiriath Sepher.)

Fig. 61. BACKGAMMON SET FROM KIRIATH SEPHER.

summoned. His courtiers warned against the direct route, ever growing narrower; his rear might still be at Arauna when the advance was already in action. They therefore recommended that he take one of the two side roads. By the first, the army would skirt the southeastern tip of the range, reach the plain by way of En Gannim, and then, with chariots in full line of battle, sweep past Taanach to Megiddo. The other, to the north of Zefti, between Carmel and the main ridge, would be a trifle more difficult, but it likewise permitted an approach to Megiddo in line of battle. Thutmose rejected their advice and swore that he would himself lead the army through the pass.

That night, the 12th of May, the royal tent was pitched at Arauna, two miles within the pass, where it opens out to a broad camping place with a spring sufficient to supply the whole army. The advance began at daybreak, but by noon the rear was just starting; had the allies fallen upon the Egyptians while marching in single file, their destruction was sure. So convinced were the Asiatics that the approach would be made by En Gannim that they had not even posted a guard in the pass.[13]

Looking down the steep descent at the mouth of the pass, Thutmose beheld the enemy forces. Their southern horn was at Taanach, their northern at the corner of the Kina, the little stream which separated Megiddo from the pass. His troops were as yet too few to justify an attack, a reverse would throw him back on troops still entangled in the pass, and the favourable opportunity was lost. Camp was pitched on the open slopes of the Kina and detachments were posted on the long gentle hills to either side as guard against surprise.

The enforced delay allowed ample time for the allies to reform their lines and to occupy the large flat-topped hill which protected Megiddo to the south where its wall was lowest. Early the next morning the Egyptians were ordered to cross the Kina valley. In their centre was the king in his electron chariot, the right was on a hill south of the stream, the left was northwest of the city. The allies drew up their forces

[13] Fig. 63.

along the slopes of the three hills opposite. Each army placed its chariots in the centre, for only there were easy grades.

Little resistance was made to the Egyptian charge. The Syrians abandoned their horses and chariots and took refuge in the city; there could have been little actual fighting, for but eighty-three dead were left behind. Then the citizens closed their gates against the fugitives; their own men were pulled up over the walls by dropping down their long girdles. Had not the Egyptian army given its heart to plundering, Thutmose sadly laments, Megiddo would have been stormed at once.

Megiddo's position was strategic. On an isolated rise, cut off from the main ridge by a bay of fertile land, its commanding site may be seen from far and near. Its massive buttressed walls, twenty feet thick and some thirty-five feet high, enclosed an area three hundred by two hundred and fifty yards. On the south and west a revetment afforded protection against the driving winter rains, there were gates at north and south. If the Kina did not furnish sufficient water, an artificial spring bubbled up on the north slope and brought water from far up the valley to distribute it through the city by conduits. Numerous other springs in the immediate vicinity made famous the Waters of Megiddo.[14]

Capture of Megiddo was capture of a thousand cities, for every chief of every northern country which had revolted was in it. Assault of so well fortified a city was hopeless; Thutmose accordingly cut down all the trees in the vicinity and constructed a wall of circumvallation. Fear of starvation brought a quick surrender, but the victory was not complete, for the kings of Kadesh and of Megiddo had escaped from the northern gate before the circumvallation was complete. Most of the citizens must have escaped with them, for but three hundred and forty captives are enumerated.[15]

There was great booty of animals, twenty thousand five hun-

[14]Figs. 62, 64; G. Schumacher, *Tell el-Mutesellim*, 1908; C. S. Fisher, *Excavation of Armageddon*, 1929.

[15]Any description of the battle must now be a mere paraphrase of the excellent study by H. H. Nelson, *The Battle of Megiddo*, 1913.

FIG. 62. MOUND OF MEGIDDO FROM THE PLAIN.
(The Oriental Institute Headquarters to the right.)

FIG. 63. THE PASS OF MEGIDDO.

dred sheep, two thousand goats, two thousand cattle, over two thousand mares, a few stallions. Chariots were taken to the number of nearly a thousand, and included that of the king of Kadesh, worked with gold and with a golden pole. His royal tent, adorned with silver, two hundred suits of bronze armor, five hundred bows were added to the spoil. From the plain below the city, yellow with harvest, more than a hundred thousand bushels of grain were garnered; this year starvation was to be the lot of the peasants.

Thutmose next advanced to Tyre, where was found every fragrant wood, and to Yanoam, Nuges, and Herenkeru. Here, in the land of Retenu, among the chiefs of Lebanon, he erected a fortress named "Thutmose is the Binder of the Barbarians," using the title regularly applied to the Hyksos. Princes favourable to the Egyptians took the place of the rebels; eighty-seven of their children were removed to the "Castle in Thebes," where they were educated to know the culture and the power of Egypt.[16]

Back in Thebes, Thutmose placed on the temple walls extracts from the formal annals, written on parchment, and also a triple list of the one hundred and nineteen countries of Upper Retenu which he had shut up in Megiddo. If all these countries were not actually conquered, the list is nevertheless a precious aid to geography, and many a name familiar from the Bible makes its first appearance.[17]

An alliance with the rising power of Assyria began the next year (1482). The second expedition was a mere promenade to collect tribute, and the same was true of the third, whose chief result was the transport back to Egypt of all the flowers and plants that grew in God's Land. Pictured in the reliefs, they form a source book for historical biology.

That all was not as Thutmose would have us believe is indicated by the course of the fifth campaign (1477). Zahi, the Phœnician coast land, was in full revolt. The prince of Tunip, an important inland state, had garrisoned Warzet; its chief

[16]Breasted, *Rec.*, II, 178 ff.; 246.
[17]David Paton, *Early Egyptian Records of Travel*, IV, 1922, pl. XLIV ff.

was taken with three hundred and twenty-nine of its inhabitants and sacrifices were offered to Amon and Harakhte. Two ships, laden with all good things, slaves, copper, and lead, were also captured.

On the return march the army entered the territory of Ardata. Very pleasant is the picture given by the Egyptian scribe: "Behold, there was found all the products of all Zahi. Their gardens were full of all their fruit, their wines were found stored in their presses as water flows, their grain on the terraces was more plentiful than the sand on the shore." Not so pleasant was what followed. The grain was confiscated, the fruit trees hewn down, and the Egyptian army was "drunk every day and anointed with oil as at a feast in Egypt"; what outrages the poor peasants suffered from the drunken soldiery may be imagined.

Next year, 1476, Thutmose landed at Simyra, marched up the Eleutherus valley, and arrived before Kadesh, the last Hyksos stronghold in Syria. Its groves were cut down and its grain harvested, and for a second time the peasants of Ardata saw their fields wasted. Thutmose returned home with an unusually large number of hostages, sons of the local chiefs.

For the seventh campaign, 1475, the Egyptian monarch sailed first to Ullaza, which was captured in one short hour; among the nearly five hundred prisoners was the son of the Tunip prince. Retenu paid tribute as usual, all the fine fragrant woods of the land. Every harbour his majesty entered was supplied abundantly with loaves of bread, oil, incense, wine, honey, and fruit, while the grain was apportioned to the royal treasury according to the tax.

Once more, in 1473, Thutmose appeared in Simyra. The march was inland to Qatna, and thence down the Orontes and into Naharina, now ruled by Saushshatar, son of Parsatata. Mitannian towns west of the Euphrates were taken and Thutmose crossed to the east bank, where he set up his boundary tablet in Mitanni proper. Returning to the left bank he erected another tablet by the side of his father's, passed south by way of Nia, and commemorated his "repelling of the foreigners of Mitanni" by a stele at Chinnereth on the Lake of Galilee.[18] Thutmose next describes the "tribute" of Assyria, Babylonia, and the Hittites; the "tribute" was in reality a gift of congratulation from powers which rejoiced to see the new Mitannian state reduced in might.

In the ninth expedition, 1472, Thutmose must return to Zahi for recovery of three towns in the district of Nuhashshe. All the harbours were filled with every good thing received by his majesty in Zahi, ships of Keftiu or Crete, of Gebal, and of the west, ships of cedar laden with poles and masts and great beams. In this same year came also the ruler of Cyprus, with four hundred pounds of pure copper and pigs of lead.

Coast-land Amor was now being supplanted by Arvad, a bare rock in the centre of a north and south line of reefs, two and a half miles from shore. A half mile long and a quarter wide, its surface rose but a few feet above the waves. The present-day settlement numbers at most some seven hundred houses; if the ancient city dispensed with flowering tree-filled courts, the number might have been doubled.

Arvad was well protected. On all sides but the east were reefs whose dangers only the local pilots knew. The bare rocks were levelled off with stones and concrete, and to west and south rose a great seawall above a moat. Massive blocks, as much as fifteen feet in length, were set in the native rock, or the rock itself was hewn out as part of the wall. Despite its massiveness, the wall was poorly constructed, vertical joints were super-imposed, and there was no mortar. Private buildings were often rock cut and cave dwellings were also in use. To the east were two rounding harbours, separated by a jetty. Water was stored in cisterns or was brought from the mainland or from a fresh-water spring which bubbled up under the sea half way to shore.[19]

Tradition ascribed the foundation of Arvad to exiles from

[18] W. F. Albright and Alan Rowe, *JEA.*, XIV, 1928, 281 ff.
[19] Figs. 65 f.; E. Renan, *Mission*, 22 ff.; R. Savignac, *RB.*, XXV, 1916, 565 ff.; Lucret., vi, 888; Plin., *Hist. Nat.*, ii, 227; v. 128; *Geoponica*, ii, 6; Arrian, *Anab.*, ii, 13, 8.

Sidon.[20] If we judge from later coins, its chief divinity was the sea god, half fish, half man, with scales and fin, long plaited hair, and pointed beard, who grasps in each hand a dolphin by the tail. Egyptian rule was witnessed by the erection of an obelisk.[21] Gebal had likewise been reduced to Egyptian vassalage, and a stele to the Lady of Gebal was a similar acknowledgment of Egyptian rule.[22]

Meanwhile, that "wretched foe of Naharina," the king of Mitanni, had not been idle. In 1471, Thutmose must fight in Araina with the numerous horses and peoples which Saushshatar had collected from the rear parts of the earth. According to the Egyptians, the enemy fled headlong, but only ten prisoners are cited, and this figure suggests a defeat. The supposition is confirmed by the events of the thirteenth campaign, that of 1468, when Thutmose must a second time overthrow the Nuhashshe district. A new king by the name of Taku was enthroned in Nuhashshe and oil was poured on his head.[23] The year following, revolt had spread to the extreme south of Canaan, the Negeb, where Thutmose must defeat the "fallen ones of the Shasu"; these nomads, there is reason to suspect, were actual Hebrews.

"Tribute" received from the "great chief of the Hittites" in 1465 may indicate formal alliance between the two powers against Mitanni, which was inciting North Syria to resistance and had placed garrisons in the cities of Kadesh. Thutmose followed the coast road and ravaged the lands of Arka, Kana, and Tunip. Three of the Kadesh cities were taken with their Mitannian defenders, six hundred and ninety-one captives, and twenty-nine hands of the slain.[24]

The campaign of 1464 is the last mentioned in the official annals, but the story may be continued through the autobiography of the general Amenemheb. Thutmose's next expedition was against Naharina, on the Heights of Wan, west of Aleppo,

[20]Strabo., xvi, 2, 13. [21]C. Virolleaud, *Syria*, V, 1924, 118 ff.
[22]K. Sethe, *Sitzungsber. Berlin Akad.*, 1906, 358 ff.; P. Montet, *Syria*, II, 1921, 263; *Byblos*, 14; 249; C. L. Woolley, *JEA.*, VII, 1921, 200 f.
[23]*K.*, 51. [24]Breasted, *Rec.*, II, 163 ff.

FIG. 64. VIEW FROM MEGIDDO

Behind the hills to the left lies Nazareth; then the peaks of Tabor and Little Hermon appear; Beth Shan is in the break leading down to the Jordan; Jezreel is on the terrace just beyond; Mount Gilboa closes the view to the right.

but Aleppo itself seems never to have been Egyptian. The Euphrates was crossed at Carchemish, though the gateway city to all appearance remained inviolate, and a crushing defeat was inflicted upon the Mitannians. Amenemheb assisted likewise at a great elephant-hunt near Nia, where a hundred and twenty of the beasts were captured. A later battle was fought at Zinzar on the Orontes, and was followed by an attack upon Kadesh. The king of Kadesh sent forth a mare to break the chariot formation; the strategy would have succeeded had not Amenemheb pursued the mare on foot, ripped her open with his sword, and presented her tail to his lord. When the city wall was at last breached, the defenders erected a counter wall, but this was in turn broken through by the Egyptians with Amenemheb in the lead. Kadesh was at last Egyptian and the Hyksos menace was past. The last known campaign of Thutmose resulted in the capture of a city named Meru, situated in Tahshe near Damascus.[25]

The king of Kadesh with his followers appeared in Egypt to pay his respects to the Pharaoh. Tunip likewise submitted and a temple to Amon was built within its walls.[26] A portrait of its prince is shown in a Theban tomb. His colour is light brown, his close-cut hair is black, his short pointed beard is stained red with henna. His nose has a strong curve with sharply undercut point. Over a long-sleeved undershirt, so thin that the flesh shows faintly through, is a long sleeveless linen dress, open all the way down the front; the seams are ornamented with red zigzags between blue lines and with a few blue and red tassels at the hem. His feet are bare. On his shoulder sits a nude child, light yellow-brown in colour, with strongly curved nose, black hair, and red-brown lock behind. The prince of Tunip has brought his infant son to be trained in Thebes; when he sits on his father's throne, he should be a loyal vassal. Thus Egypt held control of Syria.[27]

[25]Breasted, *Rec.*, II, 227 ff.; E. Meyer, *Geschichte des Altertums*, II, 1, 2 ed., 120 ff.; G. Botti, *Rend. Accad. Lincei*, XXXI, 1923, 348 ff.; N. de G. Davies, *Tomb of Puyemre*, I, 1922, 33.
[26]*K.*, 59.
[27]Fig. 67; W. M. Müller, *Egyptological Researches*, II, 20; pl. 8.

CHAPTER XI

EGYPTIANISED SYRIA

Canaan and the greater part of Syria proper were now under the political control of Egypt. Conquest had been made easy by the divided character of the land. The southern half was called by the Egyptians Kharu; it extended from Sillu, on the Isthmus of Suez, through the Sinaitic Peninsula, the Negeb, and all Canaan, as far as Ube, near Damascus. Kharu is doubtless to be connected in name with the Horites, who in Biblical times were remembered only as having been exterminated by the Edomites; it is also possible that there is some connection with the Hurrians, who formed an earlier stratum in the population of northern Mesopotamia.[1] In the native records this region is called Canaan, though the term is often extended to include Phœnicia. Phœnicia proper was Zahi to the Egyptians; to its east was Amurru, the Amorite country. North and east of Amurru were fair-sized states such as Tunip, Kadesh, Nuhashshe, Nia, Aleppo, and Carchemish.

Not only was the country divided into numerous warring states; their ruling classes were divided in race and in language. Phœnicians, if we may judge from their names and from the glosses in their letters, spoke Canaanite. Amorites also bore Semitic names, but of another family. Place-names in Canaan are almost without exception Canaanite, but the number of nobles with Canaanite names is surprisingly small.

Semitic nomenclature is virtually absent in Syria from Kadesh northward. Instead, we find a nomenclature which closely resembles the Hurrian of Mesopotamia, and names of the same type appear in Central Syria and even in Canaan, as for example, Abd Hepa, contemporary ruler of Jerusalem.

[1] Gen. 14:6; 36:20 ff.; Deut. 2:12, I Chron. 1:38 ff.; E. Chiera and E. A. Speiser, *Ann.*, VI, 1926, 75 ff.

Hittite political control, followed no doubt by racial infusion, was to be found on the northern border. Ezekiel declared that the mother of Jerusalem was a Hittite, the children of Heth were in Hebron, Esau married the daughters of Heth.[2] Whether these groups were truly Hittite, whether there was relationship to the Hittite nobles who spoke an Indo-European language, may be a question; it is certain that good Indo-Iranian names are scattered through Canaan, such as Shuwardata, "Sun given," Iashdata, Artamania, whose first element, the divine law, is the same as in Artaxerxes, Wazmania, Namiawaza, Piridashwa, "Horse owning," Piriawaza and Piridia, with reference again to the Nordic beast, Shubanda, Abiratta, Aitagama, Shatia, Iamiuta and Intauruta, blessed by the hero Yami or the storm god Indra.

Business documents in cuneiform found at Taanach give the same picture. A third of the names are those of Canaanites, who often worship El; Hurrians are numerous and reverence Teshup or Hepa; Amorites are few, but there is reference to Adad and Ashirat; Akkadian names and Nergal show Babylonian connections; Amenhotep and Amon Egyptian; others have been claimed to show Anatolian, Shumerian, Kashshite, Iranian, Aramaic, or even Indian relations.[3]

Evidence for this mixture of races is not confined to philology. The Egyptian artist had a keen eye for ethnic peculiarities; to him we owe the proof that the *marianu*—the name itself is good Sanskrit—the chariot driving aristocracy of North Syria, were predominantly Nordic, while the lower classes were as predominantly Armenoid. In the grave paintings, on the chariot of Thutmose IV, in the grave reliefs of Harmhab, such Nordics are depicted; among them we can identify the princes of Mitanni, Kadesh, and Tunip.

Racial intermixture is clear in one noble, evidently with some Nordic blood, since he is painted flesh colour, but his nose is slightly curved and hooked, with a mark at the base,

---

[2]Ezek. 16:3; Gen. 23; 25:10; 49:29 ff.; I Chron. 1:13.
[3]F. Hrozny, in E. Sellin, *Tell Taannek*, 113 ff.; A. Gustavs, *ZDPV.*, L, 1927, 1 ff.; LI, 1928, 169 ff.

his forehead is low, his head is round clear to the rear, his lips are thick. He is clad in a red and blue robe and wears a light vermilion headcloth with flap before the ear. Some of the women are also represented with decidedly pinkish skins. Their long white linen dresses are adorned with several tucks and embroidered in red and blue on the seams, a most unusual headcloth completes their costume. A linen bag on their backs carries their nude infants.

Farther south, only the two other races are represented. A grey-headed prince with yellow skin, pointed red-stained beard, projecting lips, strongly curved nose, and low forehead rising sharply to the rounded back, is dressed in a white robe with blue and red trim. His servant, on the contrary, is coloured dark red, with short pointed black beard, straight lips, straight nose slightly tilted, and a red eye. A simple skirt is all his clothing, but around his neck is a black thread which holds a white disk adorned with red circles.

Quite a different type is seen in another noble, whose skin is coloured light red. His nose is slightly curved and strongly hooked, his lower lip retreats, his forehead is low, his skull is round. His heavy black beard comes to a blunt point below the shoulder, the moustache is narrow and shaved in the centre of the lip, a very thin line of hair is left before the large ear. A red headpiece with flap before the ear and a white dress with red edging form his costume; in addition to bow and quiver he carries over his left shoulder a red copper battle axe, a semicircle with three attachments. His dark-red servant is conspicuous for his thick lips, straight nose, sloping forehead, his black hair is bunched out at front and back and is bound by a red-lined white fillet, his black pointed beard reaches the ear, but is shaved under the lip. His plain kilt is set off by elaborately ornamented shoes, a rare footgear among Syrians.[4]

Egypt owed much to Syria. Its wealth filled the Nile valley and made possible the mighty structures of the eighteenth dynasty. The tombs of the great men at Thebes are covered with reliefs or paintings depicting the tribute received from

[4] W. M. Müller, *Egyptological Researches*, II, 41 ff.

FIG. 65. JETTY BETWEEN THE TWO PORTS OF ARVAD.

FIG. 66. GREAT WALL AT ARVAD.

Retenu or Kadesh or Tunip. This heavy yearly tribute—the Retenu alone once paid nearly nine thousand pounds of white gold—was sufficiently unpleasant, but still more onerous was the tribute in men. Each year's campaign brought back huge numbers of captives. Hostages from the ruling class might be trained in Thebes, a few artisans found congenial employment in the manufacture of Syrian objects for their masters, but for the masses there was no such hope. Forced to perform the most menial tasks, they were used until useless and then thrown away. Amid the glories of the vizier Rekhmire's tomb, we behold the wretched brickmakers, Semitic in dress and in face, the "captivity which his majesty brought for the works of the temple of Amon," and the taskmaster threatens: "The rod is in my hand, be not idle." Small wonder that the earlier Egyptologists saw here the Hebrews themselves making bricks without straw under their Egyptian taskmasters.[5]

Despite the prejudice created by the Hebrew narrative, we should not forget that there were compensations for Egyptian rule. Local independence was indeed admirable for the local "kings" and for the nobility, it was not so pleasant for their subjects. Each petty king must have his court, in which he aped the greater monarchs, and the peasants paid the bill. Terrible as were the wars Egypt waged, great as were the loss of life and destruction of property, in the end it was less than that caused by the never-ending struggles of the kinglets. Once Egyptian control was established, the wars ceased, peace came with all its blessings. The fields, cultivated by the peasants without fear of attack, could well afford a higher tribute; the freedom of intercommunication within a great empire guaranteed a vast increase of wealth to the merchant class.

Our main criticism must rather be that the empire was not more efficient. A large part of Syria was never effectively subdued and revolts were constantly breaking out. Such revolts afforded much plunder to rejoice the heart of Pharaoh and his army, but they cost too large a proportion of the small body

[5] Fig. 68; P. E. Newberry, *Life of Rekhmara*, 1900, pl. XXI; Breasted, *Rec.*, II, 292 ff.; 301.

of professional soldiers, and they destroyed capital resources which might have permitted increased taxes. A true Egyptian peace would have paid.

If in fairness we should remember that efficient government of dependencies was still in the future, we should at least express surprise that the Egyptians did not copy the Hittite custom of binding their subject allies by treaties. No attempt was made to divide Syria into proper administrative units. Historic accident had produced states of the most diverse size and unity; the states were retained without change and their former kings or kinglets were continued on their thrones, provided they were loyal to Egyptian interests. Those who failed were supplanted by princes who had spent their youth at the Egyptian court; only too often claims of race proved stronger than education, especially when seconded by the great power on the north.

Certain of the local rulers retained the title of kings, others were village chiefs. At death a successor was chosen from the royal house and oil of anointing or a ring sent by the Pharaoh confirmed the investiture. By the side of the local ruler were the elders, whose independent powers were great and who might even take matters into their own hands during an interregnum. Authority of king and elders was checked by an official from Egypt whose title we may translate as "resident," though more than one city state would be under his supervision. The resident fixed tribute and acted as a court of appeal, but his chief duty was to see that his charges remained loyal. At the head of the Egyptian administration was the "governor of the north countries"; the first incumbent was Thutiy, famed in folk tale as the captor of Joppa. Strategic points were held by Egyptian garrisons, Ethiopian or Sherden mercenaries as a rule, but they were few in numbers and in strength. Now and then a city was refounded and given an Egyptian name, while a temple to Amon sought to bolster an inadequate military control by religious awe.

Intercourse between Phœnicia and Egypt was frequent by sea. A Theban tomb painting shows Phœnician ships moored

FIG. 67. THE PRINCE OF TUNIP BRINGING HIS SON AS HOSTAGE.

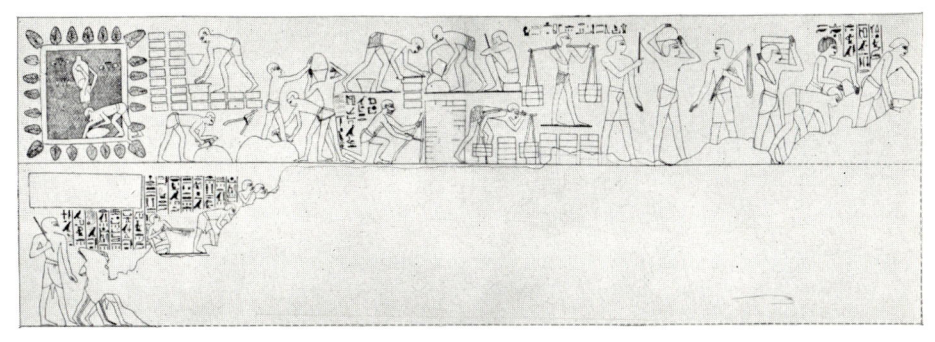

FIG. 68. SYRIAN BRICKMAKERS AND EGYPTIAN TASKMASTERS.

at the quay to trade or to pay their dues. The ships follow somewhat closely Egyptian models, the same stumpy hulls, better adapted to the Nile than to the open sea, the same stem and stern with the erect figurehead, the broad sail, set however on two yards and not on one, the many ropes to hold them, the two-oar rudders, not yet fixed. But the Phœnician shipwrights had made one great advance. Ships were built from keel and ribs on which were set the planks, the railing was made higher to protect the deck cargo in heavy seas. Among their wares are Minoan jars, hinting at a direct commerce with Crete.[6] We also hear of a wealthy Egyptian who owned a ship that traded between Syria and Egypt.

The changing art of Egypt shows definite invasion of Syrian motifs. Already under Thutmose III Syrian pottery itself began to appear in Egypt.[7] What these influences were can be surmised from the tribute. Thutmose III once lists gold in rings, "found in the hands of the artificers," two hundred and twenty-five pounds of silver in rings, nearly two hundred more represented by flat dishes of stone and gold, a large two-handled vase of Kharu work called *aggan,* a good Hebrew word, flat dishes, drinking vessels, three large kettles, eighty-seven knives. There was a silver statue in beaten work, a sceptre with a head of gold, a staff with human faces, six chairs of ivory, ebony, and carob wood, wrought with gold, six footstools, again the word is Hebrew, six large tables of ivory and carob wood, a carob sceptre wrought with gold and all costly stones, a statue of the enemy king in ebony, wrought with gold and the head encrusted with lapis lazuli. Again we hear of chariots wrought with gold and electrum and drawn with golden poles, a gold horn inlaid with lapis lazuli, a bronze corselet inlaid with gold. Of raw material, we have mention of pigs of native copper and lead, a few vessels of the still rare iron, feldspar, greenstone, precious stones, colouring matter, myrrh, incense, lapis lazuli, emery. Wine, oil, and honey added

[6]Fig. 69; G. Daressy, *Revue Archéologique,* III Ser., XXVII, 1895, 286 ff.; A. Köster, *Antike Seewesen,* 1923, 46 f.
[7]T. E. Peet, *Cemeteries of Abydos,* II, 83.

to the royal food supply. Ivory came in bulk from the herds of elephants which still roamed the north.[8]

We are no longer dependent entirely on Egyptian texts and pictures, for numerous important cities from this period have been excavated. After its destruction by Thutmose III, a fourth but smaller city arose at Lachish.[9] Kiriath Sepher had been destroyed perhaps by Ahmose; after a long period of desolation, the site was reoccupied and the walls restored, but the population was much less and much poorer, as their badly built homes and the wide spaces filled with grain pits would indicate.[10] The city wall of Beth Shemesh was rebuilt in a rough circle, seven or eight feet thick, of large stones roughly coursed with mud mortar and a filling of small stones. The gate was to the south, away from the Sorek valley, and protected by bastions in which were guardrooms and dungeons; charred wood yet remains from the flat roof.[11]

Gezer had grown, and a new wall, fourteen feet thick and at least twelve high, encircled the city for over fifteen hundred yards. Hastily rebuilt, perhaps after an Egyptian sack, it was much inferior to the former structure, which was incorporated to the east, but it was laid on the rock, scarped to receive it.[12]

Shechem's hill was entirely surrounded by a battered cyclopean wall, whose stones reached to six feet in length but were rudely dressed; it was traversed by great drainage canals. To guard against mining, the northwest city gate was fortified with heavy door sills twenty feet down. Through the west gate corridor a ramp led to the palace, set on a stone fill some twenty-five feet deep. A small irregular foreroom gave access to a hall thirty-three by twenty feet whose roof was supported by a column on a square stone block, and then a smaller room connected with a second hall thirty-three by thirty feet with ten columns and opening to the south on a court, while steps ascended to the city wall on the north.[13]

[8]Breasted, *Rec.*, II, 188, 191, 196, 206, 210 f. [9]Bliss, *Mound*, 64 ff.
[10]W. F. Albright, *ZAW.*, NF., VI, 1929, 7.
[11]D. Mackenzie, *Excavations at Ain Shems*, 1911, 1913.
[12]Macalister, *Gezer*, I, 244 ff.
[13]E. Sellin, *ZDPV.*, XLIX, 1926, 305 ff.; L, 1927, 267 f.; LI, 1928, 119.

FIG. 69. PHŒNICIAN SHIPS AT THE QUAY OF THEBES.

While life remained much the same as in former centuries there were certain marked changes, especially in the technology. Egypt had developed glaze into true glass, and the invention was transmitted to the Phœnicians, who were given credit for its discovery by the Greeks.[14] Bronze was no longer cast solid but by the lost wax process. Linen was woven into clothing for the upper classes. Scarabs fix the chronology; the earliest is that of Ahhotep, wife of Amenhotep I, but those of Thutmose III are the most numerous. Egyptian skulls, elongated ovals with parietal eminences, found at Gezer, prove that Egyptian invasion was not confined to armies and merchants.[15]

Pottery shows a widened relationship. Egyptian alabaster and glazed vases continued to be imported, but jars from the Cypriote and Minoan world were more and more in favour. Already under Thutmose III, the chief of Tinay could present as tribute a silver vessel, the work of the Cretans.[16] So great was the importation of the foreign wares, proved to be such by their foreign clays as by their design and decoration, that in another century they had almost driven the native manufactures from the market.

Base ring wares came from Cyprus. A very striking variety was a bowl with wishbone handle, which bore an exceedingly smooth and white slip, painted in a lustreless dark brown or black. Other types were the pointed juglet, smoothed by the knife and white, the tall thin red bottle with slender loop and contracted neck, and the cyma shaped bowl. Local potters attempted to imitate the prized foreign wares but without much success. They faced no such competition in the coarser wares, the big amphoræ with blunt foot for the wine or oil, the cooking pots of gritty chocolate clay, the shallow two-handled dishes, the rough juglets with ovoid mouths, the saucers and bowls of buff clay, or the saucer lamps slightly pinched at the lips.[17]

[14]Pliny, *Hist. Nat.*, xxxvi, 190; cf. v, 75.
[15]Macalister, *Gezer*, I, 60. [16]Breasted, *Rec.*, II, 217.
[17]W. J. Phythian-Adams, *QS.*, 1923, 66 ff.

While Babylonian influences were relatively rare in the material elements of culture thus far noted, there were others in which they were supreme. Egyptian writing, with its syllabary and its alphabet, had been known and employed in Syria from the earliest times, and from it had been developed, several centuries before, the alphabet used at the Sinai mines. It is therefore all the more strange that throughout all Syria during our period the natives wrote, even in their dealings with their Egyptian masters, on clay tablets, in the cuneiform character, and in the Akkadian language. Glosses are, however, frequent in the "lip of Canaan," while Canaanite grammar and idiom have often defiled the purity of Babylonian speech.

No Babylonian conquest can be invoked to explain this extraordinary circumstance; it must have been due to the Babylonian trader. To write in Akkadian meant learning a foreign language, even if not too far distant a relative, it meant opening the mind to new influences. To learn the new script and language, texts were required. Egyptian students copied stories of Erishkegal, queen of the underworld, of Adapa, who was tricked into refusing the food and water which conferred immortality, of the "king of battle," Sargon of Agade, and his exploits in Asia Minor.[18] Erishkegal survived in Egypt to be invoked in Coptic magical texts; Rib Addi of Gebal must have read the Sargon legend on its way to Egypt, for he repeatedly calls his Egyptian lord the "king of battle."[19] Another Sargon story reappears in the birth story of Moses.[20] Doubtless other Babylonian stories mirrored in our Bible first entered Canaan in this manner and at this time.

Sinai furnishes a good illustration of this mixture of elements. Ahmose, Amenhotep I, and Thutmose I dedicated vases, sistra, and the like to the Lady of Turquoise, but it was the great queen Hatshepsut who gave her especial honour. The temple had long since been extended to the edge of the incline and now it was bent to follow the hill contour. Above the stelæ which for centuries had bordered the entrance path a

[18] *K.*, 356 f.; *S.*, 193–5.
[19] *K.*, 74, 76, 79, 105, 107 f., 114, 116 f., 119, 122 f.   [20] Exod. 2.

site was levelled for a portico with four fluted columns and two pilasters; on the walls were Hathor and Soped, Snefru, the first founder, Amenemhet III, the second, and Hatshepsut, who was to be the third.

Connected with the worship of the goddess was a series of ceremonial washings. Just before the visitor reached the temple entrance he found in a corner by the gate a small oblong libation tank made from an old stele which had lost its inscription. Passing across a broad court he reached a large room in whose centre was a round basin surrounded by four pillars whose capitals were Hathor heads; we think at once of the ablution court in a modern mosque. Two other ablutions are indicated by another oblong tank in a corner and by a lesser ablution hall beyond which are sphinxes. Soped, far from master in his wife's house, possessed only a small hall before his own cave; three steps at the rear of the cave led to a rounded niche where were placed two sandstone cones with grooved base. Thutmose III extended the temple yet farther, adding a high pylon with his figure and that of the goddess. Room by room the temple grew until there were numerous tiny cells where the devotee might sleep to receive the word of the Lady of Turquoise.

The ceremonial ablutions show that, despite the outward trappings, this was no Egyptian temple but a typical Semitic high place. Incense was not offered on an Egyptian censer but on a vase altar such as is found at Taanach or at Ashur. Jars and cups yet remain to witness the sacred meals associated with the animal sacrifices; some fifty tons of the finest white ash indicate the portions of the sacrificed beast which were burned for the Lady.[21]

Sinai presents a syncretism of Egyptian and Syrian elements; Beth Shan adds elements from north and west. The city had been captured by Thutmose III, to whom its restoration was due. At times its wall was single with a maximum of ten feet, more often it was double and then it might be sixteen feet through; narrow towers projected almost nineteen

[21] Petrie, *Researches in Sinai*.

feet; within the double wall were rooms, one with a cement-lined water tank. A limestone fragment indicates a projecting parapet; a cylindrical pipe with male and female joints illustrates the drainage.

Behind the south wall was the temple. Lay visitors en-

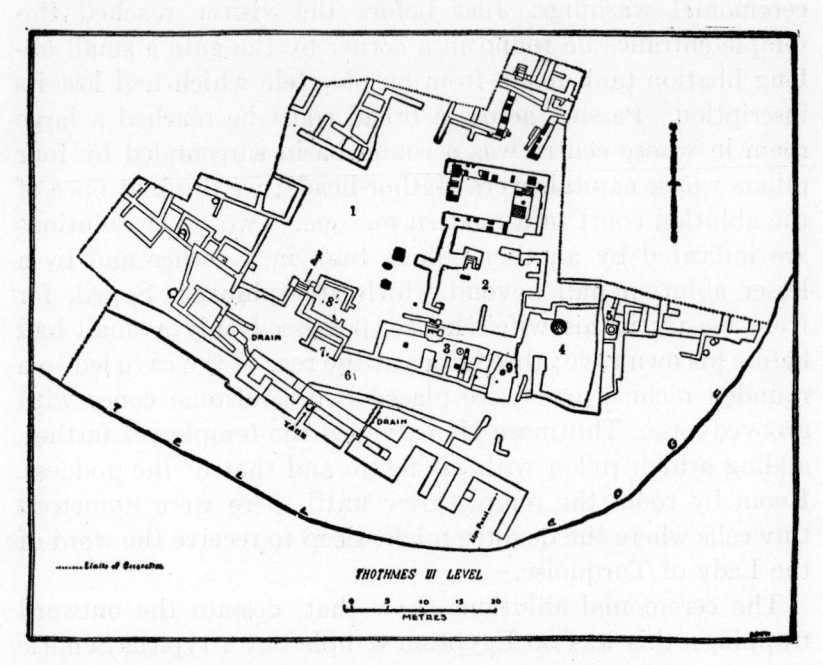

PLAN 6. BETH SHAN IN THE TIME OF THUTMOSE III.

(1) Courtyard before Inner Sanctuary.
(2) Sacrificial Altar Room.
(3) Sacred Stone.
(4) Kitchen.
(5) Well.
(6) Southern Corridor.
(7) Great Stepped Altar.
(8) Guard Room.

tered only the courtyard, eighty-four feet from east to west, a hundred and fourteen feet in the opposite direction. The bull to be sacrificed, three years old,[22] was led from his stable adorned with a heavy bronze pendant which pictured a lion leaping upon a bull, and was then perhaps paraded about. Incense was burned on a cylindrical basalt altar with hollowed top. At the south end of the courtyard was a guardroom with seat for the doorkeepers and a socketed peg to tether the guar-

[22] So also I Sam. 1:24 ff.

FIG. 70. SACRED STANDING STONE IN MEKAL TEMPLE, BETH SHAN.

FIG. 71. TEMPLE OF MEKAL AT BETH SHAN.
The view is to the southwest. To the right is the courtyard with slaughter tables, the guard room, the steps to the south corridor, and the great stepped altar; in the centre is the inner sanctuary with cult and burnt offering altars; behind is the room with the great altar of sacrifice and the room with the standing stone; to the left are the kitchen and temple well.

dian dog, which prohibited access up five steps to the southern corridor, a hundred and twenty-seven feet long and of varying width up to twenty-five feet. Four wide steps protected by balustrades led up to the great stepped altar of brick set on undressed stones, nearly seventeen feet by twelve; close by was a small basalt standing stone. In a room to the north of the other end of the corridor was the chief standing stone, again of basalt and on a base of undressed stones; the libations poured upon it were carried by a channel to a basalt bowl to the southwest.[23]

Placed against the west wall on a stone pedestal was the stele of "Mekal, great god, lord of Beth Shan," a local form of Reshuph, the fire god. Above we see the bearded deity, wearing an ornamented collar and seated on a throne. In his left hand he holds the Egyptian *waz* sceptre and in his right the Egyptian sign of life, but his conical two-horned helmet with double streamers is Babylonian. On a stand before him is a lotus; two men present him with a lotus apiece. The two men and the flower stand are repeated in the lower register; who the men are we learn from the accompanying inscription: "An offering which the king gives to Mekal, the great god, that he may give thee life, prosperity, health, keen vision, honour, and love, a prosperous mouth, the footstep in its place, until thou reachest a venerated place in peace. For the *ka* of the one favoured by his god, the builder Amenemopet, true of word, his son Pareemheb." Amenemopet was the builder of the temple who died at his post. He and his son were both Egyptians, who reverenced in their names the two chief gods of Egypt, but they had fallen under the spell of the local Canaanite god, though they treated him as another Egyptian deity.[24]

Entrance to the sanctuary, limited to the priests, was at the southeast corner of the court. By the entrance stood a basalt panel three feet high. The upper register shows in high relief a lion with a star-shaped tuft of hair on his shoulders; he is Nergal, the pest god, whose servant Atanah-ili of Taanach had professed himself centuries before, and whose "hand" was felt

[23] Figs. 70 f.   [24] Fig. 92.

by contemporary Syrian princes. Tail raised high, he fights the guardian dog. In the lower register, the dog has his teeth in the lion's back; tail between legs, the lion thinks now only of escape, the divine dog has saved his city from the plague. Mesopotamian influence is obvious in technique and in treatment, but the work itself is native; so superb a work of art once for all refutes the commonly held belief that Canaanite art was always inferior.[25]

The construction of the sanctuary walls was peculiar, a foundation of unhewn stones with a single brick course on which were set low brick pedestals, perhaps to support posts for a wooden boarding. A flight of three stone steps led to a brick altar with stone libation basin to the east. East again of this was a panelled basalt portable altar stand of Cretan form, on whose upper surface in high relief was a cross with knobbed ends; on it were placed dedications of pottery and jewelry. Before the main altar was a stone altar for the meat offering, and on it the excavators found the last sacrifice, the shoulder of a three-year-old bull.

While the main altar was in the sanctuary proper, the great brick altar was set in the north wall of a room to the south.[26] The bull was tethered to a peg and slain with a bronze dagger; his blood was carried from the altar by a channel leading to an outlet on the east and his horns were laid against the south wall. The carcass was then transported to a room on the east and roasted in a circular stone oven, six feet eight inches in diameter and two feet three in depth; with it was burned a figurine of Ashtart, wearing a wig and with left hand under breast. Ashes and charred bones were left in the oven, the liquids were carried by handled cylindrical pipes to a roughly stoned drainage pit. Basalt rubbing-stones ground the flour, water for the cakes was drawn from a brick-lined well in a small room to the east, dug forty-two feet to the virgin soil. Here doubtless the priests ate their portion; the remainder was returned to the owners of the sacrificed beast, who feasted in the courtyard at two brick tables with a small pedestal be-

[25] Fig. 72.   [26] Cf. Ezek. 40.

FIG. 72. RELIEF FROM MEKAL TEMPLE, BETH SHAN.
The pest god Nergal as a lion attempts to enter the temple, but is driven off by the guardian dog.

tween for the knives and forks to serve the meal. Mud models of the cakes were all the very poor could afford to offer.[27] Across a corridor was a northern temple, dedicated to the serpent goddess, who was often represented with breasts.

Temple finds illustrate the culture, sacred and profane. Ashtart makes a frequent appearance, sometimes pregnant, sometimes holding her breasts, sometimes with child in arms, now with wig and again with scalloped headdress and double bracelets; the material may be simple clay, ivory, or opaque green glass covered with white glaze. A flat gold pendant, with looped tang for suspension, is particularly lovely; here Ashtart is indeed nude, but she wears the Egyptian headdress and carries the *waz* sceptre.[28] A flat dish decorated with a procession of dark red gazelles reminds us that this animal was sacred to Ashtart. Ptah of Memphis holds the *waz* sceptre before the signs for life and health on a blue faience scarab. Equally Egyptian is a flat pendant in lotus form with gold wire-loop handle, or a steatite ring seal with flower design and hieroglyphic inscription, though the impossible writing proves that it was manufactured by a native imitator.

North Syrian influences are to be detected in the cylinder seals. One in blue faience shows two crossed stags, another in green glaze has the stag, sacred tree, and scroll, the hero between rampant animals and the tree appear on a white glazed cylinder, antelope and man with crossed arms on one of white steatite, two gods and a geometric design on one of lapis lazuli, a line of conventionalised birds below a crisscross pattern on one of white glaze, a god holds the sacred tree in his left hand and faces two stags and a scroll on one of blue frit. To this same northern group belongs the bronze scimitar.

A Cypriote wishbone-handled milk bowl was not disdained for the native cult, nor were two Cypriote gold pins. One altar design, we have seen, came from Crete. Hollow terra-cotta cones may have borne bull figures. A flat basalt dish still contained some of the red colouring matter; not far away was found a lump of yellow ochre. One libation cup was decorated

[27] I Sam. 2:14 ff.; Ezek. 40:42; Jer. 7:18. [28] Fig. 73.

with dark purple designs on red. Flowers offered in the fertility rites were placed on a two-handled cylinder stand, open at base and top. That the pig remained sacred is proved by a pig-headed object. A steatite mould turned out jewelry with concentric circles, an ivory cosmetic pot glimpses a lighter phase of life. In a room to the north of the sanctuary were the sacred weights of basalt.[29]

Egyptian visitors, Egyptian inscriptions, Egyptian art widely disseminated Egyptian religious concepts. Native gods were so regularly identified with Egyptian deities and so often were represented with Egyptian characteristics that we can never be quite sure whether the figures of Isis and Osiris, of Hathor and of Ptah, were intended for these Egyptian divinities or for their Canaanite brothers and sisters, the various Lords and Ladies. The ugly dwarf Bes, whose figure is so common throughout this period, may be only one of the Phoenician Kabirim, the "Great Ones." The less frequent Anubis, the jackal god, or Sebek, the crocodile, are more likely to be true Egyptian. Amon was divine king of Egypt and was worshipped as such in Syrian temples, yet even in writing to the Pharaoh himself, the Syrians regularly employed the Akkadian ideogram for the Babylonian sun god Shamash; they may have pronounced his name neither Shamash nor Amon but in good Canaanite Shemesh. Canaanite gods in their turn were recognised in Egypt, and not only through identification with Egyptian deities; as early as Thutmose III, Anath possessed a priesthood in Thebes, but the full tide of Syrian religious influence was not to flow into Egypt until the nineteenth dynasty.

Syncretism appeared in religious concepts as well as through identification of gods. Especially marked was the tendency toward unification. In the Amarna letters, *ilanu*, "gods," is employed in the general sense of "godhead," and is even given a singular verb; this usage is an exact parallel to the plural Elohim with a singular verb in our Hebrew Bibles, where we always translate "God."

[29] Figs. 74–76; plan 6; Alan Rowe, *Topography and History of Beth-Shan*, 10 ff.; *Museum Journal*, XIX, 1928, 145 ff.; XX, 1929, 37 ff.

FIG. 73. ASHTART WITH THE EGYPTIAN WAZ SCEPTER.
(Gold pendant, Beth Shan.)

FIG. 74. POTTERY STANDS.
(Ashtart Temple, Beth Shan.)

FIG. 75. RING FLOWER VASE.
(Ashtart Temple, Beth Shan.)

FIG. 76. MODEL OF SHRINE.
(Room near Ashtart Temple, Beth Shan.)

CHAPTER XII
LETTERS FROM SYRIA

CENTRAL and North Syria were in full revolt when Amenhotep II (1451-1420) became sole ruler. The rebel inhabitants of Lebanon were defeated in his second year at Shemesh Edom in Galilee and Hazor was captured. He passed Kadesh, for once quiet, and on the 12th of May crossed the Orontes at Zinzar. A few Asiatics were seen, coming on horses at the gallop, but they retreated and an insignificant booty was secured.

Alliance was made with Mitanni, whose king Saushshatar had nearly destroyed the infant power of Assyria. Amenhotep returned south by Nia, where he found the inhabitants, men and women, on the walls praising his majesty. News came that some of the Asiatics in Ikathi had planned to drive out the garrison and get the better of the loyalists; by the 5th of June the city was pacified and soon after Tunip and Qatna. Seven kings of Tahshe were carried head downward up the Nile to Thebes on the royal ship; six were sacrificed to Amon and their bodies hung on the city walls, the seventh suffered the same fate at Napata in far Ethiopia.[1]

Thutmose IV (1420-1411) found it necessary to capture Gezer, almost at the entrance of the Great Road into Canaan. Addu-nirari of Nuhashshe reminded the Pharaoh how his grandfather Taku had been made king by Thutmose IV; now the king of the Hittites is advancing against him and if the Pharaoh can not come in person, let him at least send men and chariots. Thutmose did advance as far north as Sidon, but his claim of a victorious campaign against Naharina and of tribute from Mitanni was based on a marriage with the daughter of Artatama I, the successor of Saushshatar.[2]

[1] Breasted, *Rec.*, II, 304 ff.; 317.
[2] Breasted, *Rec.*, II, 324 f.; *S.*, 22, *K.*, 51; *K.*, 85; *S.*, 12, *K.*, 29.

This marriage cemented an alliance against the Hittites, whose king Tudhaliash II had recently destroyed Aleppo on the pretense that its alliance with Hani Galbat, their name for the older Mitannian kingdom, was a sin against its former Hittite suzerain. Men of Ashtata invaded and wasted the lands of Aleppo and Nuhashshe, but the king of Mitanni came to their rescue, returned their lands, and wrote for them and sealed the tablets of their cities and regions. The alliance of Egypt and Mitanni prevented Hattushilish II, successor of Arnuwandash I as Hittite monarch, from making good his claim.[3]

Amenhotep III (1411–1375) continued the alliance and received in marriage Gilu Hepa, daughter of Shutarna (1402). Beth Shan had been partially rebuilt since the days of Thutmose III, but its strategic position demanded a thorough renovation. Foundation deposits of a scarab, a signet ring, and an amulette cartouche, all bearing Amenhotep's name, were placed under the altar steps of a new temple, his signet ring was buried under the north wall. Its plan was much the same as the early Ishtar temple at Ashur and contemporary shrines in Egypt built by Ikhnaton. A door at the west led into a tiny anteroom, whose northern exit opened into a court with low benches on three sides and a rectangular altar shaded by a roof supported by two columns with papyrus capitals. Behind the altar, steps led up to a narrow shrine, its floor of bright blue and illuminated by light holes, whose sloping topped altar was against the north wall.[4]

A limestone stele is dedicated by a woman in long flowing garment, crowned with the lotus and presenting a lotus to the goddess, who is clad in the same dress and wears the conical crown with streamer, while the two horns show she is Ashtart Karnaim, Ashtart with the two horns.[5] A model limestone altar has painted squares on the top and sacred trees on the base, a basalt model throne is of Cretan form, but on either

[3] *KBo.*, I, 6; D. D. Luckenbill, *AJSL.*, XXXVII, 1921, 188; E. F. Weidner, *Politische Dokumente aus Kleinasien*, 1923, 82 ff.; A. Götze, *Altorientalische Studien Bruno Meissner*, 1928, I, 59 ff.
[4] Fig. 77; Alan Rowe and L. H. Vincent, *QS.*, 1931, 15 f.   [5] Fig. 84.

side is the winged animal of Set and on the back the vulture with outstretched wings and the pillar whose hands hold the sign of life. A jar handle with Cretan and Cypriote signs incised shows Mediterranean relations as does a bronze spear butt with crescent end and crossed string pattern in high re-

Fig. 77. TEMPLE BUILT BY AMENHOTEP III FOR MEKAL AT BETH SHAN.
(Restoration. The view is to northeast.)

lief. A bronze Teshup, an elephant headed object, more than forty cylinders come from North Syria. A bronze axe of curved blade marked by a crescent, the grip with outstretched fingers,[5a] is exactly paralleled in the sculptures at the Hittite capital, a rude hæmatite cylinder depicts an ass and an elephant between two deities, one marked by the Hittite hieroglyph for "god." North of the temple was a room for the altar of sacrifice, two large superimposed blocks.

West was the migdol or fort which commanded the city, of large sun dried bricks laid in mud and finished with a fine mixture of clay and lime. A gate with massive sill and jambs of well dressed and fitted basalt, dovetailed into the brick wall

[5a]Figs. 93 f.

and guarded by two flanking towers, gave access to five rooms and a stairway to the roof. Floors were of rubble coated over with cement. By its side was the governor's residence, in whose court was a brick lined underground silo of over nine thousand gallons capacity for storing the tribute grain, while the migdol itself was filled with huge jars for the tribute oil.[5b]

His own records make Amenhotep a great conqueror. He is smiter of the Asiatics, his northern border is Naharina, he settles in Thebes the Kharu, children of princes. He drives his chariot over the Syrians, smiting Naharina and Upper and Lower Retenu. Amon's great bark was cut in the countries of God's Land, it was dragged over the mountains of Retenu by princes of all countries. His Nubian temple at Soleb sported columns of captives from Kadesh, Tunip, Ugarit, Carchemish, Naharina, Singara, Arrapha, Assyria, Crete, and the Hittite land; it was a wonderful extent of empire—but the half was not possessed by Amenhotep, who never in person crossed the Egyptian frontier.[5c]

The truth may be read in the letters from the archives from Amarna[5d]. In every corner of his Asiatic possessions, the native kings were in secret or open revolt. Despite its alliance with Egypt, Mitanni did not hesitate to attack North Syrian states claimed by Amenhotep. The Hittites had recovered their strength and were vying with Mitanni for the reversion of the Egyptian heritage. Farther south, a new power was growing up in Amurru.

Along the whole eastern frontier of Syria new hordes of nomads were invading the settled country. Contemporaries called them Habiru, a term long ago employed by the Babylonians for nomads and recently taken over by the Hittites. The Habiru of the Amarna letters appear to have been all

[5b] Alan Rowe, *Beth-Shan*, 19 ff.; *Museum Journal*, XIX, 1928, 145 ff.
[5c] Breasted, *Rec.*, II, 342 ff.; *K.*, 29.
[5d] Texts, C. Bezold and E. A. W. Budge, *The Tell el-Amarna Tablets in the British Museum*, 1892; O. Schroeder, *Die Tontafeln von el-Amarna*, 1915; translations, J. A. Knudtzon, *Die el-Amarna-Tafeln*, 1915; new letters, F. Thureau-Dangin, *Rev. d'Assyriologie*, XIX, 1922, 91 ff.; cf. E. Meyer, *Gesch. des Altertums*, II, 1, 2 ed., 334 ff.

Aramæans; in the Habiru who were now entering Canaan, we must see the first Hebrews.[6] Serving at times as mercenaries, at times making independent raids, the Habiru had penetrated Canaan and Central Syria and their influence became yet stronger after the return of Thutmose IV from Sidon.[7]

In more than half a hundred letters, Rib Addi of Gebal paints for his royal masters a sad picture of the situation in Syria. May the Lady of Gebal give power to the king. Gebal, the true maid-servant of the king, was once prosperous, but now the enmity of the Habiru is mighty against him. Let not the king abandon Simyra lest the Habiru take it. Pahanate, resident of Simyra, has saved Gebal, he knows its needs; food has been secured from Iarimuta.[8]

Rib Addi's greatest enemy was Abd Ashirta of Amurru. Abd Ashirta's letters to Amenhotep, in unusually bad Akkadian, begin humbly enough: "To the king, the sun, my lord, thus speaks Abd Ashirta, your slave, the dust of your feet. To the feet of the king my lord seven times and seven I bow down. Behold, I am the servant of the king and the dog of his house and all Amurru for the king my lord I guard." He has begged Pahanate, his resident, for soldiers to protect him, since all the vassal kings seek to take the lands out of his hand. Let the king ask Pahanate whether he does not guard Simyra and Ullaza. Should his request be granted, then he can harvest the grain of Simyra.[9]

Simyra was attacked by the Shehlel, who killed twenty-five of its defenders. The four who were left begged aid from Abd Ashirta; fortunately Abd Ashirta was in the nearby Arka and so could rescue them and save Simyra from being burned by the Shehlel. Yet the city chiefs have lied about him and Pahanate believes them. He had been particularly slandered by the son of Amaia, who himself was allied with the Shehlel in their assault on Simyra. He has obeyed the word of the king, let the king hear his word, for hostility is strong against him, and let him send a noble to protect him.[10]

[6]C. R. Conder, QS., 1890, 327.
[7]K., 85.   [8]K., 68; S., 32.   [9]K., 60; S., 27.
[10]K., 62; S., 28; K., 64; BB., 33.

Abd Ashirta wrote no more to the king. The reason is found in the letters of Rib Addi. Pahanate has been succeeded as resident of Simyra by his son Haia, and Rib Addi writes him: "Behold, you are a wise man at the side of the king, and because of your trustworthiness the king has sent you as resident. Why then have you delayed and not requested the king to send troops to take Simyra? What is Abd Ashirta, the slave, the dog, that he has taken the king's land for himself?" Abd Ashirta has grown strong through the mighty Habiru. Let Haia send a hundred horses and two hundred footmen to Rib Addi so that he can hold Shigata against Abd Ashirta until the regular army arrives; otherwise Abd Ashirta will collect all the Habiru and take Shigata and Ambi.[11]

Rib Addi next writes his "father" Amanappa or Amenhotep, a high official formerly stationed at Simyra, who has now returned to Egypt. Why has Amanappa not requested the king to send him with troops by which he might overrun Amurru? Does he not know that Amurru always sides with the stronger party? This is why it has gone over to Abd Ashirta, but what has he done? The city chiefs are ready to return to their loyalty should the army for which they wait day and night ever arrive. Abd Ashirta has ordered the men of Ambi to kill their lord; they have joined the Habiru and the remaining chiefs are thinking of following their example.[12]

The king knows that Gebal, the true maid-servant of the king, was prosperous from the days of his father, but now the king has permitted his faithful city to drop from his hand. Let the king examine the tablets in his father's house and see whether the official who was in Gebal was not always a faithful slave. His field is a woman without husband for lack of cultivation, his subjects must sell their sons and daughters to Iarimuta for food. All his cities, whether on the mountains or along the coast, have gone over to the Habiru; only two cities besides Gebal remain faithful. Abd Ashirta has taken Shigata, and he says to the people of Ambi: "Kill your ruler and be

[11] K., 71; S., 33. [12] K., 73; BB., 15.

like us and enjoy peace." He has ordered his soldiers to assemble and to fall upon Gebal. As birds caught in a net, so is Rib Addi in Gebal. Let the king ask Amanappa, who is now at court, and learn his necessity, then let the king give food to his servant. Day and night he asks: "What shall I do in my loneliness?"[13]

Aduna, king of Arka, has been killed, and no one has said anything to Abd Ashirta. Mia, the man of Arashni, has taken Ardata, and the people of Ambi have killed their lord. Let the king realise that the Hittite king has conquered all the lands that belonged to the king of Mitanni and the king of Naharina.[14]

Abd Ashirta has urged the people of Batrun to kill their lord, and they are going over to him. He sent a man of the Sherdan to murder Rib Addi; the assailant was killed, but Rib Addi was wounded nine times. He is now shut up in his city and cannot go out of the gate. Unless a regular army comes within two months, Abd Ashirta will secure the two remaining cities.[15]

Amanappa knew perfectly well that no help would come from Egypt, but he did his best to hold the local princes in line. Rib Addi should have followed his advice and commissioned a man to go with him to court. Had only he done so, Amanappa would have sent him with a force strong enough to hold out until the regular army arrived. Rib Addi replies that he could have sent no messenger without Abd Ashirta hearing of it, and who then would deliver him from his hand? Amanappa has bidden him send a ship to Iarimuta for money and clothing; all the men given him by Amanappa have fled. He has sent a messenger to the palace to report his attempted assassination; what can save him if another attempt is made? If he does not receive aid within two months, Rib Addi will leave his city and save his life.[16] Amanappa has asked for copper. By the Lady of Gebal, he has none, he has sent it all to the king of Tyre for aid. He is in fear of the peasants, who

[13] *K.*, 74; *BB.*, 12.
[15] *K.*, 81; *S.*, 40.
[14] *K.*, 75.
[16] *K.*, 82.

would kill him, for they are selling their children for food.[17]

The messenger to the king was deprived of his horses and the king gave him no reply. Rib Addi loses his patience and threatens that if no answer is returned he will follow the example of Iapah Addi and Zimrida of Sidon and go over to Abd Ashirta. Let the king at least send back his messenger, for his relatives are embittered and are saying day and night: "You have given our son to the king."[18] When the messenger did return, it was with empty hands and the failure of Rib Addi's efforts led Batrun to declare for Abd Ashirta.[19]

Abd Ashirta is very sick; who knows but that he will die? The time is opportune for the resident to send troops and recover the lands. It is the more necessary as the king of Mitanni is casting his eyes on Amurru.[20] One of the North Syrian princes likewise reports that the king of Mitanni has gone out with all his chariots and soldiers.[21] Shutarna had just been succeeded as king of Mitanni by Tushratta, who inaugurated his reign by an expedition into North Syria, where all the three great powers had claims.

For two years Rib Addi has been forced to measure his grain through scarcity. What can he say to his peasants? Ianhamu asserts that he has given grain, but Rib Addi demands: "What has he given me?" Money was indeed given to Iapah Addi, but he has sent no grain in return. Let the grain formerly assigned to Simyra be now assigned to Gebal. As the king lives, his subjects are friends of Abd Ashirta and the Habiru. If but one village chief would stand by him, Rib Addi would drive Abd Ashirta out of Amurru. The king of Mitanni came to Simyra and sought to capture Gebal, but there was no water for him to drink and so he returned to his own land.[22] A letter of much the same tenor was sent next year to Amanappa, who insisted that Rib Addi had received much grain of Iarimuta from Ianhamu. Rib Addi counters with the demand that Amanappa come with many soldiers to take the land of Amurru. Day and night it is angry with him, and why should

[17] K., 77; S., 36.   [18] K., 83; BB., 14.   [19] K., 87; BB., 22.
[20] K., 95; S., 48.   [21] K., 58.   [22] K., 85; S., 42.

they not be angry, so many of them have been carried captive to Mitanni.[23]

Amenhotep preferred to trust Tushratta, who brazenly described his campaign as the destruction to the last man of the invading Hittite army, and to accept the gift of chariots, horses, and captives from the Mitannian spoil.[24] Shortly after, he received a yet more precious gift, Tushratta's daughter Tadu Hepa as wife.

To save them from falling into the hands of Abd Ashirta, Rib Addi sent his sister and her children to Tyre. Soon after, Tyre rebelled and the former king and the fugitives from Gebal were slain. The new ruler had the audacity to lodge a complaint at court against Rib Addi, who must defend himself.[25] Abd Ashirta will free Gebal for a thousand minas of silver and a hundred of gold, let the king send the ransom.[26] This plain implication that Egypt could protect her vassals only by buying off their enemies was passed in silence, and Rib Addi determined to seek aid from the kings of Berut, Sidon, and Tyre. He received no answer, but Amenhotep got wind of his proposal and wrote them asking if the report was true. That the Pharaoh could inquire of suspected vassals whether a thoroughly loyal subject had shown disloyalty by seeking from them aid was proof of the utter incompetence of Egyptian administration. Rib Addi was justified in asking whether this was a gracious act.[27]

Amanappa writes that he is coming to Gebal, and Rib Addi urges him to secure from the king three hundred soldiers. If only Batrun can be taken, the people will abandon Abd Ashirta.[28] Amanappa arrived with a small force and Batrun was recovered. This roused Abd Ashirta and by his orders all the Habiru marched against Gebal. Bit Arha was captured.[29] Amenhotep awoke long enough to send a larger army under Ianhamu, who succeeded in recapturing Simyra.[30]

At last Rib Addi has good news to report. Ships of the

[23] K., 86; BB., 21. [24] K., 17. [25] K., 89; S., 43.
[26] K., 91; S., 45. [27] K., 92; S., 46. [28] K., 93; S., 47.
[29] K., 79; S., 38. [30] K., 138, 117; S., 73, 62.

Milim people have entered Amurru and have killed Abd Ashirta, since he had neither grain nor chitons nor valuable stones to give to Mitanni. Whose ships stand against him? Are they not the ships of Arvad? The king should confiscate the ships of Arvad which are in Egypt. Troops from Tyre, Sidon, and Berut have come against Amurru. To whom do these cities belong? Do they not belong to the king? Let the king place a man in each city to prevent ships from sailing against Amurru.[31]

Ianhamu has ordered Rib Addi to enter Simyra and to remain there until he comes. This is impossible, for even Ambi is hostile, and the nobles and city chiefs are on the side of Abd Ashirta's sons.[32] So far from believing Rib Addi, Amenhotep praised the ruler of Ambi for keeping his city loyal. Let him send his daughter with twenty well-favoured slaves, chariots, and well-favoured horses, and then the king will say: "My face gives you life."[33] Despite this praise or perhaps because of the demand for tribute, Ambi went over to Abd Ashirta's son, Aziru, and with it Shigata.

The long series of wailing letters is brightened by one shaft of humour, but not from Rib Addi. He had refused to admit citizens of Simyra, claiming that it was suffering from the pest. The general of the troops ironically demands: "Was it a pestilence among men or among asses? What sort of a pestilence was it among the asses?" The truth is that Rib Addi has shut his gates to prevent the recovery of asses stolen from Simyra. The asses are royal property; if the king is lord of asses, let Rib Addi seek the king's asses. The case has been reported to Amenhotep and the general awaits a reply.[34]

Pubahla, son of Abd Ashirta, has taken Ullaza; he already possesses Ardata, Wahlia, Ambi, and Shigata. The sons of Abd Ashirta are making themselves the equal of the kings of the Kashshites and of Mitanni. Rib Addi cannot go to the aid of Simyra, for he is blockaded by land and sea.[35] Simyra is shut up, on land by the sons of Abd Ashirta and on sea by

[31] *K.*, 101; *BB.*, 44.   [32] *K.*, 102; *BB.*, 23.   [33] *K.*, 99.
[34] *K.*, 96; *S.*, 49.   [35] *K.*, 104.

the people of Arvad. Rib Addi has sent three ships to Ianhamu; the men of Arvad attempted to capture them but they escaped. Their ships were permitted to leave Egypt, therefore they no longer fear. They have taken Ullaza, they seek to take Simyra, and all that belonged to Abd Ashirta they have given to his sons. They have taken the ships of the Milim people, with all their possessions, and therefore Rib Addi cannot come to the aid of Simyra. As to his feud with Iapah Addi, a court of three Egyptians headed by Ianhamu has decided the case in his favour. The Egyptian fugitives from Ullaza are with him, he has no food to give them. Iapah Addi will not allow his ships to sail to Iarimuta, and he cannot send them to Simyra on account of the ships of Arvad.[36]

Let Ahribita remain in Simyra, but let the king recall Haia and investigate his doings. Aziru is in Damascus with his brothers. Let the king send troops against him and take him, then the land will have peace. Rib Addi has plenty of charioteers, but no chariots or horses and no money to buy them. All his possessions have been spent for food.[37]

Only Simyra and Arka remain faithful to the king. Rib Addi has gone to Simyra, but Zimrida and Iapah Addi are not with him, though they were given orders by the nobles. All the guards of Simyra have fled, there are few people left in the city. Let the king send aid quickly, else no city will be left him.[38]

Amenhotep tired of these complaints and demanded why Rib Addi had sent such a tablet to the court and had wailed over Simyra more than his brothers. The unfortunate Rib Addi replies that he has written thus because he has been in trouble five years. He may wail, but he is not such a false brother as Iapah Addi or Zimrida. The resident of Simyra is dead and he is ill, he was in Simyra but all its inhabitants have fled. Let the king send a new resident, preferably Ianhamu, for he hears from the mouth of the people that he is a wise man and that all the people love him.[39]

[36] K., 105; S., 53.
[38] K., 103; S., 52.
[37] K., 107; S., 55.
[39] K., 106; S., 54.

The king has ordered him to bring Haia, the new resident, into Simyra. It cost him thirteen minas of silver and a garment to hire a man of the Habiru to take the message into Simyra. Let the king ask Haia if he was not introduced into Simyra by night.[40]

The sending of Turbiha to Arka was a blunder, for he told them: "The king hates Arka." Although their king Aduna has been killed, the citizens still profess themselves loyal. The royal resident, the man sent by the king, is attempting to make the king hostile to them, but nevertheless they guard the land. Let the king hearken to the words of his true servant, and give them gifts, while their enemies see it and eat dust. The sons of the king's enemy are trying to win them over, but they will keep shut the city gate until the king's breath comes to them. Mighty is the enmity against them, mightily, mightily.[41]

Abimilki or Abimelech guards Tyre, the great city, for the king until the mighty hand of the king comes to give him water to drink and wood to burn. The king knows that they are situated before the sea; they have no water and no wood. He has been ordered to write all that he hears in Canaan. The king of Danuna, perhaps the Greek Danaoi and the Dodanim of Genesis,[42] is dead, and his brother has become king after him and the land is quiet. Fire has destroyed Ugarit, the royal fort, the other half is no more, and the Hittite army is no more. Aitagama has become king of Kadesh and Aziru has made enmity with Namiawaza. Zimrida of Sidon has collected ships and people from the cities of Aziru against Rib Addi, day by day Zimrida writes that sinner Aziru all that he has heard from Egypt.[43]

Zimrida himself has a different story. The Egyptian army is to visit Syria and he rejoices at the news, his heart is rejoiced, his head is uplifted, his eyes are brightened, he has prepared everything against its coming. Enmity has been

[40] K., 112; S., 61. [41] K., 100; BB., 42.
[42] D. D. Luckenbill, Ztf. f. Assyriologie, XXVIII, 1913, 92 ff.
[43] K., 151; BB., 30; K., 147; BB., 29.

great against him, the Habiru have taken all the cities that the king gave him. Let the king send a general to win them back, then he can serve the king as his fathers.[44]

Iapah Addi reproaches Ianhamu for not having helped Simyra. All the lands from Gebal to Ugarit have gone over to Aziru. Simyra is blockaded by sea and neither supplies nor men can enter.[45] The position of Ugarit was difficult. Amenhotep had demanded tribute of its king Mistu and he had replied; now the Hittite king has twice complained about the tribute Mistu forwarded to Egypt, and he is in fear that the Hittites will attack him.[46] A lady who in her name honors the goddess Hepa salutes the Egyptian queen and adds a jar of spices.[47] Shama Adad would like two Ethiopian youths as a gift, also the loan of a palace physician, since there is none in his city.[48]

Qatna's wealth is illustrated by four "tablets of the treasury of the goddess Nin-egal, Lady of Qatna," and three "tablets of the treasury of the gods of the king"; the treasures of the goddess need almost four hundred lines on tablets nine or ten inches high and two new inventories were later demanded to bring them up to date. There is a profusion of gold, red, brown, single, double, triple, or quadruple, and many other kinds, not to speak of gold from the land of Tukrish; it would appear that, as in the legendary days of Solomon, silver, bronze, and copper were nothing accounted, but iron was a rarity to be set in gold. The weight of the objects is carefully noted; the majority are of but a few shekels, though two golden vases are truly impressive with a weight of eighty minas six shekels. Many are of the precious lapis lazuli or other stones, some are of glass. There are vases or objects with the heads of bulls, lions, or men, or of the horrible monster Huwawa; there are lapis lazuli lions and golden fish and eagles. Many of the unknown terms appear to be Hurrian.

Some twenty donors are named. One lot was given by Durusha, king of Kizzi or Kadesh, but when the later inven-

[44] K., 144 f.; S., 76 f. [45] K., 98; S., 51. [46] K., 45; S., 17.
[47] K., 48; S., 20. [48] K., 49.

tories were made Kadesh was no longer on good terms with Qatna and his name was eliminated. Aki Teshup may be the king of the neighbouring Tunip. Among the native kings are Nabshima, Papshima and his son Sin-atum, Addu-nirari of good Assyrian name who reigned forty-five years, his son Shalbizzalluma, and Idada, son of the official Ulashuda.[49]

Now the king of Qatna was Akizzi. He writes Amenhotep that Aitagama of Kadesh, Arzawia of Ruhuzi, and Teuwatti of Lapana have joined the Hittite king; this is the first expedition of Shuppiluliuma against Syria. Akizzi has been visited by the Egyptian messenger on his way back from Mitanni, he reports that three kings are hostile to the Hittite monarch. Aitagama has urged him to join in the alliance with the Hittite king, but he has replied that he is a servant of the king of Egypt, he will not submit to the Hittite king, even should he die, and this he has told the Hittite himself. For this reason Aitagama seeks his head. Aitagama has already caused Ube, the region about Damascus and the Biblical Hobah, to revolt; he has taken money from the house of Namiawaza. Teuwatti and Arzawia are burning Ube with fire, but the kings of Nuhashshe, Nia, Zinzar, and Tunanat are all loyal. If Arzawia and Teuwatti remain in Ube and Piridashwa in Amki or Hollow Syria, then let the king know that Ube will be no longer his land. Daily they send to Aitagama, saying: "Come, take all Ube." As Damascus in the land of Ube is at the king's feet, so is Qatna; let the king send troops, then Akizzi can enter Qatna.[50]

Qatna has been loyal to Egypt since the days of his fathers, let the king inquire of his nobles, how he gave food, drink, cattle, sheep, honey, and oil when the king's troops arrived. Six days has Aziru been in Nuhashshe; if the king does not send reinforcements they will acknowledge his suzerainty. The Hittite king has burned Qatna with fire and has carried off its inhabitants and now they dwell far from the land of his lord. Let the king provide their ransom as he has promised. "The

[49]C. Virolleaud, *Syria*, IX, 1928, 90 ff.; XI, 1930, 311 ff.
[50]*K.*, 53 f.; *BB.*, 37; *S.*, 23.

sun god, the god of my fathers, has brought it about for the king's fathers that a name should be established before him. But now the sun god, the god of my fathers, has the Hittite king made captive. Now my lord knows the deeds of the gods what they are, for now has the sun god, the god of my fathers, returned to me. So now let the king my lord give gold shekels, as many as are right, to the sun god, the god of my fathers, that a name for my lord be established as formerly before the sun god."[51] About the same time the citizens of neighbouring Tunip request Amenhotep to send them the son of their king Akit Teshup since his father has been carried off by Shuppiluliuma to the Hittite country. They fear that Aziru, now in Simyra, will do to them as he did to Nia.[52]

Namiawaza serves the king as his father Shutarna and his grandfather Saushshatar; he will protect his cities and the caravans sent by the king to Naharina.[53] As the king orders, he will go out against the enemy with his warriors, chariots, and brothers, his mercenary Habiru and Sutu.[54] Piridashwa has done a deed unheard from eternity, let the king send two hundred men until the army arrives.[55] Piridashwa has raised the city of Yanoam to revolt against him, they have shut the gate, he took chariots in Ashtaroth and gave them not to the king but to the Habiru. When they saw this, the kings of Bozrah and Halunni made agreement with Piridashwa to kill Namiawaza and to prevent him from going to Tahshe, but he escaped their hands and abides in Ube and Damascus. They acknowledge themselves vassals of the Hittite king. Arzawia has gone to Kadesh and has taken the troops of Aziru; with them he has conquered Shaddu and has given it to the Habiru. Aitagama has utterly destroyed Kadesh and Arzawia and Piridashwa have destroyed Ube. Namiawaza is protecting Kumedi, let the king renew his servant.[56]

Arahtu of Kumedi is loyal, but has neither horses nor chariots.[57] Beri of Hashabu, Andaia of Hazi, Abd Risha of

[51] K., 55; BB., 36.   [52] K., 59; BB., 41.   [53] K., 194; S., 112.
[54] K., 195.   [55] K., 196; S., 111.   [56] K., 197; BB., 43.
[57] K., 198.

Eshazi, and a fourth whose name has been lost, send identical letters to the king, informing him that they are in Amki, that Aitagama has joined the Hittites and is burning the king's cities.[58] Iamiuta of Guddashuna asks protection. The ruler of Tebah complains that his brother is inducing the city to rebel, but he can protect it if only the king will give aid.[59] Shutarna of Mushihuna, with the same name as a king of Mitanni and so perhaps of the same family, is still another who begs the king for aid.[60]

[58] *K.*, 174 ff.; *S.*, 98 f.; *BB.*, 46; Thureau-Dangin, op. cit., 94 f.
[59] *K.*, 179; *S.*, 103.   [60] *K.*, 182 ff.; *S.*, 104 f.

CHAPTER XIII

MONOTHEISM AND ITS RESULTS

NEVER was there a more sudden or more thoroughgoing revolution than when Amenhotep III was succeeded by his son Amenhotep IV, for Ikhnaton, as he later called himself, was the first known founder of a new religion. Long since the greater gods had ceased to be mere local patrons of tribes or city states; as the city states were fused into kingdoms, the god of the conquering state was accepted as divine king, the other gods were his subjects. Realisation that essentially the same divinities were worshipped under varying names led to syncretism. Identification was especially desirable with the divine head of the state. The human deputy of the god realised the advantage which accrued from the assumption by his lord of the functions of local deities; their adherents might console themselves with the assurance that the state god was their own in different guise. When foreign states were conquered, the "king of the gods" became an emperor, through whose might armies were victorious and to whom tribute was paid by foreign vassals. This stage, well called religious imperialism, had been reached in the great empires, Elam, Babylonia, Hittite, Egypt.

Egypt had worshipped the sun god Re from early dynasties, and ultimately he became its divine king. Near the beginning of the eighteenth dynasty, one of his manifestations, the sun's disk Aton, enjoyed a certain vogue. Ikhnaton made him the state god. When the opposition of the all-powerful Amon priesthood culminated in open revolt, a strict monotheism was enforced by the youthful reformer. Religious persecution followed. Amon's name was erased from every monument, the obliteration of other divinities and even of the plural "gods" was only less thorough.

No longer was the godhead to be worshipped through idols,

the Aton was depicted as the sun's disk with the life-giving rays. The all-embracing power of Aton, his loving fatherhood, extended even to foreign lands, the beauty of the nature he had created, were celebrated in a magnificent hymn. Truth was the standard by which all was measured. The evil demons who affrighted the dead were banished, prayer to the Aton alone was needed to assure a happy after life.

This was monotheism, long before it was accepted by the Hebrews. The hymn which presents the essence of the "Teaching" forms so remarkable a parallel to the one hundred and fourth psalm that some relationship cannot be denied. It is no longer possible to believe that monotheism originated with the Hebrews; is it possible that Ikhnaton's monotheism survived in Canaan to influence the Hebrew prophets? We cannot doubt that Ikhnaton attempted to propagate his religion in that Syria which is placed before Egypt in the hymn, certain passages in the Syrian letters have even been explained as references to the new teaching. However that may be, the remarkable anticipation of Hebrew monotheism and the still more remarkable parallels to the Hebrew psalm demand an adequate explanation.[1]

To escape the opposition of the Amon priesthood at Thebes, Ikhnaton founded a new capital, free from all idolatrous contamination. Fortunately for the modern historian, he transferred his father's archives to Akhetaton, the present Amarna, and here he kept his own. Wrapped in a dream of universal religion, Ikhnaton had little thought for foreign affairs. When the Hittite Shuppiluliuma congratulated him upon his accession,[2] Ikhnaton remembered Hittite intrigues in Syria and refused to reply. Yet he continued all the old Egyptian claims, and in the tombs of his servants we may see the Syrians bringing their tribute as of old.[3]

Rib Addi continues his complaints. Does it please the king that the sons of Abd Ashirta do as their hearts wish? They

---

[1]Breasted, *Religion*, 312 ff.   [2]*K.*, 41.
[3]Breasted, *Rec.*, II, 404; Davies, *Rock Tombs of el-Amarna*, II, pl. 37 ff.; III, 13 ff.

have taken the horses and chariots of the king; they have sent officers to the king of Suri, that is, Mitanni, in pledge. Rib Addi wrote to the king's father, who listened to his words and sent troops. Two messengers have been despatched to Simyra, but they must go by night on account of that dog Aziru.[4]

Formerly the king of Mitanni was an enemy of the king's fathers, and his fathers did not withdraw from Rib Addi's fathers; now the sons of Abd Ashirta capture the king's cities. They took Ardata and then Ullaza, but the king did nothing. In former times, at the very sight of a man from Egypt, the kings of Canaan fled before him, but now the sons of Abd Ashirta sneak about trying to detach the subjects of Egypt. Haia and Amanappa have abandoned Simyra.[5]

The Milim have entered Accho.[6] Aziru has seized twelve of Rib Addi's men and holds them for fifty minas ransom. The people he sent to Simyra were captured in Wahlia by ships of Tyre, Sidon, and Berut. Iapah Addi is on the side of Aziru, he has taken one of Rib Addi's ships, and is on the sea to capture the rest. It is impossible to sail to Simyra.[7]

If they say to the king: "Simyra belongs to the king," let the king realise that the sons of Abd Ashirta have taken it.[8] When Amanappa came with a small force, Rib Addi wrote the king's father and he sent a great army. At least let the king send Ianhamu and Pahor.[9] Sidon and Berut no longer belong to the king.[10] The king receives from Rib Addi a tablet on which is written all that Iapah Addi has held back, including nine thousand slaves and a hundred minas of gold.[11]

Pahor arrived with a small army and assumed the residency of Kumedi with oversight of Central Syria. Orders were sent the vassal rulers to prepare for an advance and promises of loyalty poured in. Arzawia of Ruhuzi refutes reflections on his fidelity by listing his preparation for the coming army.[12] Zer of Bashan, our first mention of that east Jordan country, is ruled by Artamania, whose good Iranian name shows the

[4] K., 108; S., 56.   [5] K., 109; S., 57.   [6] K., 111; S., 59.
[7] K., 114; BB., 13. [8] K., 116.   [9] K., 117; S., 62.
[10] K., 118; BB., 25. [11] K., 119 f.; S., 64 f. [12] K., 191.

Aryans penetrating to the very desert border; his troops too are prepared to meet the army.[13] Similar letters, some word for word identical, come from various petty princes of the region.[14] Abd Tirshi, king of Hazor, is a loyal servant, he rejoices at the coming of the king, only let the king remember what has been done against Hazor.[15] Amunira of Berut has prepared horses and chariots for the army and Berut will be safe until it arrives.[16] Abimilki of Tyre will provide ships for the Egyptian army; the man of Berut went with one ship and the man of Sidon with two, but he has gone with his whole city.[17] Zatatnia, who has succeeded his father Zurata as king of Accho, will obey the king's orders.[18]

A deed has been done against Rib Addi that has not been done forever against Gebal; the new resident Pahor has sent nomad Sutu, who have killed some of the mercenary Sherdan and he has carried off three citizens of Gebal to Egypt. How many days is the city angry against him? If the king loves him, let him return the men, then will Rib Addi live again.[19]

The king has demanded urkarinu wood. It comes from the lands of Zalhi and the city of Ugarit, where Rib Addi cannot go, for Aziru and his friends prevent his sailing by sea. He has heard that the Hittites are burning the land with fire, they are bringing Hittites to attack Gebal. Let not the king hearken to the Milim, for they have given all the silver and gold they received from the king to the sons of Abd Ashirta and they in turn to the mighty king.[20]

Only Batrun remains to him. Let the king send ships and Rib Addi will go with his gods to his lord. Aziru boasts that he does not fear Namiawaza, the resident of Ube, yet the king has not punished him. Let the king send the governors of Ube and Kumedi against him.[21] Simyra is taken, its governor Pahor slain, the men of Gebal killed. Pahanate gave him no help but did him evil. Now his son Haia has plundered and

---

[13] K., 201; S., 114.   [14] K., 191, 202–208, 211 ?   [15] K., 227 f.; BB., 47 f.
[16] K., 141; BB., 26.   [17] K., 153, 155; BB., 31;   [18] K., 233.
[19] K., 122 f.; S., 67; BB., 20.   [20] K., 126; S., 68.
[21] K., 129; S., 70; cf. Thureau-Dangin, *op. cit.*, 91 ff.

surrendered Simyra.[22] Aziru is attacking Gebal, abandoned by its gods and its inhabitants.[23]

The people of Gebal, his family, even his wife, are urging him to make peace with Aziru, but Rib Addi has refused. He has begged reinforcements from his lord, but the king has not even replied. So low in mind was he that he made a trip to Berut to secure Amunira as friend; repulsed here, he returned to Gebal, only to find himself shut out. For when the people of his house saw how his messengers returned from Egypt with empty hands, his younger brother persuaded Gebal to go over to the enemy. Two sons and two wives were handed over to Aziru. If another heart does not come to the king, Rib Addi will die. He is old and sick, his illness is due to the anger of the gods of Gebal. He has confessed his sins. Since it is impossible for him to go to Egypt himself, he has sent his son; let the king give him troops to recover Gebal. His opponents in Gebal are few, the majority of the citizens are on his side; if troops appear, Gebal will return to its allegiance. There is much silver and gold in the city and all things are in abundance in the temples; let the king do as he wishes when it is recaptured. If one objects "The city is strong," it will not be strong before the troops of his lord.[24]

For the last time Rib Addi appeals to Ikhnaton. He has lived twelve months away from Gebal. So far from offering sympathy, the king has accused him of conspiracy in Joppa. The rebels in Gebal have demanded that Amunira surrender his unwelcome guest, and to Rib Addi himself they write: "Will you not leave Berut?" Sadly he recalls the past. When Abd Ashirta took Simyra, he protected his city with his own hand. Then he wrote the king, who sent an army which retook Simyra. When Simyra again fell into the hands of Aziru, the men of Gebal demanded: "How long can we withstand the son of Abd Ashirta? All our silver has gone to the enemy." They revolted against him, but he put the rebels to death. Next they demanded: "How long will you kill us? Where will

[22] K., 131 f.; BB., 18, 24.   [23] K., 134.
[24] K., 136 f.; BB., 16.

you find men to dwell in the city?" He wrote the palace for soldiers, but none were given him. The city said: "Leave him, we will go over to Aziru." Rib Addi was firm: "How shall I go over to him and leave the king my lord?" No sooner was Rib Addi outside Gebal than his people announced: "Rib Addi is dead, we are out of his hands." Ten hours after his return from Berut, he despatched his son to court; it is now four months and he has not even seen the king's face. The men of Berut see how Rib Addi has been abandoned and they talk of revolt, then the king will have no lands at all. Rib Addi will die but his sons will live to demand of the king: "Restore our city." He ends this last pathetic letter: "Why does my lord keep himself from me?"[25]

Amunira is still awaiting the arrival of the royal troops. As for the man of Gebal, he is protecting him until the king cares for his servant. His brother in Gebal has handed over Rib Addi's children to the sinners against the king in Amurru.[26]

Abimilki of Tyre reports that Simyra has been surrendered to Aziru, who has now made an alliance with Zimrida of Sidon and the men of Arvad. They collected ships, chariots, and infantry to capture Tyre. By the aid of the king's mighty hand they did not succeed. He still holds Island Tyre, but that is all. Zimrida has taken Uzu, at the great fountains on the mainland; Abimilki has no water to drink, no wood to burn, not even a place to bury his dead. Zimrida tells all the king's words to Aziru.[27] Abimilki has sent a hundred weight of some stone to the king, let the king give him Uzu as a vessel for food and drink, for water, wood, straw, and clay. Let him send ten men as guard. The king of Hazor has left the city and joined the Habiru. The king's land has gone over to the Habiru, let the king ask his resident who knows Canaan.[28]

An unknown informant tells the king that the ruler of Accho is hostile,[29] but Zatatna himself reports that Zirdamiashta fled from Namiawaza and took refuge with the resident Shuta in Megiddo. Now he is with Zatatna and Shuta has ordered him

[25] *K.*, 138; *S.*, 73. [26] *K.*, 142; *BB.*, 27. [27] *K.*, 149; *BB.*, 28.
[28] *K.*, 148.   [29] *K.*, 236.

returned to Namiawaza, but Zatatna has refused. Accho is like Migdol in Egypt and the king has not placed him under Shuta. Let the king send a resident to receive the fugitive.[30]

Although officially a friend of Ikhnaton, Burnaburiash of Babylon makes serious complaint. The caravan of his ambassador Salmu has been twice plundered, once by Piriawaza and once by Pamahu.[31] Some of his merchants journeyed under the protection of another ambassador, Ahu-tabu, to Canaan; in Hannathon they were killed by Shum Adda, son of Paluma, and Zatatna, son of Zurata, who stole their money. Shum Adda cut off the feet of one and Zatatna placed the other on exhibition in a jar. "Canaan is your land and its kings are your servants," argues Burnaburiash, therefore Ikhnaton must punish the murderers and return the money. If they are not punished, and Burnaburiash implies his doubt of the dreamer taking action, the next time they will kill the men in the Babylonian caravans or even the Egyptian ambassadors, and so the relations between the two countries will come to an end.[32]

Shum Adda himself, from his city Shimron near the Waters of Merom, leaves no doubt as to his feelings towards his nominal master. Ikhnaton has demanded tribute of grain; Shum Adda insolently replies that it is all spoiled and beside, since the days of his father Kuzuna, no such tribute has ever been given.[33] For once Ikhnaton acted promptly. Shum Adda was deported to Egypt, where he received a letter from Iapah Addi, deploring the fact that his name had been made evil before the king, so that he could not leave Egypt, and expressing his best wishes.[34]

The Hittite menace was still threatening, and Ikhnaton determined to win over Aziru. A gracious letter was sent the former rebel, and Aziru gladly replied, for the Hittite advance was equally threatening to his independence. He is the king's servant forever, and likewise his sons, whom he gives to the king that they may do his bidding, only let the king install

[30] *K.*, 234; *S.*, 134.   [31] *K.*, 7; *S.*, 4.
[32] *K.*, 8; *S.*, 5; cf. D. D. Luckenbill, *AJSL.*, XXXV, 1919, 158 f.
[33] *K.*, 224; *BB.*, 66.   [34] *K.*, 97; *S.*, 50.

Aziru in Amurru.[35] He has always been a true vassal; the officials of Simyra were to blame for all that happened. Not the least thing has he done against the king, who should know the real sinners. He fears the attack of the Hittite king, his enemy; let the king support him with troops and chariots, then he will protect the land for the king and will give as much tribute as any of the city chiefs, only let the king answer quickly.[36]

Aziru writes his "father" Dudu, a David who sits before the king and perhaps an Asiatic; he was known at court as Tutu, "chief mouthpiece of all the foreign lands."[37] "Behold, you are my father and my lord, and I am your son. The lands of Amurru are your lands and my house is your house. And whatever is your wish, send, and I, behold, your wish I will give." Let Dudu protect him against his slanderers. "If the king does not love me but hates me, what can I say?"[38]

He is back in Amurru and will at once rebuild Simyra, then let the king grant him recognition. All the city chiefs are hostile to him.[39] One of his enemies was Ili-rabih, who with the city of Gebal reminds the king that Aziru has killed the kings of Ambi and Ardata, not to speak of Aduna, king of Arka, and the royal governor. The king should not trust anything that Aziru says, all that was reported by the governor he killed was true. Gebal is as essential to the king as Memphis, let not the king restrain himself from those who do evil.[40]

In accordance with the king's demand, Aziru has sent eight ships, urkarinu wood, and great beams. He has not yet rebuilt Simyra, for the king of Nuhashshe is hostile to him, but he will do so within the year. Let the king quickly return his messenger and he shall bring back the tribute.[41] Let not the king listen to those who slander him, when he comes to Egypt Aziru will explain all. The king has accused him of avoiding his representative Hani. Now the truth of the matter is that Aziru was at Tunip and Hani had started for Egypt before he

[35]K., 156; S., 83.   [36]K., 157; S., 84.
[37]N. de G. Davies, *Rock Tombs of el-Amarna*, VI, 14.
[38]K., 158.   [39]K., 159; S., 85.   [40]K., 139; BB., 45.
[41]K., 160.

could return. Let the king ask Hani how he was received, how Aziru's brothers and Batti-ilu stood before him, how they provided him with meat and fowl and strong drink! Horses and asses were also furnished for the return journey. To be sure, he has not yet rebuilt Simyra, but the king's messenger Hatib has induced the kings of Nuhashshe to capture his cities and Hatib himself has purloined half the objects and all the gold and silver that the king sent for Aziru. As to the reproach that he has received the Hittite king's ambassadors while avoiding the Egyptian, Aziru waxes properly indignant.[42]

At last the restoration of Simyra was undertaken, and Aziru was recognised as the Egyptian governor of Amurru. Even yet Ikhnaton was not satisfied. Rib Addi in despair had abandoned hope of Egyptian aid and had requested his ancient enemy to restore him to Gebal, promising in return the spoil of the city and its overlordship. Aziru could not forget the enmity so easily. Rib Addi was seized in Sidon and Aziru handed him over to the city chiefs. Ikhnaton angrily declares that Aziru has not told the whole truth; had he been a loyal vassal, he would have sent Rib Addi to his king. It is reported that Aziru has made alliance with Aitagama of Kadesh, who is hostile to Egypt; he has done only what he thought advantageous to himself, not to his lord. Does he not know that Aitagama is only seeking to throw him into the fire? Let him beware lest he and his family die by the king's axe. The year of grace he requested has expired, let him come to Egypt or at least send his son. Aziru has promised that if Hani shall come a second time, he will surrender the king's enemies. Hani has now arrived, let Aziru send the enemies named in the list. The names are Egyptian, perhaps they are exiles hostile to Ikhnaton's reforms and stirring up trouble in Syria.[43]

Hatib has arrived, so Aziru writes Dudu, with good words from the king. He will come to Egypt with Hatib as soon as the Hittite king returns home from Nuhashshe; there is danger that he may attack Amurru or Tunip, but two days distant from Nuhashshe. Aziru is anxious to visit Egypt, but he fears

[42] K., 161; BB., 35.   [43] K., 162; S., 86; H. R. Hall, JEA., VII, 1921, 45.

the king and Dudu, let them swear that nothing will be done to him but what is good.[44]

The troubles which marked the accession of Shuppiluliuma to the Hittite throne had permitted the revolt of Carchemish, Aleppo, and Nuhashshe.[45] Soon after, Tushratta of Mitanni invaded Nuhashshe and attempted to slay its king Sharrupsha, who sent messengers to Shuppiluliuma, saying: "Servant of the king of Hatte Land am I, save me." Aid was granted and the Mitannian invader was driven out.[46] Later, Shuppiluliuma himself invaded Mitanni and its capital Washshuganni was sacked. He then recrossed the Euphrates and overpowered Aleppo and Mukishhe. Takuwa, king of Nia, hastened to Mukishhe and entered into a covenant with the Hittite monarch, but Takuwa's brother Akit Teshup behind his back incited Nia and the mariannu nobles to revolt. Hishmia, Asiri, Zulkia, Habahi, Birria, and Niruwabi entered into agreement with Akia, king of Arahti; Shuppiluliuma defeated the allies in Arahti, took prisoner Akia and Akit Teshup, and deported them to Hatti. Qatna was taken and despoiled; the excavations show that it never recovered. Nuhashshe was next invaded, Sharrupsha was killed, and his mother, brothers, and sons were deported to the Hittite land. A servant of Sharrupsha, Takib-sharri, was made king in Ukulzat.[47] Tette was appointed king in Nuhashshe itself; by the treaty, he was to accompany his master against Hurri, Egypt, Babylonia, Ashtata, Alshe, or against any enemy of Mukishhe, Aleppo, or Kadesh.[48]

With the southward advance of the Hittites, Aziru plucked up courage to visit Egypt, since it was now definitely a choice between two masters. Even at court he was not free from attack. Ili-rabih and the men of Gebal demand why the king has sent through Aziru; he possesses Simyra and the other cities of the king, only Gebal is loyal. Even when brought to

---

[44]*K.*, 164 ff.; *S.*, 88 ff. [45]*KBo.*, I, 6. [46]*KBo.*, I, 4.
[47]*KBo.*, I, 1 f.; *KUB.*, III, 1; D. D. Luckenbill, *AJSL.*, XXXVII, 1921, 164 ff.; E. F. Weidner, *Politische Dokumente aus Kleinasien*, 1923, 2 ff.
[48]*KBo.*, I, 4, 16; *KUB.*, III, 2 f., 10; Luckenbill, *op. cit.*, 177 ff.; Weidner, *op. cit.*, 58 ff.

the king, he ordered his people to support Aitagama of Kadesh in his conquest of Amki. Let not the king of the Hittites and of Naharina and—the letter was never completed.[49]

Ikhnaton was reluctant to permit Aziru's departure. The king of Nuhashshe, the Tette enthroned by Shuppiluliuma, taunted his son: "You have sold your father for gold to the king of Egypt and when will he send him back from Egypt?" All the lands and all the Sutu have spoken thus: "Aziru does not come out from Egypt." Now the Sutu are sending messengers to say: "Your father abides in Egypt and we shall make enmity with you." Aziru's son therefore begs the Egyptian official to listen to Dudu and to send back his father.[50]

Aziru was finally released from his honourable captivity and returned to Amurru. Soured by his treatment and despairing of Egyptian aid, he promptly threw himself at the feet of Shuppiluliuma, who had mercy on him and wrote him a treaty tablet. The boundaries of Amurru remained those of his fathers, but he paid a yearly tribute of three hundred shekels of good refined gold.[51]

Through all this manœuvring for position and intriguing with each other's vassals, Egypt and the Hittites were nominally at peace and their boundaries defined by formal treaty. Zita, Shuppiluliuma's son, could even write his Egyptian "father," recalling how he sent gifts to his lord when the Egyptian envoys returned from the Hittite court, and begging for gold in return.[52] Shuppiluliuma now denounced the treaty and sent a force against Amki; the Egyptians countered with an expedition against Kadesh. Aitagama hastily sent off a letter to Ikhnaton. He has been slandered by Namiawaza, who has taken all his father's house from Kadesh and has burned his cities with fire. The royal residents and the nobles know his loyalty, he has called the noble Pahor to witness. Wherever there has been enmity against the king, he has gone with his soldiers, chariots, and brothers. Namiawaza has given

[49] *K.*, 140; *S.*, 75. [50] *K.*, 169; *S.*, 93.
[51] *KUB.*, III, 122; IV, 94; Weidner, *op. cit.*, 70 ff.; treaties with Tuppi Teshup and Bentishnia, cf. pp. 219, 226.
[52] *K.*, 44; *S.*, 16.

all the king's cities to the Habiru in Tahshe and Ube, but through the king's gods he has won them back. Let the king rejoice over his servant Aitagama forever. Ikhnaton replies that he has heard his promises, Pahor will protect Kadesh.[53]

Claiming that the Egyptians had destroyed Kadesh, Shuppiluliuma sent his generals Lupakkish and Teshup-zalmash against Amki. Baaluia and Batti-ilu write their father, detained in Egypt; Lupakish has taken the cities of Amki and those belonging to Addumi. Zitana is reported to be on the way with ninety thousand soldiers; they have read this in a Hittite document, for they give the name of Zidash, Shuppiluliuma's son, in the accusative. They cannot confirm the report; should he come to Nuhashshe, Batti-ilu will be sent to him and Baaluia will report it to his father.[54] And here the letters from the Amarna archives cease.

Just then (1358) Ikhnaton died. To his amazement, Shuppiluliuma received from the widowed Nofreteti the following letter: "My husband is dead, I have no son. You are said to have many sons. If you will give me one of your sons, he shall be my husband. I fear to take one of my slaves and make him my husband."

Suspecting that this might be a trick, the Hittite monarch despatched a messenger to learn the true state of affairs. Meanwhile, he pressed the siege of Carchemish, which had revolted under Mitannian pressure; after a seven days' assault the city was captured with 3,300 prisoners.

Nofreteti replied through her ambassador Hani. Why has Shuppiluliuma written that this is a trick? Had she sons would she have written to a foreign land? She has told the truth, she has written no other state. Let him send a son and he shall be king of Egypt as well as husband. Convinced at last, Shuppiluliuma sent his son, but it was too late. Nofreteti's son-in-law, Sakere, had secured the throne, and Shuppiluliuma's son was put to death on the way to Egypt.[55]

[53] *K.*, 189 f.; *S.*, 108. [54] *K.*, 170.
[55] *KBo.*, V, 6; J. Friedrich, *Alte Orient*, XXIV, 3, 12 ff.; E. Cavaignac, *Rev. Études Anciennes*, XXXII, 1930, 229 ff.

The Egyptian monarch reported the death to Shuppiluliuma, boasted the strength of his own army and taunted the Hittite about his reverses in Asia Minor, but declared his willingness to renew the former brotherhood. Shuppiluliuma replied that he had put down the rebels in Asia Minor and had conquered Aleppo and Carchemish. He too had soldiers and horses and the gods were on his side. He will make no brotherhood, their fathers have been enemies and so it shall continue. He will revenge the death of his son on the murderers, Egypt shall be so wasted not a bird shall be seen there.[56]

This was a declaration of war and Shuppiluliuma took up his march towards Abina or Ube, not expecting, he tells us, trouble with Kadesh. But Aitagama made good his promise to Egypt. To the astonishment of Shuppiluliuma, Shutarra and his son Aitagama advanced to give battle. Pahor gave no assistance and the men of Kadesh were defeated. They fled to Abzuia, where they were besieged and made prisoner; all were deported to the Hittite land. The year's campaign was ended by the defeat of Ariwana, king of Abina, with his nobles Uambadura, Akparu, and Artaia, likewise deported to Asia Minor.

Not long after Ikhnaton's accession Tushratta's son murdered his father, but was supplanted as king of Mitanni by a pretender, Artatama II. Artatama had formerly been a partisan of the Hittites, but now he allied himself with the Assyrians, while his son, Shutarna, in his need accepted the overlordship of Ashur-uballit. Shutarna also attempted to slay the legitimate claimant, Tushratta's son Mattiawaza. Robbed and in danger of his life in Babylonia, Mattiawaza again fled, this time to Shuppiluliuma, whose daughter looked upon the fugitive with favour and made him her husband.

Shuppiluliuma decided to reorganise North Syria. Two of his sons, Telipinush and Biashshilish, were made kings of Aleppo and Carchemish, his son-in-law Mattiawaza was restored to Mitanni. Several districts east of the Euphrates were detached from Mitanni and granted to Biashshilish in return

[56] *KUB.*, XIX, 20; E. Forrer, *Forschungen*, II, 1, 1926, 28 ff.

for the aid given Matiawaza in winning back his ancestral kingdom.[57] The prisoners taken in Syria brought back to Asia Minor the plague which raged without cessation for twenty years; Murshilish confessed to his gods that the plague was justly sent as punishment for his father's violation of the Egyptian treaty.[58]

[57]*KBo.*, I, 1–3; *KUB.*, III, 1, 17; Luckenbill, *op. cit.*, 162 ff.; Weidner, *op. cit.*, 2 ff.
[58]Forrer, *Forsch.*, II, 1, 12 ff.; A. Götze, *Kleinasiatische Forschungen*, I, 1929, 210 f.

CHAPTER XIV

HABIRU INROADS

CANAAN had remained loyal under Amenhotep III, but as the Egyptian empire in the north fell into fragments, the Canaanite princes began to dream of independence. Their hopes were not unmixed with fears, for here too the Habiru were a menace.

One man stands out as the leader of the anti-Egyptian faction. Labaia can scarcely be called a nationalist, for though his father and grandfather had ruled in Canaan before him, his name appears in a letter from Arzawa, in southeastern Asia Minor, which is written in near Hittite and this may have been the home of his ancestors. His first offense was the capture of Gitpadalla, Shunem, Bene Barak, Arraba, and Gath Rimmon, but the worst was the part he played in securing control of Shechem for the Habiru.[1]

In Shechem there lived at this time a wealthy merchant with the Hittite name of Birashshenashil. Great clay amphoræ with palm-leaf ornament stored his oil in a magazine, fourteen alabaster jugs may have held his wine. Smoothly polished stones weighed his purchases, stone spindle-whorls and loom-weights tell of his textile manufactures, a large scarab and female statuettes of Egyptian faience indicate his foreign trade. His business dealings were recorded on a clay tablet in Akkadian with seven witnesses, but that he himself was not so careful to live up to his obligations is seen from a pitiful letter: "For three years you have not sent to me to my city the grain or oil you should bring me. What is my sin? If you do not answer me, the youths who are with me will lay hands on their father and their mother." He casts himself at the merchant's feet and prays that aid be given. In his leisure, the merchant amused himself with dice of bone having one to four holes on the side. The bronze-headed spear he kept to protect his prop-

[1] K., 32; S., 202; K., 250, 289.

erty was of no avail when the Habiru took the city, for his house was destroyed by fire.[2]

To royal complaints Labaia offered the excuse that the people were too strong. The king angrily demanded: "If the people who took the city were mighty, how could the people be restrained?" Labaia answered that the city had been taken through enmity; he has been slandered to the king. Now two other cities have been taken from him.[3]

A close associate of Labaia was Milkilu of Aijalon. Adduqarradu complains that Milkilu is oppressing him and has given his servant to his father-in-law Tagi, while damage is also being done by Labaia.[4] Piridia of Megiddo has received a small detachment of Egyptian troops; since they entered his city, Labaia has shut him up so that he cannot go out of his city gate to shear his sheep. Let the king send a hundred soldiers.[5]

In response to these appeals, Ikhnaton despatched in his eleventh year a force under Hani, son of Merire, as "King's Son in the Land of Canaan." The king of Achshaph, Intaruta, a good Aryan who reveres Indra, is informed of his coming; let him obey Hani's orders. The king of Hazor rejoices at Hani's approaching visit, and has made all preparations. Shubanda, another Aryan farther south, has given Hani five hundred cattle and twenty girls.[6]

The approach of this army forced Tagi and Milkilu to make their peace with Ikhnaton. Tagi breaks forth into poetry, commonplace to be sure, as two other vassals quote the same couplets, while traces of their phraseology may be found in the Bible:

"Behold, as for us, my two eyes are on you;
If we ascend to heaven, if we descend to earth, our head is in your hand;
I looked here and looked there, but there was no light;
Then I looked at the king my lord, and it was light."[7]

[2]E. Sellin, *ZDPV.*, XLIX, 1926, 319; F. Böhl, *ibid.*, 321.
[3]*K.*, 252; *BB.*, 61.   [4]*K.*, 249; *S.*, 143.   [5]*K.*, 244.
[6]Thureau-Dangin, *op. cit.*, 100 f.; *K.*, 227; *BB.*, 47; *K.*, 301.
[7]Cf. Psalm 139:8; also *K.*, 292, 296.

Tagi attempted to collect caravans through his brother, who came within a finger of being killed; he will therefore send his caravans by the hand of his companions. When he sent his messenger to see the king's face, the king gave gifts in return.[8] Milkilu obeys the king's words, his city, given him by the king, is well. He has forwarded men and women by the hand of Haia, let the king send troops and myrrh.[9]

Labaia attempted to follow their example. He is a loyal vassal like his father and grandfather, he has never done evil, he has never sinned, he has never withheld his tribute, he has never disobeyed the resident's orders. His only sin is that he entered Gezer; then he did say: "The king has taken all my property, but where is all that belongs to Milkilu? I know the deed of Milkilu against me." He does not know whether his son Dumuia went with the Habiru, but nevertheless he has handed him over to the resident Addaia. So loyal is he that should the king demand his wife or write him: "Strike a dagger in your heart and die," he would obey. A notation by the Egyptian scribe records that the letter was received in the twelfth year.[10]

Ikhnaton, however, ordered Piridia and his brothers to capture Labaia alive and to forward him to Egypt. Piridia succeeded in his attempt and brought his captive to Megiddo. Zurata of Accho, Piridia's younger brother, then took him in charge and promised to send him to Ikhnaton; instead, he detained him for a time in his house at Hannathon, but later freed him for ransom, as he had already done with Baal-mehir of Tenni. Piridia and his brother with the equally Aryan name of Iashdata pursued after Labaia only to find that he had been murdered at En Gannim. Zurata thereupon laid the whole blame for the miscarriage on Piridia, who must send a letter of explanation.[11]

Hani's expedition, followed by the submission of Tagi and Milkilu and the death of Labaia, was success enough for Ikh-

[8] *K.*, 264 ff.; *BB.*, 70, *S.*, 151 f.
[9] *K.*, 267; *S.*, 153; *BB.*, 63.   [10] *K.*, 253 f.; *S.*, 144 f.
[11] *K.*, 245; *BB.*, 72; *K.*, 257 ff.; *S.*, 147 ff.

naton to picture the submission of the Asiatics in his twelfth year.[12] The reputation of Labaia as a determined foe of the king was lasting, and the worst accusation which could be directed against a personal enemy was that he was another Labaia. His two sons carried on their father's work, though now and then they made a pretense of loyalty. When the king sent orders through Haia for the convoy of caravans to Hani Galbat, Mut-baal declared he would follow his father's example and escort them even to Babylonia.[13]

Mut-baal informed Ianhamu that the king of Pella, Aiab or Job, had fled before the royal resident. Ianhamu doubted the accuracy of the report. "As the king my lord may live, as the king my lord may live," replied Mut-baal, "Aiab is not in Pella. Behold, two months he has been in hiding. Ask then Benenima, ask then Tadua, ask then Iashuia." Benenima is a perfectly good Benjamin, Iashuia is an equally good Joshua! Mut-baal himself has left Ashtaroth. All the cities of the Ghor, the Jordan region, Dumah, Edrei, Aroer, Meshtu, Migdol, the fount of Anab, and Zarki, are now hostile, while Hawini and Jabesh have been taken by the enemy. By the time Ianhamu returns from his journey, Aiab will be back in Pella and will obey his orders.[14] Aiab then wrote the king that he has heard the royal word sent through Athamaia, and he is carefully guarding the king's land, but he complains that the ruler of Hazor has deprived him of three of his towns.[15]

Shunem has been recovered and Piridia is plowing there with the corvee summoned from the northern Joppa and Nuribda, but the other chiefs do not plow as he does. Day and night he is protecting Megiddo, he guards his fields by day and he keeps the walls with horses and chariots, but the enmity of the Habiru is great against him. Labaia's sons have given money to the Habiru and the Kashi to go against him. Pi-

[12]N. de G. Davies, *Rock Tombs of el-Amarna*, II, 40 ff., pl. 37 ff.; III, 9 ff., pl. 13 ff.
[13]*K.*, 255; *S.*, 146.
[14]Fig. 78; *K.*, 256; *BB.*, 64; for significance of this mention of Joshua, cf. p. 197.
[15]Thureau-Dangin, *op. cit.*, 96.

ridia's brother Iashdata bemoans the cattle of which he has been robbed by the men of Taanach.[16]

Labaia's two sons are repeatedly sending to Addu-qarradu, demanding why he has handed over to the king that Gitpadalla which their father captured, and urging him to war against En Gannim, whose men killed Labaia, Addu-qarradu has refused to rebel; the king should send a noble to inquire of Namiawaza why he has not taken action against Labaia's sons, to whom Milkilu is constantly sending messengers.[17] A different story is told by the "governess" of an unknown city. The whole land is falling away to the Habiru, Zeboim has been taken, the Habiru sent to Aijalon and Zorah and just missed killing the two sons of Milkilu.[18]

Shuwardata of Keilah, who bears a good Sanskrit name meaning "Sun given," will do what the king commands him. The Habiru have invaded the land granted by the king, but he has succeeded in defeating them. All his brothers have abandoned him, only he and Abd Hepa of Jerusalem are continuing the war against the Habiru. Zurata of Accho and Intaruta of Achshaph have come to his aid with chariots; let the king send Ianhamu. Shuwardata has been invited to visit the king. Thirty cities are opposed to him, he stands alone. Let the king ask Ianhamu, with him at court, or the resident, whether there is hostility against him or not.[19]

Jerusalem is mentioned only in the letters of its king, Abd Hepa or perhaps Put Hepa. By his name he shows himself a worshipper of the Mitannian goddess Hepa, and he employs Hurrian glosses in his letters, facts which imply a foreign rule in Jerusalem. His boast is that he is not a mere city chief, he is a formally appointed royal official. Why has not the king sent a messenger? Let the king send a resident who will lead out the city chiefs with him.[20]

The lands of Gezer, Ashkelon, and Lachish have given food, oil, and all things needful to the Habiru; the deed is the deed

[16]Thureau-Dangin, *op. cit.*, 97 f.; *K.*, 243, 246, 248; *S.*, f.; *BB.*, 59.
[17]*K.*, 250.   [18]*K.*, 273 f.; *S.*, 155.
[19]*K.*, 278; *BB.*, 69; Thureau-Dangin, *op. cit.*, 98 f.; *K.*, 283; *S.*, 160.
[20]*K.*, 285; *S.*, 161.

of Milkilu and the sons of Labaia who have handed over the king's land to the Habiru. When Abd Hepa complained of the Kashi, the king thought it nothing, but now he has the evidence. Addaia, the former resident, has returned to his home in Gaza, after ordering Abd Hepa not to leave his city; let the king send him supplies until the arrival of the new resident Pauru. On its way to the king, his caravan was plundered in the open country near Aijalon. As a postscript, Abd Hepa adds that the Kashi almost succeeded in killing him in his own house.[21]

Iapahi of Gezer, Milkilu's son, has heard the word of the king and his heart is quiet. His younger brother has revolted against him and has gone to Makaz to join the Habiru, let the king attend to the matter. This was followed by his expulsion from Gezer; let the king send troops to restore him. He will then serve the king as did his father; he has heard the words of the resident Maia.[22]

Addadani, the ruler of Gath, has been ordered to obey the resident and protect the royal cities, and he has done so. He built the city of Mahanath in preparation for the arrival of the king's army, but Maia has taken it away from him and has placed his own resident in it. May his own superior, the resident Rianap, be ordered to return it. Beia has plundered Gezer many days; even the hill folk ransom a captive for thirty shekels, but Beia demands a hundred. He has captured the men sent by Addadani to protect Joppa. Widia of Ashkelon is defending his city and is preparing for the coming army; Ianbi-ilu of Lachish has obeyed all the orders of the resident Maia.[23]

Milkilu, according to Abd Hepa, has not departed from the sons of Labaia and from the sons of Arzawa. Why does not the king punish such a city chief? Milkilu and Tagi have taken Rabbah, near Kiriath Jearim, and they seek to take Jerusalem. Gath of Carmel belongs to Tagi and men of Gath garrison Beth Shan. Jerusalem may suffer the same fate, since

[21] *K.*, 287; *S.*, 163.   [22] *K.*, 297 f.; *BB.*, 50 f.; *K.*, 300; *S.*, 171.
[23] *K.*, 292; *K.*, 294; *BB.*, 71; *K.*, 320 ff.; *K.*, 328.

Labaia and the land of Shechem have given to the Habiru. Milkilu has written Tagi and his sons to furnish everything they wish to the men of Keilah. The garrison troops despatched through Haia have been taken over by Addaia and they are now in his house at Gaza, except the twenty he returned to Egypt, and Abd Hepa is left without soldiers. Pauru has likewise gone from Jerusalem to Gaza; let the king send fifty men.[24]

Milkilu and Shuwardata have hired men of Gezer, Gath, and Keilah, and have taken the land of the city of Rabbah. The king's land has fallen away to the Habiru, and now a city of the land of Jerusalem named Bethlehem has gone over to the people of Keilah. If troops are not sent, the land will fall away to the Habiru.[25]

Ikhnaton had received appeal after appeal to return the great Semite Ianhamu, now in charge of foreign affairs at the court; Ianhamu at last appeared in Canaan but accomplished nothing of account. His favourable reception by Ikhnaton did not save Milkilu from constant slander, and finally Ianhamu, under threat of death, demanded of him two thousand shekels of silver with his wife and children. Poor Milkilu can only request his royal master to order a chariot to return him to Egypt. Enmity is mighty against him and Shuwardata, let the king save his land from the Habiru; if he will not, then let the king at least send chariots to take them away, lest they be killed by their servants.[26] Iahtiri was carried off when a youth by Ianhamu; he served the king in Egypt and stood in the king's gate. Now let the king ask Ianhamu whether he watches the city gates of Gaza and Joppa.[27]

Shuwardata has broken with Abd Hepa, who is attacking his city of Keilah.[28] Keilah has fallen and the king orders Shuwardata to recapture it. This he accomplished, but then Abd Hepa wrote the men of Keilah to take silver and follow him, and thus he secured control of the city. Let the king in-

[24] K., 289; S., 165.
[25] K., 290; S., 166; O. Schroeder, *OLZ.*, XVIII, 1915, 294 f.
[26] K., 270 ff.; B., 62; S., 154.   [27] K., 296; BB., 57.   [28] K., 279; S., 158.

vestigate and see whether he has taken a man or an ox or an ass from him. Labaia, who took their cities, is dead, but Abd Hepa is another Labaia who takes their cities. Shuwardata will do nothing until he has received an answer.[29]

Abd Hepa replies to Shuwardata's accusations. What has he done against the king? He has been slandered when they say he is a rebel. In language recalling the Biblical description of Melchizedek, another king of Jerusalem, he adds: "Behold, neither my father nor my mother has set me in this place, the mighty hand of the king has led me into my father's house."[30] Why should he do harm against the king his lord? So long as the king lives, he will say to the resident Addaia: "Why do you love the Habiru and hate the city chiefs?" This is the reason why he has been slandered to the king and because he said: "All the lands of the king my lord are being lost." Ianhamu has taken all the troops and Milkilu is destroying the whole land. He would come to see the king, but the enemy is too strong; let the king send troops to convoy him, and then he will come. Not a city chief is on the king's side, the Habiru are plundering all the lands of the king; if bowmen do not arrive this year, all the lands will be lost. The letter ends with a request to the king's scribe who receives this tablet to speak fine words to the king: All the lands of the king my lord are being lost.[31]

One contemporary letter has been unearthed at Lachish. A certain Pabu writes to the noble who has headquarters in this city. Shipti Baal has united with Zimrida of Lachish and has written him: "My father, the city of Iarami has written me: 'Give me six bows and three swords; if I go out against the king's land and you are joined with me, then will I make it again obedient.' The man who made this impossible is Pabu, send him to me." For this reason, Pabu sends the information to the resident, let him give orders as to what is to be done.[32]

Despite Pabu's accusation, Zimrida remained loyal; Abd Hepa must report that Zimrida was murdered by his servants

[29] K., 280.   [30] Heb. 7:3.   [31] K., 286; S., 162.
[32] A. H. Sayce in F. J Bliss, *Mound of Many Cities*, 184 ff.; K., 333.

who wished to join the Habiru. Worse yet, Turbazu and Iaptih Adda were slain in the city gate of Sillu, on the very border of Egypt, yet Ikhnaton has done nothing to avenge their deaths. If the king will not send troops, at least let him send a resident to carry Abd Hepa and his brothers to Egypt that they may die before the king.[33]

[33] K., 288; S., 164.

CHAPTER XV

HEBREW ORIGINS

No problem of origins troubled the Hebrews. They knew that their national history began with their great ancestor Abraham, who left his home in Ur of the Chaldees and travelled by way of Harran to the Promised Land. In true nomad fashion he wandered far and wide, pitching his tent and erecting altars on the sites where his descendants were to worship his God. Abraham's son Isaac and Isaac's son Jacob lived an equally idyllic existence, at peace with the Canaanites whom their children were to dispossess. Joseph, sold into Egypt by his brothers, rose to be its master, and welcomed his father Jacob and his brothers when famine drove them to the Nile.[1]

Then there reigned a king who knew not Joseph and who set the Hebrews to task work. Led by Moses, the adopted son of the king's daughter, they escaped into the wilderness, leaving Pharaoh's army beneath the sea's waves. At Sinai they received the law, but for their sins they wandered forty years in the desert.[2]

Joshua, successor of Moses, brought them across Jordan and into the Promised Land. Canaan was subdued with extraordinary rapidity; the Canaanites were utterly exterminated, and the land was divided by lot among the tribes, the descendants of Jacob's twelve sons. No sooner was Joshua dead than the Hebrews fell into sin, but each time they repented and each time their God raised up a judge to save them. Finally, in their wickedness they demanded and received a king.[3]

Such was the epic of Israel, handed down by the fathers to the children and cited by prophet and priest on every appro-

---

[1] H. Holzinger, *Genesis*, 1898; M. Gunkel, *Genesis*, 1902; J. Skinner, *Genesis*, 1910; O. Procksch, *Die Genesis*, 1913; E. König, *Die Genesis*, 1919.

[2] H. Holzinger, *Exodus*, 1900; *Numeri*, 1903; G. B. Gray, *Numbers*, 1903; B. Baentsch, *Exodus-Leviticus-Numeri*, 1905; for Deuteronomy, cf. p. 495.

[3] For Joshua, cf. p. 201; for Judges, p. 271; for Samuel, p. 295.

priate occasion. It is a magnificent epic, but unfortunately it is not history. Like all national epics, it is composed of highly heterogeneous elements. Incorporated here and there are fragments of earlier legends which present a quite different picture, but these inconsistencies rarely troubled the minds of the hearers.

It is easy to prove that the epic is not historical, that it fits neither the earlier fragments nor the background as reported by contemporaries. To determine the truth of which the epic is the faint echo, to discover the meaning of the earlier but still far from contemporary fragments, to incorporate the few direct contemporary references, and to fix the whole into the contemporary background—this is a task to appal the conscientious historian. The best we may hope is to construct a hypothesis which shall do justice to the earlier Hebrew traditions and which shall not be in conflict with the background afforded by contemporary records.[4]

Toward the middle of the second millennium before our era, the North Arabian desert was inhabited by certain tribal groups. All were Semites by race and all spoke one Aramaic language, though with slight dialectic differences. In course of time, these various groups moved out of the desert; during the second half of the millennium, Aramæan invaders appeared in Babylonia, crossed the Euphrates into Mesopotamia, and penetrated into Central Syria and Canaan.

Their Aramæan origin was never forgotten by the Hebrews. Abraham came from Ur of the Chaldees; the very term shows that the legend grew up after the Aramæan Kaldi had seized the ancient city of the Moon God. He sojourned in Harran, another centre of the moon worship and equally a centre of Aramæan settlement. Isaac's wife Rebekah was brought from

[4]Among the most important attempts to reconstruct early Hebrew history are C. Steuernagel, *Einwanderung der israelitischen Stämme*, 1901; J. P. Peters, *Early Hebrew Story*, 1904; E. Meyer, *Die Israeliten und ihre Nachbarstämme*, 1906; F. Böhl, *Kanaanäer und Hebräer*, 1911; L. B. Paton, *JBL.*, XXXII, 1913, 1 ff.; J. M. P. Smith, *AJSL.*, XXXII, 1916, 81 ff.; E. Sellin, *Gilgal*, 1917; C. F. Burney, *Israel's Settlement in Canaan*, 1918; *Judges*, 2 ed., 1920, lv ff.; D. D. Luckenbill, *AJT.*, XXII, 1918, 24 ff.; T. J. Meek, *AJT.*, XXIV, 1920, 209 ff.; *AJSL.*, XXXVII, 1921, 101 ff.

Harran and Jacob travelled there in person to find Leah and Rachel, though an earlier form of the story sent Jacob to the Sons of the East, the nomads, and located his father-in-law Laban in Gilead. The author of Deuteronomy calls Jacob a wandering Aramæan; half a century before, the Assyrian Sennacherib had employed the same expression of contempt. In their present form these stories are doubtless late, but they recall an actual Aramæan origin, which is further witnessed by Aramaic proper names, by Aramaic vocabulary, and by Aramaisms in the early poetry.[5]

Their civilised opponents gave to these Aramæan invaders the name of Habiru, an old Babylonian term meaning nomad, bandit, mercenary. Habiru became later Ibrim, "Hebrews," now interpreted as "those who have passed over." In regular Biblical usage the term Hebrew is employed only by foreigners and the name is therefore obviously not native. Furthermore, Eber, the eponymous ancestor of the Hebrews, is the father of far more peoples than we include under that appellation;[6] it is exactly in this wider sense that Habiru is used by the writers of the Amarna letters.

Descendants of the Habiru who invaded Syria proper will once more engage our attention when, after a few centuries, they emerge again into the light of history; meanwhile, we shall confine our investigation to the Habiru of Canaan. According to our earliest Biblical narrative, the various Hebrew tribes entered Canaan in separate groups. They conquered only the villages and the open country, while all the more important cities are specifically declared to have remained in the possession of their original inhabitants.[7] This is exactly the picture presented by the Amarna letters. The list of the cities which the Hebrews were not able to conquer is virtually the list of the cities which acknowledged Egyptian suzerainty. Still more to the point, all the towns associated with the early Hebrew settlement are conspicuously missing

[5] Gen. 11:28 ff.; 12:1 ff.; 24:1 ff.; 29:1 ff.; 31:21 ff.; Deut. 26:5; cf. *History of Assyria*, 42, 157, 293; D. D. Luckenbill, *AJSL.*, XXXVI, 1920, 244 f.
[6] Gen. 11:14 ff. [7] Judges 1.

FIG. 78. LETTER OF MUT–BAAL MENTIONING AIAB OR JOB, BENENIMA OR BENJAMIN, AND IASHUIA OR JOSHUA.

(Aiab at end of sixth line, obverse, Benenima on lower edge, Iashuia in middle of third line, reverse.)

FIG. 79. TABLETS WITH A CUNEIFORM ALPHABET FROM SAPUNA.

from the Amarna correspondence. Shechem, the one exception, is the exception that proves the rule.[8]

According to the epic, Joshua led Israel across the Jordan and into Canaan. Now it is a remarkable coincidence, if coincidence it is, that a historical Joshua actually is mentioned in an Amarna letter; he is in company with other men of good Hebrew name, Job, king of Pella, and Benjamin, and he is east of the Jordan in Gilead.[9] In the epic, the crossing is located between Shittim and Gilgal, known in antiquity for its sacred images,[10] and still marked by a circle and a sacred tree, but an earlier tradition placed the crossing at Adam, southwest of Gilead.[11] Name, place, and time seem to force an identification of this historical Joshua with the Joshua of the epic.

Jericho was the first city taken; the epic remembered its walls, so mighty that they fell only when the city had been circled seven days by divine order. To be sure, Jericho's walls were now far less imposing than the fortifications of the Hyksos period. These seem to have been destroyed in the first Egyptian invasions, but soon after a new wall was built on the foundations of the still earlier wall contemporary with the twelfth dynasty. Thus the protected area was again contracted to little more than a half of the Hyksos settlement. But two or three of the foundation courses were of stone, and those of rough rocks set in mud mortar. The remainder of the wall consisted of irregularly formed mud bricks roughly coursed along the face and an interior of packed clay. The fountain was no longer included, though it was commanded by a gate tower, for the double line of wall followed the edge of the ancient mound; the outer wall was six feet thick, the inner twelve, with a space between of from twelve to eighteen feet, while at the northwest corner for forty feet this interior space was filled to support a tower.

[8]Böhl, *Kanaanäer*, 67 ff.
[9]Fig. 78; Benenima (Benjamin) on lower edge of obverse, Iashuia (Joshua) in middle of third line of reverse; *K.*, 256; cf. p. 188.
[10]Judges 3:19.
[11]Josh. 3:16.

Jericho, so the excavations prove, fell about the beginning of the fourteenth century, in other words, at the time when the Habiru were entering Canaan, and when Joshua appears in the letters. From the epic we learn that Jericho was devoted to the deity and utterly destroyed; the excavations show over the whole site houses burned to the ground, charred timbers and ashes, stones cracked and adobe turned to hard red brick by the intense heat of a great fire, the walls fallen down the slope or completely destroyed. Joshua, we are told, cursed the site; the excavations prove that only a few squatters dared the curse for half a millennium.[12]

Next the invaders advanced up the plateau to Ai, on a hill near the edge of the drop to the Jordan, guarded by rocky slopes falling away on all sides and by walls of unhewn stone. The first assault was repulsed with the loss of thirty-six men, but in a second attack the defenders were drawn out from the city by a feigned retreat and then cut off by an ambush. Like Jericho, Ai was put under the ban and made a ruined mound, a *tell;* to this day the site is uninhabited and is known as "the Tell," strewn with potsherds which date its fall to the same period as Jericho. Somewhat later its name was transferred to a not far distant site.[13]

An alliance was then concluded with a confederacy made up of Gibeon, Chephirah, Beeroth, and Kiriath Jearim, but a counter-alliance was formed by Adonizedek of Jerusalem, assisted by Hoham of Hebron, Piram of Jarmuth, the Iarimuta of the Amarna letters, Japhia of Lachish, and Debir of Eglon; this alliance was defeated at Gibeon and the allies were chased down the ascent of Beth Horon. Joshua's words on this occasion are quoted as witness to the battle:

> Sun, be still over Gibeon,
>   And Moon, in Aijalon's valley;
> So the Sun was still, the Moon stood,
>   Till the folk took revenge on their foes.[14]

[12]Fig. 80 f.; plan 7; Sellin and Watzinger, *Jericho,* 20 ff.; J. Garstang, *QS.,* 1930, 123 ff.

[13]W. F. Albright. *Ann.,* IV, 141 ff.

[14]Josh. 10:12 f.; for these early poetical fragments, cf. G. A. Smith, *The Early Poetry of Israel,* 1912.

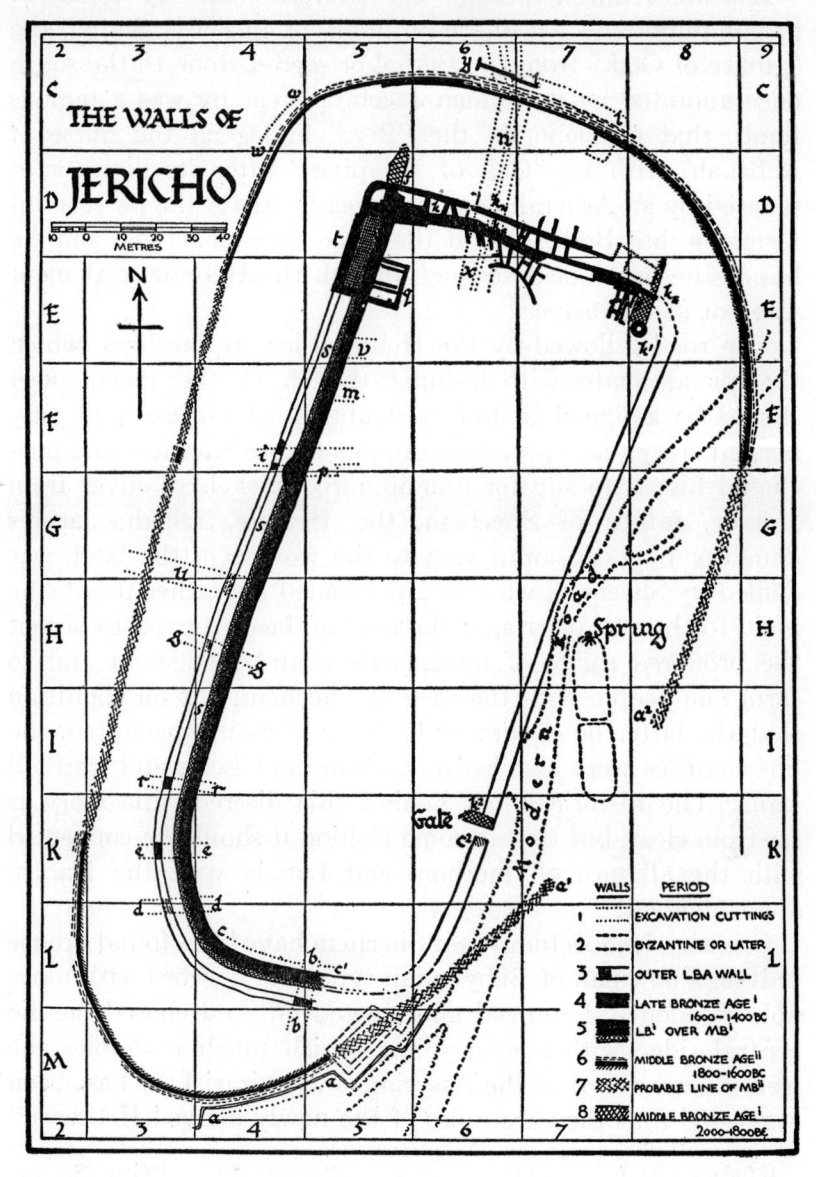

PLAN 7. THE WALLS OF JERICHO.

Luz was reduced through the enforced treachery of one of its inhabitants.[15] An alternate name of Luz was Bethel, the "House of God," from the Bethel or sacred stone to the south once anointed by its numen Jacob.[16] Near by was a famous tomb, that of Deborah, the "Bee," in legend the nurse of Rebekah, with its "Oak of Weeping," after its decay supplanted by an Asherah or sacred post.[17] Again the pottery informs us that Bethel fell at the same time as Jericho and Ai, but Bethel was not destroyed, though the Hebrew settlement was not so extensive.[18]

The road followed by the Hebrews led to Shechem, which the epic associates with Joshua,[19] though whether its conquest should be assigned to him is doubtful. A curious and very ancient story tells how Jacob camped before Shechem and purchased his camp site for four hundred shekels of silver from Hamor, father of Shechem, the Hivvite. Dinah, Jacob's daughter by Leah, on a visit to the women of the land, was defiled by Shechem, who then persuaded his father to ask the maid for him in marriage; the sons of Jacob agreed to accept the proffered rights of intermarriage and settlement and to form one people with the men of Shechem, but on condition that the latter be circumcised. While thus incapacitated, the Shechemites were assailed by Simeon and Levi, and were all slain. The historical fact behind this discreditable story is far from clear, but that in some fashion it should be connected with the alliance of Shechem and Labaia with the Habiru seems evident.[20]

Close by Jacob's tomb near Shechem have been found bronze knives, a bowman of Babylonian type, and a sword with movable wooden hilt, tanged and riveted on, and chased on the central ridge with a gold spiral, which much resembles the well-known sword of the Assyrian Adad-nirari I; it has been suggested that they are relics of the newly arrived Hebrews.[21]

---

[15] Judges 1:22 ff.
[16] Gen. 28.
[17] Gen. 35:8; Judges 2:1, 5; 4:5.
[18] W. F. Albright, *Bulletin, Amer. Schools of Oriental Research*, 29, 1928, 9 ff.
[19] Josh. 24:25 ff.
[20] Gen. 33:18 ff.; cf. p. 191.
[21] R. A. S. Macalister, *QS.*, 1909, 74.

Fig. 80. JERICHO BEFORE EXCAVATION.

Fig. 81. JERICHO'S WALLS.

Joshua was buried at Timnath Heres, where his tomb was long shown; the ruin mound is on the south side of a deep valley, watered by a clear spring from a near-by cave, and not far distant is a hamlet still called Kefr Ishua, "Joshua's Village." The modern name, the Iashuia of the Amarna letters, the Jeshua of one Biblical passage and of a Phœnician seal inscription, and the Greek transcription Jesus all imply that the well-known form Jehoshua or Joshua was later invented to make him a worshipper of the later national God Yahweh.[22]

Joshua was the hero of the tribe of Ephraim, which took its name from the wild bull it had worshipped in the desert, and thus found little difficulty in accepting the Canaanite bull cults at Bethel and the neighbouring shrines.[23] Soon Ephraim was legitimised as the son of Joseph and grandson of Jacob and Rachel, the "Ewe," whose shrine has been sought in a fertile little valley a few miles northwest of Jericho. Above abundant springs a rock-cut staircase leads to a megalithic high place, proved Canaanite by neighbouring well and shaft tombs and by pottery, bronze arrow and spear heads, axes, bracelets, and pins; the place seems to have been called Ephrath or Ephraim by the Hebrews.[24]

Thus Ephraim was settled in the hill country which took from the tribe the name of Mount Ephraim. The country was more wooded than now, but was covered with flourishing villages which had sprung up since the beginning of the second millennium. Ephraim was unusually successful in its conquest, as the silence of the Amarna letters proves; but one important city, Gezer, remained outside his boundaries. Gezer's population rapidly increased, the houses were smaller and more closely packed, the high place, no longer honoured, was covered with buildings; perhaps this was due to an influx of

[22] C. R. Conder, *Tent Work in Palestine*, 1885, 118; Neh. 8:17; Comte de Vogüé, *Mélanges d'archéologie*, 1867, 101; cf. p. 188. H. Holzinger, *Das Buch Josua*, 1901; C. Steuernagel, *Deuteronomium und Josua*, 1900.

[23] T. J. Meek, *AJSL.*, XXXVII, 1921, 119; Gen. 49:22 ff.; Is. 1:24; 49:26; Ps. 132:2, 5.

[24] II Sam. 13:23; cf. Jer. 31:15; D. G. Lyon, *Amer. Jour. Archæology*, XII, 1908, 66 f.; W. F. Albright, *Ann.*, IV, 127 ff.

Hebrews; more probably it was the result of Canaanite refugees.[25]

Own brother to Ephraim was Manasseh, originally counted the elder son of Joseph. At this time Manasseh was inferior in population and in extent of territory to Ephraim, and occupied a thin wedge north of his brother's possessions.[26]

The attractive territory occupied by Joseph, the united tribes of Ephraim and Manasseh, is well pictured by two ancient poems, later incorporated in the "Blessing of Jacob:"

> The shoot of a vine stock is Joseph,
> A vine stock shoot by the fountain,
> His branches climb over the wall.
>
> The bowmen embittered his life,
> And the archers sorely harassed him,
> But their bows by a hero were broke,
> And the tendons of their arms cut asunder.
>
> By the might of Jacob's Bull,
> By the name of Israel's Stone,
> By thy father's God, may he help,
> By El Shaddai, may he bless thee!
>
> Blessings of heaven above,
> Blessings of deep below,
> Blessings of breast and of womb,
> Blessings of father and child,
> Blessings of ancient mounts,
> Product of eternal hills,
> Let them fall on the head of Joseph,
> On the crown of the prince mid his brethren.[27]

Benjamin has already appeared with Joshua east of the Jordan in an Amarna letter. The genealogies also connect Benjamin with the Joseph tribes through their common mother Rachel. Benjamin's name is interpreted "Son of the right hand," which might mean "Son of the South"; since the

[25] Josh. 16:10; Judges 1:29; Macalister, *Gezer*, I, 21; lists of Ephraimite towns, Josh. 16:1 ff.; cf. 17:7 ff.; 18:2 f.
[26] Lists, Josh. 17:2 ff. [27] Gen. 49:22–26.

genealogy makes him the only son of Jacob born in Canaan, it has been argued that the tribe was formed in Canaan from the Joseph tribes and that the name "Son of the South" was given when Benjamin was the most southerly of the true Jacob tribes. With this would agree the fact that the ruins of the chief Benjaminite centre do not go back of the thirteenth century; the appearance of the historical Benjamin in the Amarna letter might allow some plausibility to the other old-fashioned explanation that the name came from its tribal chief, and that it was earlier in Canaan. Benjamin occupied a small extent of territory south of Mount Ephraim, between Bethel, which was Ephraimite, and Jerusalem, which remained in the hands of the Jebusites. Though few in numbers, the Benjaminites were famous as warriors, particularly their left-handed slingers, who could sling at a hair's breadth and not miss. Their bravery was celebrated in the lines:

> Benjamin is a ravening wolf,
> In the morn he devours the prey,
> And at even divides the spoil.[28]

Dan was one of the concubine tribes, which should mean that he was not of pure Hebrew blood; he was descended from Bilhah, Rachel's maid, which implies a close connection with the Joseph tribes. His blessing grants him full acceptance among the Hebrew tribes:

> Dan shall judge his folk
> As one of Israel's tribes;
> Let Dan be a snake in the way,
> A horned serpent on the path,
> That bites the hoofs of the horse,
> And back his rider falls.

Dan attempted to descend by the Aijalon route into the plain and make this boast good, but the Amorites drove him back to the hill country and retained possession of Aijalon, Shaal-

---

[28] *K.*, 256; Gen. 35:16 ff.; 49:27; lists, Josh. 18:11 ff.

bim, and the "Sun Mount" Heres, the country about Beth Shemesh, the "House of the Sun."[29]

This band of cities, to which should be added Gezer and Jerusalem, formed a complete barrier to the Joseph tribes on the south. To the north was a still more serious barrier, the great row of cities of the first class through the Great Plain and westward, Beth Shan, Ibleam, Taanach, Megiddo, Dor, which Manasseh was not able to wrest from the Canaanites.[30] North of the barrier were two tribes, Issachar and Zebulon; the genealogies made them sons of Jacob by his first wife Leah, but placed their birth after that of the four concubine sons, which might be taken to indicate that they were among the last to settle in Canaan. Issachar's name should mean "Man of Sakar," and we should then compare the Babylonian god of the same name and the Egyptian Sokar. The heart of his country was the southeastern corner of Lower Galilee, a fairly level plateau, with a row of villages clustering along the line of fountains which mark the division between the limestone and the basalt. After its exit from the lake filter, the Jordan is crystal clear, but soon the Yarmuk comes in from its gash in the eastern hills to double its flow and to muddy its waters as they run southward in frequent meanders, ox bows, and rapids. At times Issachar was able to cultivate this valley, and he also tilled the Great Plain; his blessing tells the advantage and the cost:

> Issachar is a strong boned ass,
>   Crouching between the sheepfolds;
> When he saw that rest was good,
>   And that the land was pleasant,
> He bowed his shoulder to bear,
>   And became a slave under taskwork.[31]

Zebulon took his name from his patron deity; converted to Islam, he still retains the reverence of his ancient devotees as the Prophet Sebelan. His territory was the western half of Lower Galilee, a pleasant land, with low rounded hills covered

---

[29]Gen. 30:1 ff.; 49:16 f.; Judges 1:34.
[30]Judges 1:27.   [31]Gen. 49:14 f.; list, Josh. 19:17 ff.

by a good growth of oak or cup-like fertile plains, where stood such towns as Gath Hepher, Hannathon, and Bethlehem. Not far from the northern Bethlehem was Nazareth; it is strange that the ancient lists do not mention what was to be its most famous city. His blessing praises his location:

> Zebulon dwells by the sea shore,
> And is a beach for ships,
> But he turns his back on Sidon.[32]

The blessing seems to have been no more than a pious aspiration; so far from winning the sea coast, Zebulon was not able to drive out the inhabitants of Kitron and Nahalol, well within his own hill country.[33]

Upper Galilee has fared badly at the hands of Biblical students. Few visitors have penetrated its recesses, for no sites of first-class historical importance lure them on. To the traveller who tramps up and down its paths comes a pleasant surprise; Upper Galilee is a goodly land and a beautiful.

First of all, the traveller is impressed by a sense of height. Upper Galilee is a plateau, a thousand feet or more above sea level. To the north the distant view shows no break between it and the still higher slopes of Lebanon, but the break is there. The northward advancing traveller suddenly looks down into the sheer gorge of the Litani, with its thread of green waters, broken by frequent rapids; the Litani line, drawn straight east and west as by a ruler, is a complete divider, with only a single difficult path down and across and up its gorge. The southern border of Upper Galilee is another such straight east and west line, made by a great fault which has dropped the other side of the plateau down to Lower Galilee. Its western border is slightly more irregular, but here too there is a sharp break down to the coastal plain where Hebrews never settled. Deepest of all is the boundary on the east, again the product of earth faulting.

Allied to the sense of height is the enjoyment of the views.

[32] Gen. 49:13; list, Josh. 19:10 ff.   [33] Judges 1:30.

No poet has sung the prospect from Jebel Jermak; its very name in antiquity is lost, but the view from this highest spot on the plateau should be one of the famous surveys of the Holy Land. Nowhere is the map effect more evident. Far down lies the Lake of Galilee with blue Hauran beyond. Tabor and Carmel are stunted, the rounded hills of Samaria peer above the low-lying plain of Megiddo, the sea forms the western horizon.

From the southeastern corner, Safed of many fountains, its ancient name likewise unknown, looks down on the Lake of Galilee, a few steps away in appearance, in reality thirty-five hundred feet of rough descent. The eye ranges from Carmel to the hills of Samaria, from Tabor and Gilboa through the Golan and Leja to the Hauran. From the likewise unknown Hunin, at the northeast angle, we overlook a more northerly sector of the great fault, with the Waters of Merom barely above sea level, their green marsh fringe, their tiny plain with green spots about the settlements, their little pools from which thin lines of water are sharply outlined in the morning sun as they wind to the Jordan. We realise how the lake is shut in between two ranges to the north and how the eastern mountains lose the regularity of their downward slope as they permit other peaks to show beyond. To the northeast, the view is always closed by Hermon, most lovely of mountains, especially when its peaks are outlined in rose above clouds as it is struck by the setting sun.

Our view is not confined to outside territory. Upper Galilee may be a plateau, but it is much dissected, and the traveller is constantly filling his note book with charming prospects, deep gorges, high hills, and fertile little valleys.

"And the fortified cities were . . . Ramah and Hazor and Kadesh," and the rest of the list makes dull enough reading for the easy chair. But as each is visited in turn, as one notes the position which gave one city the name Ramah, the "High," or speculates the reason for calling another Kadesh, the "Holy," as one visits the ruins and attempts to call to life again the souls who once trod the hillside paths, the visitor from far distant lands is gradually permeated by the influence of the country and begins to suspect that so large and so beautiful a portion of the territory once occupied by the Hebrews must have exerted an influence in Hebrew history which is not reflected in the pages of the Hebrew literature now extant.

Upper Galilee, for the most part, was in the possession of the tribe of Naphtali. As we traverse these upland valleys, and climb these hills where the whirr of the red-legged partridge still gives a sense of wildness, we realise how appropriate was the blessing:

> Naphtali is a hind let loose,
> Which giveth goodly young.[34]

No important roads crossed Upper Galilee, there were no industries worthy the name. Agriculture was the occupation of the little villages in their tiny but fertile plains, for wheat thrived well and barley was the staple, but there was much of hunting and the free life of the wild hind. The villages might be isolated from each other and from the outside world, but they saw this outside world from their hills, and unspoiled mountaineers could not see the prospect without envy, as we learn from a later blessing:

> Naphtali, satisfied with favor,
> And full with the blessings of Yahweh,
> Possess the Sea and the South.[35]

For Naphtali did possess the Sea and the South. Not long after his establishment in the hills he secured the southeastern portion of Lower Galilee, and from its rather bare terraces he stepped down to the Lake of Galilee.

Seen from the distance, the lake is a jewel of beauty.[36] Closer inspection is somewhat disappointing. The northwestern corner does have the plain of Chinnereth, with the Canaanite city of the same name, where there is much water and considerable cultivation, but its water is often warm and

[34]Gen. 49:21.   [35]Deut. 33:23.   [36]Fig. 82.

even sulphurous, and the beautifully clear green water of the lake itself is not without a brackish taste. To the north the Jordan winds slowly down through a marshy delta. The east shore is bare and desolate, with tame low rounded hills. Basaltic rocks close in a good part of the lake shore, their black colour giving an effect which is distinctly funereal. This impression is not entirely undeserved, for the igneous rocks are the visible sign of the underground forces which again and again have shaken the earth with terrible loss of life. By its finny wealth the lake tempts to the fisherman's struggle on its windy surface, but the health thus won is dissipated by the fevers carried by the yet greater wealth of mosquitoes. Always the visitor suffers the feeling of oppression; the shores are nearly seven hundred feet below the surface of the ocean and the abnormal atmospheric pressure, coupled to the intense and humid heat, cut the very root of effort.

For holding of this corner there was great reward. Palms and other semitropical fruit trees rewarded man's labour and then there were the roads. Unlike Upper Galilee, the lake was passed by a road, the famous Way of the Sea from Damascus to the Mediterranean.[37] Just below the exit of the lake was the Great Road itself. Yet, in the end, the fittest symbols of the lake region were the hot springs at Rakkath, gift of the fierce powers beneath the earth, and used for improving the lot of the ill, not for keeping men well and vigorous.

According to the genealogical scheme, Naphtali was the son of Jacob by his concubine Bilhah. If the original meaning of Naphtali was "Twister" or "Crafty," he was a true son of Jacob. For all his conquests, Naphtali was not able to drive out the Canaanites from Beth Anath and Beth Shemesh.[38]

"Galilee of the foreigners" was the name aptly applied to this region,[39] for Upper Galilee was shared with another of these half-Hebrew tribes, Asher, son of Jacob's concubine Zilpah. Like many another tribe, Asher took his name from the tribal deity, one of the gods of good luck, and own cousin to

---

[37] Isaiah 9:1.   [38] Judges 1:33; list, Josh. 19:32 ff.
[39] Isaiah 9:1.

FIG. 82. THE LAKE OF GALILEE FROM TIBERIAS.

FIG. 83. BAY AND CITY OF ACCHO.

Ashur, chief god and eponym of the Assyrians. An earlier settlement of the tribe may be indicated by the occurrence east of Shechem of a town named Asher, but by the days of Seti I (1313–1292) they were settled in their later home. The unfortunate fate of Qazardi, chief of Asher, when the hyena found him in the terebinth tree, had now become an Egyptian byeword.[40]

Asher's home was on the western slope of Upper Galilee, though like Naphtali he also secured a foothold in Lower Galilee. A wilderness of rocks alternates with upland meadows, deep valleys, and hills outlined in purple under the late sun. In June, every village has its threshing floor, where the women winnow the wheat in the breeze. The olive gives its oil as in the days of the blessing:

> Asher's food is fat,
> He gives dainties to kings.[41]

Even now much of the country is well wooded and with the most various trees; unfortunately in autumn the country lacks water, which must often be brought at great expense from many miles distant.

From the hill slopes there are enchanting prospects of sea and coast. For a short time Asher possessed landing places on the shore of the waters,[42] but he did not long retain them. Normally the whole coast was held by the Phœnicians. At the northwest corner and south of the Litani was Tyre, just becoming the greatest of Phœnician cities; nor was its territory confined to the few miles about the city itself. Southward its lands extended to the White Cape, and thence northeast in a quarter circle to the Litani crossing. The loss was regretted by Asher, for the Tyrian back country was pleasant, with its gentle slope up from the sea to the steep crest, within which alone Asher might consider himself more than a hopeful legatee.

[40]Josh. 17:7; W. M. Müller, *Asien und Europa*, 236 ff.; Erman, *Literature*, 230.
[41]Gen. 49:20.   [42]Judges 5:17.

South of the White Cape and the Ladder of Tyre were other foreign cities: Misrephoth-maim, where amid palms a clear spring takes its course to the sea; Achzib, with its picturesque gardens; Shimron-meron; and Accho at the north tip of the curving beach, to whose gates in our own day come long lines of camels bringing grain from the Hauran.[43] Accho's goddess naturally bore the wheat ears as her emblem, her Baal carried double battle axe and sickle, and gave his name to the near-by river, the Belus. There were also cities on the slopes, Ahlab, Helbah, Aphik, and Rehob, which were not held by Asher.[44]

East and northeast of the Lake of Galilee the country was settled by other newcomers, of whom some retained their Aramæan speech and tribal identity while others were ultimately incorporated with the East Jordan Hebrew tribes. Bashan was ruled by an Amorite king named Og, whose capital was at Edrei, where an enormous underground city proclaims a prehistoric origin; his other cities were Ashtaroth, whose name preserved the memory of the mother goddess, and Salecah, on the west border of the Hauran. Og was defeated by the Hebrews at Edrei, and his subjects were devoted to death. Later tradition made Og the last of the giants, and his iron bedstead, perhaps in reality a sarcophagus of basalt, thirteen feet long and six feet wide, was centuries after shown to wondering visitors in Rabbath Ammon.[45]

South of the purely Aramæan region was Gilead, whose northern half was occupied by Machir. He too was far from pure Hebrew, for tradition remembered that Machir, father of Gilead, was eldest son of Manasseh only by an Aramæan concubine. Gilead, Machir's son, is said to have married Maacah; Maacah is in history an Aramæan state, and when elsewhere we are told that the men of Maacah and Geshur, another Aramæan state, were not driven out but lived with the Hebrews until the rather late date at which this account was written, we realise how strong was the Aramæan element in Bashan

[43] Fig. 83.
[44] Judges 1:31; list, Josh. 19:24 ff.
[45] Num. 21:33 ff.; Deut. 3:1 ff.; Amos 2:9 f.

and Gilead.[46] When Machir took Gilead, his brother Jair, later made a "judge," whose tomb was shown at Kamon, secured the Amorite camps in Argob, on the border of Geshur and Maacah, and henceforth they were called the "Camps of Jair." Another brother of Jair took Kenath, on the western border of the Hauran, and named it Nobah, after himself.[47]

Machir's border extended from Mahanaim through all Bashan, all the towns of Jair in Bashan, and half Gilead.[48] From Gilead the route descended by an easy road to the Jabbok, a rather broad but steep valley, with flourishing trees and with oleanders by the muddy waters. The plain beyond is level and fertile and blessed by many streams; what is rare in the Near East, these upland prairies have good sward. On these prairie pastures fed the famed bulls of Bashan.

Gad, the tribe which worshipped the god of good luck with the same name,[49] was not Hebrew in the strict sense, for its ancestor was the reputed son of Zilpah, Leah's maid, and his only full brother was distant Asher, who also reverenced a god of good fortune. His most important cities were Mahanaim, where Jacob saw the hosts of God encamped, Penuel, the "Face of God," where Jacob fought the divine being, Succoth, at the exit of the Jabbok, Jogbehah, and Jazer.[50]

The territory settled by Gad was Gilead, though originally Gilead was a separate tribe.[51] Southern and eastern Gilead is level and rolling, and cultivation is general. Northward the country is more and more wooded with oaks, pines, and firs. The level continues to the west but we must cross heartbreaking gorges as we near the deep-sunk Jordan. Osha, nearly sixty-six hundred feet above the sea, is the highest mountain in Gilead, a landmark for the west Jordan country. The view is superb, the whole Jordan valley from the Dead Sea to Hermon, long stretches of the Negeb to the southwest and of Hauran to the northeast, all eastern Galilee, the plain of

[46]Gen. 46:20; Num. 36:1; I Chron. 7:14 f.; Josh. 17:1; 13:13.
[47]Num. 32:39 ff.; Deut. 3:14; Judges 10:5.
[48]Josh. 13:29 ff.; I Chron. 5:23.   [49]Isaiah, 65:11.
[50]Gen. 30:11; lists, Josh. 13:24 ff.; Num. 32:34 ff.
[51]Judges 5:17; I Sam. 13:7; II Sam. 24:5 f.; II Kings 10:33.

Jezreel to Tabor, a glimpse of the sea over Shechem, the cities of Ai, Bethel, Anathoth, Jerusalem, Bethlehem, Hebron.

Gad was followed in his invasion by the Ammonites. Lot, son of Haran and nephew of Abraham, had no sons and there was no man in all the earth to espouse his daughters; they deceived their father in the cave and from them were born Moab and Ammon.[52] In its original meaning, the incestuous union implied no shame; rather it testified to their purity of blood and to their autochthonous character. Melech, the divine "King," was the Ammonite tribal god; under his leadership they drove out before them the Zamzummim, progeny of the giants, who left behind them the megalithic palaces and tombs near the Ammonite capital.[53] This capital, Rabbath Ammon, is the only Ammonite city mentioned, and perhaps they possessed no other. The Ammonites were in perpetual warfare with the more settled Hebrews; memories of Gad's struggles to defend his heritage against Ammonite attack are preserved in a blessing whose play on the tribal name may be rendered as follows:

> Gad, guerillas shall gall him,
> But he shall gall their heel.[54]

Parallel with the Ammonites, their brothers, the Moabites invaded the desert fringe, led by their god Chemosh. They found the region occupied by the Emim, whose centre was the plain of Kiriathaim. The whole territory from the Zered to the Jabbok was soon conquered, but later they were driven back of the deep Arnon gorge by the Amorites, whose king Sihon made Heshbon his capital.

Hebrew tradition made Reuben the first born of Jacob by his first wife, Leah, the "Wild Cow"; the tradition hints that Reuben was the first tribe to settle down. The invading tribesmen, we are told, asked permission of Sihon to pass along his boundary, promising not to enter field or vineyard or even to drink from the wells. Sihon refused this slight favour and

---

[52]Gen. 11:27; 19:30 ff.   [53]Deut. 2:20; cf. pp. 27 f.
[54]Gen. 49:19.

Fig. 84. STELE DEDICATED TO ASHTART OF THE TWO HORNS. (Beth Shan.)

Fig. 85. STELE OF A MOABITE GOD OR KING.

fought the invaders in Jahaz, but was put to flight and his kingdom subdued.

Balak, king of Moab, also attempted to check the Hebrews. Such a Moabite ruler or perhaps a god is represented by a stele from approximately this period. He is nude save for his short striped kilt and helmet with long ribbon curled at the end; he holds a lance point down firmly in both hands, and behind him is what may be a lion or a bird. The kilt and the head in profile with body and eye in face are Egyptian, but the helmet and ribbon look northward or eastward.[55]

Fragments of ancient poems are cited for the invasion. There is, for example, the "Song of the Well":

> Sing, O well! To it answer,
>   Well the princes dug;
> The lords of the people delved,
>   With their sceptre, with their staff.

To this day and in this very region, a like song is chanted by the wild tribesmen as each year they clear the water pits. An extract from the Book of Yahweh's Wars is quoted as proof of the Arnon boundary of the Amorites:

> Zahab in Suphah and the gorges of Arnon,
> And the cliff of the gorge that turns to Ar's dwelling,
> And leans on the border of Moab.

The victories are commemorated by the ballad singers:

> Come to Heshbon, rebuild it,
>   Restored be Sihon's city;
> For a fire went out from Heshbon,
>   A flame from the city of Sihon;
> It devoured Ar of Moab,
>   It swallowed the Arnon's high places.
>
> Woe unto you, Moab,
>   Undone are you, people of Chemosh,
> Who his sons to flight has given
>   And his daughters to exile.

[55] Fig. 85; R. Dussaud, *Les Monuments palestiniens et judaïques*, 1912, 1 ff.

> Perished his seed
> From Heshbon to Daibon,
> Their wives without children
> From the cliff to the desert.[56]

Heshbon, Sihon's city, crowns a hill with view over the wide level; gorges are east and west, to the southwest is the ancient citadel. Medeba lies on a long low hill in the well-cultivated plain, reddish in colour when freshly plowed; by the middle of July the harvests are in and the peasants are threshing. A fine dolmen is witness that from prehistoric times the "House of Baal Meon" was a religious centre; to the west is Baal Peor, lord of a hill to which Balak of Moab summoned Balaam to curse Israel.[57] North of Baal Meon's home is Nebo, a low hill when seen from the plateau, but affording from its western cliff a fine view over Jordan. On its summit is a stone circle, perhaps the very spot to which Balaam ascended; on the north, the slopes of Pisgah, is a dolmen. In tradition this was the mountaintop from which the dying Moses viewed the Promised Land; to this day the valley to the northwest is called the "Valley of the Springs of Moses." When first we reach the gorge of the Zerka Main the water is still potable, but as streams flow in from the warm springs on the line between limestone and sandstone, the temperature rapidly rises. The pre-Israelite population, we read, was driven out by hornets;[58] hornets of colossal proportions dispute the travellers' lunch where once the Baal of Meon gave health through hot springs. Ataroth and Kiriathaim afford prospects over the Dead Sea and to Jerusalem, Bethlehem, and Gerizim. A deep gorge filled with oleanders gives access to another level plain with Daibon as its centre. Aroer, on the northern lip of the tremendous Arnon gorge, is the southernmost city of Reuben.[59]

West of the Jordan, on the later boundary between Ben-

---

[56] Num. 21:17 f., 14 f., 27–30; cf. Josh. 12:2; Judges 11:22; A. Musil, *Kusejr Amra*, 1907, 9.

[57] Num. 23:28.

[58] Ex. 23:28; Deut. 7:20; Josh. 24:12.

[59] Figs. 86–89; lists, Josh. 13: 15 ff.; Num. 32:37 f.; cf. I Chron. 5:9; Jer. 48:21 f.

FIG. 86. ENTRANCE TO THE ARNON GORGE.

FIG. 87. THE ARNON CROSSING.

jamin and Judah, was the stone of Bohan, Reuben's son. It may mark an advance of the tribe across the river, it may be connected with that grim legend that Reuben violated his father's concubine Bilhah when Israel was at the Tower of Eder. The legend is early, for it is the theme of Reuben's miscalled "blessing":

> Reuben, my first born art thou,
>   My strength and my manhood's first fruit;
> Surpassing in pride and surpassing in force,
>   Reckless as water, thou shalt not surpass;
> Thou didst climb thy father's bed,
>   Then profaned my couch thou didst climb.

Reuben, though the first born, soon lost the greater part of his possessions to Moab and to Gad; the legend explains why they were lost.[60]

This completes the survey of the tribes, whether counted later as Hebrews or not, which we have reason to believe were settled in Canaan by the fourteenth century. Other tribes, of equal importance for later history, were to enter during the following century.

[60]Josh. 15:6; 18:17; Gen. 35:22; 49:3 f.

CHAPTER XVI

HITTITE AND EGYPTIAN MASTERS

Tut-ankh-Amen (1375–1369) confesses the truth about his predecessors: "If people were sent to Syria to extend the borders of Egypt, they prospered not at all," but claims for himself tribute of Retenu, and Harmhab remembers how he was companion of his lord on the day of slaying the Asiatics. Hittite advance into North Syria and Hebrew inroads into Canaan were driving the loyalists to take refuge in the Nile valley; the fugitives say "their towns are laid waste, fire has been thrown into their grain, their countries are starving, they live like mountain goats, they know not how they shall live, and they beg that they may be received to guard the frontiers."[1]

The failure of the eighteenth dynasty brought freedom if not peace to Syria, but the accession of the nineteenth dynasty reversed this condition. Ramses I, its founder, began the construction of a new temple at Beth Shan, and prepared his faience cartouches as foundation deposits.[2] Information came to Seti I (1313–1292) in his first year that the Shasu, the Hebrew nomads, were planning rebellion; their tribal chiefs had collected on the mountains of Kharu, cursing and quarrelling, and slaying each man his neighbour, and disregarding the laws of the palace.[3]

Seti pictures for us the hundred-and-forty-mile road he followed across the desert. It began with the frontier fort of Sillu, the former "Ways of Horus," on the "Dividing Waters," the canal which separated the cultivated country from the waste; the main structure was on the Egyptian side, but a bridge led to a bridge-head on the Asiatic shore. The road then passed the outpost "Dwelling of the Lion," with a few trees

---
[1]Breasted, *Rec.*, II, 422 f.; III, 6, 12; *Religion*, 344 f.
[2]Alan Rowe, *Beth-Shan*, 24.   [3]Breasted, *Rec.*, III, 52.

Fig. 89. WATERFALL IN THE ARNON GORGE.

Fig. 88. IN THE ARNON GORGE. (Hills of Judah in the distance.)

and pools, and the Migdol or Tower of Seti with fort and wall,[4] after which there were more forts and wells until Raphia was reached. The Shasu were attacked near the Pool of Ibsekeb; they were destroyed from Sillu to The Canaan.[5]

Another messenger informed the king that Hamath had quarrelled with its next-door neighbour to the north in the Jordan valley Rehob, and with the aid of Pehel or Pella east of the river was blockading Rehob and collecting forces to attack Beth Shan. Of the four Egyptian divisions, that of Ptah was probably left at Megiddo to guard communications, that of Re was kept in reserve at Beth Shan, that of Sutekh was sent to Yanoam in the forests to watch the Hittites, and the division of Amon alone was despatched against Hamath. The enemy was overthrown in one day and a basalt stele was erected in Beth Shan near the end of the first regnal year to commemorate the victory.

A new fort was constructed and the two temples were rebuilt along the lines laid down by Amenhotep III. The only important addition was a small court west of the doorway, the entrance from the north between two columns which supported an architrave. A pottery tray with red palm and Cretan double axe, ring flower stands and cylindrical cult objects of the latest Minoan form, a Cycladic seal impression on a pot suggest that Ægean mercenaries were already in garrison.[6]

Soon after the capture of Hamath, Beth Anath and Kumedi were taken and Seti dedicated to Amon and Mut a stele at the great collection of waters, now Tell esh Shihab, east of Jordan.[7] Phœnicia had recovered its independence and he must win back Accho, Tyre, Uzu, Simyra, and Ullaza; chiefs of Lebanon were forced to cut cedar for the ark and flagstaffs of Amon, who also received his share of the looted vessels, captives, and rebels sacrificed before him.

[4]Exod. 14:2; Num. 33:7; Jer. 44:1; 46:14; Ezek. 29:10; 30:6.
[5]A. H. Gardiner, *JEA.*, VI, 1920, 99 ff.
[6]Fig. 90; Alan Rowe, *Beth-Shan*, 23 ff.; *Museum Journal*, XVIII, 1927, 25 ff.; C. S. Fisher, *ibid.*, XIV, 1923, 227 ff.; Alan Rowe and L. H. Vincent, *QS.*, 1931, 16 f.
[7]G. A. Smith, *QS.*, 1901, 347.

Seti's advance was a direct challenge to the Hittites, whose king Arnuwandash III had died after a short reign and had been succeeded by his brother Murshilish III. On his accession, Murshilish made a treaty with his brother Biashshilish

FIG. 90. TEMPLE OF SETI I AT BETH SHAN.
(Restoration. The view is to northeast.)

of Carchemish, who soon after died and was succeeded by another brother, Sharru Irah; the treaty shows the wide territory of Carchemish, down the Euphrates almost to Babylonia, a wide stretch of North Syria bounded by Mukishhe, Aleppo, Ziripa, Gargumma, and Marash.[8] Control of the territory east of the Euphrates was challenged by the Assyrian Ashur-uballit, but a show of force at Carchemish drove him off in the second campaign.[9] Early in the ninth year Sharru Irah died in camp before Kizwatna, and the Assyrians seized the oppor-

[8] *KUB.*, XIX, 27; Forrer, *Forsch.*, II, 48 ff.
[9] *BoTU.*, 50, 32 f.; Forrer, *op. cit.*, 45 f.

tunity to make trouble.[10] Murshilish proceeded down the river to drive the Assyrians from Ashtata and then returned to Carchemish, where he enthroned Sharru Irah's son Ashmisharruma.

Meanwhile, Tette, the Habiru king of Nuhashshe, had rebelled in company with Ninurtash, but Abirattash of Barga remained loyal and drove Ninurtash from his land. A general of Murshilish took the forts of Nuhashshe and the reduction of Nia followed. Abirattash then came to Murshilish and begged the return of Iaruwata, a city of Barga which the Mitannian king had taken from his grandfather and had given to Tette's grandfather; Murshilish promised to content himself with the booty and captives from Iaruwata and to grant the empty city to Abirattash. Ninurtash was destroyed with his house and land, and Iaruwata was granted by tablet to Abirattash, with his son Tuppi Teshup as heir. Disputes with the king of Carchemish were to be settled by Murshilish himself.[11]

Rimi-sharma was made king of Aleppo in place of his father Telibinu, brother of Murshilish, and a tablet was written for him.[12] Aitagama of Kadesh had remained anti-Hittite, but he was killed with his other children by his son Garma Teshup; at the approach of the Hittite general he too submitted.[13] During the revolt of Nuhashshe and Kadesh, Aziru held Amurru true to his oath; too old to lead the army himself, he sent his son Iri Teshup against the rebels. Iri Teshup died soon after his succession, leaving his kingdom to his son Tuppi Teshup, a sickly youth and still unmarried; despite this handicap, Murshilish granted him the same terms by treaty, but stressed his obligation to return the captives from Nuhashshe and Kadesh should they attempt to escape.[14]

[10]*KUB.*, XIV, 15, 29; *BoTU.*, 24; A. Götze, *Ztf. f. Assyriologie*, NF. II, 1925, 306 f.
[11]*KBo.*, III, 3; *KUB.*, XIX, 41–45; F. Hrozny, *Hethitische Keilschrifttexte aus Boghazköi*, 1919, 130 ff.; Friedrich, *op. cit.*, 19 ff.
[12]*KBo.*, I, 6.
[13]*KBo.*, IV, 4; *BoTU.*, 58, 89 ff.; Forrer, *Forsch.*, II, 1, 45 ff.
[14]*KBo.*, V, 9; *KUB.*, III, 14, 119; XIV, 5; XIX, 48; Friedrich, *op. cit.*, 14 ff.; *Mitth. vorderas. Gesell.*, 1926. 1, 1 ff.; treaty with Bentishina, p. 226.

The allies of the two powers were also dragged into the struggle. Nazi Maruttash (1321–1295) of Babylonia attempted to renew the war with the Assyrian Adad-nirari I (1310–1280), but was completely defeated. Seti fought a battle with the Hittites, who gave little aid to Garma Teshup,

FIG. 91. SETI I AT KADESH.

for Seti was able to erect in Kadesh a rough basalt monument showing him before his gods.[15] Soon after, he made peace with the new Hittite king Muwatallish.

This truce was not of long duration, for Ramses II (1292–1225) made fresh efforts to win back the lost provinces. Muwatallish renewed the stolen tablet of alliance with Rimisharma of Aleppo and made a treaty with Labu, chief elder of Tunip.[16] Bentishina of Amurru went over to Egypt and sent Murshilish this defiance: "We were your loving vassals but now we are not your vassals." Babylonia refused to continue the struggle with Assyria.

[15] Fig. 91; Breasted, *Rec.*, III, 37 ff.; M. Pézard, *Syria*, III, 1922, 108.
[16] *KBo.*, I, 6; *KUB.*, III, 5 f., 16, 21; B. Meissner, *Ztf. deutsch. Morgenländ. Ges.*, LXXII, 1918, 35 f.; Luckenbill, *op. cit.*, 188 ff.; Weidner, *op. cit.*, 80 ff.; 136 ff.

Ramses was prepared to start by his fourth year. North of Berut he reached the Dog River, which begins its course at the Honey and Milk Fountains, pours its ice cold waters under a natural bridge, and through barren gorges and by great caves hung with stalactites enters a lower canyon, where the few bits of soil are terraced with care and watered by tiny rivulets. Between the ford and the sea juts out a headland, and the stepped road turns inland to avoid the cliffs. At the highest point on the road Ramses carved the first of three rock reliefs, and thus began the long series of records, Assyrian and Chaldæan, Greek and Roman, Turkish and Arabic, French and English, which make the Dog River a veritable outdoor museum of history.[17]

Towards the end of April in the next year, 1288, Ramses left Sillu with some twenty thousand men. Ahirom, king of Gebal, accepted the title "Count of Kupna" and received in return alabaster vases with the cartouche of his master, who set up his stele in honour of the Lady of Gebal.[18] The city of Ramses Meriamon was founded in the Valley of the Cedar. Thirty days out from Sillu he reached the "Height south of Kadesh," and soon after Shabtuna, where two nomads reported that the Hittite king was delaying in Aleppo. The truth was that Muwatallish had assembled an army from Asia Minor, to which were added contingents from the North Syrian states of Naharina, Carchemish, Ugarit, and Nuhashshe. Kadesh was recaptured, and the Hittite troops, drawn up in battle array, were concealed northeast of its high mound and in the forests which then covered the land.

The Egyptians, never dreaming that Kadesh was Hittite, were marching along in open order and Ramses with the advance guard was just pitching camp when two Hittite scouts were captured; to his amazement, Ramses learned that Muwatallish was at Kadesh with his army. Before the hastily convened council of war broke up, the Hittite chariotry was upon them. The first Egyptian division ceased to exist as a fighting unit, the second was routed, the camp was invaded.

[17] Fig. 146, *History of Assyria*. [18] Montet, *Byblos*, 48 f.; 225 ff.

Ramses was almost literally fighting alone when Muwatallish launched his infantry attack.

Fortunately for Ramses, the enemy charioteers dismounted to loot. An hour later Bentishina's Amorite "Youths" arrived, and soon after the third army division. The Hittites then retired into Kadesh with the loss of a few of their higher officers. With malicious glee the Egyptian artist pictures Rimi-sharma, the "wretched chief of Aleppo, turned upside down by his soldiers after his majesty hurled him into the water."[19]

Ramses claims that he continued the battle the next day and forced Muwatallish to sue for peace. The Hittites declared that when the two kings fought for control of Amurru, Muwatallish defeated his rival and destroyed and conquered Amurru; Ramses retreated to Aba, the territory around Damascus, but Muwatallish pursued him and likewise conquered this territory. Bentishina was punished for the decisive part he had played in saving Ramses from total destruction; abandoned by his Egyptian lord, he was carried off to the Hittite capital and his place was taken by the pro-Hittite Shapilish.[20] The return of Ramses to Egypt was the signal for Canaan to revolt. Three years later he was forced to storm Ashkelon, almost on the Egyptian border, Kerpet, on the mount of Beth Anath, Merom, and Salem. He then visited the Hauran, where he dedicated a relief to Adon Saphon, the "lord of the North."[21]

Beth Shan was recovered the next year and strengthened by a fort surrounded by a double wall with corridor between; the bricks bore the impression of a left human foot, of a pig's foot, of a dog's paw, or of an anchor. Two free-standing towers of solid brick flanked on either side a chariot gate eleven and eight feet wide at the two entrances. Above the fort on a pole

[19]The classic discussion of the battle is by J. H. Breasted, *The Battle of Kadesh*, 1903; cf. *Rec.*, III, 123 ff.; J. A. Wilson, *AJSL.*, XLIII, 1927, 266 ff.
[20]*KBo.*, I, 8, 15, 19; *KUB.*, XXI, 17; XXIII, 1; A. Götze, *OLZ.*, XXXII, 1929, 832 ff.
[21]G. Schumacher, *ZDPV.*, XIV, 1891, 142 ff.; A. Erman, *ibid.*, XV, 1892, 205 ff.; W. F. Albright, *Ann.*, VI, 45.

Fig. 92. (Centre) STELE OF MEKAL, LORD OF BETH SHAN.
Fig. 93. (Right) HITTITE AXEHEAD FROM BETH SHAN.
Fig. 94. (Left) MEDITERRANEAN SPEAR BUTT FROM BETH SHAN.

Fig. 95. CYLINDER SEAL OF RAMSES II FOUND AT BETH SHAN.

FIG. 96. TEMPLE OF ANATH BUILT BY RAMSES II AT BETH SHAN.
(Restoration. The view is to southeast. The Pylon and Corridor are to the right.)

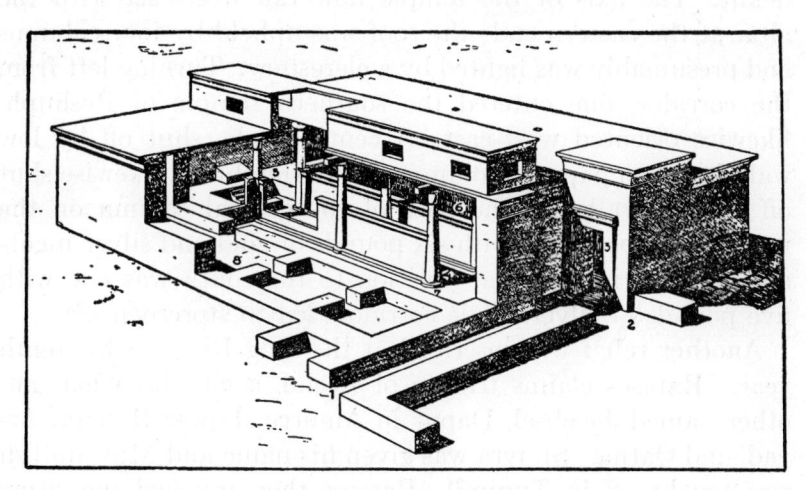

FIG. 97. TEMPLE OF RESHUPH BUILT BY RAMSES II AT BETH SHAN.
(Restoration. The view is to southeast. Part of the Pylon and Corridor to the right.)

223

floated its standard, a shield transfixed by three arrows. It is pictured on a serpentine cylinder bearing the cartouche of Ramses which was found in the temple; supported by Reshuph brandishing the scimitar, Ramses shoots arrows into two Canaanites who are tied to the pole.[22]

The new king built the usual two new temples. A great pylon was entered from the east and beyond the pylon one could see the inferior stele which Ramses set up by the side of his father's. A letter to the royal butler Menen from the royal lieutenants Ani and Bekenamen shows three such stelæ on their way to Canaan. The king has ordered his lieutenants to hasten the stelæ to the butler; they have passed the fort of Ramses in Sillu, they will unload their ships at the "Dwelling of Ramses, beloved of Amon," let the butler give further orders.

Turning right from the corridor, one entered the simple quadrangular northern temple of Antit or Anath, who is represented as a standing Ashtart on a stele for the *ka* of Hesinekht. The axis of the temple now ran west-east with the altar at the eastern end; the roof was upheld by four columns and presumably was lighted by a clerestory. Turning left from the corridor, one entered the southern temple of Reshuph, likewise oriented west-east. A central aisle, shut off by low walls between papyrus columns, led to the shrine, likewise shut off by low walls; at the base of the central column on the north was a pot filled with six pounds of gold and silver ingots and jewelry, in a similar position to the south was one with five pounds of silver. Side corridors led to storerooms.[23]

Another relief was inscribed at the Dog River in his tenth year. Ramses claims tribute of Accho, a city in Asher, another named Jacob-el, Dapur in Amurru, Lower Retenu, Arvad, and Qatna. Simyra was given his name and Muwatallish was fought off in Tunip.[24] Ramses then invoked the rising

[22]Fig. 95.
[23]Fig. 96 f.; Alan Rowe, *Beth-Shan*, 31 ff.; *Museum Journal*, XVI, 1925, 312; XVII, 1926, 298; XX, 1929, 55, 70 ff.; Alan Rowe and L. H. Vincent, *QS.*, 1931, 17 ff.; A. H. Gardiner, *JEA.*, VI, 1920, 106.
[24]Breasted, *Rec.*, III, 157 ff.; Müller, *Egypt. Researches*, I, 46 ff.

Assyrian power (1282) and Adad-nirari I replied by the capture of Carchemish.[25] Hattushilish II had just deposed his nephew Urhi Teshup and banished him to Nuhashshe, and to him Ramses sent a letter proposing a peace.

Hattushilish feared the Assyrian advance even more than Ramses, but he could not resist the temptation to put his royal correspondent in his proper place. What has been written him is not the truth. He recalls the time when the Egyptian armies took the road against the Hittite land, when one of his own armies was in Amurru and the other was in Taminta. He reminds Ramses how he was sitting on his throne when the attack was made and how he rushed about, not knowing what he was doing, while the Hittite king was carrying off the enemies of his land before the sons of Egypt and the sons of Hatte. When the enemy king came to Canaan, Ramses was exceedingly haughty towards Hatte and Kinza and Hareta. There is reference to Shamash, that is, Re, of Anna or Heliopolis, to various individuals whose seizure Ramses has demanded, to the king of Aleppo, and to the deposed Urhi Teshup. But, after putting Ramses in his place, Hattushilish agrees that there should be good condition of peace and brotherhood for Egypt with Hatte forever.[26] By the terms of the treaty (1272), each party was to respect the other's boundaries, to aid in restraining the other's Syrian vassals, and to extradite the other's enemies. The gods of Aleppo and Carchemish are listed with the Hittite gods who sanction the treaty.[27]

When Muwatallish carried off Bentishina of Amurru to his capital, Hattushilish had begged him of his brother and had given him a residence under his own protection. No sooner was Hattushilish on the throne than he returned Bentishina

[25] *History of Assyria*, 48.
[26] *KBo.*, I, 15, 19; Meissner, *op. cit.*, 37 ff.; Luckenbill, *op. cit.*, 192 f.; I have been able to utilize a new translation made by Professor Luckenbill before his lamented death.
[27] Original in Akkadian, the international language of diplomacy, *KBo.*, I, 7, 25; *KUB.*, III, 11, 120 f.; Luckenbill, *op. cit.*, 190 ff.; Meissner, *op. cit.*, 46 ff.; Weidner, *op. cit.*, 112 ff.; A. H. Gardiner and S. Langdon, *JEA.*, VI, 1920, 179 ff.; Egyptian translation, Breasted, *Rec.*, III, 163 ff.

to Amurru, married his son Neriqqa-ilim to Bentishina's daughter, and gave his own daughter Gashshuliawe to be queen in Amurru. Bentishina was granted a treaty tablet similar to that written by Shuppiluliuma for Aziru; whatever he asks of the Hittite "Sun" will not be withheld, the royal power shall remain in the family of Bentishina and the Hittite queen.[28]

Hattushilish was therefore little inclined to lend an ear to accusations directed against his son-in-law by Kadashman Enlil II (1278–1270) of Babylonia. His merchants have been killed by the people of Ugarit in Amurru, and Kadashman Enlil demands that the murderer be hanged and the goods returned to the brother of the late owner. Bentishina is indeed a curse to his land. When Hattushilish opened an investigation, Bentishina was ready with a counter complaint, the people of the city of Akkad owe him no less than three talents of silver. Hattushilish therefore advises Kadashman Enlil to bring suit against Bentishina, since he is a Hittite vassal. Bentishina shall make oath before the Hittite gods in the presence of the Babylonian ambassador Adad-shar-ilani. If the Babylonian king does not trust Hattushilish, let his servant who heard Bentishina curse the land of Kadashman Enlil come and take charge of the trial; he will then press the charge against Bentishina, for "Bentishina is my vassal, if he curses my brother, does he not curse me?" However, he must remind Kadashman Enlil that there is the matter of the lawsuit which the merchants of Carchemish have with the Babylonians; let Kadashman Enlil send an ambassador to settle this case also. Dollar diplomacy is not a modern invention![29]

Tudhaliash IV, successor of Hattushilish, made a treaty with Ishtarmuwash of Amurru, Bentishina's son.[30] According to the treaty, the king of Amurru is to be friend or foe to the kings of Egypt, Babylonia, and the Achæans as is his

---

[28] *KBo.*, I, 8; *KUB.*, III, 8; Luckenbill, *op. cit.*, 197 ff.; Weidner, *op. cit.*, 124 ff.
[29] *KBo.*, I, 10; Luckenbill, *op. cit.*, 200 ff.; letters to or referring to Bentishina, *KUB.*, XXI, 38 ff.
[30] *KUB.*, XXIII, 1; A. Götze, *OLZ.*, XXXII, 1929, 832 ff.

suzerain, but since the king of Assyria is hostile, a commercial boycott is to be established; no Amorite merchant is to enter Assyria, if an Assyrian merchant enters Amurru, even in transit, he is to be arrested and sent to the Hittite king. Tukulti Urta I replied with an inroad into Amurru.[31] Under Arnuwandash IV, Aleppo and Nuhashshe were still within the Hittite sphere of interest, though fighting was necessary to retain them.[32] With Tudhaliash V, the Hittite empire came to a sudden end.

During the last half of the sixty-seven year reign of Ramses II (1292–1225), Canaan once more was independent. Ramses was followed by his son Merneptah (1225–1215), in whose Hymn of Victory, composed in his fifth year, occurs this passage: "The kings are overthrown, saying: 'Peace.' Not one holds up his head among the Nine Bows. Wasted is Libya, Hittite Land is at peace, plundered is The Canaan with every evil, carried off is Ashkelon, seized upon is Gezer, Yanoam is made as a thing not existing, Israel is desolated, her seed is not, Kharu has become a widow."[33] This is the first reference to Israel in an Egyptian document. Israel is already in Cannan, Merneptah cannot be the Pharaoh of the Exodus; Israel is still half nomadic, for it alone is given the determinative of tribe while all the rest are settled countries. As explained by Hebrew legend, its name is no longer Jacob but Israel.[34]

From the same reign comes a letter from a frontier official who has completed the passage of the Shasu tribes of Edom through the fortress Merneptah-Hotephirma in Theku to the pools of Pithom to keep them alive and their herds in the Pharaoh's domain. The similarity to the story of Jacob's entrance into Egypt has often been noted, especially since the discovery of Israel's name in a record of this very monarch.[35]

A frontier official, stationed perhaps at Sillu, penned scribbles of great interest. The thirteenth of the ninth month of

[31] E. Forrer, *Reallexikon der Assyriologie*, I, 272 f.
[32] *KBo.*, I, 11; Luckenbill, *op. cit.*, 207 ff.
[33] Breasted, *Rec.*, III, 263 f.   [34] Gen. 32:27.
[35] Breasted, *Rec.*, III, 273; cf. Gen. 47:1 ff.

the third year Baalroi, Zippor's son, of Gaza, went up with letters for Kharu, one for the infantry captain Khay and one for Baal-remeg, chief of Tyre. On the seventeenth came to Sillu the officers of the bowmen of the Spring of Merneptah in the mountains, perhaps Menephtoah near Jerusalem.[36] A few days later arrived Thutiy, son of Zekerem, and Methdet, son of Shem Baal, both of Gaza. Sutekhmose, son of Epherdegel, of Gaza, had with him gifts and a letter for Khay; Sutekh represents a Syrian deity, *mose* is Moses, and perhaps we have here a clue to the original Moses name. The same day also went up the attendant Nakhtamon, son of Zer, from the stronghold of Merneptah-Hotephirma, which lies on the way to Upper Tyre, with two letters for Kharu, one for the infantry captain Penamon, the other for the steward of Ramsesnakht. There came also the chief hostler, Pemerkhetem, Ani's son, of the city of Merneptah, in the district of Aram, with letters for two men named Peremheb, one captain of the infantry, the other a deputy; Aram is an error for Amor, but it shows the name already in use by the Egyptians.[37] A model letter describes the search for two runaway palace slaves who passed the enclosure wall of Theku and the north wall of the "Migdol of Seti Merneptah is beloved like Set" and escaped into the desert.[38]

Semitic thought had conquered Egypt. Seti is irresistible, mighty hearted like Baal, his chariot horses are named "Anath is satisfied." Ramses II is hero of Anath, his sword is "Anath is victorious," his daughter is Bint Anath, "daughter of Anath," his dog is "Anath protects," his horses are those of his father. Anath and Ashtart are the shield of Ramses III.[39]

Persuaded by the harvest goddess, so runs a folk tale, to pay tribute to the Egyptian god, Ashtart, daughter of Ptah, the raging terrible goddess, left her home by the sea and entered the presence of the Nine Gods of Memphis. At her appearance the great gods rose up, the lesser grovelled before her, she sat

---

[36] F. von Calice, *OLZ.*, VI, 1903, 224. [37] Breasted, *Rec.*, III, 270 ff.
[38] A. H. Gardiner, *JEA.*, VI, 1920, 109.
[39] Cf. Albright, *AJSL.*, XLI, 1925, 73 ff.

down on her assigned throne. Temples of Baal and Ashtart adorned the foreign quarter of Memphis, the east quarter of Ramses was named from Ashtart. A magical papyrus calls Anath and Ashtart the great goddesses who conceive but do not bear. Numerous stelæ depict Syrian deities. Anath carries shield, spear, and battle ax, Ashtart, skirted and with hands crossed on breast, holds spear and shield and rides sidewise on a horse. Kadesh, the nude "Holy" goddess, stands on a lion with serpent and lotus in hand, her hair curled in the manner of an Egyptian Hathor. A stele of Horus on the crocodile is dedicated by a Phœnician to Ashtart. Adonis appears as Min. Reshuph, the war god, bears spear, battle axe, and shield, a conical helmet, a gazelle head on his forehead, an artificial beard, and a covering to make him invisible.[40]

Syrians with good Canaanite names occupied high places in Egypt. Ben Ozen of Bashan was chief herald under Merneptah, Mahar Baal, "Baal hastens," and his fellow Canaanites were butlers under Ramses III. Iryt, daughter of the Syrian sea captain Ben Anath, was wife of Semontu, son of Ramses II, in the forty-second year. In Ramses, built, according to tradition, by the Hebrews, there was a large Phœnician merchant colony, for not one of the weights was according to the Egyptian standard, while the majority were based on the Phœnician shekel of two hundred and twenty-seven grains.[41]

References to Syria fill the contemporary literature. Hori writes a satirical letter to Amenemopet, who does not know the Egyptian empire and in consequence has many misadventures. Amenemopet is sent at the head of an army to put down a revolt of the "Youths," the Canaanite Nearim; the nomads look askance at his careless preparation and mutter in Canaanite: "Wise Scribe!" He claims to be a Maher, a Canaanite term for "Swift"; let him learn the true meaning

[40] Erman, *Literature*, 169 f., 271; N. de G. Davies, *JEA.*, IV, 1917, 238 f.; W. M. Müller, *Egyptian Mythology*, 1918, 155 ff.; *Egypt. Res.*, I, 32 f.; Herod. ii, 112.

[41] W. Spiegelberg, *Rec. de Travaux*, XVI, 1894, 64; A. H. Gardiner, *JEA.*, V, 1918, 133; W. M. F. Petrie, *Hyksos and Israelite Cities*, 34.

of Maher. Has he gone to Hittite land or Ube? What is Simyra of Ramses like? Has he marched to Kadesh and Tebah, has he led troops against the Shasu? Has he trodden the road to Meger, where even by day the sky is dark, for it is covered with cypresses and oaks and cedars that reach the heavens, where lions are more plentiful than panthers and hyenas, and the Shasu are on every side? Has he climbed Mount Shewe, where chariot and horses must be dragged by ropes? He shrinks from climbing another mountain, so he fords its river, only to bear the chariot on his shoulder. At the evening halt he feels as if his bones are broken; waking to start before daybreak, thieves have stolen his very clothes, his groom has absconded to the Shasu with the rest.

Hori will speak of another mysterious city named Gebal. What is it like? What of its goddess? Let him give instruction about Berut and Sidon and Sarepta. Where is the Nezer, the Litani, and what is Uzu like? They tell of another city lying in the sea, Haven Tyre by name; water is carried to it in boats, it is richer in fish than in sand.

Let him learn of another misery, the crossing of Zorah; he will say it burns more than a hornet's sting. Let him indicate the road south to Accho. Where is the road to Achshaph and beside what city? Like what is the peak of User and where is the mountain of Shechem? Where does a Maher take the road to Hazor and like what is its stream? Let him indicate the road to the Hamath in the Jordan valley, to Migdol and Migdol-el, the playground of all the Mahers, let him show Yanoam. If one travels to Adummin, where does one turn the face?

Has he gone to Tahshe, Kefr Merenen, Timnath, Kadesh, Tabor, Azai, Horonaim? Has he seen Kiriath Enab and Beth Sepher? Does he know Adoraim? Does he know the name of Helez in the land of Ube, the battle ground of every warrior? Let him instruct us regarding the appearance of Kanah, acquaint us with Rehob, explain Beth Shan and Tirkel. How does one cross the Jordan? How does one pass Megiddo?

South of Megiddo is a pass, a gorge three thousand **feet**

deep, filled with rocks and sand. Amenemopet seizes the bow; "You slay like a lion, good Maher," exclaims Hori in Canaanite, but his name is like that of Qazardi, chief of Asher, when the hyena found him in the terebinth. Hidden behind bushes in the narrow pass are the Shasu, six or seven and a half feet high, fierce of face, their heart not mild, they hearken not to coaxing. Amenemopet is alone, without troops or guide; he cannot find his way, for the path is overgrown with thorns and wolf pads. On one side is the gorge, on the other the steep mountain. His horse falls and breaks the harness; to repair it, he takes it off and cannot replace it, so he continues on foot.

He enters Joppa and finds the meadow at its greenest. He forces his way into the vineyard and seduces its guardian maid; he is recognised, brought to trial, and must sell his tunic to pay the fine. While he sleeps, his bow, quiver, and knife are stolen, the reins are cut; his chariot is smashed on the slippery ground, it is repaired in the smithy.

This leader of the "Youths" and chief of the "Host," both words are Canaanite, should at least learn the way back to Egypt, from the fort of the Paths of Horus or beginning with the city of Ramses itself. Where are the various stations across the desert? Like what is the wall of Raphia, how far is it to Gaza? Let him answer and then he will be called a *marianu*. He has been told what is it to be a Maher, Retenu has been covered for him. Let him learn from this letter, some day Amenemopet may then be able to give a similar description.[42]

Perhaps this lack of experience proved his undoing, for the grave stele of an Amenemopet has been found at Beth Shan. He kneels, both hands raised, and prays that he may have a proper funeral in his town cemetery, that his soul may freely go out from its tomb to the place it desires; may he see Re while the gods adore him.[43]

---

[42] A. H. Gardiner, *Egyptian Hieratic Texts*, I, 1911, 1 ff.; Erman, *Literature*, 214; cf. W. F. Albright, *Ann.*, VI, 21 ff.
[43] Alan Rowe, *Beth-Shan*, 37 f.; *Museum Journal*, XVI, 1925, 309.

Equally unhappy is the recruit who is called for service in Syria. Not until he reaches Sillu does he find equipment. His marches take him high up in the mountain, he drinks water once in three days, and then it is brackish. Foes encompass him with arrows, but he is encouraged: "Haste thee onwards, valiant soldier, win for yourself a good name," while all the time he is barely conscious, his knee is weak, his face hurts. Should he escape alive, he must carry back to Egypt the foreign woman, faint from marching, and so exhausted is he by all these labours that henceforth he is good for nothing but servile toil.[44]

While Syrian gods travelled to Egypt, Egyptian gods passed to Syria. This is strikingly illustrated by the folk tale of the Two Brothers, supposed by many to be the prototype of the Biblical story of Joseph and Potiphar's wife.[45] Its heroes are Anubis and Bata, ancient Egyptian gods. Bata, the Egyptian Joseph, lives with his elder brother Anubis until this brother's wife attempts to seduce him. On his refusal, Bata is accused by the woman but is warned by the cattle and flees to the "Valley of the Cedar," where he spends his days in hunting and at night sleeps under a cedar in whose topmost flower he has placed his heart for safety.

By order of Re Harakhte, Khnum fashioned him a woman, earth's fairest; for her he hunted and told her his secret. The sea beheld her and attempted to take her, but must content himself with a lock torn from her head by the cedar; carried to Egypt, its marvellous fragrance led the Pharaoh to send for its owner. Bata killed the first messengers, but a second embassy, fortified by a court lady, induced the woman to visit Egypt; she revealed the secret, soldiers cut down the cedar, and Bata died.

His beer turned bad, Anubis knew what had happened. Three years search was rewarded by finding Bata's heart in the cedar flower. It was placed in water, Bata opened his eyes, he drank from the cup and rose up. He returned to

[44]A. M. Blackman and T. E. Peet, *JEA.*, XI, 1925, 292.
[45]Gen. 39:7 ff.

Egypt in the form of a bull, but was recognised by the woman and slain. A drop of his blood became two persea trees, but they were cut down. One chip flew into the mouth of the woman, who in due time bore a child, the former Bata, to be recognised as the Pharaoh's son and successor.[46] Despite the Egyptian elements, the story is essentially Syrian, and proves the deep influence exerted by the myth of Ashtart and Adonis on the simple Egyptian folk tale.

Under the long-continued foreign impact, native Syrian culture disappeared or was transformed. Egyptian influence was still strong in the south and along the coast, but Hittite and Babylonian influences were even more marked in the north. Pottery, always our best indication of cultural standards, rapidly declined, while more and more the prized specimens came from abroad, from Cyprus or even deeper in the Mediterranean world. Meanwhile, large sections had been barbarised by the intrusion of Hebrew and other Habiru tribes.

South of Mount Casius a route from the interior reached the sea at Sapuna, with a small but fine natural harbour just opposite the northeastern tip of Cyprus, whose copper mines were being exploited to the utmost by newly arrived Greeks. The site had been occupied at least as early as Hyksos times by a people who buried their dead with extraordinary variations, sometimes interred full length in the ground, sometimes in the crouching position; sometimes the flesh was stripped and placed in a jar while the legs and skull were buried by the side.

During the Egyptian domination a temple had been built, two adjacent paved courts on a raised foundation; in the northern court on a stone base stood great granite statues of the gods which imitated in style the Egyptian deities of the eighteenth and nineteenth dynasties. Here "Mami, royal scribe and overseer of the treasury," dedicated a stele on which he adored the local Baal of Sapuna in Egyptian fashion and wrote his name and titles in Egyptian hieroglyphics. When the Hittites drove out the Egyptians the new influence was re-

[46]Erman, *Literature,* 150 ff.

flected in bullæ with "Hittite" pictographs and by seal cylinders in the "Syro-Hittite" style. In close relation to the temple were shrines for other local divinities. One such is shown in a relief. On his head is the Egyptian ostrich-feather crown, but below it is the huge native horn; in his girdle is a big dagger with good-sized pommel; he rests on a spear held in his left hand, his right grasps the Egyptian hooked sceptre, but his feet are shod with the "Hittite" sandals with upturned tips.

Sapuna's rulers were buried near the tiny port in corbelled quadrangular tombs of well-dressed ashlar which were entered by a passage and down steps flanked by votive offerings of jars. The best pottery was imported from Cyprus, now in the late Mycenæan stage of culture, while terra-cotta bulls' heads and standing women decorated in red paint resemble those from Mycenæ itself. A bronze hawk wearing the crowns of Upper and Lower Egypt and a second hawk inlaid with gold and holding the uræus serpent in his claws may have been imported direct from the Nile. A seated god in short skirt and girdle has eyes inlaid with blue paste and silver. The nude goddess in Hathor headdress with lotus in each hand is on a gold plaque. Reshuph advances, his right hand raised to hurl the thunderbolt, his left extended; his high hat is wound with gold leaf, his corselet is silver, silver brassards and greaves cover his arms and legs, a gold bracelet adorns his right arm. An oval ivory jewel box has on the cover the "Mistress of Wild Beasts" seated on an altar, her bust nude, her body in flowing robes, grain stalks in each hand, and to either side a rearing goat; goddess and style alike are pure Mycenæan, and with the quantities of Cypriote pottery, the bronze tripod with down-hanging pomegranates, and the other metal work, indicate a flourishing trade with Cyprus and so with the Greek world to the west.[47] Heaps of shells include those of the famous Phœnician purple. Near the tomb entrances are the houses of the dead, filled with votive deposits of painted jars, bronze knives and daggers, gold, silver, and bronze pins, and lamps of bronze and clay. Well holes were filled with sifted

[47] Fig. 98 f.

Fig. 98. THE MYCENÆAN MOTHER GODDESS AT SAPUNA.

Fig. 99. BRONZE TRIPOD FROM SAPUNA.

earth to preserve the fine jars; the entrance was then closed by pierced stones or sealed with concrete.

Our greatest interest, however, centres, not in the temple or tombs, but in the large well-built two-story structure of freestone around a court with wells and rain-water conduit, for this appears to have been the temple school and archive. All the documents are clay tablets inscribed in cuneiform. Two are letters in the well-known Akkadian of diplomacy, one to Aki-hinni, doubtless the king of Sapuna, though his name is Hurrian rather than Phœnician; in good Amarna fashion, the writer "throws himself down at the feet of his lord." He gives news of the "man" or official of Panashta, of Urazi, "man" of Halbini, and of the "man" of Hazilu, and reports that the men of Halbini and of Hazilu have "made oath one with another," that is, have made a treaty. There are dictionaries, some of the Shumerian needed by scholars for the understanding of Akkadian, one a bilingual introducing a new language.

Far more exciting are the tablets written in a cuneiform alphabet of twenty-eight letters. The alphabetic characters invented in Sinai a half millennium before had met with little favour from the learned, who preferred the more difficult cuneiform or hieroglyphic. A century or two after its original invention, another genius had adapted this alphabet for writing with the familiar stylus on the cheaper and more durable clay tablet.

The complicated ox head for *aleph* became three parallel horizontal wedges with a short vertical stroke below; two horizontal wedges differentiated a somewhat similar sound. *Beth,* the house with one wall partly open, was exactly repeated by two horizontal wedges with two vertical wedges above. *Gimel,* the upright calyx, became a single upright wedge. *Daleth* was two long horizontal lines with three short lines placed fanwise above; the three short lines were straightened for more easy writing on the tablet, the long horizontal lines were broken into three to correspond. The head and upraised hands of the "hallelujah man" who represented *he* were turned on the side to make three parallel horizontal wedges.

Two horizontal parallel wedges represented the open hook of the *waw*, the two continuing wedges gave the handle. Sinaitic *heth* had but one sign for the two original sounds; for one, the three loops were imitated by a vertical column of three vertical wedges, for the other by a more complicated group of wedges. The hand of the *yodh* had been conventionalised to three vertical lines above and a rounding tail below; turned on its side, the three strokes were preserved as a column of three vertical wedges, the tail was broken into three more. Rounding *lamedh* could not be represented in cuneiform, so the sign was broken into three vertical wedges. *Nun,* the long curving snake, was likewise broken into three wedges, but this time they were in a vertical row. *Samekh,* the fish, was stood on his tail, a short vertical wedge, with two vertical wedges above for his body; this was the same treatment the Shumerians meted out to their fish sign when they changed from the linear writing in vertical columns and turned the signs on the side for the horizontal writing of the cuneiform. *Ayin,* the eye, had lost its pupil and had become a mere oval; this could be imitated in the cuneiform only by the short stubby wedge. *Resh,* the head, was the most complicated sign to imitate; this too was turned on the side, two rows of two or three wedges for the head proper and one for the neck. If the Sinaitic *shin* or tooth recalls our own W, so does the original form of the cuneiform, but other variants show widely differing forms, though all may be connected. Instead of the cross for *taw,* our inventor makes his mark by a single horizontal wedge. He also followed Akkadian practice by writing from left to right in horizontal lines instead of the usual vertical columns of the Sinaitic, but unfortunately he still omitted the vowels; since he also omitted the Akkadian determinatives which so greatly aid in interpreting the ordinary tablet in cuneiform, he of necessity marked off the words by a tiny vertical stroke.[48]

The language of these tablets is Phœnician, but a Phœnician

---

[48]Cf. the table of alphabets, fig. 104, and my note in M. Sprengling, *The Alphabet,* 57 ff. As the *teth* is not found in Sinai, it is not represented in the table.

definitely earlier in its grammatical forms than that found in the earliest inscriptions in the later Phœnician script. Already there is influence from the Aramaic in phonetics and from the Akkadian in vocabulary. One student employs a tiny tablet to demonstrate his ability to write words beginning with the letter *yodh*. Other tablets list personal names, followed in one case by "one," in another by "table," while on a third all begin Ben, "son of." One appears to be a deed for the "house which he built"; the house has a name to be given with the name of its *baal* or owner and of his parents. A letter mentions the wine sent by El-ner, seven jars for one man and the eighth for another. A third man departed on the second day and the addressee is advised to consult him.

For the greater part, the documents are of a religious nature; so remarkably do they anticipate Hebrew practice that they will undoubtedly be much used for Biblical illustration. El, the "God" par excellence, is the chief deity, and by his side is Elat, the "Goddess." The gods are Elim, but Elohim appears both alone and in compound, an apparent plural of majesty as in our Bibles. Baal is one of the greater gods but may also be the "Lord" of a place or a quality. Baal Zephon, the "Lord of the North," has long been known from our Bibles;[1] he now appears as the chief divinity of the city, though he is also called El Zephon or simply Zephon. A tablet lists the Baals of the various temples who were found in the temple of El, such as the Baal of the temple of Eshmun. We have Baal Kanaph, the winged Baal, the Baal of the vine, the Baal of the year and of the months. Among the other chief gods were Dagan, the grain god, Reshuph, the thunder god, and Shalem, who had given his name already to Jerusalem. Ashtart, Anat, and Asherat were naturally the chief goddesses, to whom we should add the Elat of the tower and of the enclosure, the Baalats or Ladies of the Fount and the Temple. Minor divinities are the Day and the Month, El Hokmot, god of wisdom, Alein, Baal's Son, Dinel, the "Judgment of God," Der-el, the "Wall of God," and Peger-Baal, the "Corpse of

[1] Ex. 14:2, 9; Num. 33:7.

Baal," perhaps a reference to the dead Adonis, and a whole group we cannot more closely identify.

Ritual is closely akin to the Hebrew. We hear of first fruits, sin offerings, whole burnt offerings, peace offerings "seven times according to his heart." Temple sacrifices are prescribed for the third to the seventh of the month and also for the day of the new moon, for the royal offerings, and for evening when two priests are at the king's palace. Lambs, sheep, cattle, doves form a "gift, perfect and weighty." Three times we have an offering list almost exactly repeated, a great jar, six jars of barley, a jar of bitumen, a jar of myrrh oil, a bowl of wine, a measure of sesame and one of cress, dried raisins, six hundred flowers, thirty birds, fifty homers of thorns, and once each cummin and figs. We learn of two jars of oil received yearly by one of the priests and of the *kishkanu* plant, famous in Babylonian legend.

An Egyptian story had told how the gods of Egypt welcomed the Phœnician Ashtart to her new home by the Nile; the reverse process appears in a letter. When Ashtart shall lead Horus into the king's palace, a priest shall clothe him with garments from the temple of the gods. Then another priest shall place Horus in the addressee's house. A lamb, a bull, and three sheep shall be sacrificed as peace offerings. Seven times the priest shall bow down before the gods. Then the writer turns to business: he and his colleagues will exchange for two men twenty gold shekels from the king's palace for ten shekels of good silver, face and soul. We are at once struck by the remarkable fact that at this late date gold is worth only twice the value of silver; the emphasis on "good" silver raises the suspicion that the royal shekels had been debased. In conclusion, the king is ordered to go to the sacred "Place" of the gods, seven times he shall go before them all.

Another writer orders his correspondent to burn for himself daily four peace offerings. He knows his correspondent's prince, let the daughters also pray. Horus has ascended, the star of good luck is obscured, so let him betake himself to the Lady of the Fount and there bow down. His friend's son is a

HITTITE AND EGYPTIAN MASTERS

star among the people, he is as clothed with the light of a Messenger from Heaven.

Tehem writes Regemishshab, chief of the priests, whose title also appears on five bronze sacral axes, wishing him good health. A second letter tells us that Tehem is to deliver a sliver of gold and a *log* of something.

Four recitations in slightly differing language, but alternately for men and for women, beg Meshar, prince of right-

FIG. 100. POTSHERD FROM GEZER WITH EARLIEST KNOWN CANAANITE INSCRIPTION.

FIG. 101. POTSHERD FROM LACHISH WITH NAME OF BELA.

eousness, to drive away the stranger, the man of Kadesh, the Hurrian, the Hittite, the Alashian or Cypriote, the man of Subaru or Mesopotamia, and a whole long list of unidentified peoples, those who pillage and oppress them. At the close is a reference to the Father of the Sons of God, the house of the Sons of God, and the whole assembly of the Sons of God.

An epic of nearly eight hundred lines is also reported. Taphon is the hero but more than twenty other divinities are mentioned. Perhaps after all Philo of Byblos was not so far wrong when he declared that at this very date the priest Sanchuniathon was producing religious histories.[49]

While the great majority of the learned preferred the ancient

---

[49] Fig. 79; excavations, F. A. Schaeffer, *Syria*, X, 1929, 285 ff.; *Illustrated London News*, 1930, 968 ff.; inscriptions, C. Virolleaud, *Syria*, X, 1929, 304 ff.; decipherment, P. Dhorme, *RB.*, XXXIX, 1930, 571 ff.; H. Bauer, *Entzifferung der Keilschrifttafeln von Ras Schamra*, 1930; *Ztf. deutsch. Morgenland. Ges.*, NF., IX, 1930, 251 ff. I have utilized the interpretation of Dhorme, *op. cit.*, XL, 1931, 32 ff., with the more confidence, as I had already come independently to many of his conclusions.

cuneiform or hieroglyphic and others adapted the new alphabet of Sinai to use on clay tablets, the Sinaitic alphabet found more humble admirers. A Canaanite peasant of Gezer living under Hyksos rule scratched his name, Ben Y..., on a pot in the new writing. The forms had still further evolved when Bela of Lachish incised his name on a sherd.[50]

Still more developed in form and firmly dated by associated alabaster vases with the cartouche of Ramses II are the letters in the first inscription in the true Phœnician character. It comes from the tomb of Ahirom, king of Gebal, though he also gives in Egyptian hieroglyphics his title "Count of Kupna." Under a colonaded superstructure a passage led to his tomb chamber; half way down, the intruder saw a warning cut in the rock. Three limestone sarcophagi contained the bodies of Ahirom, of his queen, and of a youthful son.

The cover of the royal sarcophagus is slightly curved, with a handle at either end in the form of a lion's head, whose body is grotesquely elongated in relief. On one side the lions is the dead man, life-sized, bearded, with generous nose, wrapped in a fringed garment and holding a lotus reversed; opposite is his son who as still in the land of the living can breathe the lotus perfume. Four lions, their growling heads and their feet projecting from the stone, support the sarcophagus. The cover is separated from the reliefs by a reversed lotus frieze, alternate buds and flowers, above a rope pattern. Ahirom sits on a backed throne borne by a female winged sphinx of lion's body and claws; his feet rest on three cushions, his right hand raises a cup, his left grasps a lotus. Before him is a table with loaves and a bull's head on plates. Facing him are seven beardless servants, their long hair filleted and knotted at the nape of the neck, and clad in long girdled robes with triple flounce. Each is a portrait: the first swings a fly-flapper over the table, the two following extend cups, the others hail the king with upraised hands and out-turned palms. At either end of the sarcophagus are four mourning women, their skirts billowing but

[50]Figs. 100 ff.; W. R. Taylor, *JPOS.*, X, 1930, 17, 79 ff.; F. J. Bliss, *Mound*, 88; W. F. Albright, *Archiv f. Orientforschung*, V, 1929, 150 ff.

FIG. 102. SARCOPHAGUS OF AHIROM, KING OF GEBAL, WITH THE OLDEST KNOWN PHŒNICIAN INSCRIPTION.

HITTITE AND EGYPTIAN MASTERS 241

tight about the feet, their upper garments dropped to expose the breasts; two beat their breasts and two their heads. On the last panel two fully clad women bear baskets on their

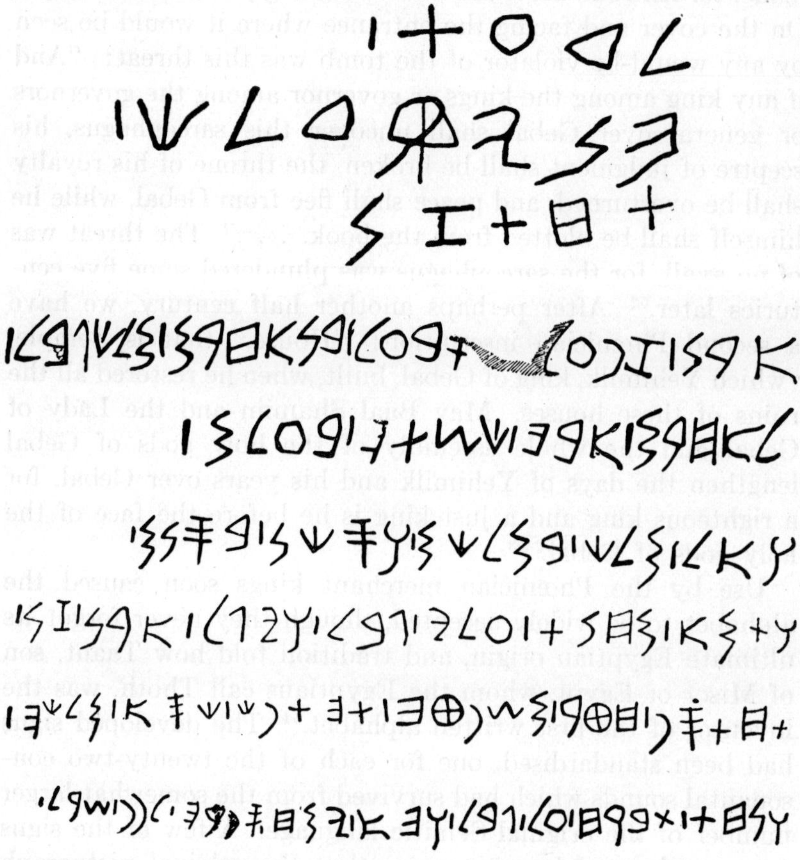

FIG. 103. INSCRIPTION OF AHIROM OF GEBAL, EARLIEST KNOWN PHŒNICIAN INSCRIPTION.

heads, mincing daintily along because of their tight skirts and balancing themselves by their extended right arms, as do two men who carry jars on their left shoulders. A bearded official leads a goat to the sacrifice, his three companions advance with upraised arms. Egyptian influence may be detected in certain details, but the whole treatment is rather North Syrian.[51]

Over the lotus band at one end is the inscription: "Sarcophagus which Ippes-baal, son of Ahirom, king of Gebal, made, for Ahirom, his father, as his resting place for eternity." On the cover and facing the entrance where it would be seen by any would-be violator of the tomb was this threat: "And if any king among the kings or governor among the governors or general over Gebal shall uncover this sarcophagus, his sceptre of judgment shall be broken, the throne of his royalty shall be overturned, and peace shall flee from Gebal, while he himself shall be blotted from the book. . . ." The threat was of no avail, for the sarcophagus was plundered some five centuries later.[52] After perhaps another half century, we have a second Phœnician inscription: "House," that is, temple, "which Yehimilk, king of Gebal, built, when he restored all the ruins of these houses. May Baal Shamim and the Lady of Gebal and the whole assembly of the holy gods of Gebal lengthen the days of Yehimilk and his years over Gebal, for a righteous king and a just king is he before the face of the holy gods of Gebal."[53]

Use by the Phœnician merchant kings soon caused the alphabet to be widely accepted, though they never forgot its ultimate Egyptian origin, and tradition told how Taaut, son of Misor or Egypt, whom the Egyptians call Thoth, was the inventor of the first written alphabet.[54] The developed signs had been standardised, one for each of the twenty-two consonantal sounds which had survived from the somewhat larger number of the original Semitic language. A few of the signs were so changed in appearance that the original pictograph was no longer recognised; new names were assigned on the acrophonic principle which approximated the list familiar

[51] Fig. 102.
[52] Fig. 103; P. Montet, *Byblos*, 215 ff.; R. Dussaud, *Syria*, V, 1924, 135 ff.; XI, 1930, 178 ff.; C. C. Torrey, *JAOS.*, XLV, 1925, 269 ff.; revision by Professor Arno Poebel.
[53] M. Dunand, *RB.*, XXXIX, 1930, 321 ff.; revision by Professor Arno Poebel.
[54] Philo Bybl., 36.

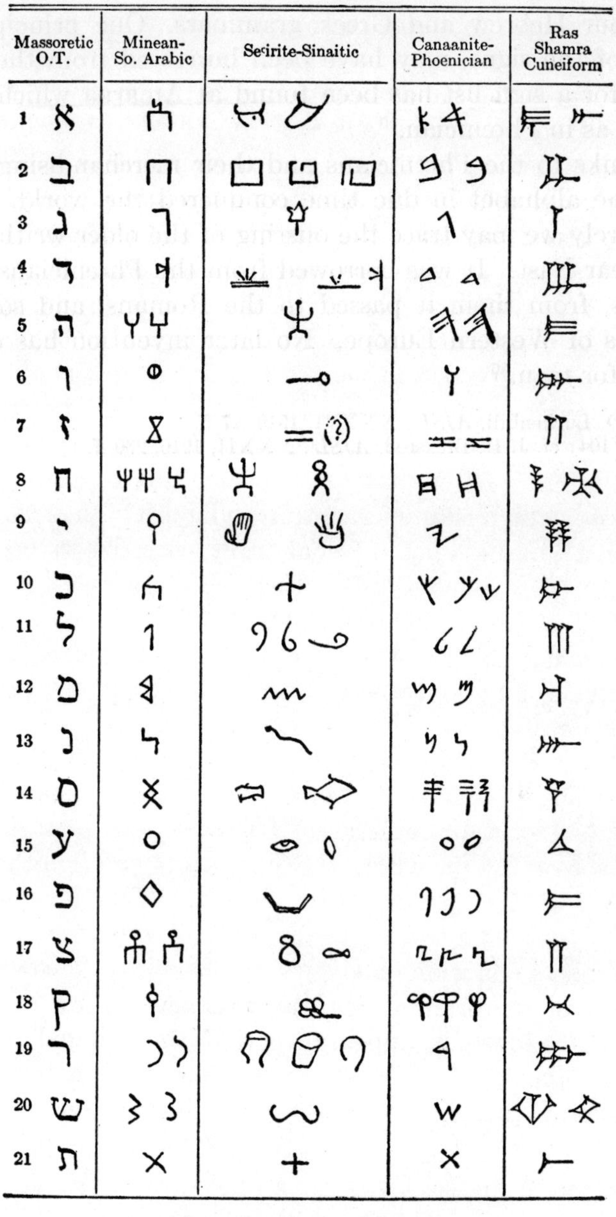

FIG. 104. EVOLUTION OF THE ALPHABET.

from our Hebrew and Greek grammars. One principle, the order of the signs, may have been borrowed from the cuneiform, for a sign list has been found at Amarna which begins with *a* as in Phœnician.[55]

Thanks to the Phœnicians and their merchandising activities, the alphabet in due time conquered the world. Slowly but surely we may trace the ousting of the older writing from the Near East. It was borrowed from the Phœnicians by the Greeks, from them it passed to the Romans, and so to the peoples of Western Europe. No later invention has done so much for man.[56]

[55] D. D. Luckenbill, *AJSL.*, XXXVI, 1919, 27 ff.
[56] Fig. 104; cf. J. H. Breasted, *AJSL.*, XXXII, 1916, 230 ff.

CHAPTER XVII

MOSES AND THE SOUTHLAND

NORTH of the Sinaitic peninsula extends the limestone plateau called by the Arabs the "Desert of the Wandering." To no portion of the earth's surface can the term "Bad Lands" be more appropriately given. It is cut by deep valleys, whose gravels have been washed down on a day of thunder-storms, but throughout the remainder of the year water is almost impossible to find. Conical hills recall our western buttes; here and there low mountains afford a wider view, but it is only a wider view of desolation.

From this "great and terrible wilderness" of Zin,[1] the home of the nomad Amalekites, the traveller suddenly comes upon the site of Kadesh Barnea. To the tourist from the grassy northlands it is a miserable hole in the ground and nothing more; one must have approached from the true desert to appreciate this unsuspected oasis. Four tiny springs flow out from under a cliff, unite, and pass down the gorge a hundred yards before they disappear. The water is sweet and never fails, a blessed change from puddles left by the rain in the rocks or the still more nauseous concoction flavoured by the goat skin in which it is contained.

A tree or two, a little real sward, some flowers in spring, the whirr of a partridge, the song of a rare bird, make a paradise when contrasted with the eternal waste to the south. A long speckled snake of deadly repute warns us to be careful. The temperature may be high, ninety-four at eight of the evening in late May, but there is a good breeze and it is almost freezingly cold before daybreak. From the plateau to the north the short but impressive gorge widens out southwest to a barren plain through which winds a long white line as witness to occasional cloudbursts. Due south the "Desert of the Wander-

[1]Gen. 21:21; Num. 10:12; 27:14; Josh. 15:1 ff.

ing" stretches in all its ghastly bareness, the horizon closed by high peaks above which the pyramid of Araif towers as landmark.[2]

At this spring we have preserved to our own day the name of Kadesh, or sacred place of the region. The spring itself was En Mishpat, the "Fount of Judgment," to which the men of the desert resorted for *toroth* or oracular decisions.[3]

Northwest from the "Sacred Fount" our route leads us through the "Gorge of the Mother of Swallowing up," where our guide warns us to beware lest we suffer the same fate; with a little good will, we might suspect a faint reminiscence of Korah's death.[4] We reach a small but fertile plain, the best in all the south country. In it are three springs. One lies in the open plain, scarcely more than a water hole, a few reeds along the sluggish stream which issues from it; the soil is infested by camel ticks brought by the beasts of the nomads. A second, the "Salty," a group of rudely stoned water holes or mere pits with a tiny stream flowing a short distance through the reeds, is in the western corner, on the road from Hebron to Egypt, whose tracks can be seen from a nearby hill sweeping far out over the level.[5] We enter a narrowing gorge, pass masses of washed-out gravel and fields of grain, and then sward with scattered acacia trees. A small mound guarded by a huge acacia, more water plants and shrubs, and we are at the source of all this fertility. Under a high cliff breaks out a spring of a force and a copiousness for which even the watercourse below has not prepared us. No wonder the valley is called the "Gorge of the Fount," for this is *the* fountain in all the southern Negeb.[6]

These are the "Waters of Meribath Kadesh," where disputes were settled; the waters came forth abundantly when Moses

---

[2]Fig. 105; the little known but widely discussed Ain Qdes, visited by us May 27, 1905, cf. N. Schmidt, *JBL.*, XXIX, 1910, 61 ff.; for our expedition to the Negeb, consistently ignored by later writers, cf. N. Schmidt, *Ann. Report Amer. School for Oriental Study*, 1904–5, 35 ff.; *Hibbert Journal*, VI, 1908, 322 ff.; A. T. Olmstead, *Western Asia in the Reign of Sargon*, 1908, 56 ff.
[3]Gen. 14:7. [4]Num. 16.
[5]Fig. 15. [6]Fig. 106.

FIG. 105. KADESH BARNEA.

FIG. 106. THE "GORGE OF THE FOUNT."

smote the rock with his mystic rod.[7] Here and at the "Fount of Judgment" are localised the stories which cluster about this Moses, in tradition a law-giver or rather an oracle-giver through the torah, the sacred lot.

According to the well-known story, Moses led the Israelites in exodus from Egyptian captivity. Earlier traditions of the tribes who settled in North and Central Canaan and across Jordan show clearly that originally they knew nothing of an exodus from Egypt, and these traditions fit badly the later story of an exodus of the whole people into which they have been incorporated. Furthermore, we have found Hebrews in Canaan long before the date of the supposed Pharaoh of the Exodus.

On the other hand, the tradition of a captivity in Egypt is so persistent, it fits so well with contemporary conditions, it is so unthinkable that any people could have invented an episode so little to their credit, that we must assume a solid basis for the belief. Now even the latest writers remembered that only seventy souls went down into Egypt, while but two midwives were required by the whole Hebrew community just before their exit from the Nile valley.[8] Such survivals of the older tradition make it plain that but a single tribe was ever in Goshen.

Moses was the leader of the Exodus and Moses was the hero of Levi; all things considered, it is most probable that it was Levi who was once in Egypt. The Hebrews were at first well received, as were other nomads introduced by frontier officials.[9] They were settled in Goshen, the present Wadi Tumilat, a triangular bit of fertile land, ten miles on the side, enclosed on two sides by the desert and on the third by a canal from the Nile to the Red Sea, which permitted its irrigation. Its area is less than a hundred square miles and not over four thousand nomads could find sustenance within its limits.[10] Later, they were forced to do task work, building the cities of Raamses and

---

[7] Num. 20:2 ff.; 27:14; 33:36; Deut. 32:51; Ezek. 47:19; 48:28.
[8] Gen. 46:27; Ex. 1:15.   [9] Cf. p. 227.
[10] W. M. F. Petrie, *Egypt and Israel*, 30.

Pithom; the former city was founded by Ramses II, who may therefore be the Pharaoh of the oppression. In the decline of Egyptian power which followed, Moses led his tribe to freedom through the desert of Zin by Mount Horeb to Kadesh.[11] The successful exodus was commemorated by a song:

> Sing ye to Yahweh, for gloriously he triumphed,
> The horse and his rider he cast in the sea.[12]

That Levi was originally a secular tribe is proved by several Biblical passages, and a place, Levi-el, "Levi is God," appears in the Egyptian lists.[13] Moses is reported to have set up a bronze serpent;[14] several of the Levite personal names are connected with serpents. It has even been suggested that Levi himself is related to Leviathan, the "coiling" monster, and that his tribal god was the snake Nahash or Nehushtan.[15]

The "Gorge of the Fount" was the most pleasant halt on the "Way to Shur," the fortress "Wall" which protected Egypt against the nomads; it appears in the story of the patriarchs and it is still called the "Way of Shur."[16] Taking its origin at the Isthmus of Suez, it passes through drifted sand, then the land roughens to culminate in a pass polished like glass by camels' feet. Flints forced from the softer rock by the feet of travellers and water holes they dug mark the route. After a broad plain the track skirts the hills to the south, comes into the upper reaches of the "Gorge of Egypt," and arrives at the "Salty Spring," the "Well of the Living One who sees me" pointed out to Hagar by the messenger of Yahweh.[17]

The road continues over hills to the plain of the "Two Wells," with some sward and a little cultivation, surrounded by thick beds of soft white sandstone full of fossil crinoids. Some distance beyond is the plain of Aujeh, with red and brown sandstones, and more crinoids. In a yet more open

[11]Cf. Ex. 17:6; Num. 20:1 ff. [12]Ex. 15:21.
[13]Gen. 34; 49:5–7; Deut. 33:8–11; Müller, *Egypt. Res.*, I, 49.
[14]Num. 21:5 ff. [15]T. J. Meek, *AJSL.*, XXXVII, 1921, 110.
[16]Gen. 16:7; 20:1; 25:18. [17]Gen. 16:7 ff.

third plain is a three hundred foot well in the shallow stream bed, the Rehoboth dug by Isaac.[18] From here the road runs over somewhat more open country to Beersheba and so to Hebron and to Jerusalem.

We are now in the territory of Simeon, full brother of Levi by Leah.[19] Obscure fragments preserved in later narratives permit a glimpse of Simeon's northward progress. We hear how he came to the entrance of Gerar, founded by Egyptians not long before to command one of the gates to Canaan,[20] seeking pasturage for his flocks. When he found that the pasturage was fat and good and the land peaceful and quiet, he ousted the former inhabitants of the house of Ham. Certain of his sons settled as far as Mount Seir. Simeon likewise smote the Amalekites and permanently occupied their country.[21]

According to another fragment, the Canaanite king of Arad, who dwelt in the Negeb, heard of the Hebrew advance and fought with them, taking certain prisoners. The exasperated Hebrews thereupon vowed to devote to death all the cities and all the Canaanites who were delivered into their hands. Zephath was captured and renamed Hormah, the "Devoted."[22] Another advance, marked this time not by devotion but by amalgamation, is witnessed by the genealogy which makes Saul, a son of Simeon, born of a Canaanite mother.[23]

The most important of Simeon's cities were along the border of cultivation. First was Beersheba, the "Well of the Oath." Abraham was said to have planted there a sacred tamarisk and to have called upon El Olam, the "Eternal God," but it was Isaac, the "Laughing," who was especially commemorated at Beersheba. The term "Laughing" may have been euphemistic, for we have the grim story of the attempted sacrifice of Isaac himself. The altar was later attributed to Isaac, and down to the time of Amos men swore "As lives thy Way, Beersheba."[24]

Also along the border were Moladah to the east, and Sharu-

[18] Gen. 26:22.   [19] Gen. 34; 49:5; 29:33.
[20] W. M. F. Petrie, *Gerar*, 1928.
[21] I Chron. 4:39 ff.; cf. Ex. 17:9 ff.
[22] Judges 1:17; cf. Num. 21:1 ff.; 14:39 ff.; Deut. 1:41 ff.
[23] Gen. 46:10; Ex. 6:15.   [24] Gen. 21:33; 26:24 f.; Amos 5:5; 8:14.

hen, where the Hyksos had made their last stand, to the west. Etam and Ain Rimmon were in Canaan proper. The majority were in the Negeb, such as Bethel, Hazar Susim, the "Enclosure of Horses," Beth Markaboth, the "House of Chariots," Hazar Shual, the "Enclosure" of the half-Canaanite son of Simeon, and Baalath Beer Ramath Negeb, the abode of the "Lady of the Well, the High Place of the Negeb."[25]

By the time when the Hebrews had entered the historic stage, Levi had ceased to exist as a separate tribe and Simeon was far in decline. According to the ancient theory of retributive justice, this must have been due to their evil habits, and the following taunt song was circulated:

> Simeon and Levi are brothers,
>   Weapons of violence their swords;
> My soul, do not enter their councils,
>   My heart, their assembly join not.
> For in anger a man they slaughter,
>   And in wantonness hock an ox;
> Cursed be their wrath, for 'tis savage,
>   Likewise their rage, for 'tis fierce.
> I will divide them in Jacob,
>   In Israel scatter them.[26]

Levi and Simeon declined before the third of the brother tribes of the Negeb, Judah. By folk etymology, Yehudah is interpreted: "I will praise Yahweh."[27] We may doubt the correctness of the verb employed in this translation, the connection with the deity remains; perhaps Yehudah really means "Yahweh knows."[28] The origins of the Yahweh worship are hidden in complete darkness and even the correct pronunciation of his name is in doubt. During the greater part of the time covered by our history it was certainly pronounced something like Yahu.[29]

[25] Lists, Josh. 19:2–8; I Sam. 30:26–31; I Chron. 4:28–33; cf. Josh. 15.
[26] Gen. 49:5–7.   [27] Gen. 29:35.
[28] M. Jastrow, JBL., XII, 1893, 69.
[29] All extra-Biblical information bearing on the pronunciation is collected, D. D. Luckenbill, AJSL., XL, 1924, 277 ff.; G. R. Driver, ZAW., NF. V, 1928, 7 ff. Assyrian transliteration of Hebrew names demands Yahu or Yeho, as do the YHW of the Elephantine papyri and the Iao and the like of Greek

Judæan writers state that Yahweh was worshipped from the days of the first man, Enosh.[30] Another passage assumes his worship by the Aramæans.[31] One of the most surprising discoveries of the last century is that of a second Judah in North Syria. Still more surprising is the discovery that one of its rulers was by his name a worshipper of Yahweh, and that two more rulers of Hamath in North Central Syria likewise commemorated the same deity in their names.[32]

> Yahweh came from Sinai,
> And rose over Seir,
> He shone from Mount Paran,
> And came to Meribath Kadesh,

chants an ancient song.[33] Here we trace the triumphant progress of Yahweh from Midian, east of the Red Sea, over Seir or Edom, then to Paran, in the eastern Sinaitic peninsula, and so to Kadesh. A far-earlier song brings him from Seir and the Field of Edom,[34] a later from Taiman, east of Edom and Mount Paran, while before his approach the tents of Kushan and Midian shake.[35] In time this was incorporated in a story of the marriage of Moses, founder of the religion, with the daughter of the Midianite priest.[36] All this implies that Yahweh was a desert god whose home was outside the later settlements of his worshippers; whether he was originally non-Hebrew is not so sure, though this has been confidently asserted. His characteristics were those of the desert, simple and austere; he was connected with the storm, on whose wings he rode; the phenomena of the epiphany at Sinai have sug-

magical papyri. In the Bible, it is Yahu, later Yah, at the end, and Yeho, later Yo, at the beginning of proper names. However, it is difficult to fit this pronunciation to the letters YHWH, and a plausible case may be made out for an original Yahwoh, cf. L. Waterman, *AJSL.*, XLIII, 1926, 1 ff. In the present uncertain state of the question, I have reluctantly employed the commonly used Yahweh, for which there is no evidence before the Christian writers, unless we count the punning allusion of Ex. 6:3. The form Jehovah is a blunder of a thirteenth century student, ignorant of the most elementary principles of Hebrew.

[30]Gen. 4:26; cf. Ex. 3:16.
[31]Gen. 31:24, 29.
[32]Cf. chaps. XXI, XXVI, XXVIII, XXX.
[33]Deut. 33:2.
[34]Judges 5.
[35]Hab. 3.
[36]Ex. 2:16 ff.

gested to some that there was also connection with volcanoes. His ritual was equally simple. As with other nomad deities, no image set forth his appearance. His abode was a tent, from which he went forth in a pillar of cloud by day and of fire by night to lead his people. Desert feasts and sacrifices and burnt offerings from the flocks and herds completed the worship.[37]

Levi appears to have accepted Yahweh very early, perhaps through union with Judah, for Levi as a separate tribe with separate territory had disappeared by the time our first records were prepared. Levites are found as resident aliens of Judæan towns,[38] and the name Levi is interpreted as from a root meaning to be joined.[39] Moses went down in tradition as the great lawgiver, who first gave the Hebrews the worship of Yahweh; the Moses stories in their earlier form centre about the Levite settlement at Kadesh Barnea, and there the Levites fought against their brothers for Yahweh, doubtless against the devotees of an older cult.[40]

To trace the early limits of Judah is difficult. We may best discover them by first noting the allied tribes who were at this date still independent, though closely related in blood and later to become an integral part of Judah. First are the Kenites, whose ancestor, Cain, the "Smith," bore the special mark of Yahweh and was a nomad;[41] to this day the Near Eastern smiths are wanderers on the face of the earth. Hobab, the Kenite, said to be the father-in-law of Moses, went up from the city of Palm Trees in the Negeb of Arad, perhaps the later Tamar in the Wilderness of Judah, to dwell with the Amalekites.[42] A fragmentary poem sings of the Kenites:

> Lasting thy abode,
>   Set on the Rock thy nest;
> Yet Cain shall be wasted,
>   . . . shall make thee captive.[43]

[37] Cf. Ex. 3:18, 5:1; 10:25 f.; Num. 10:35 f.   [38] Judges 17:7; 19:1.
[39] Gen. 29:34.
[40] Ex. 32:26 ff.; cf. D. D. Luckenbill, *AJT.*, XXII, 1918, 24 ff.; T. J. Meek, *op. cit.*, 115.
[41] Gen. 4:15.   [42] Judges 1:16; Num. 10:29 ff.; cf. I Sam. 15:6; 27:10; 30:29.
[43] Num. 24:21 f.

One of the Kenite clans was that of the Rechabites, to be in the future a strong conservative force among the Hebrews; they followed to the end the old nomad ideals, for they drank no wine, built no house, sowed no seed, planted no vineyard, but ever lived in tents.[44] Another important tribe was Jerahmeel, with Edomite connections, later made a son of Simeon.[45]

In our period, there was no close line drawn between Hebrews and Edomites. Their eponym was Esau, the "Hairy," whether from the hairiness of the nomad or from their garments of goat's hair. They too had left the desert early, for Esau was the first born of Isaac; of him was chanted this blessing:

> Away from earth's fatness shall be thy abode,
> And from dew of the heavens above,
> And by thy sword shalt thou live.[46]

In the rough country east of the Arabah, Esau found the Horites with their animal names, ass, antelope, hyena, and the like, sons of Seir, likewise the "Hairy," originally perhaps a goat divinity.[47] From him Mount Seir took his name, though the land itself was called Edom, the "Red," from the dark red of the sandstones and porphyries which form so large a part of the range. Edom was also a divinity, as were Qaus, the "Lord," and Kozah, the god of storms. Edom's southern border was at Elath and Ezion Geber, on the Gulf of Aqaba, the northern was the gorge of the Zered.[48]

In the centre of the Arabah is Jebel Maderah, presumably the ancient Mount Hor, with long low outliers of marl, seamed with watercourses; a sharp ascent over strewn debris and a broad white band of crumbling marl make difficult the climb to the long flat summit. The view is wide but monotonous, over low featureless country, reddish from the flints and shimmering in the haze. We traverse a broad plain roamed by gazelles, and a gentle rise brings us to Ain el Weibeh, with

[44] I Chron. 2:55; Jer. 35:6 f.
[45] Gen. 46:10; cf. I Chron. 2:25 ff.
[46] Gen. 27:39 f.   [47] Gen. 36:20; Deut. 2:12.   [48] Deut. 2:8; Num. 21:12.

sweet water, rushes, and a few stunted palms. We cross the Arabah by well-trodden paths and the mountains of Edom come into view; the outlying hills, low heaps of stone and debris, look for all the world like coal dumps. Over dirty yellow sandstone, where the road is so rough that the horses lose their nerve and must be unloaded, we descend to the show spot of Edom, Sela, the "Rock," more generally known by the Greek translation of Petra.

Petra lies amid a perfect network of wild gorges, their sides of banded sandstone, whose colours, rose pink, umber, purple, justify the comparison with watered silk. Through the chief gorge flows a stream of clear cold sweet water, most welcome after the brackish springs of the Arabah. There is not a little sward, intermingled with the glossy green leaves and pink blossoms of the oleander. Even in July the nights are cool and bracing. Petra's ruins, to be sure, date from the Nabatæan and Roman periods, but the site must have been a great trade centre from early times.

A gentle ascent leads the traveller out of the gorge and to the level flint-covered wind-swept steppe, the typical landscape of Edom. From the gardens and mulberry orchards of the ancient Maon, our northward progress is over broken hills and by the heads of westward-opening valleys to the steep gorge of the Zered, the northern boundary of Edom.[49]

Grandson of Esau by his father Eliphaz, though a Horite by his concubine mother Timna, was Amalek. Once the Amalekites occupied En Mishpat, well into the Negeb, but their true home was the "Desert of the Wandering." Amalek was at constant war with the Hebrews, who retaliated with this taunt:

> First of the nations was Amalek,
> But his end shall be destruction![50]

Caleb, the "Dog," our nearest approach to totemism, was a

[49] For Edom, cf. G. L. Robinson, *Sarcophagus of an Ancient Civilization*, 1930.
[50] Gen. 14:7; Ex. 17; Num. 13:29; 14:25 ff.; 24:20; Deut. 25:17 ff.; I Chron. 4:43.

son of Kenaz, the Edomite, and we remember that Edom's border once extended to Kadesh.[51] He conquered Kiriath Arba, the "City of the Four Gods," driving out three giants, sons of Anak, and changed its name to Hebron, which perhaps means "Confederacy."[52] Hebron was a city of the first importance, with its famed grapes from the valley of Eshcol, its sacred terebinths of Mamre, its altar commemorating the appearance of Yahweh to Abraham, above all, its cave of Machpelah, in the field bought from the children of Heth, where the patriarchs Abraham, Isaac, and Jacob were buried with their wives, the "Field of Abram" mentioned in an Egyptian inscription. The hero Abraham dominates the whole region, and his sanctuary, north of the town, is marked by potsherds from the third millennium to the first and its sanctity continued into Christian times.[53]

Another clan, symbolised by Othniel, younger brother of Caleb, took Kiriath Sepher, the City of the Book, or perhaps with watercourses; a sharp ascent over strewn debris and a "Oracle." Caleb gave his daughter Achshah to his brother for wife; when she reminded him that he had given her lands in the Negeb but no water, he added to his gift the Upper and Lower Gullith.[54] The excavations show that Kiriath Sepher perished by fire towards the end of the thirteenth century and its fortifications were completely razed. Before the ashes could blow away, the city was rebuilt, but the walls were of smaller stones and never more than half as thick. No more was the city crowded, for population was less and culture declined.[55]

By elimination we have found the true home of our tribe, the "Wilderness of Judah," the rough country leading down to the Dead Sea, seamed with deep gorges but with here and there a short stretch of fertile land dominated by a village on

[51] Gen. 36:11, 15, 42; Num. 20:16; 32:12; Josh. 14:6, 14; I Chron. 2:18.
[52] Josh. 14:6 ff.; Judges 1:10.
[53] Num. 13:23; Gen. 13:18; 18:1; 25:9; 49:30; 50:13; Breasted, *Rec.*, IV, 352; Joseph., *Ant.*, I, 186; *Bell.*, IV, 533; Euseb., *Onom.*, 76; A. E. Mader, *RB.*, XXXIX, 1930, 209; H. Vincent and E. J. H. Mackay, *Hébron*, 1923.
[54] Josh. 15:13 ff.; Judges 1:10 ff.
[55] W. F. Albright, *ZAW.*, NF., VI, 1929, 8 ff.

a high hill. We shall meet these villages later, when we recount the story of David's wanderings. The union of the minor clans with Judah, its rise to a commanding position in the south, its supremacy over the Hebrew tribes, all belong to later chapters.

CHAPTER XVIII

PALESTINE OF THE PHILISTINES

PALESTINE is not the land of the Hebrews but of the Philistines. Nearly half the centuries for which we have written records had passed before the land received that name. That it came to be applied to the ancient Canaan was due to events far beyond the ken of its inhabitants.

Forces akin to those which repeatedly drove the Semites from Arabia into the Fertile Crescent likewise drove hordes of Aryans from the far east and north of Europe to the happier lands around the Mediterranean. The cities which had known the glories of the Minoan culture went up in smoke before new hordes of barbarous Greeks. Broken fragments of their peoples, led perhaps by earlier Aryans and increased on the way by other groups from the crashing empires, crossed the sea into Asia Minor. "The Northerners in their isles were unquiet," say the Egyptians, "the northern countries were unquiet in their limbs." The Hittite empire disappeared in darkness, our only record of its fate a casual reference in an Egyptian list, Hittites, Carchemish, Arvad, and Cyprus, of those who could not stand before the hands of the foreigners.[1]

Carchemish was in fact, as the excavations amply show, conquered by warriors from the northern grasslands. Their victories were due in part to their superior weapons, for they were in the full iron age. Rude statuettes depict the typical Nordic animal, the horse, sometimes riderless, sometimes carrying a rider with shield, quiver, and pointed helmet. A horse with double head is intended for the led horse of the wanderer. The armour of the invaders was almost that of Athenians in the days of Pericles, tall crested helmets, with tail and neck guard, a long spear, tip down, is in the right hand, a small round shield is slung over the left shoulder. Moustache and lower

[1]Breasted, *Rec.*, IV, 24 ff.

lip are shaven, the remainder of the face is bearded, the hair descends to a plaited pigtail. A short-sleeved garment which stops above the knees is held in place by a simple girdle and the northern bow-shaped fibula or safety pin.[2]

Over the thoroughly razed older settlement a new city was built to include some two hundred and fifty acres. The line of walls was laid out with careful attention to the topography and advantage was taken of every rise or rock out-crop. An interval of thirty feet separated double walls of rubble with stone facing, seventeen feet broad; they ran in long straight lines with well-planned rectangular salients every hundred and thirty feet. Gates at the south and west were protected by flanking towers, topped by machiolations and battlements, with a raised and paved threshold and basalt door sockets and stop.

Houses were of brick with stone trimming. Roofs were flat, the gutters behind false doors of limestone decorated with red and yellow paint. Door or window lintels were flat stones or wooden beams, perhaps with a rolled projecting cornice, jambs were of stone or brick, occasionally reeded. Windows were hinged with bronze, doors were of wood with bronze binding and nails and a wooden shoe which fitted into the bowl-like basalt door socket.

A certain number of their vases may have been imports from Cyprus or the Ægean, and the native wares present close parallels to these types. Their forms may be correctly described by the Greek terminology. Bell craters slipped with white bear black geometric designs which are often of the metope style, œnochoes have the triple spout so familiar in Greece, tripod bowls and tall vessels with small mouths complete the list.

On cuneiform documents of the later Hittite kings we find seals with a new pictographic writing, which was taken over by the men of Carchemish. Henceforth it is common in North Syria and as far south as Hamath, it is dominant in eastern Asia Minor, and it is found more rarely westward to the

[2] Figs. 107–110.

Fig. 107. BRONZE FIBULA OR SAFETY PIN. (Carchemish.)

Fig. 108. CINERARY URN. (Carchemish.)

Fig. 109. CINERARY URN. (Carchemish.)

Fig. 110. FIGURINES. (Carchemish.)

Ægean. As a rule, the horizontal lines begin at the right with the signs facing the beginning, while the alternate lines run in the opposite direction with the signs reversed. Individual words are placed in short vertical columns and are generally separated by a word divider. There are about two hundred signs, the majority with ideographic value only, but some fifty appear to possess phonetic values as well, and ideographs are often followed by phonetic complements. Since the ideograph for country is known, it is possible to identify the name of the place where any given monument was erected, and this has permitted the identification of a few phonetic values. Applied to proper names, it has given individuals who also appear as rulers in contemporary Assyrian records. Such grammatical evidence as has accumulated points to a dialect of or at least influence by the Indo-European language spoken by the Hittite monarchs. In the earlier inscriptions the characters are raised and with such elaboration of detail as to indicate that the writing is still at an early stage of development; later, the characters were incised and a cursive form was evolved.[3]

The earliest sculptures from Carchemish are found at the Water Gate. A king sits on a camp stool with cushion and tassel; his beard is closely cropped, his ear sets high, he wears a long fringed robe and lifts a cup in his left hand. Before him is an X-shaped table, on which are double-handled goblet, cones, loaves of bread, and ribs of beef. An attendant, with full flat eye, outstanding ear, straight fleshy nose, and prognathous jaw, holds the fly flapper, another, whose slanting eye attracts our attention, carries in his left hand a spouted bottle. Then comes the lute player, whose instrument, decorated with ribbons and tassels, has a finger board surprisingly long for the small oval sounding box. A chariot scene with rope pattern below completes this group.

Teshup, the native weather god, if so he were called, im-

[3] Figs. 148, 149, 170; L. Messerschmidt, *Corpus Inscriptionum Hettiticarum*, 1900, 1902, 1906; A. T. Olmstead, B. B. Charles, J. E. Wrench, *Travels and Studies in the Nearer East, Hittite Inscriptions*, 1911; full bibliography with a decipherment which marks a real advance over previous attempts, by I. Gelb, *Hittite Hieroglyphic Inscriptions*, soon to be published.

pressed his might on the invaders; accompanied by his bulls, he wields the double battle axe and wears the pointed cap with crescent horns. His worshipper has banged his hair straight in front, but it falls to the neck behind; a long robe, with short sleeves, girdle, and transverse seam, descends to the fringe at the ankles. In his right hand are cords holding a basket, at his foot is a dove, a boy leads a goat to the sacrifice. Other reliefs depict mythological monsters, a maneless lion with eagle's hind claws attacking a bull, a demon with bull's legs and long tufted tail carrying a staff, a human-headed sphinx covered by scale-like feathers on breast and shoulders but with quills for wings. The lesser arts are represented chiefly by steatite or paste cylinders, no longer imported from Babylonia but of native manufacture; the engraving is poor, an archer shooting at a deer or a row of birds.

In northern fashion, the dead were cremated and the ashes interred in regular cinerary urns which were rarely painted. Over the urn was placed a rough saucer or a gilt bronze bowl, and over this again a bell crater or a bathtub inverted. Within the urn or around it were placed various objects, a column-like female holding her breasts or carrying a child, or a horse or horseman according to the sex.[4]

Not content with Carchemish, the northerners coveted the wealth of Mesopotamia. To their misfortune, Assyria was rapidly increasing its power while Babylonia enjoyed a renewal of strength under the fourth dynasty. The North Syrian "Hittites," as they were henceforth to be called by Babylonians and Assyrians, marched down the Euphrates to attack the alluvium but were beaten back by the first Nebuchadnezzar in 1143.[5]

At much the same time, allied peoples occupied Samal, at the crossing of the road from Syria through Marqasi to Asia Minor with the road from Carchemish to the sea coast and to Cilicia. For some centuries the settlement was confined to an

---

[4] D. G. Hogarth and C. L. Woolley, *Carchemish*, 1914, 1921; C. L. Woolley, *Liverpool Annals of Archæology*, VI, 1913, 94 ff.
[5] *History of Assyria*, 59.

Fig. 112. PHILISTINE CAPTIVES.

Fig. 111. WARRIORS FROM CARCHEMISH.

oval mound whose close-set houses formed the only walling; the single gate was at the south. A century or so later a cross wall was built on the citadel behind the gate, and the first city wall enclosed a hundred acres in a perfect oval. Over stone foundations, three feet deep, rose crude brick walls, four feet thick, studded by frequent towers and with other flanking towers above three gates of Syrian plan. The gate plan was repeated in the earliest palace, of large flat bricks, sun dried and mixed with straw or limestone, and held together by wood studding. Wooden columns on stone bases gave a sense of lightness to the hilani, as this style of building was henceforth called.

In the gates were the divine guardians of the city, rough hairless lions, glaring out from the wall or in partial relief. The diorite reliefs of the south gate recall the earlier art of Asia Minor, the shaven face, the short tunic, the pig-tail, the pointed shoes, the side curl, the long straight nose, the large profile eye. Scenes from daily life contrast with mythological motifs. First appears a monster, human save for eagle's wings and head. Then we see a man on horseback, in a high cap from under which drops the neck curl, and armed with a short sword; he rides without stirrups, his bare heels raised high; in his left hand he exhibits his foeman's head. Two winged monsters show a lion's body but a human face, with a pig-tail under the conical cap with knobbed tip, the brim raised before and behind. Next we find two men chatting and a bowman, accompanied by his dog, who has hung up the hare he has shot and is aiming at a stag.[6]

Something like a century later must be placed the reliefs at the citadel gate. The smooth-shaven face has given way to the Shumerian fashion of shaving the lips but leaving the chin beard, the pig-tail has been displaced by the knotted curl. Technique has distinctly improved.

A table with three curved legs is spread for the feast. On a high-backed chair sits a man, clad in skull cap, long robe, and pointed shoes, a moustache under his long straight nose; his

[6] Fig. 113.

right hand grasps the long crooked staff, he picks up food with his left. His wife, who wears the long robe bound by a six-stranded girdle and the cylindrical hat with trailing veil over the pig-tail, is seated on a lower stool without back; she prefers to use her right hand for the food, her left holds two plant stalks. A servant carries a lamb over his shoulders, a guard in ribbed cap, skirt, and strapped sandals is armed with dagger and staff, a musician sits on a stool and thrums the long-handled lute, slung by a band from the shoulder. A round-capped horseman with round shield follows a huge bull.

The weather god is in short tunic, pointed shoes, and conical cap, with pig-tail and long square-cut beard curled in rows; he is armed with the long crescent-hilted dagger, the battle axe bound by cords to the short handle, and the three-pronged thunderbolt. His consort, wearing the veiled hat, long double robe and pointed shoes, her hair curling to the neck, holds a feather in her right hand, her left grasps a round mirror with Egyptian handle. Falcons perch on the wrist of the lion-headed monster, who swings the boomerang in his left hand while with the other he raises a rabbit by its hind legs. A griffin shows a lion's body with eagle wings and head, a winged lion with tail high and open mouth wears a skull cap on its human head.[7]

While Carchemish and Samal were occupied by the advance guard of the northerners, others turned south. All Syria had been lost to Egypt, which at last was made subject by the Syrian Yarsu, its gods were degraded, their sacrifices came to an end. Yarsu was deposed by Setnakht, whose son Ramses III (1198–1167) was the last of the great Egyptian conquerors. In his fourth year, 1195, Syria was invaded, the chief of Amor was killed, and his subjects made prisoner. Three years later the Philistines set up a camp in Amor; Lebanon graves with objects of late Mycenæan style may bear witness to their temporary settlement. Sidon was destroyed and remained desolate long enough for a yard of sterile earth to accumulate above the debris; east of the city, the invaders left strange

[7] Fig. 115; F. von Luschan, *Ausgrabungen in Sendschirli,* III, 201 ff.

FIG. 113. SCULPTURES FROM THE SOUTH GATE OF SAMAL.

figurines in their tombs. Cremation burials at the fountains of Tyre have the same horsemen and animal vases as at Carchemish.[8]

One branch of the invaders, the Zakkalu, settled at Dor, where they left their finely baked pottery with metallic clink. The most characteristic forms are the amphora with sloping shoulder and the pointed pear-shaped juglet. Beautiful pebble burnishing covers the jars or they are well painted in black and red. In strainer-spouted vessels, black cross-hatched lozenges are placed between parallel red and black bands.[9]

Still the invaders pressed southward, the Peleset or Philistines, the Zakkalu from Dor, the Shekeleth, in whom some would find the ancestors of the true Sicilians, the Denyen or Greek Danians, the Weshwesh.[10] In peace, the Philistines wore the belted kilts so familiar from Cretan frescoes, their warriors were clad in scale armour and bore the helmet with feathered headdress which antiquity considered especially Carian.[11] Footmen in squads of four carried the small round shield and two spears or the leaf-shaped northern broadsword. A driver and two warriors armed with spear and shield occupied the chariots, non-combatants and supplies were transported on two-wheeled ox-carts. Another contingent followed the coast in ships of Cretan type.

Ramses III still held Beth Shan, whose inhabitants honoured him by a rude seated statue of local basalt and of local manufacture. But he held it only through the aid of Ægean mercenaries, who brought with them their imported Ægean pottery. Their features we learn from the relief covers of their cigar-shaped terra-cotta sarcophagi, interred in roughly rectangular rock chambers outside the city walls, which show strange beardless faces, prominent noses, and pierced ears; their women were perhaps native, for they are less grotesque and wear Egyptian wigs. A lozenge-shaped bit of gold foil was tied over the mouth of the corpse, Egyptian ushabtis followed

[8] C. L. Woolley, *Syria*, II, 1921, 177 ff.; G. Contenau, *ibid.*, I, 1920, 125 ff.; R. Dussaud, *ibid.*, II, 1921, 168; T. Macridy, *RB.*, XIII, 1904, 565.
[9] *Bull. British School Jerusalem*, IV, 42; VII, 81.
[10] Breasted, *Rec.*, IV, 37 ff.   [11] Alcæus, in Strabo xiv, 2, 27; Herod. i, 172.

them to the grave. These foreign mercenaries also labored on the temples and imprinted Minoan signs on the bricks. Next the great pylon they constructed a corridor under the direction of Ramses-user-khepesh, overseer of the soldiers, commander of the royal bowmen, royal scribe, and great steward, son of

FIG. 114. PHILISTINE PRISONERS.

Thutmose, fan bearer at the right hand of the king, chief of the bowmen and overseer of the foreign countries; on the door jambs he kneels with hands upraised in reverence to Ramses.[12]

Aided by similar mercenaries, Ramses went forth to Zahi "like Baal, valiant in strength," and equipped his frontier in Zahi, filling its harbour with his ships. The Philistine ships were caught by grappling irons, archers on the shore raked the fleet and picked off the fugitives who had thrown themselves into the water to escape the Egyptian boarders. The king received the prisoners at the Migdol of Ramses; it is noticeable that he ascribes the victory in large part to the Syrian divinities, Baal and Sutekh, Anath and Ashtart.[13]

[12]C. S. Fisher, *Museum Journal*, XIV, 1923, 234 ff.; Alan Rowe, *Beth-Shan*, 38 ff.; G. M. FitzGerald, *QS.*, 1931, 69 f.
[13]Figs. 112, 114–117; Breasted, *Rec.*, IV, 33 ff.; Oriental Institute, University of Chicago, *Medinet Habu*, I, 1930, pl. 29 ff.

FIG. 115. SCULPTURES FROM THE CITADEL GATE AT SAMAL.

Ramses' eleventh year, 1188, was the last time for more than two centuries that Egyptian armies were to appear in Syria. Amor must again be taken from its defenders, bearded Semites fighting behind four battlemented walls, which were topped by a crow's nest flying a triangular standard. A city surrounded by water was protected by the chariotry, but mercenary Sherdan battered the gate with axes and scaled the walls with ladders. Ereth and a companion fort were guarded by "Hittites," armed with the bow and fighting from chariots. Ramses himself battled on foot before a hill city belonging to the Setetiu. Among the kneeling and pinioned captives at his triumph are represented the chiefs of the "Hittites," of Amor, of the Philistines and Zakkalu, of the sea Sherdan, who may be on their way to Sardinia, the sea Teresh, who may be early Tyrsenians or Etruscans, and the chief of the Shasu foe, perhaps a Hebrew. In a final campaign, he fought the people of Seir of the Shasu, and plundered their tents. For the last time in many a long year captives and cattle from Syria filled Amon's temple in the Ramses city.[14]

Ramses had been successful in driving the invaders from Egypt. His ships still sailed to Phœnicia and he built for Amon in Zahi a temple called "Castle of Ramses, ruler of Heliopolis, in The Canaan."[15] His weak successors quickly lost even this slight foothold. Ramses IV (1167–1161) was the last Egyptian to leave his name at the mines of Sinai.

Repulsed from Egypt, the Philistines settled down in the fertile plain to which they gave their name. There are no true harbours, for the shore is almost mathematically straight, a waste of ever-shifting sand blown by the prevailing southwesterly winds from the Nile Delta. Travel is monotonous but the dunes afford excellent pasturage and favour the vines which produced the famed wines of Gaza and Ashkelon. Dead trees half buried in sand witness their constant encroachment, there is danger the dunes may blow out, and water seeps through easily in years of drought, but crops may be started early and some fields are sown by the end of January.

[14]Breasted, *Rec.*, IV, 68 ff.; 201.   [15]*Ibid.*, IV, 120 ff.; 167.

Beyond the coastal dunes extend fertile fields with the slightest of swells. Over the plain wind gullies with steep mud banks six to ten feet high; filled in spring with flowing water, they retain in summer only stagnant pools of liquid mud, used by the women for washing and drinking alike. Fortunately, the average village owns a deep well which descends to the underlying sandstone and is worked by a half skin and a long rope passing over a horizontal windlass. During the winter rains, the fields are a mass of mud and green grass grows on the mud roofs.

The three chief seaports fell early into Philistine hands. Gaza was the bridgehead of the desert road to Egypt and the seaport of the route by Elath to Inner Arabia. Three miles from the sea rises the ancient mound with the modern town, forty feet above virgin soil, and an hour's walk in circumference. Its circuit was much extended by the Philistines, traces of whose walls have been unearthed.[16]

Next to the north and directly on the sea was Ashkelon, its harbour a small creek. Wells of unusual depth make possible fine gardens in the midst of the sands. Pit dwellings roofed by beams or brushwood housed its earliest inhabitants. An earth rampart proves it an important Hyksos centre, and as such it was destroyed by the Egyptians, rebuilt, and again destroyed about 1400. A great bed of ashes marks the Philistine conquest but the importance of the site caused it to be quickly restored.[17]

Northwest of Ashkelon is a lake, once deep and full of fish sacred to the goddess whose shrine was built on its shore. Atargatis or Derceto was a sort of mermaid, a fish with woman's head. She offended the goddess of love, who in revenge inspired a passion for a youth; ashamed of the daughter she bore him, Derceto killed her lover, exposed her child, and threw herself into the lake, where she was transformed into a fish. For this reason, her worshippers refused to eat fish; the

---

[16] W. J. Phythian-Adams, *QS.*, 1923, 11 ff.

[17] J. Garstang, *QS.*, 1921, 15 ff.; 1922, 112; W. J. Phythian-Adams, *QS.*, 1923, 63 ff.

taboo did not hold for her priests, who offered to her boiled or roasted fish which they afterwards consumed. Gold and silver fish were acceptable offerings, but the sacrifice of goat, pig, or cow was specifically prohibited. As the "Green Lady," she yet inhabits the ruined mound; at the spring equinox, youths and maidens march to the sea in her honour and bathe nude in the waves.[18]

The third of the seaport cities was Ashdod, in an open plain three miles over blown sands to the sea, and commanding the exit from the valley of Elah. To these three was shortly added Ekron, farther inland, which controlled the valley of Sorek and the road to the highlands. Its local deity was the Semitic Baalzebub, the "Lord of Flies." Last of the five cities was Gath, whose site has been variously located.

Like the men of Carchemish, the Philistines practised incineration. Only a few graves from a later period, the representations of the contemporary monuments, and a so-called "Gentile" element among the modern Jews, permit us to describe their racial type. Skeletons found in Philistine graves were sometimes tall, one six feet three and a half inches, another five feet ten; their modern representatives are rather short. The skulls are long and ellipsoidal, forehead and nose form virtually one line, as on Greek statues, the nose is small if not actually snub and may be broad at the base, the features are small and delicate, the modern type is occasionally fair.[19]

Biblical writers trace their origin to the island of Caphtor,[20] the Egyptian Keftiu, which as a geographical designation is not to be confined to Crete but must be extended to include the opposite coast of Asia Minor. Krethi or Cretans are bracketed with the Philistines,[21] Carians also appear as mercenaries, and there was a Beth Car, "House of the god Car,"

---

[18]Herod., i, 105; Luc., *Dea Syr.*, 14; Diod., ii, 4; Athen., viii, 37; W. F. Albright, *AJSL.*, XLI, 1925, 91.

[19]Graves, Macalister, *Gezer*, I, 64 f.; modern type, R. N. Salaman, *QS.*, 1925, 40 f.

[20]Amos 9:7; Jer. 47:4; Deut. 2.23; cf. Tacit., *Hist.*, v, 2.

[21]I Sam. 30:14; II Sam. 8:18; 15:18; 20:7, 23; I Kings 1:38, 44; I Chron. 18:17; Ezek. 25:16; Zeph. 2:5.

with which we may compare the temple of the Carian Zeus.[22] In Greek times, the port of Gaza was called Minoa, Minos, the Cretan king god, is pictured on Philistine coins, or its god is identified with Crete-born Zeus.[23] Connections with Crete and with Asia Minor also appear in dress and in armour.

The Philistines were strangers in a strange land, few in numbers and hated by all their neighbours. They could preserve their identity only by military preparedness. Their five cities formed a confederacy, each ruled by a *saren,* in whom, ever since the translations of the Peshitta and the Targums, scholars have found a Tyrant in the pre-Greek sense of legitimate ruler. Together, the five tyrants formed a council which afforded a certain unity of policy; the tyrant of Gath was first among equals and occasionally he is given the title of king.

Iron was in common use,[24] though it was carefully kept from the hill men. Military equipment remained purely European. Goliath might have been one of Homer's heroes, with his crested helmet, his scale armour, his legs covered like the "well-greaved Achæans." Northern fibulæ held together their robes. Philistine temples and palaces recalled those of Crete, with their megaron ground plan, their columns, and their light wells. The Philistines still amused themselves with the same brutal games which marred Minoan culture, and they were celebrated in open courts surrounded by seat steps as at Cnossus or Phæstus.

Pottery from Cyprus, Asia Minor, and Crete had been imported since the eighteenth dynasty, and their forms and decorations had been imitated by local potters. Now these forms and ornaments were produced by men to whom they were ancestral, and the difference is clear. The commonest forms are cremation craters, cups with horizontal handles, and saucers; the shapes are the same as those found in Greece and the islands. The typical Mycenæan stirrup jar, the vase with spout, and the pilgrim bottle also occur. We know that they

[22] II Kings 11:4, 19; I Sam. 7:11; Herod., i, 171.
[23] Steph. Byz., s. v. *Gaza;* G. F. Hill, *Greek Coins of Palestine,* 1914, lxxii.
[24] Fig. 119.

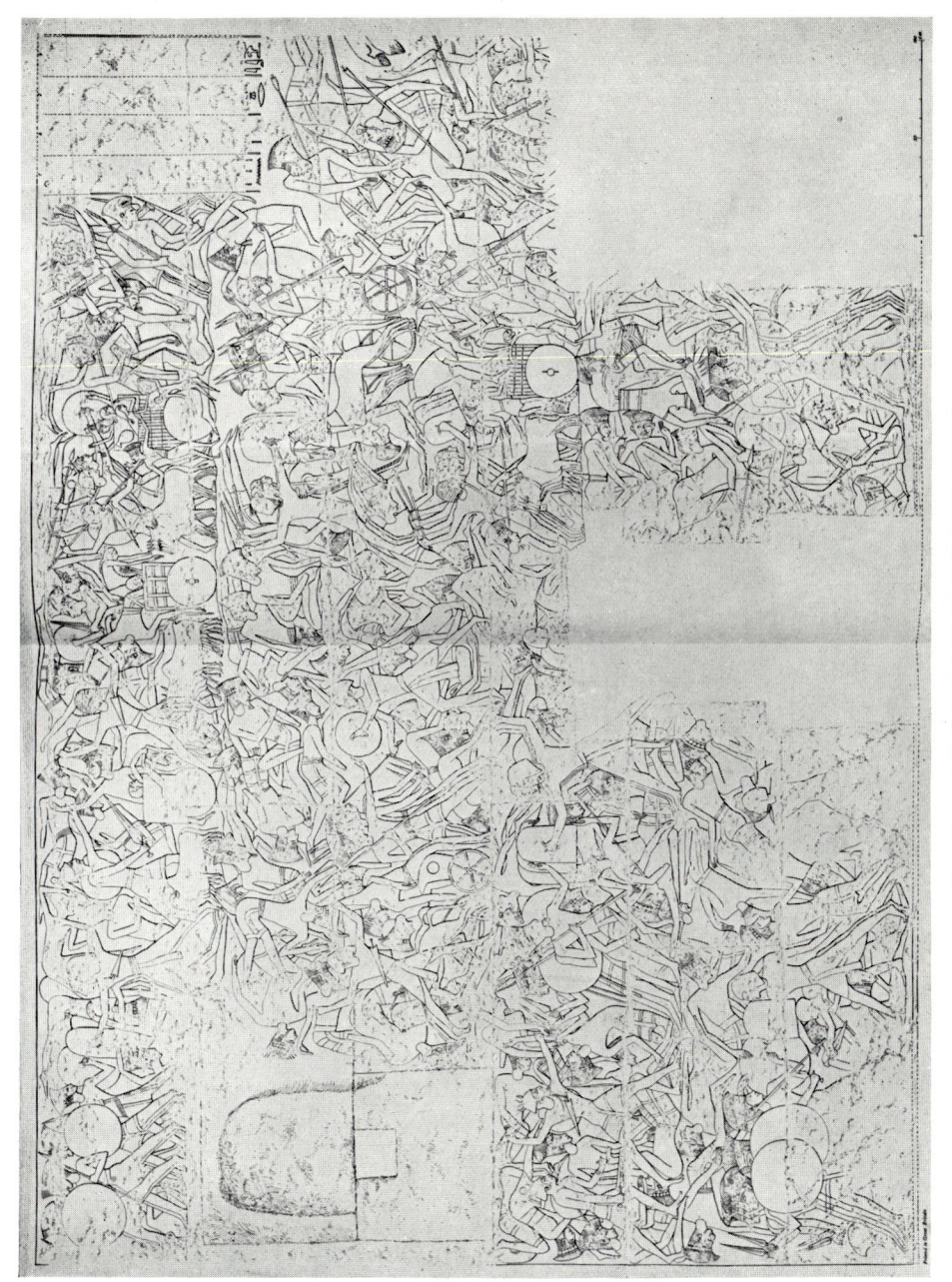

FIG. 116. LAND BATTLE WITH THE PHILISTINES.

are not imports, for they are made of the coarse local clay and their technique is inferor. Washed with white, the patterns are painted in a lusterless red or black. Among the distinctly northern motifs are the spiral, the varicolored spoked wheel, the swan, the checker board, and the swastika, which became Gaza's coat-of-arms.

Despite all effort, the Philistines gradually succumbed to the influences of the land. Painted cups and craters went out of fashion, leaving only a few bands painted in red. The middle bronze technique, a deep red paint laid on the reddish buff clay and then wheel burnished by a pebble in concentric rings, regained its sway. Handles disappeared, the interior was regularly painted.[25]

Assimilation is even more clearly shown in the sphere of religion. Objects in blue green faience from Beth Shemesh, a figurine of Isis with hieroglyphic inscription, figures of Bes and Sekhet, the sacred baboon and hippopotamus, the eye of Horus, testify to Egyptian influence.[26] The gods of their chief cities, Marna of Gaza, Atargatis of Ashkelon, Baalzebub of Ekron, were all Semitic. Their greatest divinity, Dagon, was only the Amorite grain god Dagan. In one respect alone the Philistines refused assimilation; mutilation of the body was utterly abhorrent to their minds and they never adopted the rite of circumcision practised by their neighbours. "Uncircumcised" was the worst taunt by which their enemies might assail them.[27]

[25] Fig. 121; W. J. Phythian-Adams, *QS.*, 1923, 60 ff.; *Bull. British School Jerusalem*, III, 20 ff.; W. F. Albright, *ZAW.*, NF., VI, 1929, 9 f.
[26] D. Mackenzie, *Excavations at Ain Shems*, II, 52 ff.
[27] R. A. S. Macalister, *The Philistines*, 1914; F. Stähelin, *Die Philister*, 1918; H. R. Hall, *Cambridge Anc. Hist.*, II, 283 ff.; K. B. Stark, *Gaza und die philistäische Küste*, 1852.

CHAPTER XIX

YAHWEH'S WARS

THE Hebrews found no peace in Canaan. Only the hill country was in their possession. The Great Plain which divides Canaan into two unequal portions was held by a strong line of Canaanite cities and the tribes of the south were cut off from those of the centre by the unconquered mountain fortress of Jerusalem. At no point did they reach the sea or even the fertile coastal plain.

Not only were the Hebrews divided physically, there was no sense of unity. Tribe fought tribe and there was no practical distinction between Hebrew and non-Hebrew. Even the worship of a common God was in the future, for each tribe worshipped its own tribal deity. Now that the nomads were settling down, it was necessary to add to these tribal deities the Baals and Ashtarts, the gods and goddesses of fertility, that the land might give its fruits, and with them went their fertility rituals.[1] Yahweh, God of Judah, was accepted by the Levites, who soon became in a special sense his priests, and was worshipped by Simeon when that tribe was merged with Judah. Yahweh's northward progress was slow and few of the northern Hebrews remembered him in their names. In time he became known to all the tribes but his worshippers were rarely in the majority and in no tribe was he worshipped alone.

To internal struggles were added revolts of the half-subdued Canaanites or attacks from the older culture states which could not submit to desert barbarians without an effort. Last but by no means least of the troubles suffered by the Hebrews, their own success was persuading many another desert tribe to follow their example.

The stories collected in our book of Judges were in their

[1] II Kings 17:24 ff.; Hos. 2:7 ff.; Isaiah 2:8; 5.

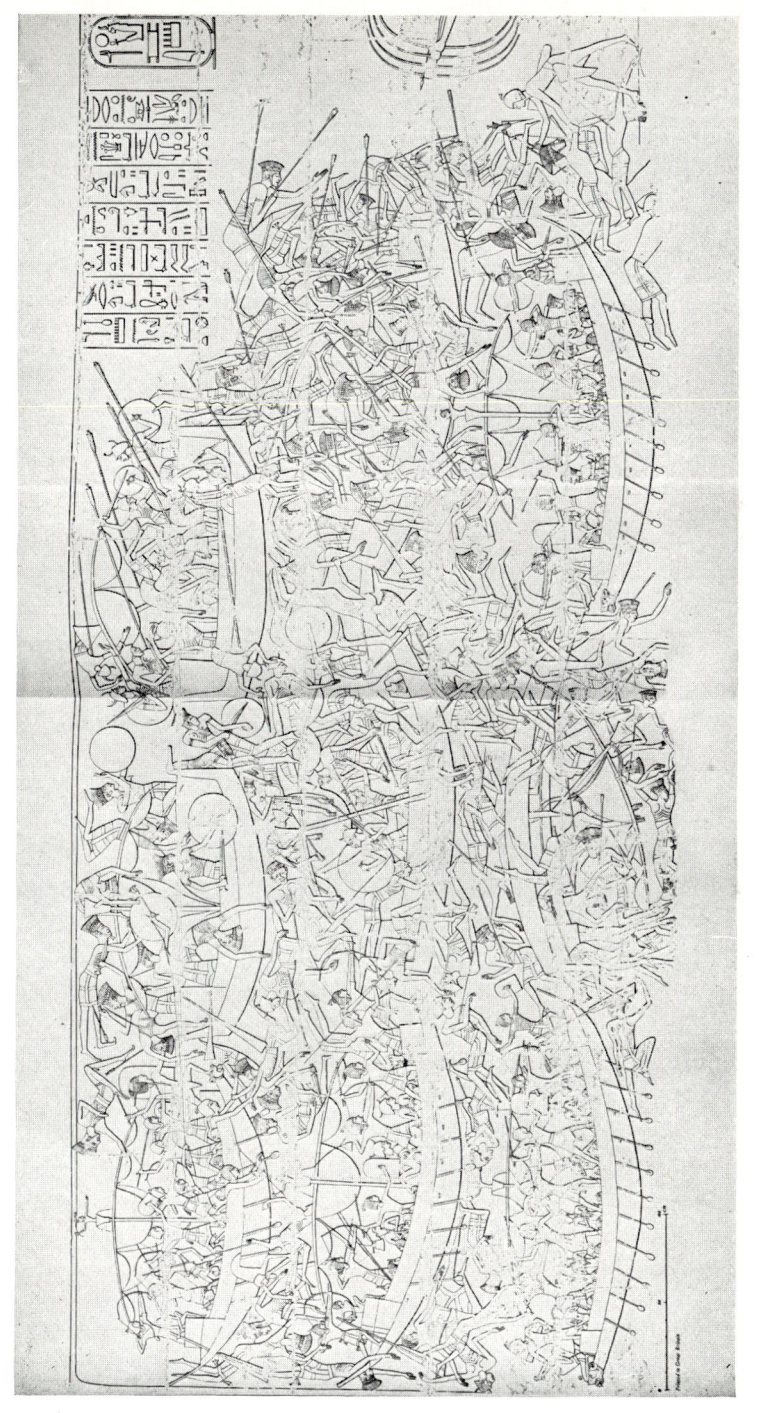

FIG. 117. NAVAL BATTLE WITH THE PHILISTINES.

original form quite without chronological indication and their relationship is in doubt. To increase our difficulty, external sources virtually cease. We can therefore only study them as fragments of a history otherwise lost.[2]

Words have their fates and there is no more curious example of perversion than that which has made "philistine" synonymous with self-satisfied ignorance. The Philistines, we have learned, were in truth a part of the wonderful Minoan world before they started on their wanderings and they settled in historic cities which had long enjoyed the closest relations with Egyptian culture. We have learned to sympathise with the Hebrews, though they too were strangers in Canaan, in whose invasion they had but little anticipated the Philistines. We should at least realise that at this time it was the Hebrews who were barbarians, that the advantages of a higher material civilisation were all on the side of their enemies.

Hebrew tribes were now settled in the Shephelah, the "Low Country." The name came from the men of the hills, from which the Shephelah does appear flat. Closer inspection proves that the Shephelah is a line of low north and south hills, paralleling the central ridge, from which it is cut off by a series of interconnecting valleys. It is a beautiful rolling country, well worth cultivation, with its reddish brown soil and its gorges of soft white chalk. The hills are breezy but the heat of the shut-in valleys is oppressive. By their occupation of the Shephelah, the Hebrews sealed the entrances up the valleys to the central range; they also prepared the way for such raids as that led by the Ephraimite Ezer and Elead, whom the men of Gath slew when they raided the cattle.[3] Their own safety demanded that the Philistines shut tightly these all too open gates; with the gates in their own possession, there was every inducement to press up the valleys to the plateau beyond.

[2]G. F. Moore, *Judges*, 1895; K. Budde, *Das Buch der Richter*, 1897; W. Nowack, *Richter, Ruth, u. Bücher Samuelis*, 1902; C. F. Burney, *Judges*, 2 ed., 1920.
[3]I Chron. 7:21.

Dan was the first Hebrew tribe with which the Philistines came into contact. Echoes of the struggle may be heard in the story of Samson. The name of Dan's great hero implies worship of the sun god Shemesh, whose traces are frequent in the nomenclature of this region. The stories themselves are filled with folk-lore motifs. But Beth Shemesh, the "Sun's House," is no astronomical *mansio* of the sun god, it is a very earthly village whose name has persisted among a little group of mud huts and whose site has been excavated. The Canaanite settlement had been burned by the Philistines, who repaired its defences and reinforced its rampart with a weaker wall. Its temple has been found, as well as a regular collection of standing stones, a socket stone, and a circular slab grooved and pitted for animal sacrifice.[4] If the "Sun's House" is not to be sought in the sky, Samson must be equally terrestrial.

Manoah, a Danite of Zorah, had no child, for his wife was barren. One day Yahweh appeared to her and announced that she was with child. Henceforth she must drink no wine or strong drink or eat anything unclean; no razor must touch the new born's head, for he was to be a Nazirite from the womb. She told her husband the message, adding that the man had the face of a god, very awful; she asked not whence he came and he told her not his name. Manoah prayed that the man return and instruct them, and his prayer was heard. He politely inquired: "What is your name that we may honour you when your words come true?" "Why do you ask my name? It is ineffable" was the disquieting reply. A kid was sacrificed on a near-by rock; as the flame ascended, Yahweh ascended with it. Full realization came to Manoah, who mourned: "We shall surely die, for we have seen a god." His wife was wiser: "Had Yahweh intended to slay us, he would not have accepted our burnt offering and given us instructions." To this day, the rock-stepped altar, covered with cup

---

[4] D. Mackenzie, *Ain Shems*, 1912–13; Elihu Grant, *QS.*, 1929, 203.

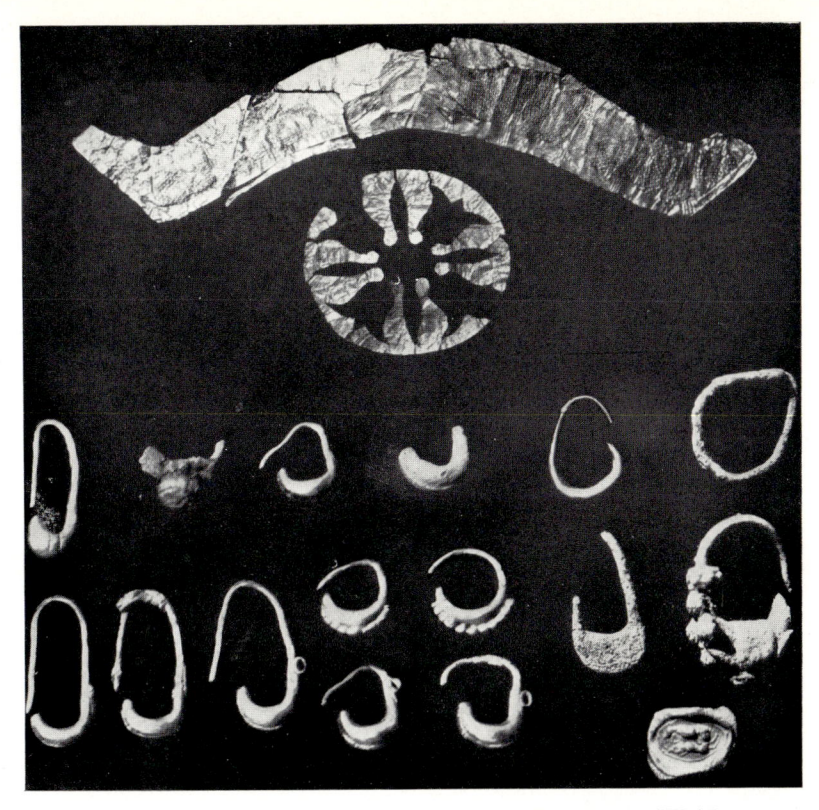

FIG. 118. GOLD FRONTLET AND GOLD EARRINGS FROM GERAR.

FIG. 119. IRON IMPLEMENTS FROM GERAR.

holes, is sprinkled with the blood of the animals sacrificed by it.[5]

In due time the son was born and named Samson. Yahweh blessed his growth and his spirit descended upon him in the Camp of Dan. On a visit to Timnath, a bare hour southwest of Zorah, he fell in love with a Philistine woman, but his father refused to ask her in marriage. A full-grown lion came roaring against him, but Yahweh's spirit rushed mightily upon Samson, and he tore the lion apart like a kid; on his return, he was amazed to find bees making honey in the carcass.

Since none of his Danite friends would attend his wedding feast, Samson chose thirty young Philistines. The feast was enlivened by a riddle:

> From eater came meat,
> From mighty came sweet.

Should it be guessed within the seven days of the feast, each attendant was to have a linen garment and festal attire; otherwise each was to pay the same forfeit. The Philistines had no intention of being beggared; they ordered the bride to learn the answer on pain of being burned with her father's house. Seven days she wept and at last Samson told her. As he was about to enter the bridal chamber, Samson was greeted with:

> What than honey is sweeter,
> What than lion is stronger?

His answer was sharp and to the point:

> With my heifer had you plowed not,
> My riddle had you guessed not.

Samson rushed back home in anger. Left in the lurch, the unfortunate bride-to-be was hastily married to Samson's best man. His anger cooled, Samson returned with a kid as gift of reconciliation. The father offered her younger and fairer

[5]Fig. 127; J. Hanauer, QS., 1885, 183 f.; R. Kittel, *Studien zur hebr. Archäologie*, 1908, 97 ff.

sister, but Samson caught three hundred foxes, tied them tail to tail with firebrands between each pair, and released them in the ripening grain. In revenge, the Philistines burned father and daughter, but Samson smote them hip and thigh.

He then took up his abode in the cleft of the rock Etam. The Philistines raided Lehi, whereupon the Judæans sent three thousand men to seize him. When he realised that his presence had excited the suspicions of their Philistine masters, Samson permitted the Judæans to bind him, only exacting an oath that they would not themselves lay hands upon him. The Philistines hurrahed at the sight of the bound hero, but Yahweh's spirit came upon him and the two new ropes melted as flax caught by the fire. Snatching up a fresh jaw bone of an ass, he smote a thousand Philistines and exulted:

> With an ass's jawbone, I made them dead asses,
> With an ass's jawbone, smote a thousand men.

Then he cast away the improptu weapon; therefore the place was called: "Throwing away the Jaw Bone."

Undeterred by his first experience of the ways of woman, Samson again fell in love, this time with a woman of Judah,[6] Delilah of the valley of Sorek. Bribed by the promise of eleven hundred shekels from each of the five Philistine tyrants, Delilah sought to discover the secret of Samson's might. First he told her it was binding with seven new bow strings, but they snapped as when a strand of tow sniffs the fire. Then it was new ropes, but he burst them like thread from his arms. Next it was weaving the seven braids of his hair into the web and beating it with the pin, but he pulled up the loom itself.

Worried to death by her importunity, Samson finally told the truth. As he slept on her knees, Delilah shaved off his seven braids and Yahweh's spirit departed from him. Deprived of his might, Samson was easily taken. His eyes were bored out and he was carried to Gaza where he was forced to turn a heavy mill in the prison.

[6] Cf. the Greek of I Chron. 4:19.

FIG. 120. MIDDLE AND LATE BRONZE POTTERY.

FIG. 121. PHILISTINE POTTERY.

At the great feast to Dagon, when their hearts were merry, the Philistine tyrants called in Samson to amuse them, while the people chanted:

> Given the god of us
> Into the hand of us
> The enemy of us
> And waster the land of us
> And who greatened the slain of us.

Samson prayed to Yahweh for vengeance for one of his two eyes. Seizing the two pillars on which the structure rested, he thrust with all the might his growing hair had restored him, and the house fell upon the tyrants and all the people gathered within. The hero was buried in his father's grave between Zorah and Eshtaol.[7]

Samson's exploits had brought Dan no safety. Philistine pressure increased and the Danites determined to migrate. Five spies were sent out from Samson's old home to look for a new abode. Their wanderings brought them to Mount Ephraim and to the house of a certain Micah.

Now this Micah by his name, "Who is like Yahweh?" was one of the rare northern Hebrews who recognised the supremacy of the southern deity. His worship of the new divinity had not raised his ethical standards, for Micah stole his mother's eleven hundred shekels of silver. His mother cursed the thief in Micah's hearing and the terrified son at once confessed. Horrified to learn that she had cursed her own son with a curse which could never be recalled, his mother first weakened the curse with "Blessed of Yahweh be my son" and then added that she had really intended to make a molten image for Yahweh but now she would dedicate it for her son. Thrift overcame her fear; nine hundred shekels were retained and but two hundred were sent to the silversmith. This was enough for an excellent molten image, fit for the private shrine in Micah's "House of Gods." To it were added an ephod or image and teraphim, the little household divinities, and over the whole was installed his son as priest.

[7] Judges 13 ff.

That the curse had indeed been averted seemed proved by the extraordinary good luck which shortly followed. A young man named Jonathan, the son of Gershom, and so grandson of the great Levite lawgiver Moses, tired of being a resident alien in Bethlehem of Judah, and set out to seek his fortune among the converts of the north. He frankly confessed that he was looking for a place and Micah was prompt in his offer: "Remain with me and be to me a father and a priest and I will give you ten silver shekels a year and a suit of clothes and your living." Such munificent terms could not be resisted; the Levite accepted and Micah thought: "Now I know that Yahweh will prosper me, for I have a Levite as priest."

When the five Danite spies reached Micah's house, they recognised the Levite's voice. To their questions, "Who brought you here? What are you doing here? What do you get here?" Jonathan proudly told them of his excellent position. Learning that he served an oracular idol, they begged him to inquire whether their journey would be successful, and were told: "Go in peace, your journey is under the watchful eye of Yahweh."

The spies reached Laish, inhabited since early bronze times, which occupied a low natural mound on the last terrace from Hermon before it sinks down to the near-by lakelet. Streams from a marsh of reeds bordered by poplars form a huge pool shaded by fine branching trees; from the pool and from smaller springs flows a clear stream to double the waters of the infant Jordan.[8] Its inhabitants dwelt in security after the manner of the Sidonians; there was no want of anything in the land but they were far from the Sidonians and they had no dealings with their neighbours, the Aramæans who had lately settled Beth Rehob. The spies returned home and reported; the land was very good and wide extending, the inhabitants were unsuspicious and unwarlike. God had already given it into their hands.

Six hundred Danite warriors set forth. Arrived at Micah's

---

[8] Fig. 122; W. F. Albright, *Ann.*, VI, 16 ff.; P. L. O. Guy, *Bull. British School Jerusalem*, VI, 75; W. J. Phythian-Adams, *Q.S.*, 1929, 59.

FIG. 122. SOURCE OF THE JORDAN AT DAN.

FIG. 123. SOURCE OF THE JORDAN AT BANIAS.

house, they decided that the oracular image which had promised them success must bring the journey to a successful conclusion. Jonathan demanded what they were doing, but the Danites had a cogent reply: "Hold your peace, put your hand on your mouth, and go with us; be *our* father and priest. What is better for you, to be priest for one man's house or to be priest for an Israelite tribe?" Jonathan saw the point. With a glad heart, he picked up the ephod, the teraphim, and the molten image, and marched away in the midst of the tribesmen. Micah collected his neighbours and pursued, but the Danites insolently demanded: "What ails you that you have collected such a crowd?" Poor Micah could only answer: "You have taken my gods that I made and my priest and gone off; what have I left and how can you ask: 'What ails you?'" For once the impetuous Ephraimites had met their match, and were forced to hear: "Let not your voice be heard among us, lest quick-tempered men fall upon you, and you lose your life and the lives of your household." Thus the curse was fulfilled and Micah lost his stolen silver.

The Danites continued on to Laish, which they found as unsuspecting as the spies had reported. Laish was burned and the inhabitants slain; perhaps at this same time Yanoam was destroyed and never rebuilt.[9] Laish was, however, restored and named Dan after the tribal ancestor. Here they set up the image with Jonathan as the tribal priest; henceforth the Danites could boast that their priests were of the blood of Moses, founder of the Yahweh religion.[10]

Jabin, king of that Hazor which played so large a part in Amarna days, led the opposition to the Hebrews in North Canaan. Jobab, king of Madon, whose thick walls of rough basaltic blocks still crown the Horns of Hattin,[11] was his chief ally, but the coalition included the kings of Shimron, Achshaph, the hill country, the Arabah south of Chinnereth, and the lowland from the heights of Dor. Strong though they were

[9] W. F. Albright, *Ann.*, VI, 23 f.   [10] Judges 17 f.; cf. Josh. 19:47.
[11] G. Dalman, *Palästina Jahrbuch*, X, 42; W. J. Phythian-Adams, *QS.*, 1929, 61.

in chariots, the allies were defeated at the Waters of Merom and chased as far as Great Sidon, Misrephoth-maim, and the valley of Mizpeh. Hazor itself was burned and its inhabitants slain under the ban. Horses and chariots were as yet unused by the Hebrews; the chariots were burned and the horses hamstrung.[12]

The Great Plain still divided the Hebrews. Early in the Iron Age the old Canaanite walled fortress which dominated the Kishon narrows was abandoned, and a new city was founded at the west end to command the spur of the Great Road which reached the sea at Accho. Harosheth "of the Foreigners," as it was called by the Hebrews, was ruled by Sisera, a non-Semitic name.[13]

Deborah, the "Bee," the wife of Lapidoth, was the moving spirit among the Hebrews. She dwelt under a palm tree and gave oracles; to this day her name is preserved by a village on a rocky ledge at the western foot of Tabor. Barak of the Naphtali Kadesh was summoned to leadership; he insisted that Deborah should accompany him and to this she agreed, but prophesied that the glory should go to a woman. Barak pitched his camp at Mount Tabor, with the hill-top city as a base, where he could receive reinforcements at the outlet of the main road from Galilee.

Word was sent to the other tribes. Judah, Simeon, and Levi were too far south for aid to be expected. Reuben too was distant and hard pressed. Three of the concubine tribes, Gad, Dan, and Asher, refused the summons. Issachar, no longer the strong-boned ass who bowed under task work, joined the northern tribes Zebulon and Naphtali, while from south of the Great Plain came Ephraim, Benjamin, and Machir, not yet reckoned a part of Manasseh.

Barak and his men rushed down from the slopes of Tabor, the other tribes advanced from the south. It was the rainy season and a sudden shower turned the plain into a morass into which the chariots of Sisera sank. The Kishon is never a

---

[12] Josh. 11; cf. Judges 4:2.
[13] *Bull. British School Jerusalem*, II, 10 ff.; cf. W. F. Albright, *Ann.*, II, 21.

great stream, its channel is rarely more than a few feet deep, but its banks are treacherous; swollen with floods, it swept away the retreating chariotry.

While Barak pursued the enemy to Harosheth, Sisera fled eastward on foot. He found refuge with Jael, wife of the Kenite Heber, and was hidden with a rug in her tent. When he begged for water, she opened a skin of soured milk and gave him a refreshing drink. Now *lebben,* as every traveller knows, is strangely soporific; no sooner was Sisera asleep than Jael pinned him to the ground with mallet and tent peg. Barak arrived to find in truth that victory had gone to a woman.

Thanks to Deborah and Barak, the danger of a disunited Israel had been at least partially averted. The list of tribes which had taken part was a roll of honour, the tribes who had refused participation felt keenly the disgrace. A contemporary immortalised the victory in a war song:

> For Israel's wide streaming locks,
> For volunteer folk Yahweh praise!
> Hear ye kings, give ear, ye mighty,
> I to Yahweh, I will sing,
> Hymn to Yahweh, Israel's God.
>
> Yahweh, in thy going from Seir,
> In thy march from Edom's field,
> Earth shook, and the heavens in tumult,
> The clouds too down dripped water,
> Mountains shook at face of Yahweh,
> At face of Yahweh, Israel's God.
>
> In days of Shamgar, son of Anath,
> In days of old, the caravans ceased;
> By crooked pathways went the travellers,
> Ceased the hamlets, in Israel ceased,
> Till thou didst arise, Deborah,
> Didst arise as a mother in Israel.
>
> Ceased the offerings to God,
> Failed the barley cakes;
> Was shield to be seen or spear

Mid Israel's forty thousand?
My heart is for Israel's rulers,
Volunteers of the folk, Yahweh praise!

Riders on tawney she asses,
Who sit on saddle blankets,
And walk the paths, speak out:
Voice of mirth makers at the wells,
There they Yahweh's justness recount,
Justness to his peasants in Israel.

Rouse thee, rouse thee, Deborah!
Rouse thee, rouse thee, chant the song!
Rise up, Barak, and lead captive
Thy captors, Abinoam's son!
Then down to the gates marched the nobles,
Marched down Yahweh's folk mid the heroes.

From Ephraim, they spread in the valley,
"After thee, Benjamin!" mid thy clansmen;
From Machir descended commanders,
From Zebulon scepter bearers;
And Issachar's chiefs with Deborah,
And Naphtali, loyal to Barak,
In the valley loosed at his feet.

Rent into factions was Reuben,
Great were his searchings of heart;
Why didst thou sit mid the sheep folds
To list to the piping for flocks?
Gilead stayed beyond Jordan,
And Dan was an alien in ships;
Asher sat still on the sea shore,
By his landing places he dwelt;
Zebulon risked his life to the dying,
Naphtali on the heights of the field.

On came the kings, they battled,
Then battled Canaan's kings;
At Taanach, by Megiddo's waters,
Gain of silver could not take;
From heaven the stars made battle,
They fought with Sisera from their paths.

The torrent of Kishon swept them,
Kishon's torrent of old;
Then hammered the hoofs of his horses,
Galloped and galloped his steeds.
"Curse ye Meroz" saith Yahweh,
"Curse ye, curse ye her folk,
"For they came not to Yahweh's assistance,
"With the heroes to give Yahweh aid."

Blessed of women be Jael,
Of women in tents most blessed,
Water he asked, milk she gave him,
In lordly bowl brought him curds.

Her hand to the tent peg she put,
And her right to the carpenter's mallet;
She hammered and shattered his head,
She smashed and pierced his temples;
Between her feet he sank, he fell,
The place he sank he lay unmoved.

From the window peers and gazes
Sisera's mother through the lattice;
"Why delays his chariot's coming,
"Why tarry his chariot hoof beats?"

Her wisest princess answers,
She herself repeats her discourse:
"Sure, they find and portion spoil,
"For each man a wench or two.

"Spoil of dyed stuffs for Sisera,
"Spoil of dyed stuffs embroidered,
"Dyed stuffs twice embroidered,
"For my neck as spoil—"

So perish all thy foes, Yahweh,
Thy friends as the rising sun in his might.[14]

Gilead had good excuse for remaining beyond Jordan, for there was constant pressure from the Ammonites. In their extremity, the Gileadites appealed to Jephthah, the son of a

[14]Judges 5.

harlot, who had been expelled by his legitimate brothers and had fled to the Aramæan Tob, where he had made his reputation as leader of a robber band. Jephthah refused to become their war chief unless he was also promised their headship in peace, and oath to this effect was taken before Yahweh in Mizpah. Then the spirit of Yahweh seized upon Jephthah and he smote the Ammonites from Aroer to Minnith, twenty cities, as far as the Meadow of Vineyards.

Before leaving home, Jephthah had vowed that if he returned in peace he would sacrifice as a burnt offering to Yahweh the first person who came out to meet him from his house. His intent was clear, he would reward Yahweh's aid with a human sacrifice, but he never suspected that his only child, a daughter, would be leading the welcoming procession with tambourine and dance. Jephthah's anguish was great, but he had opened his mouth to Yahweh, he could not turn back. His heroic daughter insisted that he must fulfil his vow; her only request was that she be permitted a respite of two months during which she and her maidens might bewail on the mountains her unmarried state. Then, still a virgin and so the most acceptable of sacrifices, Jephthah did to her that which he had vowed. Centuries later, the maidens commemorated her untimely fate by a yearly lamentation of four days.

Return to war must have been a relief to Jephthah. The Ephraimites had refused aid in the Ammonite wars, but now they crossed the Jordan to Zaphon and threatened to burn Jephthah's house because they had not been summoned! Jephthah levied his Gileadites and the Ephraimites were defeated. The Jordan fords were guarded, and when the fugitives denied that they were Ephraimites, there was one simple test; required to pronounce Shibboleth, they always said Sibboleth and were slain without mercy.[15]

Manasseh suffered from inroads of the Midianites, whose eponymous ancestor the genealogies made a son of Abraham by his second wife Keturah.[16] From their home east of the Red Sea, the Midianites worked their way north along the

[15] Judges 11 f.   [16] Gen. 25:1 ff.

desert fringe. They were defeated in the field of Moab by the Edomite king Hadad I,[17] but swept on northward up the Tent Dwellers' Road east of Nobah and Jogbehah, crossed the Jordan, and pastured their flocks in the Great Plain, even as the Bedawin did to our own day.

Salvation came from Gideon, son of Joash, of the sub tribe of Abiezer, whose home was in Ophrah, at the head of a great valley looking towards the Jordan. As he was beating out wheat in his winepress, hidden from the invaders, he beheld Yahweh seated under the sacred terebinth. "Yahweh is with you, man of might," was the greeting. "Good sir," replied Gideon, "if Yahweh is with us, why has all this befallen us?" "Go in your might and save Israel from the hand of Midian" was the unexpected answer. Gideon remonstrated: "Good sir, how can I save Israel? Behold, my clan is the weakest in Manasseh, and I am the least in my father's house." The visitor insisted: "Yahweh will be with you and you shall smite the Midianites as one man." Believing that he was facing an inferior spirit, Gideon begged him to wait for a gift. A kid and unleavened bread were made ready, the meat was placed in a basket and the broth in a pot, and the food was presented to the divine guest; at his orders, the meat and the cakes were set on a rock and the broth was poured out, doubtless in cup holes. Yahweh then touched the food with the tip of his staff, fire arose from the rock and consumed the flesh and the cakes, and Yahweh disappeared. Gideon feared, for he had seen Yahweh face to face, but Yahweh comforted him: "Peace to you; fear not, you shall not die." In honour of the divine visitation, Gideon set up the altar "Yahweh is Peace," which was in use at Ophrah for many centuries.

The Midianites encamped under Mount Moreh and at the near-by Tabor slew Gideon's brothers. To the wrongs of his people was now added the sacred duty of the blood revenge. The spirit of Yahweh clothed itself in Gideon, and he led his clan to the spring of Harod on the opposite side of the valley under Mount Gilboa. With his squire, Gideon went down by

[17]Gen. 36:35; cf. Num. 22:4 ff.

night to the enemy's camp, where a Midianite was relating a dream of a barley cake which tumbled into camp and overturned his tent; this lowly symbol prophesied that Yahweh had delivered the invaders into the hands of the Hebrew peasants. Shouting "The sword of Yahweh and of Gideon," the three hundred Abiezerites drove the nomads down to Beth Shittah.

Pursuit was continued across Jordan. To a request for a few cakes to feed his exhausted followers, the men of Succoth insolently answered: "Are the hands of Zebah and Zalmunna already in your hand that we should give food to your army?" The same reply was made by the men of Penuel. With threats of vengeance, Gideon hastened on to Karkor and captured the two Midianite kings. On his return, he caught a youth of Succoth, who wrote down for him the names of the officials and elders of the town; as he had promised, Gideon took desert thorns and thistles and carded the men of Succoth. He also broke down the tower of Penuel and slew its inhabitants.

Gideon then demanded of Zebah and Zalmunna: "Where are the men you slew at Tabor?" True to nomad character, they disdained to lie but boasted: "They were like you, each was like a king's son." Gideon's duty was clear: "They were my brothers, sons of my mother; as Yahweh lives, had you spared them, I would not kill you." Revenge was the privilege of his first born Jether: "Up, slay them!" The boy was young and hesitated to draw his sword against full-grown men. Zebah and Zalmunna protested; die they must and they were ready, but to die at the hands of a boy was eternal disgrace. "Up and slay us yourself," they begged, "for you have a man's strength." Their request was reasonable and as brave men they should be spared unnecessary indignity, so Gideon himself slew them. From the golden earrings of the slain, Gideon made an ephod or image which he set up in Ophrah, and there he ruled as shophet or war chief; it was a far cry to the civilised Phœnician shophet who ruled Citium in Cyprus or Marseilles in Gaul, in Malta and Sardinia, over the Phœnician metics in the Piræus, or the two shophets who annually headed the

Carthaginians and suggested their two consuls to the Romans.[18]

By his many wives, Gideon had seventy sons, to whom must be added Abimelech, born of a Canaanite concubine in Shechem. Shechem had remained in possession of the Canaanites, though it had accepted the overlordship of Manasseh. The older cyclopean wall with its northwest gate and western palace had been destroyed, perhaps when it was taken by the Hebrews; over the whole ruin was now packed closely a mass of marl to form a glacis to a new double wall some twelve yards inside. It was constructed of stones appreciably smaller, for only at the angles were well-coursed larger blocks, and was defended by towers and projections. The space between the walls, twelve feet, was filled with earth and stone or with casemates. The main gate was now at the east, of mud brick over well-hewn orthostate blocks, with flanking towers and a single court fifty-three feet wide. A new palace was built east of the old northwest gate, of inferior stones with white lime plaster. Next the gate were three tiny connected rooms, then a larger hall, twenty-seven by twenty-five feet, which opened into two irregular rooms to the east.[19]

The temple of Baal Berith had also changed. Three successive terrace walls had enlarged the sacred area to the city wall. Twenty feet from the temple the visitor reached a base of small stones and earth for an altar, some seven by five feet in size. Southeast of the altar and eight feet from the temple was the sacred stone of smoothed hard white limestone. rounded on the sides and perhaps on the top, five feet wide, a foot and a third deep, and at least six feet high, and set in a block of soft yellowish limestone. At either side of the temple entrance were the sacred pillars, likewise smoothed and set in limestone blocks. The ramp approach had been supplanted by stone steps. The temple itself stood on a foundation eighteen feet high and was seventy feet broad by ninety long. An en-

[18] CIS. I, 47, 165, 118, 124, 143.
[19] Plan 8; E. Sellin, *ZDPV.*, XLIX, 1926, 306 ff.; L, 1927, 207 f.; 270 ff.; LI, 1928, 119.

trance hall twenty-three by seventeen feet, flanked by two tower-like projections, led through a door to the cult room, thirty-seven feet wide by forty-five long. Two rows of wooden columns on stone bases and with Egyptian volutes as capitals

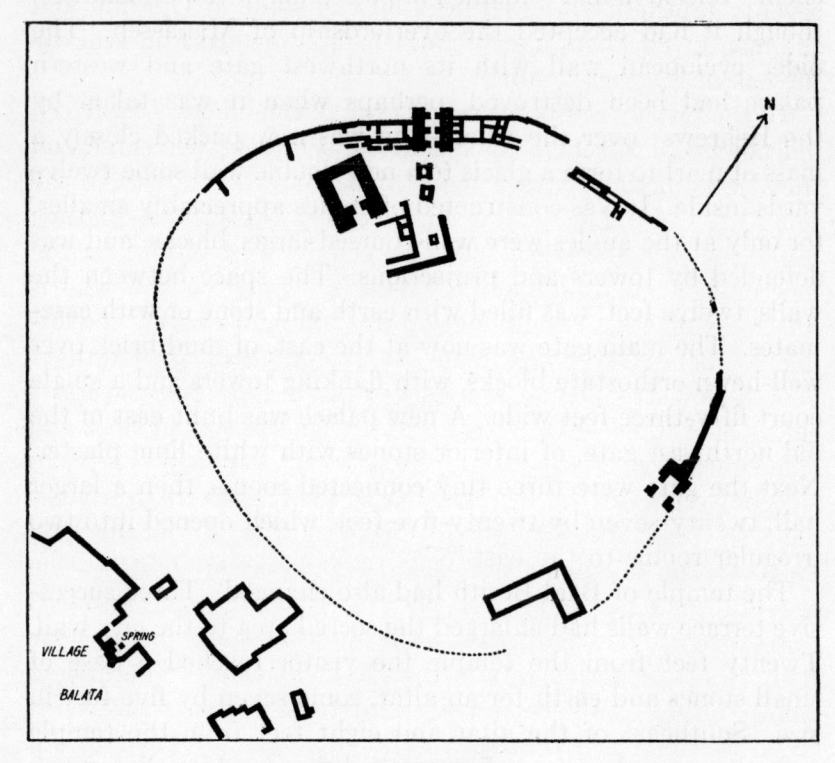

PLAN 8. SHECHEM.
City Wall, North and East Gates, East and West Palaces, Sacred Place, Terraces, and Temple of the Lord of the Covenant.

divided the room into three aisles. Between the two middle columns stood the statue of Baal Berith on a round stone base a foot and a third in diameter. A base half as large on the north side may have been for a statue of his consort, a depression to the west perhaps held the sacred pole.[20]

At his father's death, Abimelech hastened to Shechem and

[20]Fig. 124 f.; E. Sellin, *ZDPV.*, XLIX, 1926, 309 ff.; LI, 1928, 119 ff.

through his mother's brothers persuaded the citizens to accept him as of their bone and flesh in place of his Israelite half brothers. They granted him seventy shekels from the temple treasury of the Covenant Baal and he hired mercenaries. His seventy brothers were sacrificed on one stone at Ophrah, and the men of Shechem and of Beth Millo crowned him king by the oak of the sacred stone.

To the bitter disappointment of the Shechemites, Abimelech did not make Shechem his residence. Vintage time came and they trod out their grapes, made high festival, and entered the temple to eat and drink. As the wine began to take effect, they fell to reviling Abimelech. The occasion was propitious for the newcomer Gaal to demand: "Who is Abimelech and who is Shechem that we should serve him? Should not he and his deputy Zebul serve the men of Hamor, Shechem's father? Would that this people were under my hand! Then would I rid us of Abimelech and say to him: 'Increase your host and come out!'"

Zebul reported the drunken boast to Abimelech who hastened by night from Arumah. Next morning from the gate Gaal saw the advancing troops, but Zebul reassured him: "You see hill shadows and think they are men." Gaal insisted: "See, men are descending from the Navel of the Land and one body is advancing by way of the Diviner's Oak." Then Zebul taunted him: "Where now is that mouth of yours that said: 'Who is Abimelech that we should serve him?' Pray go out now and fight with them!" Shamed into action, Gaal led out the cititzens but was defeated and driven into exile. After an all-day struggle, the city was captured and the inhabitants slain. The guard of the Tower of Shechem took refuge in the cave under the temple of El Berith. Abimelech cut brushwood from Mount Zalmon, piled it over the cave, and thus killed all the men and women within. The palace and the temple of El Berith were destroyed, the temple entrance was blocked by the sacred pillars, the city was sown with salt.

Thebez was next attacked; the town was taken but the citizens fled to a strong tower in its centre. Abimelech attempted to fire its door but a woman cast down a millstone from the roof and crushed his skull. Lest it be said that a woman slew him, Abimelech ordered his squire to use his sword. Shechem was reoccupied. A small dwelling was built within the temple proper, other poorly constructed houses grew up in the sacred area, but the standing stone by the altar remained and pottery and later columns prove that the cult was still practised.[21]

A half century after Ramses III, Egyptian rule was forgotten. In the fifth year of Ramses XI, about 1114, a certain Wenamon was despatched by Hrihor of Thebes to secure cedar for Amon's new bark. Nesubenebded of Tanis promised to forward his journey and handed him over to the Phœnician captain Mengebet, with whom he descended to the Great Sea of Kharu. His first point of call was Dor.

Beder, king of Dor, sent Wenamon a guest present of fifty loaves of bread, a jug of wine, and a joint of beef. Then Wenamon's troubles began. A thief stole from his ship the money with which he was to purchase the timber. Next morning Wenamon demanded that Beder search for the money. Beder assured him that had the thief been his subject, the money would have been advanced from his own treasury; since the thief came from Wenamon's ship, he must disclaim all responsibility, though he would make search. Nine days passed and his ship lay in the harbour, so the discouraged Wenamon asked permission to depart.

Tyre was reached, and soon after Wenamon met some Zakkalu with a bag containing almost the exact amount he had lost. He took the silver and refused to return it until his own money was restored. Having thus made the Zakkalu his enemies, he sailed on to Gebal, where he hid the image of "Amon of the Way," who had thus far proved a most indifferent conductor.

Zakar Baal was now prince of Gebal; his name meant "Baal remembers," and he had not forgotten how Egyptian rulers had allowed his predecessor Rib Addi to perish. Nineteen suc-

[21] Judges 6 ff.; E. Sellin, *ZDPV.*, L, 1927, 206 f., 266; LI, 1928, 122.

FIG. 124. ALTAR AND STANDING STONE AT SHECHEM.

FIG. 125. EAST GATE OF SHECHEM AND ISRAELITE HOUSES.

cessive days he sent to Wenamon: "Get out of my harbour!" At last, Wenamon was ready to take his advice. He found a ship and had embarked all his belongings but the god when the harbour master appeared with orders to wait until morning.

That day Zakar Baal had sacrificed to his gods. A divine frenzy seized one of his youths, who ordered the prince to summon Amon and his messenger, since it was Amon who had sent him. Morning came and Wenamon was called before Zakar Baal. "I found him," writes Wenamon, "sitting in his upper chamber, and leaning his back against a window, while the waves of the great Syrian sea beat against the shore behind him." To his salutation "Kindness of Amon," Zakar Baal abruptly demanded how long since he had left the abode of Amon, and learned that it was five months and a day. Next Zakar Baal asked for the writing of Amon and of his high priest. Wenamon naïvely confessed that he had left them with the Delta prince, and was quite taken back when the wrathful Zakar Baal inquired where were the ship and Syrian crew given him by Nesubenebded, for surely he had not been handed over to a mere ship captain to be killed and thrown into the sea. Wenamon explained that it was really an Egyptian ship, since Nesubenebded had no Syrian crews, but Zakar Baal caught him up on this: "There are surely twenty ships here in my harbour which are in partnership with Nesubenebded, while at Sidon there are fifty more which are in partnership with Bereketel and sail to his house," the emporium of the great Phœnician merchant in Tanis.

This was a facer. Wenamon at this point inserts in his report the amusing aside: "Then was I silent in this great hour." Zakar Baal now asked the purpose of the visit. Wenamon was so tactless as to remind the prince that his father and grandfather had given cedar to the Pharaoh and suggested that he do the same. Zakar Baal admitted that cedar had been provided, but it had not been for nothing; the Pharaoh had sent six ships, laden with the products of Egypt, which were unloaded into the Phœnician storehouses. To prove that this was no exaggeration, he ordered the journal of his fathers to be brought and read; Wenamon was horrified to find mention of a thousand deben, nearly two hundred pounds, of silver.

Zakar Baal proceeded to rub it in: "If the ruler of Egypt had been the master of my property, and I had been his servant, he would not have sent silver and gold, neither was it a king's gift they exacted from my father. I too am neither your servant nor the servant of him who sent you." After making it perfectly clear that he was under no compulsion to provide free cedar, Zakar Baal relented: "If I cry out to the Lebanon, the heavens open and the logs lie here on the seashore." Let Wenamon furnish sails for the ships and cordage for the logs, for it is the season when Amon thunders and Sutekh raves and there is danger that the ship may break up and Wenamon perish in the waves. Egypt is the land from which civilisation came to Phœnicia, artisanship and teaching came from it to reach his abode; why then have they made Wenamon go on these miserable journeys?

Wenamon resorted to pure bluff. Every ship on the sea, the sea itself, the very Lebanon which Zakar Baal claims, all belong to Amon, yet Zakar Baal has forced the god to wait twenty-nine days while he bargained about Lebanon with its divine master. Amon was the lord of Zakar Baal's fathers, he too is a servant of Amon. His fathers indeed were given gifts, but Amon has promised Zakar Baal something far better, life and health.

Appeal to superstition as little affected the hard-headed merchant prince as the former appeal to history. Wenamon was forced to offer something more tangible. His scribe was instructed to write Nesubenebded for all that was needed. Here at last was language that Zakar Baal could understand. To show his willingness to go more than half way, he even sent an instalment of seven logs before the pay arrived. The ship returned in forty-eight days with what Zakar Baal had demanded, vessels of gold and silver, ten garments each of royal and Upper Egyptian linen, twenty measures of lentils and thirty of fish, five hundred coils of rope, five hundred rolls of papyri and the same number of "ox hides," probably parchment.

Three hundred men with three hundred oxen were appointed to fell the trees, which were left to season over winter and next summer were dragged to the shore. Zakar Baal went down to inspect them. As the shadow of the royal parasol fell on Wenamon, the Egyptian butler cracked the first recorded joke of history: "The shadow of Pharaoh, your lord, falls upon you." The joke was not particularly good nor was it exactly respectful to Zakar Baal; he sharply rebuked his underling and showed that he too could joke, though after the grimmer Semitic fashion: "Come not to contemplate the terror of the sea"—Wenamon was doubtless showing how much he wished he was already safely home across the waters—"but regard my terror also. Indeed, I have not treated you as they did the messengers of Ramses IX. They passed seventeen years in this land and they died where they were. Take him," turning to his butler, "and let him see their tombs where they sleep."

Wenamon's badly frayed nerves gave way, and "Let me not see it" he cried. Recovering a little of his courage, he reminded Zakar Baal that the messengers sent by Ramses IX were mere men, but now he was visited by a god. Let him write on a tablet all that he did for Amon and his messenger, beseeching ten thousand years of life; then, when a messenger comes from Egypt and reads his name on the tablet, Zakar Baal will receive water in the west like the gods who are there. Zakar Baal had extorted all that he could for the logs and his only comment was the dry "It is a great testimony of which you tell me."

The logs were piled on the shore when eleven Zakkalu ships appeared to arrest Wenamon and to prevent his ships from reaching Egypt. Wenamon sat down and wept. Zakar Baal knew by this time the character of his visitor. His secretary was sent to cheer Wenamon with a ram, two jugs of wine, and Tentnut, an Egyptian songstress who had migrated to Phœnicia to seek her fortune and was now in the king's employ. Then the Zakkalu were summoned and asked their business; they were informed that Zakar Baal could not arrest Amon's messenger in Gebal, but Wenamon would be given sailing orders and after that they were free to pursue him.

Wenamon escaped the Zakkalu, only to be driven to Cyprus. Men from the city came out to slay him, but finally brought him to Queen Heteb. Through a bystander who spoke Egyptian, he pled for his life, reminding her of the danger of reprisals for the slaughter of a crew belonging to the prince of Gebal. The queen bade him lie down and sleep—and the papyrus suddenly ends.[22]

Phœnician independence of and contempt for Egypt could not be more clearly expressed. So far as Egypt was concerned, Phœnicia was safe, but there was menace from the northeast. Just ten years after the ill-fated trip of Wenamon, in 1104, the first Assyrian army appeared in Syria. Tiglath Pileser I crossed the Euphrates, subdued Carchemish, and colonised Mutkinu on the right bank. Wild bulls were hunted under Mount Lebanon and cedar logs were cut for the temple of Anu and Adad at Ashur. Amurru submitted and Gebal, where perhaps Zakar Baal still was prince, Sidon, and Arvad hastened to placate the new invader by their tribute. From Arvad, he was taken over the Great Sea of Amurru to the mainland at Simyra, killing on the way a "horse of the sea," a dolphin. At the Dog River, where Ramses II had left his memorial, Tiglath Pileser carved his low squat figure with little attention to detail. Egypt still made claim of Syria and its king, presumably that Nesubenebded who had been patron of Wenamon, despatched an embassy to the Assyrian, doubtless reminding him of Egypt's former ownership. Tiglath Pileser could smile at the tribute which Thutmose III listed from a chief of Ashur; he does not even give the Egyptian's name but merely mentions the crocodile he received.

On his return, Tiglath Pileser reduced the whole Hittite land and inflicted tribute and a gift of cedar logs on Ili Teshup, king of Great Hatte, which now meant North Syria. This time, we may be sure, there was no haggling over terms. Later, he

[22] V. Golénischeff, *Rec. Travaux,* XXI, 1899, 74 ff.; Breasted, *Rec.,* IV, 274 ff.

pursued the Aramæans from Tadmar of Amurru to Anat and Rapihu on the Euphrates, the first reference to the desert route by Tadmor or Palmyra. With the retirement of Tiglath Pileser, Syria was left to her own devices for nearly two centuries. But the Assyrians were to return.[23]

[23]*History of Assyria*, 64 ff.

CHAPTER XX

SAUL, FIRST KING OF ISRAEL

SHILOH was founded by Ephraimites in the thirteenth century.[1] The site was at the upper end of a long plain, with views of Osha and over the neighbouring grey hills the blue-white frosty glow of Hermon. A temple enshrined an ark or box which witnessed the presence of Yahweh of Hosts. The ark was served by Eli, like Jonathan a Levite, and thus in a sense a missionary of Yahweh from the south. When the ark went forth before Ephraim to battle, the warriors chanted:

> Arise, Yahweh, scattered be thy foes,
> And flee thy haters before thee;

when it was brought back:

> Return, Yahweh, to the thousands of Israel.[2]

At harvest, there was a pilgrimage feast, a time of good cheer and rejoicing before Yahweh, now identified with the fertility gods. The maidens danced in the vineyards south of the town, still named the "Meadow of the Feast," and there were seized by their future husbands. Denied a child, the barren wife visited the shrine in full belief that prayer for a son would be granted. A night's sleep in the holy place might be favoured by a vision.

Philistine tyrants could not rest content in the plain when there was danger from the hills. From the territory abandoned by Dan, there was easy approach to Mount Ephraim. About 1080, the Philistines marched out to Aphek, near the great spring in the gorge leading to Shiloh, while the Ephraimites

---

[1] W. F. Albright, *QS.*, 1927, 157 f.; Hans Kjaer, *JPOS.*, X, 1930, 87 ff.; *QS.*, 1931, 71 ff.
[2] Num. 10:35 f.

and Benjaminites collected at Ebenezer. The name, "Stone of Help," was no omen, for the Hebrews were defeated. Then the ark was brought to camp by Eli's sons Hophni and Phinehas. The appearance of the Hebrew God in person sorely frightened the Philistines, but they fought with the courage of despair, slew many Hebrews including Eli's sons, and captured the ark. Shiloh was destroyed and abandoned, never to be inhabited until the Hebrews lost their independence.

The ark was placed in the Dagon temple at Ashdod, but the Philistine god fell in submission to his divine captive and was broken. Mice spread the Egyptian bubonic plague, and this was attributed to the presence of the hostile deity. The priests and diviners advised that the ark be returned with golden mice and models of the bubonic tumors to placate the offended divinity. It was placed on a new cart, drawn by two milch cows; if the cows abandoned their calves, it was proof that Yahweh had inflicted the evil.

Lowing as they went, in protest against the divine compulsion which separated them from their young, the cows took the straight path to Beth Shemesh. The men of Beth Shemesh were reaping their wheat in the valley below their hillside town, and went rejoicing to meet the ark. A great stone was set up, the cart was split for fuel, and the cows were sacrificed. But the plague followed the ark, and the affrighted citizens begged the men of Kiriath Jearim to take the dangerous cult object. The head man of Kiriath Jearim, Abinadab, placed the ark in his house and consecrated his son Eleazer as its guardian.[3]

Yahweh's ark was safe and in Hebrew territory, but the land itself was under Philistine hegemony. A Philistine governor had his seat at Gibeah of God, just east of the Bethel shrine, and thus kept watch on the north and south road along the ridge. So thoroughly had the Hebrews been disarmed that no

[3] I Sam. 3 ff.; cf. H. P. Smith, *The Books of Samuel*, 1899; K. Budde, *Die Bücher Samuel*, 1902; W. Nowack, *Richter, Ruth, u. Bücher Samuelis*, 1902; P. Dhorme, *Les Livres de Samuel*, 1910; S. R. Driver, *Notes on the Hebrew Text and the Topography of the Books of Samuel*, 2 ed., 1913; W. Caspari, *Die Samuelbücher*, 1926.

smith was left in all the land to make spear or sword. Even to sharpen their implements, the peasants must go down to the "Valley of Smiths" and pay designedly high prices. To sharpen a plowshare cost a payam, some thirty cents coin value, but a full month's wage at current rates; an axe or ox goad might be used in warfare, and their sharpening was put at eight dollars.[4]

After a full generation of Philistine oppression, salvation came from the tribe of Benjamin and the sons of the prophets. Benjamin had been forced to pay tribute to Eglon, king of Moab. One day Ehud, Gera's son, appeared with his tribute in the Moabite capital. He shortly returned alone with the promise of a divine message. Eglon dismissed his courtiers and rose in deference to the pretended oracle, when Ehud, who as a left-handed man had been able to conceal his foot-long knife on his right thigh, drove it into the body of the fat old man. Carefully locking the doors of the cool upper chamber, he escaped to the hills; then he summoned the clansmen by the trumpet, seized the fords, and slaughtered all the Moabites west of the Jordan.[5]

A still more terrible danger faced Benjamin, this time not from foreigners but from enraged fellow Hebrews. The wife of a Levite, a resident alien in Ephraim, returned to her father's home in Bethlehem. Her penitent husband followed her and won her back. His repeated efforts to start were repeatedly frustrated by her father's hospitality and it was late when he tore himself away. Two hours brought him opposite Jerusalem, where his servant wished to lodge, but Jerusalem was a foreign city[6] and the Benjaminite Gibeah was only an hour distant. The travellers seated themselves in the square where they were forced to wait until invited home by another resident alien.

While they were making glad their hearts, the men of Gibeah beat upon the door and made the demand of Sodom. The laws of hospitality evidently did not include women, for

---

[4]Cf. E. J. Pilcher, *QS.*, 1916, 77 ff.
[5]Judges 3:12 ff.   [6]Fig. 129.

the unfortunate wife was thrust outside to satisfy the lusts of the citizens. Next morning, she lay at the door, her hands on the threshold in mute appeal to laws of hospitality which applied only to her husband. "Get up, let us be going," was his brutal salutation, but she was dead. Even then, the pathos of

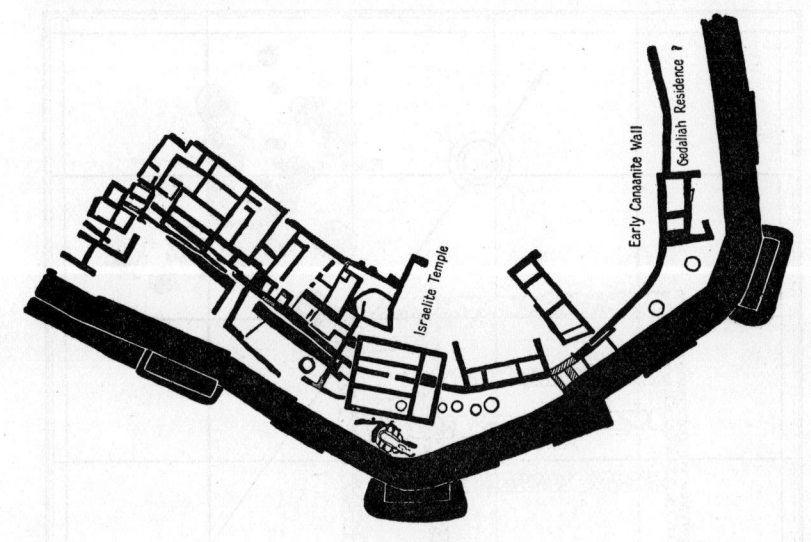

PLAN 9. MIZPAH.

her death was quite lost on the Levite, who knew only that he had been deprived of a valued piece of property. Her poor body was not given decent burial but was cut up and sent in fragments to the neighbouring tribesmen.

Thus far, the story follows the common scheme whereby a wronged woman is the cause of a war. Historical or not, it throws a lurid light on the morals of the early Hebrews. The war which followed was certainly historical. Mizpah, the "Watch Tower," was the rallying point of the tribesmen. The great Canaanite wall had not been rebuilt, but was covered with debris and a path took the place of the south gate to the spring. Population had increased and flourishing suburbs grew up on the broad level terraces east and south of the mound. Philistine pottery indicates close relations with if not conquest by the aliens on the plains.

298   PALESTINE AND SYRIA

West of the sacred cave and cup-holed rock of Canaanite times the Hebrews built their temple to Yahweh over the old city wall. The side facing the sacred "Place" formed one room, eight by thirty feet, and led to the inner shrine, ten by twenty-

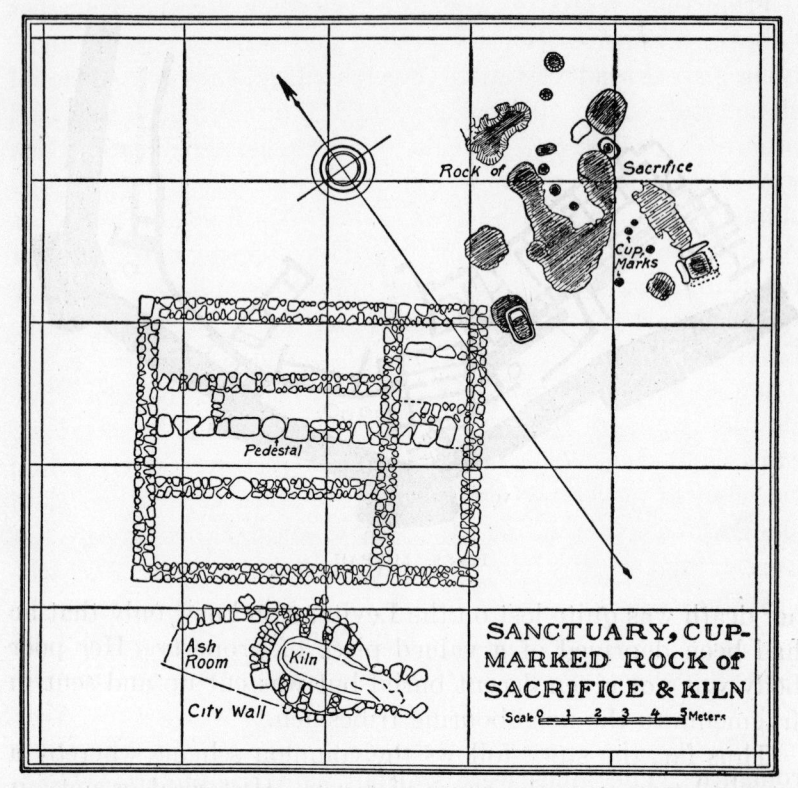

PLAN 10. PREHISTORIC ROCK ALTAR AND ISRAELITE TEMPLE AT MIZPAH.

six; in its centre and resting on a fragment of the Canaanite wall was the altar base, rounded roughly and chipped flat on top. On either side the shrine was a smaller room with storage bin, while in one were found two flint knives which may have been used for circumcision. But Yahweh did not reign alone. To the east was another temple of exactly the same plan, with a bin, a stone basin, and a table of two flat rocks in the shrine.

A clay dove, a female figurine coated with white slip and painted red, a lamp set on a triple-forked tree, all found in the temple, numerous figurines and a conical stone discovered near by, these prove beyond doubt that Ashtart was worshipped by the side and perhaps as consort of Yahweh.[7]

From the "Watch Tower" the tribesmen advanced against Gibeah, founded a century before, and protected by a high-lying two-storied fort with heavy walls of large polygonal stones, set with cypress and pine.[8] The Bethel oracle had promised success, but the first two attacks were beaten back with heavy loss by the seven hundred famous left-handed slingers, who boasted they could sling at a hair and not miss. An ambush was then laid in the little valley to the west. For the third time the Benjaminites drove the invaders north by the highroad to Bethel and by the path through the fields to Geba, but the men in hiding entered the city and set it on fire. The rising smoke was the signal for the allies to reform, while the Benjaminites fled to the rough country which breaks down towards Jordan. They were overtaken just east of Geba and the greater part destroyed. Then the allies turned back and slaughtered every living being they could find. Gibeah was burned, and to this day the stratum of ashes remains to witness the essential truth of the story.

Six hundred Benjaminites broke through the pursuit and took refuge in the caves of the tall conical rock of Rimmon, whose bare chalky top is a landmark for miles around. After four months, they were granted truce. Again the tale becomes romantic. The allies were smitten with compunction lest a fellow tribe be blotted out for lack of wives. They had sworn not to give their daughters to any Benjaminite, but the oath could be evaded. Jabesh Gilead had not joined the crusade, so it was sacked and its inhabitants killed, all but four hundred virgins reserved for the bachelors of Benjamin. Still there were not enough women, so the wifeless Benjaminites were in-

[7]Fig. 128; plan 9 f.; W. F. Badè, *Excavations at Tell-Nasbeh*, 30 ff.; QS., 1930, 8 ff.
[8]Fig. 126.

structed to seize each man his mate as the maidens of Shiloh danced in the vineyards. Thus they could return and rebuild their cities.[9]

Benjamin's destruction cannot have been as complete as the tale would imply, for a Benjaminite first united the Hebrews. His father Kish was a man of substance and Saul himself was in the prime of life and of impressive appearance. How he became king is the subject of an early story. Saul was hunting his father's lost asses. He had searched the valleys to the Jordan and circled around to the Twin Ramahs, and was ready to stop. His attendant suggested that he visit the man of God at Ramah, but Saul objected that he had no money. Fortunately, the attendant had brought a quarter of a shekel, fifteen cents, and this was enough.

The man of God had been born to Elkanah and his barren wife Hannah after she had made pilgrimage to Shiloh, a dozen miles from home. In fulfilment of her vow, Samuel was taken to the temple as soon as he was weaned and there he ministered to Yahweh before the priest Eli. One night the boy was sleeping in the shrine where the ark was kept when he heard a voice and thought it was Eli; after three calls, Eli knew it was Yahweh, and Samuel heard the terrible doom of Eli and his house. The doom was fulfilled, the family was destroyed, the ark was taken, and Samuel abandoned the ruins of Shiloh and returned home. He was no Levite and therefore did not attempt to follow Eli's priestly task, but his reputation grew as a seer. He allied himself to the newly formed prophetic bands and with them began to consider the possibility of a saviour for his sorely oppressed people.

The very day before, Yahweh had uncovered the ear of Samuel and had informed him that on the morrow would come the destined saviour, a Benjaminite. He recognised Saul at once and invited him to be his guest. The lost asses were found, but why trouble himself about them? Were not the desirable things for him and his father's house? The implica-

---

[9] Judges 19 ff.; W. F. Albright, *Ann.*, IV, 7 f., 33 ff.; cf. J. Morgenstern, *JQR.*, NS., VIII, 31 ff.

Fig. 128. ROCK ALTAR AT ZORAH.

Fig. 129. WEST GATE OF JEBUSITE JERUSALEM.

Fig. 126. GIBEAH.—PERIOD II. SAUL'S PALACE; PERIOD III. ASA'S FORT.

Fig. 127. ISRAELITE SANCTUARY AT MIZPAH.

tion was obvious, but Saul politely deprecated the importance of his tribe and clan. He was brought into the hall of the high place and given the place of honour among the invited guests; the reserved part of the sacrifice, the shoulder and fat tail, were placed before him.

At dawn, Saul was roused from his bed on the roof. Outside the city, Samuel poured a vial of oil upon Saul's head, kissed him, and said: "Has not Yahweh anointed you as prince over his people Israel? You shall reign over the people of Yahweh and save them from the enemies who surround them." Then followed signs. On the boundary of Benjamin, at the tomb of his ancestress Rachel, he should meet two men who would tell him that the asses were found and that his father was now concerned for his son. At the sacred oak of Tabor, he would come upon three men going up to worship God at Bethel; they would ask his peace, the term among Israel's neighbours for recognition of a king's sovereignty, and would offer two loaves of bread, a symbol of his gifts as ruler. A third sign would be given at Gibeah of God, the more significant as there was the headquarters of the Philistine governor. A band of prophets, prophesying under the influence of music from lyre, tambourine, flute, and harp, would be met at the city entrance, the spirit of Yahweh would likewise rush upon Saul, who would prophesy and become another man.

That very day all these signs came to pass. Priests and seers had lost their leadership, their ceremonies and predictions had become purely mechanical. A new organisation grew up, formed largely from the lower classes, and with a strong non-Semitic element. These prophets were no more respected by the higher classes than are the wandering dervishes of Islam. When the burghers with their blunt Semitic common sense beheld the hitherto respectable Saul yielding to the contagious enthusiasm of these crazy fellows, they asked in amazement: "What has come over the son of Kish? Is Saul too one of the prophets?" Saul was of good descent, that they knew, but "Who is *their* father?"[10]

[10] I Sam. 9 f.

A month later, the time came for a public appearance. Jephthah's exploits had no lasting result, and now the Ammonites were besieging Jabesh Gilead, not far from the Jordan. The inhabitants offered submission under a covenant but the Ammonite king Nahash would accept their surrender only on condition that he bore out the right eye of each. To fasten yet more firmly the shame on Israel, a seven days' respite was granted for appeal to their fellows.

Gibeah had intermarried with Jabesh Gilead, but the citizens were satisfied with weeping. Saul returned from his peasant toil in the fields and heard the news. Again Yahweh's spirit rushed upon him. He cut up his yoke of oxen and sent the fragments throughout Israel; "Whoever comes not after Saul," ran the message, "shall be treated thus." A terror from Yahweh fell upon the tribesmen and they gathered as one man in Bezek, half way between Shechem and Beth Shan. Lulled to false security by the promise of immediate surrender, the Ammonites were easily dispersed by Saul's daybreak attack. After so glorious a victory, the whole people hastened to crown Saul king before Yahweh in Gilgal (1015). It was of portent to the future that the first monarchy was elective.[11]

Election of a king was revolt against their Philistine masters. Jonathan, Saul's youthful son, smote the Philistine governor in Gibeah of God, and Saul himself captured the posts at Bethel and Michmash. The Philistines levied an army, which included a Hebrew contingent, and Saul was forced to withdraw behind the great gorge which yawns between Michmash and Geba. Its passage was guarded by a Philistine outpost on an isolated knoll half way up the ascent to Michmash. Saul with his six hundred poorly armed soldiers established his camp on the threshing floor of Geba on the southern rim of the gorge.

While the armies waited, Jonathan suggested to his armour bearer that they visit the Philistine outpost, taking the first words of the enemy as an omen. They were greeted "See, some of the Hebrews are coming out of the holes where they have

[11] I Sam. 11.

hidden themselves!" This was a good omen and they crept on hands and knees between the rock Seneh, the "Thorn," and the rock tooth Bozez, "Shining," a white cliff lit by the sun, to attack the outpost. Twenty Philistines were slain and terror fell upon the main camp.

Hebrew sentinels beheld the Philistines melting away and it was discovered that Jonathan and his squire were missing. The ephod at Nob had taken the place of the discredited ark and was borne before Israel by Ahijah, great-grandson of Eli. Before preparations could be completed for consulting the oracle, the tumult in the Philistine camp was so great that Saul countermanded the order. The battle cry was given and the bewildered Philistines attacked one another, while the commandeered Hebrews turned against their masters, aided by the Ephraimites who had hidden at their approach.

Pursuit was continued down to Beth Horon. In his excitement, Saul laid a curse upon any who ate before evening, but Jonathan had not heard it and took some honey. Informed of the curse, Jonathan replied that his father had brought disaster on the land, the slaughter would have been far greater had the people eaten of their enemies' spoil. The hungry and fainting warriors at once began to slaughter the beasts on the ground. This involved yet greater sin, eating the flesh with the blood, and Saul ordered a great stone to be rolled up as an improvised altar.

Saul proposed that the battle be continued through the night and the refreshed soldiers gave their approval, but Ahijah, smarting under the former neglect, urged "Let us draw near to God." Saul inquired: "Shall I go down after the Philistines? Wilt thou deliver them into the hands of Israel?" No answer was vouchsafed and it was clear some one had sinned. Saul then prayed: "Yahweh, Israel's God, why hast thou not answered thy servant this day? If the guilt be in me or in my son Jonathan, Yahweh, Israel's God, give Urim; but if thou say: 'It is in my people Israel,' then give Thummim." The lots were cast and Saul and Jonathan were taken. The people began to suspect what was coming and insisted that the test be stopped, but Saul could not be moved; the lots were cast again and Jonathan was taken.

Jonathan confessed and announced his readiness to die. Saul was yet under the ecstatic influence and swore: "God do so to me and more, you shall die this day." The people were equally firm: "Should Jonathan die, who has wrought this great salvation in Israel? Not one hair of his head shall fall to the ground, for he has wrought with God this day." Saul awoke to the imminence of revolt and Jonathan was ransomed. All through the tale runs a rationalism strangely out of place at so early a date. Was it sufficiently powerful to defy the curse or did the people ransom Jonathan by the substitution of another human sacrifice?[12]

Saul's kingdom was still tiny, his own Benjamin, a more or less effective control of Ephraim and of west Jordan Manasseh, perhaps the grateful Jabesh Gilead. He now rounded out his territory by subjecting the cities of the Gibeonite confederation, whose favoured position according to legend was due to a covenant secured by trickery from the invaders.[13] Jerusalem, only three miles south of Gibeah, was impregnable, but beyond it lay Bethlehem of Judah, on a low hill whose double summit is connected by a saddle, and enjoying magnificent views over the wild gorges of the Judæan desert to the Dead Sea and the hills of Moab.[14] Its chief shrine was a cave, once dedicated to the mother goddess and now to the Virgin Mother of God. Jesse, the headman of Bethlehem, barely ten miles distant from Gibeah, must have viewed with alarm the growth of a kingdom which threatened Judæan isolation. He married as an equal into the family of Nahash, the Ammonite king,[15] and such close relationship to Saul's bitterest enemy must have been deliberate. How he was led to change his attitude, whether by force or by negotiation, we cannot know; the appearance of his son David at court is sufficient proof that Jesse recognised Saul as his rightful liege, while David's high

---

[12] I Sam. 14. [13] Josh. 9:3 ff.; II Sam. 21. [14] Fig. 132.
[15] II Sam. 17:25; I Chron. 2:16; cf. A. P. Stanley, in Smith's *Dictionary of the Bible*, I, 552.

position as armour bearer indicates the importance of conciliating the Bethlehemite.

Judah's submission brought Saul face to face with the Amalekite problem. He persuaded the Kenites to abandon

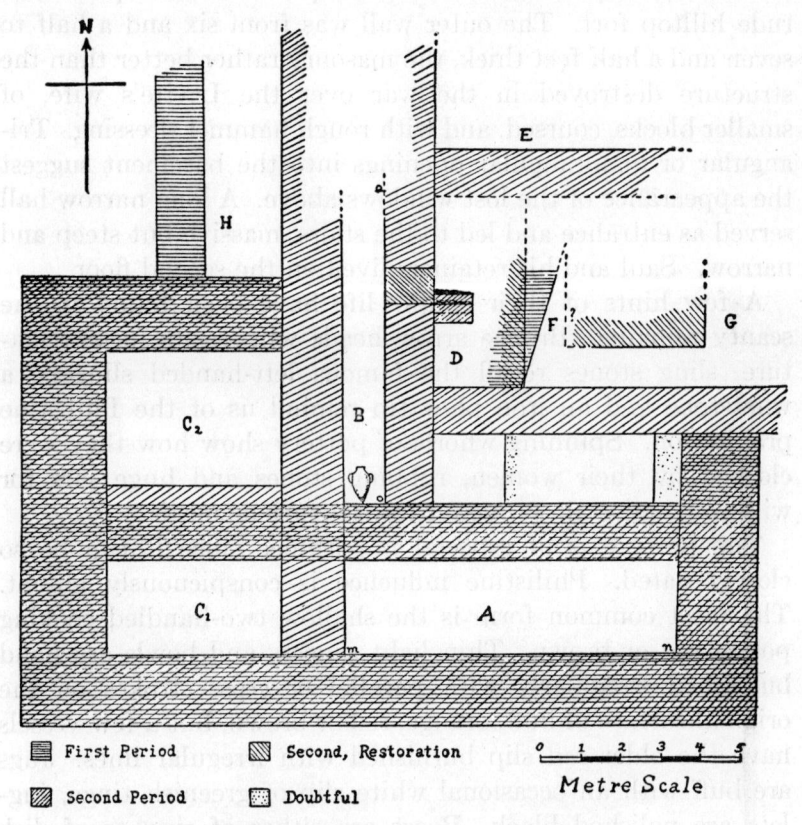

PLAN 11. SAUL'S PALACE AT GIBEAH.

their allies and ravaged the Amalekite country from Telam on the border of Edom and Moab to the Shur or "Wall" of Egypt. On his return, he set up a "Hand," a standing stone, to commemorate the victory in the Judæan Carmel. Samuel had ordered complete destruction of every living thing, and when he discovered that Saul had saved their king Agag, he hewed the captive to pieces before Yahweh in Gilgal. The break between Samuel and Saul was now complete.[16]

Gibeah, well meriting its name of "Hill," nearly twenty-eight hundred feet above the sea and steep on all sides, was made Saul's capital. On the highest point was his "palace," a rude hilltop fort. The outer wall was from six and a half to seven and a half feet thick, the masonry rather better than the structure destroyed in the war over the Levite's wife, of smaller blocks, coursed, and with rough hammer dressing. Triangular or quadrangular openings into the basement suggest the appearance of the lost windows above. A long narrow hall served as entrance and led to the stairs, massive but steep and narrow. Saul and his retainers lived on the second floor.

A few hints of their simple life have been found in the scanty remains. Bronze arrow heads witness its fortress nature, sling stones recall the famous left-handed slingers, a whetstone and an iron plow tip remind us of the Philistine prohibition. Spinning whorls of pottery show how they were clothed by their women, rubbing stones and huge jars for wine, oil, and grain prove far from luxurious meals.

The pottery is of especial importance since it can be so closely dated. Philistine influence is conspicuously absent. The most common form is the shallow two-handled cooking pot in red or brown. Thin light saucers and bowls are hand burnished irregularly with parallel or cross strokes on the original surface of buff, orange, red or brown, but a few vessels have the older red slip burnished with irregular lines. Jugs are buff with an occasional white slip of greenish tinge, juglets are polished black. Bases are either of ring or of disk form. The rare painted pottery is banded direct on the surface over a red burnished slip, or on a simple slip of white, cream, or creamy buff. The pottery alone would suffice to prove the backward state of the culture.[17]

War with the Philistines continued, and Saul's armour bearer David won such fame that the dancing women greeted

[16] I Sam. 15.
[17] Plan 11; W. F. Albright, *Ann.*, IV, 1924, 1 ff.

his return with tambourines and cymbals and sang antiphonally:

> Saul slew his thousands.
> But David his ten thousands.

Yahweh's spirit, received when he became a prophet, had departed from Saul and was replaced by an evil spirit; in modern language, his already unstable mind had been peculiarly susceptible to the prophetic enthusiasm, but now it was giving way to fits of temporary insanity. He naturally suspected David of designs on the throne, and removed him from his person. The discovery that his daughter Michal was in love with the young hero offered good opportunity to dispose of his suspected vassal. David was informed that no bride price was required, he must merely kill a hundred Philistines; this David accomplished without harm and Michal became his wife. That very night Saul despatched men to surprise David, but Michal had learned the plot and let down her husband through the window. Hiding teraphim in the bed, she pretended he was ill, and the trick was not discovered until Saul ordered that David was to be carried in his bed.[18]

David hastened to Nob, two miles away on the north end of the Mount of Olives, where Ahimelech and the priests of Yahweh had taken refuge after the destruction of Shiloh. To Ahimelech he explained that he was on a secret mission and demanded food and a sword. He assured the priest that his men were consecrated for war and therefore had kept themselves from women, and Ahimelech gave him show bread just taken from Yahweh's presence, and made inquiry of the oracle. Doeg, Saul's Edomite muleherd, was present and accused Ahimelech to the king. Saul would accept no excuse, and when his runners hesitated to risk the curse, the foreigner Doeg with his own hand slew the eighty-five priests. The destruction of Nob, the chief centre of Yahweh worship in the north, was a blow to that religion, but it was a more terrible blow to Saul. He had already broken with the sons of the

[18] I Sam. 18:6 ff., 20 ff.; 19:10 ff.

prophets; now all true followers of Yahweh must oppose his rule.[19]

David escaped to the stronghold near the cave of Adullam, where he was joined by his family and by Ahimelech's son Abiathar, who alone had escaped from the slaughter. Abiathar brought with him the ephod, and David was now the leader of those who were for Yahweh. Soon a band of four hundred fugitives had rallied around him. Remembering that his ancestress Ruth had been a Moabitess, he took his parents to Mizpeh of Moab, whose king admitted them to court.

The Philistines were robbing the threshing floors of Keilah, but David slew them with great slaughter and took their cattle. Four hundred freebooters were no improvement upon raiding Philistines, and the men of Keilah reported his presence to Saul. In words strangely reminiscent of the Assyrian liver oracles,[20] David inquired of the ephod: "Yahweh, God of Israel, your servant has heard that Saul seeks to come to Keilah to destroy the city on my account. Will Saul come down as your servant has heard? Yahweh, God of Israel, I beseech you, tell your servant." Yahweh answered: "He will come down." David then inquired: "Will the men of Keilah deliver up me and my men into the hands of Saul?" and the answer was: "They will deliver you up." He therefore abandoned Keilah and Saul returned home.

His next refuge was Horeshah in the wilderness of Ziph, but the men of Ziph promised to deliver David to Saul, and David went down to the rock in the wilderness of Maon. Saul was on one side of the mountain, David on the other, and he was in imminent danger of being surrounded when he was saved by an opportune raid of the Philistines.[21]

David saw no recourse but to seek Philistine protection. He entered the service of Achish of Gath, whom some believe an Anchises strayed from Greek lands. David pretended that he was raiding the Negebs of Judah, the Jerahmeelites, and Kenites, but in reality it was the Amalekites and Geshur which

[19] I Sam. 21 f.   [20] Cf. *History of Assyria*, 359 ff.
[21] Fig. 130; I Sam. 23.

FIG. 130. IN THE WILDERNESS OF JUDAH. THE KIDRON VALLEY AND THE MONASTERY OF SAINT SABA.

FIG. 131. THE FOUNTAIN OF GOLIATH UNDER MOUNT GILBOA.

suffered. It was a dangerous game, doubly so when based on the tyrant's residence, and David asked and was granted Ziklag in the open country.[22]

Four months later, the Philistines made a final attempt to destroy the Hebrew kingdom. David followed Achish as far as Aphek, whence the Philistines planned to march by Dothan into the Great Plain and so cut off Saul from the northern tribes. Here the tyrants, fearing that David might betray them, insisted that he be sent back. This was triply fortunate: David was saved from appearing a traitor to Hebrew independence, he was given excuse for a break with the Philistines, he hastened back to Ziklag to find the Amalekites had left it a smouldering ruin. Scattered over the country, eating and drinking and dancing, the Amalekites were easily slain and the captives and booty recovered. From the spoil, David sent a "blessing" to the elders of the chief cities of Judah.[23]

Three days after the return to Ziklag, an Amalekite appeared with clothes rent and earth upon his head. According to his story, he happened to be on Mount Gilboa;[24] Saul was leaning on his spear and the chariots and horsemen were approaching. Saul called him and ordered: "Stand over me, I beg you, and slay me, for dizziness has seized me, though I am still alive." This he did and then brought the crown and armlet to David.

Glad as David might be that his enemy was dead, he must clear himself of all suspicion and he must guard the divine character of the kingship to which he aspired. How dared the Amalekite put forth his hand against Yahweh's anointed? On his head be his blood since his own mouth had testified against him! The self-confessed assassin was put to death by the attendant youths and David and his followers mourned and wept and fasted to evening.

In the Book of the Brave, this dirge of David was to be read:

>Weep, O Judah,
>Grieve, O Israel!

[22] I Sam. 27:1 ff.   [23] I Sam. 29 f.   [24] Fig. 131.

On your heights are the slain!
　　How are fallen the mighty!

Tell it not in Gath,
　　Relate not in Ashkelon's streets;
Lest Philistia's daughters rejoice,
　　Lest the uncircumcised's daughters be glad.

Mounts of Gilboa, let no dew descend,
　　Nor rain upon you, fields of death;
There cast away is the mighty's shield,
　　The shield of Saul, unanointed with oil.

From the blood of the slain,
　　From the fat of the mighty,
Jonathan's bow turned not back,
　　Saul's sword returned not empty.

Saul and Jonathan, loved and lovely,
　　In life and death were not divided;
Swifter were they than eagles,
　　Stronger were they than lions.

Daughters of Israel, weep for Saul,
　　Who decked you with scarlet and linen,
Who placed jewels of gold on your clothes,
　　How are fallen the mighty in battle!

On your heights is Jonathan slain,
　　Anguished am I for you;
O Jonathan, brother,
　　Very lovely were you to me.

Wondrous your love to me,
　　Passing the love of women;
How are fallen the mighty,
　　And perished the weapons of warfare![25]

[25] II Sam. 1.

CHAPTER XXI

DAVID'S EMPIRE

DAVID consulted the oracle: "Shall I go up to one of Judah's cities?" The answer was affirmative, and again he inquired: "To which shall I go up?" The inevitable reply was "To Hebron," for ages the most important site in the south.[1] Soon after, about 1000, the men of Judah, which now included Simeon, Caleb, the Kenites, and other minor clans, anointed him their king.

The Philistines had dedicated Saul's armour in the temple of Ashtart and had exposed his body and the bodies of his sons on the walls of Beth Shan, but the men of Jabesh Gilead, recalling past aid, stole them by night, burned them, and buried the ashes under the sacred tamarisk. David praised their elders and promised to requite their kindness; Saul their master was dead but Judah had anointed him as king.

Jabesh Gilead did not take the hint, for it found a nearer master and one more to its liking. Saul's cousin Abner escaped to Mahanaim, east of Jordan, where once Jacob had seen the hosts of God encamped, and set up Ishbaal, a younger son of Saul. Both Ishbaal and David recognised Philistine overlordship. The boundary between the two Hebrew states was the Aijalon line. So restricted a domain could not long content David, who sent an army north under Joab, the eldest of three brothers who are never given their father's name but are always spoken of as sons of Zeruiah, David's sister. Abner was defeated by the great reservoir at Gibeon but slew Joab's brother Asahel in the retreat.

As the war continued, it became evident that the future was with David, and Abner determined to save himself before it was too late. When Ishbaal rightly objected to his marriage with Saul's concubine Rizpah, Abner proposed to transfer

[1] Fig. 133.

Israel's allegiance to David. David accepted, but he could not be overshadowed by the husband of Saul's wife, even though of the second rank; he therefore demanded the return of his former wife Michal. Michal preferred her second husband Paltiel, but she had no choice; there was no love behind the remarriage, and a quarrel soon led to complete estrangement, but David was satisfied, through Michal he now had claim to Saul's inheritance.

Abner was feasted in Hebron and the covenant was made. Joab had been sent off on a raid, but returned too soon and promptly slew Abner in the city gate. The declared reason was the blood revenge for Asahel, but his own endangered position was doubtless a contributing cause. Once more David reaped the reward without the payment. Once more there was the rending of clothes, the putting on of sackcloth, the weeping and fasting. Once more David displayed his poetical cunning:

> As dies the fool,
>   Must Abner die?
> Your hands were not bound,
>   Nor your feet put in chains;
> As falls the fool,
>   Before the ruthless you died.[2]

Abner's death left Ishbaal helpless. While he was taking his afternoon siesta, two of his officers, Rechab and Baanah of Beeroth, slipped through a door guarded only by a sleepy woman cleaning wheat for flour, and cut off Ishbaal's head. Strangely ignorant of David's practice of accepting the result while avoiding the guilt, they carried the head to Hebron, where they were promptly deprived of hands and feet and their corpses hung up by the reservoir. Ishbaal's head was buried in Abner's tomb, but David did not escape suspicion; on occasion a Benjaminite might curse him as a "man of blood."[3]

Jonathan's son Meribbaal might have contested the throne, had he not been lamed when his nurse dropped him on the

---

[2] II Sam. 1–3. [3] II Sam. 4; cf. 16:7.

FIG. 132. BETHLEHEM FROM THE CHURCH OF THE NATIVITY.

FIG. 133. HEBRON, THE MOSQUE OVER THE CAVE OF MACHPELAH.

flight from Gilboa. Through his marriage to Michal, David was therefore the only available prince connected with the former royal family. The elders of the northern tribes accordingly proceeded to Hebron and anointed David as king of Israel, but only after a covenant before Yahweh; that it was merely a personal union is shown by the royal title, "King of Israel *and* Judah."[4]

Union of all the Hebrews under an able warrior was more than the Philistines could allow. They invaded the highlands, doubtless in agreement with the Jebusites of Jerusalem, and encamped in the valley of Rephaim on the road to Bethlehem. David hastily descended to the stronghold of Adullam and Bethlehem was seized by a Philistine detachment. When David expressed the wish for a drink from the well by Bethlehem's gate, three of his mighty men broke through the Philistine camp and brought the water a dozen miles to Adullam; he won their hearts by refusing to drink and poured it out as a libation to Yahweh, the blood of men who risked their lives.[5]

To the inquiry whether he should go up against the Philistines, the oracle replied in the affirmative. The attack was successful and the Philistine gods were captured. David called the spot Baal-perazim, "Baal breaks forth," for he said: "Yahweh has broken my enemies before me, like the breaking forth of waters." Again the Philistines came up and plundered the valley of Rephaim. This time the oracle ordered: "You shall not go up to meet them; go around behind them and come upon them opposite the Balsams. And when you hear the sound of marching in the tops of the balsams, then act at once, for Yahweh will have gone out before you to smite the camp of the Philistines." David obeyed and smote them from Gibeon down the Aijalon valley to Gezer.[6]

David now took the offensive and transferred the fighting to Gath, but the Hebrews were not always successful. Once they were forced to retreat from the "Bloody Border," Ephesdamim, a small plain formed by three converging valleys an

[4] II Sam. 5:1 ff.; cf. I Kings 1:35.
[5] Fig. 132; II Sam. 23:13–17.
[6] II Sam. 5:18–25.

hour east of Gath, but Eleazer, Dodai's son, held his ground and smote the Philistines until his wearied hand clave to his sword. Again they retreated from Lehi, where not long before Samson had fought the same Philistines, and Shammah, Agee's son, made a stand in a lentil field and wrought great salvation through Yahweh. David himself was in danger of being slain by a "son of the giant" who bore a lance three hundred shekels in weight, but was rescued by Joab's brother Abishai; so narrow was his escape that his men took an oath: "You shall no more go out with us in battle, lest you quench the lamp of Israel." A series of engagements between Hebrew and Philistine champions was more successful. Sibbecai, the Hushathite, slew Saph, son of the giant; Elhanan, the Bethlehemite, Jair's son, slew Goliath of Gath, whose spear was like a weaver's beam; Jonathan, son of David's brother Shimei, slew another giant's son, a man of great stature with six fingers and six toes on each hand or foot.[7]

These isolated scraps of history have another interest, for from them was constructed one of the best known Biblical stories, as beautiful as it is unhistorical. From the story of Eleazer, its author took the location of the battle at Ephesdamim, and from that of Elhanan the name of the opposing giant, Goliath of Gath, with his spear staff like a weaver's beam. He changed the lance of three hundred shekels of bronze of the Abishai story to a spear's head of six hundred shekels of iron. The defiance of the champion was derived from the tale of David's nephew Jonathan. His one addition was the unknown shepherd lad who slew the giant with only his sling. It is a far cry from the David about to be slain to the boy champion of Israel.[8]

Hebrew independence was at last admitted by the Philistines and peace was made. The Jebusites could no longer rely on Philistine aid and David might attack that Jerusalem which so fatally divided the northern and southern tribes. Jerusalem was no new city. Where to-day the "Dome of the Rock" rises

[7] II Sam. 23:9–11; 21:15–22.
[8] I Sam. 17:1–11, 32–40, 42–49, 51–54.

in beauty was the summit of a hill. On every side the descent was steep, for the surrounding valleys had not yet been filled with debris. Under this rock summit was a cave, now called the "Well of Souls"; doubtless it was once a neolithic home, but soon it was devoted to the gods alone. Expansion to the east was prohibited by the sharp cliff of the Kidron, on the west by the almost equally precipitous "Cheesemakers' Vale"; the northern slopes were sufficiently gentle, but settlement here would permit easy access to a dangerously exposed hill top.

On the south was Ophel, a tongue of rock some two thousand feet long by four hundred wide, which combined seclusion from the now sacred hill with safe position and a good water supply on its eastern front in the intermittent Gihon spring. To the northwest was a cave, the earliest habitation on Ophel, about whose spring lie chalcolithic potsherds. A tiny valley running west formed the natural northern limit; by the third millennium it had been extended to the east by a moat ten feet wide and eight feet deep, crossed by two causeways two feet high and wide and approached by rock-cut steps. About the middle of the second millennium, the moat was filled with potsherds and beyond it was erected a rude polygonal wall, of hammer-dressed stones, one section north and south, the other at right angles, and with a tower at the corner; to the west were a towered gate and a third tower.

Towards the end of the Jebusite occupation, a better wall utilised an older rock scarp, using stones two to four feet on the side. Perhaps there was a gate on the north. The space between the two walls was kept free. Along the Kidron the city wall was forty feet thick at the base and twenty-seven at the summit. Scarping was done where needed. The face was of hammer-dressed stones in irregular courses, the joints were often straight and the corners poor, with little mortar and no plaster. The inner face had a slight batter and small stones filled the space between. At a somewhat later time, perhaps when the Hebrew threat was becoming apparent, two stepped bastions standing free from the main wall were projected fifteen feet on a great boulder base where there was no rock foundation.

Here perhaps was the original water gate to Gihon; farther south and due west of the fountain a gate of large blocks stood out from the wall. Before the end of the Jebusite period, it was decided to bring the water closer to the city. An open passage was cut from near the gate through the rock to a room over a deep shaft, then a semi-circular passage descended for a hundred and twenty-five feet, and from here the buckets could be let down a forty-four-foot shaft to where the water had been carried back fifty feet from Gihon by a canal through the rock.[9]

David's summons to capitulate was met with justifiable taunts: "You cannot enter, the lame and the blind will prevent you." Joab however managed to climb up through the water channel and was rewarded by permanent command of the army.[10] The final assault was launched from the higher ground to the north and the northern wall was breached. A temporary wall just inside closed the breach. The new wall was three and a half feet thick, with alternate courses of large and small stones, but the blocks were less massive than those in the Jebusite structure; some of the older blocks were recut, others were left where they fell to be unearthed by the modern excavators. At either side the gate was a tower. The outer face of the east wall was also restored, in the Jebusite technique, but again with smaller blocks. A new technique appears in a slight use of the comb pick and of marginal drafting and plaster was employed on a tower face.[11]

Jerusalem became the royal residence and its name was changed in accordance with oriental usage to "David's Town." The choice of a new capital was shrewd. Jerusalem was on the border between north and south, but it belonged to neither. There could be no competition with any of the ancient shrines which had long been consecrated to one or another of Israel's heroes. In every respect Jerusalem was neutral.

[9] C. Warren, *Recovery of Jerusalem*, 189 ff.   [10] II Sam. 5:6–9.
[11] Figs. 134–137; plan 12.

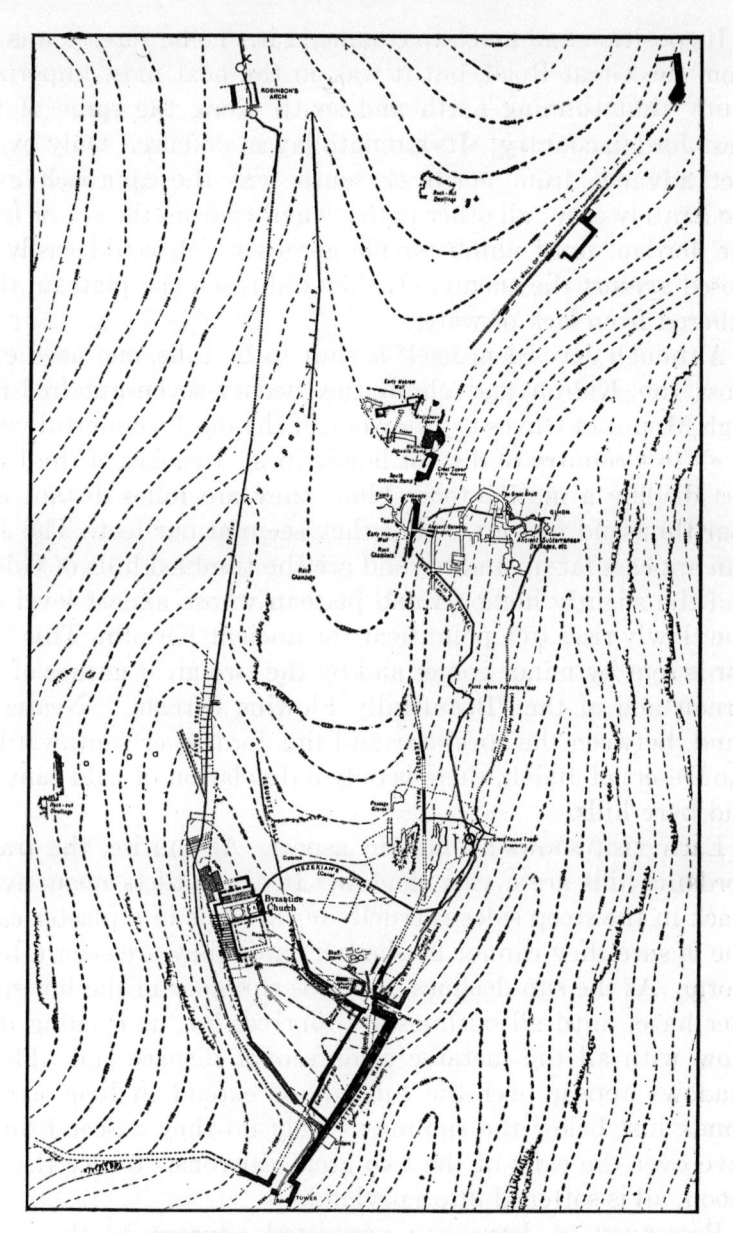

PLAN 12. JEBUSITE JERUSALEM AND THE CITY OF DAVID.

Its position had much to commend it. To be sure, it was far from the Great Road, but it was on the next most important route, that running north and south along the spine of the west Jordan country. Its strength lay in defense. Only by direct advance from north or south was the approach even moderately easy; all other paths, whether from the sea or from the Jordan, must climb terrific gorges which could easily be closed against the enemy. If they did reach the plateau, they suffered from lack of water.

Although Jerusalem itself is shut in by hills, one need only cross the Kidron and climb the twenty-seven-hundred-feet high Mount of Olives to enjoy one of the most wonderful views in all this country of distant landscapes. Reaches of the Dead Sea display a most intense blue; they are miles distant and four thousand feet lower, but they seem at our feet. The Jordan appears far up and beyond are the tumbled hills of Gilead and the slightly higher Moab plateau whose almost level sky line slowly rises to a point near the ancient Kirioth. This long bar is rent by minor gorges and by the two great gashes of the Arnon and of the "Beautifully Flowing Stream." Nearer at hand, between the spectator and the Jordan, or southward to the Desert of Judah, there is only a desolation of wild canyons and bare hills.

Each visit shows a different aspect. At sunrise, the trans-Jordanic hills are a vast shadow. In the pitiless noon, every crack in the steep sides is cruelly outlined as in a plaster cast; one is sure they cannot be sharper until they are seen after a storm. As the sun declines, the hills shimmer in the hot summer haze, until all outlines are blurred, but at evening they glow with all the metallic colours of a furnace run. Fleecy shadows appear over the hilltops or extend in long narrow bands just below the summit; rarely do they descend lower, save over the exits of the two great canyons. Under the full moon, all is softened into fairyland.

Possession of Jerusalem permitted advance to the Great Plain, whose band of important cities now for the first time became Hebrew. Beth Shan was thoroughly sacked, the temples

FIG. 134. JEBUSITE WALL OF JERUSALEM.

FIG. 135. THE BREACH IN THE JEBUSITE WALL.

FIG. 136. NORTH BASTION AND TOWER IN OPHEL WALL.

FIG. 137. DAVID'S WALL.

destroyed, the mud brick walls burned rock hard by the terrific heat from the blazing stores of grain and oil.[12] The tribes of Galilee joined the kingdom, and David was brought into contact with the Phœnicians; thus began those close diplomatic relations which for good and for ill were to continue through the following centuries.

Gebal, Amor, and Sidon had all passed their prime, and the chief Phœnician centre was now Tyre, once the farthest south of the coast cities. In a sense, Tyre is outside Phœnicia proper, for the tremendous gorge of the Litani is the natural boundary between Syria and Palestine, but the Litani is a boundary only in the hills; at its mouth is an open plain which reaches to the Ladder of Tyre, a steep cape with steps cut in the soft rock. Here is the true boundary of Phœnicia, for Tyre owned all the back country to the crest of the ridge.

Tyre's native name was Sor, the "Rock"; the original site was an isolated mass of rock which rises abruptly fifty feet from the open loamy plain a half mile from shore. On its summit was room for a tiny village, below was a sacred cave. In time of peace, an aqueduct carried water from the splendid fountains three miles to the south; for war there were rock-cut cisterns.[13]

As Egyptian sea power declined, that of Tyre increased. There was no longer need of living on a cramped rock when the city was protected by the wooden walls of the fleet. Various authors date the "foundation" of Tyre around 1200,[14] the date not far from the time when Harbor Tyre, already existing in Egyptian days, rapidly expanded as the merchants discovered that the tiny island was more convenient for their trade.

When Abibaal was succeeded by his nineteen-year-old son Hiram or rather Hirom (981–947), the capital was removed to Harbor Tyre. Expansion was easy, for there were other islands only a few yards distant, and the channels between,

[12] C. S. Fisher, *Museum Journal*, XIV, 1923, 237.
[13] Fig. 36, *History of Assyria*.
[14] Just., xviii, 3, 5; Joseph., *Ant.*, viii, 62; *Apion*, i, 126; Euseb., *Chron.*, ed. R. Helm, 55.

marked still by lines of sand, were filled. The old harbour at the north was retained and its limits set by walls over which to-day the waves break. On the west, the rocks were smoothed just below the water line and beyond there was partial protection from an outer row of jagged reefs. To the south, a smaller harbour was created by cutting down the reef to a mole. The palace and the residential section of the town were in this district, if we may judge from the immense quantity of debris. On the east, the wall ran from the harbour straight north to the present gate, inside which a slightly brackish fountain indicates the ancient sea front. As constructed by Hiram, the town was almost a perfect square, whose area was about a hundred and twenty-five acres, and whose population could not have exceeded twenty-five thousand. Huge mounds of earth filled in the eastern border to form the "Broad Square." Facing sacred Mount Hermon was the temple of Baal Melkart, "Baal, King of the city," on an island which was now united to the city by a dyke. To it Hiram made numerous dedications, including a pillar of gold.[15]

Old Tyre, abandoned as a capital, retained its sacred character. The mother goddess and her beloved Adonis were consoled by a new temple, roofed with Lebanon cedar. Baal Melkart's island temple became a Christian cathedral and lies now in ruins, but a tiny mosque yet commemorates Nebi Mashuk, the "Beloved Prophet," and his consort, and the peasants celebrate their feast in Tammuz, the month dedicated to Adonis by his alternate name.[16]

There were obvious reasons why Tyrians and Israelites should be friends. Israel had no sea-borne commerce, Tyre needed agricultural products. The first result of the new relations was a palace, built for David by Tyrian masons and carpenters with the precious Lebanon cedar. David was a "man of war," but culture began when he copied foreign palaces.[17]

[15]Dius, *Hist. Phœn.*, in Joseph., *Apion*, I, 112 ff.; *Ant.*, viii, 147 ff.; Menander, in Joseph., *Apion*, I, 117 ff.; *Ant.*, viii, 144 ff.; cf. Herod., ii, 44; Arr., *Anab.*, ii, 16; Renan, *Mission*, 569.

[16]Cf. *Sargon*, 49 n. 18; Just., xi, 10, 11. [17]II Sam. 5:11.

A capital of a united kingdom, free from earlier entanglements, permitted centralisation of religion. David was religious head of the state, his sons were priests. Yahweh had taken the place of the original tribal deities whose symbols were brought to the capital. Benjamin's ephod had come with Abiathar, Levi's brazen serpent and Judah's tent of meeting now arrived in David's Town. The first attempt to bring up Ephraim's ark from Kiriath Jearim ended in the death of its guardian Uzzah, but Yahweh so blessed its new guardian Obed Edom that David renewed the attempt. This time, the ark was carried, not on a cart but on men's shoulders, and every seven paces an ox and a fatling were sacrificed. Whirling with all his might like a modern dervish, and clad only with a linen ephod, scarcely more than a breech clout, David escorted the ark to the capital and placed it in the tent. Burnt and peace offerings were sacrificed before it and David as officiating priest ended the ceremony by a blessing in the name of Yahweh of Hosts.[18]

Returning to bless his house, David was greeted by Michal: "How honourable was the king of Israel this day who exposed himself in the eyes of his servants' maids like a crazy fellow!" "Before Yahweh was I dancing" replied David, "blessed be Yahweh who chose me above your father and all his house to set me as prince over his people." Michal had borne him no son to legitimise his rule and her disgrace was complete; she was soon to regret her anger.

Three years famine led David to inquire of the oracle, administered by Abiathar, whose whole family had been massacred by Saul; the oracle replied: "There is blood on Saul and his house." Saul had done his best to destroy Gibeon out of Israel's borders and his action could not be compounded by weregeld, the Gibeonites demanded his seven sons. Five sons of his daughter Merab and two sons by his concubine Rizpah were slain and their corpses exposed on Yahweh's Mount in Gibeon. Rizpah protected the bodies from bird and beast from the beginning of barley harvest until the rains of God

[18] II Sam. 6.

descended in sign that Yahweh was propitiated. David collected their bones and buried them in the tomb of Kish at Zela with the remains of Saul and Jonathan, returned from Jabesh Gilead; it was now safe to summon the lame Meribbaal from his exile in Lodebar east of the Jordan and to restore his father's estates.[19]

Nahash of Ammon had remained friendly to his relative by marriage when David warred with Saul and Ishbaal, and at his death a message of condolence was in order. His son Hanun was well aware of the danger to his little kingdom from the rapidly growing Hebrew state, and took the messengers for spies. Their beards were half shaved and their garments sheared to the waist; such indecent treatment of ambassadors meant war and Hanun summoned aid from the Aramæan city states of Central Syria.

Hollow Syria is definitely cut off from other portions of the great north and south depression. To the west is Lebanon, its inner slopes more precipitous than those which look to the sea. From the crest, Hollow Syria is a perfect level, dotted with orchards and vineyards and fields of yellowing grain, the junction between plain and hill sharp as though drawn with the pen. Where plain and sky merge at the watershed between Litani and Orontes is the true north limit of Hollow Syria, for beyond the country is rough and infertile. At this point is the "City of the Sun" and the colossal temple of Baalbek. On the east, Hollow Syria is bordered by Anti-Lebanon, lower and less fertile than its western mate; a deep inner valley and a sterile gravelly terrace still further cramp the plain. Majestic Hermon blocks the view to the south, while across the deep sunk valley of the infant Jordan a long narrow ridge crowds the Litani westward and forces it to carve a path through Lebanon's very roots. North of the Litani gorge the valley slowly widens to meet a narrower passage from the upper Jordan.

The junction of these two valleys is the true Litani source, a fount of such abundant waters that just below its stream is

[19] II Sam. 21:1-14; II Sam. 9.

unfordable. Ruins of the Roman Chalcis[20] strew the adjacent hillside, while half an hour distant, on an outlier to the south, a temple faces northeast and affords a wondrous view over the eight-mile wide plain. Here was Zobah, famous for its neighbouring copper mines; in the last centuries it had shared the Aramæan migration and was now ruled by Hadadezer of Beth Rehob. With him were allied other Aramæan states, at Beth Maacah in the upper Jordan valley and at Tob north of Gilead. Talmai, king of Geshur, east of the Lake of Galilee, was however allied by marriage with David, and so took no part in the war. Some hint of the "Hittite" character of this Aramæan culture may be found in the basalt lion of Sheikh Saad, which stalks along in high relief and projecting head.[21]

Hadadezer's army came within sight of Rabbath Ammon, but found Joab between them and the city. When the Ammonites sallied forth to effect a junction, Abishai held them in check, while Joab with his chosen troops attacked the relieving army and put it to flight. Hadadezer then summoned aid from the Aramæan states recently formed east of the Euphrates,[22] while David appeared at the head of the whole levy. The Hebrew army was now fully organised, from the "people," the folk levy, through the six hundred half foreign mercenaries of the body guard, the thirty lesser and the three greater "heroes," to Joab, the commander-in-chief. Once more at Helam the enemy was defeated and Shobach, the allied commander, was slain; the captured horses, all but enough for a hundred chariots, were hamstrung, and the golden shields of Hadadezer's body guard were carried as spoil to Jerusalem.

Next year, Joab opened the siege of Rabbath Ammon. In a trough on the north side of a stream which watered a broad fertile valley was the L-shaped citadel; its flat summit was separated from the plateau by a wide artificial cutting and allowed space for a good sized town, yet was isolated and difficult of access on all sides. A fine spring furnished the city

[20] Strab., xvi, 2, 10; Joseph., *Ant.,* xiv, 40; Steph. Byz., s. v. *Chalkis.*
[21] G. Contenau, *Syria,* V, 1924, 207 ff.
[22] Cf. *History of Assyria,* 65.

with water, but if this was captured by the enemy, a concealed passage led to a cistern on the west neck, where attack was most difficult.

Meanwhile, David idled away his time in Jerusalem with a discreditable intrigue. Uriah, a Hittite mercenary, was recalled to father the unborn child of his Hebrew wife Bathsheba, but refused to enter his house while the ark and Israel and Judah were in huts. He carried back a letter which instructed Joab to abandon him in the fighting and so he died. After but seven days of mourning, Bathsheba was married and at once became David's favourite wife. Her first child soon died, but a second was named Solomon, in token of the "Peace" now established with Yahweh. His education was confided to the prophet Nathan, who with Bathsheba dominated the aging king.

Joab had discovered the hidden reservoir and the fall of the city was assured; too cautious to receive its surrender, he bade David collect the levies and maliciously added: "lest I take the city and it be called by my name." The whole Ammonite population, townsman and peasant alike, was hacked by saws, harrows, and axes, or made to pass through the brick kiln. Hanun was succeeded by his brother Shobi, but only as governor. The crown of their god Milcom, a talent's weight of gold, was snatched from his head, and the precious stone in it David placed on his own.[23]

Damascus had been settled by Aramæans as early as the reign of Ramses III, whose lists already give the Aramaic spelling. When Damascus sent aid to their fellow Aramæan Hadadezer, their troops were defeated and Hebrew garrisons occupied their territory. The home land of Hadadezer was invaded and Tibhath and Berothai or Berut afforded David much bronze. Kadesh had been supplanted as chief town of Central Syria by Hamath in its deep sunk Orontes trench, and its "Hittite" inhabitants were employing the raised pictographic characters we call "Hittite." Toi its king had already warred with Hadadezer, who evidently had no intention of

[23] II Sam. 10 f.; 12:16 ff.; 17:27.

confining his kingdom to Hollow Syria, and he greeted David's victory with an embassy headed by the crown prince Joram; the gifts of gold, silver, and bronze vessels were dedicated to Yahweh, whose worship in Central Syria was commemorated in the name of the envoy.[24]

Equal success rewarded the wars of David with the other east Jordan peoples. Quite forgetful of his own Moabite blood and of the refuge granted his parents by a Moabite king, he treated the Moabite captives with unusual atrocity. Placed on the ground and measured by ropes, every two out of three Moabites were put to death.

Edom had been at first ruled by separate chiefs, each connected with a supposed descendant of Esau. About 1160, they established a monarchy. Eight of their kings are known by name, beginning with Bela, son of Beor from Dinhabah, perhaps the Balaam of legend. He was followed by Jobab, son of Zerah from Bozrah, southeast of the Dead Sea, by Husham of interior Teman, and by the first Hadad, son of Bedad, from Avith, who smote Midian in the field of Moab. After him reigned Samlah of Masrekah, Saul of Rehoboth by a stream flowing into the Dead Sea, Baal-hanan, son of Achbor, the "Mouse" clan, and the second Hadad of Pau.[25]

It would seem that the Edomites had invaded Judah, for they were defeated in the Valley of Salt. Hebrew garrisons were stationed throughout Edom, and Joab remained six months in the attempt to destroy every male. A few courtiers escaped by the round-about way of Midian and Paran, and brought to Egypt the royal child Hadad. They were well received by the reigning Pharaoh, Siamon (976–958) or Pesibkhenno II (958–945), anxious to check the upstart Hebrew state. Hadad was granted a house and estates and married to the queen's sister, while their son Genubath was reared among Pharaoh's children. The Hebrews told with glee how Esau had been cheated of his birthright as oldest son by his clever brother Jacob.[26]

[24] II Sam. 8:5–11.   [25] Gen. 36; I Chron. 1:35–54.
[26] II Sam. 8:2, 13 f.; I Kings 11:14 ff.; Gen. 27.

David's intrigue with Bathsheba set an example which was followed by his eldest son Amnon when he dishonoured his half sister Tamar. In revenge, her full brother Absalom killed Amnon and fled to his grandfather Talmai, king of Geshur and David's sole Aramæan ally. After three years of exile, he was recalled through the trickery of a wise woman of Tekoa, hired for the purpose by Joab, but two years more elapsed before he was permitted to see his father's face. He now assumed to be crown prince and prepared a chariot and fifty riders. No one was allowed to make obeisance, but all were kissed as equals; early in the morning he could be found standing in the gate and sighing because he could not do the petitioners justice.

After four years of such intrigue, Absalom begged permission to pay a belated vow for his safe return to the Yahweh of Hebron. With him he took two hundred invited guests from the first families of Jerusalem who knew nothing of the conspiracy, but Ahithophel of Giloh, one of David's most trusted counsellors, was his chief support. Emissaries were sent to all the tribes of Israel; when they heard the sound of the trumpet, they should shout: "Absalom is king in Hebron."

David thought only of flight. Accompanied by his personal court and the faithful six hundred Cherethites and Pelethites who formed his body guard, he retreated towards the Jordan fords. Zadok and Abiathar brought the ark to the Kidron, but were sent back, as was Hushai, the King's Friend. Absalom occupied Jerusalem without resistance and publicly took over the royal harem to shame his father. Ahithophel advised immediate pursuit, but Hushai craftily urged delay to collect more troops; his counsel prevailed and Ahithophel in despair went home to Giloh, made his will, and strangled himself. Hushai passed on the news to Zadok and Abiathar who relayed it through a maid servant to their sons Jonathan and Ahimaaz, in hiding near En Rogel. On receipt of the news, David crossed the Jordan to Mahanaim, with what memories of the murdered Ishbaal, who shall say?

Absalom followed with an army levied from all Israel, and took position on the Gilead hills; his commander-in-chief was the Ishmaelite Amasa, who in the *sadiqa* fashion common to foreigners had married Abigail, sister of the famous Zeruiah. David's army was inferior in numbers, though it had received additions from the east Jordan tribes, but his three generals, Joab, Abishai, and Ittai, had grown old in the making of war and his body guard was composed of seasoned warriors.

A true Battle of the Wilderness ensued. The undisciplined levies of Absalom were slaughtered and more died from the forest than from the sword. Absalom fled on his mule, but his head was caught in the thick branches of a huge oak. David had expressly ordered that his life be saved, but Joab seized three darts and transfixed his heart; the corpse was cast into a great pit and over it was raised a stone heap worthy an evil doer.

David at the gate of Mahanaim was greeted: "As the young man be the enemies of my lord king." He hid himself and wept; his weeping did credit to a father's feeling, but it was grossly unfair to men who had risked their lives in his desperate cause. Joab harshly recalled David to realities: "You have this day shamed the faces of all your servants who this very day have saved your life. You have this day declared that princes and servants are nothing to you. For I know that if Absalom were alive this day and all of us dead, it would be pleasing in your eyes. Rise, then, and speak to your servants' hearts. For I swear by Yahweh that if you do not come out this day not a man will remain with you this night, and that will be worse for you than all the evil that has come upon you from your youth until now."

Nor did David rejoice when he learned that the fugitive Israelites were asking one another why they delayed to restore their king; instead, he used their irresolution to urge the elders of Judah: "You are my brothers, my bone and my flesh; why should you be the last to restore the king?" Amasa was promised the position long held by Joab, and through his efforts Judah was persuaded to come down to Gilgal and meet the king.

This action led to renewed complaints from the Israelites:

"Why have the men of Judah, our brothers, stolen you, and brought the king and his house over Jordan? All David's men are his people." The Judæans answered: "The king is our kinsman," but Israel insisted: "We have ten parts in the king and I am the first born rather than you; why then do you despise us, for was it not my word first to bring back our king?" In the camp was a certain Sheba, of the Bichri clan of Benjamin, and so related to Saul; taking advantage of Israel's resentment, he blew the trumpet and raised the cry:

> No portion have we in David,
> No heritage in Jesse's son!
> To your tents, O Israel!

True to his promise, David made Amasa commander-in-chief, but Amasa was no Joab and he failed to raise the Judæan levy in three days. The body guard under Abishai was hurried off in pursuit and Joab accompanied his brother. When Amasa and the Judæan levy caught up with the body guard at the great stone in Gibeon, Joab kissed him and slew him.

Sheba retreated before Joab and took refuge in Abel, an important town at the foot of Lebanon and looking across the fertile upper Jordan valley to Hermon; cairns of ancient date and first bronze age pottery prove its early settlement, but now it was a part of Aramæan Maacah. A mound had been heaped up against the rampart and the wall was being undermined when a wise woman called out to Joab: "In olden times they were wont to say: 'Let them ask for the oracle in Abel or Dan,' and that settled the matter, but you are seeking to destroy a city and mother in Israel." Joab assured her that he desired only the rebel; persuaded by their wise woman, the citizens cut off Sheba's head and threw it over the wall.[27] The revolt was ended but hatred smouldered between north and south, ready to flare up at the first opportunity. Once more Joab was head of the army and virtual ruler of the kingdom, but David never forgave Absalom's murder and Joab had influential enemies, Benaiah, commander of the body guard,

[27] II Sam. 13–20.

Zadok, the priest, Nathan, the prophet, and the notorious Bathsheba.

A typical oriental administration had already been put into effect. Joab as commander-in-chief headed the list of royal officials, followed by Jehoshaphat, Ahilud's son, as prime minister. Benaiah was commander of the body guard, Ira the Jairite and David's sons were priests. The royal scribe was Shavsha, whose Babylonian name remembered the sun god Shamash and leads us to suspect that he too was a Babylonian, imported to translate foreign correspondence in the cuneiform character.

The tribal organisation was continued for administrative purposes and we have a list of the governors. Reuben heads the list, Simeon and Levi are still recognised, Manasseh and Gilead are separate. Judah is ruled by David's brother Elihu, Abner's son Jaasiel has been rewarded with Benjamin, Michael's son Omri in Issachar may be an ancestor of the great king. Local affairs were in the hands of the "heads of the fathers" or "elders of the city in the gate" or "judges." Each freeman had his "allotment" for which he must do military service. These local levies, under captains of ten, fifty, a hundred, and a thousand, were called up for a month each year under regular generals, generally from the south but with Benjamin and Ephraim represented.

Freemen were subjected to more onerous services than the military levy. Adoniram, Abda's son, was charged with the forced labour demanded for David's buildings. Oversight of the taxes collected in kind was by Azmaweth, Abdiel's son, for Jerusalem, and by Jonathan, Uzziah's son, for the fields belonging to the towns, villages, and guard towers. Ezri, Chelub's son, was over those who did the work of the field for the tillage of the ground, Shimei of Ramah was over the royal vineyards, Zabdi of Siphmoth in the Negeb over the wine paid in kind, Baalhanan of Gederah over the olives and sycamores in the Shephelah, Joash over the oil paid as tax. Shitrai of Sharon and Shaphat, Adlai's son, were in charge of the royal herds in Sharon and the valleys respectively, Obil the Ishmaelite was very appropriately in charge of the camels, Jehdeiah of Meronoth of the asses, and Jaziz the Hagrite of the flocks.[28]

To determine the military levy and to apportion the taxes, oriental monarchs needed such a census as the famous Assyrian Doomsday Book from Harran.[29] Ordered to prepare a census, Joab replied in true oriental fashion: "Let Yahweh multiply the nation a hundredfold in the king's lifetime, but why trouble with a census?" Modern methods won and the census was made; it seems to have been preserved in two lists, later assigned to the Mosaic period.

Judah has the largest population, 76,500, Simeon the least, 22,200. Benjamin has 35,500, Ephraim but 40,500, while Manasseh reaches 52,700. Reuben is still prosperous with 43,730, and Gad has 40,500. The great importance of the northern tribes appears from their statistics, 64,400 for Dan, 43,400 for Asher, 45,400 for Naphtali, 64,300 for Issachar, 66,500 for Zebulon. The total is nearly 600,000, not far from the present-day population.[30]

Gad, friend of David in adversity, announced the word of Yahweh; the census was a sin and David might choose his punishment, three years of famine, three months flight before his enemies, or three days pestilence. David chose the last. Seventy thousand perished and his messenger was stretching out his hand over Jerusalem when Yahweh relented. David was instructed by Gad to build an altar on the threshing floor of Araunah, where the messenger stayed his hand, and so he did.[31]

David's reign marks the beginnings of Hebrew literature. Stories of the fathers and of the early heroes were written in the new script adapted from the Phœnician, official chronicles told of David's wars. Poetry flourished. David himself was no minor poet, as witness the magnificent threnody on Saul's death. Early songs were collected into the "Book of Yahweh's Wars" or the "Book of the Brave." Ancient characterisations

[28] II Sam. 8:16–18; 20:23–26; I Chron. 27.
[29] Cf. *History of Assyria*, 517.
[30] Num. 26; less accurately Num. 1; cf. W. F. Albright, *JPOS.*, V, 1925, 20 ff.
[31] II Sam. 24.

of the tribes were attributed to the dying Jacob; Reuben was permitted to hold first place, though no longer "surpassing," Simeon and Levi were "blessed" with a curse and their ultimate dispersion predicted. The way was now cleared for Judah. To an older triplet:

> Judah, thee shall thy brothers praise,
>   Thy hand on the neck of thy foes,
>   Thy father's sons to thee bow,

was now added

> The whelp of a lion is Judah,
>   From the prey, my son, hast gone up;
> He crouched, he lay down like a lion,
>   Like a lioness—who dare him rouse?
>
> The sceptre shall not from Judah depart,
>   Nor the staff from between his feet,
> Till he comes, whose is the right,
>   And him shall the people obey.
>
> He binds his ass to the vinestock,
>   To the choice vine the foal of his dam,
> He washes in wine his garments,
>   His clothes in the blood of the grape;
> Dulled from wine is his eyesight,
>   And white his teeth with milk.

After this almost millennial description of David's rule, the other tribes are given briefer blessings. Joseph alone, to whom must be credited a large part of the kingdom's glory, is fully honoured. Benjamin, as the home of the deposed Saul, is placed at the very end and with the briefest blessing.[32]

A similar picture of Israel's prosperity is given in poems attributed to the diviner Balaam, who in legend was brought by Balak king of Moab to curse the invaders of his land:

> From Aram Balak has brought me,
>   Moab's king from the Mounts of the East,

[32] Gen. 49.

"Come, curse for me Jacob,
  Come, Israel condemn."
How curse him whom God hath not cursed,
  How condemn whom Yahweh condemns not?

From the top of the rocks I see him,
  Behold him from the hills;
Lo, a people by itself dwelling,
  Mid the nations counts not itself;
Who can count the dust of Jacob,
  Who can number Israel's ten thousands?

Arise, Balak, and hear,
  Give ear to me, Zippor's son;
God is not man, to lie,
  Nor a son of man, to repent;
Can he speak and not execute?
  Can he say and not fulfil?

Behold, to bless I received,
  I will bless, I cannot reverse;
No evil in Jacob I see,
  No trouble in Israel behold;
With him is Yahweh, his God,
  In his midst is the shout for a king.

From Egypt God brought him forth,
  The strength of a wild bull is his;
Like a lioness rises the folk,
  Like a lion lifts itself up;
Lies not down till he's eaten the prey,
  And drinks the blood of the slain.

Saying of Balaam, Beor's son,
  Saying of man with closed eyes;
Saying of listener to God's words,
  Who knows the thought of the Most High;
The Almighty in vision who sees,
  Fallen down, but with open eyes.

How goodly thy tents, O Jacob,
  Thy dwellings, O Israel;
Like valleys spread out,
  Like gardens by river,

Like cedars Yahweh planted,
  Like poplars by waters.

Water pours from his buckets,
  His seed is on many waters;
His king is higher than Agag,
  His kingdom highly exalted;
God brought him out of Egypt,
  The strength of a wild bull is his.

Let him eat his foes of the nations,
  Let him break their bones;
He crouched, he lay down like a lion,
  Like a lioness—who dare him rouse?
Those who bless thee be blessed,
  Those who curse thee be cursed!

I see him, but not now,
  I behold him, but not near;
A star has shone forth from Jacob,
  A sceptre arisen in Israel;
He smites through the temples of Moab,
  And the skull of all sons of pride.[33]

[33]Num. 23:7–10, 18–22, 24; 24:3–9, 15–17.

CHAPTER XXII

SOLOMON IN ALL HIS GLORY

DAVID's older sons, Amnon, Chileab, and Absalom, had all disappeared. Eldest of those surviving was Adonijah, born to the purple after his father became king in Hebron. A man of impressive appearance, he prepared a body guard of chariots and cavalry and fifty runners to precede him, fit state for a crown prince; David raised no objection while Joab and Abiathar, heads of the army and the church, actively supported his claim.

Adonijah's claim did not go unchallenged. The latest wife of an oriental monarch always enjoys the greatest favour. In the death of Bathsheba's first born, outraged public opinion had seen the punishment for the parents' sin, but since then she had borne David another son. Courtiers in plenty had wearied of Joab's unscrupulous use of his usurped power, and turned to Benaiah, son of Jehoiada from Kabzeel in southern Judah, who had been one of the three "mightiest heroes," but had now risen to command of the foreign body guard and so was closer to the royal person than Joab. Zadok, son of Ahitub, had to some extent shared with Abiathar the office of chief priest. When Joab and Abiathar declared for Adonijah, Benaiah and Zadok naturally supported his rival. Two prophets, Nathan and Shemaiah of En Halom, the "Well of Oracular Dreams," were also among Solomon's partisans.

Adonijah was alarmed and with reason. There is no definite rule of succession in an oriental monarchy, and Solomon possessed one advantage over Adonijah; not only was he born to the purple, at his birth David was king over all Israel. David was in extremis, and his death might be concealed until Bathsheba and Benaiah, supported by the royal body guard, had placed her son on the throne. Adonijah therefore summoned his partisans, David's remaining sons and all the nobles of

Judah, who collected near En Rogel, the "Fuller's Fount," and sacrificed fatlings by the "Serpent's Stone," Zoheleth, a ladder-like ascent up a broad band of exposed rock opposite the fountain.

Nathan informed Bathsheba of the danger and through their influence the dying monarch swore that Solomon should be his successor—or so it was reported. Solomon was placed on the royal mule and, accompanied by Zadok, Nathan, Benaiah, and the foreign mercenaries, was marched down to Gihon, the spring nearer the palace. Zadok anointed him with the horn of sacred oil from the tent where the ark was kept, the trumpets were blown, and the people shouted "Live King Solomon!"

The noise reached the guests at the rival coronation and they fled precipitately. Adonijah seized the horns of the altar in the sacred tent and refused to abandon sanctuary unless Solomon took oath that his life would be spared; Solomon gave the ambiguous promise: "If he shows himself worthy, not a hair shall fall to the ground; if wickedness is found in him, he shall die." By order of the new king, Adonijah was taken from the altar and brought to court where he promised loyalty.

Shortly thereafter, David passed away, and was buried in the city to which he had given his name. Immediately it was given out that David had ordered a general house cleaning. We would gladly believe that, even in his senile old age, David had not sunk so low as to order the murder of the man who made his empire and had repeatedly saved his life; that he could not have been so cowardly as to postpone his revenge until after he was safely dead. The account of these events is obviously contemporary, but quite as obviously it is propaganda history by a partisan of Solomon, and there is no reason to doubt the Chronicler's implication that it was written by Nathan.[1]

The partisan character of the history is particularly evident in the account of Adonijah's death. We are asked to believe

[1] II Chron. 9:29.

that after Solomon's warning Adonijah was rash enough to ask of Bathsheba David's cast-off wife Abishag. Despite Adonijah's flat statement that the kingdom was really his, we are further asked to believe that the shrewd queen mother never suspected that this request for a portion of David's harem was according to oriental custom a bid for the throne, that in all innocence of heart she begged this favour of her son, and that only the cleverness of a twelve-year-old boy saw through the plot. Bathsheba and Solomon alone were left to testify to the accuracy of these conversations, for the third witness, Adonijah, was promptly removed by Benaiah.

Joab heard the news and realised that he was next on the list of the proscribed. He at once took refuge at the horns of the altar and refused to obey Benaiah's summons to come forth. In fear of Yahweh's vengeance, Benaiah was reluctant to employ force, but Solomon had no such scruples; Benaiah was ordered to complete his task and Joab died at the altar whose sanctity could not protect Yahweh's suppliant.

Solomon did not quite dare kill Abiathar, who had carried Yahweh's ephod before David and had shared all his sufferings, but Abiathar was deposed and banished to his estate at Anathoth. Thus the line of Eli lost control of the ark which it had cherished from the first settlement at Shiloh; there was circulated the prophecy of an anonymous "man of God" who had predicted to Eli this disaster. The "man of God" further predicted that Yahweh would raise up in his place a faithful priest for whom should be built an enduring house and who should walk before Yahweh's anointed forever. Abiathar's office of chief priest was thereafter filled by Zadok and his descendants; the change in religious leadership was in some respects more significant than that in the state, for Zadok's descendants were high priests long after David's line had ceased to be Yahweh's anointed kings.[2]

Did Abiathar devote his enforced leisure to perpetuating the deeds of his great hero? The core of our present books of Samuel is an ancient narrative. It begins with Eli, Abiathar's

[2] I Kings 1 f.; I Sam. 2:27 ff.

ancestor, the capture of the ark, its adventures among the Philistines. Then comes Saul's relief of Jabesh Gilead, and the battle for freedom, in which Abiathar's uncle Ahimelech consults the ephod. David appears at Saul's court and marries Michal, but is forced to flee and his flight involves the murder of Abiathar's father and all his family. Abiathar escapes to David, and thereafter his consultation of the ephod is often mentioned. David becomes king and attempts to win over Jabesh Gilead, he regains Michal only to break with her. The murder of Abiathar's family is avenged indirectly by Abiathar's use of the ephod, the ark is triumphantly brought into David's Town. David enjoys foreign victories and suffers from domestic evils, and Abiathar is by his side.

Whether or not Abiathar was our historian, his work is almost a miracle to his modern successor. History such as this had never before been written. Inspired annals of a monarch's wars, lists of kings, brief dry chronicles, folk tales of past heroes, this was the best that had been produced. Suddenly and without apparent forerunners, we have a narrative which invites comparison with many present-day accounts of a reign. The author is well informed, he knows court life from the inside, he writes simply but vividly, not for a monarch's favour but for the instruction of generations to come.

What most amazes his modern successor is his complete objectivity. He shows us the youthful David whose winning ways stole the hearts of all, even the melancholy Saul, but we have the David whose lie killed the priests of Nob, who treated Nabal like a bandit, who took refuge with Israel's worst enemies and then lied again about his raids. He appreciates the remarkable task of uniting all Israel, of freeing the land from its foes, of extending its boundaries. David's religious reforms are given due attention, though there is no hint of an ecclesiastical tendency. Our author is equally careful to trace the degeneration of David's character under the influence of success and luxury, and the picture he paints, not by laboured description but by allowing the deeds to speak for themselves, is stark tragedy, true to the dramatic facts of human nature.

Unlike the poets who sang of Judah's greatness, he even foresees a little of the future's threat. His name may be lost, but his modern successor must pay tribute to this first and strangely modern historian of three thousand years ago.

Solomon was but a youth of twelve at his accession, about 955.[3] Later writers celebrated the almost millennial prosperity of his reign, but there is little of this in contemporary narratives. David had built an empire of considerable extent, but a large part was in no sense Hebrew, and the Israelite tribes still felt his dynasty to be foreign.

Solomon was not successful in his foreign relations. After the defeat of Hadadezer, his vassal Rezon, son of Eliada, collected his men and marched eastward. From Zobah, the road leaves the fertile plain and rises steeply through barren rocks; not a tree appears and for hours there is no sign of water. From the scorching red hill tops and the equally bare grey of the lower slopes, it suddenly dips into the breezy gorge of the Amana, the "Faithful," for it never fails in the hottest summer. Soon the Amana is doubled by a deep spring which pours beautiful blue white water from under noble walnuts; no wonder a temple was erected to the deity from whose bounty came all this loveliness.

From the narrow gorge exit, the wearied rider is startled by a fairy scene. The Damascus oasis is the gift of the Amana and its lesser sister, the Pharpar. From the bare limestone hills under which the modern city nestles and with which its verdure so pleasantly contrasts is a wide view. In the foreground is the plain, thirty miles long by ten wide. Behind mud walls are trees of every description and in thick profusion, brought to maturity by the rich sandy loam and the water which flows through the streets and provides fountains in every courtyard. There are evils to mar this paradise, due likewise to the waters, the heavy dew, the mosquitoes, the frequent fevers. Such must have been the ancient Damascus, but its site was eight miles due east where a mound a hundred feet high and nine hundred in diameter invites the excavator.

[3] I Kings 2:12, Greek, F. Field, *Origenis Hexaplorum*, 1875, I, 596.

Beyond the plain are the lakes in which the rivers find their death, a source of fish and the reedy haunt of the wild swine. Beyond the lake again are the Tulul, isolated conical hills of volcanic origin, and to their north the level stretches out to the sky line and to the desert. To their south the view is lost in the far distant blue of the Hauran, lower hills close in, and then Hermon dominates the scene.

Damascus is an oasis, for with all its fertility it is essentially of the desert. When desert tribes unite, it must fall, for there is no natural barrier. Damascus is middle man between the desert and the culture states, which covet the wealth thus won, but rarely cross its double mountain rampart.

Rezon founded the kingdom which was called par excellence Aram. David's death freed him from fear and all his days he was an opponent of Solomon. The Camps of Jair and Kenath were lost to Damascus or to the neighbouring Aramæan state of Geshur, no longer allied to Israel, and henceforth the boundary never extended beyond Ramath Gilead.[4] Rezon or one of his immediate successors is depicted on a limestone stele. Within a raised border, he stands in relief, one foot forward. His eye is large, his ear high set, his nose generous, his lips are shaved, below is a long pointed and curled beard. His dress is short, Assyrian sandals are on his feet. In his left hand he holds a staff, in his right is an object ending in quatrefoils.[5]

Hadad returned from Egypt and recovered the Edomite mountains, though Solomon retained Ezion Geber with its control of the Ophir trade.[6] Damascus was admittedly foreign, but Edom was closely related to the Hebrews in race and language, Edomite elements had been incorporated into Judah, early legends made Esau Jacob's brother. Hope of an ultimate incorporation was reasonable; Hadad's return put an end to this hope and began the estrangement which made "Edomite" a term of reproach to the later Jews.

[4] I Kings 11:23 ff.; I Chron. 2:23.
[5] Fig. 146; J. L. Porter, *Five Years in Damascus*, I, 383 f.; G. Contenau, *Syria*, V, 1924, 210.
[6] I Kings 11:14 ff.

About 945 the twenty-second dynasty of Libyan origin secured possession of Egypt, and Shishak (945–924) began to dream of renewed empire in Syria. His first step was to win David's weak young son. David himself had been unable to reduce Gezer, on its isolated outlier commanding the exit of the Aijalon road, but Shishak was more successful. Overawed by this exhibition of Egyptian strength at his very door, Solomon made alliance with Shishak; Egyptian kings no longer hesitated to give their daughters to foreign rulers and Solomon became Shishak's son-in-law. As part of her dowry, the partially burned Gezer[7] was handed over to the Hebrew monarch. The Egyptian queen ranked far above the other women of the harem, and Solomon found it necessary to build her a separate palace. Intimate trade relations followed the alliance and Egyptian horses were secured for re-export.[8]

The Philistines were in rapid decline, but at that Achish, son of Maacah, held Gath at another entrance to the Judæan hills.[9] Relations of a more intimate nature existed with the Phœnicians. According to the native sources, Solomon visited Tyre and worshipped in the temple of Baal Melkart, while Hiram sealed the renewal of the treaty with David by the gift of his daughter to Solomon.[10]

Egypt had long trafficked down the Red Sea to Punt. An early folk tale told of the shipwrecked sailor and the kindly sea serpent,[11] the expedition of Queen Hatshepsut was pictured on Theban walls. In this same region was Ophir, with its gold and ivory, its gum trees, and its apes.[12] Ezion Geber on the Gulf of Aqaba remained in Solomon's possession, but no Hebrew knew seafaring to take advantage of this opportunity. Solomon therefore made an arrangement with Hiram by which Phœnician sailors manned the ships built by Hebrew labour. In return, Hiram permitted Solomon to trade with

[7]Macalister, *Gezer*, I, 20.
[8]I Kings 3:1; 9:24; 10:28 f.; cf. Deut. 17:16.   [9]I Kings 2:39.
[10]Menander, in Clem. Alex., *Strom.*, i, 114, 2; cf. I Kings 11:1; Justin, *Dialog. contra Tryphon*, 34, 8.
[11]Erman, *Literature*, 29 ff.
[12]Cf. W. E. Clark, *AJSL.*, XXXVI, 1920, 103 ff.

Tarshish or Tarsus, now coming into prominence as the outlet of the silver mines north of the Taurus; the Tarsus region, Quweh or Que, exported to Solomon the famous Cappadocian stallions.[13]

An Edomite wife counterbalanced Hadad's claims, the same motive was responsible for marriages to Moabites and to the daughter of the Ammonite king Hanun; wives taken from the "Hittite" princes scattered through North Syria or from the Aramæans of Central Syria were for trade only. Horses were such a rarity in David's time that he hamstrung all but the few he could use; Solomon received horses and chariots from Egypt and Quweh and resold them through his royal factors. The kings of the desert Arabs were also in trade relations, and legend loved to tell of the visit made by the queen of the South Arabian Sheba to learn his wisdom and to behold his magnificence.[14]

It is difficult to realise the magnitude of the cultural and religious changes brought about by the empire and the changed economics. Saul's subjects were but little removed from the semi-nomadic life, his second successor was one of the great kings and his subjects were in the full flow of the Near Eastern mercantile tides. Solomon profited from his royal monopolies, but these very monopolies demanded a new merchant class. To Solomon, more than to any other single individual, belongs the credit for swerving the Hebrew genius into that path it has since followed with success. New contacts meant new imports, new needs, new points of view; from the standpoint of the great powers, the Hebrews were becoming civilised.

So far as he was able, Solomon made his court a replica of that at Thebes or Babylon or Ashur. Jehoshaphat, Ahilud's son, was still prime minister and Adoniram over the corvee. Azariah was chief priest in place of his father Zadok. Shavsha's sons Elihoreph and Ahijah followed him as royal scribes; the Babylonian father had worshipped Shamash, Ahijah pro-

[13] I Kings 10:28 f.; cf. *History of Assyria*, 144, 299, 310, 534; 125, 162, 420.
[14] I Kings 15:2; 11:1 ff.; 10.

fessed his devotion to the Hebrew deity. Another foreigner, Ahishar, was over the household as chief eunuch. Nathan's son Zabud was king's companion; another son, Azariah, was over the governors.

These titles lead us straight back to Assyria. Still more Assyrian was Solomon's provincial organisation. David had retained the tribal divisions, his son felt no need to flatter tribal susceptibilities; the entire kingdom was divided into twelve districts which corresponded but roughly to tribal division and Hebrews and Canaanites alike were treated as provincials. Over each was a governor whose chief duty was to provide provisions for the court one month each year. The list from the royal archives has been preserved, and is as instructive as the similar list in the Assyrian Chronicle.[15] Mount Ephraim under a son of Hur comes first, then the original Dan, with Makaz, Shaalbim, Beth Shemesh, Aijalon, and Beth Hanan, under Deker's son. Manasseh west of the Jordan formed the third province, with Arruboth, Socoh, and the land of Hepher, under the son of Hesed. Abinadab's son, the king's son-in-law, ruled the "Cliffs of Dor," the seacoast south of Mount Carmel. Baana, Ahilud's son, brother of the prime minister, was in charge of the Great Plain, from Jokneam through Taanach and Beth Shan to Abel Meholah, well down the Jordan valley; his capital was Megiddo where the governor's palace has recently been excavated.[16] Ahimaaz, another royal son-in-law, had charge of Naphtali; Baana, Hushai's son, was in Asher; Jehoshaphat, Paruah's son, in Issachar. Geber's son was in Gilead with his capital at Ramath Gilead; Ahinadab, Iddo's son, was farther south in Mahanaim; Uri's son was in Gad. Shimei, Ela's son, was over Benjamin. Judah was administered directly by the king through a deputy.[17]

The "Manner of the Kingdom" is described in a late prophecy placed in the mouth of Samuel, but it is accurate.[18] Their

---

[15] Cf. *JAOS.*, XXXIV, 1915, 344 ff.   [16] Cf. frontispiece.
[17] I Kings 4; cf. W. F. Albright, *JPOS.*, V, 1925, 17 ff.; R. P. Dougherty, *Ann.*, V, 23 ff.
[18] I Sam. 8:11 ff.

FIG. 138. JOPPA, PORT OF JERUSALEM.

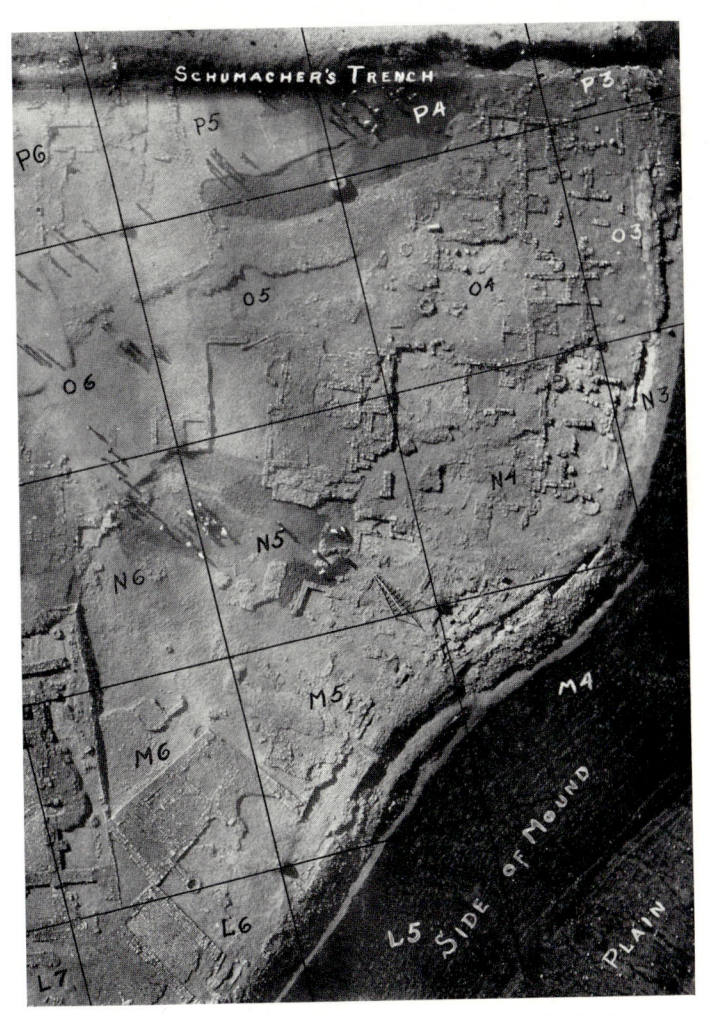

FIG. 139. THE EXCAVATION OF MEGIDDO. (Air view.)

men were levied as soldiers or for plowing and reaping the crown lands with their own animals, or for manufacturing weapons and chariots; their women were enrolled as perfumers, cooks, and bakers. The best of their fields, vineyards, and olive orchards were confiscated and granted to the king's supporters.[19] Tithe was demanded of the seed, wine, and flocks, and the "king's mowing" took the first cutting of the grass.[20] Every day the court consumed thirty cors of fine flour and sixty measures of meal, ten fat oxen, twenty pasture-fed oxen, a hundred sheep, not to mention harts, gazelles, and fatted fowl. Barley and straw must be provided for the horses, of which he had four thousand stalls, and food for the twelve thousand horsemen.[21]

With the spoils of his trade, with the labour from the corvee, with the taxes from the twelve provinces, Solomon had ample facilities for building. Gibeon was honoured by Solomon with sacrifice at its great high place in the beginning of his reign and here he received a vision. Baalath and Tamar held in check the half nomads of the wilderness. The recently acquired Gezer received a new towered wall, the Great Road was patrolled by fortifications, and stables for the horses were constructed at Lachish, Gezer, Megiddo, and Taanach. Beth Horon guarded the northern approach to Jerusalem from the sea, Hazor covered the north Jordan valley.[22]

Megiddo had outgrown its original thirteen acres on the mound summit and had extended to a terrace on the north. The new city was protected by a new wall; for thirty yards behind the wall, all buildings were destroyed to permit free movement of the defenders within, without the ground was levelled to prevent an enemy's undetected approach. Should an assault be attempted against the old city, there was a steep climb of thirty-five yards up the mound slope to the towered wall thirteen feet thick. The enemy might advance up the

[19] II Sam. 9:7; 12:8; I Kings 21:15 f.; I Sam. 22:7.
[20] Amos 7:1; I Kings 18:3 ff.   [21] I Kings 4:22 ff.
[22] I Kings 3:4 ff.; 9:15 ff.; Bliss, *Mound*, 90 ff.; Macalister, *Gezer*, I, 247; II, 406 ff.; Sellin, *Tell Taannek*, 18, 104; Guy, *New Light from Armageddon*.

curved road to the gate at the east of a court, but could he force this outer gate, he was caught in a sloping enclosure where he was in extreme danger from the defenders on the

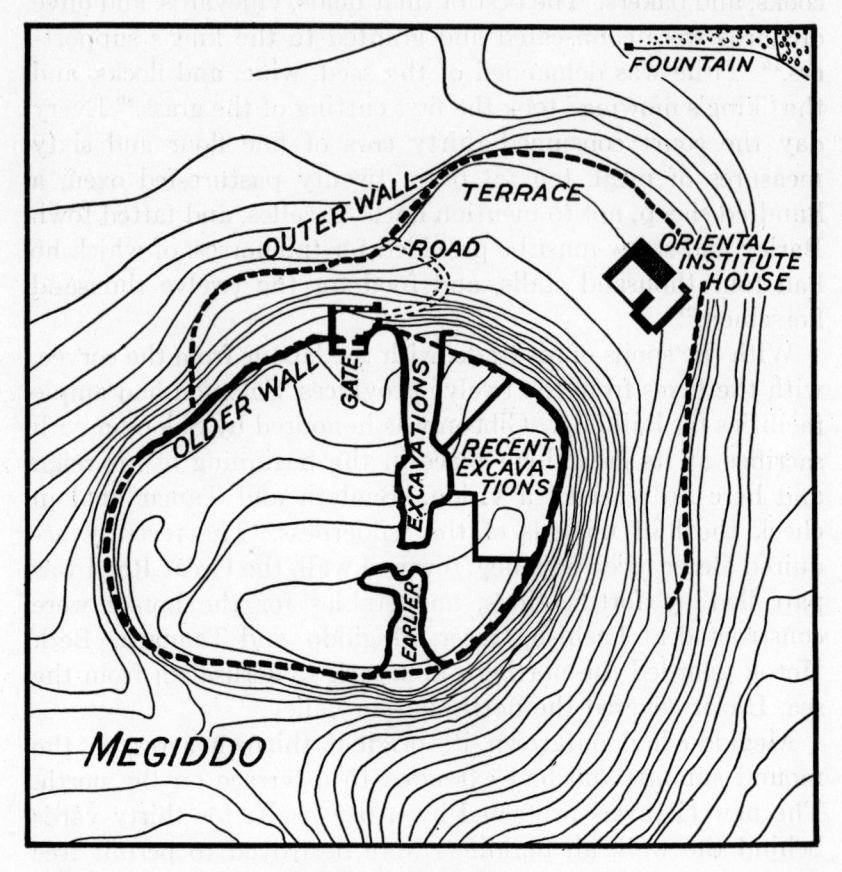

PLAN 13. MEGIDDO.

walls above. Then he must break through an inner gate to the south in the city wall, here thickened to form massive towers on either side the entrance. A stone-paved passage thirteen feet wide under which ran the city drain, covered with broad stone slabs, was guarded by double doors swung on basalt sockets and fitting into deep recesses. A second gateway was between two more towers. Three courses of carefully dressed

Fig. 140. SOLOMON'S STABLES. (Restored.)

Fig. 141. SOLOMON'S STABLES. (Present condition.)

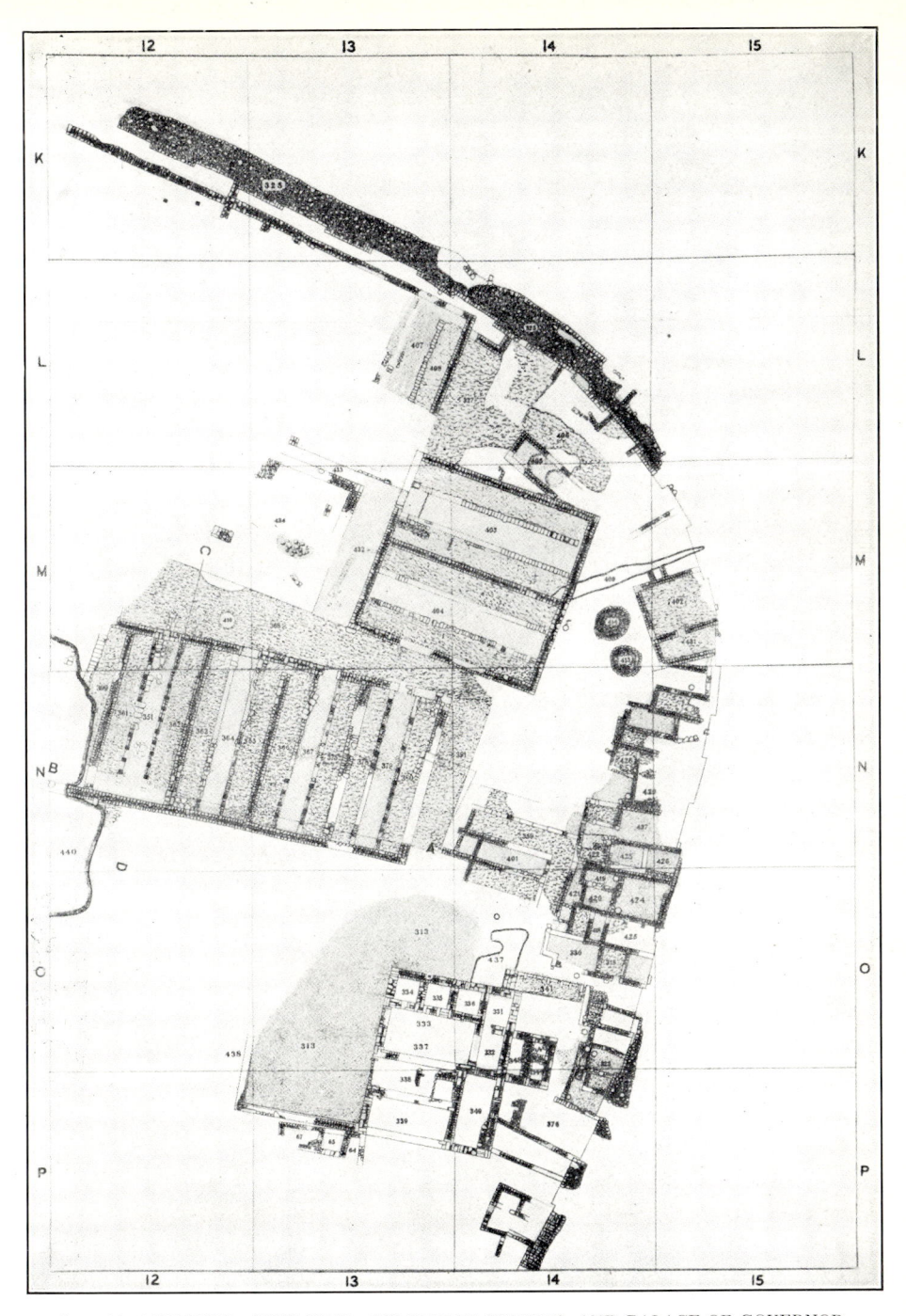

PLAN 14. MEGIDDO.—CITY WALL, SOLOMON'S STABLES, AND PALACE OF GOVERNOR.

SOLOMON IN ALL HIS GLORY

and truly laid ashlar were topped by mud brick. From the gate, the main street ran straight to the palace on the higher ground to the south; all the streets were straight and one broadened as it approached the gate.

Perhaps we may find the government house of Baana in a large building around a lime-paved courtyard, from which troops could be led up a stairway to the flat roofs of the barracks clinging along the inner face of the city wall, while an observation tower afforded a wide view over the plain. From the house, we learn the methods of Solomon's builders. Bossed blocks marginally drafted were often employed, but where the stones would show ashlar was more common. Coursing was carefully indicated by red paint lines, two headers in one course alternated with one stretcher in the next. Sections of the outer wall in rubble were presumably plastered. Over the three courses of dressed stone was a cedar beam and then mud brick, the same practice as indicated for the temple. On one block were the interlaced triangles familiar to us as David's Shield or Solomon's Seal.

Near by were the stables, carefully planned to meet the requirements of each chariot unit. Double doors hung on small stone sockets gave access from the street to a passage with fine lime-plaster pavement, and this to the rows of stalls paved with rough stone to keep the hoofs from slipping. The roofs were upheld by pillars set on large stones to equalise the downward thrust and with holes in the corners to halter the horses, while between each pair of hitching pillars was a stone manger. The largest stable consisted of five units with space for twenty-four horses each, while smaller stables brought the number of horses which could be accommodated in Megiddo up to three hundred.[23]

Solomon's constructions in the provinces paled before those in the capital. The breach in the north wall of the Jebusite city made by his father was closed by two towers, thirty-six feet by twelve, with a gate between, and was called Millo, the "Filling." Its upper story was reached by an outside staircase

[23] Figs. 139–141; plans 13 f.; P. L. O. Guy, *New Light from Armageddon*, 1931.

of stones projecting from the north side, and on one of these stones was a rude figure of Ashtart. Solomon also repaired the east wall of the city, where David's tower was raised by large well cut blocks with diagonal chisel dressing, the joints were broken, and the corner blocks were carefully bonded.[24]

In his own mind at least, Solomon was the equal of the great monarchs, and his palace must be like theirs. His palace must therefore be roofed and panelled with cedar and other sweet smelling woods of Lebanon. But Solomon was no Thutmose III or Tiglath Pileser I to receive the beams as tribute, he must come to agreement with Hiram. Each year Solomon exported twenty thousand cors of wheat and twenty thousand baths of beaten-out olive oil, yet the balance of trade turned so heavily against him that he was forced to cede twenty towns of Galilee to the Tyrian merchant prince.

Thirty thousand men were levied to work in relays, a month in the Lebanon with Hiram's subjects, two months at home engaged in their ordinary duties. After the cedars were brought down to the sea, they were formed into rafts and transported to Joppa, quite in the fashion shown on the Assyrian monuments.[25] There they were broken up and transferred by other thousands to Jerusalem. Meanwhile, more thousands were engaged in the Judæan hills, quarrying the blocks for the foundations.

North of the old city, on the hill where David had seen the destroying angel pause, was the new royal quarter. The "House of the Forest of Lebanon," so named from the forest-like columns, three rows of fifteen each, was a hundred and fifty feet long, seventy-five wide, and forty-five high. Door was opposite door and window opposite window in three rows. All the woodwork was of cedar while the stones were hewn; some of the foundation stones were twelve or fifteen feet long. Within hung three hundred bucklers and three hundred shields of beaten gold.

[24] Figs. 134–137; I Kings 9:15, 24; 11:27; Macalister-Duncan, *Excavations on the Hill of Ophel*, 56 f.; 83 ff.
[25] Fig. 138; cf. fig. 108, *History of Assyria*.

Of similar construction were his own residence, the house for Pharaoh's daughter, and the "Porch of Pillars." The "Porch of Judgment" held a great ivory throne, overlaid with gold; on each of the six steps a lion stood on guard, two more were on either side of the seat, bull's heads were at the rear.

Behind this imposing complex of buildings, on the very tip of the hill, was the tiny royal chapel, only ninety feet long, thirty feet wide, and forty-five feet high; its very existence witnessed the passing of the old belief that Yahweh could be worshipped only in a tent. Like Egyptian temples, it was oriented towards the sunrise. A porch added fifteen feet to the length, and smaller rooms in three tiers surrounded the main structure, which was set in an inner court formed by a wall of three courses of hewn stone and a course of cedar beams.

To the east on the long sacred rock was the altar. In the court were objects made by Huram-abi, a half breed whose mother was from Naphtali but whose father was a Tyrian bronze worker. Southeast of the temple was the molten sea, fifteen feet from brim to brim, and seven and a half feet high. Under its brim were two rows of gourds, cast when the sea was cast, while the brim itself was like the flower of a lily. It was supported by oxen, three looking to each of the four cardinal points, which marked the transfer of the ancient bull cult to Yahweh. Five bronze lavers, forty baths in capacity, were placed on either side of the temple. They were supported by bronze stands, resembling the contemporary stands from Larnaka and Enkomi in Cyprus,[26] six feet square and four and a half feet high; on the open frame work were lions, oxen, and cherubs, while beneath were four wheels like chariot wheels, their axle trees, felloes, spokes, and naves all cast.

In the temple porch, to right and left of the entrance, stood the pillars Jachin and Boaz. They were cast hollow, with a thickness of four fingers, a circumference of eighteen feet, and a height of twenty-seven. On them were capitals cast in bronze, seven and a half feet high, and covered with trellis-work and two rows of pomegranates. The capitals were free

[26]C. F. Burney, *Notes on the Hebrew Text of the Books of Kings*, 91.

standing and had no structural reason for being; they were cult objects pure and simple, relics of the days when standing stones were themselves objects of worship. Their immediate origin must not be sought in such crude objects; Huram-abi doubtless imitated in less expensive material the two columns of gold and "emerald" which he had seen in the temple of Baal Melkart in his home city.[27]

Huram-abi's task ended with the casting of the pots, shovels, pans, and the like, in the Jordan plain. The list of cast objects, sea, lavers, stands, columns, the minor implements of the cult, remind us of the strikingly similar list of the booty taken by Sargon from the Haldia temple of Armenian Musasir; for their forms, we may perhaps turn to the temple of Ishtar in early Ashur.[28]

Privileged visitors might enter the outer room of the temple itself, sixty feet long. In the "dim religious light" permitted by the barred windows, they noted that the room was floored with fir and panelled and roofed with cedar. At the far end stood an altar covered with gold, for the earlier regulation which allowed only stone or earth had been long forgotten.[29] Double folding doors of olive wood, carved with cherubs, palm trees, and open flowers, gave access to the inner shrine, a cube of thirty feet which imitated the primitive cave. Touching its gold-plated walls were the outstretched wings of two cherubs, winged bulls such as are found in Assyrian ruins,[30] and covered with gold. Their height was fifteen feet and this was also their measure from tip to tip of their outstretched wings; the proportions are approximately those of the average Assyrian winged bull.

Seven years of labour completed the temple. The ark was brought up from its tent in David's Town and was installed under the outstretched wings of the bulls in the inner shrine. Dedication ceremonies began during the last seven days of the old year; on New Year's Day at the fall equinox fire descended

[27] Herod., ii, 44.   [28] Cf. *History of Assyria*, 17 ff.; 238 ff.
[29] Ex. 20:24 ff.; cf. J. M. P. Smith, *AJSL.*, XXXII, 1916, 94.
[30] Cf. *History of Assyria*, figs. 60, 129, 140.

from heaven upon the altar and the new temple was ready to function.[31] The "Book of the Brave" long preserved the lines recited by Solomon at the dedication:

> Yahweh hath placed the sun in the heavens,
> He hath said he would dwell in thick darkness;
> I have built thee a house, exalted,
> The place of thy dwelling forever.

With the new temple went religious reorganisation. Temple slaves were chosen from the Canaanites, whose descendants were long after known as the "sons of Solomon's slaves."[32] The Hebrews had outgrown the unwritten custom of the desert and had taken over the Shechemite code of laws; the first truly Hebrew code was very short, a mere decalogue. Its first pentad was a calendar of five feasts: "The feast of unleavened bread you shall keep; six days shall you labour, but the seventh you shall rest; the feast of weeks you shall observe with the first fruits of the wheat harvest; the feast of ingathering you shall observe at the end of the year; the fat of the passover shall not be left until morning." The second pentad was a series of prescriptions for their proper observance: "The first of the first fruits of your ground you shall bring to the house of Yahweh your God; every first born animal is mine; every first born son you shall redeem; you shall not offer the blood of my sacrifice with leavened bread; you shall not boil a kid in its mother's milk." The basis of this code is clearly nomad, with equal clearness the three harvest feasts testify to partial assimilation to the agricultural religion of Canaan. The agricultural feast of unleavened bread has not yet been united to the nomad passover, the seven-day week and the seventh day of rest are already known, but the term sabbath is missing.[33]

To the pious of later times, Solomon's building of the temple

[31]Cf. J. Morgenstern, *JQR.*, NS., VIII, 1917, 42; *Hebrew Union College Ann.*, I, 69.
[32]Josh. 9:27; Neh. 7:57.
[33]Ex. 34:18–26; cf. Leroy Waterman, *AJSL.*, XXXVIII, 1921, 38 ff.

was his chief title to fame. Solomon himself would have been much astonished at such misunderstanding of its relative importance. He erected shrines for the Moabite Chemosh and for the Divine King of the Ammonites, nor could he have understood the monotheistic sentiments placed in his mouth by these later pietists. Neither did he reign from the Euphrates to Egypt, his father's kingdom had been far smaller, and Solomon did nothing to increase it. Before his death, the kingdom was breaking up, and it needed only his disappearance for the whole structure to crash.[34]

[34]For Kings, cf. I. Benzinger, *Die Bücher der Könige*, 1899; R. Kittel, *Die Bücher der Könige*, 1900; C. F. Burney, *Notes on the Hebrew Text of the Books of Kings*, 1903; B. Stade and F. Schwally, *The Books of Kings*, 1904; and the author's articles, *AJSL*, XXX, 1913, 1 ff.; XXXI, 1915, 169 ff.

CHAPTER XXIII

JEROBOAM AND ISRAEL'S REVOLT

Solomon was buried with his father in David's Town, and was succeeded by a sixteen-year-old son, Rehoboam, half Hebrew in blood since his mother Naamah was a daughter of the Ammonite king Hanun. There was no contest for the throne of Judah, but to be accepted by the northern tribes he must go to Shechem.

In Shechem also appeared a certain Jeroboam. His mother was a harlot, who took her name from her native city of Zeredah, his father was unknown; in later centuries, when his mother's profession was no longer considered respectable, she was made a widow whose husband was Nebat. Jeroboam was assigned to the Joseph tribes under Solomon's new system of forced labour, and rebuilt his birthplace; he was then summoned to Jerusalem, where his men repaired David's Town and constructed the Millo. His reputation grew and he brought together thirty chariots for his personal entourage; Solomon became suspicious and attempted to assassinate his too ambitious subordinate, but Jeroboam fled to Egypt where Shishak gave him his queen's sister in marriage.

Jeroboam hastened home at the news of Solomon's death, rallied his fellow Ephraimites, and built a fenced camp in Zeredah. The same Shemaiah who had once supported Solomon appeared with a word of Yahweh: "Take a new garment that has not touched water and tear it in twelve pieces; give ten pieces to Jeroboam and say to him: Thus saith Yahweh: 'Take for yourself the ten pieces to cast about you.'" Jeroboam took them and Shemaiah added: "Thus saith Yahweh: Over the ten tribes of Israel you shall reign."

Despite the prophetic influence, Rehoboam was offered his chance. Humbly enough the assembly at Shechem petitioned: "Your father made the yoke grievous upon us, and made grievous the securing of the food for his table; now therefore lighten it upon us, and we will serve you." His father's counsellors advised him to bespeak them well, but the youths who had grown up at court with him—we should remember that Rehoboam was only sixteen—urged him to reply: "My little finger is thicker than my father's loins; my father chastised you with whips, but I shall chastise with scorpions." Rehoboam followed their advice; to his astonishment, the whole assembly raised the war cry:

> No portion have we in David,
> No heritage in Jesse's son!
> To your tents, O Israel!
> This man is no leader or prince.

Adoniram, the hated official who had directed the forced labour, was stoned to death, and Rehoboam escaped a similar fate only by mounting his chariot and fleeing back to Jerusalem. Jeroboam was then anointed king of Israel. At the turn of the year, Rehoboam assembled the loyal Judæans and Benjaminites, and marched against Shechem, but was met by Shemaiah with another word of Yahweh: "You shall not go up, neither shall you fight against your brothers, the children of Israel; return every man to his house, for this thing is of me."[1]

The boundary between the rival kingdoms was drawn along the Aijalon-Michmash line, where, save on the direct road from Shechem to Jerusalem, steep gorges render crossing difficult. Beersheba was Judah's southern outpost, for the Negeb was already lost to the nomads, the Philistines occupied the plain and a good part of the Shephelah. Jerusalem, so well located for capital of all Israel, was but a dozen miles from the new frontier.

Much better was the situation of the northern kingdom. A thin line along the coast was held by Phœnicians or Philistines, but otherwise all the west Jordan land was in Israel's

[1] The original story as given in the earliest Greek translation is here followed, cf. *AJSL.*, XXX, 1913, 17 ff.

possession, as far south as Jericho with its command of the road from Jerusalem to the Jordan fords. Moab and Ammon had restored their former boundaries at the expense of declining Reuben, but Gilead was safely Israelite to Ramath Gilead. Israel was several times the area of Judah, but the disproportion was still greater in fertility, population, commerce, and wealth.

Late editors never tire of slurring the "man who made Israel to sin," but Jeroboam's revolt was no revolt against Yahweh's cult. If not instigated by the prophetic party, it met with their approval, and history proves that they were right. During the centuries which immediately followed, every fundamental advance in Hebrew religion originated in the north.

Jeroboam (935–913) rebuilt Shechem as his capital, and restored the temple of the Lord of the Covenant as that of the Lord Yahweh. The entrance was narrowed, the column bases overlaid with marl, a stone foundation for Yahweh's statue placed along the north wall, for the cult room was now under the open sky.[2] The destroyed sanctuary at Shiloh could not be rebuilt, for two reigns had confirmed Jerusalem's right to its ark, but still nearer the former capital was an even more noted shrine

Bethel's devotees told how it had been visited by their ancestors Abraham and Jacob, how Jacob had seen divine beings ascending and descending the causeway from earth to heaven, how he consecrated with oil the stone used as pillow, and named it Beth-el, "House of God." Its priests, the sons of Aaron, claimed that this ancestor had himself made a wooden core with a graving tool in the form of a bull and had plated it with gold from earrings torn by the people from their ears lest the bull be injured by the frequent kissing, had built the altar and proclaimed the festival with its burnt and peace offerings, its feasting, and its licentious sports.[3] The divine bull was no longer identified with Jacob, but with Yahweh, and to him Jeroboam rebuilt the temple and replated the bull. Follow-

[2] E. Sellin, *ZDPV*.. XLIX, 1926, 311, 316
[3] Ex. 32:2–6; Hosea, 13:2; cf. Leroy Waterman, *AJSL.*, XXXI, 1915, 229 ff.

ing Solomon's example, Jeroboam dedicated the temple on New Year's Day and as king priest offered the first sacrifice on the altar.

At the other extremity of the kingdom, by the source of the Jordan under Mount Hermon, was the rival shrine of Dan. Its priests claimed descent from Jonathan, son of Gershom, and grandson of the Levite Moses, but Moses and Aaron were not yet brothers, in fact, Aaron was not even a Levite. They too boasted a divine bull, of whose manufacture and theft we have already been informed. Dan was given the same benefits as Bethel, and the two bulls were soon honoured as the chief deities of Israel.[4]

Two groups of Hebrew tribes, whose union had been imperfect and ephemeral, whose dislike for one another had never been concealed, were now in open rivalry, yet each worshipped the same God. Through this worship alone could develop a feeling of oneness as against non-Hebrews, and this feeling must have been peculiarly strong among the leaders of the rival ecclesiastical organisations. The natural result was a more international view of Yahweh.[5]

Shishak had married his daughter to Solomon, but later another daughter had been married to Solomon's enemy Jeroboam. Solomon's son by the Egyptian princess should have been his successor; insult was added to injury when the son of a half savage Ammonitess seized the throne. To avenge this insult, Shishak invaded Syria in 931. After a battle with an unknown enemy at Lake Kemwer on the Isthmus of Suez, Raphia, the bridgehead across the desert, was occupied, as were the other key sites, Sharuhen and Lachish. A detachment appears to have swept the south country, reducing a whole group of settlements with "Field," "Stream," or "Negeb" as the first element, and then turned north into Judah, taking on the way Arad, Ziph, Adoraim, the "Field of Abram," the plot bought by the patriarch at Hebron, Beth Tappuah, Beth Anoth, Beth Zur, Etam, and Bethlehem. From Lachish, his main force traversed the Shephelah and captured Libnah, Mareshah,

[4] I Kings 12:28–32.   [5] Cf. J. M. P. Smith, *AJSL*., XXXII, 1916, 261 ff.

Gath, Adullam, Shocoh, Azekah, and Zorah, and by the ascent of Aijalon and Beth Horon and through Gibeon and Gittaim joined with the first detachment before Jerusalem. Rehoboam

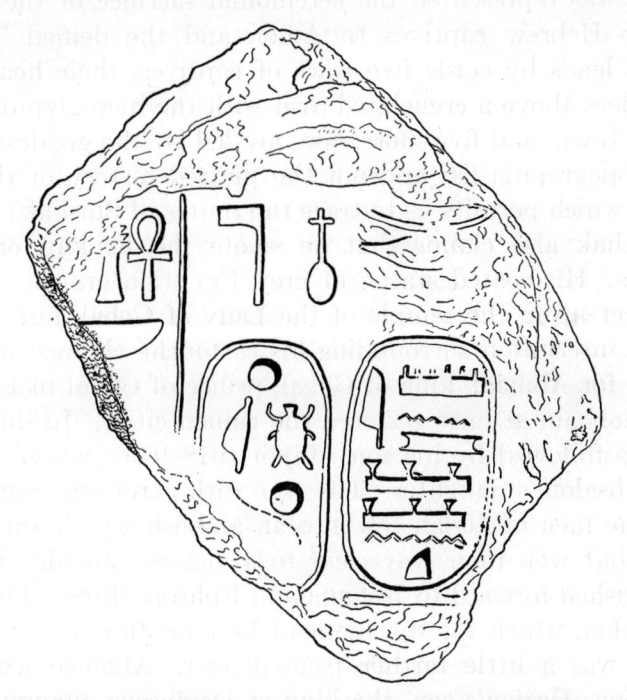

FIG. 142. FRAGMENT OF SHISHAK STELE AT MEGIDDO.

made no resistance and suffered the loss of all his temple and palace treasures.[6]

Shishak then turned against Jeroboam and by the pass of Arauna reached Megiddo, which he burned and then honoured with his stele.[7] Taanach, Shunem, and Rabbith, in or near the Great Plain, were occupied, the capture of Beth Shan permitted entrance to the Jordan valley with Rehob and Hapharaim. Jeroboam retreated across the river to Penuel,

[6] I Kings 14:25-28; the routes secured through correlation of the Shishak list with the list of II Chron. 11:5-12.
[7] Fig. 142; C. S. Fisher, *Excavation of Armageddon*, 12 ff.

which he fortified, but Shishak followed as far as Edrei and Mahanaim.

On his return to Thebes, Shishak erected a great pylon on which was represented the ceremonial sacrifice of the unfortunate Hebrew captives to Amon and the deified Thebes. Amon leads by cords five rows of captives, their heads and shoulders above a crenelated oval with the hieroglyphic name of the town, and five more rows are led by the goddess. It is this topographic list and not the pirated history of the lazy scribe which permits us to trace the routes of Shishak's army.[8]

Shishak also claims that he smote the Fenkhu or Phœnicians. His seated statue of grey Egyptian granite was indeed set up in the temple of the Lady of Gebal, but a Phœnician inscription surrounding his cartouche claimed its dedication for Abibaal, king of Gebal, prince of Gebal in Egypt.[9]

Rehoboam at once restored the ruined cities. In due time, he was followed by his son Abijah (918–915), whose mother was Absalom's daughter. The war with Jeroboam continued, and the men of Judah fell into an ambush on Mount Zemaraim, but won their way clear to a victory. Judah's frontier was pushed forward to Jeshana and Ephron, three miles north of Bethel, which for the moment became Judæan, and Jerusalem was a little farther from danger. Alliance with Tab Rimmon, Hezion's son, the king of Damascus, inaugurated a policy which was to be consistently pursued whenever Judah was independent.[10]

The accession of Asa (915–875) in Judah was followed two years later in Israel by that of Jeroboam's son Nadab (913–911), who had not yet reached his twentieth year. Gibbethon, well up in the fertile Sharon plain and on Ephraim's left flank, was still held by the Philistines, but their power was in evident decline, and Nadab hoped to celebrate his accession by its capture. No sooner was he engaged in its siege than

---

[8]Breasted, *Rec.*, IV, 348 ff.; *AJSL.*, XXI, 1904, 22 ff.; *JAOS.*, XXXI, 1911, 290 ff.; Müller, *Egypt. Researches*, I, pl. 75–87.

[9]Fig. 144; P. Montet, *Byblos*, 54 ff.; cf. R. Dussaud, *Syria*, V, 1924, 145 ff.; VI, 1925, 111; C. C. Torrey, *JAOS.*, XLV, 1925, 278.

[10]II Chron. 13:3 f., 13–17, 19; I Kings 15:19.

FIG. 143. THE GEZER CALENDAR, EARLIEST EXAMPLE OF HEBREW WRITING.

FIG. 144. INSCRIPTION OF SHISHAK AND OF ABIBAAL, KING OF GEBAL.

Baasha, son of Ahijah, from that tribe of Issachar which had so suffered from the raid of Shishak, conspired against his master and slew him. Jeroboam's whole house was blotted out, and with the loss of the royal power Ephraim sank into decline.[11]

Shishak was dead and Osorkon I (924–895) had done nothing to commemorate his reign. Like his father, he presented a statue of rose granite to the Lady of Gebal, but around Osorkon's cartouche the Phœnician ruler carved his own record: "Statue which Eli-baal, king of Gebal, made, as a dedication to the Lady of Gebal for himself; may she prolong the days of Eli-baal and his years over Gebal."[12] Nadab's war had been directed against the Philistines, whom Egypt still claimed as vassals, and Osorkon was happy to see him supplanted; doubtless it was on the invitation of Baasha that Zerah the Ethiopian, as the Hebrews called him in memory of his family's long sojourn in Nubia, invaded Judah. But Osorkon was no Shishak, and Asa defeated him in the valley north of Mareshah and pursued him to Gerar.[13]

Baasha (911–887) had meanwhile attempted to fulfil his part of the contract. Guarding his rear by alliance with Damascus, he regained Bethel and pushed across the natural frontier at the Aijalon-Michmash line to Ramah, which he rebuilt to blockade Jerusalem only five miles away. Two could play at the game of inviting Gentile aid; Asa sent all the silver and gold in temple and palace to Ben Hadad, son of Tab Rimmon, and reminded him that their fathers had been allies. Ben Hadad denounced his treaty with Baasha and destroyed Ijon, Dan, Abel of Beth Maacah, all Chinnereth, and all Naphtali. He was well along the "Way of the Sea"[14] to Accho when Baasha retreated to meet the new threat.

Asa promptly called out the corvee and carried off the timber and stone from Ramah to rebuild Mizpah and Gibeah

[11] I Kings 15:25–29.
[12] Fig. 145; P. Montet, *Byblos*, 49 ff.; cf. R. Dussaud, *Syria*, VI, 1925, 101 ff.; C. C. Torrey, *JAOS.*, XLVI, 1926, 237 ff.
[13] II Chron. 14:9–15.   [14] Isaiah 9:1.

Since its capture by the Hebrews, Mizpah had remained unfortified; the accumulated debris within the ruins of the old wall was cleared and dumped outside. On the west, the new wall rose on the remains of the great Bronze Age fortification, and was therefore twenty-six feet thick, the great tower and its revetment were reconstructed. To the north and within a rock-cut moat, a wide trench was dug to the rock and then filled two yards deep with small stones; on this was erected the sixteen-feet-thick wall of good sized blocks, coursed and laid in clay. Asa also excavated a huge cistern to supply the city with water.[15]

Gibeah had lain desolate for two centuries. The debris was roughly levelled, and served as foundation for some of the walls, while others were set on the older lines. Since the outer wall on the south was out of plumb, it was cased with a thin wall and protected by a buttress, while a revetment, roughly coursed and laid on larger blocks, followed the whole substructure. The roughly hammer-dressed building stones were quarried near Ramah, and the dressed side is often placed inward, thus proving their reuse. There was much wood employed, not of the trees found in the earlier buildings, but of the less durable almond, a good indication of the changes brought about by cultivation. Gibeah was now nothing but a quadrangular fort, and the pottery was poor, as befitted a garrison.[16]

For fifteen years, the boy Asa was ruled by his mother Maacah, who favoured the foreign culture and was supported by the higher nobility and by the commercial classes. After his victories over Osorkon and Baasha, Maacah was deposed, and with the change in court factions ensued the first of those religious revolutions which played so large a part in Hebrew history. The lower classes, the peasants especially, were his chief supporters, and their conservatism and nationalism were reflected in the insistence on the supreme position of the national God. A prominent part in the reform was taken by the prophetic party headed by Azariah, son of Oded; foreign inno-

[15]Jer. 41:9; W. F. Badè, *Excavations,* 17 ff.; *QS.,* 1930, 10.
[16]W. F. Albright, *Ann.,* IV, 17 ff., 39.

FIG. 146. A KING OF DAMASCUS.

FIG. 145. BUST OF OSORKON I WITH INSCRIPTION OF ELIBAAL, KING OF GEBAL.

vations were swept away and the Asherah, the sacred pole erected by the queen mother, was cut down and burnt at the Kidron.

With the reform went a new presentation of the religious history. It told of Moses' flight from Egypt, the theophany of Yahweh in Horeb's bush, and the promise of an Exodus from Egypt. The Exodus took place and the Israelites made pilgrimage to "Yahweh's Mount," where the laws of the covenant were promulgated and written by Moses on two tablets. The Ephraimite story of the Conquest under Joshua was joined to the southern Moses cycle by a forty years' wandering in the wilderness, and Joshua became the servant and successor of Moses. The sanctuary at Shechem had been ordered by Moses, and Joshua merely carried out his orders.

To the five decalogues of "Judgments" in the old Canaanite code of the "Lord of the Covenant" had been added four supplementary decalogues of "Precepts," and the whole "Covenant Code" was now assigned to Moses. The first of the new decalogues inculcated kindness: "A resident alien you shall not wrong; the widow and the fatherless you shall not oppress; if you lend money to your poor brother, you shall not be a creditor to him; you shall not lay interest upon him; if you take your neighbour's garment as pledge, you shall return it to him before sundown; if you meet your enemy's ox or ass going astray, you shall return it to him; if he is not near or you do not know him, then bring it to your house and keep it until he comes in search of it; you shall do the same with his ass and his garment and every lost object; if you see your enemy's ass fallen under his burden, you shall release him; if you find a bird's nest, you shall free the mother and take the young."

A second decalogue gives the rules of justice: "You shall not bear a false report; you shall not join hands with the wicked to be a false witness; you shall not follow the mob to do evil; you shall not bear witness with the mob to bring a false judgment in a case; you shall not favour the poor man in his case; you shall not change the judgment of the poor man in his case;

keep yourself from every false matter.; slay not the innocent and the righteous; do not justify the unrighteous for a bribe; you shall take no bribe."

Religious duties form the third decalogue: "You shall not make for yourselves other gods; you shall not make for yourselves gods of silver or gods of gold; you shall make for me an altar of earth; if you make me an altar of stones, you shall not build it of dressed stones; you shall not go up by steps to my altar; you shall not revile God or curse a ruler of your people; you shall not be negligent in offering of your harvest and of the outflow of your presses; the first born of your sons you shall give to me; so shall you do with your oxen, your sheep, and your asses; you shall not eat flesh torn by beasts."

Feasts are the subject of the last decalogue, which follows somewhat closely the decalogue from the Jerusalem temple: "Six years shall you sow your land and gather in the increase, but in the seventh you shall let it rest that the poor of my people may eat; six days shall you labour but the seventh you shall rest; the feast of unleavened bread you shall keep; the feast of weeks you shall observe with the first fruits of the wheat harvest; the feast of ingathering you shall observe at the end of the year; three times a year all your males shall appear before Yahweh, your God; the blood of my sacrifice you shall not offer with unleavened bread; the fat of the passover feast shall not be left until morning; the first of the first fruits of your ground shall you bring to the house of Yahweh, your God; you shall not boil a kid in its mother's milk." On the basis of this code, the people made a solemn covenant with Yahweh in the third month, presumably at the feast of the first fruits.[17]

About this same time, a peasant in Gezer scratched on a limestone fragment a list of his months, "Month of ingathering; month of sowing; month of aftergrass; month of pulling

[17] I Kings 15:9-15; II Chron. 15; code reconstructed from Ex. 20:23-26; 22:21-23:26; Deut. 22:2 f., 6 f., by Leroy Waterman, *AJSL.*, XXXVIII, 1921, 38 ff.; L. B. Paton, *JBL.*, XII, 1893, 79 ff.; J. Morgenstern, *AJSL.*, XXXVII, 1921, 261 ff.

flax; month of barley harvest; month of harvesting the rest; month of vinepruning; month of summer fruits." This earliest connected Hebrew inscription gives an interesting picture of the agricultural year.[18]

Baasha's house suffered the same fate he had meted out to that of Jeroboam, for his son Elah (887–885) lasted no longer than Nadab. While Elah was making himself drunk with the wines stored in the house of his intendent Arzah in Tirzah, the general of half his chariotry, a descendant of Saul in the sixth generation named Zimri,[19] conspired against him and slew him. The attempt to revive the Benjaminite dynasty was a failure; once more the army was encamped before that Philistine Gibbethon they had been besieging a quarter century since when Baasha revolted, and they promptly declared for their own commander Omri. Tirzah was besieged, and when escape was impossible Zimri retired to the inner keep and set it on fire. Even yet the crown was not safely Omri's, for half the people followed Tibni, son of Ginnath, and his brother Jehoram, but after four years of civil strife the men of Omri prevailed and Tibni was put to death.[20]

[18] Fig. 143; Macalister, *Gezer*, II, 24 ff.
[19] I Chron. 8:36; 9:42.
[20] I Kings 16:6–22.

CHAPTER XXIV

REPULSE OF ASHUR AND OF BAAL

TIGLATH PILESER'S raid of 1104 was a portent of coming Assyrian invasions. It was followed by a trip of Ashur-rabi II (1012–995) to Mount Atalur on the north Syrian coast.[1] Then there was a lull until 876, when Ashur-nasir-apal II (885–860), having reduced all Mesopotamia, crossed the Euphrates to Carchemish.

The warrior princes from the north had succumbed to the warmer climate and to the seductions of a higher material civilisation, and were taking advantage of their favoured location on the Great Road. Sangara bore the proud title "King of the Hittite Land," but he had quite forgotten the prowess of his ancestors; rather he showed his wealth by his tribute, twenty silver talents, a hundred of copper, two hundred and fifty of that iron which had enabled his predecessors to conquer the city, gold and copper objects, tusk ivory, furniture, blue and purple wool, linen garments. His chariotry, cavalry, and footmen were placed at the Assyrian's disposal.

The rude settlement of two centuries gone had become a city of palaces. Lower class homes had been forced outside to a southern suburb, protected by a massive river wall; the inner city was reserved for the aristocracy.

From the quay, Ashur-nasir-apal would ascend a stepped road between rows of the sculptures already described[2] to the monumental Water Gate, its outer jambs of inscribed basalt lions twelve feet long. The street within led to an open square directly under the acropolis, across which he saw a sculptured frieze of alternate black basalt and white limestone slabs raised four feet high. In the midst is a long pictographic inscription, ended by a row of sixteen hands and three heads; to one side are pairs of foot soldiers, to the other are charioteers driving

[1] *History of Assyria,* 75.   [2] Cf. p. 259.

over the prostrate foe and shooting down the fugitives. They advance towards the great mother goddess, nude and holding her breasts.

Behind this wall is her temple. In the courtyard are an altar of stone and clay, topped with ash and burnt bones, and

FIG. 147. SOUTH GATE AT CARCHEMISH.
(Restored.)

a basalt laver supported by two colossal oxen. A narrow door, with inscribed basalt jambs, leads to the Holy of Holies, some twenty-five feet on the side, the corners facing the cardinal points. Limestone blocks face the lower walls, then comes a border of white and yellow daisies, raised slightly above the blue ground of the glazed bricks, which also surrounds the doorway, and the remainder is covered with glazed bricks in wavy blue and yellow or simple blue. The roof is borne by two wooden columns on stone bases.

A palace occupies the south side of the square. On the outer wall a camel rider advances towards a group of mythological figures. A winged human figure, with short square beard and high hat but with eagle claws and scorpion tail, seizes a rearing bull by the horns while another grasps its hoof and threatens it with his mace. Two men with short skirts, round caps, and short swords seize a crouching enemy and plunge a dagger into his skull. A second winged bull is struggling with two winged sphinxes. Two animal-headed beings threaten with a boomerang two other beings between them; their human heads crowned by tall horned hats, beneath which fall long curls, their short square curled beards, their human hands leaning on spears, their bull-like lower bodies, hoofs and tails, all remind us of the Babylonian Gilgamesh. A winged and pig-tailed figure with human head on which is perched the horned and knobbed conical cap shows below a lion's head with protruding tongue and an upraised tail ending in a snake; it is one of the prototypes of the Greek chimæra. Two bulls kneel before the conventionalised tree of life. A lion places his paw on the head of a bull who apparently bears a frightened cow on his back. Two bird-headed demons, with down-pointing wings and upturned shoes, hold their hands upright. A hero has seized the paw of a rearing lion. The weather god, wearing the pointed and knobbed horned cap, raises by his hind leg a lion and brandishes his double axe, but his divine companion, in high hat with curling neck flap, has seized the lion's tail and is piercing it with his dagger. A lion springs to attack a six-spoked chariot, whose framework sides rise to the face of the charioteer and his lord. A half-kneeling figure with hair curled to the neck and square-cut beard grasps a lion by the hind foot with his right hand and with his left he holds a bull by the horn; his foot is on the hind paw of a lion and below is a crouching sphinx.[3]

We then turn the corner into a re-entrant angle for the seated figure of a god. On his head is a turban, his long beard is elaborately curled, his flowing robe bears a pictographic inscription on the hem. His hands, in one the mace and in the other the double axe, rest on his knees. On the pedestal are two lions, mouths open and tongues lolling, who are held apart by a half-kneeling demon with eagle head.[4]

In complete contrast to this ugly archaic statue are the reliefs of the re-entrant angle behind it. One side displays the wonderful march of the ten soldiers we have already found

[3] Fig. 152 f.   [4] Fig. 166.

Fig. 148. THE KING OF CARCHEMISH PRESENTS THE CROWN PRINCE. (Early Hittite Pictographs.)

Fig. 149. THE ROYAL CHILDREN AT CARCHEMISH.

occasion to describe, the other presents with equal beauty the seven high court officials. All are beardless, though whether this means they are eunuchs is uncertain. Their hair, curled round their heads in concentric circles, falls to the neck, they wear long robes with elaborate belts and sandals. All but the sixth have a long sword on the left thigh. The first bears the staff of office in his left hand and the thonged whip in his right, the second swings the fly-flapper over his right shoulder, the third holds high the sceptre, the fourth carries a spear in his right hand and a huge round shield on his left shoulder, the fifth has a staff in his left hand, the sixth a quiver over his left shoulder, and the last a spear in his right hand and a sceptre in his left.[5]

A long inscription occupies the corner and then the procession is faced by the royal family. The tall beardless king has ordered his hair crimped in concentric circles which descend to the shoulder. A triangular flap hangs down over his right shoulder and is perhaps to be connected with the long narrow sword whose sheath just appears behind, his long robe has no girdle. His left hand dips the sceptre, his right grasps firmly the wrist of the youthful crown prince before him. He too is beardless, his hair has the same elaborate coiffure, his scabbard, hung by a belt over the left shoulder, is on his left thigh, in his hand is the long staff of office. Then come the royal children, three carrying knucklebones, the youngest monkey fashion leaning on an upright staff topped with a bird. All wear their hair in short tight curls. Below we see two with whip in right hand and top in left, while two others squat by a low stool and eat greedily. The queen in round cap and long robe comes last, leading a calf and holding a very mature-looking child in her arms. Could we read the inscriptions, we should know the name of each, even of the pet animal.[6]

The line is broken by a stairway, along which one musician plays the long-handled lute, another performs on the double pipes, a third shakes the castanets, a fourth raises his hands above his head for the dance. Across the entrance a long-robed

[5] Fig. 150.   [6] Fig. 148 f.

man bears a large round shield on which the man at either side places his hands, a fourth figure blows an uplifted horn. Then the procession is renewed, with the statue of the mother goddess seated in a straight-backed chair which rests on a low-crouching lion; she wears a short-sleeved inner dress over which is a girdled gown which covers the whole head, leaves the arms free to hold a mirror, and swathes the ankles. Her chief priestess comes next, bearing in her hands a small animal for sacrifice, and then fourteen other priestesses, clad like their goddess, and carrying in their left hands some long thin object and in their right whisks or mirrors.[7] Ten beardless temple servants in short skirts and bearing sheep or goats over their shoulders close the procession.

We have now reached the main palace entrance, beyond which is a god seated above lions. Through double gates of cedar, bronze trimmed and studded, whose bronze-tipped posts swing on polished stone sockets, we pass the inscribed basalt door jambs into a courtyard, adorned with lions and stags hunted by archers. Slabs of stone cover the lower walls of the rooms, the adobe above is concealed by panels of cedar.

Returning to the square, we climb broad stairs to the acropolis. At the foot, the three great gods are represented on a huge basalt block; along the stairs are basalt reliefs, broken by doors to the lower palace rooms on the terraced slopes; the stairway ends with a monumental entrance guarded by lions, but the palace on the acropolis itself has long been destroyed.[8]

Hattina, ruled by Lubarna, still preserved the Hittite name, and its capital Kunulua is located by a "Hittite" inscription. Lubarna paid a talent of gold, twenty of silver, a hundred of lead and iron, cattle, sheep, and furniture. Gusi of Iahani, later to be known from him as Bit Agusi, paid a similar tribute. Ashur-nasir-apal then crossed the Orontes, took another city of Lubarna named Aribua, impaled the inhabitants of Luhuti, and stored their grain and chopped straw in Aribua, now resettled with Assyrian colonists.

[7] Fig. 151.
[8] D. C. Hogarth and C. L. Woolley, *Carchemish*, 1914, 1921; C. L. Woolley, *Dead Towns and Living Men*, 1920, 74 ff.

FIG. 150. OFFICIALS OF CARCHEMISH.

FIG. 151. LADIES OF CARCHEMISH.

Ashur-nasir-apal then washed the royal weapons with all due ceremony in the Great Sea of Amurru. There was no need of further advance to the south. The Phœnicians recognised that Assyria was the coming power and their fear of political conquest was less than their desire for the widened trade opportunities which submission would secure. They therefore sent rich gifts, Tyre, now ruled by Itto-baal, Sidon, giving way to its next-door rival, Gebal, whose "Hittite" inscription hints at relations with the "Hittite" states of North Syria,[9] Mahalata, Maisa, and Kaisa, one day to be amalgamated into Tripolis, Amurru, whose name was preserved in the "Westland" and in the "Great Sea of Amurru," and Arvad, whose island site permitted it to supplant Amurru after Phœnician control of the sea had freed commerce from the danger of pirate raids. Their gifts are of unusual interest, silver, gold, lead, bronze (the absence of iron is significant), linen and highly colored garments dyed with the famous Phœnician purple, bronze vessels such as are found everywhere in the Mediterranean lands to which Phœnician trade penetrated, ivory, and wood. Beams of cedar, cypress, juniper, and pine were cut on Mount Amanus, where a memorial stele was erected.[10]

Phœnician trading ventures had already been followed by Phœnician colonies. Cyprus was close at hand and its copper mines were an irresistible attraction. As early as the fifteenth century, the island had come under Minoan influence, which, as we have seen, in turn spread to the mainland. At the fall of the Minoan empire and the new barbarian invasions of Greece, the true Greeks had colonised Cyprus, whose history thereafter is that of a constant struggle between Greeks and Phœnicians. As a result there grew up a curious mixed culture; it is not easy to distinguish between Greek and Phœnician, save in the rare cases where there is an inscription in Phœnician or in the strange syllabic writing of the Cypriote Greek. Assyrian, Egyptian, and Anatolian influences are com-

[9]M. Dunand, *Syria*, XI, 1930, 1 ff.; I. Gelb, *AJSL.*, XLVII, 1931, 135 ff.
[10]*History of Assyria*, 94 f.; *JAOS.*, XXXVIII, 1918, 246 ff.

bined into a new form of art which begins to show faint traces of the æsthetic superiority of the Greeks.[11]

From Cyprus, the Phœnicians sailed into the Ægean and influenced the Greeks in their home land. In earlier days, this influence was so much exaggerated that a reaction was inevitable but the true extent of such influence is now becoming clear. It is witnessed by a long series of references to Sidonian traders and their wares in Homer, wine from Byblos or Gebal is known to Hesiod,[12] later writers admit it in ever more extreme form. The Minoan writing had been entirely forgotten and when the historic Greeks began to write, they borrowed the forms and names of the alphabet from the Phœnicians. *Aleph* became *alpha, beth* was *beta,* and so down the long list, but the Greeks made one great improvement, they employed the Phœnician characters for sounds unknown in their own language for the so highly important Indo-European vowels. Thus the *aleph-beth* of the original Sinaitic inscriptions became a true "alphabet," fitted to conquer the European world.[13]

Omri (885–874) appears to have brought Issachar to power, for an Omri was governor of that tribe under David and his own home seems to have been Jezreel.[14] His dynasty was the greatest in Israel's checkered history, and gave his kingdom international rank among the greatest of the second rank powers; long after his dynasty perished, foreigners called Israel the "House of Omri."

Alliances were the order of the day. After a thirty-four-year reign, Hiram I of Tyre had been succeeded by his thirty-six-year-old son Baal-azor I (947–930) and by his grandson Abd-ashtart (930–921) at twenty years of age. Four sons of his nurse Le-ashtart conspired against Abd-ashtart; the eldest, Methu-ashtart, aged forty-two at his accession (921–909), was

[11]J. L. Myres, *Handbook of the Cesnola Collection of Antiquities from Cyprus* (Metropolitan Museum of Art), 1914.
[12]Homer, *Iliad* vi, 290 ff.; xxiii, 743 ff.; *Odyssey* iv, 613 ff.; xiii, 272 ff.; xv, 117 ff., 403 ff.; Hesiod, *Works and Days,* 589.
[13]B. L. Ullman, *Amer. Jour. Archæology,* XXXI, 1927, 311 ff.
[14]I Chron. 27:18; I Kings 21.

FIG. 152. TESHUP AND HIS COMPANION KILL THE LION.
(Carchemish.)

FIG. 153. HERALDIC FIGURES.
(Carchemish.)

followed by two brothers, the forty-five-year-old Asirom (909–900), and Phelles, aged fifty. After nine months, the line of brothers was ended by a thirty-six-year-old priest of Ashtart named Ethbaal, or rather Itto-baal (899–867), who became the dominant ruler in Phœnicia and exchanged the title "King of Tyre" for "King of the Sidonians." Batrun, on the north coast, already known from the Amarna letters, was rebuilt, and Auza in Africa was colonised, our only hint in this weary list of the commercial activities which were sending the Phœnicians to the far ends of the Mediterranean.[15] Omri renewed with Itto-baal the alliance consecrated by David and Solomon, and the alliance of the two upstart kings was confirmed by the marriage of Itto-baal's daughter Jezebel to Omri's son Ahab. A less advantageous alliance permitted the merchants of Damascus to occupy quarters in Omri's capital without adequate return.[16]

Chemosh, patron god of Moab, so we are told by Mesha, son of Chemoshgad, was angry with his people, and permitted Omri to afflict Moab many days. Medeba, taken by the Moabites from weakening Reuben, was recaptured and colonised, Ataroth was rebuilt, other Moabite cities were levelled to the ground. During the greater part of his reign from Daibon, the "Sheepmaster" Mesha paid the huge tribute of a hundred thousand lambs and a hundred thousand rams to his Israelite suzerain.

Increased prosperity demanded a new capital. Commanding the north and south road along the central spine and the no less important route from the sea to Gilead was a long terraced hill, surrounded on all sides by ravines, but connected on the east to the Ebal range by a low saddle. From its summit was a fine view of the sea to the west and of the well cultivated plain to the east, four hundred feet below, with its numerous and well populated villages, its groves of olives and figs. Its name, Shomeron, the "Watch Tower," was well deserved, for it was impregnable to assault.[17]

[15]Menander, in Joseph., *Apion*, i, 116 ff.; *Ant.*, viii, 324.
[16]I Kings 20:24.
[17]Fig. 154.

370 PALESTINE AND SYRIA

Six years after his accession, Omri removed from Tirzah, and began a palace on the summit, where only scanty red

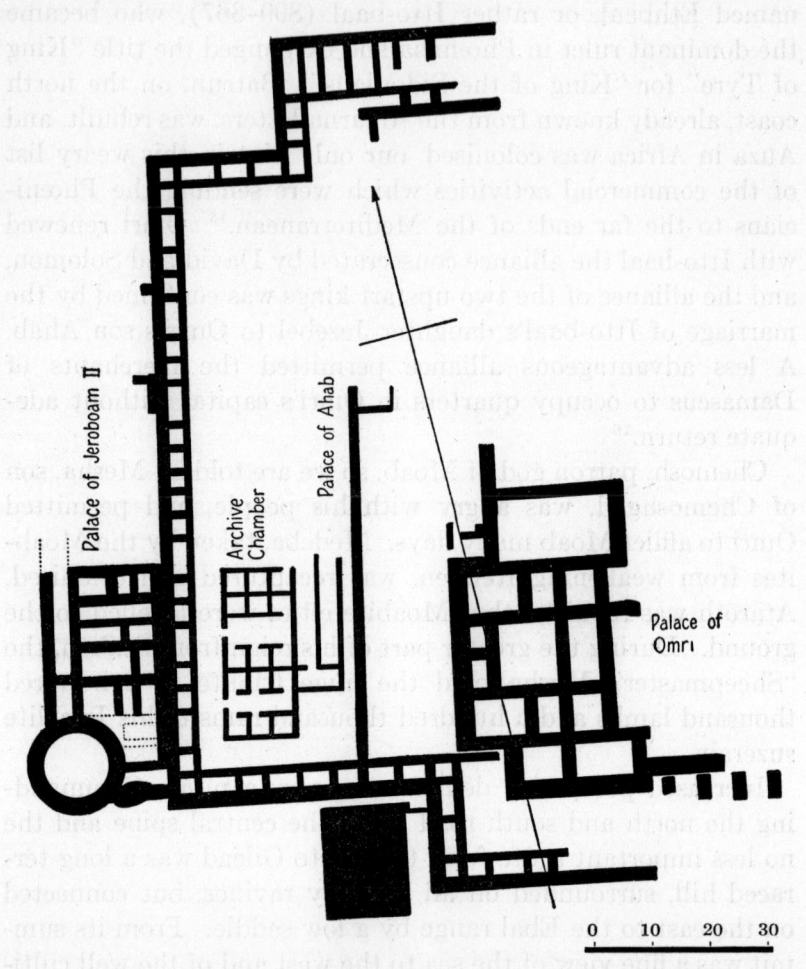

PLAN 15. SAMARIA, PALACES OF OMRI, AHAB, AND JEROBOAM II.

gravel here and there hid the rock. Building blocks were quarried from the native rock, a soft yellow limestone which hardens on exposure; channels to permit the insertion of arm and chisel roughly marked out masses a foot and a half or two

Fig. 154. SAMARIA.

Fig. 155. AHAB'S PALACE AT SAMARIA.

feet thick, which were then split off with a sharp blow or by the wetted wedge. The rock was scarped to mark the limits of construction, where the line of wall was to follow the level a shallow trench was cut, on the slopes the blocks were set in steps.

Work began at the corners. A marginal dressing with the broad adz fitted the side next the following stone. When the first course was laid, the top was dressed to receive the next course, guided by red lines made by a taut string, the plummet was used for vertical lines, and the square added for the horizontal. Below the permanent surface, rough bosses were permitted to remain, but above they were chiselled off with fine short strokes. Occasionally we find mason's marks, generally a letter of the Hebrew alphabet, or rude sketches of animals, trees, or squares, drawn by the workmen in an idle moment. Walls were set back a trifle from the scarp edge to form a gutter for the rainwater. The outer wall face was closely fitted, but behind the stones were left rough, the inner wall was also unhewn, and the space between was filled with chips from the stone dressing; the outer wall was more than eight feet thick, the inner was six. Headers and stretchers were laid skilfully, sometimes dovetailing into each other, joints were broken by alternate use of header and stretcher, stretchers were employed for the corners, intersecting walls were carefully bonded.

Omri's plan was that of the palaces at Kalhu and Babylon, open courts surrounded by smaller rooms; the largest court was eighteen yards by nine, and under it was a tunnel running west to an exit in the scarp. Channels under the rooms drained into a larger canal, and thus provided elementary sanitation. For the most part, the floors were of beaten earth, though some must have been paved with slabs as were the courts.

Along the south cliff, partly at the edge, partly on the slope, was the city wall, its face in a rock-sunk cutting, and even thicker and better dressed than that of the palace; it stood in the midst of a trench, which however did not form a moat as it was filled with well beaten debris. A rock ramp with sharp turn led to the western gate, a single large square tower commanding in Syrian fashion a narrow passage.[18]

Omri did not live to complete his palace and still greater additions were made by Ahab (874–852), whose famous Ivory House[19] was carried down the slope to the west over a surface only partially scarped. A palace platform was formed by a massive double retaining wall, three hundred and fifteen feet from north to south; the outer wall was two yards thick, the inner one, and the two-yard interval between were tied by cross walls. Along this wall ran probably a colonnade. Within this retaining wall the surface was raised by a filling of chips and debris to form the palace foundation. In the northwest of the paved court was a pool,[20] thirty-three by seventeen feet, floored with heavy slabs and covered by a grey cement mixed with wood ashes as hard as the stones themselves; from it came water for the bath, a rock-sunk room paved with large square blocks. To the south of the retaining wall was a guard tower, forty-one by fifty-three feet, with solid substructure, which commanded a narrow postern. In the southwest corner of the court was a building formed of left-overs from the quarrying, broken blocks, undressed and unfitted, mixed with chips and held together by mud mortar; it was entered by a corridor from the west and consisted of three groups of six rooms each.[21]

In these rooms were discovered the royal archives, potsherds with brief notes scribbled in carbon ink by a brush pen. They represent the flowing cursive of every-day life as opposed to the more formal characters of the inscriptions, though both were already departing from the forms of the parent Phœnician; they thus afford a clear picture of contemporary Biblical manuscripts.[22]

Through these ostraca we learn the tax system and follow a tax reform. Earlier potsherds bear such a notation as "In the

---

[18]Fig. 155; G. A. Reisner, C. S. Fisher, D. G. Lyon, *Harvard Excavations at Samaria*, 1924, 93 ff.; 120 f.
[19]I Kings 22:39. [20]I Kings 22:38.
[21]Plan 15; Reisner-Fisher-Lyon, *op. cit.*, 98 ff. [22]Fig. 156.

ninth year from the city of Geba, for Ahinoam, a jar of old wine," or a similar notation for fine or settled olive oil. Ahinoam is the under official in direct charge of the royal vineyards at Geba and the near-by Yasit, as Gedaiah is of four

FIG. 156. INSCRIBED POTSHERDS FROM SAMARIA.

similar estates west, south, and southeast of Samaria. The majority of these places are not found in the fragmentary Biblical lists, but the ostraca give us the Hebrew names of the modern villages, and thus fill out the ancient map.[23]

In the tenth year, the change begins with lists of several stewards from the same town:

"In the tenth year for Shemariah, from Beeraim, a jar of old wine;
  Rage, son of Elisha, 2;
  Uzza, son of ——, 1;
  Eliba, son of ——, 1;
  Baala, son of Elisha, 1;
  Jedaiah, son of ——, 1."

By the fifteenth year, for which the Egyptian hieratic numeral is employed, the change is complete, as "In the fifteenth year from Shemida, for Helez, son of Aphsah, Baala, son of Zakar."

[23]Cf. F. M. Abel, *RB.*, XX, 1911, 290 ff.; W. F. Albright, *JPOS.*, V, 1925, 39; R. Dussaud, *Syria,* VII, 1926, 9 ff.

There is no longer mention of old wine or fine oil, the product of the royal estates is no longer forwarded directly by the under officials but through the royal stewards, there has been a shake up of officials. In the lists of Numbers and Joshua, we hear of "sons" of Machir, Manasseh's son, and one of these left no "sons" but "daughters"; by the fifteenth year these "sons" and "daughters" of Machir have taken the place of the villages heretofore mentioned, in other words, these tribal subdivisions have become administrative units.[24]

A surprisingly large number of the personal names recall the family of Saul or the Benjaminites, others remind us of famous figures of David's times. Aha is definitely labelled "the Judæan." Nimshi might be grandfather of the future king Jehu, it is less probable that our Elisha is the grandfather of the well-known prophet.[25]

One year before Ahab's accession, Asa of Judah had died, and had been buried with a very great burning. His successor was the thirty-five-year-old Jehoshaphat (875-850), who won certain successes against the Philistines,[26] but was soon after forced to face an inroad of Ammonites and Moabites, assisted by the Meunim from Mount Seir. The invaders followed the route around the south end of the Dead Sea to Hazazon Tamar or Engedi, and were climbing the terrific ascent of Haziz when they were ambushed by the wild tribes of the neighbourhood; Jehoshaphat reached the valley of Berekah to find his work already done.[27] The East Jordan menace forced Jehoshaphat to acknowledge Ahab's suzerainty, and to marry his son Jehoram to Ahab's daughter Athaliah; as base for his east Jordan operations, Ahab rebuilt Jericho. Joshua's curse was still operative and its founder, Hiel of Bethel, must lay its foundation with his first born and its gates with his youngest son.[28]

[24]Num. 26:28 ff.; Josh., 17:2 ff.; cf. M. Noth, *ZDPV.*, L, 1928, 211 ff.
[25]Reisner-Fisher-Lyon, *op. cit.*, 227 ff.
[26]II Chron. 17:11.
[27]II Chron. 20; just below Engedi we were captured by the **Jehalin** while exploring the Dead Sea in 1905.
[28]II Kings 8:18; I Kings 16:34; Sellin and Watzinger, *Jericho,* 72 ff.

For seventeen years after the expedition of Ashur-nasir-apal, the Assyrians avoided Syria, but in 859 his son Shalmaneser III (860–825) returned. Carchemish was still ruled by Sangara, to the west was Hattina under Sapalulme, to the north in the plain around Marqasi was Gurgum under Mutallu. These three states were "Hittite" in culture, in the use of the "Hittite" character, now evolving into an incised linear, and in the names of their rulers, for Sapalulme recalls Shuppiluliuma as Mutallu does Muwatallish. South of Gurgum was Samal, where Gabbar and Bamah had been succeeded by Haya; in culture Samal was also "Hittite," but the kings were Aramæan and employed the Phœnician alphabet in writing a slightly Aramæanised Phœnician dialect. Agusi under Arame was entirely Aramæanised.

Shalmaneser first attacked the west Euphrates towns of Bit Adini, and then received tribute of Mutallu. Turning southwest to Latibu on the border of Samal, he found his path blocked by a coalition made up of Samal, Hattina, Bit Adini, and Carchemish; he claims a victory, but could not take Samal, and must content himself with placing his stele at the sources of the Saluara under Mount Amanus. He then crossed the Orontes and appeared before Alisir, a Hattinian city on the site of the later Antioch. Again the coalition blocked his way, aided now by contingents from Que or Cilicia, Hilakku or Cappadocia, and Iasbuqa under the Aramæan Bur Anate, and again Shalmaneser claims the victory and the capture of Bur Anate, but still the victory was not followed by results of consequence.

Tribute was, however, received from the "kings of the sea coast," the Phœnicians. Itto-baal's successor Baal-azor II (867–861) had just been followed as king of Tyre by the twenty-year-old Matten (861–832). Two of his merchant princes were despatched in long narrow boats, rowed without oarlocks, and with figure heads of camels at the high prows and sterns; the boats were unloaded in the shallows and the bales of dark blue wool, the cloth coloured like the precious lapis lazuli, and the ingots of gold, silver, lead, and copper were carried ashore. Shalmaneser under his parasol in his camp by the sea received the Phœnician ambassadors, clad in long clinging double robes, turbans wound round with ribbons, pointed beards, and upturned shoes; they were followed by servants bearing trays with sweet-meats, boxes over their shoulders, or big kettles on their heads like caps. Cedar logs were brought down to the sea from the near-by forests.[29]

Shalmaneser then prepared a relief on a cliff near the sea and by the side of Ashur-rabi's. The Hattinian cities of Taia, Hazazu, Nulia, and Butamu were captured; Hazazu, on a low but fair sized mound, was defended by warriors in short girdled tunics, round helmets, and neck pieces, their women wore gowns reaching to ankles and elbows, their hair hung down their backs. Tribute of Arame, son of Gusi, silver, gold, cattle, sheep, wine, a couch of gold and silver, closed the year.

The Euphrates was again crossed the next year, 858, and tribute collected from six Adini towns. The crown prince attacked Dabigu, a double-walled town with battlemented outworks in the plain, and defended against escalade or mining by archers armed with short swords. Til Bashere's gabled "Hittite" palace crowned a huge high mound, double the size of Carchemish, within oval city walls. The bearded inhabitants wore liberty caps, long double robes open at the sides, and pointed shoes, their women were long-haired and bare-legged. Til Bashere was breached by the movable ram, despite the stones dropped upon it by the defenders, who were impaled around the walls, deprived of hands and feet, or dragged off with ropes about their necks.

When Sangara's fort Sazabe was taken, the coalition made peace. The list of their tribute is a valuable contribution to North Syrian culture. Lubarna of Hattina furnished three talents of gold, a hundred of silver, three hundred of copper and of iron, a thousand vessels of copper, a thousand cloaks, twenty talents of one kind of purple wool and two of another, five hundred cattle and five thousand sheep. The reliefs picture its collection in the great Unqi swamp, entered by flat-

[29] Fig. 68 f., *History of Assyria*.

bottomed boats rowed with thong-hung oars by men clothed in fillets and little else. On a low mound in the swamp was the capital, a battlemented fortress with double gates, from which Lubarna emerged in full Assyrian dress, the long fringed robe and shawl, but his nobles retained the older "Hittite" long hair and beard, sweeping robes, and upturned shoes. Baskets and sacks, wine skins, trays of valuables, and ivory in tusks formed the spoil. Men from another swamp fort brought the same objects, but their dress was different, short robes which left the limbs free and ordinary shoes; in them we see the more recently arrived Aramæans. From a third came horses and cattle, for to this day only here do we find cattle in large numbers.

Sangara and his two youthful sons, their profile less sharp than the Assyrian, with straight nose, short hair and beard, also surrendered. The nobles were decked in the Assyrian long single robe and plain sleeved coat, but the more conservative lower classes retained the twisted conical turban, long double robes, and upturned shoes. Carchemish was not yet the richest of North Syrian cities, for the tribute was only three talents of gold, seventy of silver, thirty of copper, a hundred of iron, twenty of purple, five hundred weapons, five hundred cattle, and five thousand sheep, with a hundred maidens from the noblest families. Haya of Samal furnished ten talents of silver, ninety of copper, thirty of iron, three hundred garments, three hundred cattle, three thousand sheep, two hundred cedar beams, and two homers of cedar resin. In addition, each vassal must give his daughter with a rich dowry; the pathos of these forced marriages appears in the reliefs where the half-grown girl stretches out her hands in vain supplication to the victor. For annual tribute, Hattina gave a talent of silver, two of purple, two hundred cedar beams; Samal ten minas of silver, a hundred cedar beams, and a homer of cedar resin; Carchemish a mina of gold, a talent of silver, and two of purple.

This imposition of an annual tribute gave ample warning that Shalmaneser was no mere raider in search of booty, but had determined to form definite vassal states which might some day become Assyrian provinces. The states of Central Syria determined on united resistance. The first step was taken by Damascus where the Ben Hadad who assisted Asa had given way to an unknown son and he to a second Ben Hadad who could bring to his wars thirty-two kings. Samaria was besieged and Ben Hadad arrogantly sent word to Ahab: "Your silver and your gold are mine, likewise your wives and your children are mine." Ahab meekly replied: "According to your saying, my lord king, I am yours and all that I have." Convinced of Ahab's cowardice, Ben Hadad then announced: "This time to-morrow I shall send my slaves to search your house and the houses of your slaves, and whatever is pleasing in their eyes shall they take and carry away." Ahab summoned his elders who advised resistance, but Ben Hadad swore: "The gods do so to me and more also if Samaria's dust shall suffice for handfuls for all the men at my feet." Ahab, safe on the "Watch Tower," pointedly answered: "He who girds on his armour should not boast as he who puts it off." Ben Hadad at once ordered his men to draw up in line of battle, but a prophet counselled Ahab to make a feint with the two hundred and thirty "youths" mustered by the chief men of the provinces while the main attack was made by the seven thousand regular soldiers; Ben Hadad was caught in his tent during the noon day drinking bout and driven to flight on horseback, in the orient always a disgrace.

Ben Hadad's courtiers soon discovered the cause of his defeat: "Gods of the hills are the gods of Israel, not gods of the valley; let us fight them in the plain, then we shall be stronger than they." Warned again by the prophet, Ahab was prepared when Ben Hadad reappeared at Aphek, near the north end of the pass on the Damascus road, though the Israelites were like two flocks of little kids in comparison with the host which filled the valleys. Seven days they faced each other and then battle was joined; encouraged once more by the prophet, the Israelites were victorious and the Aramæans fled into Aphek, whose wall fell upon them, inflicting further loss.

It was sweet revenge for Ahab to hear the words of Ben Hadad: "I pray you, let our souls live." The Israelite king was a man of strong common sense, and he realised the Assyrian menace; he permitted Ben Hadad to purchase safety by restoring the cities taken by his father and by grants of Damascus bazaars for the Hebrew traders. The sons of the prophets were furious. Wounded at his own order by one of his fellows, a son of the prophets disguised himself with his helmet over his eyes and waited by the roadside. Pretending to be a soldier who had lost his captive, he tricked the king into declaring he must suffer penalty, then snatched away his helmet that Ahab might behold his prophetic mark, and pronounced the doom: "Because you have let escape from your hand the man I had devoted to destruction, your life shall be for his life, your people for his people." Ahab went his way, knowing that his action was justified.[30]

Ahab's reign is the turning point in Hebrew religion. Thus far, the religion professed by the Hebrews differed in no essential respect from that professed by their fellow Semites in neighbour lands. They worshipped as their national God Yahweh, but even in this they were not entirely unique. Yahweh was no longer the austere desert deity, he had been given the attributes of the nature gods he had but partially supplanted. He was worshipped under the form of an image, at times of a bull. Nor was he the sole God of his people; Jeremiah asserts that to his own day "as the number of your cities so your gods."[31] Rude figures of the mother goddess are the most common objects found in the strata of this period; as late as the fifth century, Yahweh had a consort among the Jews of Egypt, and we can scarcely deny that these figurines witness a similar usage at home.

Hebrew ethics were no higher than those of neighbour peoples. Religion was a matter of ritual, with no ethical content. Immorality of the grossest character was practised at the shrines and by men and women dedicated for that very purpose. Yahweh was considered a typical oriental despot, bound

[30] I Kings 20. [31] Jer. 11:13.

by no law, delighting in human sacrifice, acting at his own whim, but easily mollified by the odour of sacrifice.

The one hope of the future was the prophet. Not that the Hebrew prophet was unique. Every Semitic people had its seer to predict the future but rarely was he a man of any standing. Samuel was a mere clairvoyant, hired for an insignificant sum. The bystanders were amazed when Saul joined the prophets; he was of good lineage but who were *their* ancestors? The Philistine crisis called forth a new group of prophets, whose influence did much to hearten the enslaved Hebrews. Prophets played a large part at the courts of David and Solomon, and had not a little to do with the disruption. Prophetism in the later sense begins with Ahab's reign. It is not easy to trace the development, though it is the most remarkable revolution in religious history, but we can at least characterise the chief figures in the struggle and the principles for which they contended.

From his own point of view, Ahab was a zealous worshipper of Yahweh, in fact, he might well consider himself the first protagonist of Yahweh in north Israel. Before his day, proper names compounded with Yahweh are rare. Micah is the first certain example before Saul, who did name some of his sons after the new deity. No northern king thereafter names Yahweh until Ahab, who actually gave Yahweh names to no less than four of his children. Obadiah, "Servant of Yahweh," was a high official at court, and perhaps we have his seal where he calls himself "servant of the king."[32] The ostraca also mention Obadiah and many another who commemorates Yo, the contemporary pronunciation of Yahweh in names. When Ahab went to war, he consulted the four hundred official prophets of Yahweh.

Jezebel is an early example of a woman missionary in high places. In her youth, she had worshipped Baal Melkart, the "Lord, King of the City" of Tyre. Absence from home had only intensified her devotion and her desire that all should worship his gracious divinity. He was lord of a wealthy mer-

[32]P. Schroeder, *ZDPV.*, XXXVII, 1914, 173.

chant city, in close contact with the mightiest empires of the day; how could she condescend to worship a deity adored only by rude back-countrymen, but a few generations out of the desert?

Conversion should not be difficult. A century or two ago, none of her subjects had worshipped Yahweh, they had rather paid their devoirs to their tribal gods or to various fertility deities, whom Yahweh had conquered only by accepting their ritual and by recognising them as his divine associates. Yahweh himself was called Baal in the sense of Lord, his associates were the Baals, and identification with her Baal should be easy.

So, like many a Roman Christian lady married to a Germanic pagan, Jezebel persuaded her husband to build a temple to her more civilised god. It contained the usual altar, standing stone, and Asherah, for Ahab, though a devoted follower of Yahweh, was no monotheist. Jezebel was a forceful personality, her influence in the state was strong, it paid to be in her good graces, and there was no better way to win her favour than to worship her god. The ostraca show as many men who honoured Baal as Yahweh.

At first, the prophets were solidly behind Ahab, whom they encouraged in his wars with Ben Hadad II. The break with the "sons of the prophets" came when Ahab's recognition of the Assyrian menace returned his enemy safely to Damascus. About the same time, Jezebel was blamed for an atrocity which still further inflamed the conservatives against the foreign queen.

In Jezreel, on its shelf two hundred feet above the plain to which it gave its name, lived a certain Naboth, whose vineyard lay below where wine presses still pit the rock. Ahab desired his plot for a garden of herbs such as that owned by the Chaldæan Merodach Baladan, and offered another and better vineyard or its cash value as alternative; Sargon did exactly the same when he expropriated the lands for his new city of Dur Sharrukin.[33] Naboth, with the peasant's love for his ancestral

[33]*History of Assyria*, 523, 270 f.

lands, declined the offer, and Ahab took no action to violate ancestral rights. Jezebel, however, could not appreciate the tenacity of the free peasant, she had spent her early years in a mercantile community where everything was bought and sold, where constant seafaring had killed devotion to any one spot of land. Accustomed to the merchant's trickery, she thought it nothing to despatch orders under the royal seal to proclaim a fast. Naboth was accused to the assembled citizens by two suborned witnesses and was convicted of cursing God and the king; he was dragged from the city and stoned, and his property escheated to the king. As he descended to view his new possession, Ahab was met by Elijah: "Have you made and seized the kill? For your act hear Yahweh's oracle: In the place where swine and dogs licked the blood of Naboth shall swine and dogs lick your blood, and the harlots shall wash themselves in your blood; Jezebel also shall dogs eat in Jezreel's district."[34]

Elijah is our third great figure, dimly seen through the haze of later story. His home was Tishbeh in Gilead on the desert border, and his hairy mantle was symbol of opposition to all foreign innovations. Elijah first appears as predicting a three-years drought; the drought is historical, for Tyrian writers ascribe it to Itto-baal's reign,[35] and so it must date between the years 874 and 867. The story then tells of Jezebel's persecution of the prophets and of Elijah's challenge to the Baal priests on Mount Carmel. Baal fails to aid his devotees, fire from heaven consumes Elijah's sacrifice, the assembled people hail Yahweh as *the* God, the Baal priests are all slain, and the drought is broken by a furious storm; thus the nomad Yahweh bests the agricultural Baal in his own province.

This destruction of the Baal priests cannot be historical, for they remained in power until the destruction of Ahab's dynasty. Some of the Elijah narratives are pure folk tale, but much has been preserved that is authentic. Elijah's challenge: "How long will you limp back and forth between the

[34] I Kings 21.   [35] Menander, in Joseph., *Ant.*, VIII, 324.

two sides? If Yahweh is God, follow him, but if Baal, follow him!" is the prophetic war cry. His sneer at the Baal priests: "Cry louder! Your god is deep in thought or absent on a journey or perhaps he is only sound asleep" must often have been repeated by Elijah's partisans. In view of the prophetic attitude towards the alarming international situation, there was point to Ahab's taunt: "Is it you, you troubler of Israel?" Elijah's reply: "I have not troubled Israel; it is you and your father's house, for you have forsaken the commands of Yahweh your God and have followed the Baals," is the essence of the prophetic programme.

Ahab, for all his tolerance of foreign cults, was a true devotee of Yahweh, but Jezebel was bound by no nationalistic compunctions, and her persecution of the prophets must also be historical. Many of the prophets were put to death, others escaped only because Obadiah hid a hundred in caves and provided them with food and water. Despite the prophetic opposition to his foreign policy, Ahab was by no means in complete agreement with Jezebel's persecution, for although he knew of Obadiah's action, that high official still retained his master's confidence. Elijah had initiated the war against the interloping foreign god, but he had failed; in black despair he fled to Judah and then to Yahweh's cave at Horeb. His successor Elisha was to win the victory.[36]

The year 854 saw the Assyrian storm break on Central Syria. Tribute was received from Sangara, Arame, Haya, and Kalparunda, who now appears as king of a united Hattina and Gurgum. Shalmaneser then sacrificed to the Adad of Halman or Aleppo, and thus won divine approval for his rule in North Syria. Invasion of Central Syria began with the capture of Barga, whose tall flat-roofed and many-windowed houses rose on a low mound encircled by battlemented walls and a stream. Adennu and Argana, other towns of Irhuleni of Hamath, were taken by escalade, and the Assyrians moved up the Orontes through fig laden orchards to Qarqara, a small fort on a low mound but guarded by unusually high battlemented towers.

[36] I Kings 17 ff.

Thanks in no small degree to Ahab's statesmanlike policy and in spite of all prophetic opposition, a strong alliance had been formed to meet the Assyrian invader. At its head was Hadad-ezer of Damascus, come to the throne after Ben Hadad's defeat by Ahab, who brought twelve hundred chariots, twelve hundred cavalry, and twenty thousand infantry. Next came Irhuleni of Hamath, with seven hundred chariots, seven hundred cavalry, and ten thousand foot. Striking testimony to the relative importance of Israel is the fact that Ahab is third, with ten thousand infantry and two thousand chariots, the largest single contribution in this most aristocratic of services. Judah, Edom, and Moab do not appear, for they were Ahab's vassals and their troops must have been included in his contingent.

Osorkon II (874–853) was doubtless a prime mover of the coalition; a large two-handled jar of Egyptian alabaster, marked with his cartouche and its capacity of eighty-one hin and found in Ahab's courtyard, contained some rare unguent presented to the Israelite king when the two monarchs cemented alliance.[37] His actual aid was small, but a thousand foot soldiers. Five hundred soldiers from Que recognised the common interests of Cilicia and Syria. Matten of Tyre had already paid tribute, but the north Phœnician states were more patriotic, Arka with ten chariots and ten thousand foot, Arvad under Matten-baal with two hundred men, Usanata with the same, Shiana under Adoni-baal with perhaps a thousand. Baasha son of Rehob led ten thousand Ammonites, a thousand camel riders from Gindibu the Arab give our first indication that the true Arabs were following in the wake of their Aramæan cousins.

On the confession of the Balawat gate reliefs, Assyrian skirmishers were slain by the allies. The official annals are full of vague boasts which suddenly break off. Following events were to prove that Qarqara was a drawn battle, if not an Assyrian defeat.[38]

[37] Reisner-Fisher-Lyon, *op. cit.*, 247.
[38] *History of Assyria*, 124 ff.; *JAOS.*, XLI, 1921, 350 ff.

Assyria had been repulsed and no small part of the credit redounded to Ahab. Not a hint of this campaign appears in the Hebrew records, though it is the key to all contemporary history. Prophetic writers never hesitated to describe their monarchs' reverses, only one explanation of this omission is plausible. History had proved that Ahab was right when he defied the prophetic thunders, so they quietly dropped all mention of the Assyrian war and thus saved their reputation.[39]

Following the usual Syrian practice, the coalition broke up when the Assyrian threat temporarily disappeared. Three years after Qarqara, Ahab laid plans for the recovery of Ramath Gilead from his late ally of Damascus. Jehoshaphat of Judah approved his lord's project: "I am as you are, my people as your people, my horses as your horses," but he had no desire to hazard his life on an expedition which would bring no personal reward. Hoping for an unfavourable answer, he suggested inquiry of Yahweh. Zedekiah, head of the official prophets, made iron horns and predicted: "Thus saith Yahweh: With these shall you push Aram until they are consumed." Jehoshaphat insisted on calling another prophet, though Ahab expressed his hate for a man who always predicted evil.

While Elijah with the "sons of the prophets" was waging his war against Baal, a greater than Elijah was going his lone way. Summoned by Ahab, Micaiah son of Imlah at first gave an oracle which agreed with that of the official prophets; struck by his tone, Ahab impatiently demanded: "How many times must I adjure you to tell me nothing but the truth in the name of Yahweh?" Thus adjured, Micaiah answered:

> I saw all Israel, scattered on the mounts,
>   As sheep without shepherd; then said Yahweh:
> No master have these, let them turn,
>   Each man to his house in peace.

Ahab interrupted: "Did I not tell you that he would not prophesy good concerning me but evil?" "It is not so, it is

[39] Cf. J. M. P. Smith, *AJT.*, XXIII, 1919, 290 ff.

not from me," replied Micaiah, "from Yahweh is the word you shall hear:

I saw Yahweh, Israel's God, sitting on his throne,
   And the host of heaven standing on his right hand and his left;
And Yahweh said: 'Who will Ahab deceive,
   To make him go up to Ramath Gilead and fall?'
Then one said this and another that,
   But the spirit stepped forth and stood 'fore Yahweh's face,
'I will deceive him'; said Yahweh: 'With what?'
'I will go in his prophets a spirit of lying to be.'
'Deceive him, go forth, do thus and succeed!' "

Zedekiah smote Micaiah's jaw and wrathfully demanded: "Where is Yahweh's spirit that speaks in you?" "Lo, you shall see it on the day you enter an inner chamber and hide yourself" was the only answer. Ahab ordered the recalcitrant prophet to be imprisoned and fed with the bread and water of affliction until his return in peace, but Micaiah only reiterated: "If you return in peace, Yahweh has not spoken by me."

Ahab was still determined to make the venture, but Micaiah's prophecy had made an impression. Jehoshaphat's lukewarmness was fittingly rewarded, he was to enter battle wearing Ahab's robes, while Ahab was disguised as a common soldier. The Judæan king had no intention of becoming a vicarious sacrifice, and gave his own battle cry when attacked; orders had been given to fight only with Ahab, and when they discovered the grim joke, the Aramæans abandoned pursuit. But Ahab was not to escape his fate. An Aramæan archer idly drew his bow and let fly; the arrow pierced Ahab between the coat of mail and the jointed attachments. Ahab ordered his driver to bear him from the field, but the battle had begun in earnest and he remained propped up in his chariot until evening, when he died. At once the cry was raised: "Every man to his city and every man to his country, for the king is dead."[40]

[40] I Kings 22.

Thus died miserably Israel's greatest king and prophetic prestige was restored. He had saved his people in their greatest crisis, but patriotism and religion had clashed and Ahab had the misfortune to oppose the party which ultimately triumphed. The future was indeed with the prophets, who alone make Hebrew history more significant than that of the other second-rate Syrian states. Bitterly as the prophets hated Ahab, unkind as they were to his memory, we must nevertheless remember that it was his foresightedness alone which won for them the breathing spell needed for full development of religious beliefs of such portent for the future.

Micaiah's fate is unknown, he no longer interested Elijah's disciples when their master's policies triumphed and they in turn became official prophets, but he stands out as one of the great prophetic figures. He still admitted that the official prophets were inspired by Yahweh. His God could deceive his official mouthpiece to lead a man to his ruin, cold consolation though it was to men who might prefer to be called knaves rather than fools; it was but a step to a new conception, that these official prophets, so ready to accommodate their oracles to the wishes of their earthly lord, were in reality false prophets. Micaiah was first to believe that a true prophet must prophesy evil, he was the first to suffer because he refused to support national expansion. Elijah's sucessors ruled in temple and palace; Micaiah's spiritual successors must be sought in Amos and the noble company of prophets whose writings form the most precious contribution made to the world by Hebrew religion.

CHAPTER XXV

REFORMS OF BLOOD

AHAB's death was the end of Israel's glory, for his weakly son Ahaziah (852–850) quickly lost his foreign possessions. Mesha of Moab at once revolted. Since the first entrance of the Hebrews, conditions in the East Jordan regions had changed. Already in the days of Saul there had been inroads of the Hagar, Jetur, Naphish, and Nodab, but they were driven back and the Hebrews dwelt in their tents throughout all the land east of Gilead; three hundred years later, the Hagar appeared on the Assyrian frontier, the Jetur remained to become Ituræans.[1]

Reuben was so weakened that there was a prayer:

> Let Reuben live and not die,
> But let his men be few.[2]

As Gad was pressed south and west by the Ammonites, who had preserved their independence against Ahab, his tribesmen overflowed into Reuben's former possessions. Ataroth, almost in the centre of the ancient Reuben, had according to Mesha been held by Gad from days of old; the Biblical lists assign Ataroth, Heshbon, and Daibon without question to Gad; a little later Gad's boundary is the Arnon and Reuben has completely disappeared.[3] From these days of expansion comes the triumphant lay:

> Blessed be he who enlarges Gad,
>   Like a lioness he dwells;
>   And tears the arm and the crown of the head.
> For he chose for himself the first part,

---

[1] I Chron. 5:10, 19 ff. [2] Deut. 33:6.
[3] Josh. 13:25 ff.; Num. 32:34.

> There was the ruler's lot reserved,
> And he came to the heads of the folk.
> He executed the righteousness of Yahweh,
> And his ordinances with Israel.[4]

The tide turned when Mesha revolted. Medeba was won back, Baal Meon was restored and made a reservoir. Ataroth, rebuilt by the Israelite king, was assaulted, its slain inhabitants made a gazing stock for Chemosh and Moab, the altar hearth was dragged before Chemosh in Kerioth, the site was colonised with men from Sharon and Maharoth. Chemosh then ordered: "Go, take Nebo from Israel"; Mesha went by night and fought against it from daybreak to noon. Every soul in its midst, seven thousand men besides women, slaves, and resident aliens, was devoted to Ashtor-Chemosh, the consort of the national deity, and Yahweh's utensils were dragged before Chemosh himself. The king of Israel had rebuilt Jahaz and occupied it during his wars with Moab, but Chemosh, with the two hundred chiefs of Moab, drove him out from before Mesha's face, and Jahaz was added to Daibon. With the captured Israelites, Mesha built Kerhah, the wall of Jearim, the wall of Ophel, with its gates and towers, the king's palace, and two reservoirs since previously there had been no cisterns in the city, Aroer, the Arnon highway, the destroyed Beth Bamoth and the ruined Bezer, Medeba, Beth Diblathain, and Beth Baal Meon. Chemosh also ordered: "Go down and fight against Horonaim," and the city was recovered. Thus Chemosh saved Mesha from all his enemies and let him see his pleasure on all that hated him, while Israel perished with an everlasting destruction.

Mesha's capital Daibon was now a stronghold of the first rank. Two low hills on the plateau edge were connected by walls with a gate to the Dead Sea road; the low southern hill was fortified to prevent the enemy from overlooking the northern where the city proper was located. Three gates, on the western line of the double wall and protected by a third wall and outposts farther down the steep slope, gave access to the

[4] Deut. 33:20 f.

city, but there was also an entrance from the Arnon highway at the northeast corner, a narrow passage through double walls up a ramp with dividing paths to the city and to the palace on the east, while a wider passage ending in a cul de sac was a trap for the hostile intruder. In the southeast corner was the high place of Chemosh in Kerhah, marked by later shrine ruins and the tomb of a local saint; here Mesha set up for Chemosh the Moabite Stone, a building inscription in language which is virtually Hebrew and in good Biblical phraseology.[5]

Jehoshaphat, under the influence of the seer Jehu, son of Hanani, had been engaged in judicial reforms;[6] since Edom was ruled by his deputy, he determined to utilise Ezion Geber by resuming the lucrative Ophir trade. Ahaziah demanded a master's share, but Jehoshaphat refused, for Ahaziah was no Ahab. Unfortunately, the Judæans had not yet learned seafaring, and the ship was broken on the rocks before it could make sail.[7]

In want of issue, Ahaziah was succeeded by his bother Jehoram (850–842). Jehoshaphat died the same year and his thirty-two-year-old son, also named Jehoram, took his place (850–843). He immediately slew all his brothers, to whom his father had given the dangerous gift of Judæan forts, and with them many of the local nobility.[8] Edom revolted and set up a king in place of the former Judæan deputy. Jehoram made an expedition against Seir but fell into an ambush, his chariots were scattered, and he retreated. Henceforth Edom enjoyed her own king, who however soon found it necessary to declare himself a vassal of Israel. Libnah also revolted and went back to Philistine rule.[9]

By his name as by his marriage to Athaliah, daughter of Ahab and Jezebel, Jehoram of Judah admitted his vassalage to Jehoram of Israel. The two kings determined to attack Mesha by the road around the south end of the Dead Sea,

---

[5]Fig. 157; G. A. Cooke, *Textbook of North-Semitic Inscriptions*, 1903, 1 ff.; D. Mackenzie, *QS.*, 1913, 57 ff.
[6]II Chron. 19:2, 8 ff.
[7]I Kings 22:45 ff.
[8]II Chron. 21.
[9]II Kings 8:16 ff.

FIG. 157. THE MOABITE STONE.

where they were joined by the new king of Edom. Seven days out, water failed and the Israelite lost heart, but his brother-in-law sought for a prophet of Yahweh. Elisha, son of Shaphat, who had poured water on the hands of Elijah, was discovered, a peasant from Abel Meholah in the Jordan valley, ten miles south of the Jezreel exit. Asked to give an oracle, Elisha rudely answered: "What business have I with you? Go to your father's prophets!" Only for the sake of the Judæan king did he order a minstrel to be summoned, the prophetic ecstacy must be induced in Elisha by artificial means. He then ordered water holes to be dug; to this day sweet water rises a few hours after digging. In the rosy dawn, the water appeared as blood, and the Moabites assumed that the Edomites had fallen upon their oppressors; they rushed in disorder upon the camp and were slain.

The allies beat down the cities, filled the fields with stones, stopped up the fountains, and so harried Moab that only Kir Hareseth remained uncaptured. Kir Hareseth occupied a steep ascent under the yet higher castle hill and was surrounded on all sides by perpendicular cliffs or deep-cut moats; should the spring before the city be taken, there still remained the castle reservoir and the town cisterns, though an attempt to secure an underground water supply had failed. Slingers were attacking the city when Mesha with a hundred picked men attempted to break through the line where the Edomites were posted. The attempt failed and his case was hopeless; the supreme sacrifice was demanded by Chemosh, Mesha's eldest son, the crown prince, as a burnt offering upon the wall. The invaders were strangers in the land of a hostile god, prayer so well supported must surely be heard by Chemosh; as the record puts it "there came great wrath against Israel," and the erstwhile victors were only too glad to reach home in safety.[10]

Judah had one more loss to chronicle. The Arabs near the Kushites, that is, the nomads of Sinai, raided Judah and carried off the palace treasure together with the king's sons and wives.[11] Soon after this loss, the incapable Jehoram died, and

[10] II Kings 3. [11] II Chron. 21:10, 16 f.

his place was filled by his twenty-two-year-old son Ahaziah, who owed his throne to the citizens of Jerusalem. Related already to the house of Omri through his mother Athaliah, the connection was drawn closer by marriage to a wife from the same family.[12]

As in the case of Elijah, the career of Elisha is clouded by folk tale. From them emerges the fact that Elisha was no nomad but a peasant, called from the prosaic task of plowing. He was accepted by the "sons of the prophets" as their leader, and his miracles in behalf of their communities at Jericho and Gilgal are duly recorded. Other tales indicate the opposition to the prophetic movement. The "sons of the prophets" were little esteemed at Bethel, the centre of the bull cult, and once the youths stoned Elisha and taunted him: "Go up, you bald head, go up," perhaps in reference to a distinguishing tonsure. There are tales of a terrible famine, the blame for which was laid on Elisha by the king; the king declares that the evil is from Yahweh, why should he wait any longer for Yahweh's aid, and Elisha calls him "this son of a murderer who has sent to take my head."[13]

Royal opposition to the "sons of the prophets" resulted in conspiracy. The opportunity came when Jehoram recovered Ramath Gilead from the still weakened Damascus, but was wounded by the archers during the siege and returned with Ahaziah to Jezreel for recovery. This left Ramath Gilead and the army under the command of a certain Jehu, whose father's name Jehoshaphat shows personal worship of Yahweh. As the generals were seated together, a "son of the prophets" suddenly appeared with "I have a word for you, O general." Alone together in an inner room, the man followed Elisha's instructions, anointed Jehu as king of Israel, and fled.

Jehu's lieutenants had remarked that the man was possessed of a spirit, and uneasily they inquired whether all was well. Reassured that there was no danger to the army, they asked his message. Jehu was not quite sure how they would take it, and diplomatically answered: "You know the man

[12] II Kings 8:25 ff.; II Chron. 22:1.   [13] II Kings 2, 4, 6:25 ff.

and his message." "It is false, tell us, we pray you," and Jehu laid aside all pretense. Hurriedly they placed him upon their garments on the open stairway, blew the trumpet, and shouted: "Jehu is king."

On the high tower of Jezreel, with its far view over the plain, the watchman saw a body of men approaching. Two horsemen were sent out and failed to return, and now the furious driving was recognised as that of Jehu. Fearing that this portended the loss of Ramath Gilead, the two kings ordered their chariots to be yoked, and met Jehu with the inquiry "Is all well?" To their astonishment, Jehu replied: "How can all be well as long as the immoralities and sorceries of your mother Jezebel are so many?" Jehoram called out "Treachery, Ahaziah," and turned to flee, but was shot through the heart by Jehu, who then gave order to his third officer Bidkar: "Take him and throw him into the plot of land that belonged to Naboth of Jezreel; for I remember how, when you and I rode in company after his father Ahab, Yahweh laid upon him this oracle:

> Surely the blood of Naboth,
> And the blood of his sons have I seen;
> In this plot will I repay you,
> This is Yahweh's doom.

Now therefore take him and throw him into the plot in accordance with Yahweh's word." Thus was prophecy deliberately fulfilled.

Ahaziah fled due south by the way of Beth Gan, but was overtaken where the Jerusalem road begins to rise from the plain, on the ascent of Gur near Ibleam, and was struck by an arrow. He escaped the pursuing chariotry by transferring to horseback and rode over the rough hills to Megiddo. There he died and his servants bore his corpse to Jerusalem for burial.

With all her sins, we cannot but admire the bravery of the aged queen. Smoothing her hair and anointing her eyes with kohl as for a sacrifice, Jezebel took her position at a window. As Jehu rode through the gate, she taunted him: "Is it well, you Zimri, your master's murderer?" Just then, two eunuchs, fit instruments for so dastardly a deed, looked out, and Jehu brutally ordered: "Throw her down!" So down she was thrown and her blood spattered on the wall and on the horses who trampled her underfoot.

While her corpse was being devoured by the street curs, the callous Jehu was eating and drinking. Brought thus to a more kindly mood, he gave command: "Attend to this cursed woman and bury her, for after all she was a king's daughter." Informed that of her poor body there remained only the skull, the feet, and the palms, Jehu smugly observed: "This is the word of Yahweh, which he spoke by Elijah the Tishbite, saying:

> In the plot of Jezreel shall dogs eat the flesh of Jezebel,
> And Jezebel's body shall be ordure upon the field's face
> In the plot of Jezreel; none shall say: 'This is Jezebel.'"

This scene of horror was only the beginning of Jehu's reform. He had been ordered to destroy the house of Ahab, and there were still seventy of the family in Samaria. The chief men of the city received this message: "As soon as this letter comes to you, for your master's sons are with you, and you have chariots and horses and fortified cities and armour, choose the best and most worthy of your master's sons and place him on his father's throne and fight for your master's house!" The death of the two kings had taken all desire for fighting from the supporters of the old dynasty and the chamberlain of the palace and the prefect of the city joined with the elders and the guardians of the children in sending back word: "Your slaves are we, all that you bid us we will do; no man will we make king, do what is good in your eyes." They were ordered to cut off the heads of the unfortunate youths, pack them in baskets, and send them to Jezreel.

Next morning, Jehu strolled out to the city gate where the populace was staring at the grisly piles and exclaimed in affected astonishment: "You are righteous; true enough I conspired against my lord and slew him, but who killed all these?"

Having thus proved that there were others opposed to the fallen dynasty, he again pointed the pious moral that nothing prophesied against Ahab's house by Yahweh could fail. In further fulfilment of these predictions, he put to death all the kinsmen of the late king he could discover in Jezreel and with them the "King's Friends." Even the court priests, though worshippers of the same God as Jehu, fell victim to the prophetic reforms.

Ahab's family was now out of his path and Jehu started south for Samaria. Fortune again favoured him, for a few miles on, at Beth Eked, he met forty-two of Ahaziah's relations who were likewise slain. The way was open, Jehu might hope, to a personal union of the two kingdoms.

News of the revolt reached the ears of an ardent advocate of the ancient worship, Jehonadab, descendant of Rechab, who had warned his children to follow the desert customs without change. True to their ancestor's precepts, they still dwelt in tents and refused to build houses, sow fields, or plant vineyards, but their most stringent taboo was against that most seductive of civilised vices, the drinking of wine.[14] Jehonadab met Jehu on the road and was asked: "Is your heart as my heart?" Assured that the Rechabites would approve the new régime, the king took Jehonadab into his own chariot and bade him "Come with me and see my zeal for Yahweh."

Arrived at Samaria, Jehu instituted another massacre which wiped out the last man on whom might devolve the blood revenge for Ahab's house. He then summoned the priests and prophets of Baal with the strange assurance: "Ahab served Baal a little but Jehu will serve him much." Jehu had entered the capital with a zealous protagonist of the older Yahweh cult and this alone should have warned the Baal worshippers; nevertheless, when he announced a solemn assembly and a great sacrifice for Baal, the temple was packed. Jehu made his promise good, for he actually offered burnt offerings to Baal. Hypocrisy could go no farther.

Meanwhile, eighty men had been stationed outside the tem-

[14] Jer. 35.

ple. The completion of the sacrifice was the signal for their entrance and every worshipper within was slain. The asherah was dragged out and burned, the altar was broken up, the temple was defiled.

Jehu's hope of the Judæan throne was doomed to disappointment. Jezebel he had killed, but her daughter survived in Jerusalem, and she possessed much of her mother's ability. When Athaliah saw the corpse of her son brought back for burial, she wasted no time; the few survivors of the royal family were put to death and she seized the throne for herself. The failure of the Baal propaganda in the north only intensified her missionary zeal. No longer was Solomon's temple the royal chapel, the royal support was transferred to a Baal temple served by the priest Mattan, perhaps a relative of the Matten reigning at Tyre. Even the revenues hitherto consecrated to Yahweh were now assigned to the house of his rival.[15]

Israel was no longer protected by a willing vassal on the south. Judah was ruled by a queen who could curse Jehu for the destruction of her whole family, and this hostility was further aggravated by sharp religious differences. Tyre was hopelessly alienated, the sea and its trade were closed to Israel. Perhaps Jehu did not care, for his revolt bears the mark of a peasant reaction against Ahab's financial reforms.

Just at this moment of Israel's isolation, the Assyrians appeared. Shalmaneser had returned to North Syria in 850, had reduced the remaining cities of Sangara, and had taken by assault Arne, capital of Arame of Agusi, on its high mound with stone-covered slope and walls, but his advance towards Hamath was checked by the coalition, unbroken save for the defection of Israel. In the next year, the cities of Sangara and Arame were again raided, Mount Iaraqu was crossed, and Shalmaneser descended to the lower lying cities of Hamath. Ashtamaku, a double-walled and battlemented fort on a low mound, was taken by the crown prince's cavalry, the allies were defeated, and Irhuleni was shut up in a fort whose double walls enclosed gable houses. Irhuleni abandoned his Assyrian

[15] II Kings 11; II Chron. 24:7.

couch and his shawled eunuch wielding the fly-flapper, and came out in his long fringed draped Assyrian royal robe to beg for mercy. He and his youthful son were well treated, for they were of the blood royal, but the common folk were stripped and yoked if men, or dragged off in scanty clothing if women. On his return journey, Shalmaneser took Apparanzu, one of Arame's villages, and received the tribute of the Hattinian Kalparunda.

Hadad-ezer of Damascus still demanded a reckoning and Irhuleni thought little of his enforced loyalty. Shalmaneser therefore called out the whole Assyrian levy of one hundred and twenty thousand men, in 846, but nothing was accomplished. Some time after, Hadad-ezer died. According to a prophetic tale, Ben Hadad sent his servant Hazael to inquire of the visiting Elisha whether he would recover from his sickness; the official answer was that Ben Hadad would recover, privately Hazael was informed that he himself should be king. Acting on this hint, Hazael dipped a cloth in water and laid it on his master's face, Ben Hadad died, and Hazael became king.[16] That Elisha could give or be supposed to give so lying an oracle is a sad commentary on the low ethics of the prophetic group; whatever lies behind the tale, the ruler of Damascus was now Hazael, whom Shalmaneser calls the "son of a nobody." The coalition broke up and Jehoram took advantage of the disorders in Damascus consequent on the usurpation to recover Ramath Gilead.

When therefore Shalmaneser advanced south in 842, he found no opponent worthy of mention, until he reached the outlet of the Amana from Mount Senir, the Anti-Lebanon. Here he came upon the camp of Hazael and a great battle was fought in which six thousand soldiers were killed and one thousand one hundred and twenty-one chariots and four hundred and seventy cavalry were taken. Hazael found a safe refuge behind his walls, while the Assyrians ravaged his orchards far and wide and plundered the "countless cities" of the Hauran.

Shalmaneser returned by the plain of Jezreel and the un-

[16] II Kings 8:7 ff.

worthy successor of Ahab came out to meet him, probably at the city of that name. The scene is pictured on the Black Obelisk; Jehu is the typical Armenoid, even to his "Jewish nose," but his liberty cap, his sleeveless jacket with long fringed and girdled skirt, his short round beard, all are of nomad fashion. His followers allowed themselves additional covering, a long robe open at the left with the end thrown over the left shoulder; they brought much gold, silver, and lead in unworked ingots, golden pails, bowls, cups, ladles, a tall drinking goblet, which remind us of the Syrian tribute brought to Thutmose III, sacks of valuables, flat baskets filled with fruit, scepters, or bundles of javelins.[71]

The sea was reached at Baal's Head, perhaps Carmel, where a relief was carved. Shalmaneser then returned along the shore northward to receive tribute of Tyre and Sidon. One of the middle group of Assyrian reliefs at the Dog River may be his work, though the inscription has disappeared; across the road the rock had been levelled for the ceremonies which accompanied the carving of such a royal figure.[18]

This was the Assyrian "Farthest South" for the ninth century. A cedar cutting trip to the Amanus confirmed the success of the previous year, and was followed by a campaign against Danabi in North Syria. Matten of Tyre, Sidon, and Gebal paid tribute in 838, and four of Hazael's cities were captured, with the temple of the god Sher of Malaha, but Damascus remained inviolate. Thus ended the attempt to reduce Central Syria.

Assyrian failure in Central Syria led the states of North Syria to revolt. Arame of Agusi refused to pay tribute and his only punishment was the loss of his fort Muru in 834. The loyal Lubarna of Hattina was deposed by the usurper Surri; at his death in 831, the Hattinians surrendered his sons and supporters to the turtanu Daian Ashur who impaled them, placed Sasi on the throne, and set up an Assyrian stele in the

[17]For the Black Obelisk, cf. Fig. 77, *History of Assyria*.
[18]*History of Assyria*, 113 ff.; *JAOS.*, XLI, 1921, 369 ff.

palace at Kunulua. Then Assyria was involved in a great civil war, and the curtain drops over North Syria.[19]

Two years after the last appearance of the Assyrians in Central Syria, Jehu enjoyed a final if vicarious success. It was a strange religious situation when in the recently converted north Yahweh was the sole national deity and the old nomad cult was enforced by the secular arm, while in his original southern home Yahweh's cult had been almost submerged by that of the foreign Baal. Stranger still, this change had been brought about by a woman who in her very name invoked Yahweh. Patriotism and love for the national God united the leading spirits of Judah; at their head was Jehoiada, chief priest of the Yahweh temple, whose prestige had suffered by the rise of Mattan. Fortunately, there was available a rival candidate for the throne.

When Athaliah had completed the slaughter of the royal house begun by Jehu, Jehosheba, wife of Jehoiada and sister of Athaliah, had secreted her infant nephew Jehoash in the temple. Jehoiada now made a compact with the commanders of the Carian mercenaries who guarded the temple. During the week, one company of a hundred men was on duty, but this was doubled on the sabbath; it was arranged that the company to be relieved should be detained until the other two companies arrived, and then the whole force concentrated about the temple. With drawn weapons, the mercenaries took their position in a semicircle about the great altar. Jehoash was stationed by the pillar in the temple court, was anointed and presented with the crown and the royal bracelets. The Jerusalemites had followed the new religious fashion and were accordingly kept in ignorance, but a large body of loyal countrymen was brought in to give moral as well as physical support to the mercenaries, and they now clapped their hands and shouted: "Live the king!"

Athaliah heard the shouting and hurried to the temple. As she saw Jehoash standing by the royal pillar and surrounded

---

[19]*History of Assyria,* 137 ff.; *JAOS.,* XLI, 1921, 374 ff.

by mercenaries, she rent her clothes and screamed: "A conspiracy, a conspiracy!" Jehoiada commanded: "Take her out and kill any man who follows her, but do not put her to death in Yahweh's temple." Athaliah was dragged out to the chariot entrance of the palace and slain.

There still remained what was to Jehoiada the more essential half of the revolution. At his bidding, the solemn covenant between king and people was supplemented by the yet more solemn covenant of king and people with the national God. No longer were they to serve Baal, henceforth they were to be Yahweh's alone. Thereupon the crowd hastened to the Baal temple, tore it down, destroyed its altars and images, and slew the chief priest Mattan before his altars.

Judah's new king might be friendly to a fellow sovereign who had also driven out the foreign god and had restored the pure worship of Yahweh, but all hope of a union of the two kingdoms was gone. Jehu did not possess the army to enforce such a union, even had the religious leaders of the two states given their permission.

Jehu paid for his sins, if not in his own person, at least in the persons of his subjects. Worse than his ascent of the throne through scenes of atrocious bloodshed, he had badly miscalculated the international situation. So imposing was the Assyrian power, he could not realise that the time had come for its advance to be stopped.

Damascus was now the leader of the Assyrian opposition in the west. As soon as it became certain that Assyria would not reappear, that the revolt of Ashur-danin-apal was to sap the Assyrian strength to its foundations, Damascus undertook the punishment of the traitor to the cause of Syrian independence. It may be that Elisha had not relished so bloody a reformation, perhaps he resented the sacrifices offered, even in mockery, to Baal; some such motive may lie behind the story that Elisha was responsible for Hazael's usurpation. The story goes on to say that Elisha wept and detailed the horrors which Hazael would inflict upon the helpless Israelites. In those days, we are told by a writer who was certainly not in sympathy with Jehu's bloody reforms, Yahweh was angry with Israel; all the land east of Jordan, Manasseh, Gad, Reuben, clear to the Arnon and that Aroer which a short generation before had been won back from the Moabites, Hazael now wrested from Jehu.[20] The horrible atrocities inflicted upon the wretched peasants, and especially upon their helpless women and children, were such as to make the Assyrian inroads seem in comparison visits of mercy; a generation later, Amos felt no hatred for Assyria, but the awful misdeeds of the Damascus rulers were placed first in his terrific denunciations of foreign nations.[21]

Jehu's personal character is peculiarly repulsive. We are shocked by his bloody clearances, Jezebel's murder outrages our chivalric regard for women and for old age, we cannot repress a shudder when we read how her body was eaten by street curs. His callous explanation that this was fulfilment of prophecy appears the height of sacrilege, his hypocrisy is proved by his sacrifice to Baal, an enemy god, but nevertheless to his contemporaries a very real and living divinity. He alienated the Tyrians and no longer could there be profitable exchange of commodities and ideas between the worldly wise Phœnicians and the countrified Hebrews. A reform which laid such stress on the nomad element in religion could scarcely have made for cultural advance. He basely surrendered his country's independence, and it was unnecessary; in his own day, it lost him all the East Jordan country, it set a fatal precedent for the future.

If it is difficult to absolve Jehu, what shall we say of the prophetic writers who narrate his bloody reforms? They omit his tribute to Shalmaneser, but they repeat his crimes with gusto and with evident approbation. Their influence on later ages has been sinister; innocents have been slaughtered and crimes against women condoned in the name of a merciful God, for Jehu's story proved that the end justified the means.

Yet, before we pass final judgment, we should at least recognise that here is another case where good does come from evil.

[20] II Kings 10:32 f.   [21] Amos 1:3 ff.

Never again was the position of Yahweh as Israel's national God in danger. Israel had taken the first step on the road towards henotheism, some day there might come a true monotheism.

CHAPTER XXVI

INTERLUDE

Four years after the death of his namesake in Judah, Matten of Tyre passed away. Fearful of the growing opposition to the despotic rule of the merchants, he had married his daughter Elisa to his brother Sicharbas, the priest of Baal Melkart, in the hope that she would succeed him, but the democrats gained control, and enthroned his nine-year-old son Pumyaton or Pygmalion (832–785). At the age of sixteen, Pumyaton celebrated his majority by the murder of Sicharbas, but Elisa rescued her husband's property and sailed away to Africa to found Carthage (825).[1] Later poets identified Elisa with the "Beloved" goddess Dido and from the identification spun the tale of the Carthaginian queen and the pious Æneas.

Phœnician trade with the Greeks had awakened the old spirit of Minos. As the Greeks once more took to the sea, the Phœnicians were forced westward. In the race for the control of the Mediterranean, Greek colonies occupied South Italy and eastern Sicily, but the south shore was safely Phœnician, save for a Greek settlement in Libya. Utica was the first Phœnician settlement in Africa, though the traditional date of 1112 for its foundation is far too early. Other colonies from about this time were Zaritis, the later Hippo, Hadrumetum, and the Major and Minor Leptis.[2]

Such good seamen could not long ignore the islands off the coast of Africa, Cossura, the modern Pantellaria, Gaul, the modern Gozzo,[3] above all the splendid harbours at Malta. From these islands, it was but a step to Sicily, occupied about the same time as Carthage, for the first Phœnician objects are associated with the Proto-Corinthian pottery brought from

[1]Menander, in Joseph., *Apion*, i, 125; Trogus, in Justin, xviii, 4 ff.
[2]Strabo, xvii, 3, 16; Pliny, *Hist. Nat.*, iv, 121; v, 4, 25.
[3]Diod., v, 12; CIS., 132.

Greece by their rivals;[4] the Greeks settled the country nearest Greece while the Phœnicians colonised Motya, Eryx, Soleis, and Mahanath, to be known later as Panormus and Palermo.[5] From the ruins of these colonies, something may be learned of the architecture of the home centres, now so completely destroyed.

Italy proper was never invaded, since the Phœnicians were allied with the Etruscans, but Phœnician wares make their appearance in the eighth century. One example, the famous bronze bowl of Præneste, bears in addition to meaningless hieroglyphs of the twenty-sixth Egyptian dynasty a Phœnician inscription.[6] Alliance brought Phœnician objects to Etruscan pit graves as early as the eighth century and they continue to the middle of the sixth. Among them are cups, ivories, and imitations of Egyptian scarabs; one scarab from a grotto at Volcii bears the cartouche of Psammetichus I (663–609), a vase of Egyptian "porcelain" from Corneto has that of Bocchoris (718–712).[7]

Sardinia's mineral wealth, silver, copper, lead, early drew the Phœnicians to Sharden, the Balearic Islands[8] were stepping-stones to Spain, where Phœnician wares begin to appear in this same eighth century. Malaca, the present Malaga, was settled for its gold, Abdera for its silver, Sexti for its salt.[9] Phœnician ships passed through the straits, the Pillars of Melkart, in which their sailors recognised gigantic replicas of the pillars in the Melkart temple at Tyre.[10] On the west coast of Africa, they founded Tingis, with its temple to the Tyrian Melkart, Lixus, and three hundred trading stations.[11] About the beginning of the fifth century, the Carthaginians despatched sixty ships and three thousand men on a voyage of exploration. Several trading factories were founded north of and one south of the Sahara, strange animals were discovered,

[4]T. Ashby, *Cambridge Anc. Hist.*, II, 578.
[5]Thuc., vi, 2.   [6]Fig. 159; CIS., I, 164.
[7]R. S. Conway, *Cambridge Anc. Hist.*, IV, 393, 414.
[8]Strabo, v, 2, 7; iii, 5, 1; xiv, 2, 10; CIS., I, 144.
[9]Strabo, iii, 4, 2 f.   [10]Arrian, ii, 16, 4.
[11]Strabo, ii, 3, 4; xvii, 3, 3; Pliny, *Hist. Nat.*, xix, 4.

including gorillas which were taken for human beings, but failing provisions compelled a return when the explorers were less than ten degrees from the equator. Hanno's report is a model of a detailed geographical survey.[12]

Beyond the straits to the north was Gades, still prosperous as Cadiz, which possessed temples to El and to Melkart with the usual two pillars.[13] Tartessus had also a temple to Melkart and followed Tyrian cult practices; it cannot however be the Tarshish of the Bible for there is no trace of Phœnician trade in the Iberian peninsula for two centuries after the date of Hiram and Solomon.[14] Gradually, Phœnician trade objects and then cultural influence penetrated the interior, especially after the Carthaginian conquest. Ultimately, the natives adopted the Phœnician alphabet for their own Iberian inscriptions.[15] The farthest north of Phœnician trade relations were the Cassiterides Islands off the coast of Britain, from which came the tin and lead worked by the natives from shallow mines.[16]

Beginning in the ninth century, the force of Phœnician expansion was not lost until far later times. Greek expansion was brought to a sudden pause and in Sicily lost ground was regained. Rome's infant power was granted by treaty definite economic limits, the Etruscans were Phœnician allies. Not until the Punic wars did the western Phœnicians cease their great work of civilisation. Through this western expansion, the Phœnician capitals at home rose to wealth and glory.

No such glory brightened the period for the Hebrews. Jehu's son, Jehoahaz (814–800), was if possible more incompetent than his father. Ahab had brought to Qarqara two thousand chariots; Jehu possessed but ten chariots and fifty horsemen, for the Aramæan king had made the remainder like dust of the threshing.[17] With Israel paying tribute, Hazael could con-

[12] W. H. Schoff, *The Periplus of Hanno*, 1913.
[13] Strabo, iii, 5, 3 ff.; Diod., v, 20; Pliny, *Hist. Nat.*, ii, 242 ff.; iv, 116 ff.
[14] Aristophanes, *Frogs*, 475; Scymnus Chius, 164; Strabo, iii, 2, 11 ff.; Pliny, *Hist. Nat.*, iv, 120; Paus., vi, 19; Jul. Pollux, vi, 63.
[15] Cf. P. Bauer, *Amer. Jour. Archæology*, II Ser., XI, 1907, 182 ff.; J. Déchelette, *Rev. Archéologique*, 1908, II, 390 ff.
[16] Strabo, iii, 5, 11.   [17] II Kings 13:1, 3, 7.

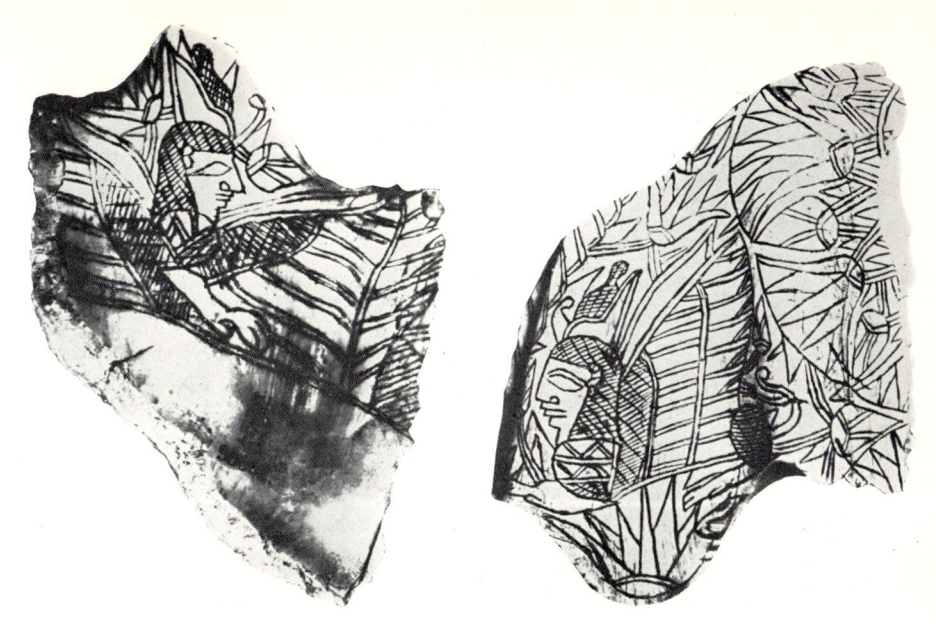

FIG. 158. PHŒNICIAN SHELL ENGRAVING FROM NINEVEH.

FIG. 159. BRONZE VASE FROM PRÆNESTE WITH PHŒNICIAN INSCRIPTION.

quer Philistine Gath and all the plain from the sea to Aphek. Jehoash saved Jerusalem from assault by sending Hazael all the palace and temple objects.[18]

Hazael seemed about to build up a great Syrian kingdom, which extended from Philistia and Judah through Israel and Central Syria clear to Hazrek. Like all similar attempts, it failed. Hazael died and was succeeded by a son, Bar Hadad III, who did not live up to the reputation of the men from whom he was named. Jehoash (800–785) became king of Israel. Hamath saw the rise of another strong king, Zakir of Laash. Worst of all, the Assyrians returned.

Incidents of the wars with Damascus are commemorated in the Elisha stories. We hear of a siege of Samaria by Ben Hadad which caused a great famine; the Aramæans fled when Yahweh made them hear the noise of a mighty army, which they supposed had been hired from the various divided Egyptian states and from the Hittite rulers of North Syria.[19] Every time an ambush was planned by the king of Damascus, Elisha informed his master, so the Aramæans sent an army to Dothan to seize the prophet; blinded at Elisha's prayer, they were led to Samaria, feted, and set free, and thenceforth Aramæan bands no longer infested Israel. By order of the dying Elisha, Jehoash shot through the open window "Yahweh's arrow of victory," which smote Aram in Aphek; three times Jehoash smote the arrows on the ground and stopped, wherefore Aram was defeated but thrice and not utterly consumed.[20]

Ben Hadad sought to retrieve in the north the laurels lost in the south. Meanwhile, Baal-shamain, "Lord of Heaven," who hears and supports him when in distress, had made Zakir to rule in Hazrek; Hazrek is the Biblical Hadrach,[21] the capital of Laash, and the expression implies usurpation. Next Zakir appears as king of Hamath and Laash, which indicates that he had conquered Irhuleni. This deposition of their old ally renewed the anti-Assyrian coalition, directed this time against Zakir; it included now seventeen kings, Hazael's son Bar Ha-

[18]II Kings 12:17 ff.
[20]II Kings 6:8–25; 13:14–21.
[19]II Kings 6:24; 7:3–16.
[21]Zech. 9:1.

dad, as he was called at home, Bar Gush of Agusi, the king of Quweh or Cilicia, the king of Umq or Hattina, the king of Gurgum, the king of Samal, the king of Meliz or Melitene, and the ten kings of the seacoast, the Phœnicians.[22] They fell upon him and laid siege to Hazrek, they raised a wall higher than its wall, and dug a ditch deeper than its moat. But Zakir lifted up his hands to Baal-shamain, who answered by the hand of seers and of men expert in numbers, and said: "Fear not, for I have made you king, and I will stand by you and will save you from all these kings who are besieging you." Then Zakir appointed men of Hazrek for charioteers and for horsemen to guard her king in her midst, he built her up and added a district to her, he made it her possession and his land. All these fortresses he filled with men, and temples he built in all his land, also he built Afish. To commemorate his deliverance, he set up his stele, written in a curious mixture of Phœnician and Aramaic, before his god El Wer; whoever destroys Zakir's name from this stele or destroys it from before El Wer, or removes it from its place, or puts forth his hand against it, Baal-shamain and El Wer and Shamash and Shahar and the gods of heaven and the gods of earth shall destroy him, with a tornado shall they smite him, both foundation and head, and shall tear out his root.[23]

Samal's king was at this time Kilamu, son of that Haya who had fought with Shalmaneser III. Except for the knobbed cap, his dress is Assyrian, a long fringed robe doubly wound about the lower body, brought up over the left shoulder, and bound by a broad girdle, over a short-sleeved vest, rosetted armlets and bracelets and sandals. His shaven upper lip contrasts with the Assyrian ringlets of his beard and hair. A lotus is in his left hand, his right is raised with pointing index finger in adoration of the divine symbols, horned cap, bridle, winged disk, sun, and moon. His servant has replaced the cap with a

[22]This restoration is due to Professor Poebel.
[23]H. Pognon, *Inscriptions sémitiques*, 1907, II, no. 86; C. C. Torrey, *JAOS.*, XXXV, 1917, 353 ff.; R. Dussaud, *Syria*, III, 1922, 176; cf. *History of Assyria*, 162 ff.

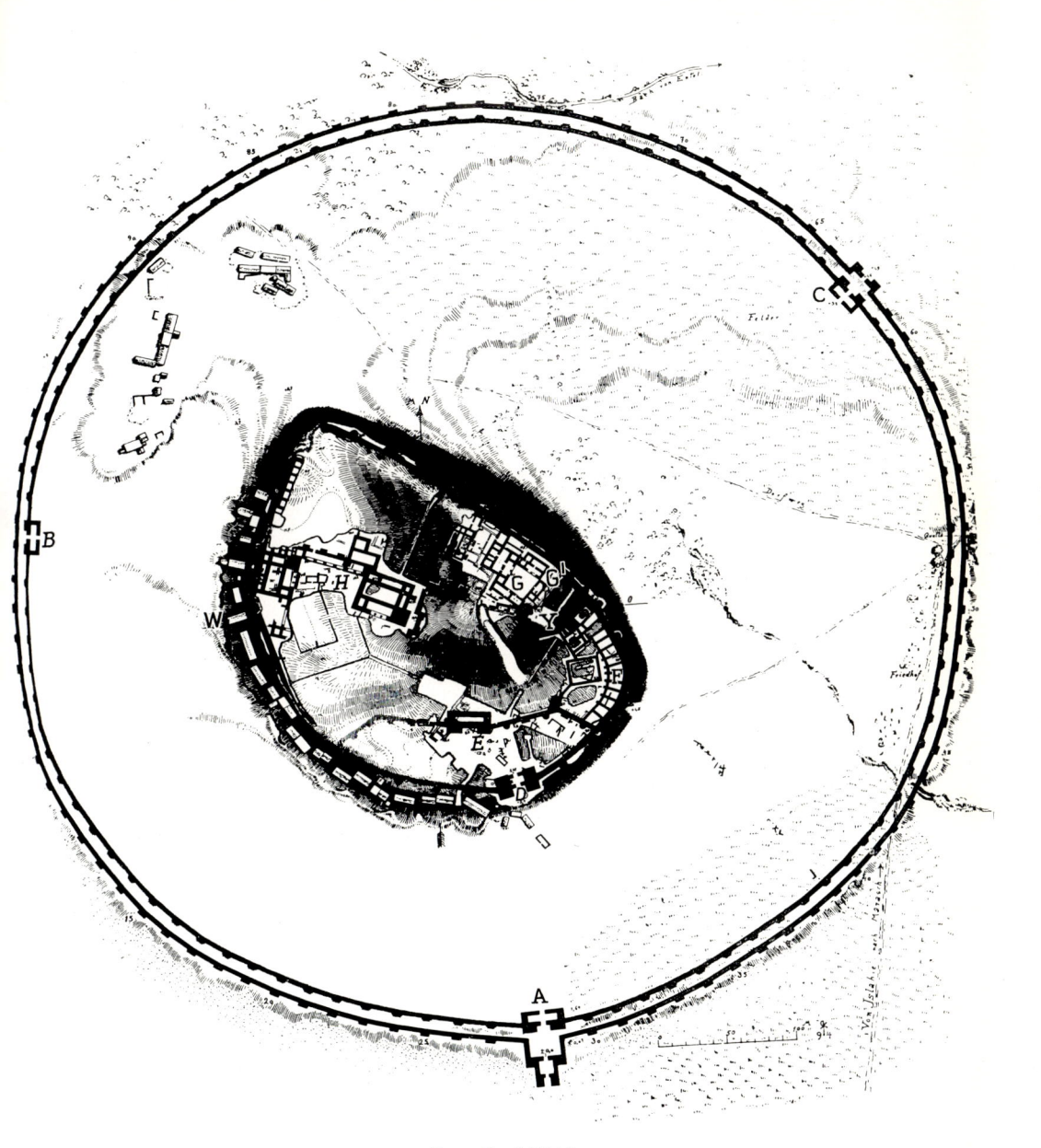

PLAN 16. SAMAL.

A. South Gate.
B. West Gate.
C. Northeast Gate.
D. Citadel Gate.
E. Gate in Cross Wall.
F. Casemates in Wall.
G. Upper Palace.
G1. Old Hilani.
H. Lower Palace.
Y. Inner Wall.

fillet, his right hand holds high a huge lotus, in his left is a small round-bottomed jug.

Kilamu's land is not Samal but Iaudi, a northern Judah; as told by Kilamu, its history is at once unconventional and naïvely humorous. He was preceded by Gabbar and Bamah, who may have represented another dynasty, and then by Father Haya and Brother Sheil or Saul; to each name he adds: "But not a thing did he!" Naturally Kilamu did what no one had done before him. At his accession, his father's house was surrounded by mighty kings, each one of whom stretched forth his hand against Kilamu to destroy him, so that he was in the hands of the kings as if in a fire that was eating his beard or as if in a fire that was eating his hand. Further, the king of the Danunim was mightier than he, yet he hired against Kilamu alone the king of Assyria! So desperate was the situation that one sold a young woman for a sheep and a hero for a garment. Then Kilamu sat on the throne of his father. Before former kings, the courtiers must sleep on their beds like dogs,[24] but he treated them like father, mother, and brother; the man who formerly had not seen a sheep he made master of a flock; he who formerly had not seen an ox, he made master of cattle and silver and gold; he who had not seen a coat from his youth was clad in Kilamu's day in fine linen. Kilamu placed their beds by his own and made them feel for him an affection like the affection of an orphan for his mother. Whoever of his sons shall sit on his throne and shall damage this inscription, may their beds not be fit for their beasts and their beasts not fit for their beds; whoever shall destroy this inscription, may Baal-semed, the god of Gabbar, and Baal-hammon, the god of Bamah, and Rekkab-el, the lord of his own house, destroy his head.[25]

This king was apparently the builder of the second hilani palace. He appears in high round cap, short-sleeved vest,

[24]Cf. II Sam. 11:9.
[25]Plan 16; F. von Luschan, *Ausgrabungen in Sendschirli*, IV, 374 ff.; correct *History of Assyria*, 184 f., by Arno Poebel, *Das appositionell bestimmte Pronomen*, 1931, 30 ff.

short belted skirt, bearded but with shaved upper lip, drawing a bow from his chariot; his driver wears a lower skull cap and wields a long whip. The small chariot with six-spoked wheels bears on the side crossed quivers and in the rear a spear, a tiny lion's head adorns the back board, the pole is high above the horses; plumes deck their heads, a griffin sits on the collar, a tassel hangs from the frontlet; halter, bits, and reins are shown. Beneath their feet is a wounded enemy in skull cap and pointed shoes who attempts to draw from his hip the royal arrow. Kilamu's warriors wear conical caps with knob and upturned brims, short fringed tunic and short-sleeved vest, broad twisted girdle, armlets, anklets, and upturned shoes; unlike their monarch, they keep the mustache, the beard is cut square in curled rows, an elaborate curl descends to the neck. Shields are of the figure eight form, the long spear has a midrib, as does the sword with its crescent hilt, notched on either side the handle, and the sheath ending in a turn.

North Judah's temple was entered through wooden columns on single or double stone bases, bearing in low relief palmettes, rosettes, intertwined rope or leaf patterns. Before the cult statue, now lost, was an altar on a mud brick foundation six feet in diameter and bound by a bronze ring with six inset handles. At the right of the little courtyard gate by the second hilani stood a huge foundation and a base where a kneeling figure in short fringed skirt and pointed shoes, with square cut beard and short sword through belt, grasps by the mane two lions with hanging tongues. On this base stood the god, both lips shaved in ancient fashion, the square beard carved in spirals, the head hair in concentric circles; a long fringed robe descends to the feet, a long tassel hangs from the girdle in which is the sword with crescent handle and ribbed blade.[26] A second base for such a statue has two horses in relief, their heads standing free; the harness is elaborately decorated with cross, rosette, sphinx, and the nude fertility goddess.

At the foot of low hills and overlooking a pleasant plain was the settlement we know only as Sakje Geuzi. Potsherds indi-

[26] Fig. 164.

FIG. 160. LIONS, MALE SPHINX, AND PRINCE.
(Sakje Geuzi.)

FIG. 161. SERVANTS WITH FLY FLAPPER AND FALCON.
(Sakje Geuzi.)

cate a continuous occupation since chalcolithic days, it became a fair-sized town before the middle of the second millennium. Under its northern and eastern walls was a small stream and a spring was approached through a postern, the main gate was to the south. The earliest wall was single, of stone, and its gate flanked by projecting towers; the second wall, contemporary with the eighteenth dynasty, was double, with baked brick superstructure and filling. In form, the town was oval.

Near the gate was a palace of the late ninth or early eighth century. Unlike most North Syrian structures, it followed the Assyrian rectangle, and in their fashion was oriented to the compass points. The walls, about 330 by 430 feet, were laid on a foundation of large rough stones, twelve feet thick, upon which was a ten-foot-thick wall of smaller stones, roughly coursed, and revetted by larger blocks. At irregular intervals, buttresses thirteen feet wide projected three feet and rectangular towers guarded the corners. The entrance gate was at the southwest with shallow flanking towers and the usual stone door socket.

A fine scene in three slabs, bordered at top and bottom by the intertwined rope pattern, decorated the gateway façade. Under the winged disk is the king in his eight-spoked chariot, drawing a bow at a retreating lion; king, driver, and horses are clad in mail. Behind him is the thunder god in a short skirt, in his right hand he brandishes the double-headed battle axe, with his left he drives his spear through the lion's rump, another divine being in Assyrian helmet and coat of mail thrusts with both hands the spear into the lion's brain.[27]

Within the gateway, the path turned slightly to the right; paved first with slabs and then cobbles, it broadened to two steps of large blocks at the entrance. On either side was a lion in high relief with free standing head and forequarters, in the centre was a column base, a row of fingers with nails upward, resting on two female sphinxes with full faces and inset eyes; the head was covered by a wig in plaited rows, hair fell

[27] K. Humann and Otto Puchstein, *Reisen in Kleinasien und Nordsyrien*, 1890, 372 ff.

in ringlets before and behind the ears, down covered the breasts, the wings were closely folded to the sides, the body was a lion which according to Assyrian taste had been presented with a fifth leg.[28]

Facing the right-hand lion was a monster with human body, four wings, eagle head, bare feet, short skirt, and plaited hair; in one hand was a cedar cone, in the other a basket. Then came the tree of life, quite changed from its Assyrian original, with a palm base, three pairs of curving branches like Ionic volutes, and a palmette at the top. The divine figures either side the tree were also much changed from their Assyrian ancestors. In facial features, square-cut curled beard and hair, short skirt under fringed garment, high in front but almost touching the ground behind, they were quite Assyrian, but they were not winged, they wore the flat-knobbed hat and pointed shoes, in one hand was the curved knife, the other extended the seed to the winged disk above; from a twelve petalled rosette representing the sun over the crescent hung, not the older bird's legs, but other volutes dropping in slender filaments to the seeds.[29]

Behind each lion was a long-bodied male sphinx, with round-knobbed hat and bird's heads at the tip of the tail. Behind the sphinx again marched the prince, whose small nose contrasted with his thick lips, clad in vest and loose robe passed over the shoulder and held tight in the left hand, Assyrian sandals and bracelets; his hair, bound with a fillet ornamented with concentric circles, is curled in rows and heavily bunched at the neck, in his right hand he carries the long-stemmed cup. His servants also wear the long robe, fringed some distance above the hem, the fillet dropping in a fringed bow, and slightly pointed sandals; one raises the fly-flapper and bears the fringed towel over his shoulder, the other has a falcon on his right wrist and in his left hand the lure to recall him.[30]

The palace proper was some seventy-five feet square, with outer stone walls five feet thick, above which the building was of burnt brick. From the long shallow entrance hall, a flight of

[28] Fig. 163.   [29] Fig. 162.   [30] Fig. 160.

FIG. 162. LION, WINGED DEMON, AND GOOD GENII.
(Sakje Geuzi.)

FIG. 163. PILLAR BASE SUPPORTED BY FEMALE SPHINXES.
(Sakje Geuzi.)

slabs decorated with rosettes descended to the guard room. Beyond the entrance was the great hall with other rooms

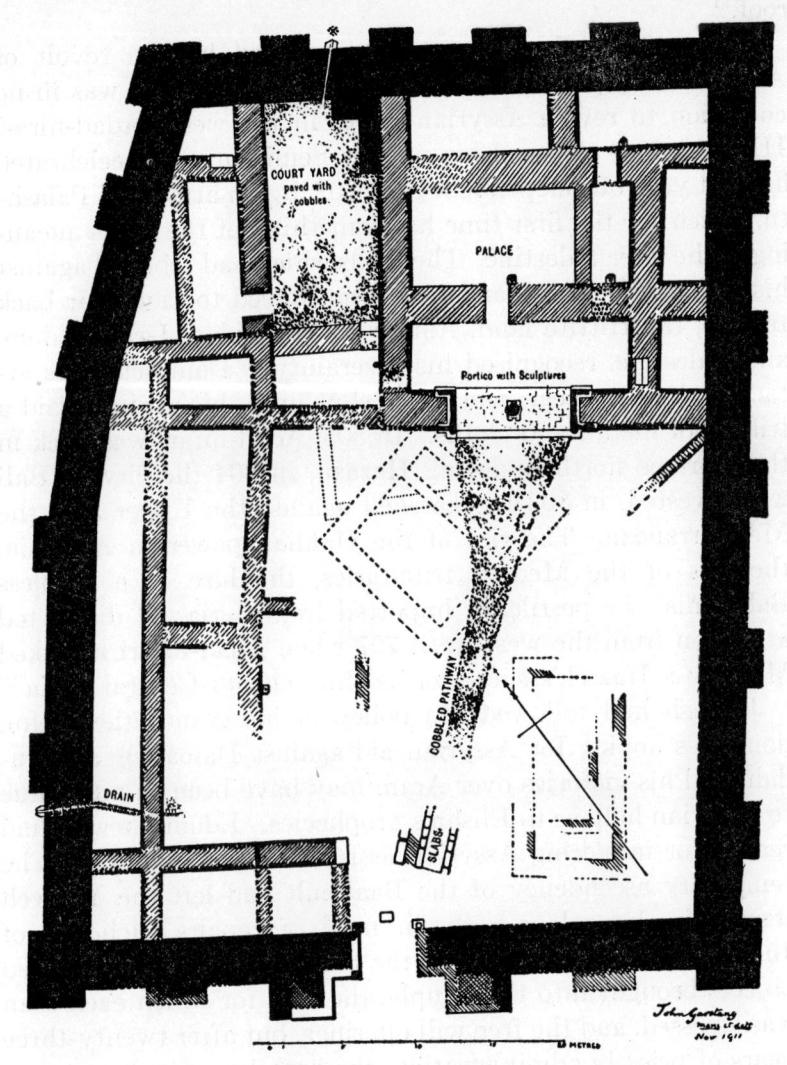

PLAN 17. PALACE ENCLOSURE AT SAKJE GEUZI.

along the outside wall, to its left was a cobble-paved courtyard from which steps ran up to the enclosure wall, other rows of rooms were right and left of the main court. Differing levels led the rainfall to regular stone drains whose outlets projected from the enclosure wall, stone gutters served the roof.[31]

Shalmaneser's last days were darkened by the revolt of Ashur-danin-apal, and Shamshi Adad V (825–812) was in no condition to revive Assyrian hopes in the west. Adad-nirari III (812–782) deposed his mother Semiramis and celebrated his first year of independent rule, 807, by an attack on Palashtu, which for the first time has something of the wider meaning of the later Palestine. The lands which had rebelled against his father, Arpad in particular, were forced to pay their back tribute, the Hittite land, Amurru, Tyre, Sidon, Israel, Edom, and Palestine, recognised his suzerainty. Damascus was attacked the next year, and Mari, shut up in his capital, paid a tribute of metals and cloths. In 805, Adad-nirari was back in the extreme north besieging Hazazu, in 804 the city of Bali was invested, in 803 he marched against the Upper Sea, the Mediterranean. The rise of the Haldian power in Armenia, the loss of the Median tributaries, the lure of a helpless Babylonia, the pestilence imported from Syria, all distracted attention from the west until 797 when Adad-nirari attacked Mansuate, Hazrek's successor as chief city of Central Syria.[32]

Jehoash had followed the policy of his grandfather Jehu, doubtless hoping for Assyrian aid against Damascus and Judah, and his victories over Aram may have been as much due to Assyrian help as to Elisha's prophecies. Edom likewise had reason for imploring Assyrian assistance against Judah. The temporary ascendency of the Baal cult had left the Yahweh temple in Jerusalem sadly in need of repairs. Jehoash of Judah therefore appropriated the money from the consecrated objects brought into the temple, the sum for which each man was assessed, and the free will offerings, but after twenty-three years of priestly administration, the breaches were as open as before. Jehoash then forced the priests to hand over the fu-

[31] Plan 17; J. Garstang, *Liverpool Annals*, I, 1908, 97 ff.; V, 1912, 63 ff.; *Hittite Empire*, 1930, 262 ff.; cf. E. Pottier, *Syria*, V, 1924, 1 ff.
[32] *History of Assyria*, 159 ff.

ture income from these sources to the more honest secular authorities; all the money brought to the shrine was placed in a chest with hole in the lid, set at the pillar by the entrance, the king's scribe took the money and sealed it, and from this the carpenters, builders, masons, and stone cutters were paid. Jehoiada died, and Jehoash, disgusted by the priestly dishonesty, went over to the opposition represented by the princes; despite the solemn covenant, Judah once more served the asheras and the idols. Jehoiada's son Zechariah reproached the king for his apostasy: "Because you have forsaken Yahweh, he has forsaken you," and fulfilment of this prophecy was found in the invasion of Judah by the Aramæan Hazael. Zechariah was stoned by the king's commandment in the temple court, but this outrage roused the priests; they had made Jehoash king, they could unmake him, and Jehoash was murdered by two of his servants.[33]

Amaziah (799–782) found difficulty in securing his father's throne, but finally the "kingdom was established in his hand," and the assassins were slain; it is noted that he exempted their children from punishment, an unusual mercy in those hard days. A great success further stabilized his throne. Taking advantage of Judah's troubles, an Edomite army made a raid, but was caught in the Valley of Salt, south of the Dead Sea, and pursued back up into the hills; their rock-girt metropolis Sela was taken and the prisoners hurled to their death from the top of the cliffs.

An Israelite writer tells how the youthful Amaziah, he was only twenty-five, sent a message to the equally youthful Jehoash: "Come, let us look one another in the face." Jehoash replied: "The thistle in Lebanon sent to the Lebanon cedar, saying: 'Give me your daughter to my son as wife.' But a Lebanon wild beast passed by and trod down the thistle. You have, to be sure, smitten Edom, and your heart is uplifted; glory in it but stay at home, for why should you provoke calamity and fall and Judah with you?" Another story speaks obscurely of a body of Ephraimite mercenaries, hired by Ama-

[33] II Kings 12:4–12, 17 f., 20–21; II Chron. 24:15–18, 20 ff.

ziah but later dismissed, who in retaliation plundered the cities of Judah as far as Beth Horon. Whatever the cause, the two kings did look one another in the face at the unwalled Beth Shemesh commanding the direct route to the capital, Amaziah was captured and carried to Jerusalem; the city was plundered, the wall broken down for two hundred yards from the Gate of Ephraim at the present Damascus Gate to the gate at the northwest corner, and the covering fort at Gibeah was also destroyed. Amaziah remained on his throne, but as a vassal prince, and hostages were taken to ensure his fidelity.[34]

Amaziah's rule had not been pleasing to the conservatives, who raised a conspiracy against him in Jerusalem. He fled to Lachish, on his way to refuge in Egypt, but the rebels sent after him and he was slain. His corpse was brought on horseback to the capital, the lack of chariot roads is to be noted, and was buried with his fathers in the City of David. Azariah, his sixteen-year-old son, was then enthroned by the conspirators.

Towards the end of his reign, Adad-nirari saw his revenge on Damascus. Seated in the palace of the Ben Hadads, he received Mari's tribute, twenty talents of gold, three hundred of silver, three thousand of copper, five thousand of iron, with linen, an ivory bed, and a litter inlaid with ivory. With the rich booty went an unrecognised curse, the pestilence, which, as Amos puts it,[35] Yahweh had sent among the Hebrews from the road of Egypt. Assyria was now in rapid decline. The bubonic plague was prevalent in the Assyrian homeland, Haldians penetrated within twenty-five miles of Nineveh, the conquests in the mountains were lost, Babylonia slipped away into anarchy, yet the Syrian expeditions were continued by Shalmaneser IV (782–772), who reached the cedar lands in 775 and in 773 marched against Damascus. Even as late as Ashur-dan (772–755), Hazrek was attacked in 772 and 765, but the bubonic plague was again virulent and the Syrian adventure was definitely abandoned.[36]

[34]II Kings 14:1–14; II Chron. 25:6–13; W. F. Albright, *Ann.*, IV, 53.
[35]Amos 4:10. [36]*History of Assyria*, 169.

CHAPTER XXVII

HIGH LIGHTS AND SHADOWS

ASSYRIA's breakdown gave new opportunity to the second-rate states and they were not slow to profit by it. The long reign of Azariah, more commonly called Uzziah (782–751), marks an upward trend in Judah's fortunes. Tribute was paid by the Ammonites, attacks of the Arabs in Gur-baal and of the Meunim near Sela were repulsed, Edom was invaded and Elath with its Red Sea trade facilities won back. Philistine Gath had threatened too long Judah and was destroyed, the walls of Jabneh and Ashdod were torn down, only a remnant of the Philistines was left. Gibeah was again fortified against Israelite invasion.[1]

Uzziah could count two thousand six hundred heads of families, men of wealth, among his subjects. He hewed out many cisterns, for he had much cattle in the Shephelah and the table land, he loved husbandry and possessed husbandmen and vine dressers in the mountains and in the fertile fields. To protect his flocks in the wilderness, he built towers, which exist to this day, securely dated by their potsherds.

In the "Gorge of the Fountain," a little distance down from the spring associated with Moses, is a ruined mound, the only one of its sort in the Negeb proper.[2] Excavation has shown it a fort, nearly two hundred feet long by over a hundred and thirty wide, with skewed towers at the corners and in the centre of each side. Up to ten feet, the walls were built solid, of small stones and mud, and faced with carefully selected, more or less regular rocks; above this height, there were small rooms

[1] II Kings 14:22; II Chron. 26:6–8; Amos 6:2; 1:8; Albright, *Ann.*, IV, 53.
[2] Fig. 106; discovered by our party May 28, 1905; first mentioned, *Western Asia in the Reign of Sargon*, 1908, 61; first published, N. Schmidt, *JBL.*, XXIX, 1910, fig. 11; correct accordingly statement of priority, C. L. Woolley and T. E. Lawrence, *Wilderness of Zin*, 1914, 64 n. 2.

418   PALESTINE AND SYRIA

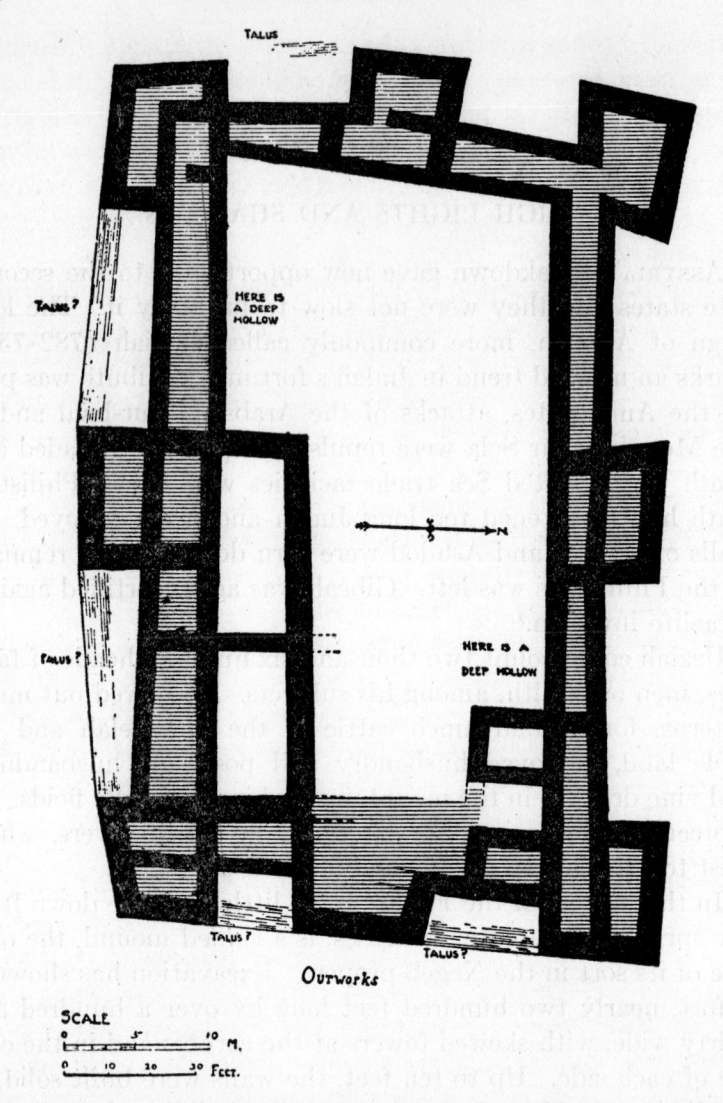

PLAN 18. FORT OF AZARIAH IN THE NEGEB.

in the wall and the interior. Two lesser forts commanded the little plains to the north on the "Road to Shur."

Under the protection of these forts lived the herdsmen in circular or quadrangular stone shelters, roofed by bush or a bit of goat's hair cloth. Even thus late, implements were all of flint, and bronze appears only as a rare ornament. Much of the pottery, especially the burnished hæmatite ware, was hand made, though the wheel was used for the large greyish green jars; the most characteristic ware was hand made from very gritty clay, baked in an open hearth so that the jars were red on the outer surface and black or grey within, but surprisingly thin and hard.

Their dead were buried within circles near each of the three springs. The corpse was laid flat on the back, the hands at the side, the head turned to the west; sometimes a shaft was dug, sometimes a larger stone in the circle marked the position of the head and feet. A bit of bronze, a few sherds completed the funerary equipment.[3] Not so many years ago, many scholars believed that in this region and at this very time there existed a kingdom of Musri so powerful that it contested the rule of the Near East with Assyria and was later confused with the similarly named Misraim or Egypt![4]

The disruption of Solomon's kingdom had put an almost complete end to building, but the weakening of the north permitted Judah's growth and this was soon reflected in an architectural revival. Fortified towers were constructed at the Corner Gate, the Valley Gate, and the Angle. We possess the seals of two high officials of Uzziah, "Abiyo, servant of Uzziyo," and "Shebaniyo, servant of Uzziyo." Although both officials like their master reverence in their names Yahweh in the older form Yo, they do not hesitate to employ foreign religious motifs to ornament their seals; Abijah, as he would have been called later, chose the child Horus, crowned with the sun disk between horns and kneeling on the lotus, Shebaniah has adopted Assyrian garb, raises his right hand in adoration and rests on a flower-tipped staff, while his name and office are protected by an Egyptian sun disk above and an Assyrian sun disk below.[5] Towards the end of his life, Yahweh

[3] Plan 18; Woolley-Lawrence, *op. cit.*, 41 f.; 64 ff.; for date, Albright, *Ann.*, IV, 18.
[4] Refutation, *Western Asia in the Reign of Sargon*, 56 ff.
[5] H. Blau, *Zeitschrift der deutsch. Morgenland. Gesell.*, XIX, 1865, 535; L. Delaporte, *Catalogue des Cylindres Orientaux*, 1923, II, pl. CIV, 37.

smote Uzziah and he became a leper, dwelling at liberty in his own house, but the affairs of the kingdom were administered by his son Jotham as regent.[6]

In the few lines grudgingly vouchsafed by the editor of Kings to Jeroboam II (785–745), we glimpse one of the mightiest rulers of Israel. Fortunately, we have other sources to prove the extraordinary prosperity of his long reign. At Samaria, he extended his palace to the west of that built by Omri and Ahab and with the same fine construction; at the southwest corner rose a mighty tower, round, and no less than eighty-one feet in diameter.[7] To what heights art had advanced is shown by the magnificent lion with gaping jaws and upraised tail which appears on the jasper seal of "Shema, servant of Jeroboam," in Megiddo, while the lapis lazuli seal of Asaph from the same city betrays Egyptian influence in the winged griffin with the crowns of Upper and Lower Egypt and the hieroglyphic signs for "life" and "beloved" within a cartouche in addition to the Hebrew inscription.[8]

The changed situation of the tribes is pictured in a series of "blessings" imitated from the "Blessing of Jacob" and assigned to Moses. Reuben still holds first place but is about to perish. Simeon has disappeared without trace, but there is hope that Judah will again unite with Israel:

> Hear, Yahweh, the voice of Judah,
> And bring him to his people;
> With thy hands contend for him,
> Be thou a help against his foes.

Levi has ceased to be a local tribe and has become the sacred priestly order which traces its descent from the Levite lawgiver Moses:

> Give to Levi thy Thummim,
> And thy Urim to thy beloved,
> Whom thou didst prove at Massah,
> And strove with at Meribah's waters.

[6] II Kings 14:19–22; 15:5, 7; II Chron. 26:6–12.
[7] Reisner-Fisher-Lyon, *Harvard Excavations at Samaria*, 117 ff.
[8] Figs. 174 f.; C. Watzinger, *Tell el-Mutesellim*, II, 64 ff.

It is now an association chosen from all classes:

>Who of his father says:
>I have not seen him;
>His brethren he does not acknowledge,
>Nor doth he know his children.

Levi has usurped the power of the elders to give toroth or oracles:

>For they guard thy word
>   And thy covenant keep,
>They show thy judgments to Jacob,
>   Thy oracles also to Israel;
>Incense they place in thy nostril,
>   Whole offerings on thy altar.

But the power of the new priestly class is not yet secure, and they have opponents:

>Bless, O Yahweh, his means,
>   And the work of his hands accept;
>Smite his foes through the loins,
>   His haters so they ne'er rise.

Benjamin is now famous only for his shrine at Bethel:

>Yahweh's beloved
>   Dwelleth securely,
>He covereth him all day,
>   And between his shoulders he dwelleth.

For Joseph, our author can only repeat the ancient blessing,

>The shoot of a vine stock is Joseph,
>   Blessed of Yahweh his land,
>With the choice things of heaven above,
>   From the deep that croucheth below,
>With the choice things of the sun's crops,
>   With the choice things of the moon's yield,
>With the choice things of ancient mounts,
>   With the choice things of eternal hills,
>With the choice things of earth to its full,

And the favour of the Dweller in the Bush,
Let them fall on the head of Joseph,
On the crown of the prince mid his brethren.

Ephraim is now the glorious brother, Manasseh has somewhat declined:

First born, a bull majestic,
His horns are the wild bull's horns,
With them the peoples he pushes,
And drives to the ends of the earth;[9]
These are Ephraim's ten thousands,
And these Manasseh's thousands.

Zebulon had virtually absorbed Issachar:

Rejoice, Zebulon, in thy outlets,
And Issachar in thy tents;
The peoples they call to the mountain,
Right sacrifice offer there;
For they suck the sea's abundance,
And the treasure hid in the sand.

Gad has much improved his position, thanks to the wars with Damascus. Dan is well established in the north:

Dan is the whelp of a lion,
He leaps out from Bashan.

Naphtali has at last won down to the Sea of Galilee and the Great Plain. Asher is as fortunate as his name, but this fortune has brought dangers:

Blessed above sons be Asher,
Let him be the favoured of his brethren,
Let him dip his foot in oil.
Iron and bronze be thy bolts,
And as thy days thy strength.[10]

Taking advantage of the prostration of the Central Syrian states through the Assyrian inroads and of the subsequent de-

[9]Cf. I Kings 22:11. [10]Deut. 33:6–25.

cline of the Assyrians themselves, Jeroboam drove back Damascus, took the east Jordan Lodebar and Karnaim, and made a census of the recovered east Jordan tribes,[11] and extended the borders of Israel from Libo of Hamath to the Sea of the Arabah. In this he was encouraged by a prophet, Jonah, son of Amittai, whose native home was the Galilean Gath Hepher, a bare three miles from that Nazareth which was to produce a yet greater prophet. "Thus," says a writer from the northern kingdom, "he turned away the wrath of Yahweh from Israel. For Yahweh saw the bitter affliction of Israel, for there was none shut up or left at large, nor was there any helper for Israel. Nevertheless, Yahweh had not declared that he would blot out the name of Israel from under the heavens, but he saved them by the hand of Jeroboam, son of Jehoash."[12]

There was another prophet, not from protected Galilee but from hostile Judah, who thought quite differently. He gives us our best picture of the prosperity of Jeroboam's reign, but he also draws the shadows, and they are deep.

Six miles south of Bethlehem lay the little village of Tekoa. To the northwest was a fertile plain, an unusual feature in this barren land, twenty-seven hundred feet above the Mediterranean, on other sides there were swift descents with views over the sterile desert of Judah, the Dead Sea, and Moab. Rehoboam had made it one of his line of fortified cities, its "wise woman" had tricked David.

In Tekoa lived a certain Amos, a shepherd of flocks such as might find a living on this high wind-swept plateau. By his seminomad life, he was largely cut off from human associations and from the joys of family life, and there was little opportunity to develop his emotions. Nor was there anything in the stern scenes constantly before his eyes to soften his character.. Protecting his flocks from savage wild beasts or from men scarcely less savage, he grew an extreme individualist, bold and hardy in spirit, with little patriotism and no realisation of the complexities inherent in a fuller material

[11] Amos 6:13; I Chron. 5:17.
[12] II Kings 14: 23–28.

civilisation. As he felt himself at the mercy of the elemental forces, the fatalism latent in all orientals became extreme.

Now and then he descended to the lower slopes and added to his scanty wages by tending the sycamores, whose spreading shade was more appreciated than their stunted woody fig-like fruit. Back in his desert solitude, he meditated on the evils he had witnessed in the populous cities to the north. Though not a professional prophet, he was deeply in sympathy with their programme and with the nomad religion for which they fought. He had listened to their outpourings until he had absorbed their spirit as well as their poetic mode of expression, from them he had learned stories of the older time, the far views from his native country and his journeys had given a wider knowledge of what was going on in the great outside world.

Israel was now enjoying unparalleled prosperity and wealth was pouring in from Jeroboam's successful wars. As the general wealth increased, it was natural that the increase should be divided very unevenly, and there grew up that feeling, so familiar to the historian of every period of success, that the rich were growing richer and the poor growing poorer, at least by comparison. As always, there was much hardship and injustice in the process of economic readjustment.

It was inevitable that the shepherd should be shocked, and in truth there were shadows enough on the picture of material prosperity. The old desert customs were no longer observed, the desert morals were no longer binding. Amos had learned of a great far-away power, which had once sent its armies to Israel, and was threatening to come again. Once Israel had submitted to the Assyrian king, and in consequence the antique nomad religion preached by Jehonadab the Rechabite had driven out the intruding Baal. Assyria had come no more and the nomad simplicity which heralded the dynasty of Jehu had given way to a cult which took its whole colouring from the worship of the old Canaanite deities. Strange to relate, the Israelites were satisfied. Did they only bring Yahweh enough offerings, were the services elaborate and costly, Yahweh must meet his part of the contract and grant them a continuance of the prosperity they now enjoy. As to the old desert morality, what did that have to do with religion?

His mind full of such matters, Amos began to see visions:

Thus the lord Yahweh showed me:
  For behold, he was forming locusts
    At the first of the aftergrowth's shooting;
  But when they were making an ending
    Of eating the grass of the country
  Then said I: Forgive Yahweh, I pray thee!
    How can Jacob stand, for he's tiny?
  Of this thing Yahweh repented,
    It shall not come to pass, said Yahweh.

Then the lord Yahweh showed me:
  For behold, he was calling to judgment
    By fire—it was the Lord Yahweh—
  And the great abyss it was eating
    And would the plowed land have eaten.
  Then said I: Cease, Yahweh, I pray thee!
    How can Jacob stand, for he's tiny?
  Of this thing Yahweh repented,
    This too shall not be, said Yahweh.

Thus the Lord Yahweh showed me:
  For behold, Lord Yahweh was stationed
    On a wall, in his hand a plumb line,
  And he said: See, I'm setting a plumb line
    In the midst of Israel, my people,
  And will not again grant him pardon.
    For Isaac's high places lie wasted,
  And destroyed Israel's holy places,
    'Gainst the house of Jeroboam will I rise up with the sword.

Thus the Lord Yahweh showed me:
  For behold, summer fruits in a basket!
    And he said: What seest thou, Amos?
  I replied: Summer fruit in a basket.
    Then unto me spake Yahweh:
  The end has come to my people,
    Ne'er again shall I pass by them!

Spurred on by these visions of doom, Amos hastened to Bethel, now the religious capital of the northern kingdom. At first, his hearers received his prophecies with complacence, for they condemned the foreign nations for their sins:

> Thus hath Yahweh said:
>   For three revolts of Damascus,
>   And for four I will not avert it,
>   Since they threshed Gilead with iron sledges.
>
>   So fire I send in Hazael's house,
>   And it eats the palaces of Ben Hadad,
>   And I shall break the bars of Damascus.
>
>   And I cut off the dwellers from Aven's valley,
>   And holder of scepter from Beth Eden,
>   And Aram's folk to Kir shall be deported.
>
> Thus hath Yahweh said:
>   For three revolts of Gaza,
>   And for four I will not avert it,
>   Since they deported them to deliver to Edom.
>
>   So fire I send in Gaza's wall,
>   And it shall her palaces eat up,
>   And my hand I will turn against Ekron.
>
>   And I cut off the dweller from Ashdod,
>   And the scepter holder from Ashkelon,
>   And the Philistine remnant shall perish.
>
> Thus hath Yahweh said:
>   For three revolts of Tyre,
>   And for four I will not avert it,
>   Since they delivered them captive to Edom.
>
>   And forgot the covenant of brothers,
>   So fire I send 'gainst Tyre's ramparts,
>   And it shall eat up her palaces.
>
> Thus hath Yahweh said:
>   For three revolts of Edom,

And for four I will not avert it,
Since he pursued with the sword his brother,

And kept his anger forever.
So fire I send in Teman,
And it eats the palaces of Bozrah.

Thus hath Yahweh said:
For three revolts of Ammon,
And for four I will not avert it,
Since they ripped pregnant women in Gilead.

So fire in Rabbah's wall I kindle,
And it shall consume her palaces,
With a shout in the day of battle,

With a storm in the day of tempest.
So their king shall go into exile,
He and his princes together.

Thus hath Yahweh said:
For three revolts of Moab,
And for four I will not avert it,
Since they burned the bones of the king of Edom.

So fire I send in Moab,
And it eats the palaces of Kerioth,
With a shout, with the sound of the trumpet.

And Moab shall die in a tumult,
For her judge in her midst I cut off,
And I slay with him all her princes.

Thus hath Yahweh said:
For three revolts of Judah,
And for four I will not avert it,
Since Yahweh's law they have rejected.

So fire I send in Judah,
And it eats Jerusalem's palaces,

. . . .

By this time, his hearers were becoming suspicious; Judah like Israel was Hebrew, it worshipped the same God whose laws Judah was said to have rejected. So they were prepared for the climax:

> Thus hath Yahweh said:
> For three revolts of Israel,
> And for four I will not avert it,
> Since they sell for silver the righteous,
> And the poor for a pair of sandals.
>
> They tramp on the head of the needy,
> Push aside from the path the humble,
> Yea, a man and his sire go to harlots,
> Thus to profane my name holy.
>
> On pledged clothes they recline by each altar,
> Drink wine from those fined in God's temple,
> Yet 'twas I brought you up out of Egypt,
> To possess the Amorite's country.
>
> Yet 'twas I smote the Amorites before you,
> Whose height was the height of the cedars,
> And strong was he like the oak trees,
> But his fruits I smote down from above,
> And his roots from beneath.

Israel alone has Yahweh known of all earth's peoples, therefore shall be visited upon them all their transgressions. He chose some of their sons to be prophets, their youths to be Nazirites, but the Nazirites they made drink wine and bade the prophets be quiet. Israel was proud of its elaborate ceremonies and was sure that Yahweh would reward them for their zeal; Amos cites early history to prove that Yahweh was not always worshipped in this vain fashion:

> Brought you offerings to me in the desert,
> Forty years, O house of Israel?
> Yet you lift up the shrine of your King
> And the image you made of your God.

It is not Yahweh who is worshipped at the various shrines; Amos anticipates the modern historian who has learned that these gods were honoured long before Yahweh was introduced to Canaan:

> Who swear by the Sin of Samaria,
> And say: As thy god, Dan, liveth,
> And: As liveth thy way, Beersheba.

There is nothing ethical in such service:

> Come to Bethel—and sin,
>   To Gilgal—and sin the more;
> Your offering bring each morn,
>   Each third day your tithes;
> Burn thank offerings from leavened bread,
>   Proclaim freewill offerings, make them known.

but this is only doing what they really love. Amos will show them a better way:

> Seek me and live,
> But to Bethel seek not,
> And to Gilgal enter not,
> And to Beersheba cross not.
> For Gilgal goes captive,
> And Bethel becomes nothing.

> I hate, I despise your feasts,
>   And will not in your festivals smell,
> Though you offer burnt offerings to me,
>   Meal offerings too I will not accept.
> Take from me the noise of your songs,
>   Your harp's music I will not hear,
> But let justice roll as the waters,
>   And right as a running river.

All the coming woe is due to the outrageous conduct of the wealthy:

> Woe to those who are careless in Zion,
>   And secure in Samaria's mount,
> Who make themselves chiefs of the nations,
>   Spoil Israel's house for themselves,

> Who recline on ivory couches,
>   And stretch themselves on their divans,
> Who eat of the flocks the lamblings,
>   And calves from the midst of the stall,
> Who sing to the sound of the harping,
>   Like David make instruments for song,
> Who drink down wine in caldrons,
>   With the best of oils them anoint.

The women, "cows of Bashan" Amos contemptuously calls them, are as bad as their husbands; they oppress the poor and crush the needy, and bid their lords: "Bring, let us drink." A day is coming when a hook shall lift them by the nostrils, a harpoon by the back; dragged shall they be through the breaches in the wall and cast on the dung heap.

The rich turn justice to wormwood, they trample the weak and take from him levies of grain, they accept bribes and turn aside the poor in the gate. They tread on the needy and destroy the poor peasants; impatiently they ask: "When will the new moon be over that we may sell grain, and the sabbath, that we may open the grain sacks?" They make small the ephah and great the shekel, with false balances they deal deceitfully. Justice is turned into poison and the fruit of righteousness into wormwood. Let them seek good and not evil; then "Yahweh will be with you," as you say.[13]

Jonah of Gath Hepher had prophesied that Jeroboam would restore the border of Israel from Libo of Hamath to the Sea of the Arabah; Amos scornfully reverses the prediction:

> Behold, I am raising against you,
>   O House of Israel, a nation
> Which shall crush you from Libo of Hamath
>   To the gorge of the Arabah.

Men vividly remembered the great solar eclipse of June 15, 763,[14] when Yahweh made the sun set at noonday and brought darkness on earth in clear daylight, and about the same time there had been a great earthquake when all the earth trem-

---

[13] Cf. Song of Balaam, Num. 23:21.   [14] *History of Assyria*, 172.

bled. There was lack of bread and clean teeth in all Israel's cities. Yahweh withheld rain and two cities staggered to one to drink water and had not enough. They were smitten with blasting and mildew, their gardens and vineyards were wasted, locusts ate up their figs and olives. Plague by the road from Egypt[15] was sent by Yahweh, the sword slew their young warriors, the camp stench ascended to their nostrils. Cities were cast down as Yahweh cast down Sodom and Gomorrah, but always there is the refrain: "Yet ye turned not to me, saith Yahweh."

Israel had found courage in his misfortunes through a belief in the "Day of Yahweh," when the national God would descend to wreak his vengeance on his people's foes; now that Jeroboam was all victorious, many were convinced that the "Day" had arrived. To Amos, the "Day" had quite another meaning:

> Woe to you who desire the Day of Yahweh!
> What have you to do with the Day of Yahweh?
> As if a man fled from a lion,
> And a bear tore him,
> Or entered a house and leaned hand on wall,
> And a serpent bit him!
> Is not Yahweh's Day darkness, not light,
> Deep darkness with no light in it?

Israel is no better than the Ethiopians, Yahweh brought the Philistines from Caphtor and the Aramæans from Kir as he did Israel from Egypt. Not a fugitive shall escape, though they descend to Sheol or ascend to heaven, though they hide on Carmel's summit or in the depths of the sea. Proclaim in the palaces of Ashur and Egypt to collect on Samaria's mount and behold the great tumults within. The winter house shall fall on the summer, the ivory and ebony palaces be destroyed. Bethel's altar horns shall be broken, Yahweh himself has commanded to smite the capitals that the sills be shaken.

Amaziah, chief priest of Bethel, remembered how under the preceding dynasty the prophets had opposed the constituted

[15] *History of Assyria*, 164, 169.

authorities; he therefore informed Jeroboam: "Amos has plotted against you in the midst of Israel; the land is not able to bear all his words, for he has said: 'By the sword shall Jeroboam die and Israel shall go into exile out of his land.'" Amos was bidden: "O seer, go flee to the land of Judah, for there you may secure bread by your prophecies, but prophesy no longer at Bethel, for it is the king's holy place and the House of the Kingdom." The answer of Amos contains the essence of the new prophecy: "No prophet was I nor a prophet's son, but a shepherd and a sycamore tender, yet Yahweh took me from following the flock and said: Go, prophesy against my people Israel." Amaziah had ordered him to cease preaching against the house of Isaac, this was the word of Yahweh: "Your wife shall be dishonoured in the town, your sons and daughters fall by the sword, your land shall be divided by the rope, you yourself shall die in an unclean country, for Israel shall go into exile out of his land."[16]

[16]Cf. W. R. Harper, *Amos and Hosea*, 1905; *The Structure of the Text of Amos*, 1904; K. Marti, *Das Dodekapropheton*, 1904, 144 ff.; W. Nowack, *Die Kleinen Propheten*, 3 ed., 1922, 110 ff.; E. Sellin, *Das Zwölfprophetenbuch*, 2 ed., 1930, 179 ff.; R. S. Cripps, *The Book of Amos*, 1929.

CHAPTER XXVIII

ASSYRIA'S RETURN

Assyria's return was delayed beyond the expectation of Amos. The solar eclipse of 763, to Amos the sign of Yahweh's wrath, had been interpreted by the Assyrians in like manner, and a revolt had placed on the throne a stronger monarch, Ashur-nirari V (755–746). His very first year, Ashur-nirari attempted to win back Hazrek, and in his second he forced Mati-ilu of Arpad to swear to a treaty of vassalage.[1] The Haldians were now more powerful than the Assyrians and it was not difficult for their king Sardurish II to persuade Mati-ilu to forget his oath. Sardurish then assumed the title "King of Syria."

Another revolt brought to the throne one of the greatest Assyrian kings, Tiglath Pileser III (746–728). In 744, he fell upon Sardurish and his vassals Mati-ilu of Arpad, Sulumal of Melidia, Tarhulara of Gurgum, and Kushtashpi of Qummuh. In Aleppo an Aramaic inscription was prepared on which Mati-ilu and his companions were cursed by the Assyrian gods. Mati-ilu as one forsworn realised that he could expect no mercy and held out for three years; his terrible punishment was long remembered by the Hebrews.[2]

Tiglath Pileser's reorganisation of the provinces was applied to the recently conquered Syrian states. A small corner of North Syria, just across the Euphrates, had belonged to Bit Adini and had been made a part of the province of Kar Shulmanasharidu when Shalmaneser had destroyed Bit Adini in 856, but had been lost in the period of decline. Tiglath Pileser in 740 formed the eastern half of North Syria into the province of Arpaddu or Arpad. Tutamu of Hattina, or rather Unqi

---

[1]*History of Assyria*, 172 ff.; Luckenbill, *Records*, I, 265 ff.
[2]II Kings 18:34; 19:13; Isaiah 36:19; 37:13; R. Dussaud, Comptes Rendus Acad. Ins., 1930, 155 f.

as it was now called, hid in his swamps, but Tiglath Pileser set up his throne in the capital Kunulua or Calneh.

While in Arpad, Tiglath Pileser received homage from Kushtashpi and Tarhulara, as well as from Pisiris of Carchemish, Rezon of Damascus, and Hiram II of Tyre. After Pum-yaton's death in 785, the Tyrian king list is lost but a new series begins with Hiram II, whose rule as "King of the Sidonians" over the Cypriote Carthage through his sakan or governor is proved by certain bowls, dedicated as the first fruits of the bronze to the Baal of Lebanon.[3]

After Kilamu, Quril or Cyril ruled Samal about 800 and was followed by his son Panammu I, who set up for Hadad a statue nine and a half feet high; the god was represented with double-horned cap, curled and rounded beard, inset eyes, arms outstretched in blessing, body in columnar form, and below the girdle an inscription. Already in his youth, the gods Hadad, El, Rekkab-el, Shemesh, and Reshuph had favoured him and had placed in his hand the sceptre of rule. When Quirl had asked anything of the gods, Hadad had not granted him permission, but when Panammu desired to build he was always granted permission, and he built all his days; we think at once of Nathan's refusal to permit David to build the temple and its erection by David's son Solomon.[4] His land is a land of barley, wheat, and garlic, where men till the soil and plant vineyards, for in his days Yaudi both ate and drank. His own grave "place" is close to Hadad's statue, so when his son sacrifices to the gods, let him say: "May the soul of Panammu eat with Hadad and his soul drink with Hadad, let it rejoice in the offering like Hadad." He has built a house for the gods in his city, wherefore they have given him seed. The inscription ends with curses against those who disobey his injunctions.[5]

Bar Sur followed his father, but was killed in the conspir-

---

[3] CIS., I, 5; cf. *History of Assyria*, 182 f.
[4] II Sam. 7.
[5] Fig. 165; F. von Luschan, *Ausgrabungen in Sendschirli*, I, 49 ff.; Cooke, *Text-Book*, 159 ff.; Poebel, *Das appositionell bestimmte Pronomen*, 40 ff., cf. *History of Assyria*, 185 f.

FIG. 164. EARLY HADAD STATUE AND BASE.   FIG. 165. HADAD STATUE WITH INSCRIPTION OF PANAMMU I.

acy which Panammu had feared. The usurper was a certain Azariah, of the same name as a recent king of the southern Judah, and by that name he professed himself a worshipper of Yahweh.[6] This is not the only appearance of Yahweh in Syria, for a Joram was crown prince of Hamath in David's time and Iaubidi was king of Hamath under Sargon. That a devotee of Yahweh came to the throne through a conspiracy, taken in connection with the fear manifested by Panammu and his emphasis on the worship of Hadad, raises the suspicion that we may have a religious reform parallel to Jehu's. We should then understand why Hadad was angered when the usurper raised his sword against Panammu's house and showed his wrath by a great dearth of wheat and barley, so that a peres of wheat and a shatrab of barley and an esnab of oil stood at the shekel. Unable to cope with the usurper by his own might, Panammu the younger summoned Tiglath Pileser.

Azariah's allies failed him and he was bested by the Assyrians. Panammu the younger was appointed over his father's house, the prisons were opened, the captives set free. Wheat and barley, millet and spelt were plentiful in his days, for lowness of cost his people ate and drank. Tiglath Pileser appointed lords over villages and lords over chariots, but Panammu was esteemed among the mighty kings. He ran at the chariot wheel of his lord, in the campaigns which he waged from east to west, even to the four world quarters.[7]

The other rebels were deposed and their lands divided, while cities from the border of Gurgum were added to the territory of the fortunate Panammu. The name of Judah disappears and henceforth we hear only of a "King of Samal"; we cannot but wonder whether the name Judah was abandoned because of its connection with the southern Judah and the Yahweh worship.

---

[6] One is tempted to compare the contemporary chalcedony seal, adorned with a bull, of "Shemaiah, son of Azariah," bought in Aleppo, Comte de Vogüé, *Mélanges d'archéologie orientale*, 1868, 131 f., but it may have been carried in recent days from Palestine. E. Meyer, *Gesch. Altertums*, II, 2, 1931, 427 ff., actually claims that Azariah and Iaubidi were Hebrews.

[7] Von Luschan, *op. cit.*, I, 55 ff.; Cooke, *op. cit.*, 171 ff.

Eniel of Hamath possessed a considerable kingdom, extending well to the sea. When his provinces revolted, he made cause with Azariah, and therefore they were not returned to him; instead, they were formed into four Assyrian provinces, Kullania or Calneh along the coast south of the Orontes, and including the Phœnician city of Gublu or Gebala, Simirra or Simyra, farther south, with the Phœnician Arka, Zimarra, and Usnu, Hatarikka or Hazrek, and Mansuate in the Orontes valley between Aleppo and Hamath (738). Simyra was administered by the crown prince Shalmaneser, who was given general oversight of all North and Central Syria.

Previous Assyrian monarchs had made use of deportation, but Tiglath Pileser first employed it on a large scale. In the words of the younger Panammu, the daughters of the east did Tiglath Pileser bring to the west and the daughters of the west to the east. He himself tells us that thirty thousand inhabitants of the Simyra region were removed to Que or Cilicia and to Ulluba on the newly conquered Armenian frontier. In their stead came prisoners from the south and east, twelve thousand Ahlame Aramæans from the region about the Lower Zab, fifty-four hundred from Der in Babylonia, others from Lulume on the Median border or from Nairi on the Armenian. Others again, a few hundred here and there, were settled in the Phœnician cities. At the same time came tribute from other rulers, Eniel of Hamath, Sibitti-baal of Gebal, and Menahem of Samaria.

Israel had already forgotten the glorious days of Jeroboam II, so vividly pictured by Amos. In a sense, Hosea was the successor of Amos, but in temperament they were almost exact opposites. Amos viewed Israel from without, Hosea was a respected citizen of the northern kingdom. Both were sturdy opponents of the abuses connected with the current economic and social system, both predicted speedy ruin at the hands of Assyria, but Amos saw ruin without hope, Hosea retained his belief in Yahweh's loving-kindness. This difference in temperament was due in part to their different environment, for Amos was a shepherd in the far places while Hosea lived the common life and knew men, but the determining factor in Hosea's prophetic career is to be sought in his home.

Hosea, son of Beeri, married Gomer, daughter of Diblaim. He had already felt the prophetic call, for when his first son was born he named him Jezreel, in obedience to the divine oracle: "Call his name Jezreel, for in a little while I shall avenge the blood shed at Jezreel on the house of Jehu, and will bring to an end the kingdom of the house of Israel." Hosea thus publicly aligned himself with Amos and the prophetic group who had come to realise the evils inherent in Jehu's bloody reforms, evils still further accentuated by the formalism of Elisha's successors.

Hosea and his wife were both intensely religious, but in different fashion: he was a prophet of the new school; Gomer, with the conservatism inherent in woman, clung to the older customs. These customs included religious prostitution. To Gomer, such a "sacred marriage" was absolutely demanded to secure the blessing of fertility, and she felt her devotion rewarded when another child was born; to Hosea, such religious prostitution was utterly abhorrent, a sacrifice of chastity to the Canaanite Baals who still inhabited the local shrines under the mask of Yahweh. Far from rejoicing over the new-born daughter, Hosea could not even be sure he was the father. In his wife's mistaken religious fervour, he found a parallel to Israel's apostasy from her God, and there came an oracle: "Call her Not-Loved, for I will no longer love the house of Israel nor in any manner pardon them." A third child was born and Hosea heard the word of Yahweh: "Call his name Not-my-People, for you are not my people, therefore I will not be your God."

Suddenly there came to Hosea an amazing realisation. His wife was an honest woman according to her lights. Despite all her mistakes, Hosea loved her with a new, passionless love; human love could be no greater than divine, Yahweh must love Israel despite her sins. In his soul he heard the word of Yahweh:

    Go again and love this woman,
    Loving lover, an adultress,

As loves Yahweh Israel's children,
Though to other gods they turn them,
And are lovers of raisin cakes.

He would redeem Gomer, even against her will. No longer should she be permitted to frequent the licentious rites of the sanctuary, she should remain at home without sin and without relations with any man, even her husband. Thus likewise should it be with the Israelites, many days should they remain without king or prince, sacrifice or pillar, ephod or teraphim.[8]

With sadly mingled feelings, love for his erring wife and sorrow for his sinning countrymen, Hosea pleads for reform. Their mother has become a harlot, has gone after the lovers who gave her the bread and water, the wool and flax, the oil and drink, nor did she know that it was in truth Yahweh who gave her the grain, wine, and oil, who increased for her the silver and gold they used to make Baal. Therefore Yahweh will take back the grain and wine, the wool and flax given to cover her body, will stop the mirth of her feasts, new moons, sabbaths, and festal assemblies.

Yahweh has a quarrel with the Israelites. There is no truth, no mercy, no knowledge of God in the land, but cursing and lying and killing and stealing and adultery, they break out and blood touches bloodshed. The people are like their shavelings, a people not knowing and ruined; the priest shall stumble by day and likewise the prophet. Israel is destroyed for lack of knowledge, they have rejected Yahweh's knowledge, he has rejected their priesthood; they have forgotten the law of their God, he has forgotten their sons. They feed on the people's sin, the priest has become no better than the commons; of their wood they ask counsel, and their staff gives them answer. Harlotry, wine, and new wine have sapped their hearts, they sacrifice on the tops of the mounts and on the hills burn incense beneath the terebinths, oaks, and poplars. Do not enter Gilgal and do not ascend to Beth Aven, and say

---

[8]This interpretation of Hosea's marriage follows that of Leroy Waterman, *JBL.*, XXXVII, 1918, 193 ff.

not "As Yahweh liveth," for Israel acts like a stubborn heifer. Ephraim is wedded to idols, leave him alone, a band of drunkards. Let the priests and the royal household give ear, for they were a snare in Mizpah and a net spread on Tabor and have dug a pit in Shittim.

> In his guilt shall Israel stumble,
>   And Judah shall stumble with them,
> They shall go to seek for Yahweh,
>   But not find, for he has gone from them;
> They have not kept the faith with Yahweh,
>   For they have begotten strange children,
> Now the new moon eats them with their portions.

Jezreel, name of ill omen, was not long of fulfilment. Zechariah, son of Jeroboam II, lasted but six months, when he was murdered by Shallum at Ibleam; as prophecy had declared, the line of Jehu became extinct in the fourth generation. After eight days of rule, Shallum was killed in Samaria by Menahem (744–735), who came from the old capital of Tirzah. Tapuah refused to open its gates. Menahem slew all who were within, and stained his memory forever by the same horrible cruelty to expectant mothers of which Amos had accused the Ammonites. News came that Tiglath Pileser had entered North Syria in 744. Hosea proclaimed:

> Blow the horn in Gibeah,
>   And the trumpet in Ramah;
> Cry aloud in Beth Aven:
>   After thee, O Benjamin!

Menahem, however, was too canny to fight. A special assessment of fifty shekels each was levied on the sixty thousand wealthiest men in the state, and thus were secured a thousand talents of silver to send as tribute to Tiglath Pileser.[9]

To Hosea this was only a respite, Yahweh's punishment is sure. The princes of Judah have become removers of landmarks, Ephraim breaks down the right; therefore Yahweh

[9] II Kings 15:8–20.

will be a moth to Ephraim and decay to the house of Judah. When Ephraim saw his sickness and Judah his sore, Ephraim went to Ashur and Judah sent to the "mighty king." Destruction is sure, but after there is hope:

> I will go and return to my place,
> Till confounded my face they seek,
> In affliction will seek unto me,
> Saying: Come, let us turn unto Yahweh,
> For he has torn but will heal us,
> After two days will revive us,
> The third day will upraise us,
> Let us follow to know Yahweh,
> If we seek him so shall we find him,
> He will come as the winter rain,
> As the spring rain that waters the earth.

CHAPTER XXIX

ISRAEL'S FALL

"In the year that king Uzziah died," Isaiah begins his narrative, "I saw Yahweh sitting upon a throne, high and exalted, and his skirts filled the temple. Seraphim," once perhaps serpent godlings, but now guardians of the threshold, "were standing about him; each had six wings—with two he covered his face, and with two he covered his feet, and with two he flew. And one called to another and said:

> Holy, Holy, Holy is Yahweh of Hosts,
> Full is all earth with his glory.

The threshold foundations shook and the temple was filled with smoke. Seraphs covered their faces before the dazzling countenance of their divine master, and Isaiah cried out: "Woe is me, I am lost! I am a man of unclean lips and I dwell among a people of unclean lips, yet have I seen the King, Yahweh of Hosts." But a seraph brought a live coal from the altar and placed it on Isaiah's lips, saying: "Your iniquity will depart and your sin be expiated." The voice of Yahweh was heard: "Whom shall I send and who will go for us?"

Consecrated for service, Isaiah eagerly cried out: "Here am I, send me," and received this commission:

> Hear ye, hear ye, but understand not!
> See ye, see ye, but perceive not!
> Make fat the heart of this people,
> Make its ears heavy, its eyes plaster,
> Lest it see with its heart and hear with its ears,
> Understand with its heart, and I turn and heal them.

Amazed to learn that his people would not hearken to the word of their God, Isaiah inquired: "How long, Yahweh?" and received the terrible reply:

> Until they lie waste,
> Cities without citizens,
> Houses without men,
> And ground left desolate;
> And Yahweh move men to a distance,
> In the land many places abandoned;
> Though but a tenth remain in it,
> It must be consumed again.[1]

Isaiah returned from his glorious vision in the temple to take up the hard life of a prophet. No attention was paid to his predictions of evil, there was no return to a purer religion. To emphasise his certainty of the coming doom, Isaiah named his first born Shear-jashub, "Only a remnant shall return."

Yahweh has rejected his people, the house of Jacob, for the land is full of Philistine-like diviners from the East, and many strange children have been born to the people. The land is indeed full of silver, horses, and chariots, but it is also full of idols. Yahweh has a Day against the proud and haughty, against the Lebanon cedars and the oaks of Bashan and all ships of Tarshish. Yahweh alone is exalted, the idols shall pass away.[2]

Jotham passed easily from the regency to the kingship and his reign (751–736) was most prosperous. He was successful in his wars with the Ammonites, who paid him a tribute of a hundred talents of silver and ten thousand cors each of wheat and barley. With his wealth he built the upper gate of the temple, restored the wall of Ophel, founded new settlements in the hill country of Judah, and erected castles and towers in the rough thicket regions. Isaiah's predicted doom seemed far away.

Jehoahaz (736–721) as his full name is given by the Assyrians, Ahaz, as his name is abbreviated in the Biblical writings, was thoroughly incompetent. Isaiah declares that now

---

[1]Isaiah 6; cf. K. Marti, *Das Buch Jesaia*, 1900; B. Duhm, *Das Buch Jesaia*, 4 ed., 1914; G. H. Box, *The Book of Isaiah*, 1908; G. B. Gray, *Isaiah*, 1912; K. Fullerton, *JBL.*, XLI, 1 ff.; E. König, *Das Buch Jesaja*, 1926; O. Procksch, *Jesaia*, I, 1930.

[2]Isaiah 2:6–19.

ISRAEL'S FALL

Yahweh is taking from Jerusalem and Judah stay and staff. Youths are given them as princes, caprice overrules them, children are their oppressors, and women reign over them. Thanks to this regency of the queen mother, so terrible shall be the destruction that if a man has in his father's house so much as a mantle, they shall seize him and say: "Come, be our chief, let this ruin be under your hand," but he shall answer: "I will not be a healer, in my house is no bread or a mantle, I will not be chief of this people."

Yahweh is about to enter in judgment with the elders and princes:

> It is you who have eaten my vineyard,
>   In your house is the plunder of the poor;
> What mean you that you crush my people,
>   And grind the face of the poor?

Jerusalem's ladies found no favour in Isaiah's eyes:

> Because they are haughty, the daughters of Zion,
>   And walk with outstretching of necks and ogling of eyes,
>   Walking and tripping as they go and tinkling with their feet,
>
> Yahweh shall scab their skulls and lay bare their shame,
>   For balsam shall be corruption and for girdle a rope,
>   For hair well dressed, baldness, for rich robes, sack.
>
> And seven women shall seize a single man,
>   Saying: Our bread we shall eat, our robe we shall wear,
>   Let us only be called by your name, take away our reproach.[3]

At one of the vineyard festivals, Isaiah began what sounded at first like a cult song to the Dod, the "Beloved" fertility divinity:

> Let me sing, I pray, of my Loved One,
> My Beloved's song of his vineyard:
>
> My Loved One had a vineyard on a fruitful hill,
>   He dug it and he cleared it and he planted choice grapes;

[3] Isaiah 3:1–15; 16–17, 24; 4:1.

And he built in its midst a tower, a wine vat he also hewed,
    And he looked to its bearing grapes, and it bore—wild grapes!

So now you Jerusalem dwellers and men of Judah,
    Judge, I beseech you, between me and my vineyard;
What should yet have been done for my vineyard I did not?
    Why, when I looked for grapes, did it bear wild grapes?

And now, I pray, let me tell what I'll do to my vineyard:
    I shall take out its hedge, it shall be consumed;
I shall break down its wall, it shall be trampled,
    I shall lay it waste, it shall not be pruned or hoed.

Thistles and briars shall it grow,
    The clouds shall I order that they rain not upon it;
For the vineyard of Yahweh of Hosts is the House of Israel,
    And the men of Judah the plant he delights in;
He looked also for justice, but behold bloodshed,
    And for righteousness, but lo, a cry!

Having thus turned the apparent fertility chant into a bitter parody, Isaiah then denounces woes against those who add house to house and field to field until there is no room and the rich dwell alone in the land, against those who rise early at dawn to follow strong drink and linger till nightfall when wine inflames them; in their feast are the lute and the harp and wine, but the work of Yahweh they do not regard.

    Woe to the heroes—in drinking wine!
        And the men of might—who mix strong drink!
    Who acquit the guilty for a bribe,
        And the right of the righteous set aside!

The fertility goddess descends to the Land of No Return to bring back her dead lover; Sheol has increased its capacity, says Isaiah, to contain her dead worshippers.[4]

Ahaz rapidly lost the possessions won by his father. Elath, with its access to the Red Sea trade, thereafter belonged to the Edomites. Philistines raided the Judæan Negeb and the Shephelah, and took Beth Shemesh, Aijalon, Gederoth, Tim-

---

[4] Isaiah 5:1–14; cf. Cant. 8:11; W. C. Graham, *AJSL.*, XLV, 1929, 167 ff.

nah, and Gimzo; Beth Shemesh was burned and never again occupied. Isaiah's doom was in process of fulfilment.[5]

Damascus and Israel were ancient foes, and it was natural to assume that Israel's destruction was to come from the Aramæans or from the Philistines:

> A word hath Yahweh sent against Jacob,
>   And it falls upon Israel;
> All the people shall know it,
>   Ephraim and Samaria's dwellers.
> For they spoke in pride
>   And in greatness of heart:
> Bricks have fallen, with hewn stone we'll rebuild,
>   Sycamores cut down, with cedars we'll replace them.
> But Yahweh has raised up the princes of Rezon,
>   His enemies incited;
> Aram on the east, Philistines on the west,
>   With open mouth shall Israel devour.
> Spite all this turned not his anger,
>   And his hand is outstretched still.

Three times this refrain ends the long stanza which describes the coming woes and its manifold causes, the prophets who see lies and the guides who make them stray, and

> Those who decree orders hurtful,
>   And who writing trouble write,
> To turn from justice the needy,
>   And to rob the rights of the poor,
> To make the widow their booty,
>   And to make the orphan their prey.

The poem closes with this terrific prediction:

> Then a flag he'll raise to far nations,
>   For it hiss from the ends of the earth;
> And behold, they shall come with speed quickly,
>   None shall weary or stumble of them.
> Not loosed from their loins is their girdle,
>   The thong of their sandals not snapped;
> Sharpened are their arrows,
>   And all their bows are bent.

[5] Mackenzie, *Ain Shems*, II, 11.

> Like flint are the hoofs of their horses,
> Like whirlwind accounted their wheels;
> Like a lioness is their roaring,
> Like young lions shall they roar;
> They shall growl and seize hold the booty,
> Drag off with none to save.[6]

Isaiah's expectations of a war between Damascus and Israel were disappointed. At the death of Menahem, his son Pekahiah held the throne for a year, when his general Pekah collected a body of fifty Gileadites and slew him within the palace at Samaria.[7] Once more Israel was definitely anti-Assyrian. Hosea had professed no love for Menahem, but he had still less for the latest usurper:

> Gilead is a city of evil doers,
> It is tracked with blood;
> As robbers a man may ambush,
> The priests hide themselves on the road;
> They murder those going to Shechem,
> For wickedness they do.

Chaos has covered the whole land, the thief enters and robbers roam about; the cause is the frequent change of rulers:

> In their wickedness kings they anoint,
> In their treacheries princes,
> All of them are unfaithful.
> On the day of our king they are sick,
> The princes with heat of wine,
> He extended his hand to lewd fellows.
> For their hearts do burn as an oven,
> All night their anger sleeps,
> But at morn it blazes like fire.
> All of them glow like an oven,
> They devour those who judge them,
> Fallen are all their kings,
> For none of them calls on me!

---

[6] Isaiah 9:8–21; 10:1–4; 5:26–29; cf. K. Fullerton, *AJSL.*, XXXIII, 1916, 9 ff.
[7] II Kings 15:22–25.

> They made kings,—but not from me,
>   Made princes—I knew them not!
> With their silver and gold made they idols,
>   Against them my anger is kindled!

Again and again Hosea recalls the early Hebrew epic so recently set down in writing:

> When Israel was a child, I loved him,
>   From Egypt I called him;
> 'Twas I taught Ephraim walking,
>   I took him in my arms.
> 'Twas I, Yahweh thy God,
>   Brought thee up from the land of Egypt;
> No other God did you know,
>   Nor was there a saviour beside me.
> I shepherded thee in the desert,
>   In the land of dryness;
> When they fed, they filled themselves full,
>   Exalted their heart, they forgot me.

From their earliest days, witness the sin of Baal Peor, Israel's fathers were wicked; the beginning of sin was the establishment of Saul's kingdom:

> From the days of Gibeah is the sin of Israel,
> Against me then stood the children of Israel,
> In Gibeah shall not war overtake them?

Hosea likewise knows the "Blessing of Jacob," where Joseph is "the shoot of a vine stock, his branches climb over the wall";[8] he paraphrases: "A luxuriant vine is Israel, his fruit he increases for himself," but this increase of his fruit has only been for increasing Ephraim's heathen altars. Instead of the blessings of heaven above and deep beneath, of breast and womb, of father and child, there shall be neither birth, pregnancy, nor conception, they shall be given a miscarrying womb and dry breasts. Ephraim's root is withered, they cannot bear fruit; if they do beget children, Yahweh will slay the beloved of their womb.

[8] Gen. 49:22 ff.; cf. p. 202.

In the days of Jeroboam II, Israel was the greatest of the Syrian powers:

> When Ephraim spoke, they trembled,
>   He was a ruler in Israel;
> Then he sinned through Baal and died,
>   Yet still they continue to sin!
> They make for themselves from their silver,
>   Idols after their model,
> All of it work of the smith,
>   But "God" is what they call it!

Israel has forgotten its earlier simplicity. Its isolation has been replaced by closer political relations to the great powers, and there has come a new culture mixed with foreign elements:

> Ephraim—with the peoples he is mingling!
>   Ephraim—he has become a cake unturned!
> Strangers eat his strength, he knows it not,
>   Grey hairs sprinkled on him, he knows it not!
>
> Ephraim is a dove, silly, without understanding,
>   To Egypt they call, to Ashur go;
> As they go, I will spread my net o'er them,
>   Bring them down as a bird of the sky.
>
> Israel is mid the nations,
>   For they have gone to Ashur;
> A wild ass, roving alone,
>   To Egypt gives love gifts.

Ephraim has multiplied altars, but they are altars only for sinning; they sacrifice flesh for the eating, how can this delight Yahweh? Though he wrote his laws by the myriads, Israel would count them as those of a stranger. Nor do they respect Yahweh's prophet, the fowler's snare is in all his paths, they dig for him a pit in the house of his God; they shall learn that their own prophets are fools and the man with the spirit is mad. Because of their guilt, they shall return to Egypt, where Memphis shall bury them, or eat unclean food in Ashur.

What then can they do on the day of assembly, on the day of Yahweh's feast?

Yahweh is still compassionate and sighs:

> How can I give thee up, Ephraim?
> How can I cast thee off, Israel?
> My heart is turned within me,
> My compassions are kindled together.

Love may redeem Israel in days to come, but the immediate future must bring punishment; Hosea's last words lament that Samaria is laid waste for her sin against her God, by the sword shall they fall, their children be dashed to pieces and their women ravished.[9]

Forgetful of the Assyrian menace, Pekah and Rezon united against Judah. Not far from Jerusalem, they fell upon Ahaz and defeated him; an Ephraimite hero named Zichri slew the king's brother Maaseiah, the chamberlain Azrikam, and Elkanah, second in command under the king. Gibeah, the first outpost to the north of the capital, was destroyed, and sling shots, skulls, and traces of an intense fire bear witness to the horrors of its siege.[10]

Small wonder that the hearts of king and people trembled as the trees of the forest before the wind. With his son Shearjashub whose ill-omened name had been only too well justified, Isaiah met Ahaz at the end of the conduit of the Upper Pool, on the road of the fuller's field, where he planned to hide the city water supply. This was the message:

> Take care quiet to remain,
> Fear not, nor let your heart faint,
> For these two smouldering firebrand tails,
> Rezon and Remaliah's son.

The allies had purposed to set up Tabeel's son in Judah, but Yahweh decreed it should not come to pass:

[9]Cf. W. R. Harper, *Amos and Hosea*, 1905; Marti, *Dodekapropheton*, 1 ff.; Nowack, *Die Kleinen Propheten*, 2 ff.; Sellin, *Zwölfprophetenbuch*, 6 ff.; O. R. Sellers, *AJSL.*, XLI, 1925, 243 ff.

[10]II Chron. 28:7; W. F. Albright, *Ann.*, IV, 53.

> For Aram's head is Damascus,
>   And the head of Damascus is Rezon;
> And Ephraim's head is Samaria,
>   And Samaria's head Remaliah's son;
> If you believe not,
>   You shall be established not.

"Ask a sign of Yahweh, deep in Sheol or high above," Isaiah demanded, but Ahaz replied evasively that he would not tempt Yahweh. Isaiah was not deceived: "Hear now, O house of David! Is it a small thing for you to weary men that you should also weary my God? Yahweh himself will give you a sign." Paraphrasing the well-known prediction to Hagar of the birth of Ishmael,[11] he continued:

> Behold, the young woman shall conceive and bear a son,
> And you shall call his name Immanuel;
> For before the child shall know
> To choose the good, refuse the evil,
> The land whose kings you dread shall be forsaken.

The young woman who was to bear the child "God with us" was doubtless the wife of Ahaz; this was acceptable enough, but there was an addition: From the day that Ephraim should depart from Judah, Yahweh would bring upon him days such as had never come before, the king of Assyria in person.[12]

By divine order, Isaiah took a great tablet and wrote on it in the common character "For Maher-shalal-hash-baz," as if on a seal; as witnesses he took the chief priest Uriah and Zechariah, son of Jeberechiah. When his second son was born, Isaiah gave him this ominous name, "Hurry spoil, hasten booty!" "Before the child knows how to cry 'My father' or 'My mother,' the riches of Damascus and the spoil of Samaria shall be carried off before the king of Assyria."

> Since this people have refused Siloam's softly flowing waters,
>   Lo, Yahweh is making to rise the waters, strong and many of the River;

---

[11] Gen. 16:11; cf. J. M. P. Smith, *AJSL.*, XL, 1924, 292.
[12] Isaiah 7:1–17; cf. K. Fullerton, *AJSL.*, XXXIV, 1918, 256 ff.

ISRAEL'S FALL

It shall flood over all its channels and overflow all its banks,
 It shall sweep onward into Judah and shall reach unto the neck.[13]

These prophecies made no impression on Ahaz. He sacrificed his eldest son by fire, but the danger remained. In utter despair, he took the silver and gold from palace and temple and sent them to Tiglath Pileser: "I am thy servant and thy son, come and save me."[14]

The next year, 734, the Assyrians descended, the sixteen provinces of Damascus were overrun, Kurussa, Irma, and Metuna were captured. Rezon was shut up in the city which saw its orchards and gardens destroyed, but the siege dragged. Panammu of the Northern Judah died in the Assyrian camp, mourned by the whole army; Tiglath Pileser honoured him with an elaborate funeral feast, escorted his body home for burial, and filled his place with his son Bar Rekkab. At last, Damascus was taken and Rezon was put to death while the inhabitants were deported to Kir (732).

Isaiah exulted over the removal of this threat:

> Behold, Damascus is removed as a city,
> It shall be a ruin, forsaken forever;
> Flocks shall her cities possess,
> They shall lie down with none to affright.
> And the fortress shall cease from Ephraim,
> And the kingdom shall pass from Damascus,
> And the remnant of Aram shall be
> Like the glory of Israel's sons.
>
> Diminished the glory of Jacob,
> And the fat of his flesh become lean;
> As when harvester plucks grain still standing,
> Gleans ears in the Giant's Vale;
> There remain, as at beating of olive,
> Two or three berries on topmost bough,
> Four or five on the branch of the fruit tree,
> 'Tis the oracle of Yahweh, Israel's God.[15]

[13] Isaiah 8:1–8; cf. K. Fullerton, *JBL.*, XLIII, 1924, 253 ff.
[14] II Kings 16:5 ff.   [15] Isaiah 17:1–6.

At the conclusion of the siege, Tiglath Pileser held a review of his vassals, and among them was Ahaz. As in all newly organised provinces, the cult of Ashur and the king had been established in Damascus, and the vassal rulers were ordered to follow this example. Ahaz sent the altar pattern to Uriah, the chief priest, who had witnessed Isaiah's prediction that Damascus would fall, and when Ahaz returned the altar was ready. A throne for the divine king was built in the temple and the outer royal entry was turned to the house of Yahweh from before the face of the king of Assyria, presumably represented in stele form. The new great altar was to have the burnt and meal, drink and peace offerings, in fact, all the sacrifices formerly given to Yahweh; henceforth Ashur and the deified Assyrian king were to be Judah's chief divinities. The bases were cut up, the panels removed, the sea taken down from the twelve supporting bronze oxen and set on a stone pedestal; no longer could the oxen suggest the might of Yahweh. Yahweh was degraded to a minor deity, deprived of all regular sacrifices, his only function was to deliver oracles at the bronze altar brought from the temple forefront and placed north of the new altar.

Ahaz had made the supreme sacrifice and Yahweh had not saved him; by the logic of the times, Assyrian gods were more powerful, for they and not Yahweh were the cause of his salvation, and they deserved to supplant a deity so obviously without power. We may understand this logic, but as students of history we must realise that here was a crisis of the first magnitude; had Ashur and the king retained their position, our religion to-day would have been far different.

To the six Assyrian provinces of North Syria were added seven from the central regions. Hollow Syria became Supite or Zobah, with an indefinite expansion into the desert. Damascus itself was the seat of a second province. South of Damascus was a third, Qarnini, whose centre was probably Ashtaroth Karnaim. Assured of Judæan support in Israel's rear, Tiglath Pileser sallied forth to attack Rezon's ally Pekah. A short march brought him to Pekah's home in Gilead, to

ISRAEL'S FALL 453

Argob, and to the Camps of Jair. The entire east Jordan country was detached from Israel and formed into three provinces, Hamath in the Jordan valley, Haurina or Hauran, the capture of whose city Ashtaroth is depicted on one of the slabs, and Galaza or Gilead. Among the captives was Beerah, prince of Reuben, our last reference to an independent Reuben.[16]

Then the Assyrians crossed the Jordan and took Ijon, Abel of Beth Maacah, Janoah, Kadesh, Hazor, Aruma, and Merom, the wide land of Naphtali, and all were made a province ruled from Magidu or Megiddo which stood as an Assyrian guard post against an Israel confined to the few square miles about Samaria; the new administrative connection of Galilee with Megiddo endured for many centuries. The entire sea coast, as far south as Rashpuna just north of Joppa, became the province of Duru or Dor. There were now thirteen Assyrian provinces in Syria.[17]

Pekah was not allowed to retain even this terribly decreased Israel; Hoshea conspired against him with Assyrian backing, and paid ten talents of gold and many of silver from his tiny kingdom, but at that he must witness Israelites deported from Gabara, Hannathon, Cana, Jotapata, and Iron (732). To save Ahaz from the threatened Philistine attack, Tiglath Pileser continued south. Mitinti of Ashkelon died in a conflagration and his son Rukibti appeared in the Assyrian camp to make homage. Hanun of Gaza fled to Egypt, but when a stele and a royal image were set up in his palace in sign that Gaza was to be made a fourteenth province, Hanun returned and accepted Assyrian rule. Tribute was received from Matten-baal of Arvad, Sanibu of Ammon, Shalman of Moab, Iauhazi or Jehoahaz of Judah, and Chemosh-nadab of Edom. Matten II of Tyre seemed plotting revolt; the Assyrian commander-in-chief appeared in 728 and Matten won forgiveness only by payment of a hundred and fifty talents of gold. Damascus also rebelled but was crushed the next year.

[16] I Chron. 5:6.
[17] Cf. E. Forrer, *Die Provinzeinteilung des assyrischen Reiches,* 1920; A. Alt, *ZDPV.,* LII, 1929, 220 ff.

Tiglath Pileser died and his son came home from Simyra to reign as Shalmaneser V (728–722); his absence from Syria allowed new revolts to be stirred up by Sibu or So, perhaps one of the Egyptian Delta kings, and Tyre, Sidon, and Accho rebelled. Tyre had been a harsh mistress to the Phœnician states, which gladly welcomed Shalmaneser and furnished sixty ships and eight hundred oarsmen, but the Tyrian fleet of twelve vessels defeated their rivals and took five hundred prisoners. A blockade from the shore cut off the island from the streams and springs on the mainland, but Tyre possessed wells within her walls and held out for five years. In the end, the Assyrian great king was compelled to offer terms to Luli or Elu-eli; after his successful defiance of the empire, Elu-eli found no difficulty in winning back the rebel Citium of Cyprus.[18]

At the first appearance of Shalmaneser, Hoshea (732–723) of Israel had paid his tribute. Later, he sent messengers to So and neglected to forward the yearly payments. Shalmaneser therefore imprisoned Hoshea, but Samaria itself, thanks to its impregnable hill, held out for three years, and was reduced only by blockade. Thus ended the kingdom of Israel as the prophets had foretold.[19]

[18] Menander, in Joseph., *Ant.*, ix, 283 ff.
[19] II Kings 17:1 ff.; 18:9 ff.; cf. *AJSL.*, XXI, 1905, 179 ff.

CHAPTER XXX

ISAIAH AND HEZEKIAH

SARGON, by his deposition of Shalmaneser, received as legacy the Syrian problem. The disturbances which accompanied his usurpation gave renewed hope to the Syrian peoples. In the south, the revolt was headed by Hanun of Gaza, in the north by Hamath under Iaubidi, who shows in his name the same reverence for Yahweh as did Azariah of the Northern Judah.

For his own and his father Panammu's righteousness, his lord Rekkab-el and his lord Tiglath Pileser had placed Bar Rekkab upon his father's throne in Samal. His father's house had prospered more than all others and he had run at the chariot wheel of his lord, the king of Assyria, in preference to great kings, lords of silver and lords of gold; thus he was able to make his father's house more glorious than that of one of the mightiest kings and all the kings his brothers envied the glory of his house. His predecessors, the kings of Samal, had never possessed a fine house but had only the house of Kilamu and the winter and summer palace;[1] Bar Rekkab did in fact build a third hilani as a summer house looking to the north and a portico to connect it with the second hilani. Through the usual entrance, with two lion column bases, one came to the rectangular hall, traversed a narrow passage way to a larger hall, and reached the small private rooms in the rear, where a canal brought water for the bath.

Bar Rekkab appears in the portico which connects the two hilanis, seated on a throne scarcely less magnificent than that of his Assyrian lord; it rests on cedar cones with bull's heads at the four corners of the seat, his feet are on a stool of like ornamentation. He wears the long looped fringed Hittite robe and knobbed cap, but his beard and hair fall in Assyrian curls, a lotus is in his left hand, his right is raised palm open.

[1] Poebel, *op. cit.*, 46 ff.

Before him is the sun and moon symbol on a support with two down-hanging tassels; the accompanying inscription mentions the Baal of Harran, otherwise known to the Assyrians as Sin and to the Aramæans as Si. A beardless secretary attends Bar Rekkab, his right hand raised, while under his left arm is the ivory or wooden tablet, in his left hand is the Egyptian writing-box with places for ink and reed pens.[2]

With Bar Rekkab are his beardless attendants. One holds up for inspection a Greek-looking œnochoe, decorated above with a band of zigzags and below with a row of lotus flowers. The next presents arrows and carries a quiver with long hanging tassel and a short thick compound bow ending in ducks' heads; the three-fingered glove through which the arrows slipped and the square leather guard for the bow hand hint at the force demanded for this compound bow. A third servant holds a short sword point downward, a bearded warrior shows a stout dagger.

Another group depicts the musicians in long robes bound by thick girdles with elaborate buckles and tassels. A bearded man beats the tambourine as does a long-haired boy or woman who stands on his shoulders. Two beat tambourines and two play small harps, one with level top, the other at an angle; one of each group has straight hair and beard, the other's is elaborately curled. The procession is closed by an attendant with goat. Traces of blue and red show that the reliefs were picked out in colours.

Once again we see Bar Rekkab, standing before the double-horned cap, the bridle, the winged disk, the star in the circle, and the sun and moon symbol. Before him is the inscription which tells of his father's death and his own accession, behind him is the servant with fly-flapper and napkin. Another inscription is on the drapery of the statue he erected for his father Panammu, a standing figure in long heavily fringed robe, coming down to the tips of the laced shoes.

Bar Rekkab boasted of honours from Tiglath Pileser, he could expect none from the murderer of his benefactor's son.

[2] Fig. 91, *History of Assyria*.

ISAIAH AND HEZEKIAH

He too rebelled and his example was followed by Arpad and Simyra. Elu-eli of Tyre felt no longer bound by the agreement with Shalmaneser, Damascus revolted for the second time since the loss of its independence in 732, Samaria was once more its ally. The whole provincial organisation of Tiglath Pileser was crumbling.

Sargon acted quickly. Bar Rekkab's cool summer palace was burned, Northern Judah was made a province under the name of Samal, a small residence for the governor was constructed on the ruins of the first palace. Iaubidi was defeated on the historic battle ground of Qarqara and was flayed alive, while two hundred of his chariots and six hundred of his cavalry were added to the Assyrian army. Hamath became a province and was colonised with six thousand three hundred Assyrians. All inland Syria was henceforth under direct Assyrian administration.

Zechariah, son of Jeberechiah, exults over the fall of Hadrach, Damascus, and Hamath; the Phœnicians and Philistines are to follow:

> The ruthless has come to Hadrach,
>   And Damascus is his camp,
> For his is the "Eye of Aram,"
>   And Hamath on its frontier.
> Also Sidon, though it be so knowing,
>   Though Tyre a tower has built,
> And heaped up like dust the silver,
>   And gold like the mud of the streets;
> Behold, Yahweh will impoverish,
>   And cast in the sea her wealth.
>
> Ashkelon sees and is fearful,
>   Gaza too and is pained,
> And Ekron, shamed her reliance,
>   From Gaza perished her king,
> Ashkelon shall not be dwelt in,
>   And a bastard in Ashdod sits.
> Philistine pride I cut off,
>   But I camp about my house,

> To guard against comer and goer,
> No taskmaster comes against them.[3]

The first half of the prophecy was fulfilled. Hanun was defeated at Gaza and fled to the advancing Egyptian army led by Sibu. From a long low rise, the Assyrians had their first view of Raphia, a fine rolling plain with more grass than is usual in this barren country and well fitted for cavalry; a well marked a station on the Great Road which was shut off from the sea by lagoons and sand dunes. Sibu was defeated and fled back to Egypt, Raphia was destroyed, and nine thousand thirty-three captives were taken. Hanun was carried in chains to Assyria, but his memory has been preserved to this day by Beit Hanun, the "House of Hanun," a village on a low elevation northeast of Gaza which prides itself on the shrine of the "Prophet Hanun." Five years later (715), peace was made with Bocchoris who for a short time made the Saite dynasty supreme in Egypt; Sargon describes the royal gifts as tribute of Pharaoh, King of Egypt!

Central Syria had now been incorporated within the empire, and but two states of North Syria retained a nominal independence. It was obvious to their rulers that this anomaly would not be long permitted. Knowing the lure of his wealth to Sargon, Pisiris of Carchemish entered into alliance with Midas of Phrygia, but no effective aid was forthcoming and Carchemish fell in 717. Pisiris and his family were carried off in chains, his fifty chariots, two hundred cavalry, and five hundred foot swelled the Assyrian forces. The booty was enormous: eleven talents, thirty minas of gold, two thousand one hundred talents, twenty-four minas of silver. Carchemish was settled with captives and made a province, ruled from a great fort on the acropolis whose foundations thoroughly destroyed all earlier constructions. In a recess of the south gate, the Assyrians found a colossal seated statue of white limestone, almost marble in its fine texture, which represented a

---

[3] Zech. 9:1 ff.; cf. Isaiah 8:2; E. G. H. Kraeling, *AJSL.*, XLI, 1924, 24 ff.; 194.

FIG. 167. A KING OF CARCHEMISH.

FIG. 166. GOD THRONED ON LIONS.
(Carchemish.)

king of Carchemish, perhaps Pisiris himself, in short-sleeved tunic, heavy fringed mantle, head cloth, and turban; they shattered it into fragments but even in its lamentable state the combination of broad effect and refined detail proves it a masterpiece of late "Hittite" art.[4]

Gurgum in the extreme north was after the fall of Carchemish the only vassal state in Syria proper. Its capital Marqasi, still flourishing as Marash, commanded from its citadel a narrow fertile valley with at least twenty-one settlements and the great trail from Syria north into the recesses of the Anti-Taurus. No less than seventeen sculptures in the round or in relief testify to its "Hittite" culture, and often they are accompanied by "Hittite" inscriptions. A great lion is covered with the early raised pictographs. Various slabs depict the meal of men or women. A woman in the long robe and high cylindrical headdress sits in a high-backed chair with a child on her knees, in one hand a mirror and in the other a bird-topped lyre, while before her is a cross-legged table with six flat globes and a goblet. Another shows a beardless figure, in scantier dress and holding goblet and palm leaf, communing across a table with a larger god in the long fringed garment; underneath two smaller figures hold a lance or lead a horse by the bridle.[5]

So long as the pro-Assyrian Tarhulara sat on the throne, Gurgum was safe, but when he was murdered by his son Mutallu, Sargon had the desired excuse for intervention. Mutallu was carried off to captivity and Gurgum became the province of Marqasi (711). All North Syria, all Central Syria, with the exception of the Phœnician coast, all Palestine, save the four Philistine cities, Judah, and the trans-Jordanic Ammon, Moab, and Edom, were under direct Assyrian administration.

We can trace the workings of this administration most clearly in Samaria. Fifty chariots were added to the royal army and 27,290 captives deported; when we compare this with the sixty thousand landholders of the far greater Israel

[4] Fig. 166; Hogarth-Woolley, *Carchemish*, 92.
[5] Figs. 168–170; H. H. von der Osten, *Metropolitan Museum Studies*, II, 1929, 112 ff.

a few years before,[6] it is evident that a clean sweep was made of the higher classes and thus the land was left without effective leadership. The deported Israelites were settled in Gozan, Halah, and along the Habor river in Mesopotamia proper; an Assyrian letter to one of the later kings deals with affairs in Gozan, and mentions Halbishu, the man from the land of Samaria, Neriah, the rab nikashi official, the property custodian, and another official Paltiah who is in close relations with the subgovernor.[7] Perhaps we may find their traces in other letters and documents which tell of serfs on the great estates of this region; one group refers to settlers in Kannu, which some have thought a transplanted Canaan.[8] Since these deported captives did represent the higher classes, they swung the weight of Hebrew influence to Mesopotamia, which long remained a centre of the best Hebrew thought.

Bit Humri, the "House of Omri," became the province of Samaria, and its surviving inhabitants were treated as Assyrians, subject to the usual taxation; a tablet of Arihi to his "son" Nabu-dur-usur reports that there is no information as to whether the tribute grain of the men of the land of Samaria has been received.[9] The gaps in the population were filled by deported captives. Four such deportations to Syria are reported in Sargon's annals alone. Two Aramæan tribes from Der in Babylonia were settled in 720, the Biblical writings add captives from revolted Hamath in the same year. Damascus received two "Hittite" tribes in 717, two Arab tribes were assigned to Samaria, Deioces of Media and Itti of Allabria were interned in Hamath. Men from Cutha and Babylon were transported in later reigns.

Sargon tells how he rebuilt Samaria and made it greater than before. On the summit was the fort for the Assyrian garrison, irregular in plan, its west wall just outside and

---

[6] II Kings 15:19 f.; restoration of Sargon's Annals for this section, *AJSL.*, XLVII, 1931, 262 f.

[7] Leroy Waterman, *Royal Correspondence of the Assyrian Empire,* 1930, I, 440 ff.

[8] C. H. W. Johns, *Proc. Soc. Biblical Archæology*, XXX, 1908, 107 ff.

[9] Waterman, *op. cit.*, II, 330 f.

FIG. 168. WOMAN WITH CHILD.
(Marqasi.)

FIG. 169. SCENE OF WORSHIP.
(Marqasi.)

FIG. 170. LION WITH PICTOGRAPHIC INSCRIPTION.
(Marqasi.)

parallel to the wall of Ahab, its north and south walls cut obliquely through his palace. Portions of the ruined palace were still occupied, the remainder was used as a quarry and Ahab's magnificent blocks were cut down for the foundations. Above were the back and front walls with tie walls between, the rest was nothing but rough mud-laid rubble. New buildings were yet ruder; for the room angles and the door jambs there were large well-dressed stones, bonded alternately into each wall, but the remaining face was of roughly squared blocks on a rubble interior, here and there held together by headers. Even the probable house of the governor had but three rooms. The city wall was of the same rough type. Nothing could more clearly indicate Israel's decline in material culture after independence was lost.[10]

Occupation by an Assyrian colony is further proved by the writing. A cuneiform tablet, in part a palimpsest, is sealed with the round stamp bearing what appears to be an altar and the beginning of a Hebrew name, Ab. . . . .; it reads: "If by the tenth day of Ab, Nergal-tallim shall say: 'Abiahe to the governor of the cities shall give six oxen and twelve sheep,'" and the rest is missing. A letter seal, with a line of cuneiform above and below, is addressed "To Ashur-. . .-iddin."[11]

Soon the Assyrian king received a message: "The nations which you deported and placed in the cities of Samaria do not know the law of the God of the land; therefore Yahweh has sent lions among them, and behold they are slaying them, because they know not the law of the God of the land." This was a reasonable complaint, and Sargon gave order: "Carry there one of the priests whom I brought from there, and let him go and dwell there, and let him teach them the law of the God of the land." The priest was settled in the old religious centre of Bethel, and there he taught the new colonists the ancient cult. Yahweh, nonetheless, was no longer supreme in his own land. Each nation made gods of its own and established them in the houses of the high places built by the Sa-

[10]Reisner-Fisher-Lyon, *Harvard Excavations at Samaria*, 123 ff.
[11]*Ibid.*, 247.

maritans; the men of Babylon made Succoth-benoth, whoever that was, the men of Cutha made Nergal, those from Hamath made Ashima and the Avvites Nibhaz and Tartak, perhaps Atargatis, while the men of Sepharvaim burnt their children to Adrammelech and Anamelech. In the word of the narrator, "They feared Yahweh but made priests for the high places from their own people to sacrifice for them on the high places; they did indeed fear Yahweh, but they also served their own gods after the manner of the nations from whose midst they had been carried away."[12] On this basis was formed the mixed people of the later Samaritans.

Isaiah had predicted that the new-born son of Ahaz would be named Immanuel, "God is with us"; actually, he was named Hezekiah, "Yahweh strengtheneth," in memory of the accomplished salvation. His reign (721-693) was one of the most important in Judah's history. Ahaz had been pro-Assyrian and had worshipped Ashur and the deified king; his son took advantage of Assyria's troubles to declare his independence.

From Moresheth of Gath in the Shephelah, from whose hills could be seen the marching Assyrian armies, a new prophet named Micah arose to support Isaiah's teaching:

> Hear, all ye nations,
>   Heed, earth, and all your peoples;
> Yahweh is witness against you,
>   The Lord from his holy temple.
>
> Lo, Yahweh goes forth from his place,
>   Has gone down and treads on earth's heights;
> The hills melt before him,
>   The valleys cleave asunder.
>
> This has come for the wrongs of Jacob,
>   For the sins of the house of Judah;
> The wrong of Israel? Samaria!
>   And the sin of Judah? Jerusalem!
>
> I made for this Samaria a field mound,
>   As places for planting vineyards;

[12] II Kings 17:24-33; cf. Ezra 4:2.

> Her stones poured down to the valley,
> Her foundations laid open.
>
> For her wounds cannot be cured,
> Now it has come to Judah,
> It reaches my people's gate,
> Jerusalem it approaches.

Micah like his predecessors finds the cause of this coming destruction in the lack of simple morality. There is woe for those who devise iniquity on their beds and execute it in the morning, who covet fields and houses and seize them and oppress a man and his heritage. Yet such is the utter hypocrisy of these men that

> Prophesy not, they demand,
> Such things one should not predict;
> This reproach of a babbler
> Will not touch the house of Jacob.
> Is Yahweh's temper short,
> Are such his accustomed doings?
> Are not his sayings gracious
> To him who walks uprightly?

Micah replies that this is not so, they rise up like an enemy against those who think they are walking in safety and tear off the robe from the peaceful passerby; they drive the women from their pleasant houses and take from their young children the glory forever. If a man should walk in wine and falsehood and lie, and say: "I will prophesy wine and strong drink," he would be the right prophet for this people!

> Hark, Yahweh cries to the city!
> Hear, tribe and city assembly!
> Can I forget the wicked's house treasure,
> The short measure that is accursed?
>
> Can I make pure her wicked scales,
> Her bag of weights unlawful?
> Her riches of violence full,
> Her inhabitants speaking falsehood?

> Thou hast followed the statutes of Omri,
> All the works of the house of Ahab,
> So I make thee a desolation,
> Ye shall bear the reproach of the nations![13]

To the days of Jeremiah, the noble partisans of that prophet recalled how Micah had predicted:

> Zion shall be plowed like a field,
> And Jerusalem become heaps of stone,
> And the temple mount as wooded heights,

how Hezekiah hearkened to him and entreated Yahweh, and how God had repented of the evil he had pronounced against them.[14] At the same time, the young Hezekiah—he was barely fifteen—was sick unto death. Isaiah brought him Yahweh's oracle: "Set your house in order, for you shall die and not live." Hezekiah wept sore and besought Yahweh, who sent word through Isaiah that his prayer had been heard and that fifteen years would be added to his life; in token, the shadow should turn backward ten steps on the sun dial staircase of Ahaz.[15]

Thus incited by Micah and Isaiah, Hezekiah followed up his declaration of independence by a religious reformation. Once more Yahweh was the national God, the images of Ashur and the king were broken up, the asherah cut down, and the high places removed. Nehushtan, the bronze serpent to which Judah burnt incense, according to tradition made by Moses to save his people from a plague of snakes,[16] was likewise destroyed. The great altar had been defiled by sacrifice to Ashur and the king, whose images had equally defiled the temple itself, and rites of purification were demanded. Through union of the old nomadic spring feast and the agricultural feast of unleavened bread held at the same time, the passover was assuming its later form; a great passover celebrated the puri-

---

[13]K. Marti, *Dodekapropheton*, 258 ff.; J. M. P. Smith, *Micah, Zephaniah, and Nahum*, 1911; W. Nowack, *Die Kleinen Propheten*, 195 ff.; E. Sellin, *Zwölfprophetenbuch*, 302 ff.
[14]Jer. 26:16 ff.
[15]Isaiah 38:1-8; II Kings 20:1-11.   [16]Num. 21:4 ff.

fication of the temple, and the inhabitants of the former northern kingdom were invited to take part in the hope that Judah's influence might thus be extended. Perhaps at this time began the collection of the northern religious literature

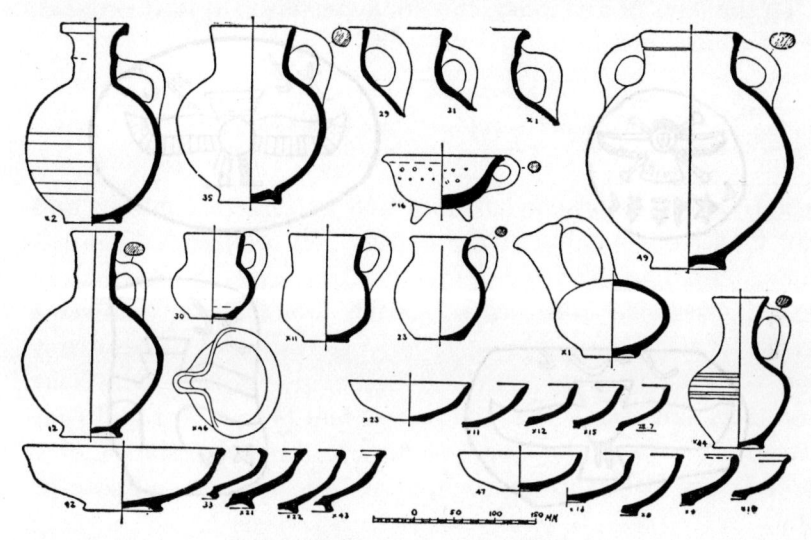

FIG. 171. HEBREW POTTERY, 800–600.

for future use in the south. Shrines outside the capital were destroyed and religious centralisation brought one step nearer.[17]

Fiscal reorganisations followed. Royal storehouses for the tax in grain, new wine, and oil were built, and royal potteries for the jars in which the tribute was to be forwarded were established at Netaim and Gederah where excellent clay was to be found. Fragments of these jars are numerous; they bear a scarab with four wings and are inscribed "For the king" with the addition of Hebron, Socoh, Ziph, or Memshath, the capitals of the four provinces formed by Solomon in southern territory.[18]

Shortly thereafter, Hezekiah received an embassy from the

[17] II Kings 18:1 ff.; II Chron. 29 ff.
[18] Fig. 172; II Chron. 32:28; I Chron. 4:23; cf. W. F. Albright, *JPOS.*, V, 1925, 44 ff.

466   PALESTINE AND SYRIA

Chaldæan Merodach Baladan, who had recently usurped the throne of Babylon and had met Sargon in what was at least a drawn battle. Alliance with the most successful of Sargon's opponents was certainly worldly wisdom, and Hezekiah showed

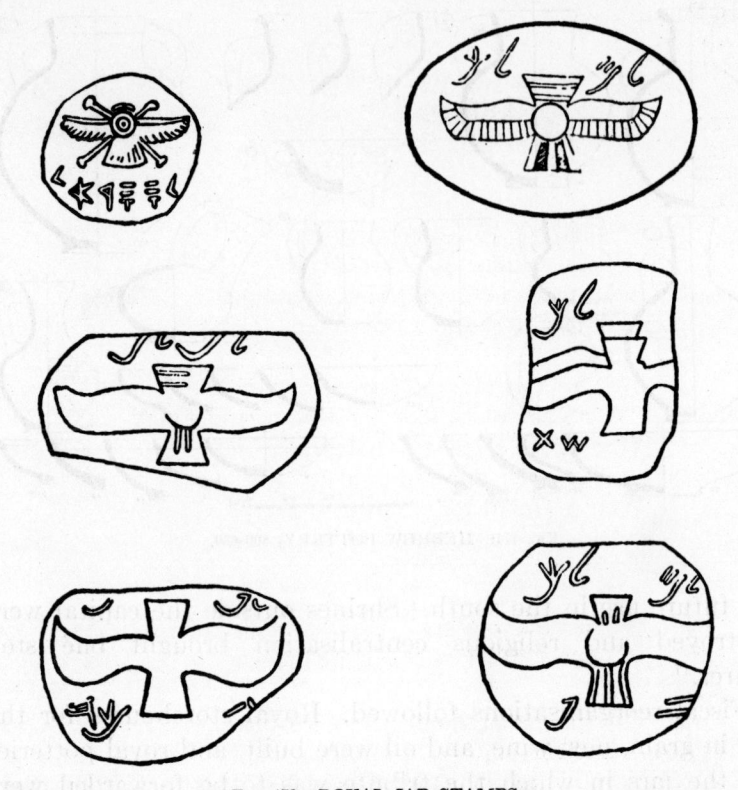

FIG. 172. ROYAL JAR STAMPS.

the ambassadors all his wealth and his armory. Much as Isaiah urged political and religious independence, he was opposed to foreign entanglements; should Judah remain neutral and trust in Yahweh, Yahweh would bring salvation. When Hezekiah admitted his exhibition of his resources, Isaiah declared that all these treasures in days to come should be carried to Babylon, but the young king selfishly replied: "Good is the

[19] Isaiah 39; II Kings 20:12-19.

word which Yahweh has spoken, provided only there is peace and righteousness in my days."[19]

Egypt was now ruled by the Thebans returned from Ethiopia,[20] and once again the Syrians were hoping for Egyptian assistance. Isaiah was no more pro-Egyptian than pro-Babylonian:

> Ah, the land of the rustling of wings,
>   Beyond Ethiopia's rivers,
> That messengers sends by the sea,
>   Papyrus boats on the waters.
>
> Depart, ye swiftest envoys,
>   To a nation tall and smooth,
> To a people fearful, down treading,
>   Whose land the rivers divide.[21]
>
> Woe to the rebel children,
>   Who complete a purpose—not from me!
> Who strike a treaty—not my spirit!
>   That they may add sin to sin!
> Who set forth to go down to Egypt,
>   But have not asked of my mouth,
> To flee to Pharaoh's fortress,
>   Take refuge in Egypt's shade;
> So your shame shall be Pharaoh's fortress,
>   Your confusion be Egypt's shade!
>
> For though at Zoan are his princes,
>   And his envoys to Hanes come,
> Yet all shall be shamed by a folk that cannot aid them,
>   That bring no help but shame and disgrace.
> By the beasts of the land of the Negeb,
>   Through a country of distress and trouble,
> From whence come the lioness and lion,
>   The viper and the flying dragon,
> They bear on asses' backs their riches,
>   Their treasures on the humps of camels,
> To a people that cannot aid them,
>   For Egypt's help is vain and to no purpose.

[20]Breasted, *History of Egypt*, 537 ff.   [21]Isaiah 18:1–6.

Such language to men who were expecting speedy aid from Egypt could not be popular. As Isaiah puts it, they said to the seers: "See not," and to the prophets: "Prophesy not to us right things, speak to us smooth things, predict illusions; leave the way, turn aside from the path, abolish out of our sight the Holy One of Israel." Therefore the Holy One of Israel says: "Because you reject this word and trust in wile and guile, this guilt shall be to you a breach ready to fall, bulging out in a high wall, whose breaking comes suddenly in an instant." He shall break it like a potter's vessel, there shall not be found among the pieces a sherd large enough to take fire from the hearth or dip water from the cistern. In returning and rest should they have been saved and in confidence should have been their strength but they would not. They said: "No, but we will fly on horses," therefore shall they flee, "We will ride on the swift," so swift shall be their pursuers. A thousand shall flee at the shout of one or five, till they be left as a pole on a mountain top or a signal on a hill.[22]

"Woe to those who descend to Egypt for help and rely on horses, who trust to chariots because they are strong, but do not ask oracle of Yahweh. Yet he too is wise and can bring evil to pass, will not recall his words but will rise against the evil-doer's house. The Egyptians are men and not gods, their horses are not spirit; when Yahweh stretches out his hand, he that helps shall stumble and he that is helped shall fall and they shall all be consumed together. As the lion with his young cub growls over his prey and though a multitude of shepherds be called forth against him he will not be dismayed by their shout or cast down by their noise, so Yahweh of Hosts shall come down to fight against Mount Zion and upon its hill."[23]

Shebna, the Aramæan chamberlain of the palace, was the leader of the pro-Egyptian party; as a foreigner and presumably a eunuch, Isaiah pours out his wrath against him: "What right have you to be here and whom have you here as kinsman, that you are hewing a tomb on high and carving a

[22] Isaiah 30.   [23] Isaiah 31.

home in the rock? Lo, Yahweh will hurl you, O man, will hurl you away into a wide extending country and there you shall die; there shall be your glorious tomb, you shame of your lord's house! I shall thrust you down from your station and you shall be pulled down from your office; then I shall call my servant Eliakim, Hilkiah's son, and clothe him with your robe and bind him with your girdle, your authority I shall commit to his hand, he shall be a father to Jerusalem's inhabitants and the house of Judah, the key of David's house shall I lay on his back, he shall open and none shall shut, shall shut and none shall open. I shall drive him as a peg into a sure place, he shall be a seat of honour to his father's house; on him shall they hang all the honour of his father's house, offspring and issue, all small vessels from the bowls to the flagons." Before long, the prophecy was fulfilled, Shebna was demoted to the secretariate while Eliakim was made chamberlain.[24]

The treaty of Bocchoris with Assyria did not prevent Egyptian intrigue in Palestine. Azuri of Ashdod withheld his tribute in 714, but the Assyrians placed his brother Ahimiti on the throne. Ahimiti in turn was deposed by Iamani, the "Ionian" from Cyprus, the first appearance of a Greek in the history of Palestine. Ashkelon was held loyal by Rukibti, but Gath, Judah, Moab, and Ammon joined the rebels. Isaiah naturally opposed Hezekiah's action; as sign of the coming deportation, he loosed the sackcloth from his loins and the sandals from his feet and thus half clad went about Jerusalem three years. This was the oracle: "As my servant Isaiah has walked naked and barefoot for three years, a sign and an omen against Egypt and Ethiopia, so shall the king of Assyria lead away the captives of Egypt and the exiles of Ethiopia, young and old, naked and barefoot, the shame of Egypt; they shall be dismayed and ashamed because of Ethiopia their expectation and of Egypt their boasting."[25]

Sargon hastily despatched his turtanu Ashur-isqa-danin with the four hundred and twenty soldiers of his body guard. Azekah, behind massive walls on a steep broad-topped hill

[24] Isaiah 22:15 ff.; cf. 36:3.   [25] Isaiah 20.

commanding a splendid level plain covered with grain and olives and with a view over the whole Philistine plain, was quickly captured. Ashdod was in the open plain, but the Ionian had surrounded it with a trench and brought water from outside; when he heard of Azekah's fall, he fled to Egypt, but was returned by the Egyptian monarch, not yet ready to try conclusions with Assyria. Men in long robes and helmets with neck pieces defended Ekron on a low hill by the water, but in vain. Other Philistines in fringed blankets which covered the head and fell down over the left shoulder defended the high isolated rock which was the acropolis of Gezer's Baal, but the eunuch general constructed a ramp up which two rams were driven and the acropolis was taken. Ashdod was made a province, the Philistine cities were rebuilt and resettled with colonists, Sargon claims that he possessed all the desert to the dry river bed of Egypt. The four hundred and twenty men of the body guard were too few to attack Hezekiah, so this time Judah and the trans-Jordanic states escaped punishment.[26]

[26]For this chapter cf. *History of Assyria,* 206 ff.

CHAPTER XXXI

THE ROD OF YAHWEH'S ANGER

SARGON's death in battle (705) brought new hope to Syria. Hezekiah levied an army, introduced mercenary Arabs into Jerusalem, and renewed the alliance with Tyre, whose king Elu-eli was now the dominant personality in southern Phœnicia. Ashdod ejected its governor and re-established the kingship with Mitinti, and Zedekiah of Ashkelon followed his example. Padi of Ekron held steadfast to his oath, but his subjects placed him in fetters and sent him to Hezekiah for safekeeping.

With the exception of Ashdod, the provinces remained quiet. Menahem of Shimron-meron, Uri-milk of Gebal, and Abd-elot of Arvad held the north Phœnician cities true. The east Jordan peoples, Ammon under Bodel, Moab under Chemosh-nadab, and Edom under Melech-ram, now were partisans of Assyria, for they feared no danger to their desert borders and they hoped for revenge against their Hebrew foes. Within the revolted territory itself there was far from unanimity. A pro-Assyrian party under Ittobaal of Sidon contested south Phœnicia with Tyre. Padi had his partisans in Ekron; Sil Bel of Gaza refused to join with the other Philistine cities. In Judah itself, the prophet Isaiah was, if not pro-Assyrian, at least opposed to Judæan participation in the war of independence. While Padi was being brought in chains to Jerusalem, Isaiah issued an oracle against the Philistines:

> Rejoice not, united Philistines,
>   That the rod which smote you is broken;
> Comes an asp from the root of the serpent,
>   His fruit is a snake fiery and flying.
>
> Howl, O gate! cry, O city!
>   Let united Philistia faint!

> From the north a smoke is coming,
> No straggler is in his ranks.[1]

The "asp" made his appearence in 701. Merodach Baladan had been driven into the swamps, an Assyrian nominee was on his throne, the Babylonian question was apparently settled. Sennacherib first fired the summer house of Elu-eli in the Lebanon, a palace of well-cut ashlar with open balcony among two and three story residences with flat roofs, square doors, and numerous tiny upper windows; its vineyards were trampled down, its furniture and vases, horses and chariots were spoiled.[2] The Assyrians then climbed the higher slopes, working their way up by spears or clubs and resting under the cedars, to a castle on the tree-clad summit, whose prisoners were led manacled to Sennacherib, enthroned in his camp. A rock sculpture was cut on the cliffs by the Dog River, and Ittobaal surrendered Sidon with its suburbs, Lesser Sidon and Beth Zeth, the "House of Oil." Zarephath, where Elu-eli had stored food and drink for his garrisons, surrendered without fighting. Tyre was besieged, and the Assyrian archers from behind their wicker shields rained arrows upon the battlemented shield-hung citadel at the mountain foot. No aid came from Egypt. Elu-eli therefore handed over his children to his wife, who was already on board ship by the arched water gate flanked by four Ionic columns; embarking himself on one of the biremes, he set sail for Cyprus, where he died some time before 694.

Now Isaiah might hope that Hezekiah would make terms with the invader; his oracle on the fall of Tyre is a veritable pæan:

> Howl, ships of Tarsus, destroyed is your haven,
> From the land of Cyprus 'tis revealed to them;
> Be dumb, coastland dwellers, merchants of Sidon,
> Who cross the sea, merchants on the waves;
> Whose harvest is the grain of Horus' Waters,
> Whose revenue is the nations' trade.

[1]Isaiah 14:29, 31; cf. K. Fullerton, *AJSL.*, XLII, 1926, 86 ff.; W. A. Irwin, *AJSL.*, XLIV, 1928, 73 ff.
[2]Fig. 122, *History of Assyria*.

Be shamed, Sidon, for the sea has spoken,
    The stronghold of the sea:
I have neither travailed nor brought forth,
    Neither nourished youths nor brought up maids;
When the report comes unto Egypt,
    They will be for Tyre sorely pained.

    Cross to Tarsus and howl,
        Inhabitants of the coast!
    Does it fare with you thus, joyous one,
        Of origin from ancient days,
    Whose feet once carried her
        Afar off to sojourn?
    Who has purposed this
        Gainst Tyre, bestower of crowns,
    Whose merchants were like to a prince,
        Whose traders the honored of earth?

    Yahweh of Hosts it has purposed,
        To profane all glorious pride,
    To disgrace all of earth's honoured.
        Overflow your land as the Nile,
    O daughter of Tarsus,
        No longer a girdle have you!
    He has stretched out his hand o'er the waters,
        He has shaken the kingdoms,
    Yahweh has commanded of Canaan
        To destroy her fortified towers.

    No more shall you rejoice,
        Ravished virgin daughter of Sidon,
    Rise up, to Cyprus cross,
        Even there you shall find no comfort.

From the flight of Elu-eli, Isaiah turns to the flight of Merodach Baladan, late ally of Hezekiah:

    Consider the land of the Chaldæans,
        This people no more exists,
    For the Assyrians have it appointed
        As the abode of desert jinns.
    They set their siege towers against them,
        Their palaces hurled into ruin,

> So howl, you ships of Tarsus,
>   For thus is your fortress laid waste.[3]

In reward for his loyalty, Ittobaal was given Tyre. Mahalliba, Ushu, Achzib, and Accho surrendered. The few remaining Syrian kings made their homage at Ushu, and with them the repentant Mitinti of Ashdod. Tyrian, Sidonian, and Cypriote shipbuilders constructed the Assyrian fleet of 694 at Nineveh and sailed it across the Persian Gulf to Elam.

Isaiah was torn between his patriotism and his prophetic duty; his changing attitude appears clearly in his next oracle:

> Woe to you, Ashur, rod of my anger,
>   Staff, in whose hand is my indignation!
> 'Gainst an impious nation I sent him,
>   And 'gainst the people of my wrath,
> To make spoil and seize prey gave him order,
>   And to trample them like mire of the streets.

But Ashur does not so limit his plan; in his heart is to destroy and to cut off not a few nations. He says: "Are not all my princes kings? Is not Calno as Carchemish, Hamath as Arpad, Samaria as Damascus? As my hand found the kingdoms of idols, though their images excelled those of Jerusalem and Samaria, shall I not, as I've done to Samaria and her idols, so do to Jerusalem and her idols?"

> By the strength of my hand have I done it,
>   By my wisdom, for I have understanding;
> I have moved the bounds of the peoples,
>   Have cast down like a hero the rulers.
> My hand has found as a nest,
>   The riches of the peoples;
> As one gathers abandoned eggs,
>   The whole earth have I gathered;
> There was none that fluttered a wing,
>   Or opened a beak or chirped.

So closely does Isaiah's language parallel the inscriptions of Sennacherib that we are almost convinced the prophet must

[3] Isaiah 23:1-14.

THE ROD OF YAHWEH'S ANGER

have read his boast of his wisdom and of how through his own understanding new technological processes were invented;[4] Isaiah has his reply: "Shall the axe boast itself against its wielder? Shall the saw magnify itself against the one who draws it? As if a rod could move its lifter! As if a staff could lift up one not wood! Yahweh of Hosts will send leanness against his fattest parts, under his glory will be kindled the burning of fire, which shall consume the glory of thicket and field, and the remnant of his forest trees shall be so few that a child may write them down."[5]

Isaiah expected the invader to advance along the hill road direct upon Jerusalem, and he gives a vivid description of the expected march: "He has gone up from Pene Rimmon, he is coming to Ai, he is passing through Migron, at Michmash he is storing the baggage, they are crossing the gorge, they are lodging at Geba. Ramah is trembling, Saul's city of Gibeah is in flight, cry aloud, daughter of Gallim, listen, O Laishah, Anathoth, answer her. Madmenah is a fugitive, the inhabitants of Gebim are fleeing to save their goods. He is halting in Nob, he is shaking his fist against the mount of Zion's daughter, the hill of Jerusalem."[6]

The prophet was forgetting the awaited doom in his patriotism:

> Behold, the Lord Yahweh of Hosts
> Will lop off the boughs with a terrible crash,
> And the high of stature shall be hewn down,
> And the lofty shall be brought low.
> With iron shall he cut down the forest glades,
> And Lebanon shall fall through a Glorious One.[7]

"Surely as I have planned so shall it come to pass, and as I have purposed, so shall it stand, to break the Assyrian in my land, and on my mountain tread him under foot. This is the purpose which is purposed concerning the whole earth, and this is the hand that is outstretched over all the nations; it is

[4] *History of Assyria*, 320 ff.
[5] Isaiah 10:5–19.
[6] Isaiah 10:27–32; cf. W. F. Albright, *Ann.*, IV, 134 ff.   [7] Isaiah 10:33 f.

Yahweh of Hosts who has purposed and who can annul it, his the outstretched hand and who can turn it back?"[8]

Jerusalem however enjoyed a brief respite, for Sennacherib did not follow the expected route but passed without opposition through the province of Dor into the plain of Sharon, where he captured Beth Dagon, Joppa, Bene Barak, and Azur, once Danite and now possessions of Ashkelon. He found the Egyptian army led by a youth of twenty, Taharka, Shabaka's nephew,[9] and ensconced behind the protection of the Jamnia stream at Eltekeh; they were defeated and the commanders of the Egyptian and Ethiopian chariotry together with the sons of the Egyptian kings fell into his hands. The capture of Eltekeh and Timnah was followed by that of Ekron; the rebels were killed and their bodies hung about the cities on poles, their followers were made captive, the pro-Assyrian party was again placed in power. Padi was still imprisoned in Jerusalem, and must be recovered, but Sennacherib had no time to waste on the mountain fortress and the rab shaqe or commander-in-chief was sent to negotiate.

Hezekiah had made his preparations. Missiles and weapons had been made in abundance. Millo in the City of David was strengthened, the ruinous Jebusite wall was restored with towers; closely parallel to this was a new outer wall, the polygonal face neatly plastered and with stone and earth filling, but so hastily built that the foundations rested as a rule on the soil and not on the rock.[10] Hezekiah then took counsel with his advisers and determined to stop the waters of the fountains outside the city and the brook that flowed through the midst of the land, for they said: "Why should the king of Assyria come and find much water?" So Hezekiah made the pool and the conduit and brought water into the city, he stopped the upper springs of the waters of Gihon and brought them straight down on the west side of the City of David.[11]

---

[8] Isaiah 14:24–27. [9] Breasted, *Rec.*, IV, 455 ff.
[10] II Chron. 32:5; Macalister-Duncan, *Excavations on Hill of Ophel*, 65 ff., 87.
[11] II Chron. 32:2–4; II Kings 20:20; cf. Isaiah 22:9–11.

Thus was constructed the tunnel, winding over seventeen hundred feet through the rock directly underneath Ophel. Just inside the southern entrance was the inscription: "Behold the piercing through! And this was the manner of the piercing through: While yet the miners were lifting up the pick, each toward his neighbour, and while yet there were

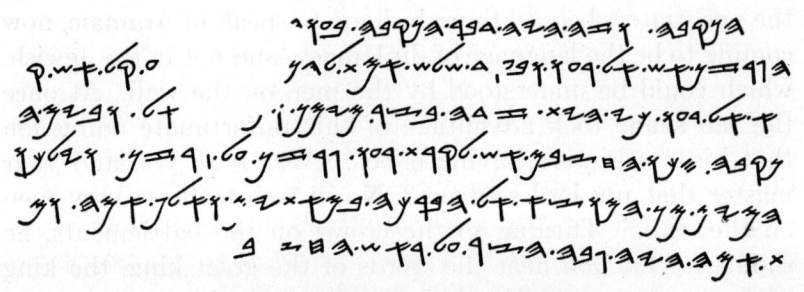

FIG. 173. THE SILOAM INSCRIPTION.

three cubits to be pierced through, there was heard the voice of each calling to his neighbour, for there was a fissure in the rock on the right hand. And on the day of the piercing through the miners smote each so as to meet his neighbour, pick against pick, and the waters flowed from the source to the pool, twelve hundred cubits, and one hundred cubits was the height of the rock over the heads of the miners."[12]

The rab shaqe took his stand by the conduit of the upper pool on the highway of the fuller's field, where Isaiah had encountered Ahaz. There he was met by the Judæan ambassadors, Eliakim, Hilkiah's son, who had succeeded Shebna as ruler of the household, Shebna himself, now royal scribe, and Joah, Asaph's son, the chancellor. Shebna may have written down the rab shaqe's speech, which presents the essence of Assyrian imperial theory: "Say to Hezekiah: Thus says the great king, the king of Assyria: In what have you trusted? Is not your strength for war but useless talking together and vain words? On whom do you trust that you have rebelled against me? Behold, you have trusted to Egypt, this staff of a

[12]Fig. 173; Cooke, *Text Book*, 15 ff.

shattered reed, which has pierced the hand of him who leaned upon it. But if you say: 'It is Yahweh, our God, in whom we trust,' then exchange pledges with my lord the king, and I will give you two thousand horses if you can place riders upon them. In truth, it was by order of Yahweh himself that I have come up against this land to war against it."

Horrified at this claim of approval by the national deity, the negotiators begged the rab shaqe to speak in Aramaic, now coming to be the language of diplomacy, and not in the Jewish, which could be understood by the men on the wall. At once the rab shaqe took advantage of this unfortunate admission that his words were having effect: "Was it to you and your master that my lord sent me? No, it was to these very men on the wall." Turning to the crowd on the battlements, he shouted: "Do *you* hear the words of the great king, the king of Assyria? Let not Hezekiah deceive you with empty words, for he cannot deliver, neither let him tell you that the gods will deliver you so that this city will not fall into the hands of the king. For he says: Make a treaty with me and every man shall eat of his own vine and fig tree and drink the water of his own cistern until I come and take you away to a land like your own, a land of grain and wine, of bread and vineyards. Let not Hezekiah seduce you by saying that the gods will deliver you. Has any of the gods of the other nations delivered his land from the hands of the Assyrian king? Where are the gods of Hamath and Arpad? Where is the god of Sepharvaim? Have their gods delivered Samaria out of my hand? Who of all these nations has delivered his land out of my hand that the gods should deliver Jerusalem out of my hand?"

By the king's order, the men on the wall made no reply, but they had heard the offer and they might purchase peace by the murder of their monarch. Hezekiah rent his garments, covered himself with sackcloth, and entered the temple to beg aid, while the elders, with Eliakim and Shebna, were sent to Isaiah: "This day is a day of trouble and punishment and contumely and wrath. Perchance Yahweh your God will hear the words of the rab shaqe, sent by the king of Assyria, and will deal punishment for the words which Yahweh your God has heard; therefore lift up your prayer to Yahweh your God for the remnant that is left."

The actual presence of the enemy at the gate completed the change in Isaiah, and he responded with one of his finest prophecies:

She hath despised thee and scorned thee, the virgin of Zion,
   Behind thee her head hath shaken, Jerusalem's daughter.
Against whom hast thou brought reproach, thy voice uplifted?
   Thou hast lifted on high thine eyes, against Israel's Holy,
By the hands of thy slaves made reproach against Yahweh, saying:
   I, with my chariots massed, will act like a hero,
Will ascend to the heights of the hills, to Lebanon's corners,
   Will cut down its highest cedars, its cypresses choicest.
I have digged and have drunk from waters foreign,
   With the soles of my feet will dry all the rivers of Egypt.

Hast thou not heard how long ago I made it,
   From days of old it fashioned, but now have brought it,
To make desolate heaps of ruins from fortified cities,
   And their dwellers were weak of hand, dismayed and confounded?
They became as grass of the field, as the herb in its greenness,
   As green grass on the roofs, as grain blasted before it was standing.
Before me thy rise and returning, thy in and outgoing,
   Thy raging I know, to my ears there cometh thy uproar.
I will put my hook in thy nose, in thy lips my bridle,
   And will turn thee back on the road by which thou camest.

As sign: "This year you shall eat the aftergrowth, the second year what grows by itself, the third year you shall sow and reap and plant vineyards and secure the fruits." The Assyrian king "shall not come into this city nor shoot an arrow there nor shall he come before it with shield nor build a mound against it; by the way he came, by that shall he return, saith Yahweh."[13]

Sennacherib boasts how he shut up the strong and proud Hezekiah like a bird in a cage in Jerusalem, how he threw up earthworks against him and turned back to his misery any

---

[13]Isaiah 36–39; II Kings 18:13–20:19; cf. *AJSL.*, XXXI, 1915, 196 ff.

who attempted to leave by the gate, how his picked troops and mercenary Arabs deserted Hezekiah. The horses, mules, asses, camels, cattle, and sheep were carried off, with ramps, siege engines, mines and tunnels forty-six walled cities and their numberless suburbs were taken, two hundred thousand one hundred fifty prisoners were made; the whole population of the western slope was not so great, and the one hundred and fifty to which the huge round number is affixed is nearer the truth. Next year we find one of these captives sold in Assyria.

Sennacherib himself continued the reduction of the other Philistine cities, whose portly inhabitants wore the long robe with many-folded girdle, their hair bunched on the neck with the headdress of high feathers worn by their first ancestors. Outside Ashdod were rock gardens planted with rows of trees and a hanging garden supported by entablatures and proto-Corinthian columns. Double-headed ferry boats and skin rafts floated in Iamani's canal, drawn from a deep river, arched gateways and ramps led from the outer wall to the inner. Mitinti again made his submission, Zedekiah of Ashkelon was deported and his place filled by Rukibti's son Sharru-ludari, the loyal Sil Bel of Gaza received his lord, and Sennacherib advanced the sixteen miles to Lachish.

Sennacherib pitched his camp by the water holes on the tongue of land between the two dry stream beds. His opponents, protected by round shields and pointed helmets with ear lappets, increased the height of their walls by wooden platforms hung with the same round shields, knocked down the men raising scaling ladders, and threw stones and lighted torches on the wicker shields and wooden sheds of their assailants. Behind a line of kneeling archers and another of crouching footmen the main assault was prepared, supported by spearmen and slingers, with horsemen and chariots in reserve. Ten ramps were constructed for the seven "tanks" with inclosed battering rams. Lachish was taken and destroyed, the prisoners were impaled, flayed, or decapitated, and the survivors were carried off in their ox-drawn carts.[14]

[14]Figs. 123, 126, 127, *History of Assyria*.

From Lachish, the Assyrians advanced upon Libnah, but while besieging that city news arrived that Taharka was coming up with fresh forces. According to the Hebrew writer, the angel of Yahweh smote in the Assyrian camp a hundred and eighty-five thousand warriors, and Sennacherib broke camp and departed. Herodotus reports an Egyptian story to the effect that when the two armies came face to face at Pelusium field mice ate up the quivers, bow strings, and shield straps, and the invaders, unable to use their weapons, were slaughtered.[15] Angel of Yahweh and field mice alike are elsewhere connected with the pest, and the actual cause of the Assyrian retreat may have been that bubonic plague, which more than once before had stopped Assyrian advance in the west.

Whatever the cause, Sennacherib abandoned hope of further conquest, and negotiated a treaty with Shabaka. No attempt was made to create new provinces, Ashdod was permitted to retain its king. Jerusalem had not been taken, but Hezekiah had seen his whole countryside laid desolate; he was allowed to retain his throne and his Judæan possessions, but the territory he had won from the Philistines was returned to Mitinti, Padi, and Sil Bel. He paid up the tribute in arrears, and after Sennacherib's return to Nineveh sent a contribution of thirty talents of gold, eight hundred of silver, precious stones, antimony, carnelian, ivory seats and couches, elephant hides and raw ivory, maple and box wood, coloured woollen cloths and linen chitons, violet and purple wool, metal vessels, chariots, shields, lances, armour, iron daggers, bows, arrows, and spears.

Sennacherib's policy was justified. Egypt kept the peace and there were no fresh revolts. Isaiah's prestige was high and Jerusalem, saved from the foe and thus proved the special protégé of Yahweh, tended to supplant the ravaged older shrines in the minds of the people. This was a long step towards monotheism.

[15] II Kings 19:35 ff.; Herod., ii, 141.

CHAPTER XXXII

REACTION

SENNACHERIB's retreat had placed the seal of Yahweh's approval on the prophecies of Isaiah, and Hezekiah continued faithful to Assyria. In this respect, Manasseh (693-639) followed in the footsteps of his father.[1] Hezekiah's religious policy was less successful. Isaiah, Micah, and their companions had progressed far beyond the thought of the conservative countrymen, whose influence was strong with the twelve-year-old Manasseh. The high places were rebuilt, an asherah set up, an altar raised for Baal as a manifestation of Yahweh, once again the shaveling priests burnt incense in the villages. Manasseh himself made his sons pass through the fire, the sacrifice in Tophet to the god king Melech. As a loyal servant of Ashur, his worship was reintroduced with that of the Assyrian king, and this in turn added to the prestige of Melech. Altars were built on the roof of the upper chamber of Ahaz in connection with the stepped sun dial, altars for the sun, moon, zodiacal signs, and all the host of heaven were to be found in the temple and its court. There were processional chariots dedicated to the sun under the charge of the chamberlain Nathan Melech, whose father had thus designated his son as the gift of the king god. Ishtar, the Babylonian mother-goddess, appeared as the Queen of Heaven, whose obscene images were produced in great numbers, her son and lover Tammuz was bewailed by the Jerusalem women.[2]

Isaiah's partisans in the capital naturally opposed this reaction. Manasseh, we are told, shed innocent blood very much, until he had filled Jerusalem from one end to the other, which meant that there was renewed persecution of the

[1] Cf. L. E. Fuller, *Reign of Manasseh*, 1912.
[2] II Kings 21:5; 23; Jer. 7:17 ff.; 44:15 ff.; Ezek. 8:14.

prophets. Some recollection of these persecutions may be preserved in the late tradition that Isaiah was sawn asunder.[3]

Manasseh remained loyal throughout the reign of Sennacherib (705–681) into that of his son Esarhaddon (681–668). Esarhaddon's accession had been marred by the war with his parricide brothers, while in Egypt Shabataka (700–688) had been deposed by his abler cousin Taharka (688–663). Trusting in Egyptian aid, Abd-melkart of Sidon revolted, and it was not until 677 that his city was taken and its wall cast into the waters. Abd-melkart fled to the midst of the sea but was drawn out like a fish and decapitated. Looted alabaster vases which once contained oil from his palace may yet be seen. Sidon was removed from the reef to the mainland and renamed Kar-Ashur-ahi-iddina, "Esarhaddon's Fort," which became the capital of the "Sealand" province; to it were assigned the former Sidonian possessions, the cities about Biru or Beirut, such as Bit Supuri, Inimme, Hildua; Gebal with its dependency Batrun remained independent, but to the north the province continued with Kilme or Calamus, Bitirti or Bruttus, Sagu, the Amarna Shigata, and Ampa, the Ambi of the Amarna letters.[4]

Among the kings of the Hittite land and seacoast who assisted in the siege was Sidon's deadly rival, Baal of Tyre. He was rewarded with the gift of the former Sidonian cities, Marub and Zarephath, and a treaty was granted him. Should Baal sin against the oath, the gods will punish him: Gula, the healing goddess, is to inflict sickness, the seven war gods are to strike him down with their weapons, the Bethels and Anath are to abandon him to the claws of a hungry lion. The great gods of heaven and earth, the gods of Assyria and Akkad, with the gods of Ebir Nari, the land "Across the River," will curse him with a curse that cannot be turned. Baal of the heavens, Baal Melkart, the Baal of the North, will send evil winds against the ship, break the cables, smite down the mast, sink the ship in the mighty flood, bring a hurricane upon

[3] Talmud Bab., Jabmuth, iv, 13; cf. Hebrews, 11:37.
[4] V. Scheil, *Le Prisme S d'Assaraddon*, 1914; cf. Forrer, *Provinzeinteilung*, 65.

them. Milkili and Eshmun will destroy the land, lead its inhabitants into captivity, destroy the food for their mouths, the crumbs for their bodies, the oil for their anointing. Ishtar will break their bows in battle, bring them under the feet of their foes, make them captive. Baal is to obey the resident who has authority over him. If Baal smites a ship, whether his own or of Arvad, in Palestine or on any Assyrian border, everything in the ship belongs to Esarhaddon, but the people on board are to be freed. Regulations are also made for the land trade with Arpad, Accho, Dor, now an Assyrian province in the land of Palestine, the cities on the Assyrian border, on the seacoast, Gebal, Mount Lebanon, the cities on the mountain.[5]

Syria could never be quiet while Egypt was independent, and Esarhaddon determined on its subjugation. The bridgehead to Egypt was secured by the capture of Arza at the Nahal Misri, the "Dry River Bed of Egypt," where before the Great War Egypt held an advanced post at Arish, and its ruler Asuhili was made captive. Raids into the North Syrian desert cleared the flank from Arab menace.[6]

When Esarhaddon had begun his armory, some time after 677, the twelve seacoast kings made their contribution. Baal of Tyre and Manasseh of Judah head the list as the two most important. In addition to Baal we find Mattenbaal of Arvad, Milk-asaph of Gebal, and Abi-baal of Shimron-meron among the Phœnicians, four Philistine cities, Ashdod under Ahimelech, Ekron under a second Achish, Ashkelon under Mitinti, and Gaza under Sil Bel, retained their autonomy; these coast kings had been allowed independence, since their trade might be destroyed and their tribute suffer were they reduced to provinces. With the exception of Judah, all the interior was administered directly by Assyrian governors. East of the Jordan, and permitted to retain independence because they held the border against the desert, were Pudiel of Ammon, Musuri, the "Egyptian," of Moab, and Chemosh-gaber of Edom. A

---

[5]Correct *History of Assyria*, 375, from Luckenbill, *Rec.*, II, 229 ff.
[6]*History of Assyria*, 374 ff.

letter to the Assyrian king reports that the royal governors have brought two manas of gold from the men of the house of Ammon, one mana of gold from the Moabites, ten manas of silver from the Judæans, about twelve manas of silver from probably the Edomites, and an unknown contribution from the men of Gebal.[7]

Once Egypt was Assyrian, the days of even a theoretical independence for the Syrian princes were numbered. Yakin-el, Matten-baal's successor at Arvad, Baal of Tyre, the king of Ashkelon, and Manasseh all determined to ally themselves with Taharka. Manasseh built an outer wall to David's Town on the west side of Gihon in the valley at the entrance to the Fish Gate, Ophel was surrounded by a wall and raised to a great height, valiant captains were placed in all the cities of Judah. Manasseh's son was named Amon in honour of the greatest Egyptian god; its significance was political rather than religious, for nationalistic revolt was once more accompanied by nationalistic religion. The foreign gods and the idol, among which we must include the images of Ashur and the king, were removed from the temple and all the altars to foreign divinities were taken away from the capital. The altar of Yahweh was rebuilt and the usual peace and thank-offerings were again sacrificed. Judah was commanded to serve Yahweh, the God of Israel.[8]

Esarhaddon collected the troops of the Syrian states which had remained true to their allegiance. Nergal-ballit informed his lord that the Philistine contingent organised by the king was still loyal and was stationed at Lachish.[9] Egypt was invaded in 675, but two years later the Assyrians were badly defeated and were forced to retire. The disaffection in Syria became more pronounced. Nabu-shum-iddina reported that the men of Ebir Nari would not come.[10] Esarhaddon inquires of his god whether, if he goes against Ashkelon, the Egyptians and their allies will fight in Ashkelonite territory; if he goes

[7] Waterman, *Royal Correspondence*, I, 440 f.; *AJSL.*, XLV, 1929, 284 f.
[8] II Chron. 33:14–16.
[9] Waterman, *op. cit.*, I, 148 f. [10] *Ibid.*, 48 f.

to Ebir Nari, will he again return from Ashkelon to his house? Ishtar-shum-eresh the astrologer has observed Mars return from the head of Leo and pass over Cancer and Gemini; this signifies end of the rule of the king of Amurru.[11] Akkullanu likewise observes that when Gemini approaches Mars there will be war in Amurru, brother will slay his brother in the palace. The prince, who is a wall of protection to the land, shall go to another land. Through the wicked revolt of its king, his gods shall cause him to hasten against his enemy.[12] A solar eclipse on the 20th of Tabitu, January, observed by Mar Ishtar, concerns the land of Amurru, whose king will die, his land will be reduced, a second time it will be destroyed. An army will immediately proceed against Amurru. Whoever speaks to the king about the land of Amurru or the land of the Hittites, whoever brings him this sign against the land of the Hittites or the Arabs, it is well, the king shall attain his wish.[13] By king of Amurru did they mean Baal of Tyre or Manasseh of Judah?

Baal remained safe on his island and Judah in her highlands, even Ashkelon was ignored. Esarhaddon plunged at once into the desert, passed Aphek of Simeon, Raphia, and the Dry River Bed of Egypt, and after incredible sufferings reached the Nile and conquered Egypt.

On his return, Ashkelon capitulated. Manasseh was carried captive to Babylon, where Esarhaddon loved to dwell. To Isaiah's Immanuel prophecy was now added: "Within sixty-five years shall Ephraim be broken to pieces, so that it shall not be a people"; sixty-five years from Pekah's invasion brings us to that of Esarhaddon. Doubtless Manasseh did not go into captivity alone; the waste territory was filled by Esarhaddon with other captives, who soon took up the worship of Yahweh. After a term of imprisonment, the chastened Manasseh was, in accordance with good Assyrian custom, returned to his throne.[14]

The task of punishing Tyre was assigned to Bel Harran-

[11] *Ibid.*, 364 f.   [12] *Ibid.*, 466 ff.   [13] *Ibid.*, 438 f.
[14] II Chron. 33:11–13; Isaiah 7:8; Ezra 4:2.

shadua, governor of Sidon. Earthworks on the mainland shut up Baal on his island and cut him off from food and drink. His favoured commercial treaty no longer held, the Greek kings of Cyprus were winning his commerce, his mainland cities were reduced and formed into the province of Dur Bel Harran-shadua, the "Wall" of the governor who was carrying on the siege. Baal was forced to make peace, to pay up his back tribute, and to hand over his daughters; thereafter he was confined to his island, for the mainland was occupied permanently by the Assyrians. Yakin-el surrendered Arvad and his daughter. Esarhaddon then carved his relief in the outdoor museum at the Dog River and told of his conquest of Egypt and the surrender of Ashkelon and Tyre. Samal was restored, with casemates for the Assyrian garrison, while a stele in the city gate depicted Esarhaddon holding a rope by which Baal and Taharka were ringed through the nose.[15]

The reign of Ashur-bani-apal (668–626) marked the height of Assyrian expansion. Shortly after the death of Taharka, 663, his successor Tanutamon drove the Assyrians from Egypt proper and Necho's son Psammetichus fled to Syria. Here he was subject of complaint by Ashipa, who had oversight of the border Arabs, but Ashur-bani-apal could do nothing. Egypt was recovered by the Assyrians, Thebes was sacked, and Assyrian rule established for a short time, but soon Psammetichus began his long and prosperous reign, which he counted from 663.

Ashur-bani-apal lists the same twelve Syrian states as his father, but Yakin-el is now king of Arvad and Ammi-nadab of Ammon. A seal of Adoni-pelet, servant of this same Ammi-nadab, ranks with the best from antiquity; the strong Assyrian influence exercised on even this border dependency is seen in the winged being with clawed feet and tightly curled tail who holds in his left hand a dagger and stands between crescent moon and sun. Elimaaz, son of Elisha, from Rabbath Ammon, bearded, in long girdled robe and Assyrian headdress,

[15]Fig. 146, *History of Assyria;* G. Smith, *Assyrian Eponym Canon,* n.d., 167 ff.; von Luschan, *Ausgrabungen in Sendschirli,* I, 11 ff.; pl. 1–5.

raises his right hand in prayer to the conical cap, half moon, and star on his seal. A terra cotta from Rabbath Ammon shows an Amazon-like woman with single breast, the other mutilated in Amazon fashion. Chemosh-yehi of Moab has placed his name under the protection of the winged disk.[16]

How Assyria was losing its grip on the Phœnicians is illustrated by a letter from the Assyrian fiscal agent Itti Shamash-balatsu, stationed at Arvad. He was not permitted to visit the island harbour, but must remain at the Assyrian harbour by Amurru, on the mainland. Yakin-el, he complains, will not allow ships to anchor at the king's wharf, but kills all the captains who sail there and destroys their ships. The merchants, even the king's companions, must bribe Yakin-el to secure commercial privileges. Yakin-el's death for the moment restored Assyrian control as his sons contended for the throne. Azi-baal was given royal approval, the others were kept in honourable captivity at court as rival candidates should Azi-baal attempt revolt.

Contemporary Phœnician art is well represented by objects of tribute or trade found in Nineveh or Ur. An ivory figure from the centre of an inlaid panel is at first sight pure Egyptian, with its wig supporting the uræus, its garment with projecting skirt accentuating rather than concealing the body, but the hands on breast prove it the Syrian mother-goddess. Fragments of ivory plaques show the Egyptian bud and lotus or a man whose belted tunic is bordered with varicolored lozenges of paste. Shells were engraved with winged sphinxes wearing the Egyptian double crown or with chariot horses. One from Sippar bears within a human head whose wings are cleverly fitted to the curve of the shell, without a god rises from a solar disk between two men on horseback.[17] From Ur comes an ivory pyxis where, under a garland of pointed leaves

---

[16] Fig. 176; C. C. Torrey, *Ann.*, II–III, 103 ff.; R. Brünnow, *Mitth. und Nachr., Deutsche Palästinaverein*, 1896, 4; Florence Bennett, *Amer. Jour. Archæology*, II Ser., XVI, 1912, 480 ff.; Comte de Vogüé, *Mél. arch. orientale*, 89.

[17] Fig. 158; L. W. King, *JEA.*, I, 1914, 107 ff., 237 ff.

Fig. 174. (*Upper Left*) SEAL OF ASAPH. (Megiddo.)
Fig. 175. (*Upper Right*) SEAL OF SHEMA, SERVANT OF JEROBOAM. (Megiddo.)
Fig. 176. (*Lower Left*) SEAL OF ADONIPELET, SERVANT OF AMMINADAB, KING OF AMMON.
Fig. 177. (*Lower Right*) SEAL OF ELISHAMA, SON OF GEDALIAH, WITH FIGURE OF YAHWEH.

Fig. 178. CYLINDERS, SEALS, AND JEWELER'S MOULD.
(Carchemish.)

beautifully carved and thoroughly Egyptian, dancing girls hold hands around the curved surface. The temple of E-nun-mah has given the lid of an ivory jewel casket which, according to the Phœnician inscription, was dedicated to Ashtart by Amat-baal, daughter of Pat-es; she reverences the Phœnician Baal, her mother, the Egyptian Isis. Another room presents the dedication of an ivory toilette set, plain comb, comb with beautiful bull engraving, sphinx paint pot, lotus column mirror handle, a second of white shell, tubular kohl pot and kohl stick, and lid of circular unguent box decorated with large flower rosette.[18]

The revolt of Shamash-shum-ukin, supported by the kings of Amurru and Egypt, seriously weakened Assyria in the west, but Ashur-bani-apal still had in his army men from Amqa, the great North Syrian swamp, and from Samaria; Sidonians could still be employed for shipbuilding on the Persian Gulf; there were captives from the Hittite land.[19] As Assyrian power declined, Syria was more and more subject to Arab attacks. Yatha, the most important Arab chief, had once acknowledged Assyrian overlordship, but later he aided Shamash-shum-ukin and now was plundering Syria. All along the border, from Edom and Seir, through Moab, Ammon, the Hauran, Hezron, to Zobah and Iabroda north of Damascus, local contingents or tributaries were fighting the nomads. Nabu-shum-lishir, the Assyrian governor, in a series of letters reports on the war with Ammuladi, king of Kedar, and his raids on the subject kings of Amurru; finally Ammuladi was captured by Chemosh-halteh, the new Moabite ruler. Other letters deal with the condition of Central Syria or report that all is well with the desert of Hamath. In the days of David, Zobah had been a powerful state in Hollow Syria; civil wars and Assyrian deportations had so reduced the population that its governor, Bel-liqbi, speaks of villages without inhabitants and urges that its fertile territory be occupied by Assyrian colonists. The reverse side of the picture is given by the book of Ezra, which

[18] C. L. Woolley, *Antiquaries Journal*, V, 382; VII, 410.
[19] Waterman, *op. cit.*, I, 480 f.; II, 58 f.; 202 f.

tells of men from Uruk, Babylon, and Susa, of Dahha and Elamites deported to Samaria and Across the River by Ashurbani-apal.[20]

Towards the end of the reign a last attempt was made to quell the nomads. From Damascus as a base an Assyrian force penetrated deep into the desert; the report is elaborate but the results were small. Ushu and Accho, doubtless at the instigation of Psammetichus, withheld their tribute; the men of Ushu were killed or made captive, the leaders at Accho were impaled and the citizens forced into the Assyrian army. Never again did Assyrian armies appear in Syria.[21]

Manasseh slept with his fathers, and his twenty-two-year-old son Amon (639–638) reigned in his stead. Amon remained true to Assyria and in religious affairs was a conservative; supported apparently by the reformers, his servants put him to death in his own house. Again the men of the country showed their opposition to the reforming movement by killing all the conspirators and placing the eight-year-old Josiah on the throne of his slain father.[22]

A new prophet was heard, Zephaniah, a descendant of Hezekiah, and so of the nobility. Nevertheless, he too preached a message of doom. Yahweh is about to consume utterly all things from the face of the ground, man and beast, birds of the sky and fish of the sea. He will stretch out his hand against Judah and Jerusalem and cut off Baal's last remnants and the name of the shaveling priests, those who worship heaven's hosts on the house tops, those who worship Yahweh but swear by Milcom.

Quite in the older prophetic fashion, Zephaniah believes in the "Day of Yahweh." The "Day" is at hand, Yahweh has prepared his sacrifice and consecrated his guests, but it is for punishment of the princes and king's sons, the prophet's own close relatives, and all who clothe themselves with foreign apparel, all who leap over the threshold and fill their master's house with violence and deceit. There shall be a cry from the

[20]Ezra 4:9.   [21]*History of Assyria,* 415 ff.; 426 ff.
[22]II Kings 21:19 ff.

Fish Gate, wailing from the New City, a great crashing from the hills, wailing from the Mortar. Men think "Yahweh does no good but neither will he do evil," but their scepticism shall be rewarded.

> Near is Yahweh's great day,
>   Near and hastening fast,
> Near is Yahweh's bitter day,
>   Hastening faster than the hero.
> That day is a day of wrath,
>   A day of trouble and distress,
> A day of desolation and waste,
>   A day of darkness and gloom,
> A day of clouds and thick dark,
>   A day of trumpet and alarms,
> Against the fortified towns,
>   Against the battlements high.

The doom is extended to the Philistines, nation without shame; Gaza shall be forsaken, Ashkelon be a waste, Ashdod driven out at noon, Ekron be rooted up. Yahweh is against the coast dwellers, nation of Cretans, the coast shall become pastures and folds for flocks, shepherds shall feed their flocks in Ashkelon's palaces and lie down there in the evening. Moab shall be as Sodom and the Ammonites as Gomorrah. The Kushite rulers of Egypt shall Yahweh's sword slay, he will stretch out his hand to the north and destroy Ashur. Nineveh shall be made desolate, dry like the desert, herds shall lie in her midst and all beasts of the field, screech owls and porcupines shall lodge in her capitals, owls hoot in the windows and ravens on the threshold. Jerusalem herself is a rebel city, defiled and an oppressor, she has obeyed no voice and received no correction. Her princes are roaring lions, her judges are evening wolves who leave naught till the morn, her prophets are reckless and treacherous, her priests profane the holy and violate the law. But Yahweh within her is righteous, no iniquity does he do, but morn by morn he establishes justice and light does not fail.[23]

[23]Marti, *Dodekapropheton*, 357 ff.; Norwack, *Die Kleinen Propheten*, 285 ff.; J. M. P. Smith, *Micah, Zephaniah, and Nahum*, 1912; Sellin, *Zwölfprophetenbuch*, 414 ff.

Events of world magnitude were in the making. Ashur-bani-apal died in 626, and Assyria sank still more rapidly than before. No successor to her power was in sight, a better opportunity for regaining independence could not be asked.[24]

Northeast of Jerusalem an hour, but completely hidden from it, lay Anathoth, the village of the Anath goddesses, on a high hill isolated on all sides. Its view south and west to the civilised portions of Judah was cut off, but to the north was a good share of Benjamin with Ramah, Geba, and Ophrah. Here was a fine play of colours, but poor when compared with the stretches of the Dead Sea and Moab; all are pale when the eye looks due east to a violently upthrust mass, which glows a molten old rose and old gold that baffles description. Civilisation in Jerusalem might never exist, but the savage country eastward was an always present influence.

In Anathoth lived a young priest named Jeremiah.[25] The impending crisis brought to him the conviction that he was called of Yahweh to be a prophet. Assyria might appear in full decline, but he remembered how a similar decline had not prevented Amos from prophesying doom to Israel, and his prophecy had come true. Assyria must return again. The word of Yahweh came: "Before I formed you in the body I knew you, before you came from the womb I had sanctified you, a prophet to the nations I had appointed you." Jeremiah feared he could not speak, for he was but a youth, but Yahweh touched his mouth: "Behold, I have set you this day over nations and kingdoms to pluck up, break down, and destroy."

Jeremiah was asked what he saw; it was an almond branch: "Well have you seen, for I watch over my word to perform it." A second time he saw a symbol, a boiling cauldron facing the north: "From the north shall evil boil over." Yahweh is calling all the nations of the north, they shall each set his throne at Jerusalem's gates, for her inhabitants have burnt incense to

---

[24] *History of Assyria,* 627 ff.
[25] N. Schmidt, "Jeremiah," *Encycl. Biblica;* B. Duhm, *Das Buch Jeremia,* 1901; C. H. Cornill, *Das Buch Jeremia,* 1905; F. Giesebrecht, *Das Buch Jeremia,* 1907; P. Volz, *Der Prophet Jeremia,* 1922; G. A. Smith, *Jeremiah,* 1923; J. Skinner, *Prophecy and Religion,* 1923.

other gods and worshipped the works of their hands. Jeremiah has been made a fortified city against the whole land, against Judah's kings and princes, her priests and her people.

Blow a trump in the land, cry aloud: "Assemble in fenced cities," raise a standard against Zion, for Yahweh is bringing evil and great destruction from the north. It is a hot wind from bare desert heights but not to winnow or cleanse. He is bringing a nation from afar, whose tongue they know not nor understand what they say; they come from the northland, a nation stirred from earth's ends, they lay hold of bow and javelin; cruel and without mercy are they, like the sea their voice roars, upon horses they ride. The whole land flees from the noise of the horsemen and bowmen, they enter caves, hide in thickets and climb the rocks; all the country is forsaken, not a man dwells therein. Though Jerusalem clothes herself in scarlet and decks herself in golden trinkets, though she lengthens her eyes with kohl and makes herself fair, her lovers despise her, they seek, not her favours, but her life.[26]

[26] Jer. 1; 4–6.

CHAPTER XXXIII

JOSIAH'S REFORM

Josiah began his reign as a religious conservative, and Jeremiah could detect no difference between his reign and that of his father. His picture of these early days is the same as that painted by earlier prophets. Yahweh remembers the troth of Israel's youth and her love as a bride, how she followed her lord through the desert, the land unsown; not then did she ask: "Where is Yahweh who brought us from Egypt, who led us through desert, land of waste and pits, land of drought and barren, where no man dwells?" Yahweh brought her into a garden to eat its fruit, but she defiled his land, the priest did not ask for Yahweh, the givers of law knew him not, the shepherds transgressed against him, the prophets predicted by Baal. Cross to Cyprus' isle and see, send to Kedar, consider with care; has there ever been such a thing that a nation has changed its gods, even if not true? Men of Memphis and Daphne have abused her, why should they take the road to Egypt to drink Nile water, or to Ashur to drink from the Euphrates? Under every green tree, on every high hill she has bowed down and played the harlot. How can she say: "I am not defiled, I have not gone after Baals"? Kings and princes, prophets and priests call a tree "My father," and say to a stone "You brought me forth"; according to the number of Judah's cities are their gods, according to the number of Jerusalem's streets are those who burn incense to Baal, her own sword has devoured her prophets.[1]

Despite Jeremiah's insistence, Josiah continued his preparations for revolt. Jeremiah demanded: "Why are you gadding about to change your ways? You shall be ashamed of Egypt as you were of Assyria; from thence you shall go forth in the same fashion, with your hands upon your head, for Yahweh

[1] Jer. 2.

has rejected those you trust and you shall not prosper with them."[2]

By the eighteenth year of Josiah, 621, the time appeared ripe for revolt. As sign of independence, the shrine of Yahweh was to be rehabilitated, for neglect had allowed breaches to appear in the temple itself. Shaphan the scribe was sent to discover how much money had been collected by the threshold keepers from the temple visitors, and was met by Hilkiah the chief priest with the astonishing news: "I have found the book of the law in the house of Yahweh."

The code was ascribed to the lawgiver Moses, but in reality it had been composed not long before, and it is difficult not to suspect that Hilkiah himself was perfectly aware of its origin. Much useless discussion has raged over the ethics of this transaction; the historian need only observe that Hilkiah was simply following the usual custom of antiquity when he ascribed the code to a great lawgiver of dimly remembered times. So far as content and influence are concerned, Hilkiah needs no apology; the laws marked a great advance over those previously obeyed, the religion preached was attractive and bracing. Behind its teaching lay the prophetic movement, but political and priestly motives were yet more pronounced and not all the prophets approved the new laws.

This code forms the core of our book of Deuteronomy. It is more than a law book. The laws themselves are almost lost in the exhortations by which they are emphasised, while for introduction and conclusion we have veritable sermons, now and then a little repetitious, but often rising to flights of a somewhat artificial but powerful oratory.

The early stories which had long floated about regarding Israel's origins had been brought together in various collections and finally into one narrative, which forms the basis of our Genesis, Exodus, and Numbers. From this and similar sources our author selects episodes, but always to point a moral. The heart of his teaching is that wonderful Shema, which Judaism has well taken as its profession of faith: "Hear,

[2] Jer. 2:36 f.

O Israel, Yahweh our God is one God; and thou shalt love Yahweh thy God with all thy heart and with all thy soul and with all thy might."[3] Even an imperfect monotheism was still a new belief of the intellectuals and our author must repeatedly insist that Israel must not go after other gods. Let them keep all Yahweh's commandments, statutes, and ordinances, that their days may be long in the land they go to possess. They must kill all the inhabitants of the promised land; our author knows this was not done, so he adds they must make with them neither covenant nor marriage, lest they be led to worship other gods. Canaanite altars must be torn down, their pillars broken, their asherahs hewn up, their graven images burned. They are a people holy to Yahweh, they must keep his covenant, then they shall be blessed with fruitfulness of body and earth, and shall be free from all sickness. Let them not think Yahweh has given them the land for their righteousness, they have always been a stiff-necked people.

"Yahweh thy God is bringing thee into a good land, a land of brooks of water, of fountains and springs, flowing forth in valleys and hills; a land of wheat and barley and vines and fig trees and pomegranates; a land of olive trees and honey; a land in which thou shalt eat bread without scarceness, thou shalt lack nothing in it; a land whose stones are iron, and out of whose hills thou mayest dig copper." It is not like the land of Egypt from which they came out, where they sowed the seed and watered it with the foot like a garden of herbs, but it is a land of hills and valleys which drinks the water of heaven, for Yahweh's eyes are always upon it from the beginning of the year to the end.[4]

The "statutes and ordinances" repeat or expand provisions of the Covenant Code, but the atmosphere is entirely different. The earlier code showed no interest in trade; the new code was adapted to an advanced civilisation. The cult was much more elaborate. New also was an intensely humanitarian spirit, with constant reference to the widow, orphan, and resident alien.

Since the fall of the northern kingdom, there had developed

[3] Deut. 6:4 f.   [4] Deut. 8:7–10; 11:10–12.

a growing recognition of the essential unity of all Israel. Now there was actual hope that this unity might be restored as under David. The new nationalism demanded a new emphasis on the national God. All local shrines must be destroyed, the worshipper of other gods is to be stoned, heretic cities must be devoted. Heathen practices, such as cutting the person or making oneself bald for the dead, are prohibited. All burnt offerings, sacrifices, tithes of grain, new wine, or oil, heave offerings, vows, freewill offerings, firstlings of herd and flock, are to be brought to one chosen place, where they shall eat in joy before Yahweh. Clean animals may be eaten at home without special ceremony, provided the blood is poured on the ground; unclean flesh, pork in particular, is stringently prohibited. Tithes which cannot be taken to Jerusalem must be sold and the money brought to the city, where it may be spent for what will rejoice the heart before Yahweh, even to wine and strong drink. Every three years the tithe is to go to the Levites. Every seven years there shall be a year of release of debtor to creditor, though this does not extend to foreigner or Hebrew bond-servant. All male firstborn of herd and flock are sanctified to Yahweh, they shall be neither worked nor sheared. Blemished beasts must not be sacrificed.

Three times each year every male must appear before Yahweh in Jerusalem, and not with empty hands. Passover and Feast of Unleavened Bread are one and are in memory of the exodus from that Egypt which was now threatening them. Sacrifice is to be made at evening of the first day, no flesh is to remain unto morning; six days unleavened bread is to be eaten, the seventh is a solemn assembly to Yahweh. Seven weeks from the time the sickle is put into the standing grain is the feast of weeks with a freewill offering. The feast of booths is for seven days after they have brought in from threshing-floor and wine-press. Vows are not compulsory, but when made must be performed.

Levi has long ceased to be a secular tribe; he has no more portion or heritage in Israel. Yahweh is his inheritance, but he has more substantial rewards, the shoulder, cheeks, and maw of the sacrificed sheep or ox, the first fruits of the grain, new wine, oil, and wool. Should any Levite wish to take his place with the priests in Jerusalem, he may minister with them and share their dues.

Male and female prostitutes still filled the temple. This shocking survival is condemned and no vow from their hire may be brought into the temple. No self-mutilated eunuch, no illegitimate child, no son of Moabite or Ammonite is to be admitted to Yahweh's assembly to the tenth generation; Edomites or Egyptians may be admitted in the third.

A king shall be chosen by the people; he must not be a foreigner or increase his horses, wives, silver, or gold. He must rather prepare a copy of this law and read therein all the days of his life. Since the local oracles are to be destroyed and the aristocratic elders are little favoured, judges and officials by tribes must be set in all the gates, with appeal to the judge in the capital. No man may be punished on the testimony of one witness; false witness is punished according to the law of talio.

Three cities of refuge are to be appointed for the involuntary homicide to which he may flee from the avenger of blood, but murderers must be surrendered. Slave stealing is punishable by death. A stubborn son is to be taken before the elders and stoned. Father and child shall not be punished for the other's sins. Beatings must not exceed forty stripes. Justice shall not be wrested in the case of the resident alien or the fatherless. If a criminal is hung, his body shall be taken down before sunset lest the land be defiled. If a corpse be found and the cause of death be unknown, the elders of the nearest city shall take an unworked heifer and bring it to an untilled valley with running water; they shall break her neck, wash over her their hands, and pray that the innocent blood be expiated.

Just weights must be employed, not one great and one small. Landmarks must not be removed. Interest must not be taken from fellow Hebrews, but is allowed from foreigners. A widow's garment or a millstone may not be taken in pledge, the pledged garment of the poor must be returned at night that he may sleep in it; no man may enter a house to seize his pledge. To make safe the house, battlements are obligatory. Escaped slaves are not to be returned to their masters, women as well as men slaves are freed and not with empty hands; a hired servant must be paid regularly. Overlooked sheaves, olives, grapes, must be left for the resident alien, widow, and orphan. Grapes may be eaten and grain plucked from a neighbour's vineyard or field, but must not be carried off. The ox must not be muzzled when he treads out the grain, the young in a bird's nest may be taken, but the mother must be freed.

Judah had revolted and there was promise of territorial expansion to the Euphrates, but Egypt was threatening and all were thinking of preparation for the coming war. The army is to be a folk levy which choses its own officers. Those with new houses or vineyards or betrothed wives are excused from military service, the newly married husband for a year to cheer his wife. Before a city is attacked, terms of surrender are to be offered; if accepted, the inhabitants are to be made tributary. If they resist, all the males are to be slain and the women and children made captive. Fruit trees must not be cut down in a siege. The woman captive is to be granted a month for mourning, then her captor may marry her; he may later divorce her, but cannot sell her into slavery.

Provisions of the Covenant Code are exactly repeated for accusations of unchastity and the like. No man may marry his father's wife. If a woman no longer pleases her husband, he may divorce her when she marries the man of her choice, but her husband can never take her back. Should a man die without issue, his brother must marry the widow and the first son must bear the dead man's name. The victim of leprosy must follow priestly direction. One sex must not wear garments of the other, a man must not sow two kinds of seed, plow with an ox and an ass yoked together, wear clothes of mixed wool and linen; fringes must be on the four borders of the garment.

Shaphan read the book before the king, who rent his clothes when he heard the terrific denunciations of those who had not obeyed the law. Hilkiah and his companions were ordered to consult the prophetess Huldah, wife of the wardrobe keeper, who dwelt in the New Quarter to the north, and received this oracle: "Behold, I will bring evil upon this place and all its inhabitants, all the words of the book which the king of Judah has read; because they have forsaken me and have burned incense to other gods, that they might provoke me to anger with all the work of their hands, therefore my wrath shall be kindled against this place and it shall not be quenched." This was quite in the manner of the older prophets, but there was consolation for Josiah: "Because your heart was tender and you humbled yourself before Yahweh when you heard what I spoke against this place and its inhabitants, I also have heard you. Therefore, behold, I will gather you to your fathers and you shall be gathered to your grave in peace, neither shall your eyes see all the evil I will bring upon this place."

A solemn covenant was made with all the people to obey the law. All the vessels made for Baal, the asherah, and the host of heaven were taken out of the temple and burned in the Kidron fields. The shaveling priests, ordained by former kings to burn incense on the high places of the villages, with those who burned incense to Baal, the sun, moon, zodiacal signs, and heavenly host, were burned themselves. The asherah was brought from the temple and burned at the Kidron, its dust cast on the graves of the commons who worshipped it. The house of the male prostitutes in the very temple precinct, where women wove tunics for the asherah, was torn down, as were the high places of the satyrs at the gate of Joshua, governor of the city. Tophet in the valley of the children of Hinnom, where human sacrifice was offered to the divine King, was defiled and the chariots of the sun committed to the flames. Rejection of Assyrian overlordship was indicated by the destruction of the altars on the roof of the upper chamber of Ahaz and those made by Manasseh in the two temple courts. The high places on the right of the Mount of Destruction, where Solomon had erected altars to Ashtart, Chemosh, and Milcom, were defiled, and the place of the pillars and asherahs was filled with dead men's bones. A passover, for the first time celebrated according to the new rules, fittingly closed the reform.

Josiah's reform has come to be in the eyes of modern students the central point in Hebrew history. Undoubtedly it is an outstanding landmark on the long road to monotheism; there is great advance in ethics and a growing kindliness. Nevertheless, we shall misunderstand its true meaning if we disregard its secular aspect.

Centralisation of the cult had begun when David took as his capital Jerusalem, an alien city with no previous religious associations for the Hebrews, and collected there the various tribal cult objects. Here Solomon built a royal chapel, attached to the palace and under the direct control of the monarch who sacrificed in person as both high priest and king. Changes in religion were due to the ruler's initiative, the temple funds were at his disposal, it was he who checked priestly peculation. Added to the tendency towards centralisation inevitable from the royal character of the shrine was the movement towards political centralisation which, checked by Jeroboam's revolt, found new life with the fall of the northern kingdom.

The new law contemplated a king who was by no means free from priestly control,[5] but the actual reform was carried out by Josiah, who put into effect such provisions as he saw fit. If Yahweh was now supreme in his land, so was his vicegerent the king; if Jerusalem was the unique centre of Yahweh worship, no less was it the sole Hebrew capital.

The effect of the reform on religion was twofold. A single sanctuary demanded a single deity and thus it was an aid to the monotheism rapidly developing among the higher classes. Its effect on the peasantry was most deplorable. The regular priests, now called Levites, were permitted by the code to come to Jerusalem and share equally in the cult privileges with the local priesthood. Few appear to have taken advantage of the offer and those who did were not granted the promised rights, but sank into dependents of the priestly aristocracy

[5] Cf. Deut. 17:14 ff.

who distinguished sharply between priests and Levites. The shaveling priests of the Judæan high places were burned to death. So far as authority could effect that result, the peasant had been robbed of his religion.

It is only too true that this worship of the countryside was far from ideal. "On every high hill and under every green tree" were performed those rites in which sexual impurity found a place, and the prophets had long remonstrated against other abuses. But all was not unclean. At Hebron and Beer-sheba lingered traditions of a loved and glorious past, when Abraham had been friend of God. If the worship of Yahweh as a young bull at Bethel had provoked the indignation of the advanced thinkers, few could forget that here Jacob saw the road to heaven, and the burning of human bones on its altar was pure sacrilege. To many a thinking and pious Hebrew, Josiah's reform must have appeared the utter negation of all that was best in the nation's past.

Among the village priests who settled in Jerusalem under the new regulations was Jeremiah. There was much in the code which was in exact agreement with his own teaching, and at first he was inclined to be sympathetic, even going so far as to denounce those who did not accept the words of "this covenant."[6] Residence in the capital and the failure to grant the promised rights led him to exclaim: "Run through Jerusalem's streets and seek in her squares to see if you can find a man who does justice and seeks truth that I may grant pardon. They say 'As Yahweh lives,' but they swear falsely, you smite them but they do not grieve, you consume them but they do not take correction, their face is harder than rock, they refuse to return." "Then I said: These are the poor and foolish, they do not know Yahweh's way or the law of their God; I will go and speak with the great, for they know Yahweh's way, the law of their God. But they too have all broken the yoke and burst the bonds, their revolts are many and frequent their backslidings," so they shall be punished.[7]

The Jerusalem temple is now the sole shrine of Yahweh, and

[6] Jer. 11:1 ff. [7] Jer. 5:1–6.

its devotees are convinced that, whatever their private conduct, no calamity can approach them. Jeremiah fiercely attacks this complacency: "Amend your ways and your doings and then I will make you dwell in this place. Trust not in lying words, saying: 'The temple of Yahweh, the temple of Yahweh, the temple of Yahweh are these.'" "You trust in lying words that cannot profit; will you steal, murder, commit adultery, swear falsely, burn incense to Baal, and walk after other gods you have not known, and then come before me in this house and say: 'We are delivered'? Has my house become a den of robbers in your eyes?" Long ago there was another temple which was thought inviolate: "Go now to my place which was in Shiloh, where I caused my name to dwell at the first"—he is quoting the very phrase which the new law used for Jerusalem—"and see what I did to it for the wickedness of my people Israel." They too have sinned, "therefore I will do to the house which is now called by my name, in which you trust, as I did to Shiloh; I will cast you out of my sight as I cast out all your brothers, the whole seed of Ephraim."[8]

The code was introduced by the story of Moses and the Exodus from Egypt. Jeremiah flatly denies its truth: "Add your burnt offerings to your sacrifices and eat flesh; for I spoke not to your fathers nor did I give them commands concerning burnt offering and sacrifices. This one thing alone I did command them: Hearken to my voice and I will be your God and you shall be my people; walk in all the way I command you that it may be well with you."[9] After this emphatic condemnation of the whole sacrificial system of the code, we are not surprised to find even more emphatic condemnation of the work as a whole: "How can you say: 'We are wise and Yahweh's law is with us'? Lo, the scribe's false pen has wrought falsely! Shamed are the wise, dismayed and taken, since Yahweh's word they have rejected, where is their wisdom?"[10] "An astonishing, horrible thing has come to pass in the land; the prophets predict lies and the priests bear rule at their

[8] Jer. 7:1–15.   [9] Jer. 7:21–23.
[10] Jer. 8:8 f.

hand. My people love to have it so, but what will you do at its end?"[11]

There was truth in Jeremiah's savage condemnation. Religion had been a vital part of the peasant's life. Slaughter of a sheep was sacrifice to Yahweh, and his simple meal might be blessed by the presence of his God; when he brought to the local shrine his first fruits, he "rejoiced before Yahweh's face." His priests were of his own class, the local seer found his strayed asses at small cost, the "man of God," scarce more than a wandering dervish, shared his frugal meal and blessed him.

Now all was changed. His friends, the local priests, were dead or nonentities in the capital, his first fruits eaten by strangers. By the new mode, he could be religious only in Jerusalem and then only at the three yearly feasts. He must tramp the unspeakable trails on foot and under the blazing sun at an expense which, however small, was too great for his scanty means, and then worship with strangers. Intimate relation between official religion and the home life was broken and forever. The peasant became a "pagan," one of the "people of the land," as they were stigmatised by the officially "Pious." All opportunity for influence by the advanced thinkers was lost when Josiah's reform snapped the connection between the official cult and the daily life of the peasant.[12]

[11] Jer. 5:30 f.   [12] Cf. *Amer. Historical Review*, XX, 1915, 566 ff.

CHAPTER XXXIV

JEREMIAH THE PESSIMIST

HULDAH the prophetess had predicted that Josiah should be gathered to his grave in peace. He had obeyed Yahweh's word as presented in the new-found law, he might expect the long life and prosperity there promised as reward. That his fate was far other was due to the rapidly changing international situation.

Assyria was indeed steadily declining. Her last known governor ruled Tyre in 648, Samaria and Damascus about 645, Simyra a little later.[1] Media, Egypt, and Babylonia were already planning to seize the inheritance. Babylonia had been ruled at intervals by Chaldæans, an Aramæan tribe settled in the alluvium since the ninth century; in 626 Nabopolassar declared his independence of Assyria and by 616 he had freed all Babylonia.[2]

Meanwhile, Psammetichus I (663–609) was laying in Egypt the foundations of the vigorous twenty-sixth dynasty. Gerar was garrisoned with a great square fort and numerous grain pits, thirty feet deep, below the occupied rooms.[3] Ashkelon was quickly taken, Ashdod was secured after a twenty-nine-year siege, a naophorus statue with his name was left in Arvad.[4] Psammetichus had no desire to see a weakened Assyria succeeded by a strong Babylonia; leaving Judah aside for the moment, he advanced to the aid of the Assyrians and drove Nabopolassar from Mesopotamia. Sin-shar-ishkun was about to win back the revolted provinces when, late in 615, Cyaxares, who had just united the scattered Medes, intervened in favour

[1] C. H. W. Johns, *Assyrian Deeds and Documents,* I, 1898, 569 f.
[2] *History of Assyria,* 627 ff.; "The Chaldæan Dynasty," *Hebrew Union College Annual,* II, 29 ff.
[3] W. M. F. Petrie, *Gerar,* 4 ff.
[4] Herod. i, 105; ii, 157; Renan, *Mission,* 26 f.

of Babylonia. Nineveh was destroyed by the allies in June of 612, and Nahum, an Israelite exile in Elkosh, celebrated its fall in a savage poem. Ashur-uballit escaped to Harran, but was ousted by the Medes in 610, and fled across the Euphrates. Psammetichus had just been succeeded by his son Necho II (609–593), who sent Ashur-uballit back into Mesopotamia with Egyptian reinforcements, only to suffer a crushing defeat.[5]

Once more in 608 Necho set out. Meanwhile, Josiah had prospered and the promises of the newly found book seemed in process of fulfilment. At his accession, his kingdom had reached from Geba to Beersheba,[6] but a list of his provinces and their dependent towns from the middle of his reign shows a wide increase of his territory. Twenty-nine villages of the Negeb, towards the border of Edom, the old territory of Simeon, appear to have been under Beersheba. Fourteen of the Shephelah were under Adullam or perhaps rather Socoh, and included Jarmuth and Azekah, while Lachish was the centre of sixteen towards the plain. Libnah, Keilah, and Mareshah were among the ten villages of the next group. Eleven in the hill country would be supervised by Debir, the ancient Kiriath Sepher, whose captor was the Kenazite Othniel. Hebron was the obvious capital of the nine Calebite towns, another group of ten included the Kain of the Kenites. Six cities were under Beth Zur and eleven under Bethlehem; this was the true Judah in the narrower sense. The four cities of the old Gibeonite confederacy and the other near-by towns were directly administered from the capital; the frontier was soon advanced northward, the temple at Mizpah was destroyed,[7] and with the minor villages now secured fourteen were under Jerusalem. A further advance permitted the desecration of the altar at Bethel, whose diluted worship of Yahweh was no longer protected by the Assyrian king, the frontier now stood north of Ophrah, and Jericho and the lower Jordan valley were added to the new province of twelve towns. In

[5] *History of Assyria*, 634 ff.; C. J. Gadd, *The Fall of Nineveh*, 1923.
[6] II Kings 23:8.   [7] Badè, *Excavations*, 36 f.

the earlier days of Ashur-bani-apal, Ekron was still independent under its own king Achish,[8] but Josiah brought it under his control, though the three seacoast Philistine cities and Joppa were never taken, while Hadid, Ono, and Lod or Lydda seem to have been added later.[9] The long irregular province of seventeen cities extended northward through Gibbethon and touched the sea at Rakkon, north of Joppa.[10]

Josiah had invited the inhabitants of the former northern kingdom to partake of his passover and he now marched north to occupy the whole of Ephraim and Manasseh. Confident that Yahweh would reward his faithful servant and repeat the victory of Moses over the Egyptians, he drew up his army at Megiddo, where long since the Syrian princes had attempted to block the advance of Thutmose III along the Great Road and into the Great Plain. Necho desired to waste no time on a minor king and attempted to persuade Josiah that the expedition was by special order of Yahweh, but in vain; the mail-clad Greeks in the Egyptian army proved too much for the more lightly armed Judæans, and Josiah was carried home to die.[11]

Josiah's eldest son was the twenty-five-year-old Eliakim, who as crown prince had adopted a policy the direct opposite of his father. The anti-Egyptian "people of the land" therefore passed him by and chose Shallum, two years his junior, who on his accession took the name Jehoahaz, "Yahweh has seized." Necho received the submission of the Phœnician cities and took up his position at Riblah, an excellent camping-ground in the midst of a fertile, well-watered plain, at the crossing of the Great Road and the road from the sea through the gap between Lebanon and Bargylus to the open desert. Here he learned of the accession of Jehoahaz; after reigning but three months, the unfortunate youth was brought in chains to Riblah and later sent to his death in Egypt.[12]

[8] Cyl. C. I, 30; cf. Zeph. 2:4.   [9] Cf. Ezra 2:33.
[10] Josh. 15:21 ff.; 18:21 ff.; A. Alt, *Palästinajahrbuch*, XXI, 1925, 100 ff.
[11] II Chron. 35:20 ff.; II Kings 23:29 ff.; cf. Herod, ii, 159.
[12] II Kings 23:30–34.

Jeremiah broke his long silence to sing a dirge:

> Weep not for the dead nor bemoan him,
>   Weep sore for the exile, no more to return,
>   Nor see the land of his birth.
>
> For thus saith Yahweh of Shallum, who went from here:
>   In the place they led him captive, there shall he die,
>   And shall see this land no more.[13]

The pro-Egyptian Eliakim was now permitted to ascend the throne denied him by the popular party, but the land had sinned, and he must pay a hundred talents of silver and ten of gold, more than two million dollars in coin value. Judah's treasury was empty, and Eliakim must tax his subjects for this enormous sum. Some whim of Necho changed his name from Eliakim to Jehoiakim.[14]

Nabopolassar considered himself the legitimate heir of Assyria in the west. Already in his last illness, his eldest son Nebuchadnezzar was placed in charge of the Chaldæan army. Passing up the right bank of the Euphrates, Nebuchadnezzar fell upon the Egyptians at Carchemish; Jeremiah's picture of the battle is full of color:

> Prepare the buckler and shield,
>   And draw near to battle;
> Harness the horses, rise up, you horsemen,
>   Stand forth with your helmets;
> Furbish your spears,
>   Put on your coats of mail.

The Egyptians are dismayed and turned back, their mighty men are beaten down, they have fled and look not back, in the north, by the river Euphrates, have they stumbled and fallen. Egypt rises up like the Nile and his waters toss like the rivers, he thinks to rise and cover the earth, to destroy cities and their inhabitants. Let the horses go up and the chariots rage, let the men of might go forth, Cush and Put that handle the

[13] Jer. 22:10–12.   [14] II Kings 23:34 f.

shield, and the Lydians who bend the bow; this is the Day of the Lord, Yahweh of Hosts, a day of vengence on his foes, his sword shall devour and be satiated and drink its fill of blood, for Yahweh has a sacrifice in the north land by the Euphrates.

> Ascend into Gilead, take balm,
> O virgin daughter of Egypt!
> In vain do you use many drugs,
> For you there is no healing!
> The nations have heard of your shame,
> The earth is full of your weeping,
> For hero gainst hero has tripped,
> Both together have fallen.[15]

Excavations tell more of the story. The chief man of Carchemish occupied a pleasant house of well-plastered mud brick above a two-foot course of hard, carefully dressed limestone; a porch and a large entrance hall gave access to a guard room on the right, the main reception-room on the left, and a series of other apartments. Clay impressions with Necho's name, statuettes of Isis and Horus, a bronze Osiris much "Hitticized" with huge ears, protruding eyes and lips, a fleshy nose, alabaster bowl and flask with Egyptian inscriptions, a painted mask of white steatite with inlaid eyes and brows, prove strong Egyptian influence as against the few signs of Babylonian. In his ruined house was found the owner's body, with a ring whose bezel bore the cartouche of the first Psammetichus, a gift to his friend of Carchemish. The violence of the struggle is shown by swords dropped where their owners fell, numerous javelins and hundreds of bronze and iron arrow heads, their points often blunted or broken off by the force with which they were hurled against the walls. A shield of Ionian design but with orientalising tendencies marks the passing of a Greek mercenary in Necho's army. The terrible punishment meted out to the rebel city is seen in the carbonised timbers and reddened brick work.[16]

Necho's army ceased to exist and all Syria fell to the Chal-

[15] Jer. 46:3–12.   [16] Fig. 177; Hogarth-Woolley, *Carchemish*, 123 ff.

dæans. Jeremiah exulted: "Hamath and Arpad are confounded, they hear evil tidings, on the sea is sorrow, it cannot be quiet; Damascus is feeble, she turns to flee, trembling has seized upon her."[17] "The fathers look not back to their children, their hands are feeble, for the Day has come to destroy all the Philistines and to cut off from Tyre and Sidon every remaining helper. Yahweh shall destroy the Philistines, remnant of Caphtor's isle. Baldness has come upon Gaza, Ashkelon is made naught! Remnant of Ekron, how long will you cut yourself? Sword of Yahweh, how long ere you will be quiet? Put yourself in the scabbard, rest and be still; how can you be quiet since Yahweh has charged you? Against Ashkelon and the seashore has he appointed it."[18]

Phœnicia and Philistia were taken by the Chaldæans and Jeremiah turned to Egypt: News of the great defeat comes to Migdol, the border fort, and then to Memphis; the Greek mercenaries say: "Arise, let us go to our own country, Pharaoh is but a noise." Egypt is a fair heifer, her hired men are like calves of the stall, they flee and do not stand. Egypt's daughter shall be delivered into the hands of the people of the north.[19] Egypt lay helpless before Nebuchadnezzar and the prophecy was about to be fulfilled, but at the Dry River Bed of Egypt the crown prince received news of his father's death in May or June of 604. Handing over his troops with the Syrian and Jewish captives to his "friends," Nebuchadnezzar hurried across the now blazing desert by way of Palmyra to Babylon, where he found his right to the throne had been respected.

Jehoiakim had submitted to Nebuchadnezzar, but he had not forgotten the Egyptian friend who had given him the throne. Shortly after his accession, Jeremiah took his stand in the temple court and proclaimed to the visiting citizens of the Judæan towns that unless they repented they should become like Shiloh. The priests and prophets whose future was thus summarily disposed of were naturally displeased; Jeremiah was seized and threatened with immediate death. Power

[17] Jer. 49:23 f.   [18] Jer. 47:3–7.   [19] Jer. 46:14–24.

of life and death was not however in the hands of priests and prophets but of the princes; hearing of Jeremiah's arrest, they came up from the palace and took their seat in the entry of the new temple gate. Before this tribunal Jeremiah was accused by the religious leaders as one worthy of death for speaking against the city, and the prophet professed himself ready to endure whatever punishment should seem right in their eyes, but he warned them that they would bring upon themselves and their city the curse of innocent blood, for in truth Yahweh had sent him.

The odium theologicum felt by the priests found no echo in the hearts of the secular leaders, the majority of whom were probably anti-Egyptian in secret. They decreed that Jeremiah could not be punished, for he had indeed spoken in the name of Yahweh. However unwelcome this quasi-official recognition of the inspiration of Jeremiah's prophecies, worse was to come. In the assembly of the people, certain elders of the land reminded their hearers how Micah the Moreshathite had prophesied the destruction of Jerusalem in the days of Hezekiah and how the king, far from putting him to death, besought Yahweh, who repented of the evil he had threatened.

Jeremiah escaped, largely through the aid of Ahikam, son of Josiah's high official Shaphan, but Uriah, son of Shemaiah, of Kiriath Jearim, was less fortunate. When he attempted to imitate the denunciation of the better-known prophet, Jehoiakim ordered his death. Uriah fled to Egypt, but Necho had no use for such prophets and delivered him up to the Judæan messengers; Uriah was slain in the king's presence and his corpse thrown out into the potter's field.[20]

Jeremiah now turned his attention to Jehoiakim himself: "Woe to him who builds his house with injustice and his upper chambers with wrong, who uses his neighbour's services without wages and gives him not his hire." He thinks: "I shall build me a house, wide and with airy rooms, I shall cut windows and panel it with cedar, I shall paint it with vermilion." Is this the way he should reign, striving to excel the

[20] Jer. 26.

cedar? His father Josiah certainly did eat and drink, but did he not also do justice and righteousness? He judged the cause of the poor and needy and then all was well. But now Jehoiakim has evil eyes and heart, he covets and sheds innocent blood and does oppression and violence. The time is coming when Jehoiakim must die. He shall have no proper lamentation: "Ah my brother, ah my sister, ah my lord, ah his glory!" He shall be buried with the burial of an ass, drawn and cast outside Jerusalem's gates.[21]

Jehoiakim might not have been so strongly pro-Egyptian had more authentic news come out of Egypt. In his first terror, Necho had begun to dig a great trench through the Isthmus of Suez. The official explanation was a desire to move the Egyptian fleet at will from sea to sea; we who in our own day have seen its successor check the Turko-German invasion will not need be told that a like defence was intended. Nebuchadnezzar's hasty return restored Necho's confidence. A new fleet was built to control the sea and to prevent the coast cities from falling into Chaldæan hands. Gebal was regained and its king made a dedication for Necho, who granted the Phœnicians a trading centre in Memphis and employed Phœnicians to make the circumnavigation of Africa.[22]

As the Chaldæans advanced southward, Jeremiah prophesied:

> Go up to Lebanon and cry,
>   Lift up your voice in Bashan,
> Also from Abarim cry,
>   For destroyed are all your lovers;
> O you, who Lebanon inhabits,
>   Who makes your nest in the cedars,
> How you'll groan when pangs come upon you,
>   The pain of a woman in travail.[23]

Nebuchadnezzar did go to the "Lebanon, the cedar mountain of the luxuriant forests of Marduk, whose scent is

---

[21] Jer. 22:13–19.
[22] Herod., ii, 112, 158 f.; iv, 42; F. L. Griffith, *Proc. Soc. Biblical Archæology*, XVI, 1894, 90 f.
[23] Jer. 22:20–23.

pleasant, whose cedars are tall." An enemy stranger had possessed it and had carried off its product, so that its inhabitants had fled far away. Nebuchadnezzar set his troops in battle order and defeated that enemy above and below; he rejoiced the heart of the land, its scattered inhabitants he collected and restored them to their place. What no former king had done, he cut through the high mountains and opened up passageways, a path for the cedars he prepared. Before king Marduk, the great cedars, tall and stately, whose favour was precious and splendid their dark appearance, were removed with no more difficulty than if they had been reeds, they were brought overland to the Arahtu canal and so to Babylon. The men of Mount Lebanon were made to dwell in peace, no enemy might go against them. That none might harm them, Nebuchadnezzar made an eternal image of his majesty by the passageway he had cut and beside it he inscribed his name, with a curse against all who might damage it.

We may still follow the trail which ascends the Wadi Brissa. Half way up, the gorge bends and narrows, and we catch a last glimpse of the Riblah plain. A spring under a tree once invited a tiny hamlet, but to-day not a soul is in sight, though there are traces of charcoal burners. The cedars are all gone and only a few scrub oaks survive. Even in July, the cold at night is intense.

On either side the valley is a smoothed rock face. On one, Nebuchadnezzar stands before a cedar, on the other he wards off a springing lion, a motif which is repeated on the near-by Mount Akrum.[24] With the second Wadi Brissa relief is an inscription in archaic characters, the other is in the current style. A few words near the close speak of his timbering operations and hint of warfare, the major part is devoted to recital of his building operations in far-away Babylonia. We may well ask how this could interest the few inhabitants of this hidden nook in Lebanon, granted even that they could interpret the complicated cuneiform.[25]

[24] H. Lammens, *Musée Belge*, VI, 1902, 37 f.; *RB.*, XII, 1903, 600 f.
[25] S. Langdon, *Die Neubabylonischen Königsinschriften*, 1912, 174 ff.

Nebuchadnezzar continued south to the Dog River. Three Egyptian and four Assyrian reliefs already occupied the choice positions along the road which climbed the cliff to the south of the stream. On the north bank was a low sandstone rock which had not been pre-empted, and on this Nebuchadnezzar caused to be inscribed a duplicate of the inscription at the cedar mountain.[26]

At Nebuchadnezzar's approach, Jehoiakim once more made formal submission (600), but after three years he rebelled. Judah always had enemies in plenty, ready to take advantage of any opportunity, and soon raiding parties of Edomites, Moabites, and Ammonites were driving settlers and nomads alike behind the walls of Jerusalem for safety.[27] Among the nomads were the Rechabites, whose leader Jehonadab had aided Jehu in his bloody reforms. Their ancestor Rechab had made them forswear houses, agriculture, and wine, sure signs of apostasy from nomad simplicity. Driven into Jerusalem, they had perforce abandoned tent life, but wine they abhorred. Well knowing their answer, Jeremiah took Jaazaniah and his brethren into the temple and there set bowls of wine before them. Here if anywhere, as part of Yahweh's worship, wine might be drunk, but the Rechabites refused in horror. Then came the obvious application: The Rechabites still obeyed to the letter the commands of their earthly father, the men of Judah had not followed the ordinances of their God.[28]

Already Jeremiah had been threatened with death, and he determined to preserve in writing for posterity all that he had thus far prophesied; perhaps he could not write, at any rate he dictated them to Baruch, Neriah's son, who henceforth was his faithful scribe. Since it was no longer safe for Jeremiah to appear in public, Baruch was ordered to read the roll in the temple on the ninth month of the fifth year when the people had proclaimed a fast to Yahweh. This was reported to the princes who feared for their friend and bade Baruch hide him-

---

[26] Langdon, *op. cit.*, 35 f.; squeezes of the Wadi Brissa and Dog River inscriptions secured by us are now in Cornell University.
[27] II Kings 24:1 f.
[28] Jer. 35.

self and his master, while they themselves would bring the roll to the king.

Jehoiakim commanded Jehudi to read, but before he had passed the fourth column the king seized the roll and, despite the entreaties of the princes, cut it in pieces with a pen knife and cast the fragments into the brazier burning before him. He likewise gave orders to seize Jeremiah and Baruch, but they were well concealed. Jeremiah then prepared a new roll, with this addition: "He shall have none to sit upon David's throne, his dead body shall be cast out to the heat by day and the frost by night, I will punish him and all his seed for their iniquity, I will bring upon him all the evil I have pronounced."[29]

The prophet was disappointed, for Jehoiakim died in peace and was buried in the garden of Uzzah (597). He was succeeded by a child of eight, Jeconiah, now to be known as Jehoiachin. We possess the seal of his younger brother, "Asayo, son of Yokim," or Jehoiakim, with the youthful Egyptian Harpocrates rising from the lotus very appropriately carved on the other side. One of Jehoiachin's officials, "Eliakim, youth of Yokin," impressed his beautifully carved seal on jar handles at Kiriath Sepher and Beth Shemesh which were to contain wine or oil sent to the king.[30]

Nehushta, the queen mother, was the real monarch, but Jeremiah was no more favourable to this "regiment of women": "Humble yourselves and sit down, your glorious crown from your head is taken; shut up are the Negeb cities, and there is none to open; Judah is all carried captive, it is wholly taken captive."[31] "As I live, saith Yahweh, though Coniah were the signet on my right hand, I would pluck him off. I will give you to those who seek your life, to those you fear, into the hands of the Chaldæans, I will cast you out with the mother who bore you, to a land not of your birth, there shall you die. Is Coniah a despised vessel in which none takes

[29] Jer. 36.
[30] W. F. Albright, *ZAW.*, NF., VI, 1929, 16; Cooke, *Text Book*, 362.
[31] Jer. 13:18 f.

delight? Why is he hurled into a land he knows not? Earth, earth, earth, hear Yahweh's words: Write this man childless, no more having seed to sit on David's throne or to rule in Judah."[32]

This prophecy was quickly fulfilled. Egypt brought no aid and after but three months of rule Jehoiachin saw the arrival of Nebuchadnezzar in person. Accompanied by his mother and all his officials, the boy king went out the gate in hope of mercy; mercy was granted to the degree that no one was slain, but Jehoiachin was carried off to Babylon with his mother, his whole court, seven thousand of his soldiers, and a thousand of his craftsmen and smiths. Mattaniah, the twenty-one-year-old uncle of the deposed king, was given the vacant throne, but his kingdom was strictly limited to the territory about the capital and this remained the Judah of later times. He was forced to swear a solemn oath by Yahweh to be loyal to his new lord; that he might be ever mindful of his oath, his name was changed to Zedekiah, "Righteous is Yahweh."[33]

[32] Jer. 22:24–30.
[33] II Kings 24:10–12, 15–18; Jer. 34:7; 13:19; Ezek. 17:13.

CHAPTER XXXV

THE FALL OF JERUSALEM

ZEDEKIAH (597–586) was at first loyal to Nebuchadnezzar. His anti-Chaldæan subjects, the wealthy landholders, were in exile, his peasants joyfully declared: "They are far from Yahweh, to us is this land given for a possession."[1] The exiles themselves were of a different mind, for their prophets assured them of a speedy return home. When Zedekiah sent an embassy to his lord, Jeremiah sent with it this message to the exiles: "Build houses and dwell in them, plant gardens and eat their fruits, take wives and beget sons and daughters. Seek the peace of the land to which I have exiled you, pray to Yahweh for it, for in its peace you shall have peace. Let not your prophets and diviners deceive you, hearken not to the dreams they dream, for they prophesy falsely in my name, I have not sent them." Two prophets are singled out for condemnation, Ahab and Zedekiah; they are to be slain by Nebuchadnezzar before the exiles, whose worst curse henceforth shall be: "Yahweh make you like Zedekiah and Ahab, whom the king of Babylon roasted in the fire."[2]

A more serious opponent was Shemaiah of En Halom, the "Well of Oracular Dreams," descendant of those Shemaiahs who had escorted David with the Ark, opposed Solomon, assisted Jehoshaphat with his legal reforms, and taken part in the reforms of Hezekiah and Josiah. He had good family reason for believing himself a true representative of Yahweh, especially against a Jeremiah who had opposed Josiah's reform. From his exile he wrote in good Babylonian style a letter to Zephaniah, son of Maaseiah: "Yahweh has appointed you priest in place of the priest Jehoiada, to be an official in the house of Yahweh, for everyone who is mad and makes himself a prophet, to put him in the stocks and in the collar. Why

[1] Ezek. 11:15.   [2] Jer. 29:1–9, 21–22.

then have you not stopped Jeremiah of Anathoth, who is making himself a prophet for you? He has sent to us in Babylon, saying: 'The captivity will be long, build houses and dwell in them, plant gardens and eat their fruit.'" Censorship could not have been strict when so treasonable a letter could have been smuggled out. Proud of his new office, Zephaniah had no intention of submitting to outside dictation, and read the letter to Jeremiah who sent this reply: "Because Shemaiah has prophesied to you, though I did not send him, and has made you trust in a lie, behold, I will punish Shemaiah and his seed, they shall not have a man left to see the good I will do you."[3] Nevertheless, another Shemaiah lived in the days of Nehemiah and was an opponent to that doughty governor.

Jeremiah saw a vision of figs, some very good, some so bad they could not be eaten. The good represented the exiles in Babylonia, who some day were to return, the bad Zedekiah, his nobles, the remnants of Jerusalem, and the refugees in Egypt, against whom were to come sword and famine and pestilence until they should be utterly consumed.[4]

There were indeed among the exiles men who did not agree with Zedekiah, Ahab, and Shemaiah, in particular the priest Ezekiel, son of Buzi. Five years after his deportation, Ezekiel saw the vision of the cherubs, and was instructed not to fear, even though briars and thorns were to be his portion and he was to dwell among scorpions. He ate the offered scroll, filled with lamentations, and found it sweet to his taste. Led by Yahweh's spirit, he came to the captives at Tell Abib, an ancient site dated by popular tradition to prediluvian times and situated on the Chebar, the "Great" canal in central Babylonia which ran through Nippur. After seven days of silence, Ezekiel received orders to draw a city plan on a tile and make its wall an iron plate; the mimic city was to be besieged in regular manner by building a tower, throwing up a mound, establishing camps, and setting battering rams round about. A hundred and ninety days, the days of the siege, he was to lie on his left side and then forty on his right, the years Judah was

[3] Jer. 29:24-32.   [4] Jer. 24.

to bear its punishment. Food and water were to be weighed and measured as Yahweh was to break the staff of bread in Jerusalem. Next Ezekiel shaved his head and beard with a razor-sharp sword and weighed the hair in a balance; a third he burnt in the city, a third he smote round about, a third he scattered to the winds, a remnant he bound in his garment, only to throw part into the fire. Then he prophesied against the mounts and gullies, the hills and vales, whose sun pillars were to be broken, their altars defiled by their worshippers' bones.[5]

These prophecies gave Ezekiel high place in the "Captivity." The elders of Judah waited upon him at his home the following year and the hand of Yahweh came upon him; it carried him by the hair of his head to Jerusalem, where in the north gate of the inner temple court he was shown the image which caused Yahweh's wrath and was responsible for Yahweh leaving his land. He was taken to the wall and ordered to dig. A door was found, leading to the secret room on whose walls were painted every species of serpent and wild beast —we think at once of the lions, bulls, and dragons along Nebuchadnezzar's festival street[6]—and before them stood Jaazaniah, Shaphan's son, and the seventy elders, censer in hand. In the north doorway were women weeping for the dead god Tammuz, but the worst scandal was at the very entrance to Yahweh's temple, where other Jerusalemites adored the sun god, their faces to the east and their backs turned contemptuously to the temple. Wrathfully the divine guide shouted: "Approach, executioners of the city, every man with slaughter weapons in his hand!" The divine scribe appeared, clad in linen and with an inkhorn; he was ordered by Yahweh's Glory to pass through the city, marking with a *tau* or cross the forehead of all who sorrowed over the abominations they wit-

[5]Ezek. 1–7; cf. C. H. Cornill, *Das Buch des Propheten Ezechiel*, 1886; A. Bertholet, *Das Buch Hesekiel*, 1897; R. Kraetzschmar, *Das Buch Ezechiel*, 1900; C. H. Toy, *Book of the Prophet Ezekiel*, 1899; J. W. Rothstein, *Das Buch Ezechiel*, 1922; J. Herrmann, *Ezechiel*, 1924; G. Hölscher, *Hesekiel*, 1924; C. C. Torrey, *Pseudo-Ezekiel*. 1930.

[6]R. Koldewey, *The Excavations at Babylon*, 1914, 38 ff.

nessed. After him went six executioners under instructions to slay without pity old and young, youth and maid, child and woman, and they began with the elders before the temple. Finally, the man in linen scattered live coals over the doomed city.[7]

Again the spirit lifted Ezekiel and showed him the east gate of the temple, where Jaazaniah, son of Azzur, and Pelatiah, son of Benaiah, were devising iniquity. Ezekiel was commanded to bring against them the men they had slain in the streets; he did as he was bidden and Pelatiah died. Yahweh's Glory arose and took its place on the Mount of Olives in token that Yahweh had abandoned his temple. The vision was translated to the people by another symbol. Ezekiel dug through the mud brick wall of his house and thus brought out his personal property, covering his head so he could not see the ground; so Judah's prince was to come captive to Babylon and yet not behold it.[8]

This group of prophecies was delivered in 591. Time passed and they were not fulfilled. A saying gained currency: "The days are prolonged and every vision fails." Ezekiel sharply retorted: "I will stop this saying, no more shall they use it as a proverb in Israel; say rather to them: 'At hand are the days and the fulfilment of every vision.'" The people did not dare dispute the prophet's inspiration, but they comforted themselves: "The vision he sees belongs to a time many days distant, it is of times afar off that he is prophesying."

Like Jeremiah, Ezekiel protests against the lying prophets, who stand like jackals on the ruins and howl their own thoughts, who see visions that are false and divine lies. These pacifists cry "Peace" when there is no peace, and whitewash the mud brick walls to protect them against the driving rains and hail of the Babylonian winter! Even women dare to be prophets; they sew amulets on men's wrists and place fillets on their heads, they hunt men's souls, and all for the few handfuls of barley and the few scraps of bread they receive in payment! Israel has abandoned herself to idols; though

[7] Ezek. 8–10. [8] Ezek. 11–12.

THE FALL OF JERUSALEM

Noah, Daniel, and Job were there in person, they could but save their own lives.[9]

Jerusalem is a woman, abandoned on the day of her birth by her Amorite father and her Hittite mother. She lay in her blood, ready to die, when Yahweh passed by and took pity, he cared for her until she was grown and then made her his wife. But she did not appreciate the kindness which had permitted her beauty to develop, rather she entered a life of shame. In place of Yahweh, she received as lovers the Egyptians, great of flesh, the Assyrians and the Chaldæans, inhabitants of a land of merchants, and slew her children as sacrifices before her images. She proves the proverb "Like mother, like daughter," in fact she has excelled in evil her elder sister Samaria and her younger sister Sodom.[10]

There were two sisters, Oholah and Oholibah, Samaria and Jerusalem. In their youth, they were unchaste in Egypt, yet Yahweh married them. Oholah sinned with the Assyrians, nobles clad in purple, prefects and governors, all stately youths, knights on horseback. Abandoned by Yahweh to her lovers, she found them enemies who imprisoned her children and slew her with the sword. Her fate became a warning to women, but not to Oholibah, for she too sinned with the Assyrians and after them with their successors, when she "saw men portrayed upon the walls, portraits of Chaldæans painted in vermilion, girdled with girdles upon their loins and with fillets on their heads, all of them princes to look upon." Therefore all the Babylonians and Chaldæans, the Aramæan tribes of the Pekod and Shoa and Koa, shall come up against her with chariots and wagons, she shall drink the cup of her sister, large and deep, the cup of astonishment and desolation.[11]

Once there was a great eagle, with long wings and broad pinions, full feathered and varicoloured, who came to Lebanon and carried off the top of a cedar to the land of traffic, the city of merchants. Its seed he took and planted in fertile soil, by plenteous streams of water he set it out as a slip, that it might grow and become a spreading vine of low stature. But another

[9] Ezek. 12–13. [10] Ezek. 16. [11] Ezek. 23.

eagle attracted the vine, which bent its branches towards it for water; shall not he who planted it now pull it up, shall it not wither when touched by the hot east wind? If the "Captivity" does not understand this riddle, Ezekiel will explain. The king of Babylon came to Jerusalem and deported king and princes, another of the royal family he took by covenant that the kingdom might be lowly, not exalting itself; nevertheless, the king sent to Egypt for horses and troops, though Pharaoh and his hosts cannot avail when mounds and forts are set up. The king took the oath in Yahweh's name, now he has forsworn himself; his sin is against Yahweh, in Yahweh's net shall he be caught.[12]

Two high roads are marked out for the sword of Babylon's king, one against Rabbath Ammon and one against Jerusalem, he stands at the cross road by the sign post and makes divination with the shaken arrows, the teraphim, and the inspected liver, the lot of Jerusalem comes out in his right hand. Let Judah's wicked king remove his miter and take off his crown, no more shall they be used until he comes whose right they are.[13]

With unwonted solemnity Ezekiel dates the word of Yahweh, the ninth year, the tenth month, the tenth day of the month: "Son of man, write the name of this day, for on this very day the king of Babylon has drawn near to Jerusalem. Set on the caldron and fill it with water, gather in it the choice cuts, thigh and shoulder, pile under it wood and boil the choice bones. Woe to the bloody city and the rusty caldron, for her blood is in her, she has placed it on the bare rock and has not poured it on the ground or covered it with earth. Therefore wrath shall arise to take vengeance, Yahweh has likewise set her blood on the bare rock, not to be covered."[14]

Ezekiel's wife, the "desire of his eyes," died on the evening of one of his visions. The bereaved husband shed no tears, re-

---

[12]Ezek. 17; cf. the net of Ningirsu of Lagash, J. B. Nies, *JAOS.*, XXXVI, 1917, 137 ff.
[13]Ezek. 21:19–27; for liver divination, cf. *History of Assyria*, 358 ff.
[14]Ezek. 24:1–8.

fused to tear off his headdress and footgear, did not cover his lips, or eat the food provided for the funeral. Yahweh, he explained, was about to profane his sanctuary, the prize of their power, the desire of their eyes; news would soon come that their children left behind in Judah had been slain, yet they would not be able to mourn in public the death of public enemies.[15]

Back in Judah, a certain Habakkuk made complaint: "How long, Yahweh, must I cry, and thou not hear, cry 'Violence,' and thou not save, why show me iniquity, on trouble make me look? Before me is destruction and violence, strife and contention, the law is benumbed, justice goes not forth, the wicked circumvent the righteous, justice is perverted." Yahweh replies:

Lo, I raise up Chaldæans, fierce and hasty nation,
    Marching the breadth of earth, taking homes not his;
Terrible, dreadful is he, from him goeth out judgment,
    Swifter than leopards his horses, they are fiercer than wolves;
His horsemen come from afar, vultures hastening to eat,
    All for violence come, captives gather as sand;
He scoffs at kings and princes are his derision,
    He laughs at every fort, heaps earth and takes it;
His purpose he changes, he passes along,
    And raises an altar to his god.

Punishment of wicked Judæans is understandable but why should the wicked Chaldæans prosper? Yahweh replies that they are to be destroyed, but the righteous shall live by his faith.[16]

Psammetichus II (593–588) invaded Palestine in 590 and gave the Tyrian throne to Ittobaal III (589–574). The kings of Edom, Moab, and Ammon joined with Tyre and Sidon in sending to Zedekiah ambassadors urging him to revolt. Jeremiah presented the ambassadors with bonds and neck bars for

---

[15] Ezek. 24:15–24.
[16] B. Duhm, *Das Buch Habakuk*, 1906; W. H. Ward, *Habakkuk*, 1911; Nowack, *Die Kleinen Propheten*, 258 ff.; Marti, *Dodekapropheton*, 326 ff.; Sellin, *Zwölfprophetenbuch*, 377 ff.

their lords and a message that Yahweh had granted the earth to Babylon's king. Their prophets and diviners were saying: "Do not serve the king of Babylon," but this was a lie, whose only result would be their removal to a far country. Yahweh will punish the nation that does not put its neck under the yoke of Babylon's king, but the nation that submits will be permitted to remain in its own land.[17]

Hananiah of Gibeon, Azzur's son, one of the official prophets, predicted in Yahweh's name to the crowds assembled in the temple: "I have broken the yoke of Babylon's king, within two full years will I bring back to this place all the vessels of Yahweh's house; also will I bring to this place Jeconiah and all the captives of Judah." Jeremiah replied: "Amen, so may Yahweh do, may Yahweh accomplish what you predict; nevertheless, hear now this word that I speak in your ears and in the ears of all the people: The prophets of old who were before me and before you prophesied war against many countries and great kingdoms; as for the prophet who predicts peace, when his words come to pass, then it shall be known that Yahweh in truth has sent him." Hananiah snatched the bar from Jeremiah's neck and broke it, saying: "Thus saith Yahweh: Thus will I break the yoke of Babylon's king from off the neck of all nations." Jeremiah went his way, but soon came the word: "You have broken the bars of wood, you have made iron bars in their stead; a yoke of iron have I put on the neck of all those nations that they shall serve Babylon's king. Yahweh has not sent you, but you make this people trust a lie; lo, I have sent you away from earth's face, you shall die this very year," and so it came to pass.[18]

Prophets who predicted the return of his rival Jehoiachin found little favour with Zedekiah, and when Nebuchadnezzar began the siege of Jerusalem on the tenth day of the tenth month of 588, Zedekiah sent messengers to Jeremiah begging him: "Inquire for us of Yahweh, I pray you, for the king of Babylon is warring against us; perchance Yahweh will do his wondrous work, that he may depart from us." The soft words

[17] Jer. 27:2–11.   [18] Jer. 28.

of the weak king turned not away wrath, for Jeremiah only repeated: "I will turn back the weapons of war with which you fight the Chaldæans, I will collect them in this city. The way of life and the way of death have I set before you; he who remains in this city shall die by the sword and by famine, he who goes out and passes over to the Chaldæans shall live." Lachish and Azekah, the only cities still in Jewish possession, were besieged by Nebuchadnezzar, and again Jeremiah assured Zedekiah that he should be made captive and should speak with Nebuchadnezzar mouth to mouth.[19]

The loss of Judah meant nothing to Apries or Hophra (588–569), but when Nebuchadnezzar also began the siege of Tyre in 587, the Egyptians at last appeared in Palestine. Nebuchadnezzar went out to meet him and the siege of Jerusalem was raised. There was great rejoicing—for all but the slaves. In the first terror of the siege, Zedekiah had made a covenant with the officials, priests, and people, that all slaves of Hebrew birth should be freed according to the new law, and had confirmed it by marching between the two halves of the sacrificial calf as had Abraham; no sooner were the Chaldæans out of sight than the masters revoked their promise. Swift was Jeremiah's rebuke: "You have not hearkened to me, to proclaim every man freedom to his neighbour; lo, I proclaim to you freedom—to the sword, the pest, and famine!" They shall be given to the hands of their enemies, their bodies shall be food for the birds of the heaven and the beasts of the earth; Yahweh will command the Chaldæans to return, and will give them the city to burn with fire. The Egyptians are the ones who will return home, let not Zedekiah deceive himself; though he smite the whole Chaldæan host and only the wounded remain, they shall rise up and burn the city.[20]

Jeremiah attempted to utilise the temporary raising of the siege to settle an ancestral estate in Anathoth. A grandson of Hananiah was on duty at the Gate of Benjamin and Jeremiah was seized on suspicion of deserting to the Chaldæans. De-

---

[19] Jer. 21:1–10; 39:1–7.
[20] Jer. 34:8–10, 17–22; 37:3–10; cf. Gen. 15; Herod., ii, 161; Diod., i, 68.

spite his denial, he was brought before the princes who ordered his imprisonment in the house of the scribe Jonathan. Zedekiah summoned him secretly and anxiously inquired whether there was any new word from Yahweh; the only answer was that he should go to Babylon. "Where now are your prophets," Jeremiah with reason demanded, "who prophesied to you: 'Babylon's king shall not come against this city or this land'?" He did beg Zedekiah not to send him to his death in his former prison, and the king had the decency to order him committed to the court of the guard where each day he was given a loaf of bread until the supply in the city ceased.[21]

Here Jeremiah continued to give defeatist prophecies until his former friends, the princes, urged the king to slay him as weakening the hands of the men of war. Poor Zedekiah could only answer: "See, he is in your hand, for the king can do nothing against you." Jeremiah was lowered into a mud-filled pit in the court of the guard, but Ebedmelech, the Ethiopian servant of the king, informed his master, who sent thirty men to pull Jeremiah out and bring him into his presence. For the last time, Zedekiah made inquiry; Jeremiah, still covered with mud, was naturally suspicious: "If I declare it to you, will you not surely put me to death? Even if I do give you counsel, you will not listen to me." But the king swore secretly: "As Yahweh lives, who made us this soul, I will neither put you to death nor deliver you into the hand of these men." For the last time, the prophet placed before him the alternatives, surrender with safety or resistance with capture. Zedekiah excused himself with the fear that he might be delivered into the hands of the Judæans who had deserted to the Chaldæans and be mocked, but Jeremiah swept away this excuse and implored him to think of the terrible fate in store for the women of his harem, but to no avail. The best he could secure was a promise of remaining in the court of the guard if he would conceal the interview. Ebedmelech was promised that his life would be spared.[22]

On the ninth day of the fourth month of the eleventh year,

[21] Jer. 37:11–21. [22] Jer. 38; 39:15–18.

586, the walls were breached. Zedekiah and his men of war fled that night by the gate between the two walls at the southeast corner near the king's garden and the pool of Siloam; they hoped to reach the Arabah and so pass to the east Jordan country, but were overtaken at Jericho. Zedekiah was carried to Nebuchadnezzar at Riblah, where his sons were slain before his eyes and then he was blinded that his last sight might be the end of his hopes of posterity.

A month later, Nabu-zer-iddina, captain of the guard and a king's companion, returned to Jerusalem, burned the temple, palace, and all other buildings and broke down the wall. The few remaining nobles were deported, among them the chief priest Seraiah, the second priest Zephaniah, the three threshold keepers, the head of the army, five royal companions, the scribe of the captain of the host who mustered the people of the land. Only the poorest peasants were left behind as vinedressers and husbandmen.[23] The whole line of prosperous Shephelah towns, Azekah, Shocoh, Adullam, Keilah, Kiriath Sepher, and the rest, were utterly destroyed and never reoccupied during our period.[24] Gedaliah, son of Ahikam and grandson of that Shaphan who had been a power under Josiah, was appointed governor of such Jews as remained, and took up his residence at Mizpah in a great tower and three thick-walled rooms built against the inner city wall.[25]

Jeremiah had considered himself a true patriot, but Nebuchadnezzar realised how valuable had been his services in weakening the morale of the rebels, and he therefore gave Nabu-zer-iddina specific orders to treat him well and to execute his every wish. Nabu-zer-iddina, Nabushazban, the rab saris, and Nergal-shar-usur, the rab mag and governor of the city Sin-magir, soon himself to be king of Babylon, brought out the prophet from the court of the guard and invited him to go in honour to Babylon; Jeremiah declined and was then sent with gifts from Ramah, where the captives had been collected, to Gedaliah at Mizpah.[26]

[23] II Kings 25:1–12, 18–21.   [24] W. F. Albright, *ZAW.*, NF., VI, 1929, 16.
[25] Badè, *Excavations*, 25 f.   [26] Jer. 39:14; 40:1–6.

If the seal of "Elishama son of Gedaliah" actually refers to our governor, then Gedaliah was no radical in religion, for on it Yahweh is depicted as a bearded god in long robe and high crown with uplifted right hand which apparently brandishes the thunderbolt; he is seated on a throne with footstool between seven parted palmettes raised on stands and is borne along on a ship ending at stem and stern in birds' heads.[27] Soon the leaders of the bands wandering about in the open country came in to Gedaliah, who urged them to settle in the abandoned towns they had occupied and to gather in the wine, summer fruits, and oil. Fugitives from Edom, Moab, and Ammon swelled the remnant. The leaders were indeed in captivity, but something like three-quarters of the population remained, and there was hope for the future.

Baalis, the Ammonite king, sent Ishmael, son of Nethaniah, of the seed royal, to assassinate the new governor. Johanan informed Gedaliah and offered to put Ishmael out of the way secretly, but Gedaliah refused to believe what he considered a base slander. Three months after Jerusalem's fall, Ishmael arrived with ten followers and was received with all hospitality; to his eternal disgrace, Ishmael violated the sacred laws of hospitality and murdered Gedaliah and all the Jews and Chaldæans in Mizpah. Two days later, eighty pilgrims from Shiloh, Shechem, and Samaria appeared with beards shaved, clothes rent, and bodies mutilated, the rites of mourning for the dead, and bearing meal offerings and frankincense to the ruined temple at Jerusalem. Ishmael met them, weeping hypocritically for the destruction of the temple, invited them within in Gedaliah's name, and slew them, all but ten men who purchased their lives with stores of wheat, barley, oil, and honey hidden in the fields, and their bodies filled the great pit which Asa had made in fear of Baasha. Then, taking the few Jews remaining in Mizpah, including the daughters of the late king, the renegade Ishmael departed to take up his abode among the children of Ammon.

[27] Fig. 177; G. Dalman, *Palästinajahrbuch*, II, 1906, 44 ff.

Word of the outrage reached Johanan and the other captains. Ishmael was pursued to the great waters of Gibeon and the captives were recovered and brought to the Lodge of Chimham near Bethlehem, but Ishmael escaped with eight of his ten men. Gedaliah's body was taken from the cistern under the citadel and the polluted cistern was carefully sealed.[28] Jeremiah was asked for an oracle and the leaders took oath that they would obey; after ten days of anxious waiting, they were ordered to remain. Fearing the vengeance of the Chaldæan army encamped before Tyre, they angrily declared that Jeremiah had lied, that he had been influenced by the pro-Babylonian Baruch who wished them to be deported to Babylonia and slain.

Johanan and all the Jews in Mizpah fled to Tahpanhes in Egypt. Even in the Nile Delta, Jeremiah continued to show his anti-Egyptian feelings. Taking great stones, he mortared them at the palace entrance with this prophecy: "Behold, I will send and bring Nebuchadnezzar, and set his throne on these stones I have laid; he shall spread his royal pavilion over them when he comes and smites Egypt." "He shall break the obelisks in the House of the Sun," Heliopolis, "the house of Egypt's gods shall he burn with fire."[29]

Settled in Pathros, the Jews continued their worship of other gods. Jeremiah reproached them in their assembly, but they had a reply which was from their point of view unanswerable: "We will not listen to the word you have spoken to us in the name of Yahweh, but will certainly perform every word that has gone out of our mouth, to burn incense to the queen of heaven and to pour out drink offerings to her as we did, we and our fathers, our kings and our princes, in the cities of Judah and on the streets of Jerusalem, for then we had plenty of bread and were well and saw no evil. But since we ceased burning incense to the queen of heaven, we have been in want of all things and have been consumed by the sword and by famine. For when we burned incense to the queen of heaven and poured out drink offerings to her, did we make cakes to

[28]Badè, *l. c.*   [29]Jer. 40–43.

worship her and pour out drink offerings to her without our husbands?"

Jeremiah could only reiterate his belief that Yahweh had made them desolate because he remembered these very misdeeds. Not even in Egypt shall they find safety; as Zedekiah was given into the hands of Nebuchadnezzar, so shall Pharaoh Hophra be given into the hands of his enemies. With this last prediction of evil, the words of Jeremiah end.[30]

[30]Jer. 44:15-22, 30.

CHAPTER XXXVI

BY BABYLON'S RIVERS

By Babylon's rivers, there we sat down,
    Yea, we wept, remembering Zion;
On the poplars in its midst we hung up our harps,
    For there our captors asked of us singing,
Our tormentors asked of us mirth:
    Sing us one of Zion's songs.
How sing Yahweh's songs in a foreign land?
    Jerusalem, if I forget you, let my right hand forget,
Let tongue cleave to mouth's roof, if I remember you not,
    If I prefer not Jerusalem above my chief joy!
Remember, Yahweh, Jerusalem's Day against Edom's sons,
    Who said: Rase it, to its foundations rase it!
Babylon's daughter, about to be destroyed,
    Happy he who rewards you as you have served us;
Happy he who takes and dashes
    Your little ones against the rock.[1]

Such was the sad lament of the Jewish exiles in Babylonia. The homesickness so beautifully expressed in the first stanza almost but not quite makes us forget the savage hatred expressed in the last. Other poets grieved no less for the past and hoped for the future:

When Yahweh returns Zion's exile, we'll be as dreamers,
    Our mouth filled with laughter, our tongue with song;
They shall say mid the nations: Great things doth Yahweh,
    When Yahweh doth great things, we shall rejoice.

Yahweh, return our exile, as streams in the Negeb,
    They who sow in tears shall reap in joy;
He who goes forth with weeping, with seed for sowing,
    Shall return with joy, bringing his sheaves.[2]

Not all the Jews in Babylonia were anti-Babylonian. Many were prospering in business, at Tell Abib and Ahava on the

[1] Psalm 137.   [2] Psalm 126; cf. Psalm 85.

Chebar near Nippur, at Casiphia or Ctesiphon. A few at least had become good Babylonian citizens. Even after Nebuchadnezzar had destroyed his old home, Ezekiel continued loyal to his new master, but his whole prophetic fervour was transferred to the neighbouring peoples which rejoiced over Jerusalem's fate and sought to win advantage from it. Warning of their coming ruin and reprobation of their savage rejoicing brought from his lips prophecies which glow and refute the general opinion that Ezekiel is a dull writer. Against Ammon comes this word:

> Because you said Aha over my profaned shrine,
> And Israel's land when it was made desolate,
> And Judah's house when it went into exile,
> Lo, I give you to Kedem's sons as a possession,
> They shall pitch their tents and set their homes in you,
> They shall eat your fruit and drink your milk,
> Rabbah will I make a camel pasture,
> Ammon a grazing place for flocks,
> And you shall know that I am Yahweh.
>
> Because you clapped your hands and stamped your feet,
> With despite of soul over Israel's land,
> Lo, my hand I will stretch out against you,
> And deliver you as spoil to the nations;
> I will cut you off from the peoples,
> Make you perish out of the countries,
> I will destroy you,
> And you shall know that I am Yahweh.

Other dooms follow in like manner. Moab has said: "Judah's house has become like all the nations"; Moab's flank shall be laid open from his frontier cities to the land's glory, the capital, and like Ammon shall be given to the nomad children of Kedem. Edom took vengeance against Judah; therefore shall man and beast be cut off, from Teman to Dedan shall they fall by the sword. The Philistines have taken vengeance with scorn of soul to destroy with a perpetual hatred, the Cretans shall be cut off and the remnant of the seacoast be destroyed.[3]

[3] Ezek. 25.

Nebuchadnezzar had begun the siege of Tyre in the year before the capture of Jerusalem, but Ittobaal III yet retained his independence. Tyre, safe on her island, has gloated over the fall of her rival Jerusalem: "Aha, she is broken, the gate of the peoples, she is open to me, I shall be full, now that she is laid waste." Ezekiel devotes his best poetical powers to predicting the success of his Babylonian master:

> Behold, I am against you, O Tyre,
> Will make many nations come up against you,
> As the sea makes its waves to come up!
> Tyre's walls shall they destroy, and break down her towers,
> I will scrape her dust from her, make her bare rock.
> A place for the spreading of nets in the midst of the sea,
> A spoil to the nations shall she be;
> Her mainland daughters with the sword shall be slain,
> And they shall know that I am Yahweh.[4]

There follows a description of Tyre's commerce which is a distinct contribution to the history of ancient trade. Tyre dwells at the entrance of the sea, the merchants of the peoples to many isles. Her anchorage is in the sea's midst. All her planks have been fashioned of cypresses from Senir or Anti-Lebanon, cedar from Lebanon makes her mast. Her oars are from oaks of Bashan, her deck of ivory inlaid with boxwood from the isles of Cyprus. Her sail is fine linen with Egyptian embroidery, such an ensign as we find on her later coins, her awning is the blue and purple of Elishah or Greece. Men of Sidon and Tyre were her rowers, wise men of Tyre were her pilots, skilled workmen from Gebal caulked her. Persia and Lydia and Phut were mercenaries in her army, men of Arvad and Cilicia were on her walls and men of Kumedi on her towers.

Tarsus was her merchant, they traded for Tyre's wares the silver, iron, tin, and lead of the famous mines of Asia Minor.[5] Javan, the Ionians, and the Asia Minor tribes of Tubal and Meshech[6] were her traffickers, who traded bodies of men and vessels of copper[7] for her merchants. The house of Togarmah,

---

[4] Ezek. 26:1–6. [5] *History of Assyria*, 534, fig. 79.
[6] *Ibid.*, 63, 80, 125, 143, 221. [7] *Ibid.*, 534.

the Assyrian Til-Garimmu, traded horses, war steeds, and mules, such as the famous Cappadocian stallions.[8] Men of Rodan or Rhodes were her traffickers, many coast lands were marts of her hand, they brought tribute of ivory tusks and ebony from far distant Africa. The Aramæans, who monopolized the internal trade as did the Phœnicians that of the maritime shores, traded purple, embroideries, fine linen, jasper, and the pearls from the Persian Gulf.[9] Judah and Israel purchased her manufactures with agricultural products, wheat of the Ammonite Minnith, pannag, honey, oil, and balm of Gilead. Damascus supplied the wine of Helbon, from the slopes of Anti-Lebanon, which Nebuchadnezzar had just immortalised by inclusion on his famous "wine card," and which was to continue the favourite of Persian kings,[10] together with white wool from the flocks of the near-by desert. Uzal sent iron, cassia, and calamus. Arabian Dedan was her merchant for saddle cloths, Arabia and all the princes of Kedar were traders controlled by her hand and sold her their lambs, rams, and goats. Even far distant Sheba in southwest Arabia exchanged the most precious spices, all sorts of precious stones, and gold. From Mesopotamia, the cities of Harran, Canneh, Eden, Ashur, and Chilmad, came choice garments, mantles of blue, embroidered work, stuffs of varied colours, strongly bound skeins. Ships of Tarsus were caravans for her merchandise.

Yet for all her wealth, her rowers have brought her into vast stretches of water, the east wind has broken her in the midst of the sea. Who was glorious like Tyre in the midst of the sea? When her wares went forth on the waters, she supplied many peoples and enriched the kings of the earth; now all the men of the coast lands are dismayed at her fall, their kings are horribly affrighted.[11]

Tyre's heart was uplifted, she said in her pride: "I am a god, I sit in the seat of the gods in the sea's midst." She is

[8]*Ibid.*, 225, 311, 518; 276, 320.   [9]*Ibid.*, 54, 180, 256.
[10]Langdon, *Königsinschriften*, 90 f., 154 f.; Strabo, xv, 3, 22.
[11]Ezek. 27.

wiser than Daniel, no man is her equal, by her wisdom has she secured wealth, her heart is like that of a god. She was in Eden, God's garden, adorned with every precious stone, but she became unrighteous and was filled with violence; therefore Yahweh has cast her out from the Mount of God as profane, the cherub has driven her from the midst of the fiery stones.[12]

Ezekiel's hopes were disappointed. Ittobaal held Tyre for thirteen years against the Babylonian armies; we possess a receipt for flour for the men who brought food to the king and the soldiers who went forth with him against the land of Tyre. Like their Assyrian predecessors, the Chaldæans were poor seamen and were unable to accomplish anything against Tyre, which remained safe on its island, protected by its large and efficient navy, and supported by that of Egypt. Finally in 574 there was a compromise; Ittobaal gave way to Baal II (574–564), and Tyre admitted a nominal Babylonian suzerainty.[13] Henceforth, Tyrian business documents were dated by the years of Nebuchadnezzar. In his thirty-fifth year, sesame is sold at Tyre and men of Arvad are mentioned. Five years later, the governor of Kadesh, Milki-idri, buys cattle. Next year, Innina-zer-ibni, Rimut's son, acknowledges his indebtedness to high officials in Uruk for the great sum of three manas eight shekels of silver; the witnesses are headed by the shandabakku or royal commissar Enlil-shapik-zer, sent by Baal, king of Tyre, who certifies his action by his seal. The year following, the same Innina-zer-ibni buys a quantity of dates in Uruk for the nobles of Tyre. About the same time, Nebuchadnezzar prepared a list of his high officials which ends with the kings of the lands of Tyre, Gaza, Sidon, Arvad, Ashdod, and two unknown cities.[14]

The Egyptian fleet was under Greek direction, the best in the world, and in 570 it fought a battle with the recreant Tyrians, supported by the other Phœnician states of the sea-

[12]Ezek. 28:2–19.   [13]Menander, in Joseph., *Ant.*, x, 228; *Apion*, i, 156.
[14]R. P. Dougherty, *Archives from Erech*, 1923, 94, 151, 169; E. Unger, *Theologische Literaturzeitung*, L, 1925, 481 ff.; *ZAW.*, NF., III, 1926, 314 ff.

board and of Cyprus. The allies were put to flight and Sidon was stormed; Ezekiel's prediction of Sidon's destruction was fulfilled, though not quite as he had expected. This was followed by the submission of the other Phœnician states, and an Egyptian garrison stationed at Gebal began the erection of a temple to the local Lady whom long before they had identified with their own Hathor.[15]

A defeat in Libya followed by a revolt supplanted Apries in the next year by Amasis (569–525). Nebuchadnezzar attempted to take advantage of the opportunity, and Ezekiel, though disappointed at the failure of his predictions concerning Tyre, still hoped for a reward for his royal master. Nebuchadnezzar had caused his army to endure hard service against Tyre, every head was made bald and every shoulder was galled from the armour worn so continuously, yet he had no wages; now he will be given Egypt as wages for his army and recompense for his service.[16]

Yahweh is against Pharaoh, king of Egypt, great monster who lies in the midst of his river, who says: "My river is my own for I made it." Yahweh will put hooks in his jaws and draw him out with all the fish of the river sticking to his scales, and will cast him out into the desert to be food for the beasts of earth and the birds of the heavens. Pharaoh has been a staff of reed to the house of Israel; when they seized his hand, he broke and made all their loins shake. Egypt shall be utter desolation from the border fort of Migdol to Seveneh or Syene on Ethiopia's frontier where already Jews had settled as mercenaries.[17]

Let the Egyptians wail, near is Yahweh's Day; her supporters, Ethiopia, Put, Lydia, the Arabs and Cretans, shall fall and be desolate, even among desolate regions. This shall be accomplished by Nebuchadnezzar and his people, most terrible of nations, they shall fill the land with the slain; the river shall be made dry, the land shall be sold into the hands of hard men. Nobles shall cease from Memphis, no more shall there

[15] Herod., ii, 161; Diod., i, 68; Ezek. 28:20–23; Renan, *Mission*, 26 ff.; 179.
[16] Ezek. 29:17–20. [17] Ezek. 29:3–10; cf. chap. XLI.

Fig. 180. GRAVE MONUMENT OF AN ARAMÆAN IN EGYPT.

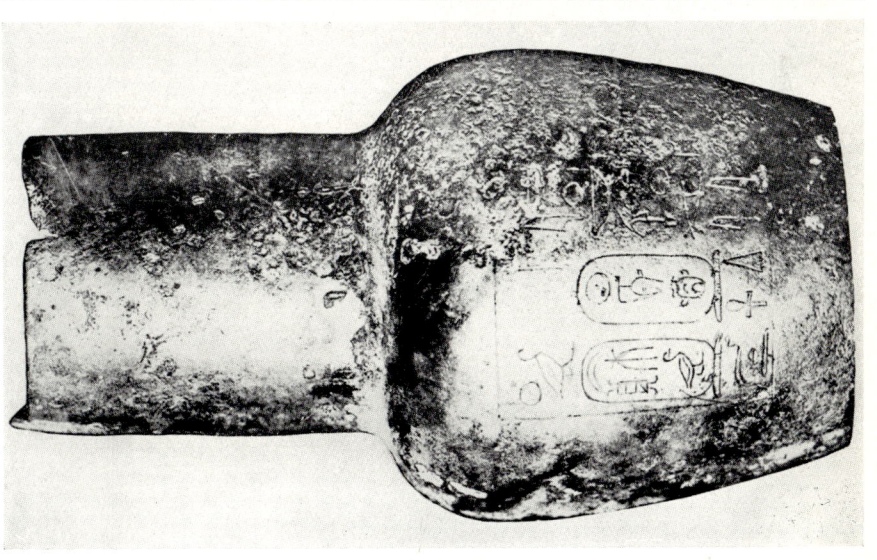

Fig. 179. BRONZE VASE OF AMASIS FROM SIDON.

be a prince in Egypt. Yahweh shall make Pathros desolate and kindle a fire in Zoan, he shall execute judgment on Thebes, and Syene shall be in great anguish, Thebes shall be breached, the walls of Memphis shall be cut through. The young men of Heliopolis and Pi-beseth shall fall by the sword, the cities shall go into captivity. In Tahpanhes, where the exiles had taken Jeremiah in their wild rush for safety, the day shall be dark when Yahweh breaks the yoke of Egypt. Her pride of power shall cease, a cloud shall cover her, her daughters shall go into exile. Pharaoh's arm he has broken, it cannot be bound up, no medicine or bandage can strengthen it enough to hold the sword; it is Nebuchadnezzar's arms which Yahweh shall strengthen, it is his hand into which Yahweh shall place his sword, but Pharaoh with broken arm shall groan before him, with the groanings of a man deadly wounded. The Egyptians shall be scattered among the nations, and they shall know that he is Yahweh.[18]

"Whom are you like in your greatness?" Ezekiel asks of the Pharaoh, and he draws the comparison with the Assyrian cedar, so glorious but now hewn down.[19] Egypt too shall be brought down with the trees of Eden to the Underworld, and shall lie with the uncircumcised, those slain by the sword.[20] Amasis has likened himself to a young lion among the nations; in truth he is but a sea monster, who spouts water from his nostrils, troubles the water with his feet, and fouls the rivers. Yahweh shall drag him up with his net, he shall be cast into the uncultivated field, and all the birds of the heavens shall settle upon him; all the beasts of the field shall be satiated feeding upon him, his flesh shall be exposed upon the mountains, the valleys shall be filled with his corpse. When he is extinguished, the heavens shall be covered, the sun shall be dark, Yahweh shall cover the sun with a cloud and the moon shall not give her light, all the bright lights of heaven shall be made dark, and darkness shall descend upon his land. Yahweh shall destroy all the beasts that dwell beside Egypt's many waters, they shall be no longer troubled by foot of man or hoof

[18]Ezek. 30.   [19]Cf. *History of Assyria*, 643 f.   [20]Ezek. 31.

of beast, their waters thus untroubled shall settle, their rivers flow smooth as oil.

    Wail for Egypt's inhabitants and cast them down,
        You and the daughters of mighty nations,
    Into the Underworld,
        With them that go down to the Pit.

    Whom in beauty do you surpass?
        Descend, with the uncircumcised lie down,
    Among those slain by the sword,
        Lie down, you and all your folk!

    Mighty warriors to him shall speak,
        With his helpers from Sheol's midst,
    Descend, with the uncircumcised lie down,
        With those who are slain by the sword!

    Ashur is there with her army, round about her grave,
        All of them slain, fallen by the sword,
    Whose graves are set in the Pit's utmost part,
        For they caused fear in the land of the living.

    Elam is there with all her army, round about her grave,
        All of them slain, fallen by the sword,
    Who uncircumcised to the Underworld have gone down,
        For they caused fear in the land of the living.

    Meshech and Tubal are there with their army, round about
        their grave,
        All of them uncircumcised, slain by the sword,
    Now their shame they bear, with those who go to the Pit,
        For they caused fear in the land of the living.

    They lie not with heroes, the uncircumcised fallen,
        Who went down to Sheol with their weapons of war,
    Swords under their heads, shields over their bones,
        For the terror of their might was in the land of the living.

    Edom is there, all her princes and her kings,
        Who in might are laid with the slain by the sword,
    With those uncircumcised shall they lie,
        With them that go down to the Pit.

There are all the princes of the North,
 All the men of Sidon, gone down with the slain,
In the terror of their might with the uncircumcised lie,
 With those who are slain by the sword.

Then Pharaoh shall see, take comfort for his host,
 For he too caused fear in the land of the living,
He too shall be laid, the uncircumcised among,
 With those who are slain by the sword.[21]

At first, it seemed as if these hopes were to be realised. Sidon was held loyal by gifts, two bronze jars with the cartouche of Amasis and a votive sistrum.[22] Two years after his accession, in 567, Amasis collected his troops, which included contingents from Pittacus of Lesbos and other Greeks from far distant regions in the midst of the sea. The armies of Egypt advanced to make battle but Nebuchadnezzar claims their overthrow;[23] the victory was certainly not decisive, perhaps the claim is false, for three years later, in 564, there was a revolution in Tyre. The pro-Egyptian oligarchs deposed Baal and abolished the kingship in favour of shophetim or "judges." Hekinni-baal, son of Baal-sakkun, the first judge, lasted but three months. He was supplanted by the son of Abdæus, Kelbis, whose name, "Dog of Isis," showed his Egyptian sympathies, for ten months, and by the high priest Abi-baal for three. Then the oligarchs determined to follow the example of their daughter Carthage and elected two suffetes or shophetim to head the state; these two, Matten and Ger Ashtart, son of Abd-elim, ruled six years (563–557).[24]

Nebuchadnezzar had devoted much treasure to reconstruction of Babylonian temples, but his attitude was distinctly anti-hierarchical. Amel Marduk (562–560) abandoned his father's policy and followed the priests. His first act was to free Jehoiachin from his thirty-seven years of captivity and to place his throne above those of the other subject kings.

[21] Ezek. 32. [22] Fig. 179; M. Dunand, *Syria,* VII, 1926, 123 ff.
[23] Langdon, *Königsinschriften,* 206 f.; cf. H. Winckler, *Altorientalische Forschungen,* I, 511 ff.
[24] Menander, *l. c.*

Jehoiachin was permitted to marry and thus the Davidic line was perpetuated; in memory of this unexpected mercy, Jehoiachin named a son Pedaiah, "Yahweh has ransomed." Thus Jeremiah's prediction that he would be childless was proved false and the exiles might hope for the fulfilment of the prophecy by Jeremiah's rival Hananiah according to which Jehoiachin was to return with the exiles to Jerusalem. Shortly thereafter, and perhaps in preparation for the expected return, a member of the prophetic party wrote a history of the Hebrew kingdoms, an earlier edition of our present Kings, in which each monarch was charactised as good or evil according to the extent with which his actions coincided with the prescripts of the code enforced by Josiah.[25]

This action of Amel Marduk was much more than recognition of a petty frontier king, it was a direct break with his father's political policies. The militarists therefore promptly supplanted him by Nebuchadnezzar's son-in-law Nergal-shar-usur (560–556). Militarists in power meant renewed interest in the west, and the oligarchic suffetes in Tyre were overthrown by the democrats and the kingship restored in the person of Baalator (557–556). Nergal-shar-usur's son Labashi Marduk supported the priests a few days, but again the King's Friends conspired and placed on the throne the Babylonian Nabu-naid, who definitely proclaimed himself the political successor of Nebuchadnezzar and Nergal-shar-usur.

[25] II Kings 25:27 ff.; I Chron. 3:17 ff.; Jer. 22:30; 28:4; cf. p. 524, and *AJSL.*, XXXI, 1915, 169 ff.

CHAPTER XXXVII

PROPHETS OF HOPE AND OF HATE

EZEKIEL had been a true Babylonian patriot, rejoicing in Nebuchadnezzar's success and deploring his failures. He had advised his fellow Jews to make their peace with their captors, to settle down and share the daily life of their neighbours, and many had taken his advice. His policy seemed justified when Amel Marduk rescued Jehoiachin from prison and assigned him a high position at court. The exiles began to dream of restoration to their homeland under their own king. All too quickly Amel Marduk was deposed, his memory condemned, his friends disgraced; we are not informed of Jehoiachin's fate, but a man so distinguished by the fallen monarch can scarcely have escaped. The intense patriotism of the faction which had enthroned Nergal-shar-usur and Nabu-naid left little hope for Jewish dreams. The utter hopelessness of the exilic plaint by Babylon's rivers almost justified their savage expectation of Babylon's fall.

There were other Jews who were not content with hopeless weeping. One Hebrew poet had studied that Babylonian masterpiece, the Descent of Ishtar to the Land of No Return,[1] but with little sympathy; in a savage parody, even to the pentameter rhythm, he announced Babylon's coming shame:

> How has ceased the oppressor, has ceased the raging!
> He has broken the wicked's staff, the tyrant's scepter,
> Smiting the peoples in wrath with continual smiting,
> Trampling the nations in anger, with unchecked trampling:
> All earth is at rest and quiet, they break out singing,
> O'er you the fir trees rejoice and the Lebanon cedars;
> Since you were laid low no woodcutter comes against us.
>
> Sheol from its depths is shaken to meet your entrance,
> Evokes for you the shades, of earth all the leaders,

[1] R. W. Rogers, *Cuneiform Parallels to the Old Testament*, 1912, 121 ff.

Raises up from their thrones all kings of the nations,
All of them speak to you, to you give answer:
You too, are you weak like us, hast come in our likeness?
Dragged down to Sheol your pomp, the sound of your lutestrings,
Beneath you a couch of worms, your blankets of maggots!

How are you fallen from heaven, morn's son, the day star!
How are you hurled down to earth, prostrate mid corpses!
Who said in your heart: I will rise up to the heavens,
Above the stars of God my throne will establish,
Will sit on the Mount of Assembly, the north's far limits,
Will ascend o'er the heights of the clouds, like the High me making;
Yet shall you go down to Sheol, to the Pit's distant borders.

Who sees you shall stare at you, you shall consider:
This the man who shook earth and made kingdoms to tremble?
Made a desert of earth, and threw down its cities,
His captives freed not, all the kings of the nations?
All of them sleep in glory, each in his dwelling,
But you, from your mound cast down, like branch abhorrèd,
Clothed with the clothes of the slain, with the sword are you piercèd,

Who descend to the stones of the Pit, a corpse downtrodden,
Not placed in the grave with your sires, your land destroyèd,
Your people you kill, so your seed be named never,
Slaughter prepare for his sons, for sins of the father,
Lest they rise and seize the earth and fill its cities.[2]

Cyaxares the Mede had united with Nabopolassar in the destruction of Assyria, but his son Astyages (585–550) was not so friendly. It was obviously fear of Median aggression that caused Nebuchadnezzar to surround Babylon with such mighty fortifications. His death was followed by internal struggles which brought four kings to the throne in six years and offered Astyages unhoped for opportunity to attack. Jewish exiles began to dream that destruction would come upon Babylon from this quarter.

One exile had long studied Jeremiah's prophecies, especially those predicting destruction from the north; quite in his master's manner, he begins:

[2]Isaiah 14:4 ff.; cf. F. Vanderburgh, *AJSL.*, XXIX, 1913, 111 ff.

On bare mountain set up a standard, raise to them the voice,
Wave the hand that they enter the gate of the nobles;
I have commanded my men, consecrated for war,
Have summoned my heroes for my wrath, my men proudly exulting.
A sound of tumult on the mounts, appearance of many peoples,
A sound of confusion of kingdoms, the assembled nations,
Yahweh of Hosts has summoned the host to battle;
They are coming from distant lands, from the ends of heaven,
Yahweh and his weapons of wrath to destroy the whole earth.

Behold, I am bringing against them the Medes,
Who silver regard not, in gold take no delight,
Their bows shall shatter the youths, not pity the fruit of the womb;
And Babel, the glory of kingdoms, the beauty of Chaldæan pride,
Shall be as the overwhelming of Sodom and Gomorrah by God.
No more shall it be dwelt in, occupied from age to age,
No Arab shall pitch his tent there, nor shepherds there rest their flocks;
The desert beasts shall rest there, their houses full of jinns,
Ostriches shall dwell there, and there shall satyrs dance;
Jackals shall wail in their castles, and hyenas in their palaces of pride,
For near to come is her time, and her days shall not be prolonged.

This hymn of hate found an echo in the breasts of Jewish exiles:

Declare among the nations, set up a standard, do not conceal it, but say: Babylon is taken, Bel is put to shame, Marduk is broken down. Flee from Babylon's midst, depart from Chaldæa, be as goats before the flocks. Yahweh is stirring up against Babylon many nations from the north, and they set themselves in array against her. The sad fate of Israel is contrasted with the punishment of her oppressors; Israel is a scattered sheep, the lions have driven him away; first Assyria's king devoured him, now Babylon's king has broken his bones. Nonetheless, Yahweh will punish Babylon's king as he punished the king of Assyria, he will bring Israel back to his pasture and make him feed on Carmel and Bashan, his soul shall be satisfied on Ephraim's hills and in Gilead.

The Nar Marrati or Sealands and the Aramæan tribe of the Puqudu are to be reduced.³

> Go up against the Sealands,
> And against the men of Pekod,
> Slay them and devote them,
> Do all that I have commanded.

Nations are coming from the north, from the uttermost parts of the earth:

> They lay hold on bow and spear,
> They are cruel and have no mercy,
> Their voices roar as the sea,
> Also they ride upon horses,
> Every one set in array,
> As a man going to battle.

A note of sadness creeps in; the exiles have lived long in Babylon, and would gladly have saved her, had that been possible:

> Flee from Babylon's midst,
> And save every man his life,
> In her wickedness be not cut off,
> For 'tis Yahweh's time of revenge.

> Suddenly fallen is Babel,
> And destroyed, so wail for her,
> Balm do you take for her suffering,
> If so she may be healed.

> We would have Babylon healed,
> But healed is she not,
> Forsake her and let us go,
> Each to his own land.

Our poet recalls Median exploits, how they have already subdued the northern peoples who so long were a threat to Assyria;[4] now their troops will be found in the Median ranks, the men of Urartu, the Mannai, the Ishguza or Scythians:

³Cf. *History of Assyria*, 167, 480; 178, 445.
⁴Cf. *History of Assyria*, 50, 75, 360, 425.

> Set up a standard in the land,
> Blow the trump among the nations;
> Sanctify the nations against her,
> Call together the kingdoms against her,
> Ararat, Minni, Ashkenaz.

Babylon's heroes have foreborne to fight, they remain in their strongholds, their might has failed, they have become as women. Her dwelling places are fired, her bars are broken. One post runs to meet another, one messenger to meet the next, to show to Babylon's monarch how his city is taken in each quarter. There is hope for escape since Babylon is divided into factions: "My people, go out from her midst, save yourself from Yahweh's fierce anger; let not your hearts faint, fear not for the tidings heard in the land, for tidings shall come in one year and tidings in another, violence is in the land and ruler against ruler."

> The sound of a cry from Babel,
> From Chaldæa great destruction,
> For Yahweh lays waste Babel,
> Destroys from her the great voices.
> The destroyer has come upon her,
> Her men of might are taken,
> Their bows in pieces are broken,
> For a God of reward is Yahweh.[5]

Nabu-naid began his reign with an empire which extended to the Egyptian frontier at Gaza. Traces of the Chaldæans are frequent in Syria. At Nerab in the north we find the priest—the same word is used as for the heretical priests killed by Josiah—of the moon god Sahar whose good Assyrian name Sin-zer-ban honours a better-known moon god. Raising his hands in prayer, he tells us that this is his image and threatens despoilers by Sahar, Shamash, Nikkal, and Nusku. Another priest of Sahar is Agbar, who sits before an altar and presents a libation while his servant holds a fan. "For my righteousness before him, he established for me a good name and lengthened my

---
[5] Isaiah 13; Jer. 50 f.; cf. Isaiah 21; this section has been revised in the light of studies made in Median history by my pupil, Mr. G. G. Cameron.

days. In the day that I died my mouth was not closed from words, and with my eyes—what do I see? Sons of the fourth generation! They wept for me and were distracted, but they did not place with me any vessel of silver or bronze, with only my garment they placed me, so that you should not plunder my couch. Whoever you are who shall injure me—may Sahar and Nikkal and Nusku make evil his dying and may his posterity perish!"[6]

Business documents of the common Babylonian type have been found in this same Niribu. They are dated from the first year of Nebuchadnezzar to the sixteenth of Nabu-naid; those from the last reign also have Aramaic dockets. Loans, with or without interest, and generally of grain, slave sales or hiring of workmen, form their subject. Niribu has relations with Babylon, Hit, and Hamath. A basalt duck weight is eight manas according to the Babylonian standard. Nude females hold their breasts in Babylonian fashion, but the female with nude abdomen and flower at breast wears a peplos over her shoulder and covers her lower body with a pleated tunic and so must be Cypriote. Bronze fibulæ, bracelets, earrings, mirrors, weapons, all find Babylonian analogies.[7] The typical neo-Babylonian seal, a priest standing before the sacred symbols, is found in the Hamath region while Qatna shows Babylonian ceramics.[8]

At Nabu-naid's accession, the Tyrians requested the return from Babylon of Mar-baal (556-552) as king and this was granted. His first full year, 555, Nabu-naid marched against the rebels, in his second he took the mountain road, the road of death, against the "Hittites"; here he became ill but recovered in Hamath. Babylon held the west by a dangerously thin line, for the greater part of Mesopotamia was in Median possession, and Astyages was no longer friendly. In the Median vassal state of Anshan, Teispes, Cyrus, and Cambyses had been suc-

---

[6]Cooke, *Text-Book*, 186 ff.

[7]B. Carrière and A. Barrois, *Syria*, VIII, 1927, 126 ff., 201 ff.; P. Dhorme, *ibid.*, 213 ff.

[8]L. Speleers, *Syria*, IV, 1923, 195 f.; R. D(ussaud), *ibid.*, X, 1929, 81 f.

ceeded in 559 by a second Cyrus, who six years later revolted, in all probability with the promise of Chaldæan aid. Nabu-naid at once seized Harran and the line to Syria was broadened.

In May of this same third year, 553, Nabu-naid marched forth from Babylon, and in August he reached Mount Ammananu, the Anti-Lebanon, where he found orchards with every fruit. The men of the city Ammananu were decapitated and their bodies hung up, captives were carried to Babylon. Again Nabu-naid was ill but recovered. In December, he once more collected his troops, something happened to an unknown and to Nabu-Bel-dan-usur, who were perhaps kings of Amurru, and the Chaldæans camped against the city of Dumah, well into the Arabian desert. The next year, Nabu-naid advanced from Dumah still deeper into the desert to Teima, slew its king and people, built there a palace after the Babylonian fashion, and made it his residence. Mar-baal of Tyre had shown Egyptian tendencies, and Hiram III (552–532) was sent from Babylon to take his place.[9]

While Nabu-naid was dallying in Teima and Belshazzar was the virtual ruler of Babylon, the storm was gathering. Astyages was captured by Cyrus in 550 and the Median empire disappeared; Cyrus was now King of Persia. Babylon was his next objective, but thanks to Nebuchadnezzar's vast projects, the whole region around the capital was a huge fortified camp, which could not be starved, for within its outer walls were fields sufficient to feed the entire population. Cyrus therefore determined on a policy of encirclement, hoping that meanwhile the disaffected elements within Babylon itself might revolt. Crœsus of Lydia was attacked and Sardis fell in 547. In June of the next year, an Elamite general of Cyrus entered north Babylonia and a Persian governor was established in Uruk, the most important city of the south.

Nabu-naid and Belshazzar had restored the cults of the older

[9] *Hebrew Union College Annual*, II, 1925, 43 ff.; R. P. Dougherty, *Nabonidus and Belshazzar*, 1929; Sidney Smith, *Babylonian Historical Texts*, 1924, 27 ff.; E. F. Weidner, *Jour. Soc. Oriental Research*, VI, 1922, 117 ff.

Babylonian cities at the expense of Babylon and its great lord Marduk. Nabu-naid's long absence in Teima robbed its citizens of the great New Year's festival, when the king recognised the overlordship of Marduk by taking his hands. All these slights alienated the Marduk priests, who began to look upon Cyrus as the coming saviour. In this at least they were followed by certain Jewish exiles.

The greatest of these, one of the greatest of Hebrew prophets though his name to-day is unknown, begins his prophecy with an astonishing promise:

> The desert and dry land shall be glad,
>   The waste joy and bloom like the crocus;
> Abundantly shall it bloom,
>   Shall rejoice with joy and singing.
> Lebanon's glory shall be given it,
>   The majesty of Carmel and Sharon;
> They shall see the glory of Yahweh,
>   The majesty of our God.
>
> Strengthen the hands that are weak,
>   Make firm the feeble knees;
> Say to those fearful of heart:
>   Be strong, fear ye not!
> Behold, your God will avenge,
>   God's recompense will come,
>   He will come to save!
>
> Then the eyes of the blind shall be opened,
>   And the ears of the deaf be unstopped;
> Then the lame shall leap up like the hart,
>   And the tongue of the dumb shall sing.
> In the wilderness streams shall break out,
>   In the desert rivers appear;
> The mirage shall become a true pool,
>   And the thirsty land be a fount;
> The jackal's abode be a marsh,
>   With reeds and rushes for grass.

But the most wonderful sight in this transformed wilderness is the road by which the exiles are to travel back to Jerusalem.

Like the great Processional Road made by Nebuchadnezzar in Babylon, it is to have a name, not Aibur-shabu, but Road of Holiness. Like its prototype, it may be trod only by the ceremonially clean, like Aibur-shabu it shall be so straight that even the half-witted cannot lose their way. As the visitor passed along Aibur-shabu, he saw on either side coloured enamelled bricks which bore representations of stalking lions, savage bulls, or, more horrible still, the *mushrush,* a composite creature with horned viper's head, forked tongue, and scaly body, hairy mane, stinged tail, the forefeet ending in lion's claws, the hind feet in those of an eagle.[10] Nothing like this will be found on the Road of Holiness, neither lion nor ravenous beast shall affright. On this highway

> The ransomed of Yahweh shall return,
>   And with singing to Zion come,
> Eternal joy on their heads,
>   Gladness and joy they obtain,
>   Sorrow and sighing shall flee.
>
> Comfort ye, comfort ye my people saith your God,
>   Speak to Jerusalem's heart, cry to her,
> For finished is her servitude, pardoned her sin,
>   For her sins she received double from Yahweh's hand.
>
> The voice of one cries in the desert,
>   Prepare ye Yahweh's Road,
> In the wilderness make it level,
>   A highway for our God.
>
> Each valley shall be exalted,
>   Each mount and hill be made low,
> The uneven shall be made level,
>   The rough places made a plain.
>
> Thou who tellest good tidings to Zion,
>   On a mount that is high get thee up!
> Who tellest Jerusalem good tidings,
>   Thy voice uplift with strength!

[10] Fig. 181 f.; Koldewey, *Excavations at Babylon,* 31 ff.; cf. the apocryphal book, Bel and the Dragon.

> Say to the cities of Judah:
> Behold thy God!
>
> He will feed his flock like a shepherd,
> He will gather the lambs in his arms;
> He will carry them in his bosom,
> He will lead those with young.

Again and again Second Isaiah repeats his pure monotheism: "I am Yahweh who maketh all things, who extended the heavens alone, who fixed firm the earth, who is there by my side?" "I am Yahweh, there is none else, I form light and create darkness, I am Yahweh who doeth all things." Again and again he ridicules the senseless idols. In one amusing passage, he tells us how these idols are manufactured; one part of the wood is used to bake the workman's bread or roast his meat, another keeps him warm, what is left is made into an image before which he falls down and prays for deliverance. It is Bel Marduk who bows down and Nabu who stoops; even when they make their appearance on the great New Year's festival, their images can march in procession through the city only as a load on the backs of wearied beasts. They cannot deliver their worshippers, for they themselves have gone into captivity. No more shall the virgin daughter of Babylon be called tender and delicate, she must sit in the dust and grind meal. When Yahweh was wroth with his children, he delivered them into her hand, but she showed them no mercy; in a moment shall come upon her loss of children and widowhood because of her sorceries.[11]

Yahweh has raised up a saviour from the east and north, one who calls upon Yahweh's name has come from the rising sun. He confirms the word of his servant and brings to completion

---

[11] Kittel, *Geschichte des Volkes Israel,* III, 222 ff., suggests that the "Servant of Yahweh" commemorated by the songs inserted in the writings of the Second Isaiah was the man, presumably of Davidic descent, whom he expected to lead the exiles home; Isaiah 53 would then tell how he was betrayed to the Babylonian authorities and put to death for treason. The view is attractive and might explain Second Isaiah's hatred of Babylon and his appeal to Cyrus.

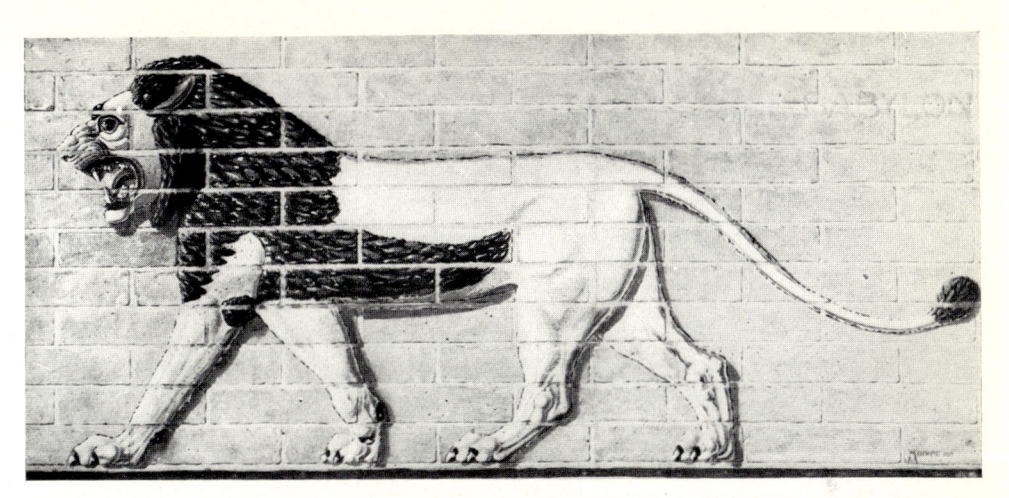

FIG. 181. LION ON THE PROCESSIONAL STREET OF BABYLON.

FIG. 182. DRAGON OF THE ISHTAR GATE AT BABYLON.

the counsel of his messenger; Cyrus he calls "My shepherd," for he shall perform all Yahweh's pleasure, he says of Jerusalem "She shall be rebuilt," and of the temple "Thy foundation shall be laid."

> Thus saith Yahweh to his Anointed,
> To Cyrus, whose right hand I hold,
> To subdue the nations before him,
> And loosen the loins of kings,
> To open the doors before him,
> And the gates shall not be shut,
> I will go before thee,
> And make the rough places smooth;
> The doors of bronze will I shatter,
> Cut asunder the iron bolts,
> I will give thee the treasures of darkness,
> The secret hoards long hid.[12]

Cheered by these and similar predictions, doubtless forwarded to him in secret, Cyrus was back in Babylonia by 540. A battle was fought at the Tigris and the kings of the Sealand against which the Jewish poet had prophesied were brought under control. It began to be suspected that the evils suffered were due to Marduk's wrath; Nabu-naid reappeared in Babylon and took Marduk's hands at the New Year's Feast. Southern Babylonia was abandoned, and, the emergency foreseen by Nebuchadnezzar having arrived, the whole territory within the lines was isolated by flooding the surrounding country. All the gods of the cities outside the lines were brought within.

Cyrus executed works which reduced the flow of the waters and broke through the lines. In October, he fought a battle at Opis on the Tigris and burned the city. Sippar surrendered on the fourteenth and Nabu-naid saw that further resistance was futile. He fled and the general Gobryas entered Babylon without fighting. Unable to escape, Nabu-naid returned to his capital and was made prisoner.

[12] Isaiah 35, 40–55; cf. *Hebrew Union College Annual*, II, 1925, 53; *JAOS.*, XLIV, 1924, 174; C. C. Torrey, *The Second Isaiah*, 1928.

Jewish hopes were in part disappointed. Babylon was not rased, Bel and Nabu were not cast down, in fact, Cyrus worshipped Marduk and Nabu with far more zeal than Nabu-naid or Belshazzar had ever shown. Nevertheless, the enthronement of Cyrus was the end of Babylonian independence. For a time, the priests of Marduk saw no difference; the difference became apparent when the tolerant Cyrus and his two sons Cambyses and Bardiya were succeeded by the usurper Darius, ardent propagandist for the new religion of Ahuramazda. Babylon then revolted time and again and was punished with ruthless ferocity until at last Xerxes destroyed Marduk's temple. Marduk slowly but surely slipped down to that limbo into which the kings who worshipped him had already descended. In the final analysis, Ezekiel's pupil was justified in predicting that Babylon would follow Assyria and Egypt to the depths of Sheol.

CHAPTER XXXVIII

THE FIRST ZIONISTS

Cyrus entered Babylon on the third of November and established peace. At once he began a deliberate campaign of propaganda against the memory of Nabu-naid and Belshazzar. In his own official inscription, he tells us that a weakling was appointed to the lordship of his land, a man in his image he established over them. Ur and the other cities were made like Esagila, Marduk's shrine, in his hostility Nabu-naid allowed the regular offerings and the worship of the king of the gods Marduk to cease, daily he showed his enmity towards Marduk's city, he brought all Marduk's people to ruin through servitude without rest. Because of their complaints, the lord of the gods was furiously angry and abandoned their land; the gods who dwelt among them left their abodes in wrath because he had brought them into the midst of Babylon.

The same hostility appears in the seemingly objective chronicle which told of Nabu-naid's last days. Before long, there came a more literary form of propaganda, composed in verse that it might the more easily remain in men's memories. Nabu-naid had been seized by an evil spirit, he executed no righteousness but slew the weak by his weapon, he closed the way to the merchant and took from the peasant his field, he sent men to prison and destroyed their property, truth was no longer in the land and men ceased to rejoice. His greatest sin was the erection of an abomination, a shrine that was no shrine, for the god he wrongly called Sin, in imitation of Marduk's temple Esagila, until it was completed he made the New Year's feast at Babylon to cease. When he went to Teima, he entrusted the kingship to his eldest son, who likewise showed himself unrighteous.

This propaganda of Cyrus was successful. The same picture of an impious monarch who met his death during wild revels was transmitted to the Greek world by Herodotus and Xenophon.[1] Another Persian legend, likewise passed on to the Greeks, told how the great Nebuchadnezzar had been possessed by a god and had predicted that a Persian mule, "aided by your own deities as allies," would enslave the Babylonians, and then Nebuchadnezzar disappeared.[2]

This same Persian propaganda also affected a Jewish writer in Babylonia who composed in Aramaic tales of a certain Daniel. As a youth, Daniel had been deported to Babylon by Nebuchadnezzar and had been chosen to serve the king. With his three Jewish companions, Daniel refused to eat the heathenish foods offered, but they nevertheless excelled ten times all the magicians and enchanters in the realm. Nebuchadnezzar dreamed and forgot his dream; none of his experts could recall it, but Daniel gave both the dream and the interpretation. In consequence, Daniel was made governor of the whole province of Babylon and became head of the wise men as well as a member of the King's Gate or chancellery. Summoned to interpret a second dream, Daniel this time predicted that the king would become insane and live as a beast; here we may cite the story of Nebuchadnezzar's possession as a parallel. On his recovery, Nebuchadnezzar praised the God of the Hebrews.

Belshazzar the king made a great feast while his city was besieged; we have the same story of the impious king revelling in time of danger, but our Jewish writer knows as the Greeks did not Belshazzar's true name and the fact that he was actually granted the kingship. In his impiety, Belshazzar drank wine from the vessels once sacred to the Jerusalem temple; his impiety was rewarded by the sight of the fingers of a man's handwriting on the plaster. Again the Chaldæan wise men failed in their interpretation, and the queen urged that the aged Daniel be summoned. This was Daniel's interpretation:

[1] Herod., i, 190 f.; Xen., *Cyrop.*, vii, 5.
[2] Megasthenes in Abydenus in Euseb., *Præp. Evang.*, ix, 41.

Mene: Measured hath God thy monarchy and ended;
Tekel: Tested by scales art thou and found wanting;
Peres: Partitioned thy monarchy and given to the Persians.

That very night was Belshazzar, king of the Chaldæans, slain, but Daniel lived on to the first year of Cyrus.[3]

Marduk, Cyrus goes on to say in his inscription, searched through all lands seeking a righteous prince, the desire of his heart, whom he took by his hand and called by his name, for princeship over all he appointed him. Marduk gave him Gutium, the Medes, and Babylonia, with truth and righteousness Cyrus cared for them. Marduk, the great lord, the protector of his people, looked with joy on his deeds of piety and his upright heart, to his city of Babylon his march he ordered, he made him to take the road to Babylon, as a friend and companion he went at his side. Without conflict or battle, he made Cyrus enter Babylon, Nabu-naid, the king who did not fear him, he delivered into his hand. The men of Babylon, all Shumer and Akkad, rejoiced at his kingship, their faces shone. The gods who dwelt in Ashur, Susa, Agade, Ashnunak, Zamban, Me Turnu, Der, as far as the border of Gutium, as well as the gods of Shumer and Akkad whom Nabu-naid had brought into Babylon, by Marduk's command Cyrus returned in peace to their shrines, and he gave them an eternal habitation.[4]

There were others in Babylonia who deserved well of Cyrus. The Second Isaiah had proclaimed Yahweh's summons to Cyrus in words strangely reminiscent of Cyrus' own language. Whatever the actual aid furnished by the Jews, their prophets had hailed Cyrus as Yahweh's anointed and had predicted that he would return the Jews to their ancestral homes and would re-establish the worship of their God. Cyrus was already committed to the return of captive gods to their temples, but he

[3] Daniel 1:1–5:30, much revised in Hellenistic times; cf. A. A. Bevan, *Short Commentary on the Book of Daniel*, 1892; J. D. Prince, *Critical Commentary on the Book of Daniel*, 1899; K. Marti, *Das Buch Daniel*, 1901; J. A. Montgomery, *The Book of Daniel*, 1927; R. H. Charles, *The Book of Daniel*, 1929.

[4] For bibliography, cf. p. 547.

had stronger reasons for fulfilling prophecy. He claims that all the palace-dwelling kings from the Upper Sea and all the tent-dwelling kings of Amurru brought their heavy tribute to Babylon and kissed his feet, but Syria was yet to be given Persian administration, and beyond the isthmus lay Egypt. Belesus was appointed governor of Assyria and Syria and Hiram III was permitted to rule Tyre until 532, but the loss of Hiram's Cypriote cities to Amasis quickly brought home to Cyrus the Egyptian danger. A Jewish community in Palestine which owed its existence to Cyrus would form an effective counterweight to the pro-Egyptian faction which past history had shown might always be expected in Syria. Furthermore, there were Jewish communities in Egypt which should feel kindly towards the ruler who restored the worship at their ancestral sanctuary.

Shortly after Cyrus had celebrated his first full year as king of Babylon, he removed to his summer home in Ecbatana, and from there issued the following decree: "Concerning the house of God which is at Jerusalem, let the house be built, the place where they offer fire sacrifice continually; its height shall be sixty cubits and its breadth sixty cubits, with three courses of great stones and one of timber. And let its expenses be given out of the king's house. Furthermore, let the gold and silver utensils of the house of God, which Nebuchadnezzar took out of the temple which is in Jerusalem and brought to Babylon, be restored, and brought again to the temple which is in Jerusalem, each to its place. And you shall put them in the house of God."[5]

The parallelism of this decree to official documents quoted above is obvious. There was no image of Yahweh to correspond to the returned images of Assyrian, Gutian, Elamite, and Babylonian gods, so Cyrus returned the utensils from the despoiled temple. He had restored Babylon's wall and the shrines of the returned gods, he would do the same for Jerusalem. The utensils were handed over to Sheshbazzar, who was to be the governor of the new commonwealth; his name is the

[5] Aramaic decree, Ezra 6:3–5; cf. 5:14–16 and 1.

Babylonian Shamash-apal-usur, but whether he was of Jewish descent is uncertain.

With Sheshbazzar went some exiles, few in numbers, for the majority of the Jews had made themselves comfortably at home in Babylonia. Many had become wealthy if we may judge from the numerous Jewish names found in the business documents, not a few assumed Babylonian names reverencing Babylonian gods, and were rapidly assimilated to the surrounding population.

Much as they may have sympathised with the hopes of their more pious brethren, we may be sure that few of the rich and noble returned to Zion. Those who went were the zealots, whose chief interest was in religion, not politics or trade. Their leaders were not from the official priesthood but from the laity and few of these were of noble birth. Unlike their comrades, absence from the temple worship had only intensified their observance of such ceremonies as could be still performed, circumcision, sabbath keeping, prayer and fasting, study of the Law. To meet the new needs, there was promulgated a new code, the Law of Holiness.

Like Deuteronomy, the code mingled its laws with admonitions, such as "You shall be holy as I, Yahweh your God, am holy," from which the code has been given its modern name. Sacrifice must not be made to he goats, or seed given to the king god. They must not turn to familiar spirits or wizards, they must not use enchantments or practise augury, round the corners of their heads or mar the corners of their beard, make cuttings of their flesh for the dead or tattoo themselves. They shall not dedicate their daughters as sacred prostitutes, they shall not turn to idols nor make molten gods. The sabbath rest is repeatedly urged, every seven years there shall be a sabbath for the land. Passover comes on the fourteenth of Nisan, the next day is the feast of unleavened bread, the feasts of first fruits, pentecost, and booths are assuming their permanent form. Sharp distinction is made between clean and unclean beasts, the food of the latter must not be eaten. Blood must not be eaten but poured out, for the soul of the flesh is in the blood. Near relatives by blood or marriage are forbidden to marry, laws against various forms of unchastity are severe. Kindness should be shown to the resident alien, for such were the Jews in Egypt. Corners of fields and gleanings of vineyards should be left for the poor. There should be just balances and weights, ephah and hin. It is forbidden to steal, deal falsely, lie, swear falsely, oppress or rob neighbours, keep till morning the wages of the hired, curse the deaf or put stumbling block before the blind, respect poor or rich in judgment; vengeance should not be taken, one must love one's neighbour as one's self.[6]

Difficulties at once met the new arrivals, for Palestine was not a vacuum in which the Jewish commonwealth could be created. A good half was in the possession of peoples who were in every sense Gentiles. The Edomites had been forced out of their earlier home by fresh hordes of Arabs, the Nabataeans, and had taken refuge in the Judæan homelands, the Negeb and south Judah as far as Hebron; the Calebites in turn had been forced north to Bethlehem.[7] The Shephelah was occupied by the Philistines. Numerous bodies of deported captives had been settled by the Assyrian kings, Sargon, Esarhaddon, and Ashur-bani-apal, and they occupied some of the most fertile regions once tilled by the Hebrews. Naturally they all resented the return of the exiles.

Nor was this all. The Hebrews deported by Sargon and Nebuchadnezzar had indeed represented the leaders, those eminent by reason of birth, of religious position, of religious thought. Nevertheless, they were but a minority, at most a quarter of the population. Not all who claimed distinguished ancestors had been deported, and these new leaders could have had no liking for intruders who claimed prior rights. Religion itself was not the exclusive prerogative of the returned Zionists. Priests still existed by the ruined temple, fasts had been instituted to mourn its destruction. The lamentations sung over the wasted city are in themselves sufficient to prove that

[6] Lev. 11, 17–26. [7] I Chron. 2:50 ff.

poets of great force and beauty were still to be found in Judah, and more than one prophet had predicted the coming of freedom.[8] Were the newcomers so superior that they should be conceded precedence?

The eighteen years which followed the return to Zion were years of complete disillusion. No sympathy was expressed by the native Hebrews, the foreigners were suspicious or definitely hostile. Little or nothing was done to rebuild the temple, for there were no funds; the exiles were struggling for a bare existence on the worn-out soils of Palestine, so inferior to the rich Babylonian alluvium.[9]

Meanwhile, Cyrus had met his death in 529 and had been succeeded by his son Cambyses (529–522). Preparations for the conquest of Egypt were at once begun. Phœnicia, where Hiram III had died in 532, decided it was high time to make a formal submission; its possession gave the Persians command of the sea and afforded a base from which the fleet could support the land army. Cyprus followed the example of Phœnicia and revolted from the Egyptians. Gobryas, already satrap of the Babylon he had captured, had been given in addition the province "Across the River," the Ebir Nari of the Assyrians and Babylonians and the Abar Nahara of the Aramaic. In November of Cambyses' second year, we find Gobryas in camp with the king in the city of Amanu in the Amanus region, to which he ordered sheep from the folds of the goddess Innina of Uruk to be brought for army supply.[10] The final mustering of the army took place at Accho. Camels

---

[8] Lam. 1:4; Zech. 7 f.

[9] For Ezra-Nehemiah, cf. E. Meyer, *Entstehung des Judenthums*, 1896; H. H. Howorth, *Proc. Soc. Bibl. Archæology*, XXIII, 1901, 147 ff., and following; C. A. Siegfried, *Esra, Nehemia, und Esther*, 1901; A. Bertholet, *Esra und Nehemia*, 1902; C. C. Torrey, *Ezra Studies*, 1910; L. W. Batten, *Ezra and Nehemiah*, 1913; for Persian history, G. Rawlinson, *Five Great Monarchies*, n.d., III, 84 ff.; G. Maspero, *Histoire ancienne des peuples de l'Orient classique*, III, 1899, 569 ff.; E. Meyer, *Geschichte des Altertums*, III, 1915; Percy Sykes, *History of Persia*, 2 ed., 1921; R. W. Rogers, *History of Ancient Persia*, 1929.

[10] C. E. Keiser, *Letters and Contracts from Erech*, 1917, no. 169; R. P. Dougherty, *Ann.*, V, 1925, 42 ff.; for Ebir Nari, cf. *History of Assyria*, 376.

were hired from the king of the Arabs to supply water while the troops were crossing the desert between Palestine and Egypt. Egypt was reduced without much difficulty; it may be that the Jews of Palestine did Cambyses some favor, the Jews of Egypt may have regarded him as the coming deliverer, quite as the Second Isaiah had regarded his father, at any rate when Cambyses destroyed the Egyptian temples, that of Yahu at Elephantine was spared.[11]

Cambyses died at Ecbatana near Mount Carmel,[12] and was succeeded by his brother Bardiya. Bardiya was received by the empire without sign of dissatisfaction, but when he was murdered by the devotee of Ahuramazda, Darius I (522–485), the provinces broke out in a perfect orgy of revolt.

Syria was one of the outlying provinces. Thus far, it had remained peaceful, but it might easily follow the example of the other rebels. Many of the Jews were subject to these rebels, and the Jews in Babylon itself were ruled from October of 521 to February of 520 by the rebel Nebuchadnezzar III. Darius therefore resolved to follow the example of Cyrus and to settle more Jews in Palestine. At his court was a young man of about twenty-one, Zerubbabel or Zer Babili, the "Seed of Babylon," whose father Shealtiel was the eldest son of king Jehoiachin.[13] Zerubbabel was ordered to Jerusalem as governor, and in his extremity Darius was willing to promise much. Jerusalem was to be rebuilt, the Edomites were to surrender the villages they had taken, the territory was to be free from tribute, no official was to enter their doors. The governors of the province Across the River and the officials in Lebanon were ordered to furnish cedar to rebuild the city, a sum of money was granted for the restoration of the temple, and for the burnt offering on the altar which had been set up among the temple ruins. It goes without saying that these emergency orders were imperfectly obeyed.

Darius had issued his decree in the beginning of 520, imme-

---

[11]Strabo, xvi, 2, 25; Herod., iii, 4 ff., 19; cf. chap. XLI.
[12]Herod., iii, 62 ff.; Pliny, *Hist. Nat.*, v, 75; Steph. Byz., *s.v.*
[13]I Chron. 3:17.

diately after the recovery of Babylon, and Zerubbabel at once started for Jerusalem with a party large enough to require the escort of a thousand horsemen.[14] Shortly after his arrival, on September 28, there appeared a prophet named Haggai; he may have been one of Zerubbabel's party, for there is an extraordinary parallelism between his expressions and those of Gudea, well-known governor of the Babylonian Lagash seventeen hundred years before.[15] Eighteen years after the return of the first exiles, the people were still saying: "The time to build Yahweh's house has not arrived." Haggai appealed to Zerubbabel and to Joshua, son of Jehozadak, the last head priest at Jerusalem, who now bears the new title of high priest: "Is it time for you yourselves to dwell in panelled houses, while this house is in ruins?" Let them consider their present case: "You have sown much but bring in little; you have eaten, but not to repletion; you have drunk, but not to drunkenness; you have clothed yourselves, but not to warmth; he who worked for wages—for a purse with holes!" "You looked for much, but it became little; you brought it home, and I blew upon it. Why? Because my house is in ruins, while each of you runs about his own house. This is why the heavens withhold rain and the earth withholds its fruits, why I called for a drought upon the land and grain and new wine and oil and all the land brings forth, and upon man and beast and all the work of their hands." To change this, let them go up into the mount, cut wood, and build the temple, that Yahweh take pleasure in it and show his glory.

Thus incited, Zerubbabel and Joshua began the work twenty-four days later. A permanent altar took the place of the former temporary structure and henceforth the continual burnt offerings, the burnt offerings for the sabbaths, new moons, and set feasts, and the free-will offerings were regularly sacrificed upon it. Money to begin the work was granted the masons and stonecutters, while supplies of food, drink, and oil were sent to the Sidonians and Tyrians who were to bring cedar timbers from the Lebanon to Joppa. Levites twenty

[14] I Esdras, 4:47 ff. [15] Cf. J. A. Bewer, *AJSL.*, XXXV, 1919, 128 ff.

years and over were appointed to do the actual work on the temple. At the foundation exercises, there were responsive singing and much shouting; the old men who had seen the former house in its glory and in whose eyes the present structure was as nothing, wept with a loud voice, but their weeping was drowned by the shouts of the rejoicing multitude.[16]

To counteract this too conspicuous disparagement, Haggai appeared on the twenty-first of the seventh month with this promise: "Who is there among you who saw this house in its former glory and how do you see it now? Is it not in your eyes as nothing? Nevertheless, be strong and work, for I am with you, and my spirit abides among you. Fear not! For thus says Yahweh of Hosts: Yet a little while and I will shake the heavens and the earth and will shake all nations. Likewise the treasures of all nations shall come and I will fill this house with wealth. Mine is the silver and mine the gold; the future wealth of this place shall be greater than in the past, and in this place will I give peace, says Yahweh of Hosts."

The next month, Haggai was supported by another prophet, Zechariah the priest, Iddo's son. Haggai had already hinted of coming freedom as a result of the revolts against the Persians, but skeptics might cite the news of one success of Darius after another. Zechariah appeals to the older prophets, whose writings already were almost canonical: "Be not as your fathers, to whom the former prophets preached: 'Thus saith Yahweh of Hosts: Turn now from your evil ways and your evil deeds,' but they did not hearken to me. Your fathers, where are they? And the prophets, do they live forever? But my words and my statutes, which I commanded my servants the prophets, did they not overtake your fathers?" They must admit: "As Yahweh of Hosts has purposed to do to us, according to our ways and our doings, so has he done to us."

News that the "Sons of the Captivity," the returned Zionists, were building a temple came to the ears of their neighbours. A deputation appeared before Zerubbabel and the heads of fathers' houses and offered to aid in the work, for

---

[16] Ezra 3.

they had sacrificed to the same God ever since they had been colonised by Esarhaddon. The offer was most opportune and was about to be accepted when on the twenty-fourth of the ninth month Haggai made clear the true issue: "Ask the priests for an oracle: If a man carries holy flesh in his skirt and touches with his skirt bread or pottage or wine or oil or any other food, does it become unclean?" The priests answered "No." "If one unclean from a dead body touches any of these, will it be unclean?" The answer was in the affirmative. Haggai then drew the obvious conclusion: "So is this people and so is this nation before me and so is every work of their hand and what they offer there is unclean." Before one stone was laid upon another in the temple, "when one came to a heap of twenty measures, there were but ten, when one came to the wine vat to draw off fifty measures, there were but twenty." The autumn rains have come, the seed has been sown, "is the seed yet in the storehouse? The vine and fig tree and pomegranate and olive have not yet borne, but from this day I will bless you." As a result of this protest, the overtures were rejected; the faith continued undefiled by half-heathen practices, but the proffered friendship was turned into bitter enmity. The more lax among the aristocrats and priests remained on good terms with the descendants of the Assyrian colonists and even married into their families, but the Samaritans were henceforth a constant thorn in the flesh to the more pious.

Haggai had promised the shaking of all nations, but Zerubbabel was too canny to rebel against his benefactor, whose strength he had had full opportunity to realise. This same day a second oracle was directed to him: "I will shake the heavens and the earth and will overthrow the thrones of the kingdoms; I will destroy the might of the nations and overturn chariots and riders; the horses and their riders shall go down, each by the sword of his brother." Jeremiah had employed the symbol of the plucked-off ring to predict Yahweh's abandonment of Jehoiachin; Haggai reversed the symbol for his grandson: "In that day, says Yahweh of Hosts, I will take you, O Zerubbabel, my servant. and will make you a signet, says Yahweh of Hosts."[17]

This last prophecy was purposely obscure. More clear were the visions of Zechariah, with whom begins apocalyptic in the stricter sense. Cut off from active participation in the political life of far distant Babylon, there was opportunity only for dreams. Yahweh recedes farther and farther from the prophet's consciousness, the direction of affairs is increasingly in the hands of angels, as we may at last properly translate the word previously rendered as messenger.

Meanwhile, about October, 520, a second rebel against Darius in Babylon had announced himself as Nebuchadnezzar IV. Shortly after, four men left the Jewish community in Babylonia and brought the news to Jerusalem. Not long after their arrival from their four months' journey, on March 16 of 519, Zechariah began to see visions. A man appeared among the myrtles in the hollow and behind him were horses, bay, chestnut, white, and piebald. "What are these?" Zechariah inquired of the angel with whom he was talking. The answer came from a horseman who reported the whole earth was at peace and quiet, a peace unfavourable to Jewish hopes. "How long, Yahweh of Hosts," expostulated the angel, "will you continue to refuse compassion to Jerusalem and the cities of Judah which you have cursed these seventy years?" Through the angel, Zechariah was bidden to proclaim: "I am jealous for Jerusalem and for Zion with a great jealousy, but I am angry with the too confident nations; I was but a little angry, but they helped forward the evil. I will return to Jerusalem in compassion, and my house shall be built in it and the building cord shall be once more stretched out over Jerusalem."

Four horns that scattered Judah so he could not uplift his head appeared in the second vision, but four smiths cast down the horns. In his third vision, Zechariah saw a man with a measuring rod, who was attempting to discover the extent of

---

[17] H. G. Mitchell, *Haggai and Zechariah*, 1912; Marti, *Dodekapropheton*, 378 ff.; Nowack, *Die Kleinen Propheten*, 307 ff.; Sellin, *Zwölfprophetenbuch*, 444 ff.

the new Jerusalem; the angel checked him and informed him that the city was to be inhabited after the fashion of open villages because of the multitude of men and of cattle who were to be within. No wall was needed, for Yahweh himself was to be in her, a wall of fire about her and a glory in her midst.

Next Zechariah saw the high priest Joshua, standing before Yahweh's angel and clad in soiled clothes, as befitted a prisoner at the bar of justice. By him stood the Satan, the Adversary, as prosecuting attorney; as in the contemporary book of Job, Satan was still in good standing, a member of Yahweh's court. The angel refused to hear the Satan's accusation: "Yahweh rebuke you, O Adversary! Is not this a brand plucked from the burning?" He then commanded that Joshua's soiled garments be removed and that he be clothed in robes of state and a clean turban placed on his head. The angel stood up and delivered this charge: "If you will walk in my ways and will guard my orders, then shall you rule my house and guard my courts, and I will give you access to those who stand here." Joshua and his companions are men for a sign; a precious stone with seven eyes or facets has been delivered to Joshua, Yahweh himself will engrave the inscription and in one day will remove all inquity from the land. Accusations, we may suspect, had been directed against the high priest by those who wished Zerubbabel to possess all the religious rights formerly held by the king; Zechariah grants Joshua full powers in religious affairs, though Zerubbabel is to remain the secular head. Thus began that growth of the high priestly power which was to become supreme after the failure of the royal line to function.

As from sleep, Zechariah was awakened by the angel, and saw a lamp of gold with seven lights about a bowl fed by seven pipes, while on either side was an olive tree. The seven lights, he learned, were Yahweh's eyes which go about the earth, the olive trees represented the "sons of oil," the anointed ones, who stand by the Lord of the whole earth; there was no need to explain that these were Joshua and Zerubbabel.

"Not by might nor by strength, but by my spirit, says Yahweh of Hosts. Who are you, great mountain? Before Zerubbabel become a plain! He shall bring out the capstone with shouting: 'Grace, grace to it!' Zerubbabel's hands have laid the temple foundations, his hands also shall complete it. Who has despised the day of small things? They shall rejoice to see the plummet in Zerubbabel's hands."

A flying roll, thirty feet by twenty, was the curse that courses over the whole earth, it enters the house of the thief or false witness and abides there until it has consumed the house with its timbers and stones. Zechariah then saw something he could not name; it was explained as an ephah, a measure of about a bushel capacity. A lead disk was lifted and the woman Wickedness was seen inside; she was thrust back unceremoniously into the ephah and the disk of lead was placed upon its mouth. Two women with stork's wings lifted it high in air; they were going, said the angel, to build her a house in Babylonia and place her on her pedestal.

These two visitations cleansed the land of all sin and prepared for the last vision. Four chariots, the four winds, came out between the two bronze mountains which stood before the divine residence; here the prophet borrowed from Babylonian mythology, where the sun god Shamash comes out from the great mountain, the place where fates are decided, where heaven and earth meet, from the foundation of heaven, and the great gods come out to meet him for judgment. Each chariot had horses of a different color, black, white, piebald, and grey, and each went to a different point of the compass. Those who went north, said Yahweh, brought his spirit to rest in the north country; this was a hint, perhaps as definite as Zechariah dared make it, that destruction from the north was coming upon Persia.

The four men from Babylon bore gifts from which a crown was to be made for Zerubbabel; with a play on Zerubbabel's name, "Seed of Babylon," Zechariah gave this oracle: "Thus says Yahweh of Hosts: Behold the man whose name is the 'Shoot'; for he shall shoot up and shall build the temple of

Yahweh. He shall assume majesty and rule on his throne, and Joshua shall be priest on his right hand." Perhaps friction had already developed, for the prophet adds: "There shall be counsel of peace between them."

Haggai and Zechariah were not the only prophets who were hoping for an "Anointed One." From an unknown comes one of the most beautiful of Biblical prophecies:

> The people who walked in darkness
>   Have seen a great light;
> The dwellers in the land of death's shadow,
>   Light has shone upon them.
>
> You have multiplied the nation,
>   You have increased their joy;
> They rejoice before your presence,
>   As in harvest men rejoice.
>
> For the yoke of his burden,
>   And his shoulder bar,
> The rod of him who drives him,
>   You have broke as in Midian's Day.
>
> For each shoe worn in tumult of battle,
>   And the mantle rolled in blood,
> They shall be for the burning,
>   As food for the fire.
>
> For to us a child has been born,
>   To us has been given a son,
> On his shoulder dominion shall be,
>   And his name shall be called:
>
> Wonderful Counsellor,
>   Mighty God,
> Father Eternal,
>   Prince of Peace.
>
> Mighty his rule,
>   Peace without end,
> On David's throne,
>   And through his realm.

> To establish it and uphold it,
> > In righteousness and peace,
> > From henceforth and forever,
> > This Yahweh's zeal shall accomplish.[18]

Perhaps from the same pen came another beautiful prediction of a glorious future:

> A Shoot shall come forth from Jesse's stump,
> > And a branch from his roots bear fruit;
> > The spirit of Yahweh shall rest upon him,
> > A spirit of wisdom and insight.
>
> By the sight of his eyes he'll not judge,
> > Nor decide by what his ears hear;
> > But he'll judge with righteousness the poor,
> > And decide with justice for the meek.
>
> And he'll smite the ruthless with the rod of his mouth,
> > Slay the wicked with the breath of his lips,
> > Righteousness shall be the girdle of his waist,
> > And faithfulness the cloth about his loins.
>
> Then the wolf shall be guest of the lamb,
> > And the leopard lie down with the kid,
> > The calf and young lion together shall graze,
> > And a little lad shall drive them.
>
> The heifer and bear shall be friends,
> > Together their young shall lie down,
> > Like the ox shall the lion eat straw,
> > The suckling on cobra's hole play.
>
> On viper's den shall the weaned put his hand,
> > In all my holy mount they shall not harm;
> > With the knowledge of Yahweh shall the earth be filled,
> > As the waters covering the sea.[19]

Still a third prophecy rejoiced men's hearts:

> Behold, in righteousness shall reign a king,
> > And princes in justice shall rule;

[18] Isaiah 9:2–7.   [19] Isaiah 11:1–9.

> And a man shall be as a shelter from the wind,
> And shall be a refuge from the storm;
> As streams of water in the steppe,
> As the shadow of a rock in a fainting land.
>
> The eyes of those who see shall not be closed,
> And the ears of those who hear shall attend,
> The heart of the rash shall discern to understand,
> And the stammerer's tongue speak clear;
> No more shall the fool a nobleman be called,
> Or the miser be said to be free.[20]

Such prophecies were nothing less than treason against the Persian king. To make matters worse, the false Nebuchadnezzar IV had been put down at the beginning of 519, actually before the date of Zechariah's vision, though before the news could reach him. Soon western Asia was at peace.

Some inkling of the crown may have come to the ears of Ushtanni or Tattenai, who combined the satrapies of Babylon and Across the River as Gobryas had done before him.[21] He appeared in Jerusalem and demanded of the Jewish elders: "Who gave you permission to build this house and to complete this foundation?" They replied that Cyrus had given them this permission, that Sheshbazzar had laid the foundation, and that the temple had been in process of building since then. In the face of this assurance, Tattenai did not dare forbid the work, but he obtained their names and with his scribe Shetherbozanai and his associated Persians, he sent a letter to Darius, requesting that search be made as to the truth of the claim and that the king indicate his pleasure in the matter. The implication was plain, Tattenai did not believe that the work should be continued.

Darius therefore gave order that search be made in the treasure house where were stored the records from Babylon, and there was found in the citadel at Ecbatana a roll with a memorandum of Cyrus' decree. Western Asia for the moment

[20] Isaiah 32:1-5.
[21] J. N. Strassmaier, *Inschriften von Darius*, 1892, no. 27, 82; cf. the Hystanes of Herod., vii, 77; B. Meissner, *ZAW.*, XVII, 1897, 191 f.

was at peace, but the loyalty of Egypt was dubious, and the Jews were on his flank should he find it necessary to send an army to the Nile. Furthermore, Darius had but recently usurped the throne, and it was necessary to deal carefully with any decree claiming the authority of the empire's founder. He therefore issued a decree, warning Tattenai and his fellows to keep away from the place and to allow the governor and elders of the Jews to continue building the temple to the God of Heaven. The expenses of the temple shall be met from the provincial revenues, bulls, rams, and lambs shall be furnished for the burnt offerings, wheat, salt, wine, and oil shall be given daily as the priests desire, that they may pray for the life of the king and his sons. If any man alters this decree, let a beam be pulled out from his house and let him be impaled upon it, let his house be a refuse heap forever. He closes: "I Darius have made this decree, let it be executed with all diligence." After such a warning, Tattenai could only obey, while the elders of the Jews built and prospered.[22]

Scholars in recent years have almost unanimously declared these decrees to be forgeries. Placed against their contemporary background, the decrees are justified. They are not in Hebrew but in Aramaic, which had already been employed in Babylonia and Assyria as early as the eighth century,[23] and by now had largely supplanted the cuneiform in Babylonia and the hieroglyphics in Egypt. Aramaic legends are common on the seals of Babylonia and Syria, the coins of eastern Asia Minor are regularly inscribed in the same language, the papyri from the Jewish community at Elephantine include official rescripts in Aramaic, copies of the official Aramaic translation of Darius' own Behistun inscription, the Wisdom of Ahikar which had come from a cuneiform original through or influenced by the Persian. The Jewish archives proper show the same official formulæ, the same use of Persian words, the same Hebraisms, and the same textual errors. In language, however, the rescripts quoted in Ezra show closer agreement with the eastern

[22] Aramaic decree, Ezra 5:1–6:15; Chronicler's account, Ezra 6:16–22.
[23] *History of Assyria*, 178, 392, 544.

THE FIRST ZIONISTS 571

Aramaic found in the official translation of the Behistun inscription and the Wisdom of Ahikar, and this too adds to the presumption of their authenticity.

Contemporary parallels to the decree are numerous and significant. Cyrus prays to Babylonian gods for himself and his son Cambyses.[24] Cambyses drove the intruding Greek mercenaries from the temple of Neith in Sais, purified the temple, restored the offerings and re-established the revenues. Darius, while still in Aram or Syria, likewise restored the temples with their feasts and revenues.[25] The imprecation in the Ezra rescript resembles the imprecation placed by Darius near the end of his own Behistun Inscription, and we know he punished by impalement.[26]

But that this action of Darius was no isolated favour but represents his determined policy is best proved by a Greek inscription: "The king of kings, Darius, son of Hystaspes, to his slave Gadatas thus speaks: I have learned that you do not in all respects obey my injunctions. In so far as you cultivate my land by transplanting the fruits of Across the Euphrates to the parts of Lower Asia, I commend your purpose, and because of this there shall be laid up for you great favour in the king's house; nevertheless, because you are setting at nought my policy towards the gods, I will give you, if you do not change, a proof of my injured feelings. For you have enforced tribute from the holy gardeners of Apollo and have ordered them to dig unhallowed ground, not knowing the mind of my forefathers towards the God, who told the Persians the whole truth."[27]

Gadatas was keeper of the royal paradise or park near Magnesia on the Mæander, as was Asaph in the days of Nehemiah. He had brought plants from Across the Euphrates,

[24] Prism 34 ff.
[25] Inscription of Wazhor, Petrie, *History of Egypt*, III, 360 ff.
[26] Behistun ins., 67; Herod., iii, 159.
[27] G. Cousin, and G. Deschamps, *Bulletin de Correspondance Hellénique*, XIII, 1889, 529 ff.; W. Dittenberger, *Sylloge Inscriptionum Græcarum*, 3 ed., 1915, no. 22; C. J. Ogden, in G. Botsford and E. G. Sihler, *Hellenic Civilization*, 1915, 162; cf. E. Meyer, *Entstehung des Judentums*, 19 ff.

an alternative name for Across the River, but in his excessive zeal he had encroached on Apollo's lands. Apollo had shown himself pro-Persian in Magnesia as he had at Branchidæ and at Delphi, and as had the Second Isaiah and other Jewish prophets in Babylon. The action of Cyrus settled the matter as it did Tattenai's complaint. The rescript to Gadatas was preserved in Apollo's archives as the rescript to Tattenai was preserved in Yahweh's temple; one was copied by the Aramaic compiler, the other was reinscribed by the priests in the days of the emperor Hadrian. Thus neither is an autograph; one sceptical scholar has denied the authenticity of the Gadatas rescript, numerous Biblical students deny the authenticity of the other. The Ezra rescripts show contamination from post-Christian Aramaic, the Apollo priests went farther and attempted to turn their rescript into good Koine Greek; one word and one construction alone prove the Ionic original of the Gadatas rescript, the language of the Ezra documents is much closer to contemporary writings. In each case, the determining proof of authenticity is not language but the formulæ and the agreement with known historical facts.

Zechariah's last dated prophecy was in December, 518. The temple was well on its way to completion, and the men of Bethel sent their representatives to inquire of the prophets and priests whether they should continue to weep in the fifth month for the destruction of Jerusalem. They were not of the returned exiles but of the "peoples of the land," they came from Jerusalem's ancient rival where the priest had taught the worship of Yahweh to the strangers deported by the Assyrians. Zechariah's reply was by no means flattering, it shows only too clearly the gulf he felt to exist between the returned Zionists and men whose mixed race was proved by the very names of their messengers. "When you fasted and mourned in the fifth and seventh months," the anniversary of Gedaliah's murder, "and behold it is now seventy years, was it to me you fasted? And when you eat and drink, is it not you yourselves who are eating and drinking?" Zechariah had no small measure of truth in this contemptuous answer, for these fasts were in reality ancient fasts for Adonis which had retained much of their former character, but he alienated the "peoples of the land."

For all his apocalyptics, Zechariah was a true successor of the former prophets in his demand for ethical living: "Execute true justice and show kindness and compassion, each to his brother. Oppress not the widow or orphan or the resident alien or the poor, and do not plan evil in your hearts against your brother." Their fathers made their hearts adamant, refusing to hear the oracle given by the former prophets; for this came wrath and scattering among nations they had not known.

Now, however, there are promises. Yahweh will return to Zion, and will abide in Jerusalem, now to be called the "City of Truth," while the mountain of Yahweh will be "Holy Mount." In the new community, the inhabitants were naturally for the greater part men and of active age; the time will come when old men and old women shall sit in the open squares, each with staff in hand because of great age, while these squares will be also full of playing boys and girls. Even in these days, when all revolts have been put down and the foreigner's yoke seems more tightly riveted than ever, though it appears impossible to the remnant of this people, is it impossible for Yahweh? He will save his people from the lands of the rising and setting sun, he will bring them home and be to them their God in truth and righteousness.

"Let your hands be strong, you who are hearing in these days these words from the mouths of the prophets. For before these days," he is almost imitating Haggai now, "there was no hire for man or beast, and there was no safety for him who went in or came out on account of the enemy," who may be Cambyses on his march through Palestine to Egypt. No longer will Yahweh be against the remnant of this people as in former days. He will sow the seed of peace and the vine shall give its fruit, the earth its produce, the heavens their dew, and all these shall the remnant of this people inherit. As the house of Judah was formerly a curse among the nations, so now shall it be a blessing. As Yahweh in the past determined to do evil because their fathers provoked him to anger, so now he has determined to do good to Jerusalem. To win this favour, righteousness is demanded; let every man speak truth to his neighbour, execute judgment of peace in the gates, devise not evil in their hearts against their neighbours, or love a false oath.

Zechariah's last prophecy ends with a note of joy. Not only the fasts of the fifth and seventh month, those of the fourth and tenth as well, the anniversaries of Jerusalem's fall and the beginning of the siege, shall become cheerful feasts. Many people, inhabitants of many cities, shall come, the men of one city shall go to another, saying: "Let us go to entreat Yahweh's face," and the answer will be "I too will go." For in those days, is the prophet's closing promise, "ten men from all the tongues of the nations shall seize the skirt of a Jew, saying: 'We will go with you, for we have heard that God is with you.'" Beautiful words, but they testify to the failure of nationalistic aspirations. Judah's future was not to be in the sphere of worldly politics but in religion.[28]

A greater than Zechariah has given this belief in Judah's future its classic form:

> It shall be at the end of days,
>   That the mount of Yahweh shall be fixed,
> The house of our God on the crest,
>   Exalted above the hills;
> All peoples shall stream to it,
>   Many nations shall go and say:
>
> Come, ascend to Yahweh's mount,
>   To the house of Jacob's God,
> That he may teach us his ways,
>   That we may walk in his paths,
> For from Zion instruction goes forth,
>   From Jerusalem Yahweh's word.
>
> He will judge between many peoples,
>   Give decision for mighty nations;

[28] For bibliography, cf. under Haggai, p. 564.

They shall beat their swords into ploughshares,
Their spears into knives for pruning,
No nation raise sword against nation,
Nor shall they learn war any more.[29]

[29]Micah 4:1-3; Isaiah 2:2-4.

CHAPTER XXXIX

THE YOKE OF THE LAW

EVERY Jew in the world lived in a single empire, but it was not Jewish. Their leaders were still in Babylonia, and many a Jew appears in the business documents dated by the reigns of Darius I, Artaxerxes I, and Darius II. Yahweh was generally worshipped, as is shown by names with the elements Iahu or Yahu and Iama or Yawa. Nevertheless, names compounded with other gods prove that syncretism was taking place. Bali Iama tells us that Baal or Bel is the same as Yahweh! Mannu-danni Iama insists "Who is mighty like Yahweh?" but his father is Shulum Babili. Bel-aba-usur invokes the "Lord" Marduk to protect the father, but his daughter Bii Iahu and his grandson Gadal Iama or Gedaliah invoke Yahweh. Tiri Iama worships Yahweh but christens his son Shamash-uballit, begging the sun god to grant life. The good Hebrew Rahimiel gives his son the Persian name Udarna, but Udarna's son is Hanani Iama or Hananiah. Nana-iddina is the gift of the mother goddess of Uruk, but his son is Igdal Iama.

Not all the Babylonian Jews had prospered. Hanana, Menahem, and Berechiah are slaves. Kimni-anni, son of Bel-aba-usur, his sister Bii Iahu, Ishia, Natina, Tab-shalam, Zabad Iama, son of Hinni Bel, are poor fishermen, who must pay five hundred fish for five nets bought from the slave Ribat. Mannu-danni Iama, despite his boastful name, is only a tender of sheep and goats, who must promise to make proper return. Hanani son of Menahem is over the king's birds.

Another Menahem is paqdu official of Labashi. Taddanu, son of Tiri Iama, is shaknu or under governor of the Gimirrai or Cimmerians. Already in the third year of Darius I, Ishribi Iama, son of Pillu Iama, governor of the Shushanu folk, receives of the treasury from Rimut Ninurta, son of the famous banker Murashu, two manas of silver, the tax for a man of the

THE YOKE OF THE LAW

king, the king's meal, tax, and gift for the king's house for the bow land. The same banker in the next year gives a mana to Iadah Iama for a mortgaged field. In the fifth year, Minaimen, son of Bel-aba-usur, official of the tax gatherer of the Bel-aba-usur canal, receives barley from Rimut Ninurta.[1] Prediction that they should lend to many nations but not borrow was being fulfilled.[2]

Darius I completely reorganised the Persian empire and divided it into permanent satrapies. Abar Nahara became the fifth satrapy, and included Palestine, Syria, and Cyprus; it paid an annual tribute of three hundred and fifty talents, not too much for the Phœnician merchant princes to pay.[3] Zerubbabel disappeared, perhaps he was deposed when Darius passed through Palestine in 517 to put down Aryandes, viceroy of Egypt. Zerubbabel left children,[4] but none was ever permitted to serve as governor, and henceforth Judah was ruled by a Persian.

His disappearance brought no ill results to the Jewish community or to the temple, which was completed April 9, 515. The Jewish colony of mercenaries at Elephantine had presumably taken part in Cambyses' ill-fated expedition against Ethiopia, it doubtless formed a part of the garrison established by Darius on that frontier; as token of his regard, Darius sent these Jews a copy of the official Aramaic translation of his Behistun inscription, and so much did they value it that when it became frayed with age, new copies were prepared.[5]

Messianic hopes had proved delusions. Jewish history was henceforth to be a mere episode in the history of Persia. The little community was exposed to the overwhelming influences of a mighty empire with all its higher material culture. That the Jews were not completely assimilated was due to their religion. As in the modern Near East, where nationalism is preserved only in the religious communities, where a man denies his nationality when he apostatises from the faith, so

[1] A. T. Clay, *Business Documents of Murashu Sons of Nippur*, 1904.
[2] Deut. 15:6. [3] Herod., iii, 91. [4] I Chron. 3:19 ff.
[5] Herod., ii, 30; Cowley, *Aramaic Papyri*, 248 ff.

Jewish nationalism found its only outlet in the cult. If Zerubbabel was gone, the high priest Joshua remained and his power was on the increase. Judah had ceased to be a nation and had become a church. The leading spirits no longer sought a career in politics but in religion.

Exile had shifted the whole point of view. Idolatry was gone and forever, personal religion was in process of development. The new religion centred about the sanctuary, whose services were confined to those of the stricter belief. This greater strictness was doubtless necessary to preserve Jewish nationalism, but the price was great. There arose a much increased emphasis on the cult and on the legal prescriptions. Those who were less strict in their observances, whether the "peoples of the land," the descendants of the older Hebrews, or children of exiles deported from other parts of the Assyrian empire, were excluded from the Jewish community.

Phœnicia flourished under the Persians. The system of roads, the coined money, the almost universal use of Aramaic, all assisted Phœnician trade. Phœnicians were specially privileged, for their fleet formed the core of the Persian navy and they gladly used their ships against their natural maritime rivals, the Greeks. The struggle was especially severe in Cyprus, where Citium was the Phœnician base; coins on the Persian standard with the couchant lion and smooth reverse appear before the end of the sixth century, but are soon succeeded by coins having the seated lion with the Egyptian sign of life on the reverse.

Perhaps the Ionic Revolt was caused by Persian favours to Phœnicians at Greek expense; at any rate the Phœnicians struck the first blow by transporting Persian troops to revolted Cyprus. Defeated in the first sea fight, they nevertheless still retained Citium and Amathus, and ultimately the land army they had ferried over conquered the island (497). Their fleet, where triremes had supplanted the older pentecontors, won the sea fight at Lade which ended the Ionic Revolt (494).[6]

[6]Herod., v, 108 ff.; vi, 6.

The reign of Xerxes (485–465) began with Egypt in revolt. It was natural for the Jews to hope for independence and it was more natural for their enemies to attribute to them such longings. At the very beginning of the reign, three of these enemies, Bishlam, Mithradates, and Tabeel, sent Xerxes a letter of complaint against the Jews. We do not know the result, but we hear no more of the Jewish community during the next twenty years.

Xerxes had no desire to face a Jewish problem, for he was preparing the great invasion of continental Greece. Two hundred and seven Phœnician ships headed his fleet; the ruling kings were Tetramnestus, son of Anysus, of Sidon, Matten, son of Hiram, of Tyre, and Marbaal, son of Agbaal, of Arvad.[7] Phœnicians showed their skill in digging the canal at Mount Athos, for they alone allowed for the angle of the slope, a Sidonian trireme won the contest at Abydos. At Artemesium, the Phœnicians introduced the strategic "breaking the line," they held first place at Salamis and opened the battle. Enraged by their defeat, Xerxes beheaded the first captains who approached him, and the others returned home at once with their ships. Soon after, Baal-milk I of Citium, on whose coins Melkart fights with club and bow, attacked Idalium with Persian aid, but on the return attack Citium was captured by the Greeks.[8]

Edom had been closely related to Judah in the early days and Jacob and Edom had been brothers. Even Josiah's code permitted Edomites to be admitted to the assembly in the third generation. But Edomites had taken part in the destruction of Jerusalem, and a hatred had been engendered which never weakened. Towards the end of the sixth century, the Edomites had been driven from Mount Seir and Sela by the Nabatæans.[9] The catastrophe was celebrated by Obadiah:

---

[7] Herod., vii, 98.
[8] Herod., vii, 23, 44, 84, 89, 100, 128; Æschyl., *Persæ*, 408 ff.; Diod., xi, 3, 7; 19, 4; Sosylus, in F. Bilabel, *Die Kleineren Historikerfragmente*, 1923, 10; H. Collitz, *Sammlung Griech. Dialektinschriften*, I, no. 60.
[9] Diod., xix, 94 ff.; Arrian, ii, 20, 4.

We have heard an oracle from Yahweh,
    And a messenger is sent among the nations;
Gather and rise up against her,
    And rise up for battle;
I have made you small among nations,
    Despised are you among men!

The pride of your heart has betrayed you,
    Who dwells in the cleft of the Rock,
Who holds the height of the Mountain,
    Who says: Who shall bring me to earth?
If you make your nest high like the eagle,
    Yahweh says, from there shall I bring you!

If gleaners of grapes came to you,
    Would they not leave some of the grapes?
If thieves in the night came to you,
    Would they not steal only enough?
How is searched out Edom,
    His hidden treasures sought!

They have driven you out to the Border,
    All the men allied with you;
Men at peace with you have betrayed you,
    They have planted beneath you snares;
For the wrong to your brother Jacob,
    You are covered with shame and forever cut off!

On the day that you stood aloof,
    And strangers entered his gates,
O'er Jerusalem gambled by lot,
    You too were one of them;
As you did, so 'tis done to you,
    Your reward returns on your head![10]

All this, declared another prophet, was Yahweh's own revenge:

    Who is this who comes from Edom,
        With blood red garments from Bozrah?

[10] J. M. P. Smith, *AJSL.*, XXII, 1906, 131 ff.; J. A. Bewer, *Obadiah and Joel*, 1911; Marti, *Dodekapropheton*, 228 ff.; Nowack, *Die Kleinen Propheten*, 171 ff.; Sellin, *Zwölfprophetenbuch*, 274 ff.

THE YOKE OF THE LAW

> This, the glorious in apparel,
>   Marching in the greatness of his strength?
> I who in righteousness speak,
>   Mighty in power to save!
>
> Why is red your apparel,
>   And your garments like the treader in the wine vat?
> I have trodden alone the winepress,
>   No man of the peoples was with me,
> For I trod them down in my anger,
>   And trampled them in my wrath!
>
> Their life blood is sprinkled on my garments,
>   And all my raiment have I stained;
> In my heart was the day of vengeance,
>   And the day of my redeeming was come;
> For I looked, and there was no helper,
>   And I wondered there was none to support.
>
> So my own arm wrought salvation,
>   And my wrath supported me,
> And I trod down the peoples in my anger,
>   And made them drunk in my wrath,
> And I poured out on earth their life blood,
>   . . . . [11]

Added to the danger from their enemies was dire poverty. The temple was built, but the promised plenty had not come, and men began to doubt the love of Yahweh. An unknown prophet, whom we know only as Malachi, retained his faith. How can they doubt Yahweh's love when of the two brothers he has loved Jacob and hated Esau, whose mountains have been made a desolation and his inheritance given to desert jackals.

He turns to the priests: "A son honours his father and a slave fears his lord; if I am a father, where is my honour, if I am a Lord, where is the fear of me?" The priests have despised Yahweh's name, offering unclean food, the blind, the lame, the sick, upon the altar; let them offer such a gift to their Persian governor, will he accept them? Yahweh's name is great

[11] Isaiah 63:1–6; the last line is lost.

among the nations, from the rising to the setting sun, and in every sacred "place" a pure offering is ascending to his name; only in Jerusalem is his name profaned, there the priests say: "Yahweh's table is unclean, his food is contemptible," they complain of the ritual: "What a bore!"

Once Yahweh made a covenant of life and peace with Levi; true oracle was in his mouth and many he turned from evil. The lips of a priest should keep knowledge and men should seek oracle at his mouth as Yahweh's messenger; present-day priests have turned from the way and made many to stumble through their oracles, they have violated the covenant with Levi and have shown partiality in their oracles. Yahweh has therefore made them contemptible, he has brought them low before all the people.

Will a man rob God as they have been doing? Let them bring the whole tithe to the storehouse that there may be provision in Yahweh's house; then let them see whether Yahweh will not open the windows of heaven and pour them out a blessing! The locust will be rebuked for their sake, he shall not destroy the fruit of the ground, nor shall the vine blast its grapes. All nations shall call them fortunate, they shall be a land of delight.

Judah has profaned the loved sanctuary of Yahweh and has married the daughter of a foreign god, and then they wonder why Yahweh no longer turns to their offering or receives it from their hand! They may cover the altar with their tears, but Yahweh has witnessed Judah's treason to the wife of his youth.

The prophet has witnessed the defeat of Xerxes at Salamis and Platæa and Mycale, the crushing of the Phœnicians at the Eurymedon in 464,[12] perhaps the revolt of Egypt under Inarus (462–454) was on at the time. He is full of hope. Yahweh is sending his messenger to prepare the way before his face, the Lord they are seeking will suddenly arrive in his temple. Do they realise what they are hoping? Who can endure the day of his coming? He is like a refiner's fire or fuller's soap; he

[12] Diod., xi, 60 ff.

will cleanse the sons of Levi and refine them like gold and silver until they can once more offer their sacrifices in righteousness.

Sceptics declare "Every evil doer is favoured in Yahweh's eyes," and demand "Where is the God of Justice?" Even those who truly fear Yahweh are saying: "It is vain to serve God; what profit have we for keeping his charge and walking in mourning before him? It is the arrogant we call fortunate, for evil doers are built up and those who tempt God escape." Yahweh has heard and a book of remembrance has been written before him; he will not forget them on the day he is bringing to pass, he will save them as a man saves the son who serves him. On that day they shall be able to distinguish between those who serve God and those who do not. When that day comes, it will burn like a furnace, it will burn up the arrogant and evil doers like stubble. For those who fear Yahweh's name, the sun will rise with healing in his wings, they shall go forth and gambol like stall-fatted calves. But the wicked shall be trodden like ashes under the foot of the righteous.[13]

In 458, a certain Ezra appeared before Artaxerxes I (464-424) with a new project for Jewish colonisation. Ezra was a priest, a descendant of that Seraiah who had been chief priest under Zedekiah, but he is more generally known as a scribe. Before the exile, a scribe had been a mere secretary, now he was a man "skilled in the law of Moses which Yahweh had given." To the three earlier codes had been added a fourth, which we call that of the Priests, for in it there was a more emphatic emphasis on the high functions and the corresponding duties of that class. Far more attention was devoted to the minutiæ of the cult, often of high antiquity and non-Jewish origin, but now tied into the post-exilic religion. Side by side had grown up new presentations of the older legendary history, with special attention to chronology and genealogy, but here again the chief interest was in the cult, which according to these priestly writers had been given by God to Moses in its

[13] J. M. P. Smith, *Malachi*, 1912; Marti, *Dodekapropheton*, 456 ff.; Nowack, *Die Kleinen Propheten*, 404 ff.; Sellin, *Zwölfprophetenbuch*, 586 ff.

full post-exilic form. In both history and law, the process of addition was slow, and some of the latest elements were not incorporated until the beginning of the Macedonian period.

It was in knowledge of this new code that Ezra was skilled, in fact, later tradition made him its editor.[14] Zealots in Babylonia had accepted it, but it was quite unknown in Palestine and Egypt. It was no time to emphasise Jewish exclusiveness in Egypt, blazing with an intense and for the moment successful nationalism under Inarus (465–454), but Palestine promised a more fertile field. Ezra therefore begged authorisation to enforce this new code on his fellow religionists in Jerusalem; such an appeal to a Gentile monarch confessed the bankruptcy of Jewish nationalism.

Artaxerxes granted a formal decree which authorised Jewish volunteers to accompany Ezra. He was to carry the offerings made by the king and his counsellors and any free-will offerings, and to buy with them temple offerings. Other contributions he was to dispose as he saw fit. Further needs were to be met from the royal treasury and all the treasurers of the province Across the River were to give Ezra what he desired to a maximum of a hundred silver talents, a hundred cors of wheat, a hundred baths of wine, and salt without limit. Priests, Levites, singers, porters, Nethinim, and temple servants were to be free from tribute in money, tax in kind, or toll. Since Ezra had been sent by the king and his seven counsellors to make an inquiry about Judah and Jerusalem according to the law of his God, he was therefore, according to the wisdom of his God, to appoint magistrates and judges to judge all the Jews in the province and Across the River, all who knew the law of his God, and to teach those who did not know it. Whoever will not obey the law of his God and the law of the king shall have justice executed upon him, death, banishment, confiscation of goods, or imprisonment.[15]

New Year's Day saw the start. A fast was proclaimed to seek a straight road, for, as Ezra confesses: "I was ashamed to

[14] II Esdras, 14:19 ff.; Talmud Babli, *Sukkah*, i, 11.
[15] Aramaic decree, Ezra 7:11–26.

ask the king for a body of soldiers and horsemen to help us against the enemy on the way, since we had told the king: The hand of our God is upon all who seek him for good." He lists the family chiefs, the most important of whom was Hattush, fifth descendant of Zerubbabel, and numbers the sixteen hundred males; he also lists the offerings and utensils, quite in the fashion of the contemporary Elephantine inventories. The king had been generous and the Babylonian Jews also gave freely from their acquired wealth.

The Mesopotamian plains were in their full spring beauty, and Ezra must often have recalled Second Isaiah's prophecy that the desert would blossom like the crocus. No enemy hindered their passage and Jerusalem was reached on the first of the fifth month. Two months later, the first of the seventh month and the religious New Year's, the Zionists assembled at the square before the Water Gate to hear the new code. Ezra mounted a wooden pulpit and the first synagogue service in Jerusalem began. As he opened the sacred volume, the people rose in reverence, he blessed Yahweh and the congregation answered "Amen," they lifted up their hands and bowed their heads to the ground in worship. From day break to mid-day the law was read section by section, while the Levites translated it from Hebrew to the better understood Aramaic.

There was much in the new law that had never been observed, and the people wept that it had remained unheeded since the days of its author Moses. Ezra and the Levites comforted them: "This day is holy to Yahweh, your God, mourn not nor weep; go, eat the fat, drink sweet drinks, send portions to those who have nothing." Assembled again on the third day, they learned of the feast of the seventh month when they were to dwell in booths. They brought from the hills branches of the olive, wild olive, myrtle, and palm, and made booths, each man on the flat roof of his house or in his court, or in the temple courts and the squares before the Water Gate and the Gate of Ephraim if he did not live in the capital.

Joy soon turned to mourning. Ezra was informed by the princes that even the nobles, priests, and Levites had intermarried with the peoples of the land. Ezra rent his garments and mantle, pulled out the hair from his head and beard, and sat stunned until the time of the evening offering, when he fell upon his knees and prayed. A great crowd collected and began to weep. Their spokesman was Shecaniah, whose father Jehiel was one of the culprits; he admitted their sin but promised a covenant by which they would put away their foreign wives and children.

Ezra took their oath to carry out their promise, and went to the house of Johanan, son of the high priest Eliashib, who had succeeded Joiakim, son of Joshua,[16] where he remained fasting. Proclamation was made that whoever did not assemble to Jerusalem within three days—the short time allowed is eloquent testimony to the meagre territory occupied by the returned Zionists—should have his property devoted while he himself should be expelled from the assembly of the captivity. Accordingly they assembled in the open place before the temple and replied to Ezra's demand that they would do as he wished, but it was the rainy season, the people were shivering in the autumnal downpours, and furthermore it was not the task of a day or two since very many had thus sinned. They requested that the princes represent the congregation and that definite times should be appointed for the sinners from the different cities to be heard. Open opposition to Ezra's plan was voiced by Jonathan, son of Asahel, and Jahzeiah, son of Tikvah, as well as by the Levites Meshullam and Shabbethai, but the congregation as a whole agreed and Ezra chose heads of fathers' houses to examine the matter. The board began its sitting on the first of the tenth month and by the next New Year's Day the task was completed.

Ezra lists the sinners, headed by four of the high priest's own family; because of their prominence, they were required to sacrifice a ram as sin offering. Thirteen more of the priests, six of the Levites, two of the singers, three of the porters, eighty-three of the nobles show how wide-spread were mixed marriages among the first families. On the twenty-first, the

[16] Neh. 12:10 f.

Jews assembled fasting, clad in sackcloth and covered with earth, confessed their sin, and separated themselves from their foreign wives and children.[17]

In his prayer, Ezra had given thanks that he had been granted opportunity to repair the ruins of Zion and had been given a wall in Judah and Jerusalem. It would seem that Ezra did actually attempt to rebuild the walls. Rehum, the reporter, Shimshai, the scribe, and their companions in Samaria and in Across the River wrote Artaxerxes. The Jews who had come up from him have arrived and are rebuilding Jerusalem, the wicked and rebellious city, they are completing the walls and have already laid the foundations. If this city is rebuilt and its walls completed, the Jews will no longer pay tribute in money or tax in kind or toll, and the king's revenue will thus be decreased. Because they eat the salt of the palace and it is not right to see the king being stripped, they have sent and ask that search be made in the record books of his fathers; he will find that this city has been rebellious, damaging kings and provinces, that the Jews have been rebellious and from days of old made insurrection in it, and for this reason was the city laid waste. If this city is rebuilt and its walls completed, the king will have no territory in the province Across the River.

Egypt was still in revolt and Artaxerxes was naturally of a suspicious disposition. His reply confirmed all the charges and ordered that the building be stopped. Rehum and his companions hurried off to Jerusalem and compelled the Jews to cease their building by force.[18]

[17] Ezra Memoirs, Ezra 7:27–8:34; 9; Ezra Story, Ezra 7:1, 6, 9; 8:34–36; Neh. 7:70–73; Ezra 10; Neh. 9:1–5.
[18] Aramaic Document, Ezra 4:7–23.

CHAPTER XL

BUILDING THE WALLS

NEHEMIAH, son of Hacaliah, was a cup bearer before Artaxerxes I, and was therefore presumably an eunuch. While thus serving the king in the citadel at Susa, his brother Hanani brought to him certain returned Zionists. They reported that Jerusalem's wall had been broken down, its gates burned with fire, the survivors of the captivity treated with contempt and in great distress. At this news of the recent catastrophe, Nehemiah mourned and fasted many days.

When his turn came to present wine to the king, Nehemiah's face still showed signs of his grief. Artaxerxes demanded the cause of this sadness of heart. "Let the king live forever!" answered Nehemiah, "Why should not my face be sad when the city, the place of my fathers' sepulchres, lies ruined and its gates consumed by fire?" This was dangerous, for court etiquette prohibited a show of sadness before the king, but Artaxerxes continued: "For what are you making request?" Thoroughly frightened yet determined to make trial of the king's generosity, Nehemiah whispered a prayer and requested that he be sent to rebuild his native city.

The twelve years which had elapsed since Ezra's departure had totally changed the situation in the empire. Inarus and his Athenian allies in Egypt had been utterly crushed by the Phœnicians. Megabyxus, satrap of Syria, had revolted in 450, but had been taken prisoner and forgiven. Next year the half century of warfare with the Delian League was brought to a close by the so-called Peace of Callias. Azbaal of Citium had at last won the Idalium his father Baal-milk was unable to capture. The empire was entering the period of unbroken peace within and without which characterised the second half of the reign; his queen Damaspia was sitting by his side and Artaxerxes felt in a mood for generous action.

BUILDING THE WALLS

Artaxerxes accordingly inquired how long Nehemiah wished leave of absence and a time was set. Nehemiah then requested letters of safe conduct to the hostile governors of Across the River and orders to Asaph, keeper of the king's paradise or park southeast of Jerusalem, to furnish timber for the beams of the temple citadel, to be famous as the Tower of Antonia as the paradise became the "Gardens of Solomon,"[1] for the city wall, and for the governor's palace.

Even with the royal safe conduct, Nehemiah must be protected by troops. The governors of Across the River were given the royal letters and at Samaria he met his future opponents, Sanballat and Tobiah. Sanballat of Beth Horon, then governor of Samaria,[2] bears an Assyrian name, Sin-uballit, "Sin gives life," and was probably a descendant of men deported by Assyrian kings. Tobiah is called by Nehemiah an Ammonite slave, though both he and his father reverence Yahweh in their names, and later the family owned a palace east of the Jordan and occupied a prominent position in Judaism. Both according to Nehemiah were exceedingly troubled that a man had come to seek the welfare of the children of Israel. A third enemy was the Arab Gashmu, perhaps a descendant of an Arab tribe such as the Tamud whom Sargon deported to Palestine.[3]

Three days after his arrival at Jerusalem in 444, Nehemiah arose in the night. He told no man what his God had put in his heart to do for Jerusalem, but with a few personal followers he viewed the walls which in places were so ruinous that he must proceed on foot. Then he summoned the leaders and urged them to rebuild the fortifications; the practical courtier took no stock in Zechariah's theory that Yahweh's presence in Jerusalem dispensed with the need of walls.

Nehemiah's enemies professed great amusement but asked if he was planning revolt against the king. Nehemiah answered that the God of Heaven would prosper them, also the king had given permission to his loyal servants, but Sanballat and his

[1] Joseph., *Ant.*, viii, 186; I Macc., 13:52; Acts 21:37; 22:24.
[2] Cowley, *Aramaic Papyri*, 30.   [3] *History of Assyria*, 210 f.

companions would have no portion, authority, or remembrance in Jerusalem. Construction was pushed rapidly, the high priest Eliashib undertook one of the gates, other gates or sections of the wall were the portion of the more prominent, such as Shemaiah, Zerubbabel's descendant. With Rephaiah and Shallum, each ruler over half Jerusalem, are bracketed as of equal importance the goldsmiths Uzziel and Malchiah and the perfumer Hananiah, thus showing the incursion of the new nobility of trade into the old nobility of birth. The other goldsmiths and merchants repaired another section, and Levites and priests each took their part. A few outside villages were also represented, Jericho, Gibeon, Mizpah, the seat of the governor of Across the River, Beth Haccherem, Beth Zur, Keilah, the Jordan plain, and Tekoa, though of these last it must be reported that their nobles did not put their neck to the work of their lord.

Before the army of Samaria and his brothers Sanballat mocked: "What are these feeble Jews doing? Are they depending on God? Will they accomplish it by sacrificing? Will they complete it in a day? Will they bring back to life the burned stones from the rubbish heaps?" Tobiah also added his contribution to the assembly's wit: "What they are building, if a fox went up on it, he would break down their stone wall!" Ezra's failure gave some excuse for their scepticism, but Nehemiah was no Ezra.

He did indeed have recourse to prayer: "Hear, O our God, for we are despised, and turn back their reproach upon their own head, and give them up as spoil in a land of captivity," but he also pushed the work while the people were in the mood. When the wall reached half its intended height, Sanballat planned to attack the scattered workers and kill them, but if Sanballat had his friends in Jerusalem Nehemiah received information from the neighbouring villages. Half his personal body guard was constantly under arms, the trumpeter stood by the governor's side, the workmen carried weapons. Every one labored from sunrise to the coming out of the stars and Nehemiah's personal followers, prepared for all alarms, did not even undress at night, while the men from the outlying villages slept in the city.

All but the gates had been completed when Sanballat changed his tactics. He suggested a conference at Cephirah in the plain of Ono, but Nehemiah was not deceived; he replied that the work was so great he could not delay it by his absence. After four such attempts, Sanballat sent an open letter: "It is reported among the Jews, and Gashmu confirms it, that you and the Jews are planning to rebel, that this is the reason you are building the wall, and that you are to become their king. Furthermore, that you have instigated prophets to proclaim concerning you in Jerusalem: 'A king is in Judah!' This is sure to be reported to the king, so come down and let us consult together." Nehemiah's reply was characteristically short and to the point: "No such things have been done as you say; you have invented them from your own hearts."

Sanballat then tried to work on Nehemiah's fears. Pretending that he could not go out to deliver his message, Shemaiah induced Nehemiah to come to his house and begged him: "Let us meet together in the inner temple shrine and shut the door, for they are coming in the night to kill you." Nehemiah was no man to seek refuge in sanctuary, especially as recent laws made it a crime for a common man to enter the inner shrine; no prophet who suggested a violation of the divine law could be anything but a false seer. He naturally suspected that Sanballat had bribed Shemaiah and replied: "Should such a man as I run away? Should a layman like myself enter the temple, even to save his life? I will not go in!" Nehemiah also pays his respects to the prophetess Noadiah and the rest of the prophets who tried to make him afraid.

Fifty-two days after its beginning, the wall was completed on the twenty-fifth of Elul. This was extraordinarily quick work, even if much of the wall had remained intact. Recent excavations prove how badly the work was done, for the breaches were filled with stones of all sizes, set in plenty of mud mortar.[4] Poor as it was, it sufficed. General oversight

[4] J. G. Duncan, QS., 1924, 128.

was given to Nehemiah's brother Hanani and to Hananiah, captain of the citadel. Guards were appointed to watch the section opposite each man's house, the gates were opened only when the sun was hot and closed while the sun was yet in sight.

Starting from the Valley Gate, at the southwest corner of the city, two processions circled the walls, one to the left, the other to the right, and met at the temple where the dedication ceremonies were brought to an end. Another problem remained. Few houses had been built within the walls, those of the nobles only, for the peasants preferred the country where they were close to their fields. Nehemiah called an assembly and one out of ten was chosen by lot to dwell within the walls; nothing is said as to the means by which they were to secure their sustenance. There were still alarms, for many of the nobles were hostile to their new governor. Tobiah in particular had his partisans, for he had married a daughter of Shecaniah while his son Jehohanan had espoused the daughter of another prominent citizen named Meshullam. All Nehemiah's words were promptly reported to Tobiah by his Jerusalem friends, who attempted to persuade the governor that after all Tobiah was a good man. When this failed, Tobiah sent letters to Nehemiah to frighten him.

Nehemiah now had time for social reform. Taxes were high, previous governors had oppressed the people, no doubt requisitions had been made when the Persian armies marched on Egypt. Rich Jews had taken advantage of the plight of their poorer brethren, crops had failed, the situation had been aggravated by the necessity of dropping all work at a critical time in the agricultural year to build the wall.

There was a great outcry from the people. Some complained: "We, our sons and our daughters are numerous; give us grain that we may eat and live!" Others declared: "We are mortgaging our fields and vineyards and houses to secure grain in the famine." Still others were in yet worse case: "We have borrowed money to pay the king's tribute; our flesh is as the flesh of our brothers, our children as their children, yet we must make our children slaves. Furthermore, some of our daughters have been kidnapped and we cannot redeem them, for our fields and vineyards belong to the nobles."

Nehemiah was exceedingly angry. He called the nobles and rulers, rebuked them for taking interest from their fellow Jews, and laid upon them a great curse; according to his means, he had been redeeming his brothers sold to the Gentiles, must he now buy back those who had been sold by their brother Jews? He and his followers had loaned money and grain without interest, they too must return the property they had seized and with it the interest they had taken. Under the circumstances, the creditors were forced to agree; lest they later change their minds, Nehemiah summoned the priests and made them take oath. He also shook out the fold of his garment, saying: "So may God shake out from his house and from the fruit of his labour every man who does not fulfil this promise; even thus may he be shaken out and empty." All the assembly said "Amen" and praised Yahweh; it is not reported what the creditors said.

Nehemiah thus sums up his twelve years of rule (444–432). In all that time, he and his brothers never ate the governor's bread, the perquisites of his office, though former governors had been a burden to the people, taking from them daily forty shekels for bread and wine, and allowing their servants to oppress them; rather he gave free meals to the hundred and fifty Jews and rulers who sat at his table, beside those who came from surrounding nations. Each day he slew one ox, six choice sheep, and fowls, and once in ten days wine was given in abundance for all the people. He refrained from oppression because of his fear of God; he concludes: "Remember to me for good, O my God, all that I have done for this people." His own summary characterises the man and his very justifiable self-satisfaction, his courage and honesty, his very genuine piety coupled with that rare perception that "God helps those who help themselves."

In 432, Nehemiah returned to his royal patron. The walls had been built, his enemies had been defeated, justice and mercy had been established. Some time later, not long before the death of Artaxerxes in 424, bad news came from Palestine. He returned to find much of his work undone. The high priest Eliashib was a backslider; he had cleared out the meal offering and frankincense from the temple storehouse and had handed over the room to his relative Tobiah. "It displeased me greatly," says Nehemiah, "so I threw out all the utensils of Tobiah's house from the room." The chamber was then purified and restored to its former use.

He also found that the Levites had not been given their portions and had been forced to retire to their fields to gain a living. "Why is the house of God neglected?" he demanded of the rulers. The Levites were again collected and all Judah was induced to bring the tithes into the storerooms. To prevent further peculation, officials were appointed to distribute the portions and priests and Levites were set over the wood offerings and the first fruits.

Recent days had witnessed an increased emphasis on the sabbath. The sabbath had long ceased to be the fifteenth of the month, the time of danger when the moon reached its full, and had become the first day of a seven-day week. Recent codes had emphasised its sanctity as had one of the ten commandments attributed to Moses. Now its origin was pushed still farther back, to creation itself. In imitation of the Babylonian seven tablets of creation, the creative activity of God was carried through six days of labour, and on the seventh God rested and blessed the day and hallowed it.[5]

To his amazement and horror, Nehemiah found men treading winepresses, bringing in heaps of grain, loading asses with wine, figs, grapes, and produce, and carrying them to Jerusalem, all on the sabbath. Merchants from Tyre were also to be seen in the capital, selling fish and all sorts of wares on the holy day. Again the nobles came in for rebuke and Nehemiah quoted examples from past history to show how Yahweh had punished their fathers for like sins. As it began to grow dark in the gates on the day before the sabbath, the doors were

[5] Gen. 1.

closed and guarded by Nehemiah's servants. The merchants then took position just outside the walls and continued their thriving business. Nehemiah threatened them with personal violence, and they came no more.

The protests of Malachi and Ezra against mixed marriages had borne little fruit. Nehemiah was shocked to find half-breed children who spoke no Jewish, but only the Ashdodite of their mothers. Nehemiah adopted more direct methods. He cursed and beat and pulled out the hair of these renegade fathers and put them under oath not to repeat the offence, but he did not have the heart to follow Ezra's orders to divorce the wives and to inflict the stigma of illegitimacy on innocent children. Even with this concession, Nehemiah failed as utterly as Ezra. Jews still intermarried with Philistines, and a Philistine type of body and even of mind has been claimed for one portion of the present-day Jews.[6]

Foreign marriages were not confined to the lower classes. Eliashib the high priest was allied to Tobiah, and his grandson Manasseh, Jehoiada's son, had married Nicaso, daughter of Sanballat, Nehemiah's ancient foe. This was too great a provocation, and Nehemiah drove him out without mercy.[7]

Sanballat received the fugitive gladly and built for him a new temple on the age-old sacred place on the summit of Mount Gerizim, overlooking the fertile vale of Shechem.[8] This was the origin of the Samaritan schism, but a complete break was long in coming. The "Pious" refused indeed to recognise them as true worshippers of Yahweh, but the higher classes, above all the leaders of the official cult, were in close and friendly contact. In a sense, in matters religious Shechem was but a dependency of Jerusalem, and this close relationship continued into the Macedonian period. Of the Jewish scriptures, now becoming canonical, the Samaritans took over only the first five books attributed to Moses, but these they preserved

---

[6]So R. N. Salaman, *QS.*, 1925, 37 ff.; 68 ff.
[7]Memoirs of Nehemiah, Neh. 1–4; 6; 12:31–32, 37–40; 7:4 f.; 11:1 f.; 5; 14:4–31.
[8]Joseph., *Ant.*, xi, 303.

in such form as to show that even after the Greek translation was made some two hundred and fifty years before our era they were correcting their copies from those held sacred in Jerusalem.[9]

As a result of Nehemiah's efforts, the people came together to make a covenant accepting his reforms. Nehemiah's name heads the list, but the name of the high priest Eliashib is conspicuously missing. Twenty-two priests, seventeen Levites, forty-four chiefs of the people follow. Then come the regulations which the assembly accept under curse and oath. They will not intermarry with the peoples of the land. They will not buy produce of the peoples of the land on a sabbath or holy day. They will forego cultivation of the soil and the exaction of debt in the seventh year. Each year they will give a third of a shekel for the temple services, for the show-bread, the continual meal and burnt offerings, for the sabbaths, new moons, and set feasts, for the holy things and the sin offering to make atonement for all Israel, and for all the work of the temple. Priests, Levites, and people have cast lots for the bringing in of the wood offering at stated times in the year, to burn upon the fire altar. They will bring in the first fruits of their ground and the first fruits of all kinds of trees year by year to the house of Yahweh. They will bring the first-born of their sons and of their cattle, as it is written in the law, and the firstlings of their herds and flocks to the temple, to the priests who serve there. They will bring the best of their coarse meal, the fruit of all kinds of trees, the new wine and the oil, to the priests in the temple chambers. They will pay the tithes of their land to the Levites. They will bring, both children of Israel and the children of Levi, the offerings of grain, new wine, and oil, to the chambers where are stored the sanctuary utensils and where are the serving priests, porters, and singers. They will not neglect the house of their God.[10]

This covenant is of extraordinary interest. Least important is its close agreement with the reforms narrated in Nehemiah's

[9] *AJSL.*, XXXIV, 1918, 151; cf. J. A. Montgomery, *The Samaritans*, 1907.
[10] Neh. 9:38–10:39.

memoirs. These Jews determine the future of the temple and of its cult, not as a result of a written law, not at the suggestion of a cold if not hostile high priest, but through a free-will agreement proposed by a layman and ratified by the whole people. The majority of the provisions trace back to Josiah's code or even to the Code of the Covenant. There is a certain knowledge of provisions in the Priestly Code, but it is evident our present complete codification is still in the future.

CHAPTER XLI

THESE FROM THE LAND OF SINIM

ELIASHIB soon after Nehemiah's return was succeeded by Jehoiada as high priest and he shortly by Johanan.[1] Near the end of 411, Johanan received a letter from Egypt. It came from a community of Jewish mercenaries settled at Yeb, the later Elephantine, which with its sister garrison of Sun or Syene across the river guarded the southern border at the first cataract.[2] We are told that they first entered Egypt "in the days of the kings of Egypt"; Psammetichus I had a garrison at Elephantine as early as 640, and there is reason to believe that these Jews had migrated before Josiah's reform of 621. Psammetichus II used them in his campaign against the Ethiopians about 590.[3] Ezekiel threatens these, from his point of view, apostate Jews, when he declares that "those who uphold Egypt shall fall, from Migdol," on the Syrian frontier, "to Seveneh," Syene, on the opposite border.[4] When the Second Isaiah was prophesying return to Zion, he included among the returning Zionists those from the north, those from the west, and those from the land of Sinim or Syene.[5] Like the Greeks and other mercenaries in Egyptian service, these Jews were hated by the natives. They may have heard the words of Second Isaiah, they may have learned the kindly treatment of their coreligionists by Cyrus, they may have even revolted to Cambyses in 525, for their temple was spared the general destruction of Egyptian shrines. They were loyal in the revolt

[1] Neh. 12:10 f., 22.
[2] A. H. Sayce and A. Cowley, *Aramaic Papyri discovered at Assuan*, 1906; E. Sachau, *Aramäische Papyrus und Ostraka aus Elephantine*, 1911; A. Ungnad, *Aramäische Papyrus*, 1911; M. Sprengling, *AJT.*, XXI, 1917, 411 ff.; XXII, 1918, 349 ff.; A. Cowley, *Aramaic Papyri of the Fifth Century B.C.*, 1923.
[3] Letter of Aristeas, 13; cf. Herod., ii, 30; and perhaps Deut. 17:16.
[4] Ezek. 30:6.   [5] Isaiah 49:12.

of 486 and Darius rewarded them with the official Aramaic version of his Behistun inscription.

Their documents are all written in Aramaic, the official language of the Persian government in its dealings with the west and the common speech of commerce. The characters approach the square forms familiar from our printed Hebrew Bibles. In many respects, these documents afford a close parallel to the documents in Ezra with closely similar language and phraseology, the same Hebraisms, even the same mistakes.

Members of the community are "the Jews," "the Jewish army," more rarely "Aramæans of Syene." They form a permanent garrison, under a "chief of the army," and are divided into "standards" whose commanders always bear Persian or Babylonian names, and these in turn into "hundreds." Each man is identified by his "standard"; some are only "lords of a standard," mere soldiers, others are full "citizens." As a regular garrison, their families are with them and they enjoy a full community life.

In civil affairs they were ruled by a "chief" with his "associates, the priests." There were no Jewish courts and regular civil courts were held at Syene or more rarely in Elephantine, presided over by the "chief of the army," assisted by the royal judges; next above this was the court of the fratarak, subgovernor of the nome of Teshteres, and final appeal might be made to the satrap.

The documents, which begin in 495, are generally of a business nature. Babylonian formulæ familiar from the cuneiform tablets are closely followed. First comes the date, the year of the reigning king, with double indication of the month, the Babylonian name now beginning to be employed by the Jews, and the native Egyptian. Technical Babylonian terms are common, the penalties for non-fulfilment of contracts are also Babylonian. The document ends with the witnesses, who often sign their names, thus showing a rather considerable literacy. Witnesses are often Gentile, for there was no ghetto, and the various races lived together; for instance, an Egyptian priest of Khnum and Sati, deities of the cataract, actually lived under the shadow of the Jewish temple. On the outside was the endorsement, in the Aramaic already long familiar from Assyrian and Babylonian tablets. The papyri were rolled up, tied, sealed, and preserved in a box.

As in the Assyrian times, the standard of weight was the "royal stone." Units of counting were Babylonian. Ten hallurin, the Babylonian halluru, made a quarter; four quarters made a shekel, about our quarter dollar; ten shekels made a karash; six kerashin or sixty shekels, as in Babylonia, made the mina or "pound."

We may examine a few of these documents. Soldiers, though living in their own houses, received regular rations. A list dated 419 indicates that the "army of Syene" received a money payment and one, one and a half, or two ardabs of barley per month.[6] From 484, we have an agreement by which Espemet, "boatman of the difficult waters," the cataract, gives Hosea and Ahiab eleven ardabs of beans and forty-four ardabs of barley, worth ten shekels the ardab, rations for eleven men of the "hundred" of Bethel-teqem, five ardabs for two men, and half an ardab of beans and the same number for the "hundred" of Nabu-shalliv. They will deliver it to the army and make their reckoning with the King's House and the scribes of the Treasury.[7] Fields are sometimes held in common by the "standard."[8]

One family may be traced through many years. In 471 a certain Mahseiah, son of Jedoniah, an Aramæan of Syene, though living in Yeb or Elephantine, of the standard of Warizath, granted permission to Coniah of the same standard to build a buttress wall at his own gateway, but reserved title to the land, right of egress, and air rights to erect a structure above.[9] All through these documents we find ample evidence that the lands were held, not by the Egyptian servile tenure, but by the fee-simple tenure common in Babylonian free

---

[6]Sachau 21 f.; Ungnad 20; Cowley 24.
[7]Sachau 25 f.; Ungnad 27; Sprengling 1; Cowley 2.
[8]Sachau 7; Ungnad 7; Cowley 16.
[9]Sayce-Cowley A; Sprengling 23; Cowley 5.

cities.[10] Six years later, Mahseiah appears before Damidata and his associated judges and by their orders takes oath by Yahu that he rightly occupies land claimed by Dargman, a Persian from Khorassan, and Dargman must sign a quit claim.[11] In 460 this property is given by Mahseiah to his daughter Mibtahiah, who is to marry his next-door neighbour Jezaniah, and with it goes the quit claim of Dargman.[12] The same property is then granted to Jezaniah; in return for developing it, he is to have right of possession but no right of disposal. If Mibtahiah divorces him, he is to continue in possession as trustee for their children; if he divorces her, it is to be divided half and half.[13] Mahseiah is a witness in 455 when Egypt was in revolt[14] and in 447 he gives Mibtahiah the house secured from the money lender Meshullam in return for goods given him when he was an official in the fortress; he cannot pay her and therefore gives the land, bounded on one side by the temple of Yahu, and with it Meshullam's old deed.[15]

Meanwhile, Mibtahiah had divorced Jezaniah, and had married a certain Pi, an Egyptian contractor of Syene. This marriage likewise proved a failure, and in 441 she divorced him. According to agreement, they divided their property, silver, grain, garments, bronze, and iron, and he surrendered the marriage agreement by which perhaps he had secured some rights to her property. Mibtahiah, lax enough Jewess to marry a Gentile, had no scruple to taking oath by the goddess Sati as imposed by the court. Perhaps she had been disowned by the Jewish community, for all the witnesses are Gentile.[16]

Apparently she already had in mind another Egyptian contractor who in his name As-hor honoured the god Horus. He may have become a Jewish proselyte to obtain the rich heiress, for he later appears with the good Hebrew name of Nathan. In view of her past matrimonial adventures, he was surely optimistic when he declared: "I came to your house that

[10]Cf. *Amer. Hist. Rev.*, XXXII, 1926, 9.
[11]Sayce-Cowley B; Cowley 6.   [12]Sayce-Cowley D; Cowley 8.
[13]Sayce-Cowley C; Cowley 9.
[14]Sayce-Cowley L; Ungnad 88; Cowley 11.
[15]Sayce-Cowley E; Cowley 13.   [16]Sayce-Cowley F; Cowley 14.

you might give me your daughter to wife; she is my wife and I am her husband from this day forever!" Nonetheless, his optimism did not prevent his making ready for all possible eventualities. He carefully notes the five shekels he gave her father as bride price, and as carefully lists his presents to his wife and their cash value: one karash, two shekels for her outfit; a brand new striped woollen garment, dyed on both sides, twelve by seven and a half feet in size, worth two kerashin, eight shekels; a closely woven mantle, equally new and of the same size, worth eight shekels; a fringed robe nine by six feet, worth seven shekels; a bronze mirror worth a shekel and a half; a bronze tray of the same value; two bronze cups worth a shekel each; a bronze bowl worth half a shekel. The total value is carefully summed. He also lists but without their value her gifts to him, including a reed bed with four stone legs and a new cosmetic box of ivory which makes one suspect he was a bit of a fop. If either dies without issue, the other shall inherit all that is on the face of the earth. If Mibtahiah stands up in the congregation and says: "I divorce As-hor my husband," the cost of the divorce shall be on her head, she shall go back to the scales and weigh out to As-hor seven and a half shekels, the bride price with fifty per cent interest, and surrender all that he gave her. Then she may go where she will without suit or service. If he divorces her, he forfeits the bride price, but all the rest must be returned. If however he drives her out by force, he must pay twenty kerashin, the contract is cancelled, and she retains all his gifts. He may have no other wife or children; should he disobey, he must pay her twenty kerashin and he cannot take away her property, under further penalty of twenty more kerashin.[17]

Mibtahiah was by now at least thirty years of age and had learned at last how to live the married life. Fear of lack of issue proved groundless and in due time her third marriage was blessed by two sons, named from her grandfather and father, Jedoniah and Mahseiah. As-hor died about 420 and his sons were sued before the fratarak Damandin and the army

[17] Sayce-Cowley G; Cowley 15.

chief Vidarnag by Meshullam's sons Menahem and Ananiah for return of property deposited with As-hor by their grandfather Shelomem and including wool and cotton, clothing, bronze, iron, wood, and ivory vessels. Settlement was made and they gave quittance.[18]

Another Jedoniah, nephew of Mibtahiah's first husband Jezániah, appeared in 416 before Vidarnag and claimed the house of his uncle. Again Jedoniah and Mahseiah were successful and the other Jedoniah must give a quit claim.[19] The much-married Mibtahiah died in 411, and her sons divided the property. Each took a slave marked by the letter yodh on the arm to the right of the Aramaic marking "To Mibtahiah," but the mother of the slaves and her infant son were left to be settled later.[20]

Interesting as are these glimpses into the life of this faraway Jewish community, the most significant revelations are in the field of religion. These exiled Jews brought with them their religion, but it is by no means what we have been accustomed to call Hebrew. They do worship the Hebrew national deity, but they call him Yahu in agreement with the evidence for the earlier pronunciation of his name, and in their dealings with foreigners they call him "God of Heaven," as in our book of Ezra. Yahu possessed a temple in Yeb as early as 525 and it continued in use over a century. Josiah's reform had attempted to suppress all other sanctuaries in favour of the temple at Jerusalem, but the reform had not touched Yeb. As at Jerusalem, the Yeb temple had an altar on which were presented meal offerings, incense offerings, and whole burnt offerings. There is no mention of feasts until near the end, no Sabbath stops their labour, the Law is unknown, neither Moses nor any other of the early heroes is commemorated in their names. They have priests but there is no hint that they were considered sons of Aaron or even of Levi.

Especially instructive are the oaths. When Mahseiah is accused of stealing fish, he is ordered by the court to prove

[18]Sayce-Cowley H; Cowley 20.   [19]Sayce-Cowley J; Cowley 25.
[20]Sayce-Cowley K; Cowley 28.

his innocence through oath to Yahu,[21] but when Menahem is accused by Meshullam of wrongly retaining possession of half a she ass, the oath of compurgation is by Yahu, Anath Yahu, and the temple, the practice prohibited by Matthew.[22] Malchiah is ordered by the court to swear by his god, and the oath is taken, not by the Yahu honoured in his name, but by Harem-bethel.[23] Harem-nathan is the son of Bethel-nathan and grandson of Jonathan; the grandfather was "given" by Yahu, the father by Bethel, the grandson by Harem![24]

In 419, there was a contribution of two shekels each by a hundred and fifty-nine persons. The list states at the beginning that the contributions were made to Yahu the God, but at the close we find that it was divided. Of the total of thirty-one kerashin eight shekels, only twelve kerashin six shekels go to Yahu, seven kerashin go to Ishum-bethel, and twelve kerashin, almost as much as Yahu's portion, to Anath-bethel.[25] Obviously, the Jews of Yeb were no monotheists, and when in the documents we find the word "gods" we may be sure they meant just what they say. In addition to Yahu, they worshipped Anath-bethel or Anath Yahu, the old mother goddess Anath who had become Yahu's consort, Ishum-bethel or Ashima,[26] and Harem-bethel.[27]

Into this sleepy little outpost of earlier, tolerant Judaism there came in 419 a certain Hananiah with startling news. Darius II, like his predecessors whose decrees are preserved in the book of Ezra, had been busying himself about matters of Jewish religion. Unfortunately the letter transmitting his rescript is badly damaged, but it may be restored about as follows: "To] my [brothers, Jedo]niah and his associates, the ar[my of the J]ews, your brother Hanan[iah.] The peace of my brothers may the gods [seek.] And now this year, the

[21]Sachau 32; Ungnad 34; Cowley 45.
[22]Sachau 32; Ungnad 33; Cowley 44; cf. Matt. 23:16.
[23]Sachau 26; Ungnad 28; Cowley 7.
[24]Sachau 33; Ungnad 36; Cowley 18.
[25]Sachau 17 ff.; Ungnad 19; Sprengling 15; Cowley 22.
[26]II Kings 17:30; cf. Amos 8:14.
[27]Cf. J. M. P. Smith, *AJSL.*, XXXIII, 1917, 322 ff.

fifth year of king Darius, a message was sent from the king to Arsha[m, saying: 'In the month Tybi let there be a passover for the army of the Je]ws.' Now therefore do you count fou[rteen days of the month Nisan and kee]p [the passover,] and from the fifteenth day to the twenty-first day of [Nisan are seven days of Unleavened Bread. Do you] be clean and take heed. And do [n]o [work on the fifteenth day and on the twenty-first day. Also drink n[o beer,] or anything at all [in which i]s leaven, [do not eat from the fifteenth day from] the setting of the sun to the twenty-first day of Nis[an, seven days let it not be seen among you. Do not br]ing it into your chambers, but seal it up during those day[s. Thus let it be done as ki]ng [Darius commanded."[28] Despite its damaged state, this letter is of extraordinary interest. The Passover is not expressly mentioned in the part preserved, but its mention is demanded by the context and an ostracon from Yeb does actually refer to it.[29] The Feast of Unleavened Bread which follows the Passover is introduced into Yeb for the first time, and by orders of a Persian king.

Hananiah's visit put new religious zeal into the Jews of Yeb, and the great collection was made for Yahu's temple. Perhaps they were more zealous in their faith, perhaps they offended the Egyptians by their animal sacrifices, perhaps they began to tell what they had just learned in the Law of Moses about the mistreatment of their fathers by the Egyptians, their punishment by the God of Israel, and Israel's triumphant exodus. Perhaps nothing more is demanded than the usual hatred of the Egyptians for foreigners, especially when they were mercenaries employed by a foreign power to hold them in subjection. Jewish popularity was not increased by their refusal to join some revolting native standards a little later.

Arsham, the Persian satrap, visited the king in 411, and the natives took advantage of his absence to revolt. The priests of Khnum, successors of that priest who had dwelt in the shadow of the Yahu temple, bribed Vidarnag, now chief of the

[28] Sachau 6; Ungnad 6; Sprengling 4; Cowley 21.
[29] Sachau 77, 2.

army, and his followers destroyed the king's stores in the fortress of Yeb and built a wall in the midst of the fortress. The garrison well of ever-flowing water was stopped up by the priests. Vidarnag sent a letter to his son Nephayan, who had succeeded his father as chief of the army in Syene, and ordered the demolition of the Yahu temple in Yeb. Nephayan led out the natives and foreign troops in July, they came to the fortress with their weapons, they entered the temple, and rased it to the ground. They broke up the stone pillars and destroyed the five gateways, built of hewn stone, with the doors and bronze pivots. The cedar roof and the furniture were burned, the movable property, including the gold and silver bowls, they stole.

The Jews with their wives and children put on sackcloth and fasted, their wives were as widows, they neither anointed themselves with oil nor drank wine. They prayed to Yahu, God of Heaven, and he permitted them to see their desire on Vidarnag; the dogs tore off the anklet from his feet, his riches were taken away, all the men who sought to do harm to that temple were killed.

Revenge had been secured, but the temple was in ruins. Their Persian masters may have suspected that they were not without blame for the disturbance. The Jews of Yeb therefore began to write letters of appeal, copies of which were fortunately preserved. One was to Johanan, high priest at Jerusalem, his associates, Austan, brother of Anani, and the nobles of the Jews. Johanan had been a supporter of Ezra, who had found lodging in his house,[30] and he naturally felt no desire to aid his schismatic coreligionists, in fact, he must have considered the destruction of their temple a just reward for their heresy. He accordingly returned no answer.[31]

Furthermore, Johanan had troubles of his own. His brother Joshua was on friendly terms with Bagohi, the Persian successor of Nehemiah as governor of Judah, who had promised

---

[30] Ezra 10:6.
[31] J. Euting, *Mém. Acad. Ins.*, XI, 1903; Sachau 75; Ungnad 2; Sprengling 10; Cowley 27.

Joshua the high priesthood. Joshua was imprudent enough to quarrel with his brother in the temple precincts; Johanan might support Ezra's reforms, but that did not prevent him from murdering his brother in the very temple itself. Bagohi thereupon invaded the temple and when the pious Jews protested, he sarcastically demanded whether he was not more pure than the corpse of the man slain in the sanctuary. As punishment, he inflicted the payment of fifty shekels for every lamb used in the daily offering, and this payment was enforced for seven years.[32]

When no satisfaction could be obtained from Johanan, Jedoniah and his associates turned to his enemy Bagohi. A first letter produced no result and in 408 they tried again: "To our lord Bagohi, governor of Judah, your servants Jedoniah and his associates, the priests who are in Yeb the fortress. The peace of your lordship may the God of Heaven seek bounteously at all times, and give you favour before Darius the king and the sons of his house more than a thousand times, and may he give you long life and may you be happy and prosperous at all times." They recall their suffering at the hand of that cursed Vidarnag, and close: "If it seems good to our lord, let him take an interest in that temple to build it, since they will not permit us to build it. See, there are men under obligation to you for your kindness and your favours here in Egypt; let a letter be sent to them about the temple of the God Yahu, that it be built in Yeb the fortress as it was built before, and we shall offer the meal offering and the incense offering and the burnt offering on the altar of the God Yahu in your name and we will pray for you at all times, we and our wives and our children and the Jews, all who are here. If you will do this so the temple shall be built, then you will have greater merit before Yahu, God of Heaven, than a man who offers him burnt offering and sacrifice to the value of a thousand talents." Jedoniah and his associates did not rely solely on promise of divine reward, they added a guarded hint that a bribe might be forthcoming: "As to the gold, we have

[32] Joseph., *Ant.*, xi, 297 ff.

sent information." They have likewise sent information to Delaiah and Shelemiah, sons of Sanballat, governor of Samaria, and they end with the assurance that the satrap Arsham knew nothing of what had taken place.[33]

Bagohi, governor of little Judah, could only deal cautiously with the mighty satrap Arsham. He sent no letter in reply to Jedoniah, but gave a verbal message which the unskilled messenger wrote down as best he could: "Memorandum of what Bagohi and Delaiah said to me: Memorandum, that is, you are to say in Egypt before Arsham about the altar house of the God of Heaven which was built in Yeb the fortress of old, before Cambyses, which that cursed Vidarnag destroyed in the fourteenth year of king Darius, to build it in its place as it was before, and to offer upon that altar meal offerings and incense offerings as it was before done."[34] The cult was not to be complete, for burnt offerings of animals were tacitly prohibited. Bagohi was evidently a good Zoroastrian, to whom pollution of fire by burning bodies of slain animals was sacrilege; in his setting the tax on animals sacrificed at Jerusalem so high as to be prohibitive, he may have been following the same policy.

Jedoniah and his four associates thankfully replied that they would no longer offer sheep, oxen, or goats as burnt offering, but only incense, meal offering, and drink offerings. Even for the lesser boon, if his lordship will give orders to that intent, they will pay his lordship's house a certain sum in money and a thousand ardabs of barley.[35] A damaged letter to Jedoniah and his colleagues tells of the progress of the negotiations with Arsham. The petitioners have friends at the satrap's court, but the Egyptians are likewise giving bribes, and "we fear robbery because we are so few." They have found a man to speak before Arsham, but some one is filled with wrath against them. Some one has given the writer twelve staters—it is surprising to find the Greek term so early in a Hebrew writing.

[33] Fig. 183; Sachau 1 ff.; Ungnad 1; Sprengling 8; Cowley 30 f.
[34] Sachau 4; Ungnad 3; Sprengling 9; Cowley 32.
[35] Sachau 4; Ungnad 4; Sprengling 12; Cowley 33.

FIG. 183. ARAMAIC PAPYRUS FROM ELEPHANTINE.

Petition of the Jewish community in Yeb to Bagohi, Persian Governor of Judah, for restoration of their Temple.

Zeho and Hor have been pardoned. Letters have come, evidently from Jedoniah, and they will do the thing suggested.[36]

Before much could be done towards rebuilding the temple, Egypt revolted under Amyrtæus II (404–398) and the natives took their revenge on the Jews. Jedoniah and his colleagues were seized with their wives and children in the gate of Thebes as they were attempting flight, were imprisoned, and presumably put to death; their property was taken but later returned in part. The unlettered writer implies that the Persians will no more have authority in Yeb and ends: "Peace to your house and your children until the gods permit us to see our desire upon them."[37] Their desire was not fulfilled. We possess one more document which shows a standard of Jews still in garrison in the fifth year of Amyrtæus, about 400, and then the curtain drops.[38]

There were those in Palestine who did not consider the sad events at Yeb with the same complaisance as Johanan. Joel prophesied: "Egypt shall be a desolation and Edom a desolate wilderness, for the violence done to the children of Judah, because they shed innocent blood in their land."[39] An anonymous prophet is more specific. Yahweh is riding on a swift cloud and will come to Egypt, whose idols shall tremble in his presence. He will stir up Egyptian against Egyptian, city against city, and kingdom against kingdom, he will give the Egyptians into the hands of a harsh lord and a mighty king shall rule them. Zoan's princes are fools, those of Memphis are deceived, they have led Egypt astray. But in that day there shall be five cities in Egypt that shall speak the language of Canaan, and one shall be called "City of Righteousness." In that day there shall be again an altar to Yahweh in the midst of Egypt and a pillar at its border to Yahweh, it shall be a sign and a witness to Yahweh of Hosts in Egypt's land. For they shall cry to him because of the oppressors and he will be to them a saviour and a defender, and he will deliver them.

[36]Sachau 11; Ungnad 10; Sprengling 11; Cowley 37.
[37]Sachau 15; Ungnad 16; Sprengling 13; Cowley 34.
[38]Sachau 34; Ungnad 37; Sprengling 14; Cowley 35.   [39]Joel 3:19.

Then Yahweh shall be known in Egypt and the Egyptians shall know Yahweh in that day; again shall they worship with sacrifice and oblation, they shall vow to Yahweh and perform it. Then Yahweh will bless them, together with the Assyrians and Israel, and they shall say: "Blessed be Egypt, my people, and Assyria, the work of my hands, and Israel, my inheritance."[40]

[40]Isaiah 19.

CHAPTER XLII

LAST DAYS

LITTLE is known of Syrian history during the last century of Persian rule. Jewish sources abruptly stop about 400. Henceforth we must attempt to construct a narrative from a few brief and uncertainly dated Phœnician inscriptions, a few inscribed coins,[1] a few incidental references in Greek writers. It is equally difficult to form a picture of the culture from the scattered fragments found in the excavations.

For instance, about 425 we find Baal-milk II, son of Azbaal, son of Baal-milk I, still king of Citium and Idalium.[2] Now and then the Phœnicians appear in Persian service. Their fleet did much to end the Peloponnesian War, when under the influence of the younger Cyrus Persia for the moment was anti-Athenian, but when Persia resumed its normal foreign policy, Phœnicians assisted in restoring the walls of Athens as their ships restored its sea power.[3] Thenceforth Athens was regularly pro-Persian and therefore pro-Phœnician. Phœnician metics resided in Attica in large numbers. In a suit with the inhabitants of Phalerum for the possession of a temple to Poseidon, they employed the famous Athenian orator Deinarchus. The Phœnician metic colony continued in the Piræus and in Athens itself into the Hellenistic period, when we have several inscriptions in Phœnician or in Greek and Phœnician of metics who set up altars to their gods, identified with good Greek deities, translated their names into Greek, and were buried under tombstones carved by Greek artists.[4]

Among the Hebrew "Rolls" is the story of Esther; the events

[1]CIS. I; Cooke, *Text-Book*, 18ff.; G. F. Hill, *Catalogue of the Greek Coins of Phœnicia*, 1910; *Cyprus*, 1904; *Palestine*, 1912.
[2]P. Berger, *Comptes Rendus, Acad. Ins.*, XV, 1888, 203 ff.
[3]Thuc., i, 110; Xen., *Hell.*, iii, 4, 1; iv, 3, 11.
[4]Dionys. Hal., *de Dinarch.*, 10; CIS., I, 115–121; cf. p. 617.

narrated took place under king Ahasuerus, whom the Greek translation identifies with Artaxerxes, doubtless the second king of that name (404–358). Although the story is almost universally condemned as unhistorical, it fits so well the events of this reign that the verdict must be reconsidered.

Artaxerxes could not "sit on the throne of his kingdom" until his third year, by which time he had disposed of his rebel brother Cyrus. He did go to winter in Susa according to the usual custom and there he celebrated his victory by a great feast.[5] During his earlier years, his only wife was Stateira, whose Persian name may be represented roughly by the Hebrew Vashti. He insisted on retaining her when her whole family was put to death by his father, though he thereby incurred the wrath of his mother Parysatis, who thenceforth plotted to secure the throne for his younger brother Cyrus. Stateira was in continual feud with her mother-in-law, who at last brought about her fall; the Greeks were not quite sure how it happened, but thought she was poisoned by Parysatis.[6] According to the Hebrew narrative, Vashti refused to expose her face in public and the drunken monarch divorced her on the advice of the "Seven"; to prevent his recall of the beloved queen, it was suggested that a new queen might be found among the levy of maidens.

Among the Jews of Susa, the story continues, was a Benjaminite whose ancestor Kish suggests descent from Saul and who had been deported with Jehoiachin; his name was Mordecai or Marduka, abbreviated from some Babylonian name which honored Marduk. With him lived his niece Esther, whose Babylonian name invoked the goddess of love Ishtar, her Persian name was Hadassah, which might be the Greek Atossa. Artaxerxes loved her, we are told, and made her his queen, for Esther concealed her race.

Some time after, we learn, the prime minister Haman introduced certain reforms which threatened the Jews. Suggestions as to the character of these religious changes may be

[5] Xen., *Anab.*, i; *Cyrop.*, viii, 2, 6.
[6] Ctes., *Pers.*, 29; Plut., *Artox.*, ii, 2 f.; v, 6; xix ff.

found in Gentile sources. Since the days of Darius I, Ahuramazda had been the sole official god recognised by the empire; Artaxerxes II was the first Persian king to worship with him the sun god Mithra and the mother goddess Anahita, two old Daevas whom Zoroaster had bitterly opposed. He was also the first to set up statues of the sacred prostitute Anahita in Babylonia, Susa, Ecbatana, Persia, Bactria, Damascus, and Sardis; Persian capitals found in Damascus may have come from the Anahita temple quite as well as from the local Persian palace.[7] If an attempt was made to enforce this religion, pious Jews would have been in the same position as were the Christians when brought face to face with Roman emperor worship and in like manner their refusal would have been construed as treason. That Haman cast lots on New Year's of the twelfth regnal year to determine when persecution should begin becomes explicable when we remember that Marduk and the gods met on this same New Year's, the vernal equinox, in the chamber of fate to determine men's lot for the year. The lot came out for the month Adar and thus eleven months were allowed the Jews to submit.

Mordecai was a lukewarm Jew, but threat of persecution brought him to Jewish consciousness. Esther was ordered to use her influence to set the decree aside. Meanwhile, the king passed a sleepless night and commanded the "book of the records of the chronicles" to be read; if the eunuch who found the place was a Jew, we can explain the "accident" by which reading began with the story of Mordecai. Two eunuch guards of the gate had conspired against the king at the second gathering of virgins; the Greek record says a servant revealed the plot,[8] the Hebrew ascribes it to Mordecai, a guard at the palace gate. Mordecai was honoured, the queen gained her request, Haman was hanged.

Mordecai was made prime minister, and Esther petitioned

---

[7] F. Weissbach, *Die Keilinschriften der Achämeniden,* 1911, 122 ff.; Berossus, fr. 16; Plut., *Artox.,* xxvii, 3; C. Watzinger and K. Wulzinger, *Damaskus,* 1921, 41.
[8] Plut., *Artox.,* xxix.

the king for a reversal of Haman's rescripts; this was impossible under Persian law, but the Jews were permitted to defend themselves and the officials were ordered to assist them. The Jews were victorious on the fateful thirteenth of Adar. An account of these events was sent to all the Jews of the empire, who were commanded to celebrate the fourteenth and fifteenth of Adar as days of deliverance; the festival was to be called Purim, the "Lots," in memory of the lots cast by Haman. We then have the significant statement that Mordecai was "accepted by the majority of his brethren," which obviously implies that there were many who did not approve and among them must have been all of the stricter faith. Even if salvation did come through Esther, she had violated the first principle of true Judaism by marrying an unbeliever. Mordecai and Esther were therefore forced to write a second letter "by authority." Our author cannot refrain from telling us of the greatest exploit of Artaxerxes while Mordecai was "second to the king," how Artaxerxes "laid a tribute upon the land and upon the isles of the sea"; the reference is to the infamous King's Peace of 387, five years after the events just mentioned, and the language recalls the complaint quoted from Artaxerxes' court physician Ctesias, that the Spartans surrendered to the Persian great king "all the Greek cities of Asia and the islands, as many as are next Asia, to possess them on payment of tribute."[9]

The Jewish story fits exactly the facts presented by Gentile authors. We may find it difficult to believe that a Jewess could have been a Persian queen and a Jew become prime minister, but there are even more serious difficulties if we refuse to credit the narrative. How then can we explain the origin of Purim, accepted before long by even the most orthodox? How can we explain the close agreement with undoubtedly historical events? Above all, how can we explain how a story of two exceedingly lukewarm Jews, who bore transparently pagan names invoking pagan deities, of a Jewess who violated the principles for which Malachai and Ezra and Nehemiah had

[9] Plut., *Artox.*, xxi.

contended, a story which did not even once mention the national God, could have crept into the Biblical canon?[10]

Somewhere about the turn of the century, Uri-milk was king in Gebal. His son Yehar-baal did not reign, but his grandson Yehaw-milk has left us a stele. Under the Egyptian winged disk and clad in the long Persian robe and flat round cap, Yehaw-milk raises his left hand in adoration and presents with his right a bowl to the Lady of Gebal, who sits enthroned with all the attributes of the Egyptian Hathor, a lotus-topped sceptre in her left hand, a vase extended in her right. Yehaw-milk tells us that the princess, the Lady of Gebal, has made him king over Gebal. Whenever he has called upon her, she has heard his voice, wherefore he has made for her that bronze altar which is in this court, and that golden stele which is opposite this stele of his, and this gold uræus which is in the midst of the stone . . ., which is above that gold stele, and this portico and its pillars and the capitals which are upon them and its roof; he is referring to the temple whose scanty ruins have been laid bare in recent excavation. May she bless him and give him life and lengthen his days and his years over Gebal, for a righteous king is he. May she give him favour in the eyes of the gods and in the eyes of the people of this land. If any king or common man makes additions and in so doing erases the name of Yehaw-milk, then the Lady of Gebal shall destroy that man and his seed.[11]

Henceforth, our history is the recital of Phœnician relations to Persian masters, to friendly or hostile Greeks, and to rebel Egyptians. For a time, the adventures of the Greek Evagoras lend a certain unity to our story. A Phœnician exile had driven his ancestors from Salamis of Cyprus, Abdemon drove out his fellow Phœnician, but Evagoras returned in 411 and soon ruled a large part of the island.[12] Belesys, satrap of Syria, was shortly before 400 succeeded by Abrocomas, who opposed

---

[10]This is essentially the view of J. Hoschander, *The Book of Esther in the Light of History*, 1923; older literature, L. B. Paton, *The Book of Esther*, 1908.
[11]CIS. I, 1; Cooke, *Text-Book*, 18 ff.; Poebel, *Das appositionell bestimmte Pronomen*, 11 ff.
[12]Isocrates, *Evagoras*; *Panegyricus*.

the march of Cyrus the younger.[13] Amyrtæus II (404–398) had freed Egypt to rule as the twenty-eighth dynasty, Nepherites began the twenty-ninth in 398. Two years or more later, the Persians collected three hundred ships in Phœnicia to sail against Egypt, but nothing came of it. Amathus, Citium, and Soli requested help of Persia against Evagoras in 391; the king of Citium and Idalium was Milk-yaton (392–361), son of a private man named Baal-ram, who first introduced coinage in gold. In his second year, Milk-yaton gave his god Reshuph-Mekal in Idalium a gold plating because he heard his voice and a statue because with his aid he conquered those who came out and their helpers.[14]

Evagoras revolted in 389 and the Egyptian Hakkoris (390–378) gave him aid. Tyre was captured with a great fleet and Evagoras raised to revolt the Syrian Arabs, while Hakkoris left his inscription in the Eshmun temple north of Sidon.[15] Aided by the Athenian admiral Chabrias, Demonikos for the years 388–387 drove Milk-yaton from Citium and employed Attic standards in his coins alongside the common Phœnician. Evagoras was shut up in Salamis by 386. Soon after, Abrocomas and the other satraps prepared another expedition against Egypt, but again the attempt was a failure. Evagoras won an honourable peace about 380. Nectanebo I (378–361) began the thirtieth dynasty and four years after his accession faced a huge army collected in Syria by Pharnabazus and Chabrias, but faced them successfully.

Evagoras died in 374 and was followed by his son Nicocles, who vied in reputation for luxury with the second man whose career gives a little unity to our dull details, Abd-ashtart (370–358) of Sidon, whom the Greeks knew as Strato.[16] When the Athenians sent ambassadors to the Great King in 367, Strato forwarded their journey to the best of his ability, and the grateful Athenians rewarded him by decree with the gift of the

[13]Xen., *Anab.*, i, 4, 10; 3, 20; vii, 8, 25.
[14]CIS. I, 90 f.; cf. 13, 17 f., 39, 77, 88 f.; Cooke, *Text-Book*, 75 ff.
[15]Isocrates, *Panegyr.*; Diod., xiv, 98; Ctes., frag. 29, 63; W. von Landau, *Mitth. Vorderas. Ges.*, 1904, 5, 64 ff.
[16]Theopompus, fr. 111.

LAST DAYS

proxeneia and freed his subjects from the usual taxes imposed on resident aliens.[17] Strato's philhellenism was further shown by a dedication, in Phœnician and Greek, of images of Tyre and Sidon brought from Tyre by a sacred embassy in honour of the Delian Apollo.[18]

Abd-ashtart took part in the great revolt of the satraps in 366. Tachos (361–359) of Egypt gave him aid and invaded Syria with forces led by the Spartan Agesilaus and the Athenian Chabrias. Agesilaus deposed Tachos in favour of Nectanebo II (359–343), but Nectanebo quickly abandoned the Syrian enterprise.[19] Milk-yaton of Citium had added to Idalium the important city of Tamassus by 363 and his subject Menahem, son of Ben-hodesh, dedicated a statue to Reshuph Eliyath in that city; in an accompanying inscription in the ancient Cypriote syllabary, he appears as Manases, son of Nomenios, and his god is Apollo Elites.[20] Milk-yaton's son Pum-yaton (361–340) seems to have lost Tamassus for a time, but was again in possession by 341.[21] El-paal was a contemporary king of Gebal. Palestine witnessed another abortive attempt to secure Egypt in 359, when Ochus was compelled to return home on the death of his father Artaxerxes II (358). The same year Abd-ashtart died and was succeeded by Tennes. A second invasion by Ochus, now Artaxerxes III, was likewise a failure.

This failure led to the revolt of Tennes. Nectanebo sent him four thousand Greek mercenaries under the Rhodian Mentor, and with their aid Tennes drove out the Persian garrisons, burned the cavalry supplies, and destroyed the paradise or park on the hill slopes east of Sidon with the Persian palace whose bull capitals have survived to our day.[22] Tyre, Sidon, and Arvad had recently united the three small towns, Maha-

---

[17]*Inscriptiones Grœcœ*, II, ed. 2, 141; W. Dittenberger, *Sylloge Inscriptionum Grœcarum*, ed. 3, 1915, no. 185; E. L. Hicks and G. F. Hill, *Greek Historical Inscriptions*, 1901, no. 111.
[18]CIS. I, 114.   [19]Diod., xv, 92, 5.
[20]Cooke, *Text-Book*, 88 ff.
[21]CIS. I, 10; Cooke, *Text-Book*, 55 ff.
[22]G. Contenau, *Syria*, IV, 1923, 276 ff.

lata, Maisa, and Kaisa, into a new city, called by the native coins something like Athar and by the Greeks Tripolis, the "Triple City," but each town retained its own wall and its own local organization. Here met the three hundred delegates to the Phœnician common assembly and here was the seat of the viceroy.[23] It was now captured by the allies, who defeated Belesys, satrap of Syria proper, and Mazdai, satrap of Abar Nahara and of Halak or Cilicia, and drove them out of Phœnicia. The nine chief Phœnician cities then expelled the Persians and declared themselves free under their own kings.

Artaxerxes assumed personal charge of the punitive expedition, but opposed to him were more than a hundred Phœnician ships, triremes in part, in part the newly invented quinquiremes with five banks of oars. Six thousand additional Greek mercenaries arrived, the citizens of Sidon were drilled, the wall was raised, and Sidon was encircled by a triple ditch. Prospects for a successful resistance were bright when Tennes and Mentor suddenly determined to betray the city. Tennes first handed over to Artaxerxes a hundred of the leading citizens, who were at once slain by javelins. Five hundred more citizens left the gate with boughs of supplication in their hands, but they too were slaughtered. Then the Persians were admitted, but the surviving Sidonians fired their ships, shut themselves with their families in their houses, and forty thousand perished in the flames. Speculators paid Artaxerxes a huge sum for the treasure hid in the ruins. Mentor was taken into Persian pay, but Tennes, contrary to the royal promise, received the merited reward for his treachery.[24] Sidon was taken late in the spring; the story is continued by a Babylonian tablet: "Fourteenth year of Ochus whose name is called Artaxerxes, month October, the prisoners whom the king made prisoner in the land of Sidon into Babylon and Susa entered. That month, day thirteen, a few soldiers among them into

---

[23] Fig. 185; Scylax, 104; Diod., xvi, 41; Strabo, xvi, 2, 15; Pliny, *Hist. Nat.* v, 78; Mela, i, 12; Steph. Byz., *s.v.*; Hill, *Phœnicia*, cxvi ff.
[24] Diod., xv, 45.

FIG. 184. PHŒNICIAN SHRINE IN ARTIFICIAL LAKE.
(Marathus.)

FIG. 185. TRIPOLIS.

Babylon entered. Day sixteen, the numerous women, prisoners of the land of Sidon, whom the king to Babylon sent, on that day into the palace of the king entered."[26]

A Minæan caravan, trading with Egypt, Assyria, and Abar ha-Nahar, Across the River, was caught in the war between the lords of the north and south, the war between the Medes and Egypt, but their gods brought them safely out of Egypt. In memory of their deliverance, they dedicated an inscription to the gods, which throws an interesting light on contemporary trade with southwest Arabia along the great incense routes through Gaza and Petra and through Tyre and Damascus.[26]

Two years after the fall of Sidon, Artaxerxes finally reduced Egypt to obedience (343) and Phœnician rebels could no longer hope for aid from the Nile. For a brief period, Evagoras II, a grandson of the first Evagoras, was allowed to rule Sidon, but soon his place was taken by Abd-ashtart II (342–333). Mazdai continued to command the Persian troops in Syria (351–333) and issued coins in his own name with the Sidonian types but with Aramaising characters. Pum-yaton of Citium recovered Tamassus by 341.

Archæology tells but little of culture during the Persian period. Native pottery of the late iron age shows definite decline with only a simple linear ornament.[27] This was in part due to the economic decline of the interior, in part to the invasion of Greek wares. Greek influence makes its appearance during the sixth century at Lachish in an inscription whose letters are much like those of the contemporary Greek settlement at Naucratis in the Nile Delta. Typical Greek ware of the fourth century is also found at Lachish. The poor seventh city was thoroughly destroyed by fire, leaving the charred barley, sesame, pulse, grapes, and snails on which the inhabitants subsisted. It was followed by an eighth city which was abandoned just at the end of our period.[28]

[25] S. Smith, *Babylonian Historical Texts*, 148 f.
[26] H. Winckler, *Mitth. Vorderas. Ges.*, 1898, 1, 20 ff.
[27] H. Vincent, *Syria*, V, 1924, 83.
[28] Bliss, *Mound of Many Cities*, 122, 133 f., 137.

Megiddo was an unwalled town, whose small irregular houses followed narrow rubble-paved lanes with shallow covered gutters in their centre and clustered around a large rectangular fort. A strongly walled passage led to a north gate with jambs of large well-dressed blocks, but the facing of the walls was of roughly dressed stones chinked with smaller against a rubble core. Within were three courts surrounded by barracks and stables. To this succeeded a last Megiddo, a still poorer town. The fort remained in part on the older foundation stones, but with decreased area, a narrow paved road led to the western entrance. The houses, for the most part of poor rubble, no longer followed streets but sprawled everywhere. This last Megiddo was destroyed about 350, perhaps during the invasion of Artaxerxes III.[29]

Shechem has a Persian stratum with potsherds inscribed in Aramaic and an agate seal with Aramaic legend.[30] Jericho's tiny settlement is of interest only because of potsherds with the name Yahu in late Hebrew characters.[31]

Coast Philistia was in better condition. Gaza late in the period possessed a rude glacis.[32] Its commercial importance is shown by the coins. After the Peloponnesian War, Athens no longer had the wealth to issue her famous "owls" which had hitherto been the trade money of the Near East, and Philistine and Phœnician coins began to take their place. Some of the Philistine coins bear the name of Gaza in Aramaic, other mint names cannot be certainly attributed. The earliest imitate closely the archaic helmeted Athena, the sitting owl within an incuse square, the ATHE of the Athenian mint, while the weight is not much below the Attic standard. Later the Egyptian Bes and Isis or local types make their appearance. One coin shows on the obverse a bearded helmeted god, on the reverse a god seated on a winged wheel; the inscription Yahu proves that it is the Hebrew deity.[33]

[29]Fisher, *Excavation*, 16, 61 f., 68.
[30]E. Sellin, *ZDPV.*, XLIX, 1926, 232.
[31]Sellin and Watzinger, *Jericho*, 79 ff.; 158 f.
[32]W. J. Phythian-Adams, *QS.*, 1923, 13.
[33]Hill, *Greek Coins of Palestine*, lxxxiii ff.

In describing the late Persian culture of Phœnicia, our greatest difficulty is in determining whether any given group of monuments is really late Persian or early Hellenistic, as, for example, the famous group of the Eshmunazer dynasty of Sidon. We are on safest ground with the coins, for these can often be assigned to Persian vassal kings whose story we have already told.

The anthropoid sarcophagi from Sidon also date, at least in part, from Persian times. A shaft, later filled with stones, leads to rounded chambers on east and west some six feet high. The dead are buried in sarcophagi of native workmanship but imitating in Greek style Egyptian mummy cases. On one the foot is roughly carved, there are handles, the head sunk down into the shoulders lies flat on the heavy oval lid, the ears are covered by a roll of hair, the face is square, the lower jaw heavy. Colour is lavish, dark red for the hair, flesh colour for the face, vermilion for the lips, the white of the eye is tinged with blue, the inner corner is touched with vermilion, the iris is a deep brown, the outer circles are outlined in black, the colour of the pupil, the eyelashes are drawn in fine lines. The sarcophagus of a youth with creased forehead and humorous mouth shows a blue iris. Sarcophagi of apparently somewhat later date have reddish brown hair or a vermilion band around the hair, hair on either side the shoulder in good Egyptian fashion, and one of these took with him a good seal ring of Greek character and with the Greek letter delta.[34]

Perhaps a little earlier are the masks and statuettes from Sidon, which in spite of their rudeness add their bit to the account of Phœnician culture. If they are not caricatures, deliberate or due to lack of skill, the physical type is peculiar. Heads projecting from shoulders, far outjutting jaws, big teeth, and high gorilla-like eyebrows are almost Neanderthal, but the sloping forehead, huge nose, lips, ears, and neck in a straight line up with the back of the head make it probable that Armenoids are intended. Some of the males are bearded and wear strange bonnets or caps, the females are veiled. Deities are

[34] Fig. 186; C. C. Torrey, *Ann.*, I, 1 ff.

well represented. A mask with wig and double beard of Osiris and heads of Bes are Egyptian, though Bes sometimes is horned. A smiling bearded and horned faun may have a Greek origin. The nude goddess pressing her breasts is Babylonian but the goddess with diagonal wound tunic exposing the breasts is Cypriote. Melkart with the lion skin may have been influenced by the Greek Heracles. Egyptian again is the painted terra-cotta shrine with uræus frieze above winged disk and palmette. Horsemen, horses, birds, dogs, mules, goats, camels, asses, masks of oxen and cows who are given the same outjutting jaws as their human masters complete the list.[35]

When Alexander appeared in 332, the Phoenicians were still more or less willing Persian subjects. Their kings, Ger Ashtart of Arvad, Ainel of Gebal, and Azmilk of Tyre, had already aided in the defense of the Asia Minor coast, but when Alexander succeeded in reaching Syria, he was met by Ger Ashtart's son Strato, who handed over Arvad, the great and flourishing Marathus, Sigon, and Mariamme. Strato was deposed as pro-Persian and his place was taken by Abdalonymus. From Marathus, Parmenio was despatched to seize the treasure in the royal palace at Damascus. Gebal surrendered at Alexander's approach, and Sidon, remembering her destruction by Artaxerxes, sent ambassadors to promise submission.[36]

Tyre was willing to make terms but refused the request of Alexander to sacrifice to Melkart in his island temple; they suggested he content himself with sacrifice in the more ancient Melkart temple at Old Tyre. When Alexander insisted, the Tyrians sent their old men, women, and children to Carthage, manned their eighty ships and collected others, covered the walls with engines, and armed the whole citizen body.[37]

Alexander determined to build a mole. The shallows underlaid with mud made the first progress easy, but farther out the sea was deeper, the waves were high and the current strong. The Tyrians attacked the workers with their triremes, and a

---

[35] G. Contenau, *Syria*, I, 1920, 216 ff., 305 ff.
[36] Arr., ii, 13, 7 f.; 15, 6f.; 20, 1.
[37] Arr., ii, 16; 24, 5; Curt., iv, 2 ff.; Diod., xv, 73, 4; 77, 4; xvii, 41; Just., xi, 10.

FIG. 186. (*Left*) ANTHROPOID SARCOPHAGUS FROM SIDON.
FIG. 187. (*Right*) HADAD IN THE PERSIAN PERIOD.

fire ship, aided by a storm, destroyed the greater part of the mole. Then Alexander rebuilt the mole at an angle to the southwest to break the prevailing wind. Eighty Sidonian, Gebalite and Arvadite ships had deserted from the Persians and were now at Sidon; they came over to Alexander as did a hundred and twenty-five from the Cypriote kings and the whole fleet was now two hundred and twenty-four strong. With this overwhelming superiority, Alexander could blockade the two ports. Moles a hundred and fifty feet high of huge blocks set in gypsum reached the walls, which were battered by engines placed upon the moles. An attack of the Tyrians on the fleet blockading the narrow entrance of the Sidonian harbor almost succeeded, but at the last moment Alexander brought up a new fleet. Bags of sea weed broke the force of the rams, rapidly moving wheels caught the missiles, grappling hooks tore down the men from the bridges, hot metal and hot sand scorched the attackers, scythes hacked the ropes of the rams. When the wall began to give way, the defenders built an inner wall. Then the Macedonians placed their engines on board ships and breached the wall near the Egyptian harbour; the assault at this weak point was successful as were attacks on the harbours. Fighting continued on the streets and roofs, a last stand was made at the temple of Agenor. Azmilk and the chief officials took sanctuary in the temple of Melkart and were spared, others were concealed on Sidonian ships, but two thousand prisoners hanged about the walls and thirty thousand women, children, and slaves sold at public auction showed how thin was the veneer of Alexander's culture. Alexander celebrated his victory by a sacrifice in the Melkart temple; the temple was oriental but the celebration was Greek and Melkart was identified with the Greek Heracles. It was an omen of the mixed culture which was to dominate the Hellenistic age.[38]

After this exhibition of Macedonian savagery, all Palestine submitted with the exception of Gaza, where the eunuch Batis had hired Arab mercenaries and had taken refuge on the high

[38] Arr., ii, 18 ff.

mound surrounded by strong walls. Alexander was wounded but at last the wall was undermined and breached or taken by escalade. The garrison fought to the death, but the wives and children were sold and Batis was dragged around the walls in imitation of Achilles' treatment of Hector.

The way was open to Egypt, and to the foundation of Alexandria. Arbela was fought and Babylonia and Persia fell. Once more all the Jews in the world were under one rule, but a new rule which opened a new book in their history.

CHAPTER XLIII

COMING JUDAISM

We have traced the history of the Jews under Persian rule as it is presented by our scant narrative sources. We have quoted such prophecies as can be dated with relative assurance. There remains to be considered a group of contemporary productions, some of them fragmentary and dull, some of them masterpieces of Hebrew literature, but all casting light on the religious and intellectual development of the Jewish people during the period of Persian control.[1]

It would be a serious mistake to assume that there was religious unity during this period. On the contrary, this was the very time when Judaism began to break up into the sects whose barriers were to be raised yet higher in centuries to come. At one extreme were those who had been definitely excluded from the reorganised Jewish community. Some were descended from the exiles settled in Palestine by the Assyrian kings, others were "People of the Land" who, since the great break made by Josiah's reform, had grown more and more out of sympathy with the official cult.

Although recognised as "brethren," Jews of a sort, they are brethren who hate the orthodox; in reality, they are sons of the sorceress, the adulteress, and the harlot, for they still reverence their local divinities and follow the ancient cult practices. They purify themselves to enter the gardens of Adonis, they march in the sacred procession behind the leader of the mysteries, they sacrifice in these Adonis gardens and burn incense upon the brick altars, they celebrate rites for the dead among the graves and spend the night in secret caverns. Among the terebinths and under every green tree they celebrate

[1]In so far as these sources afford the needful background for the history of the Greco-Roman Orient, it is hoped to give them more adequate study in a later volume.

the sacred marriage, they sacrifice their first born in the valleys under the rock clefts, they pour out drink offerings and make meal offerings to these dumb stones, then they sacrifice on the high mountains. The abominable symbol of their fertility cult is placed behind their doors and door posts, they prepare a table for Gad, the Luck of the old tribe of that name, they mix drinks for Meni or Fate. They eat pork and creeping things and even the mouse, they drink broth prepared from animals that defile, and then they dare say: "Stop where you are, do not come near me, for I am holier than you!" They open wide their mouths and stick out their tongues at the pious and even expel them because they insist on the pure worship of Yahweh; Yahweh has been patient but now their fate is upon them.[2]

Yet from these backward and despised "People of the Land" came into our Bible an anthology of wonderfully beautiful poems of love. Long centuries before, the Canaanites had honoured their dead and risen "Lord" at the spring equinox by hymns which sang the passionate love of the Shulamith, the fertility goddess, for her "Beloved," the Dod. Under Babylonian influence, the hymns were recast, Babylonian hymns to Ishtar and to her beloved Tammuz were closely imitated, Babylonian words were employed in the technical cult meaning. In process of time, their original religious significance began to be forgotten and they could be sung as mere secular love ditties at feasts or even in taverns. Ultimately, the dim memory of their original religious significance won them a place, though not without a struggle, within the sacred canon.[3]

Only to a degree less conservative than the "People of the Land" were the priests. They now claimed descent from Aaron, once the reputed founder of the bull cult at Bethel, but now made the brother of the great lawgiver Moses. No longer

---

[2] Isaiah 57; 65 f.

[3] T. J. Meek, *AJSL.*, XXXIX, 1922, 1 ff.; *The Song of Songs*, edited by W. H. Schoff, 1924, 48 ff.; W. Wittekindt, *Das Hohe Lied*, 1925; cf. N. Schmidt, *The Messages of the Poets*, 1911; M. Jastrow, *The Song of Songs*, 1921; K. Budde, in K. Budde, A. Bertholet, and G. Wildeboer, *Die fünf Megillot*, 1898, 1 ff.

was it high honor to be a Levite, a follower of Moses; the line between priests and Levites was ever more sharply drawn, to the Levites were assigned the more menial tasks about the sanctuary, and at that they could not be always sure of receiving their scanty dues.

The priests were indeed strict monotheists, for one Temple demanded one God, but they were too close to the altar to cherish illusions. Their one chief interest was the extension of the cult. Down to the days of the last Persian king and beyond, additions were being made to the Code of the Priests, but we no longer find the broad humanitarianism of the older laws, the later editors were only anxious to define more minutely the cult prescriptions. Significant of the innate priestly conservatism is the fact that it is just this Priestly Code which is most often cited for the survival of pre-Hebrew religious concepts and practices, while the close parallels to the contemporary Carthaginian tariffs of sacrifices[4] have often been noted. It is equally significant that the growing hope of a personal immortality which warmed the hearts of the pious left the priests entirely cold.

Hopes that Zerubbabel would prove the expected "Shoot from Jesse's Stump" had been rudely dashed and nationalism all but flickered out. In the absence of a prince from David's line, such leadership as was exercised over the Jews fell to the high priest. As his political responsibilities increased, as the foreign monarchs more and more treated him as the representative of his people, political expediency tended to control his actions at the expense of deep personal religious emotion. A Johanan, for example, might realize how Ezra's reforms would strengthen the priestly power, but Ezra's law did not restrain him from the murder of his brother. As the leader of his people, the high priest was in constant contact with the leading Gentiles; this contact induced a broad toleration but it also induced him to follow foreign customs and it opened his mind to foreign thought. Members of the high priestly family even intermarried with Gentile aristocrats.

[4] CIS. I, 165 ff.

As Jeremiah had proved, the nobles were never particularly favourable to the priestly hierarchy. Strengthened now by the new nobility of trade, they became ever more worldly. This was particularly true of the Jews of the Dispersion. Jewish mercenaries at Elephantine were not even monotheists, much less did they know of Josiah's reforms, and a wealthy Jewish heiress could marry a Gentile and take oath by an Egyptian deity. Jews in Babylonia did not hesitate to invoke pagan gods in their names. Many of the Dispersion were undoubtedly lost entirely to the Jewish community. Often these lax Jews retained a certain amount of Jewish consciousness, and in time of crisis might, like Esther and Mordecai, make definite if unorthodox sacrifice for their people.

This class might be lacking in formal religion, but they were not uneducated, and they thought seriously about the problems of life. Modern pessimism is anticipated by the writer we name Ecclesiastes, the "Preacher." Stripped of the accretions added later to fit it for a place in the sacred canon, we have merely the reflections of a man who has found that life is fleeting and death is sure, that moderation in all things is advisable, and who concludes that we should enjoy such good things of life as come our way until our account is closed by death. Ecclesiastes has well been called a "Gentle Cynic."[5]

Sometimes they presented their conclusions in hard dry practical proverbs. Collections of such proverbs are ascribed to Solomon and to the men of Hezekiah, and doubtless proverbs of pre-exilic date are preserved in our book of that name. Taken as a whole, the book is no such collection of popular proverbs, but a series of reasoned arguments in praise of wisdom, the knowledge of the right way, which is personified almost in the manner of the Greek "Mind." The cult as such is quite ignored; God is by no means left out of account, but he functions through the Divine Wisdom.

Late in Egyptian history, a certain Amenemopet followed long past precedent and indited a series of Admonitions to his

---

[5] G. A. Barton, *The Book of Ecclesiastes*, 1908; M. Jastrow, *A Gentle Cynic*, 1919; G. Wildeboer, in Budde, Bertholet, Wildeboer, *op. cit.*, 109 ff.

youthful son. The manuscript fell into the hands of a Jewish thinker who found little difficulty in adapting its teaching to his own purpose, especially as Amenemopet's thought was not far from a tacit monotheism.

"Give thine ears, hear the words that are said, give thy mind to interpret them; to put them in thy heart is good." "They will be a mooring post in thy tongue." Our Jewish thinker paraphrases: "Incline thine ear, and hear my words, and apply thy heart to know them; for it is pleasant if thou keep them within thee, if they be established as a peg on thy lips; that thy trust may be in Yahweh," he inserts, "I have made known to thee this day the path of life," following Amenemopet's "to direct him to the path of life." "See for thyself these thirty chapters, they please, they educate," is turned into "Have I not written thee thirty sayings, they consist of counsels and knowledge." "Knowledge how to answer a statement to its pronouncer, and return a report to one that has sent him" becomes "That thou mayest make the truth known to him that speaketh, that thou mayest bring back words to him that sent thee." "Beware of robbing a poor wretch, of being valorous against the man of broken arm" is now "Rob not the poor because he is poor, nor oppress the afflicted in the gate," with the addition "For Yahweh will plead their cause, and despoil of life those who despoil them."

"Do not associate to thy self the passionate man, nor approach him for conversation"; "leap not to cleave to that fellow, lest a terror carry thee away" is the advice of Amenemopet. "Do not associate to thy self a man given to anger, nor go with a man of passions, lest thou learn his ways and get a snare to thy soul," is the advice of the Hebrew proverb maker, but he cannot resist adding a warning against becoming a surety for debt. "Remove not the ancient landmark which thy fathers have set" repeats "Remove not the landmark on the boundaries of the sown."

Himself a scribe, Amenemopet can conceive of nothing more honourable than to be a success in that profession: "As a scribe who is experienced in his office, he will find himself worthy to be a courtier"; "seest thou a man diligent in his business? He shall stand before kings, he shall not stand before obscure men" is the natural paraphrase of our writer. "Eat not bread in the presence of a noble, nor apply thy mouth at the beginning; if thou art satisfied with false munchings, they are a diversion of thy saliva; look at the cup that is before thee, and let it do thy need" becomes in the Hebrew: "When thou sittest to eat with a ruler, consider diligently what is before thee; and put a knife to thy throat, if thou be a man given to appetite; be not desirous of his dainties, seeing they are deceitful food."

"Labour not to seek increase, thy needs shall be secure for thee; if riches be brought to thee by robbery, they shall not stay the night with thee; day dawneth and they are not in thy house, their places shall be seen but they are not there; the earth hath opened its mouth, it adjusts it and swallows it, and has sunk them in Tei; they have made for themselves a great breach of their measure, and they have sunk themselves in the corn store; they have made themselves wings like geese, they have flown to heaven." This is abbreviated: "Labour not to be rich, cease to prepare violence; doth it not take to itself wings and is not? Surely it makes itself wings, like an eagle it flies to heaven."

"Covet not the property of a dependent, nor hunger for his bread; verily the property of a dependent is a choking of the throat, a vomiting for the gullet; when he has obtained it by false oaths, his desire is perverted by his belly." "The too great mouthful of bread, thou swallowest it and vomitest it, thou art emptied of thy good." "Eat not thou the bread of one that hath an evil eye, nor desire thou his dainties"; " 'eat and drink,' saith he to thee, but his heart is not with thee. The morsel thou hast eaten must thou vomit up, and must lose thy dainties" repeats our author. "Empty not thine inmost soul to everybody nor spoil thereby thy influence" is now "Speak not in the hearing of a fool, for he will despise the wisdom of thy words." "Remove not the ancient landmark," our writer is repeating himself, "and enter not the fields of the fatherless, for their avenger is mighty, he will plead their cause against thee"; he is now following more closely Amenemopet: "Remove not the landmark on the boundaries of the sown, nor shift the measuring rod's position, covet not a cubit of land, nor throw down the boundaries of the widow." "Beware of throwing down the boundaries of the sown, lest a terror carry thee away." With few exceptions, each sentence of this long Hebrew composition is closely paralleled by the Admonitions of Amenemopet; parallels to his Admonitions and to other Egyptian gnomic writings in other Biblical writings testify equally to an Egyptian origin.[6]

The most splendid literary production of the period is the book of Job. If Proverbs shows in places undoubted indications of an Egyptian origin, Job follows closely a Babylonian composition from the time of the Third Dynasty of Ur. Tabi-utul Enlil was a rich and respected citizen of Nippur, noted for his piety towards the gods and his goodness to men. Undeserved poverty, terrible suffering, rejection by men came upon him, his case was like those who had not feared the gods. When he cried unto God, God showed not his face. With deep sympathy and complete understanding, our Babylonian author presents the case of the just man who suffers undeservedly and who cannot reconcile his sufferings with the justice of the gods; in the end he falls back upon the divine vision, through whose prescriptions the sufferer is cleansed of his sins and freed from his pains.[7]

Our Hebrew poet knew an old folk tale in which a certain Job was accused by Satan before Yahweh as serving his God only for what he could gain by such worship. To prove Satan mistaken, Yahweh gave him permission to afflict Job with loss

[6]Prov. 22:17–23:11; E. A. W. Budge, *Facsimiles of Egyptian Hieratic Papyri*, 2 Ser., 1923; *The Teaching of Amen-em-apt*, 1924; A. Erman, *OLZ.*, XXVII, 1894, 241 ff.; *Sitzungsber. Berlin Akad.*, 1924, 86 ff.; H. O. Lange, *Das Weisheitsbuch des Amenemope*, 1925; H. Gressmann, *ZAW.*, NF. I, 1924, 272 ff.; L. Keimer, *AJSL.*, XLIII, 1926, 8 ff.; F. L. Griffith, *JEA.*, XII, 1926, 191 ff.; D. C. Simpson, *ibid.*, 232 ff.; cf. G. Wildeboer, *Die Sprüche*, 1897; C. H. Toy, *The Book of Proverbs*, 1899; W. O. E. Oesterley, *The Book of Proverbs*, 1929.

[7]S. Langdon, *Babylonian Wisdom*, 1923.

of family, friends, and health. Job endured the trial and in the end was blessed more than before.

Our poet throws the story into rough dramatic form. Job's three friends assert that his sufferings are caused by his sins. In a series of magnificent poems, unsurpassed in the world's literature, Job replies. He insists that he has never sinned, he challenges God to meet him as man to man and to answer his charge; so sympathetic and so understanding is our poet's treatment that many have assumed that it represents his own point of view. Yahweh answers Job out of the whirlwind. He disdains to answer Job's complaint or to accept his challenge. He simply points to nature as his complete justification, and Job, like his Babylonian predecessor, has no answer. To our poet, the problem of undeserved suffering is insoluble, he can only say that God is righteous and that somehow all his works are justified.[8]

Over against the reactionary peasants, the time-serving priests, and the worldly aristocrats of birth and of business, stood the Hasidim, the Pious. They too reverenced the temple and the cult but their chief delight was to meditate on the Law of the Lord day and night. Fulfilment of the Law was not to be sought primarily in temple and cult but rather in the ordering of their lives in minute detail according to its provisions. Perhaps now and then they irritated their less observant fellows with a too openly expressed sense of superiority, their piety may have been a trifle narrow, but theirs none the less was a genuine piety which must command our deepest respect and even admiration.

Their finest outpourings of soul and their highest aspirations are found in our Psalter. Not all the Psalms bear their mark. Some present remarkable parallels to the earliest Shumerian hymns, especially in their sense of sin. A few are of pre-exilic

[8] K. Budde, *Das Buch Hiob*, 1896; B. Duhm, *Das Buch Hiob*, 1897; N. Schmidt, *Messages of the Poets*, 1911; E. C. S. Gibson, *The Book of Job*, 3 ed., 1919; M. Jastrow, *The Book of Job*, 1920; H. Torczyner, *Das Buch Hiob*, 1920; S. R. Driver and G. B. Gray, *The Book of Job*, 1921; C. J. Ball, *The Book of Job*, 1922; P. Dhorme, *Le Livre de Job*, 1926; E. König, *Das Buch Hiob*, 1929.

date and have been plausibly assigned to the worship at the Jerusalem temple or even to the cults at Bethel and at Dan. Washed-out reminiscences of the ancient mythology have survived. But as a whole, the Psalter is a hymn book, collected for the use of the average man; there is little of theology in the narrow sense, but true worship and the religious emotion of the individual heart. It is just this appeal to the religious feelings of the average man which has made these psalms fit vehicles for the expression of true religion throughout the ages.[9]

History was rewritten from this new point of view by the Chronicler. From the great general history of the Hebrew people and from other sources he brought together various genealogical lists as introduction. He began his narrative with the death of Saul, whose failure to found an enduring kingdom was a foil to his great hero David; to David as founder the Chronicler assigned the whole cult as he found it in his own day. He then told the story of Solomon and of Judah, but the northern kingdom was outside his view, save when it came into contact with the south. Often he copied his source, an earlier form of Samuel or Kings, with literal fidelity, but at intervals he rewrote his story on the assumption that the religious practices of his own time had always been observed. While using these "Chronicles of the Kings of Judah and Israel" in good oriental fashion as his main source, he now and then amplified this material by extracts from other sources which he is careful to name; long under the suspicion of the critics, of late this added material has often been proved correct by new archæological or literary data. He knew or cared little about the exile, but he glorified the return to Zion, he incorporated without troubling to translate them the Aramaic rescripts of the Persian kings, as well as the autobiographies of Ezra and Nehemiah. His latest reference is to Johanan's

---

[9] F. Baethgen, *Die Psalmen,* 1904; C. A. and E. G. Briggs, *The Book of Psalms,* 1906; R. Kittel, *Die Psalmen,* 1914; S. Mowinckel, *Psalmenstudien,* 1921–22; J. P. Peters, *The Psalms as Liturgies,* 1922; B. Duhm, *Die Psalmen,* 1922; H. Gunkel, *Die Psalmen,* 1926; J. M. P. Smith, *The Psalms,* 1926.

son Jaddua, contemporary of Darius the Persian, and his book must have been written not long after Darius II died in 404. Much as he misinterprets the older times, he has preserved valuable source material and his work illustrates the thought of his own day.[10]

Prophecy was waning, and the majority of prophetic effusions deserve the title of "Minor." The names of a few prophets have been preserved, but in general the prophetic literature is anonymous. Inferior as a whole, yet here and there are passages of great beauty such as some already quoted or the poems preserved in the last eleven chapters of Isaiah. One of the latest prophets himself predicts the disappearance of prophecy. Should a man still dare to prophesy, his own parents will kill him as one speaking lies in Yahweh's name. The prophet will be ashamed of his vision, no more shall he deceive by wearing Elijah's hairy mantle. Accused of being a prophet, he will insist that he was a bound serf from his youth; asked about the wounds between his hands, he will reply that they were received in the house of his friends.[11]

In a sense, the older prophecy had already become canonical, but not to the degree that its content was hard and fast. These older prophets had been prophets of doom. Their dooms had been fulfilled, the descendants of their hearers had learned their lesson and had turned to Yahweh with all their heart. Although the Pious were more and more attentive to minute ritual requirements, although the temple cult had never been so carefully regulated, the Jews of Palestine were not prosperous. There was dire need of comfort and encouragement and there were scribes ready to give this comfort. Passages of doom in the older prophecies were supplemented by more recent productions which sought to turn the curse and to give hope for the future. To this future men were more and more turning

---

[10] *AJSL.*, XXX, 1913, 1 ff.; XXXI, 1915, 169 ff.; I. Benzinger, *Bücher der Chronik*, 1901; R. Kittel, *Die Bücher der Chronik*, 1902; E. L. Curtis and A. A. Madsen, *Books of Chronicles*, 1910; J. W. Rothstein and J. Hänel, *Das erste Buch der Chronik*, 1927.

[11] Zech. 13:3–6.

their attention. True apocalyptic first appears in the visions of Zechariah; a whole apocalyptic literature was to grow up under Macedonian and Roman rule.

While Ezra, Nehemiah, and the Pious were striving to drive out the foreign element, men of equal piety were striving to enlarge the bounds of Israel. For all his intense nationalism and his opposition to the "People of the Land," Zechariah had prophesied of strangers coming to Jerusalem that they might entreat the face of Yahweh, of ten men from all the tongues of the nations saying to the Jew that they would go with him since they had heard that Yahweh was with him. A contemporary had told of all peoples streaming to the temple to learn Yahweh's ways. Malachi contrasts priestly profanation of the Jerusalem temple with the pure offerings rising to Yahweh's name in every sacred place, he rejoices over the greatness of Yahweh's name among the nations from the rising to the setting sun.

One prophet declared that the "aliens resident among you, who beget children among you, shall be to you as born in the country among the children of Israel, they shall have an inheritance among you among the children of Israel."[12] If here these privileges are confined to Palestine, another prophet goes much farther: "Also the sons of the foreigner who join themselves to Yahweh to serve him and to love the name of Yahweh, to be his servants, every one who keeps the sabbath from profaning it, and takes hold of my covenant, even them will I bring to my holy mountain, and make them joyful in my house of prayer, their burnt offerings and their sacrifices shall be accepted upon my altar, for my house shall be called a house of prayer for all peoples."[13]

These noble sentiments were enforced by stories which showed the justification for such proselytism. Ezra had outraged the deepest feelings of the human heart when he had compelled his converts to divorce their wives of foreign birth and to send away the innocent children of such marriages. To some Jews, the actions of Ezra and Nehemiah, the preaching

[12] Ezek. 47:22.   [13] Isaiah 56:6 f.

of Malachi, could not be left without answer, and they took up the cudgels for defense. In a brief tale of great beauty, one writer retold the story of David's ancestry. His heroine was Ruth, the Moabitess, whose descendants according to Josiah's law could not enter the assembly until the tenth generation; Ruth's great-grandson was David, Israel's greatest hero and in contemporary belief the true founder of their cult. There was no need of labouring the moral.[14]

The moral was more obvious in the story of the prophet Jonah. Ordered to preach repentance to those worst of all sinners, the Assyrians, he preferred flight to the hateful duty. Punished by imprisonment in the body of the whale, he finally brought himself to preach to the Ninevites, who turned from their evil way and averted the wrath of God. Like many another of Ezra's persuasion, the proof that Yahweh's mercy extended even to these wicked Gentiles left Jonah exceedingly displeased and angry; he regretted the loss of the gourd which had sheltered him for the day, he regretted still more the failure of his prediction, though fulfilment meant the destruction of a mighty city. The moral comes in Yahweh's final question: "You care for the gourd, though you neither laboured for it nor made it grow, which sprang up in a night and perished in a night; should not I then care for Nineveh, that great city, in which are more than a hundred and twenty thousand persons who cannot distinguish between their right hand and their left beside much cattle?"[15]

We must do justice to the innate conservatism of the peasant who retained the faith of his fathers. We should realise that nobles and business men played their part in laying the foundations of the social and economic structure of the Jewish community. We must admit that, had not the high priests in their worldly wisdom kept the Jews united and protected them against the foreigners, there would have been no separate Jewish community. Nevertheless, had these groups alone set

---

[14] A. Bertholet, in Budde-Bertholet-Wildeboer, *op. cit.*, 49 ff.
[15] J. A. Bewer, *Jonah*, 1912; Marti, *Dodekapropheton*, 241 ff.; Nowack, *Die Kleinen Propheten*, 181 ff.; E. Sellin, *Zwölfprophetenbuch*, 1922, 237 ff.

the tone for the community, we should have found no occasion to study Jewish history.

Two parties alone had significance for the future. In due process of time, the Pious became the Pharisees. After the destruction of Jerusalem and the disappearance of even the most attenuated nationalism, these successors of the Pious constructed the vast edifice of mediæval Judaism, which has preserved the Jews as a "peculiar people" to our own day. The liberal party carried its proselyting activities far into the Gentile world; from this party came the missionary zeal which has brought the western world to worship the Christ.

INDEXES

INDEX OF PROPER NAMES

Names of kings of important countries or city-states are in small capitals; names of countries or cities ruled are abbreviated as follows: A = Assyria; B = Babylonia; C = Carchemish; D = Damascus; E = Egypt; G = Gebal; H = Hittite; I = Israel; J = Judah; M = Mitanni; P = Persia; S = Sidon; T = Tyre. Other proper names are thus indicated: C = city; G = god; L = land; M = mountain; P = prophet; R = river; T = tribe.

Aaron, 353, 626
ABDALONYMUS (Arvad), 622
ABD ASHIRTA (Amurru), 159 ff., 172, 174
ABD ASHTART (T), 368
ABD ASHTART (S), I, 616 f.; II, 619
ABD-ELOT (Arvad), 471
Abdera (C), 405
ABD HEPA (Jerusalem), 140, 189 ff., 193
ABD-MELKART (S), 483
ABD TIRSHI (Hazor), 174
Abel of Maacah (C), 30, 46, 328, 357, 453
Abel Meholah (C), 342, 392
ABI (G), 97
Abiathar, 308, 321, 326, 334 ff.
ABI-BAAL (Berut), 100
ABI-BAAL (G), 356
ABI-BAAL (Shimron-meron), 484
ABI-BAAL (T), 319
Abiezer (T), 283
ABIJAH (J), 356
ABIMELECH (Shechem), 285 ff.
ABIMILKI (T), 166, 174, 176
ABIRATTASH (Barga), 219
ABI-SHEMU (G), 95, 97
Abner, 311 f.
Abraham, 83, 194 f., 212, 249, 255, 353, 502, 525
Absalom, 326 ff., 356
Accho (C), 132, 173 f., 176 f., 187, 189, 210, 217, 224, 230, 278, 357, 454, 474, 484, 490, 559
Achæans, 226
ACHISH (Gath), I, 308 f.; II, 340
ACHISH (Ekron), 484, 507
Achshaph (C), 186, 189, 230, 277
Achzib (C), 210, 474
Across the River, 483, 485 f., 490, 559 f., 569, 572, 584, 587, 589 f., 618 f.
Adad (G), 82, 141, 383
ADAD-NIRARI (A), I, 200, 220, 225; III, 414, 416
Adam, 101
Adam (C), 197

Adapa, 148
ADDADANI (Gath), 190
ADDU-NIRARI (Nuhashshe), 155
Addu-qarradu, 189
Adennu (C), 383
Admah (C), 59
ADONI-BAAL (Shiana), 384
Adonijah, 334 ff.
Adonis (G), 70 ff., 75, 94, 97, 102, 229, 233, 320, 573, 625
Adonis (R), 70
ADONIZEDEK (Jerusalem), 198
Adon Saphon (G), 222
Adoraim (C), 230, 354
Adullam (C), 308, 313, 355, 506, 527
Aduna (Arka), 161
Ægean, 263, 368
Æneas, 404
Afish (C), 408
Agade (C), 148
AGAG (Amalek), 305, 333
Agenor, 623
Agesilaus, 617
Agusi (L), 375, 397, 408
AHAB (I), 369, 372 ff., 378 ff.
Ahab (P), 517
AHASUERUS (P), 612
Ahava (C), 531
AHAZ (J), 442 ff., 464
AHAZIAH (J), 393 f.
AHAZIAH (I), 388, 390
Ahijah, 303
Ahikar, 570
Ahimelech, 307
AHIMELECH (Ashdod), 484
AHIROM (G), 221, 240 ff.
Ahithophel, 326
Ahlab (C), 210
Ahlame (T), 436
AHMOSE (E), 129 f., 146, 148
Ahuramazda (G), 560, 613
Ai (C), 198, 212, 475
Aijalon (C), 85, 127, 186, 189 f., 198, 203, 311, 313, 340, 342, 352, 355, 444
AINEL (G), 622

641

INDEX OF PROPER NAMES

AITAGAMA (Kadesh), 166, 168 ff., 179, 181 ff., 219
AKI-HINNI (Sapuna), 235
AKIT TESHUP (Tunip), 168 f.
AKIT-TESHUP (Nia), 180
AKIZZI (Qatna), 168
Akkadian, 50, 83, 99, 141, 148, 185, 235
Aleppo (C), 3, 47, 117, 119, 138 ff., 156, 180, 183, 218 ff., 225, 227, 383
ALEXANDER (Macedon), 622 ff.
Alexandria (C), 624
Alishar (C), 116
Alisir (C), 375
Amalekites (T), 245, 249, 252, 254, 305, 308 f.
Amana (R), 338, 398
Amanappa, 160 ff., 173
Amanus (M), 3 f., 10, 79, 367, 399, 559; Gates, 47
Amarna letters, 158 ff.
Amasa, 327 f.
AMASIS (E) 536 f., 556
Amathus (C), 578, 616
AMAZIAH, (J), 415 f.
Amaziah, 431
Ambi (C), 160 f., 164, 178, 483
AMEL MARDUK (B), 539, 541
AMENEMHET (E), I, 86; II, 88; III, 89, 95, 149; IV, 90, 96
Amenemopet, (1), 229; (2), 628 ff.
AMENHOTEP (E), I, 130, 147 f.; II, 155; III, 156, 217; IV, cf. Ikhnaton
Amki (L), 168, 170, 181 f.
AMMI-NADAB (Ammon), 487
Ammon (L), 5, 25, 281 ff., 302, 322 ff., 341, 350 f., 353, 374, 388, 417, 427, 442, 453, 469, 471, 484 f., 487, 489, 491, 498, 523, 528, 532, 534, 589
Amnon, 326
Amon (G), 97, 132, 136, 139, 141, 143 f., 154 f., 158, 171, 217, 288 ff., 356
AMON (J), 485, 490
Amor (C), 74, 79, 81, 118, 137, 262, 265
Amorites, 87, 127, 140 f., 203, 210 ff., 428, 521
Amos (P), 249, 416, 423 ff., 436
Amu, 55, 84 f., 87 f., 98, 118, 130
Amurru (L), 74, 79, 81, 140, 158 ff., 162, 164, 176, 178 f., 181, 219 f., 224, 262, 265, 292, 367, 414, 486, 488, 556
Amurru (G), 81
AMUNIRA (Berut), 174 ff.
AMYRTÆUS II (E), 609, 616
Anahita (G), 613
Anak, 23, 255
Anath (G), 65, 103, 123, 154, 224, 228 f., 237, 264, 483, 492
Anath Yahu (G), 604
Anathoth (C), 212, 336, 475, 492, 525
Anchises, 308

Anshan (L), 546
Anti-Lebanon (M), 4, 6, 10, 47, 49, 72, 78, 322, 398, 533 f., 547
Anti-Taurus (M), 47, 459
Anubis (G), 69, 154, 232
APEPI (E), I, 122; II, 123; III, 129
Aphek (C), of Lebanon, 70; of Bashan, 46, 378; of Ephraim, 294, 309, 407; of Simeon, 486
Aphik (C), 210
Apollo (G), 571, 617
Apparanzu (C), 398
APRIES (E), 525, 536
Aqaba, 49, 253, 340
Ar (C), 213
Arabah, 253 f., 423, 430
Arabia, 8, 35, 266, 534, 619
Arabs, 35, 341, 384, 392, 417, 460, 471, 480, 484, 489, 536, 543, 558, 560, 589, 616, 623
Arad (C), 249, 252, 354
Arahti (L), 180
ARAHTU (Kumedi), 169
Araina (C), 138
Aram, 228, 331, 339, 385, 407, 571
Aramæans, 159, 195 f., 210, 293, 322 ff., 341, 377, 431, 436, 460, 534
Aramaic, 81, 141, 195 f., 237, 478, 546, 554, 570, 577 f., 585, 599, 620
ARAME (Agusi), 375 f., 383, 397 ff.
Ararat (L), 545
Arauna (C), 133, 355
Arbela (C), 624
Ardata (C), 136, 161, 164, 173, 178
Argana (C), 383
Argob (L), 211, 453
Aribua (C), 366
Arka (C), 73, 85, 138, 159, 161, 165 f., 178, 384, 436
Armenia, 3, 19, 116
Armenoids, 19 ff., 50, 81, 141, 399, 621
Arne (C), 397
Arnon (R), 127, 212 ff., 318, 388 ff., 402
ARNUWANDASH (H), I, 156; III, 218; IV, 227
Aroer (C), of Moab, 214, 389; of Gilead, 188, 282
Arpad (C), 414, 433 f., 457, 474, 478, 484, 510
Arsham, 605, 608
ARTATAMA (M), I, 155; II, 183
ARTAXERXES (P), I, 576, 583; II, 612 ff.; III, 617 ff.
Arumah (C), 287
Arvad (C), 137, 164 f., 176, 224, 257, 292, 367, 384, 453, 471, 484 f., 487 f., 505, 533, 535, 579, 617, 622
Aryans, 115, 118, 174, 186, 257
Arza (C), 484
Arzawa (L), 185, 190

INDEX OF PROPER NAMES

Asa (J), 356, 374
Ashdod (C), 23, 267, 295, 417, 426, 457, 469, 471, 480 f., 484, 491, 505, 535
Asher (T), 81, 208 f., 211, 224, 231, 330, 342, 422
Asher (G), 81, 208
Asherah (G), 81
Asherat (G), 237
Ashima (G), 604
Ashirat (G), 81, 141
Ashkelon (C), 85, 120, 189 f., 222, 227, 265 f., 269, 310, 426, 453, 457, 469, 471, 476, 480, 484 ff., 491, 505, 510
ASHMI-SHARRUMA (C), 219
Ashtamaku (C), 397
Ashtaroth (C), 169, 188, 210, 453
Ashtart (G), 23, 65, 73, 102, 152 f., 228 f., 233, 237 f., 264, 270, 299, 311, 489, 500
Ashtart Karnaim (G), 23, 156
Ashtaroth Karnaim (C), 23, 452
Ashtata (L), 156, 180, 219
Ashtor-Chemosh (G), 389
Ashur (G), 81, 209
Ashur (C), 88, 448, 534
ASHUR-BANI-APAL (A), 487 ff., 507, 558
ASHUR-DAN (A), 416
ASHUR-NASIR-APAL (A), 362 ff.
ASHUR-NIRARI V (A), 433
ASHUR-RABI II (A), 362
ASHUR-UBALLIT (A), I, 218; II, 506
Asia Minor, 3, 32, 47, 50, 79 f., 116, 148, 267 f.
ASIROM (T), 369
Assyria, 47 f., 50, 81, 135, 137, 155, 158, 183, 218 ff., 227, 260, 292, 362 ff., 375 ff., 383, 397 ff., 416, 433 ff., 451 ff., 455 ff., 472 ff., 483, 487 ff., 506
ASTYAGES (Media), 542, 546
Atalur (M), 362
Atargatis (G), 266, 269, 462
Ataroth (C), 214, 369, 388 f.
ATHALIAH (J), 374, 390, 393, 397, 400 f.
Athens (C), 588, 611
Aton (G), 171 ff.
Atossa, 612
Avaris (C), 120, 123, 129
Avith (C), 325
AZARIAH (North Judah), 435 f.
AZARIAH (J), 416 ff.
Azariah (P), 358
AZBAAL (Citium), 588, 611
Azekah (C), 355, 469, 506, 525, 527
AZI-BAAL (Arvad), 488
AZIRU (Amurru), 164 ff., 219, 226
AZMILK (T), 622 f.
Azur (C), 476
AZURI (Ashdod), 469

Baal (G), 65, 210, 228 f., 237, 264, 270, 382 f., 396, 489, 494, 500

BAAL (T), I, 483 ff.; II, 535
Baalat (G), 92
Baalath (C), 343
Baalath Beer (G), 32
Baalath Gebal (G), 67
BAALATOR (T), 540
BAAL-AZOR (T), I, 368; II, 375
Baalbek (C), 118, 322
Baal Berith (G), 106, 285
Baal Gezer (G), 470
Baal-hammon (G), 409
BAAL-HANAN (Edom), 325
Baal Harran (G), 456
Baal Hazor (G), 78
Baal Hermon (G), 77
BAALIS (Ammon), 528
Baal Kanaph (G), 237
Baal Lebanon (G), 434
Baal Markod (G), 75
Baal Melkart (G), 320, 340, 348, 380, 404, 483
Baal Meon (G), 214, 389
BAAL-MILK (Citium), I, 579, 588; II, 611
Baal Peor (G), 214, 447
Baal Sapuna (G), 233
Baal-semed (G), 409
Baal-shamain (G), 407 f., 483
Baal Shamim (G), 101, 242
Baal Tamar (G), 103
Baalzebub (G), 267, 269
Baal Zephon (G), 237, 483, cf. 233
BAASHA (I), 357
BAASHA (Ammon), 384
Babylonia, 37, 47 f., 50, 79, 81, 137, 490, 531, 541 ff., 618
Baghdad (C), 122
Bagohi, 606 f.
Bair, wells, 37
Balaam, 214, 325, 331 ff.
BALAK (Moab), 213 f., 331
Balearic Islands, 405
Barak, 278
BARDIYA (P), 560
Barga (L), 219, 383
Bar Gush, 408
Bargylus (M), 4, 7, 73, 118, 507
BAR REKKAB (North Judah), 451, 455 ff.
BAR SUR (North Judah), 434
Baruch, 514 f., 529
Bashan (L), 23, 25, 78, 104, 127, 173, 210 f., 229, 422, 430, 442, 512, 533, 543
Bast (G), 97
Bata, 232 f.
Bathsheba, 324, 329, 334 ff.
Batrun (C), 161 ff., 174, 369
BEDER (Dor), 288
Beeroth (C), 198, 312

INDEX OF PROPER NAMES

Beersheba (C), 32, 45, 249, 352, 429, 502, 506
Beit Jibrin (C), 23
Bel (G), 543, 550
BELA (Edom), 325
Belshazzar, 547, 554
Benaiah, 328, 334 ff.
Bene Barak (C), 476
BEN HADAD (D), I, 357; II, 378 ff., 398; III, 407 f.
Benjamin (T), 188, 197, 202 f., 214, 278, 296 ff., 321, 328 ff., 342, 421, 439
Benjamin, 188, 197, 202 f.
BENTISHINA (Amurru), 220, 222, 225 f.
Berut (C), 7, 74 ff., 100, 103, 163 f., 173 f., 221, 230, 324, 483
Beruth (G), 102
Bes (G), 154, 269, 620, 622
Beth Anath (C), 208, 217, 222
Beth Anoth (C), 354
Beth Aven (C), 438 f.
Beth Car (C), 267
Beth Dagon (C), 476
Bethel (C), 19, 30, 200 f., 203, 212, 295, 299, 302, 353, 356, 393, 421, 426, 429, 431, 461, 502, 506, 572, 623, 626
Bethel (G), 86, 102, 483, 604
Beth Haccherem (C). 590
Beth Horon (C), 198, 303, 343, 355, 416, 589
Bethlehem (C), of Judah, 212, 214, 276, 296, 304, 313, 354, 506, 558; of Galilee, 205
Beth Maacah (L), 323, 357
Beth Millo (C), 287
Beth Rehob (L), 276, 323
Beth Shan (C), 46, 88, 127, 132, 149, 156 f., 190 f., 204, 216 ff., 222 f., 230 f., 263, 311, 318, 342, 355
Beth Shemesh (C), 124, 146, 204, 269, 272, 295, 342, 416, 444, 515; of Galilee, 208
Beth Shittah (C), 284
Beth Tappuah (C), 354
Beth Yerah (C), 46, 120
Beth Zur (C), 354, 506, 590
Bezek (C), 302
BIASHSHILISH (C), 183, 218
Bilhah, 203, 208, 215
Bit Adini (L), 375 f., 433
BOCCHORIS (E), 405, 458, 469
BODEL (Ammon), 471
Bohan, 215
Bostrenus (R), 75
Bozrah (C), of Edom, 325, 427, 580; of Hauran, 169
Bridge of Assembly, 43 ff.
Brissa, Wadi, 573
BURNABURIASH (B), 177
Butamu (C), 376

Cabeiroi (G), 75
Cadiz (C), 406
Cain, 102, 252
Calamus (C), 73
Caleb, 254 f., 311
Calebites, 506, 558
Calneh (C), 436
Calno (C), 474
CAMBYSES (P), 559 f., 571, 573, 577, 598, 608
Cana (C), 453
Canaan (L), 50, 66, 76, 140, 166, 173, 176 f., 185 ff., 194, 217, 225, 227, 265, 460, 473
Canaanite language, 81, 90, 140, 148, 229, 231, 609
Canneh (C), 534
Canticles, 19 f., 626
Caphtor (L), 267, 431, 510
Cappadocia (L), 116, 341, 375, 534
Carchemish (C), 21, 79 ff., 117, 139 f., 158, 180, 182 ff., 218 f., 221, 226, 257, 262, 292, 362, 375, 377, 434, 458, 474, 508
Caria (L), 263, 267, 400
Carmel (C), 305
Carmel (M), 20, 45, 58, 78, 104 f., 206, 382, 399, 431, 543
Carthage (C), 285, 404, 622, 627; of Cyprus, 434
Casiphia (C), 532
Casius (M), 3 f., 102, 233
Casius (G), 101
Cassiterides Islands, 406
Caucasus (M), 116, 130
Cedar, Valley of, 221, 232
Chabrias, 616 f.
Chalcis (C), 323
Chaldæans, 466, 473, 505, 523
Chebar (R), 518, 532
Chemosh (G), 212 f., 350, 369, 389 f., 392, 500
CHEMOSH-GABER (Edom), 484
CHEMOSH-HALTEH (Moab), 489
CHEMOSH-NADAB (Edom), 453, 471
Chephirah (C), 198, 591
Cherethites, 326
Chinnereth (C), 60, 137, 207, 277, 357
Chronicler, 633 ff.
Cilicia (L), 47, 260, 375, 384, 408, 436, 533, 618
Cilician Gates, 47, 79
Cinyras, 70 f.
Citium (C), 284, 454, 578 f., 588, 611, 617 ff.
Cnossus (C), 122
Cold River, 73
Cossura, 404
Crete, 122, 137, 145, 147, 156, 158, 217, 263, 267 f., 491, 532, 536

INDEX OF PROPER NAMES

CRŒSUS (Lydia), 547
Ctesias, 614
Ctesiphon (C), 532
Cush (L), 508
CYAXARES (Media), 505, 542
Cyclades, 117, 217
Cyprus, 137, 233 f., 257 f., 268, 292, 347, 367, 472 f., 487, 494, 533, 536, 556, 559, 578, 623
CYRUS (P), I, 547 ff., 553 ff., 569, 571; II, 611, 616.

Dabigu (C), 376
Dagan (G), 82, 237, 269, cf. Dagon.
Dagon (G), 102, 269, 275, 295
Daibon (C), 214, 369, 388
Damascus (C), 19, 43, 46, 78, 119, 139 f., 165 f., 168 f., 208, 222, 324, 338 ff., 356 f., 369, 378, 384, 393, 398, 401, 407, 414, 416, 422, 426, 434, 445, 451 f., 457, 460, 474, 490, 505, 510, 613, 619, 622
Dan (T), 203, 272 ff., 277 f., 294, 330, 342, 422
Dan (C), 277, 328, 354, 357, 429, 633
Dan, Camp of, 273
Danabi (C), 399
Danaoi, 166, 263
Daniel, 521, 535, 554 f.
DARIUS (P), I, 560 ff., 576, 599; II, 576, 599, 604 ff., 634
DAVID (I), 23, 256, 304 ff., 430, 633, 636
Dead Sea, 1 f., 5 f., 46, 48 f., 59, 104, 127, 211, 214, 255, 318
Debir (C), 198, 255
Deborah, (1) 200; (2) 278 ff.
Dedan (L), 532, 534
Delian League, 588
Delilah, 274
Delta of Egypt, 44 f., 83 f., 120, 265
DEMONIKOS (Citium), 616
Der (C), 436, 460
Derceto (G), 266
Desert of Wandering, 245, 254
Deuteronomy, 108, 196, 495 ff.
Dido, 404
Dinah, 200
Dod (G), 443, 626
Dog River, 3, 16, 74, 221, 224, 292, 399, 472, 487, 514
Dor (C), 204, 263, 277, 288 ff., 342, 453, 476, 484
Dothan (C), 309, 407
Dry River of Egypt, 44, 484, 486, 510
Dudu, 178, 180 f.
Dumah (C), of Gilead, 188; Arabian, 547
DURUSHA (Kadesh), 167

Ebal (M), 104, 369

Ebenezer, 295
Eber, 196
Ecbatana (C), 556, 569, 613
Ecclesiastes, 628
Eden, 534
Eder, 215
Edom (L), 1 f., 140, 227, 251, 253 f., 279, 283, 325, 339, 341, 390, 392, 414 f., 417, 426 f., 444, 453, 471, 484, 489, 498, 514, 523, 532, 538, 558, 560, 580
Edrei (C), 23, 188, 210, 356
Eglon (C), 127, 198
EGLON (Moab), 296
Egypt, 7 f., 21, 52 ff., 67 ff., 83 ff., 117 ff., 129 ff., 216 ff., 247 ff., 262 ff., 288 ff., 332, 339 ff., 351, 354 ff., 384, 428, 431, 447 f., 454, 458, 467 ff., 476, 481, 483 ff., 494, 498 f., 505 ff., 521 ff., 529 f., 535 ff., 559 f., 577, 579, 582, 598 ff., 615 ff.
Ehud, 296
Ekron (C), 267, 269, 426, 469, 471, 476, 484, 491, 507, 510
El (G), 67, 73 f., 85, 102, 141, 237, 406, 434
El Hokmot (G), 237
El Olam (G), 249
El Shaddai (G), 202
El Wer (G), 408
Elah, Vale, 267
ELAH (I), 361
Elam, 21, 99, 490, 538
Elat (G), 237
Elath (C), 253, 266, 417, 444
Eleutherus (R), 136
Elephantine (C), 560, 570, 577, 585, 598 ff., 628
Eli, 294 ff., 300, 336
Eliakim, 507
Eliashib, 586, 590, 594 f., 598
ELI-BAAL (G), 357
Elijah (P), 382 ff., 634
Elim, 102
Elisa, 404
Elisha (P), 392 ff., 398, 401, 407
Eliun (G), 102
EL-PAAL (G), 617
Eltekeh (C), 476
ELU-ELI (T), 454, 457, 471 f.
Emim, 23, 212
Engedi (C), 374
En Halom, 334, 517
ENIEL (Hamath), 436
En Rogel, 326, 335
Endor (C), 30
En Gannim (C), 132 f., 187, 189
Enki (G), 127
En Mishpat, 32, 246, 254
Enosh, 101, 251
Ephes-dammim, 313

INDEX OF PROPER NAMES

Ephraim (T), 201 f., 271, 275, 278, 282, 294, 304, 321, 329 f., 342, 415, 422, 543
Ephrath (C), 201
Ephron (C), 356
Eres (G), 102
Erishkegal (G), 148
Eryx (C), 405
ESARHADDON (A), 483, 558, 563
Esau, 101, 141, 253 f., 325, 339, 581
Eschol, 255
Eshmun (G), 75, 103, 237, 616
ESHMUNAZAR (S), 621
Eshtaol (C), 275
Esther, 611 ff., 628
Etam (C), 250, 274, 354
ETHBAAL (T), 369
Ethiopia, 93, 144, 431, 467, 536, 577
Etruscans, 265, 405
Euphrates (R), 21, 47, 79, 81, 88, 130 f., 139
Eurymedon (R), 582
EVAGORAS (Salamis), 615 f.
EVAGORAS (S), 619
Eve, 101
Ezekiel (P), 127, 141, 518 ff., 532 f., 541
Ezion Geber (C), 253, 339 f., 390
Ezra, 583 ff., 627, 635

Face of God (M), 72, 74

Gaal, 287
Gabara (C), 453
Gad (P), 330
Gad (G), 211, 626
Gad (T), 211 f., 215, 278, 330, 342, 388, 402, 422
Gadates, 571
Gades (C), 406
Galilee, 2 f., 48, 78, 155, 204 ff., 211, 319, 346
Galilee, Lake of, 9, 12, 43, 49, 60, 78, 137, 206 f., 323
Galilee, Man of, 9, 13, 37
Galli, 75
Ganesh (C), 116
Gargumma (L), 218
GARMA TESHUP (Kadesh), 219 f.
Gath (C), 23, 190 f., 267 f., 271, 308, 310, 313 f., 340, 355, 407, 417, 469
Gath Carmel (C), 190
Gath Hepher (C), 205, 423
Gaul, 404
Gaza (C), 23, 45, 59, 124, 132, 190 f., 228, 231, 265 ff., 274, 426, 453, 455, 457 f., 471, 480, 484, 491, 510, 535, 545, 619 f., 623 f.
Geba (C), 299, 302, 373, 475, 506
Gebal (C), 45, 67 ff., 70, 83, 85 ff., 94 ff., 102, 115, 118, 137 f., 148, 159 ff., 221, 230, 240, 242, 288 ff., 356 f., 367 f., 399, 436, 471, 483 ff., 512, 533, 536, 615, 617, 623
Gebal, Lady of, 67, 69, 94, 97 f., 102, 138, 159, 221, 356, 615
Gedaliah, 527 ff., 572
Gederah (C), 329
Gederoth (C), 444
Genesis, 103
Gerar (C), 249, 357, 505
GER ASHTART (Arvad), 622
Gerizim (M), 30, 104, 595
Geshur (L), (1) 210 f., 323, 326, 339; (2) 308
Gezer (C), 17 f., 22, 31, 61 f., 93, 98, 100, 122, 124, 132, 146 f., 155, 187, 189 ff., 201, 204, 227, 240, 313, 340, 343 f., 360
Ghor, 188
Gibbethon (C), 356, 361, 507
Gibeah (C), 296, 299 ff., 304, 306, 357 f., 416 f., 439, 447, 449, 475
Gibeah of God (C), 295, 301 f.
Gibeon (C), 127, 198, 311, 313, 321, 328, 343, 355, 524, 529, 590
Gibeonite confederacy, 304, 506
Gideon, 283
Gihon, 315 f., 335, 476, 485
Gilboa (M), 206, 283, 309
Gilead (L), 104 f., 196 f., 210 f., 318, 353, 382, 388, 426, 446, 452 f., 509, 534, 543
Gilgal (C), 30, 197, 302, 306, 327, 393, 429, 438
Gilgamesh, 364
Giloh (C), 326
GIMIL SIN (B), 79
Gimzo (C), 445
Gittaim (C), 355
Gobryas, 551, 559
Golan (L), 6, 25, 78, 206
Goliath, 23, 268, 314
Gomorrah (C), 49, 59, 431
Gorge of Fount, 417
Goshen (L), 120, 247
Gozan (L), 460
Gozzo, 404
Great Plain, 204, 270, 278, 283, 309, 318, 342, 507
Great River, 74
Great Road, 43 ff., 58, 120, 132, 208, 278, 318, 458, 507
Greeks, 257, 367 f., 487, 507 ff., 533, 579, 617
Gublu (C), 436
Gudea, 79, 561
Gula (G), 483
Gurgum (L), 375, 383, 408, 433, 435, 459
Gusi (L), 366
Gutium (L), 555

INDEX OF PROPER NAMES 647

Habakkuk (P), 523
Habiru, 158 ff., 176, 182, 185 ff., 196, 219, 233
Habor (R), 460
Hadad (G), 82, 85, 103, 434
HADAD (Edom), I, 283, 325; II, 325; III, 325, 339, 341
HADADEZER (Zobah), 323 f., 338
HADADEZER (D), 384, 398
Hadid (C), 507
Hadrach (C), 407, 457, cf. Hazrek
Hadrumetum (C), 404
Hagar, 248, 450
Haggai (P), 561 ff.
Haia, 160, 165 f., 173 f., 187 f., 191
HAKKORIS (E), 616
Halah (L), 460
Haldians, 433
Halunni (C), 169
Ham, 249
Haman, 612 ff.
Hamath (C), 47, 251, 258, 324, 383 f., 397, 407, 436, 455, 457, 474, 478, 489, 510, 546
Hamath of Jordan (C), 46, 85, 217, 230, 453
Hammon (C), 102
HAMMURABI (B), 107
Hamor, 106, 200, 287
Hananniah (P), 524; (2) 540; (3) 604
Hanes (C), 467
Hani, 186 f.
Hani Galbat (L), 130, 156, 188
Hannathon (C), 177, 187, 205, 453
Hanno, 406
HANUN (Ammon), 322, 341, 351
HANUN (Gaza), 453, 455, 458
Harajel (C), 16
Harakhte (G), 136
Haran, 212
Harem (G), 604
HARMHAB (E), 141, 216
Harod, well, 283
Harosheth (C), 278
Harpocrates (G), 94
Harran (C), 194 ff., 506, 534, 547
Hatarikka (C), 436
Hathor (G), 57, 69, 86, 90, 92, 98 f., 149, 154, 229, 234, 536, 615
HATSHEPSUT (E), 131, 148, 340
Hattin (M), 277
Hattina (L), 366, 375 f., 383, 398 f., 408, 433
HATTUSHILISH (H), I, 117; II, 156, 225
Hauran (L), 4, 6, 78, 206, 210 f., 222, 398, 453, 489
Hawini (C), 188
HAYA (North Judah), 375, 377, 383
HAZAEL (D), 398, 401 f., 406 f., 426
Hazazon Tamar (C), 127

Hazazu (C), 376, 414
Hazor (C), 155, 174, 176, 186, 188, 206, 230, 277 f., 343, 453
Hazrek (C), 407 f., 414, 416, 433, 436
Heber, 279
Hebrews, 118, 128, 138, 159, 194 ff., 216, 265, 271; language, 50, 81
Hebron (C), 19, 23, 59, 127 f., 141, 198, 212, 246, 249, 255, 311 ff., 326, 334, 354, 465, 502, 506, 558
Helbah (C), 210
Helbon (C), 534
Heliopolis (C), 529, 537
Hepa (G), 141, 167, 189
Herenkeru, 135
Heres (M), 127, 204
Hermon (M), 6, 12, 46, 49, 72, 77 f., 105, 127, 206, 211, 276, 294, 320, 322, 354
Heshbon (C), 19, 24, 212 ff., 388
Hesiod, 368
Heth, 255
HEZEKIAH (J), 462 ff., 471 ff., 490, 628
Hilakku (L), 375
Hilkiah, 495
Hippo (C), 404
HIRAM (T), I, 319 f., 340, 346, 368; II, 434; III, 547, 556, 559, 579
Hit (C), 546
Hittites, 116 f., 130, 137 ff., 141, 155 f., 158, 161, 163, 166, 172 ff., 177, 216, 218, 239, 257
"Hittites," 260, 323, 341, 375, 407, 521
Hivites, 200
Hobab, 252
Hobah (C), 168
HOHAM (Hebron), 198
Hollow Syria, 6, 47, 49, 72, 78, 118, 168, 322, 452
Homer, 368
Homs (C), 82
HOPHRA (E), 525
Hor (M), 253
Horeb (M), 248, 359, 383
Horeshah (C), 308
Horites, 140, 253 f.
Hormah (C), 249
Horonaim (C), 389
Horus (G), 99, 229, 238, 269, 419, 509
Horus, Ways of, 57, 84, 216, 231
Hosea (P), 436 ff., 446 ff.
HOSHEA (I), 453 f.
HRIHOR (E), 288
Hur, 93
Hurrian, 116, 130, 140 f., 167, 180, 189, 235
HUSHAM (Edom), 325
Huwawa, 167
Hyksos, 97, 106, 117, 132, 135, 139, 250, 266

INDEX OF PROPER NAMES

Iahani (L), 366
IAKIN-ILU (G), 86
IANBI-ILU (Lachish), 190
Ianhamu, 162 ff., 167, 173, 188 f., 191 f.
Iapah Addi, 162, 165, 167, 173, 177
IAPAHI (Gezer), 190
IAPA-SHUMU-ABI (G), 95 f.
Iaptih Adda, 193
Iaraqu (M), 397
Iarimuta (L), 85, 159 ff., 165, 198
Iarmuti (L), 79
Iaruwata (C), 219
Iashdata, 189
IAUBIDI (Hamath), 435, 455, 457
Ibla (L), 79
Ibleam (C), 132, 204, 394, 439
Idalium (C), 579, 588, 611, 616 f.
Ieud, 67
Ijon (C), 357, 453
IKHNATON (E), 171 ff.
Ilat (G), 93
ILI TESHUP (Hatte), 292
INARUS (E), 582, 584, 588
Indo-European, 116, 141
Indo-Iranian, 130, 141
Indra (G), 130, 141, 186
INTARUTA (Achshaph), 141, 186, 189
Ionians, 469, 533
Ionic Revolt, 578
Ipuwer, 83
Iranian, 173
Iranian plateau, 51, 86
IRHULENI (Hamath), 383 f., 397, 407
IRI TESHUP (Amurru), 219
Iron (C), 453
Isaac, 194, 249, 253, 255
Isaiah (P), 441 ff., 449 ff., 471 ff., 483
ISHBAAL (I), 311
Ishmael, 450
Ishmaelites, 327, 329
Ishtar (G), 482, 484, 626
ISESI (E), 58
ISHTARMUWASH (Amurru), 226
Isin dynasty, 81
Isis (G), 69, 71, 154, 269, 509, 539, 620
Israel, 227, 327 f.
Issachar (T), 204, 278, 329 f., 342, 357, 368, 422
ITTO-BAAL (T), I, 367, 369, 382; III, 523, 533, 535
ITTO-BAAL (S), 571
Iturea (L), 78, 388

Jabbok (R), 104, 127, 211 f.
Jabesh Gilead (C), 188, 299, 302, 304, 311, 322
JABIN (Hazor), 277
Jabneh (C), 417
Jacob, 30, 123, 128, 194, 196, 200 f., 208, 212, 227, 255, 311, 325, 332, 339, 353, 442, 502, 581
Jacob, well of, 106
Jaddua, 634
Jael, 279
Jahaz (C), 213, 389
Jair, 211, 339, 453
Jaita (C), 16
Janoah (C), 453
JAPHIA (Lachish), 198
Jarmuth (C), 127, 198, 506
Jazer (C), 211
Jebusites, 59, 125, 203, 313 ff.
Jedoniah, 604, 607
JEHOAHAZ (I), 406
JEHOAHAZ (J), cf. Ahaz
Jehoahaz, 507
JEHOASH (J), 400 ff., 414 f.
JEHOASH (I), 407, 414 f.
JEHOIACHIN (J), 515 f., 524, 539 ff., 560, 563, 612
Jehoida, (1) 400; (2) 598
JEHOIAKIM (J), 508 ff.
Jehonadab, 396
JEHORAM (J), 374, 390 f.
JEHORAM (I), 390 ff., 398
JEHOSHAPHAT (J), 374, 385 ff., 390
Jehoshaphat, (1) 329; (2) 393
JEHU (I), 393 ff.
Jehu, (1) 374; (2) 390; (3) 437
Jephthah, 281 ff.
Jerahmeel (T), 253, 308
Jeremiah (P), 464 ff., 492 ff., 502 ff., 540, 563
Jericho (C), 30, 46, 60, 98, 125, 197 ff., 353, 374, 393, 506, 527, 590, 620
Jermak (M), 206
JEROBOAM (I), I, 351 ff.; II, 420 ff.
Jerusalem (C), 19, 23, 30, 85, 125, 127, 140, 189 ff., 198, 203 f., 212, 214, 237, 249, 270, 296, 304, 313 ff., 352, 416, 419, 481, 501, 506, 527, 587
Jeshana (C), 356
Jesse, 304
Jesus, 201
Jewish language, 478, 595
Jezebel, 369, 380 ff., 394 ff.
Jezreel (C), 368, 381, 393 ff., 399, 437; plain, 212, 398
Joab, 311, 323 f., 334 ff.
Job, (1) 188, 197; (2) 521
Job, book of, 631
JOBAB (Madon), 277
JOBAB (Edom), 325
Joel (P), 609
Jogbehah (C), 211, 283
Johanan, (1) 529; (2) 586, 598, 606 f., 609, 627, 633
Jokneam (C), 132, 342
Jonah (P), 423, 430

INDEX OF PROPER NAMES

Jonah, book of, 636
Jonathan, (1) 276 f., 354; (2) 302, 310, 312, 322
Joppa (C), 124, 131 f., 144, 175, 190 f., 231, 346, 476, 507, 561; northern, 188
Joram, 325, 453
Jordan, 4, 6, 8, 30, 43, 46, 49, 58, 104, 132, 194, 204, 206, 230, 276, 322
Joseph, 23, 106, 201 f., 232, 331, 421
Joshua, (1) 188, 194, 197 ff., 359; (2) 561 ff., 565, 578; (3) 606 f.
JOSIAH (J), 490, 494 ff., 505 ff.
Jotapata (C), 453
JOTHAM (J), 420, 442
Jotham, fable of, 105
Judah (T), 3, 78, 215, 250 ff., 270, 274, 278, 309, 311, 321, 327 ff., 342, 420; wilderness of, 48, 255, 318
Judah, North Syrian, 251, 409

Kabirim (G), 75, 102 f., 154
KADASHMAN ENLIL II (B), 226
Kadesh (C), 47, 87, 132, 134, 136, 139 ff., 155, 158, 166 ff., 179 f., 219 f., 239, 535
Kadesh of Galilee (C), 206, 230, 278, 453
Kadesh (G), 119, 229
Kadesh Barnea (C), 245 f., 248, 252, 255
KALPARUNDA (Hattina), 383, 398
Kamon (C), 211
Kana (C), 138
Kanah (C), 230
Karkor (C), 284
Kashshites, 141, 164
Kedar (T), 489, 494, 534
Keftiu (L), 137, 267
Keilah (C), 189, 191, 308, 506, 527, 590
KEMOSE (E), 129
Kemwer, 86, 354
Kenath (C), 211, 339
Kenaz, 255
Kenites (T), 252 f., 279, 305, 308, 311, 506
Kerioth (C), 389, 427
Keturah, 282
Kharu, 132, 140, 145, 158, 216, 227 f., 288
KHASEKHEMUI (E), 68
KHIAN (E), 122
Khnum (G), 599, 605
KHUFU (E), 54, 68
Kidron (R), 315, 318, 326, 359, 500
KILAMU (North Judah), 408 f., 455
Kina (R), 133
Kinza, cf. Kadesh
Kir (L), 426, 431, 451
Kir Hareseth (C), 392
Kiriath Arba (C), 255, cf. Hebron

Kiriath Enab (C), 230, cf. Kiriath Jearim.
Kiriath Jearim (C), 190, 198, 295, 321, 511
Kiriath Sepher (C), 58, 124, 127, 146, 230, 255, 506, 515, 527
Kiriathaim (C), 212, 214
Kirioth (C), 318
Kish, 300, 322, 612
Kishon (R), 4, 132, 278, 281
Kizwatna (L), 218
Korah, 246
Kozah (G), 253
Kullania (C), 436
Kumedi (C), 169, 173 f., 217, 533
Kunulua (C), 366, 400, 434
Kupna, cf. Gebal.
Kurds, 131

Laash (L), 407
Labaia, 185 ff., 190 ff., 200
Laban, 196
LABARNA (H), 117
LABASHI MARDUK (B), 540
Lachish (C), 60, 124, 127, 132, 146, 189 f., 192, 198, 240, 343, 354, 416, 480, 485, 506, 525, 619
Lady of Fount, 237
Lady of Turquoise, 52, 57, 86, 88 f., 90, 92, 148 ff.
Lagash (C), 79
Laish (C), 46, 276 f.
Lapana (C), 168
Latibu (C), 375
Leah, 196, 200, 204, 211 f., 249
LE-ASHTART (T), 368
Lebanon (M), 1, 3 f., 6, 10, 19, 47, 49, 68 ff., 74, 76, 78 f., 88, 105, 118, 130, 135, 205, 217, 262, 290, 292, 322, 346, 415, 484, 507, 512 ff.
Lehi (C), 274, 314
Leja, 78, 206
Leptis (C), 404
Lesbos, 539
Levi (T), 200, 247 f., 278, 321, 329, 331, 420, 582
Leviathan, 248
Levites, 252, 270, 276, 296, 420 f., 497, 501 f., 561, 584, 590, 594, 627
Libnah (C), 354, 390, 481, 506
Libo (C), 118, 423, 430
Libya, 536
Lihyanian, 93
Lisan, 59
Litani (R), 76 ff., 205, 209, 230, 319, 322
Lixus (C), 405
Lod, 507
Lodebar (C), 322, 423
Lot, 212
LUBARNA (Hattina), 366, 376 f., 399

INDEX OF PROPER NAMES

Lugal-zaggisi (B), 79
Luhuti (L), 366
Luz (C), 200
Lydda (C), 57, 507
Lydians, 509, 533, 536

Maacah (L), 210 f., 328
Machir (T), 210 f., 278, 374
Machpelah, cave, 19, 23, 255
Maderah (M), 253
Madon (C), 277
Maghareh, Wadi, 55 ff., 93
Magnesia (C), 571
Mahaliba (C), 474
Mahanaim (C), 211, 311, 326 f., 342, 356
Mahanath (C), 190; of Sicily, 405
Maia, 190
Makaz (C), 190, 342
Malaca (C), 405
Malachi (P), 581, 635 f.
Malta, 284, 404
Mamre, 127, 255
Manasseh (T), 202, 204, 210, 278, 282, 285, 304, 329 f., 342, 374, 402, 422
Manasseh (J), 482 ff.
Manetho, 123, 128
Mannai (T), 544
Mansuate (C), 414, 436
Maon (C), 254
Marash (C), 218, 459
Marath (C), 74
Marathias (R), 74
Marathus, 74, 622
Mar-baal (T), 546 f., 579
Marduk (G), 543, 548, 553
Mareshah (C), 354, 357, 506
Mari (L), 79, 81, 88
Mari (D), 414, 416
Marqasi (C), 47, 260, 375, 459
Martu (L), 74
Marub (C), 483
Massah, 420
Mati-ilu (Arpad), 433
Mattan, 397, 400 f.
Matten (T), I, 375, 384, 397, 399, 404; II, 453; III, 579
Matten-baal (Arvad), I, 384; II, 453; III, 484
Mattiawaza (M), 183
Mazdai, 618
Medeba (C), 214, 369, 389
Medes, 436, 460, 505, 542 f., 555, 619
Mediterranean, 5 f., 48, 74, 79, 208
Mediterranean race, 35
Megiddo (C), 124, 127, 132 ff., 176, 186 ff., 204, 217, 230, 342 ff., 355, 394, 453, 507, 620; plain of, 3 f., 45, 48, 104, 206; waters of, 134, 280
Mekal (G), 151, 616

Melchizedek (Jerusalem), 192
Melech (G), 212, 482
Melech-ram (Edom), 471
Melkart (G), 103, 405 f., 622
Memphis (C), 178, 228 f., 448, 510, 512, 536 f., 609
Memshath (C), 465
Menahem (I), 436, 439
Menahem (Shimron-meron), 471
Menephtoah, 228
Menes (E), 53
Meni (G), 102, 626
Menkuhor (E), 58
Menkure (E), 68
Mentiu, 84
Mentuhotep (E), 84
Meribath Kadesh, 246, 251, 420
Meribbaal, 312, 322
Merikere (E), 84
Merneptah (E), 227 f.
Merodach Baladan (B), 381, 466, 472
Merom (C), 222, 453; waters of, 78, 177, 206, 278
Meronoth (C), 330
Merpeba (E), 54
Mesha (Moab), 369, 388 ff.
Meshar (G), 239
Meshech (T), 533, 538
Mesopotamia, 47, 79, 116, 140
Methu-ashtart (T), 368
Mibtahiah, 601 ff.
Micah (P), 462
Micah, (1) 275; (2) 511
Micaiah (P), 385 ff.
Michal, 307, 312 f., 321
Michmash (C), 302, 352, 475
Midas (Phrygia), 458
Midian (L), 93, 251, 282, 325
Migdol (C), of Egypt, 177, 217, 264, 536, 598; of Bashan, 188
Milcom (G), 324, 490, 500
Milim (T), 164 f., 173 f.
Milk (G), 85
Milk-asaph (G), 484
Milkili (G), 484
Milkilu (Aijalon), 186 ff.
Milk-yaton (Citium), 616
Millo, 345, 351, 476
Min (G), 229
Minæans, 93, 619
Minnith (C), 282
Minoa (C), 268
Minoan, 145, 147, 217, 264, 271, 367
Minos, 268
Mishtu (C), 188
Misor (G), 102
Misrephoth-maim (C), 210, 278
Mistress of Beasts, 234
Mitanni (L), 130, 136 ff., 155 f., 161 ff., 168, 173, 180, 183, 219

INDEX OF PROPER NAMES 651

Mithra (G), 130, 613
MITINTI (Ashkelon), 453, 471, 474, 480 f., 484
Mizpah (C), 18, 59, 124, 297, 357 f., 439, 506, 527 ff., 590
Mizpah of Gilead, 282
Mizpeh, 278
Mizpeh of Moab, 308
Moab (L), 5, 23, 25, 104, 212 ff., 283, 296, 308, 318, 325, 331, 333, 341, 350, 353, 369, 374, 388 ff., 427, 453, 469, 471, 484 f., 489, 491, 498, 523, 532
Moladah (C), 249
Mordecai, 612, 628
Moreh, 283
Moreshath (C), 462
Moses, 93, 148, 194, 214, 228, 246 ff., 276 f., 354, 359, 417, 420, 464, 495, 503, 583, 594, 605, 626 f.
Motya (C), 405
Mugharet el Wad, 13
Mukishhe (L), 180, 218
MURSHILISH (H), I, 117; III, 184, 218 f., 220
MUSURI (Moab), 484
Mut (G), 217
MUTALLU (Gurgum), I, 375; II, 459
Mut-baal, 188
Muth (G), 102
Mutkinu (C), 292
MUWATALLISH (H), 220 ff.
Mycenæ (C), 234, 262, 268

Nabatæans, 254, 558, 579
NABOPOLASSAR (B), 505, 508
Naboth, 381 f., 394
Nabu (G), 550
NABU-NAID (B), 540, 545 ff.
NADAB (I), 356
Nahalol (C), 205
Naharina (L), 130, 132, 136, 138, 155, 158, 161, 169, 181, 221
Nahash (G), 248
NAHASH (Ammon), 302, 304, 322
Nahum (P), 506
Namiawaza, 166, 169, 174, 176 f., 181, 189
Naphtali (T), 207 f., 278, 330, 342, 347, 357, 422
Nathan (P), 324, 329, 334 ff., 434
Nazareth (C), 48, 205
NAZI MARUTTASH (B), 220
Nazirite, 272, 428
Neanderthal man, 9 f.
Nebat, 351
Nebo (M), 19, 25, 214, 389
NEBUCHADNEZZAR (B), I, 260; II, 508, 510, 532 ff., 542, 554, 558; III, 560; IV, 564, 569
NECHO II (E), 506 ff., 511

NECTANEBO (E), I, 616; **II,** 617
NEFERHOTEP I (E), 97
Neferrohu, 85
Nefud, 38
Negeb (L), 5, 45, 49, 127, 138, 140, 211, 246, 249, 252, 308, 352, 354, 417, 444, 467, 506, 515, 531, 558
Nehemiah, 588 ff., 635
Nehushtan (G), 248, 464
NEPHERITES (E), 616
Nergal (G), 99, 141, 151, 462
NERGAL-SHUM-USUR (B), 527, 540
NESUBENEBDED (E), 288
Nia (C), 131, 136, 139 f., 155, 168 f., 180, 219
NICOCLES (Salamis), 616
Niha, Twins of, 76
Nikkal (G), 545
Nile (R), 6, 44 f., 85
Nin-egal (G), 83, 167
Nineveh (C), 488, 506, 636
Ninurtash, 219
Nippur (C), 518, 532, 631
Niruwabi (C), 180
Nisatya (G), 130
Noadiah, 591
Noah, 521
Nob (C), 303, 307. 475
Nobah (C), 211, 283
Nofretete, 182
Nordics, 115, 131, 141
Nuhashshe (C), 137 f,. 140, 155 f., 168, 178 ff., 182, 219, 221, 225, 227
Nulia (C), 376
NUSERRE (E), 57 f.
Nusku (G), 545

Obadiah, 380, 383
Obadiah (P), 579
OG (Bashan), 23, 210
Olives (M), 307, 318, 520
OMRI (I), 329, 361 ff., 368 ff., 460, 464
Ono (C), 507, 591
Ophel, 59, 315, 442, 477, 485
Ophel of Moab, 389
Ophir (L), 339 f., 390
Ophrah (C), 283 f., 287, 506
Opis (C), 551
Orontes (R), 47, 72, 82, 118 f., 136, 139, 155, 322, 366, 383
Orthosia (C), 73
Osha (M), 105, 211, 294
Osiris (G), 71, 97 ff., 154, 509, 622
OSORKON (E), I, 357; II, 384
Othniel, 255

PADI (Ekron), 471, 476, **481**
Pahanate, 159, 174
Pahor, 173 f., 181 ff.
Palermo (C), 405

INDEX OF PROPER NAMES

Palestine, 257, 484
Palmyra (C), 293, 510
PANAMMU (North Judah), I, 434 f.; II, 436, 451, 456
Panormus (C), 405
Pantellaria, 404
Paran, 251, 325
Parysatis, 612
Pathros, 529, 537
Pauru, 191
PEKAH (I), 446, 449, 452
PEKAHIAH (I), 446
Pekod (T), 521, 544
Pelethites, 326
Pella (C), 46, 188, 197, 217
Peloponnesian War, 611
Pelusium (C), 481
Penuel (C), 211, 284, 355
People of Land, 572, 578, 625
PEPI (E), I, 58, 69; II, 69
Persia, 8, 533, 547 ff.; Gulf, 79, 534
PESIBKHENNO II (E), 325
Petra (C), 37, 254, 619
Pharisees, 637
Pharnabazus, 616
Pharpar (R), 338
PHELLES (T), 369
Philistines, 257, 262 ff., 271 ff., 308, 311, 313, 340, 352, 374, 390, 431, 480, 620 ff.
Philo Byblius, 67, 100 ff., 239
Phœnicia, 135, 140
Phœnicians, 8, 45, 50, 66 ff., 130, 209, 319 f., 340, 352, 367, 404 ff., 578, 611 ff.; language, 66, 81, 375; ships, 144 f.
Phrygia, 458
Pi-beseth (C), 537
Pillars of Melkart, 405
Pious, 632 ff.
Piræus, 611
PIRAM (Jarmuth), 198
Piridashwa, 168 f.
PIRIDIA (Megiddo), 186 ff.
Pisgah (M), 214
PISIRIS (Carchemish), 434, 458
Pithom (C), 227, 248
Pittacus, 539
Platæan, 582
Potiphar, 232
Præneste bowl, 405
Proverbs, 628
Psalms, 632
PSAMMETICHUS (E), I, 405, 487, 490, 505, 509, 598; II, 523, 598
Ptah (G), 75, 92, 97, 153 f., 217, 228
Pubahla, 164
PUDIEL (Ammon), 484
PUM-YATON (Citium), 619
Purim, 614
Put, 508
PYGMALION (T), 404

QA (E), 54
Qadisha (R), 72
Qarqara (C), 383 ff., 457
Qatna (C), 82, 88, 119, 136, 155, 167 ff., 180, 224, 546
Qaus (G), 253
Qazardi, 209, 231
Qedem, 87
Qode (L), 132
Que (L), 341, 375, 384, 436
QURIL (North Judah), 434

Raamses (C), 247, cf. Ramses
Rabbah (C), 190 f.
Rabbath Ammon (C), 28, 127, 210, 212, 323 f., 487 f., 522, 532
Rachel, 196, 201 f., 301
Rakkath (C), 208
Rakkon (C), 507
Ramah (C), 300, 329, 357, 439, 475, 527; of Galilee, 206
Ramath Gilead (C), 339, 342, 353, 385 f., 393 f., 398
Ramman (G), 82
RAMSES (E), I, 216; II, 220 ff., 240, 248, 292; III, 262 f., 324; IV, 265; IX, 291, XI, 288
Ramses (C), 229, 231
Raphia (C), 231, 354, 458, 486
Rashpuna (C), 453
Re (G), 69, 97, 171, 217, 231 f.
Rebekah, 195, 200
Rechabites, 253, 396, 514
Red Sea, 3, 5, 12, 49, 251, 282, 444
Rehob (C), 46, 217, 230, 355
Rehob of Asher, 210
REHOBOAM (J), 351 ff., 423
Rehoboth (C), 249
Rehoboth of Edom, 325
Rekhmire, 143
Rekkab-el (G), 409, 434, 455
Rephaim, Vale of, 313
Reshuph (G), 101, 151, 224, 229, 234, 237, 434, 616 f.
Retenu, 89, 130 f., 135 f., 143, 158, 216, 224, 231
Reuben (T), 212, 214 f., 278, 329 ff., 353, 369, 388, 402, 420, 453
REZON (D), I, 338 f.; II, 434, 445, 449, 451
Rhodes, 534
RIB ADDI (G), 148, 159 ff., 172 ff., 288
Riblah (C), 118, 507, 527
RIMI-SHARMA (Aleppo), 219 f., 222
Rimmon (G), 82, 299
RIYIN (G), 97
Rizpah, 311, 321
Rome, 406
Ruhuzi (L), 168, 173
RUKIBTI (Ashkelon), 453, 469

INDEX OF PROPER NAMES 653

Russia, 95, 115 f.
Ruth, 308, 636

Sabæans, 93
Safaitic, 93
Safed (C), 206
Sahar (G), 545
SAHURE (E), 57 f.
Sakar (G), 204
SAKERE (E), 182
Sakje Geuzi (C), 20, 410 ff.
Salamis (C), 579, 582; of Cyprus, 615
SALATIS (E), 122
Salecah (C), 210
Salem (C), 222
Salt, Valley of, 325, 415
Saluara (R), 375
Samal (C), 260 ff., 375, 377, 408, 434, 455, 457, 487
Samaria (L), 2 f., 48, 206
Samaria (C), 369 ff., 395 ff., 407, 420, 429, 436, 439, 446, 454, 457, 459 ff., 474, 478, 489, 505, 528, 587, 589, 608
Samaritans, 462, 563, 595
SAMLAH (Edom), 325
Samson, 272 ff.
Samuel, 300 ff., 305, 342, 380
Sanballat, 589, 608
Sanchuniathon, 100, 239
SANGARA (Carchemish), 362, 375 f., 383, 397
SANIBU (Ammon), 453
Sanin (M), 16
Sanskrit, 141, 189
SAPALULME (Hattina), 375
Sapuna (C), 233 ff.
Sardinia, 265, 284, 405
Sardis (C), 547, 613
SARDURISH II (Haldia), 433
Sarepta (C), 230
SARGON (B), 79, 148
SARGON (A), 381, 455 ff., 558
Satan, 565, 631
Sati (G), 599, 601
Saturn, 67
SAUL (I), 300 ff., 321 ff., 330, 380, 388, 612, 633
SAUL (Edom), 325
SAUSHSHATAR (M), 136, 138, 155
Sazabe (C), 376
Scythians, 544
Sealands, 544, 551
Sebek (G), 154
Seir, 93, 249, 251, 265, 279, 374, 390, 489, 579
SEKENENRE (E), 129
Sekhet (G), 269
Sela (C), 1, 37, 254, 415, 417, 579
SEMERKHET (E), 54
Semites, 35, 41, 50, 195; language, 36

SEMTI-DEN (E), 53
SENEKHT (E), 54, 56
SENNACHERIB (A), 196, 472 ff.
Serabit, Wadi, 57 ff., 85, 93
SESOSTRIS (E), I, 87 f.; II, 88; III, 89
Set (G), 71, 157
Setetiu, 53, 84, 86, 88, 265
SETI I (E), 209, 216 ff., 220, 228
SETNAKHT (E), 262
Sexti (C), 405
Shaalbim (C), 127, 203, 342
SHABAKA (E), 476, 481
SHABATAKA (E), 483
Shahar (G), 408
Shalem (C), 237
SHALLUM (I), 439
Shallum, 507 f.
Shalman, 453
SHALMANESER (A), III, 375 ff., 383, 397 ff., 433; IV, 416; V, 436, 454
Shamash (G), 408, 545, 566
SHAMASH-SHUM-UKIN (B), 489
Shamgar, 279
Shamim (G), 102
SHAMSHI ADAD (A), I, 88; V, 414
Shaphan, 495
SHAPILISH (Amurru), 222
SHAR-GALI-SHARRI (B), 81
Sharon, 105, 329, 356, 476, 548
Sharon of Moab, 389
SHARRU IRAH (Carchemish), 218
SHARRU-LUDARI (Ashkelon), 480
SHARRUPSHA (Nuhashshe), 180
Sharuhen (C), 130, 249, 354
Shasu, 131, 138, 216 f., 227, 230 f., 265
Sheba, queen of, 341
Sheba, 328
Shechem (C), 30, 89, 104 ff., 124, 127, 146, 185 f., 191, 197, 200, 209, 212, 230, 285, 351, 359, 446, 528, 595, 620
Shehlel, 159
Sheikh Saad (C), 323
Shemaiah (P), (1) 334, 351; (2) 517; (3) 591
Shemesh (G), 85, 93, 154, 272, 434
Shemesh Edom (C), 150
Sheol, 444, 450, 538, 541
Shephelah, 5, 271, 329, 352, 354, 417, 444, 506, 527, 558
Sherdan, 144, 174, 265
Sheshbazzar, 556 f.
Shiana (C), 384
Shigata (C), 160, 164, 483
Shiloh (C), 294 ff., 300, 336, 353, 503, 510, 528
Shimron (C), 177, 277
Shimron-meron (C), 210, 471, 484
SHISHAK (E), 340, 351, 354 ff.
Shittim (C), 197, 439
Shocoh (C), 355, 506, 527

INDEX OF PROPER NAMES

Shukbah, 13
Shulamith (G), 626
SHUM ADDA (Shimron), 177
Shumerians, 50, 90, 103, 141; influence, 79 f., 632
Shunem (C), 185, 188, 355
SHUPPILULIUMA (H), 168 f., 172, 180 f., 226
Shur, Way of, 248, 305, 418
SHUTARNA (M), 156, 162, 183
SHUWARDATA (Keilah), 189, 191 f.
SIAMON (E), 325
SIBITTI-BAAL (G), 436
Sibmah (C), 24
SIBU (E), 458
Sicilians, 263
Sicily, 404
Sid (G), 76, 101
Sidon (C), 7, 74 ff., 138, 155, 159, 162 ff., 166, 173 f., 176, 179, 205, 230, 262, 278, 292, 367, 399, 414, 454, 457, 471 ff., 483, 487, 489, 510, 523, 535 f., 539, 561, 579, 616 f., 619, 621 ff.
Sidon (G), 103
Sidonians, 368
SIHON (Heshbon), 212 f.
SIL BEL (Gaza), 471, 480 f., 484
Sillu (C), 132, 140, 193, 216 f., 221, 224, 227 f., 232
Siloam, 450, 477, 527
Simeon (T), 200, 253, 270, 278, 311, 329 ff.
Simirra (C), 436
Simyra (C), 74, 159 f., 162, 173, 178 f., 217, 224, 230, 292, 436, 457, 505
Sin (G), 85, 93, 456, 553
Sinai, 1, 5, 19, 44, 52 ff., 84, 86, 140, 148, 194, 245, 251 f., 265, 392
SIN-SHAR-ISHKUN (A), 505
Sinuhe, 86, 117
Siphmoth (C), 329
Sippar (C), 488
SISERA (Harosheth), 278
Smiths, Valley of, 296
SNEFRU (E), 54, 57, 85
So (E), 454
Socoh (C), 465
Sodom (C), 49, 59 f., 431; mount, 6
Soleis (C), 405
Soli (C), 616
SOLOMON (I), 324, 334 ff., 465, 500 f., 628. 633
Soped (G), 57, 149
Sorek, vale of, 146, 267, 274
South Arabia, 81
Spain, 405
Stateira. 612
STRATO (Sidon), 616
STRATO (Arvad), 622
Succoth (C), 284

Suduk (G), 75, 102
Susa (C), 21, 490, 612 f., 618
Sutekh (G), 123, 129, 132, 217, 228, 264, 290
Sutu (T), 169, 174, 181
Syene (C), 536 f., 598 ff.
Syrian Desert, 38
Syrian Gates, 47

Taanach (C), 46, 124, 132 ff., 141, 189, 204, 280, 342 f., 355
Tabor (M), 78, 206, 212, 230, 278, 283, 439
TAB RIMMON (D), 356
TACHOS (E), 617
Tadmar (C), 293
Tagi, 186 f., 190 f.
TAHARKA (E), 476, 481, 483, 485, 487
Tahpanhes (C), 529, 537
Tahshe (C), 139, 155, 169, 182, 230
Taia (C), 376
TAKU (Nuhashshe), 138
TAKUWA (Nia), 180
TALMAI (Geshur), 323, 326
Tamar, 326
Tamar (C), 252, 343
Tamassus (C), 617, 619
Tammuz (G), 482, 519, 626
Tanis (C), 122, 128, 288, cf. Zoan
Tanit (G), 102
TANUTAMON (E), 487
Tapuah (C), 439
TARHULARA (Gurgum), 433, 459
Tarshish (C), 341, 406, 442
Tarsus (C), 341, 472 f., 534 f.
Tartessus (C), 406
Tattenai, 569
Taurus (M), 6, 341
Tebah (C), 170, 230
Teima (C), 547
Tekoa (C), 326, 423, 590
TELIBINU (Aleppo), 219
TELIPINUSH (Aleppo), 183
Tell Abib (C), 518, 531
Teman (L), 325, 427, 532
TENNES (S), 617
Terraces of Turquoise, 53
Teshup (G), 141, 157, 259
TETI (E), 69
TETRAMMESTUS (S), 579
TETTE (Nuhashshe), 180 f., 219
TEUWATTI (Lapana), 168
Thamudæan, 93
Thebes (C), 129, 132, 135, 154, 537, 609
Thebez (C), 287 f.
Thoth (G), 100, 242
Thutiy, 131 f.. 144
THUTMOSE (E), I, 130, 148; II, 131; III, 131 ff., 149; IV, 141, 155 f., 159
Tidanum (L), 79

INDEX OF PROPER NAMES

Tiglath Pileser (A), I, 292; III, 433 ff., 451 ff.
Til Bashere (C), 376
Timnah (C), 230, 273, 444, 476
Timnath Heres (C), 201
Tingis (C), 405
Tirzah (C), 361, 370, 439
Tishbeh (C), 382
Tob (L), 282, 323
Tobiah, 589
Togarmah (L), 533
Toi (Hamath), 324
Tophet, 482
Tripolis (C), 72, 367, 618
Troglodytes, 54, 86
Tubal (L), 533, 538
Tudhaliash (H), II, 156; IV, 226; V, 227
Tukrish (L), 167
Tukulti Urta I (A), 227
Tunanat (C), 168
Tunip (C), 135 f., 138 ff., 143, 155, 158, 168 f., 178 f., 220, 224
Tuppi Teshup (Amurru), 219
Turquoise, Lady of, 57, **86, 90, 92**
Tushratta (M), 162 f., 180, 183
Tutamu (Hattina), 433
Tut-ankh-amon (E), 216
Tyre (C), 77 f., 101, 135, 161, 163 f., 166, 173 f., 176, 209 f., 217, 228, 230, 263, 288, 319 f., 340, 367, 375, 380, 384, 399, 414, 426, 453 f., 457, 471, 486, 505, 510, 523, 525, 533, 535, 539 f., 546 f., 556, 561, 579, 594, 616 f., 622
Tyre, Ladder, 210, 319
Tyrsenians, 265

Ube (L), 140, 168 f., 174, 182 f., 230
Ugarit (C), 158, 166 f., 174, 221, 226
Ullaza (C), 85, 136, 159, 164 f., 173, 217
Uni, 58
Unis (E), 69
Unqi (L), 376
Ur (C), 81, 100, 194 f., 488
Urartu (L), 544
Urhi Teshup (H), 225
Uriah, 450, 452
Uriah (P), 511
Uri-milk (G), I, 471; II, 615
Uruk (C), 79, 490, 547
Usanata (C), 384
Ushu (C), 85, 474, 490, cf. Uzu
Usnu (C), 436
Utica (C) 404
Uzu (C), 176, 217, 230, cf. Ushu
Uzziah (J), 417, 441

Varuna (G), 130

Washshuganni (C), 180
Way of Sea, 208
Wenamon, 288 ff.
White Cape, 209
Widia (Ashkelon), 190

Xerxes I (P), 579 ff.

Yahu (G), 250, 560, 601 ff., 620
Yahweh (G), 250 f., 270, 325, 379, 389, 496, 528, 576
Yakin-el (Arvad), 485, 487 f.
Yam (G), 103
Yanoam (C), 46, 135, 169, 217, 227, 230, 277
Yarmuk (R), 12, 104
Yarsu (E), 262
Yehaw-milk (G), 615
Yehem (C), 132
Yehi-milk (G), 242
Yinnaten (G), 97

Zadok, 326, 329, 334 ff.
Zaherani (R), 76
Zahi (L), 135 ff., 140, 264 f.
Zakar Baal (G), 288 ff.
Zakir (Hamath), 407 f.
Zakkalu, 263, 265, 288, 291 f.
Zalmon (M), 287
Zamzummim, 212
Zaphon (G), 282
Zarephath (C), 472, 483
Zaritis (C), 404
Zatatna (Accho), 174, 176 f.
Zeboim (C), 59, 189
Zebul, 287
Zebulon (T), 204 f., 278, 330, 422
Zechariah (I), 439
Zechariah (P), (1) 415; (2) 450, 457; (3) 562 ff., 572 ff., 635
Zedekiah (P), (1) 385 f.; (2) 517
Zedekiah (Ashkelon), 471, 480
Zedekiah (J), 516 ff.
Zela (C), 322
Zemaraim (M), 356
Zemer (C), 74, cf. Simyra.
Zephaniah (P), 490 f.
Zephaniah, 517
Zer (E), 53
Zer (C), 173
Zerah (E), 357
Zered (R), 212, 253 f.
Zeredah (C), 351
Zerqa Main (R), 24, 214
Zerubbabel, 560 ff., 585, 627
Zeruiah, 311, 327
Ziklag (C), 309 f.
Zilpah, 208, 211
Zimarra (C), 436

INDEX OF PROPER NAMES

Zimri (I), 361, 395
Zimrida (Lachish), 192
Zimrida (S), 162, 165 f., 176
Zin, 245, 248
Zinzar (C), 139, 155, 168
Zion, 429, 464, 468, 475, 479, 493, 549, 573, 587
Ziph (C), 308, 354, 465
Ziripa (C), 218

Zoan (C), 128, 467, 537, 609, cf. Tanis
Zoar (C), 59
Zobah (C), 323, 338, 452, 489
Zoheleth, 335
Zorah (C), 189, 230, 272, 275, 355
Zoroaster, 613
Zoroastrianism, 608
Zoser (E), 54
Zurata (Accho), 174, 177, 187, 189

INDEX OF SUBJECTS

Acacia, 55
Acheulean, 9
Acorns, 62
Adz, 60, 371
Agricultural religion, 32
Agriculture, 18, 31, 35, 60
Alabaster, 69, 95, 98 f., 122, 384
Alignments, 25
Almonds, 75, 358
Alphabet, 90 ff., 148, 235, 240, 368, 406
Altar, 59, 64, 90, 94, 100, 106, 149 ff., 157, 224, 255, 272, 285, 330, 335 f., 347, 360, 363, 381, 410, 452, 464, 482, 561, 615
Ambassador, 177, 179, 226
Amber, 2
Amethyst, 88, 95 ff.
Amulet, 19, 65, 520
Anemone, 71
Angel, 564
Anklet, 63
Anointing, 311, 335
Antelope, 10, 38, 153
Antimony, 481
Ape, 4, 69, 340
Apocalyptic, 564, 635
Apricot, 75
Arch, false, 52
Archers, 118, 202, 261, 264
Architrave, 217
Ark, of Amon, 217; of Yahweh, 294 ff., 321, 326, 335 ff., 353
Armlet, royal, 309
Armour, 135; scale, 263, 268
Army, 499
Arrow, 16, 22, 53, 64, 87, 201, 224, 306
Asherah, 200, 357, 381, 397, 482, 496
Ashlar, 345, 472
Asphalt, 2
Ass, 57, 89, 157, 164, 204, 280, 300, 330 f., 448
Assault, 109
Assembly, 618
Augury, 34, 557
Awl, 13, 16, 60, 108, 115
Axe, 10, 16, 64, 80, 87, 157, 179, 201, 239, 265, 324; double, 217, 364, cf. battle axe

Baboon, 69, 94, 269
Backgammon, 127
Badger, 62, 93
Bag, 288

Baker, 343
Balm of Gilead, 509, 534
Balsam, 443
Balustrade, 82, 94, 151
Bark, 69, 98, 288 ff.
Barley, 18, 22, 33, 62, 87, 207, 238
Basalt, 2 ff., 55, 60, 65, 99
Basin, 82, 94
Basket, 84, 132, 241
Bastion, 146, 315
Bath, 372, 455
Batter, 125, 315
Battle-axe, 60, 142, 210, 229, 260, 262, 411
Battle cry, 386
Battlements, 258, 265, 376, 499
Bazaar, 379
Beads, 14, 53, 63 f., 69, 80, 95
Beam, 178
Beans, 62, 600
Bear, 8, 13, 57
Beard, 54, 88, 139, 142, 258 f., 262
Bed, 23, 210, 602
Beef, 95
Beer, 232
Betrothal, 113
Bison, 8, 13
Bitumen, 238
Blood guilt, 110
Blood money, 110
Blood revenge, 39, 284
Boar, 8, 13, 38, 65, 70
Boat, 375, 377
Body guard, 323, 328 f., 334
Bolts, 82
Booths, feast of, 34, 497, 585
Borer, 8, 10, 63
Boss, 119
Bow, 22, 89, 130, 135, 142, 310, 456, 493
Box, 12, 64
Boxwood, 533
Boycott, 227
Bracelet, 53, 63, 96 ff., 153, 201, 234, 400
Brassards, 234
Brazier, 515
Bread, 56, 62, 87, 136
Brick kiln, 324
Bride price, 307, 602
Broadsword, 263
Bronze, 60, 64, 80, 94 ff., 122, 147, 324
Broom, 55
Brush, paint, 64
Buckler, 346
Buffalo, 22, 62

657

INDEX OF SUBJECTS

Bull, 22, 110, 118, 150, 152, 201 f., 260; of Amu, 98; of Bashan, 78, 211; wild, 292, 332; gold, 353 ff.
Burial, 14, 41, 52, 59 f., 65, 67, 79 f., 87, 115, 122, 127, 233, 260, 262 f., 419, 434, 523, 545
Burnishing, 20, 46, 61, 63, 80, 99, 117, 126, 263, 269
Burnt offering, 238, 252, 607
Bustard, 38
Butler, 291
Buttons, 63

Cairn, 25, 30, 88, 328
Cakes, 438, 529
Calendar, 33
Cambrian, 1
Camel, 70, 330, 363, 375, 467, 559
Camps, 118 f.
Canal, 316, 371
Cannabalism, 14
Cap, knobbed, 261
Capital, 347; papyrus, 156; bull, 617
Caravan, 177, 187 f., 279
Carboniferous, 1
Carnelian, 63, 80, 94, 96, 481
Carob, 145
Casemates, 285
Cassia, 534
Castanets, 365
Cattle, 57, 64, 168; humped, 62
Causeway, 120
Cavalry, 334, 343, 384
Cave, 2, 9 f., 14, 17, 19, 23, 30, 64, 94, 149, 298, 304, 319, 383; burial, 59; temple, 67, 77, 90
Cedar, 12, 47, 68, 72, 78, 82 f., 105, 131, 217, 230, 289 ff., 320, 333, 345 ff., 366 f., 376, 399, 415, 442, 445, 479, 512 ff., 560
Celt, 64, 80
Cement, 158
Cenozoic, 3
Census, 330, 423
Cerastes, 55
Chair, 145
Chalcolithic, 21
Chamois, 13
Champagne glass, 80
Chariot, 118, 123, 132 f., 135, 141, 145, 169, 259, 263, 278, 323, 341, 364, 384, 394, 396, 410, 442, 459, 482, 500
Cheese, 38
Chellean, 7, 37
Cherries, 75
Cherubs, 347 f., 518, 535
Chimæra, 364
Chisel, 16, 56, 64, 370; dressing, 80, 346
Chiton, 164

Circle, 24, 52, 60, 77, 88, 90, 197, 214, 419
Circumcision, 41, 67, 200, 269, 298
Cistern, 23, 61, 64, 137, 358
Clabber, 38
Clerestory, 224
Cloisonné, 70, 96
Clothing, 8, 14, 38, 88, 95, 130, 139, 142, 240, 259, 276 f., 365 f., 399, 408 f., 411 f., 456, 602
Club, 89
Cobra, 64
Coffin, 122
Coins, 570, 578, 611 ff.
Collar, 96 f., 115, 151
Colonization, 366
Colossi, 94, 233
Column, 82, 94, 146, 149, 217, 224, 261, 268, 286, 346, 363, 410 f., 472, 480
Comb, 489; comb facing, 46, 61, 63, 99; pick, 316
Concubine, 109, 285
Conduit, 134, 235
Cone, 149
Coney, 77
Cook, 343
Copper, 1, 21, 44, 52 ff., 60, 64, 122, 136 f., 145, 362, 496, 533; Asiatic, 131; Cypriote, 233; mines, 323, 367
Core, 8, 30
Corselet, 145, 234
Cosmetics, 127, 154, 602
Court, 28, 82, 90, 94, 146, 217, 371
Covenant, 40, 312 f., 360, 401, 500, 525, 582, 596
Crab, 75
Crane, 62
Creation, 594
Cremation, 19, 26, 59, 260, 263, 267, 311
Cress, 238
Cretaceous, 2
Crocodile, 154, 229
Cross, 152
Crown, 309, 324, 400
Crucible, 56
Crystal, 63, 80, 94
Cummin, 238
Cuneiform, 81, 86, 141
Cup bearer, 588
Cup holes, 18 f., 59, 64, 77, 272, 283, 298
Curse, 198, 275, 303, 360, 382, 593
Cushion, 240
Cylinder seal, 69, 81, 95, 99, 117, 127, 153, 157, 234, 260
Cypress, 230, 299, 367, 479, 533

Dagger, 16, 64, 80, 89, 117, 122, 152, 234, 262, 365
Dance, 33, 65, 294 300
Dart, 327

INDEX OF SUBJECTS

Dates, 38
Debt, 108
Deer, 8, 10, 13, 64, 100
Deportation, 436, 460
Desert, 6, 35, 43, 49, 195
Devotion, 249, 278
Diadem, 95 f.
Dice, 185
Dictionary, 235
Diorite, 98 f., 261
Disk, 69
Ditch, 119
Divination, 34, 40, 101, 442, 522
Divorce, 114, 499, 601 f.
Dog, 62, 87, 151, 222, 261
Dolmen, 24 ff., 214
Dolphin, 138, 292
Donkey, 62 f., 76, 89
Dove, 62, 238, 260, 299
Dowry, 114
Drainage, 46, 124, 150, 152, 344, 413 f.
Dream, 41
Drink, strong, 179
Dungeon, 146
Dye, 281

Eagle, 77, 100, 118
Earring, 63, 80, 122, 284, 353
Ebony, 145
Eclipse, 430, 433, 486
Elders, 31, 114, 144, 313, 329, 498, 519
Electron, 133, 145
Elephant, 8, 139, 146, 157
Elm, 12
Emerald, 96
Eocene, 3 f.
Eolith, 5
Ephod, 275, 284, 303, 308, 321, 336
Epic, 239
Eunuch, 71, 75, 342, 395, 498, 588
Exodus, 128, 227, 247, 497, 503, 605

Falcon, 262, 412
Fast, 33, 382, 572
Feasts, 33, 40, 65, 252, 294, 349, 360
Feather headdress, 263, 480
Feldspar, 145
Fennel, 74
Fibulæ, 258, 268, 546
Fig, 44, 58, 62, 72, 75, 87, 105, 238, 383, 496
Figure head, 145
Figurines, 69
Fillet, 142
Fir, 211, 348
Fire drill, 63
Fire tray, 63
First fruits, 238, 349, 557, 594
Fish, 73, 95
Fist hatchet, 7 ff., 13

Flag staff, 131, 217
Flax, 18, 274, 361, 438
Flint implements, 2, 20, 30, 52, 60
Floor, 157
Flute, 301
Fly flapper, 240, 259, 398, 456
Footstool, 94, 145
Forced labour, 329, 352
Forests, 3, 33, 58, 66, 201, 221
Fork, 96
Foundation deposit, 94, 115, 216
Fowl, 87, 179, 343
Fox, 13, 274

Garden, 381
Garlic, 434
Gate, 31, 61, 80, 82, 94, 119, 146, 157, 258, 261, 285, 316, 344, 363
Gazelle, 13, 38, 55, 62, 100, 153, 253, 343
Giants, 23, 212, 314
Girdle, 115, 134, 258, 262
Glacial periods, 5
Glaciers, 10, 12
Glass, 147, 153, 167
Glaze, 147, 363
Gneiss, 1
Goad, 296
Goat, 22, 38, 49, 52, 57, 62, 64, 135, 234, 241, 260; wild, 8, 10, 13, 55
Gold, 70, 94 ff., 145, 167, 181, 234, 263, 324, 340, 590
Gorilla, 406
Gourd, 347, 636
Grain pits, 146
Granite, 1, 55, 96
Grapes, 23, 33, 62, 87
Greaves, 234, 268
Greenstone, 145
Griffin, 262, 410, 420
Grouse, 38
Gum trees, 340
Gutter, 258
Gypsum, 2 f., 6

Hæmatite, 55, 80, 157
Hair dressing, 54
Hairpins, 127
Hammer, 8, 13, 61, 64, 75; dressing, 80, 125
Harbour, 320
Hare, 14, 38, 62, 261
Harem, 82
Harlot, 428
Harness, 231
Harp, 301, 429, 444, 456
Harpoon, 14, 430
Harrow, 324
Hart, 343
Harvest, 33
Hat, 262

INDEX OF SUBJECTS

Hawk, 95, 234
Hazel, 12
Hearth, 10, 52, 59, 62
Hedgehog, 38
Helmet, 151, 213, 229, 257, 263, 268, 376
Henna, 139
Herdsmen, 98
High place, cf. Place
High priest, 627
Hilani, 261, 409, 455
Hinge, 82, 258
Hippopotamus, 269
Hoe, 18
Honey, 87, 136, 145, 168, 273, 303, 496, 534
Hook and line, 101
Horn, 366
Hornet, 214
Horse, 13, 115, 118, 123, 135, 203, 257, 278, 281, 323, 340 f., 343, 345, 442, 459, 498, 534, 564, 566
Hospitality, 39, 296
Hostages, 136, 143
Hot springs, 208
Houses, 21, 62, 70, 258
Hyena, 38, 56, 62, 209, 230 f.

Ibex, 38, 62
Ibis, 94
Immortality, 627 f.
Impalement, 570
Incantation, 101
Incense, 95, 136, 145, 149 f., 500, 529, 607, 619, 625
Ingathering, feast, 33 f., 349
Ink, 91, 372, 456
Interest, 359, 498, 593
Interpreter, 55, 90
Inventories, 167
Iron, 1, 145, 167, 210, 257, 268, 306, 362, 376, 496, 533
Irrigation, 46, 58
Ivory, 20, 53, 95, 98, 127, 145 f., 234, 340, 347, 362, 377, 488, 533 f.

Jackal, 62, 154
Jasper, 420, 534
Javelin, 87, 399, 493
Jerboa, 62
Jewel box, 234
Jewelry, 154
Judges, 194, 270, 329, 498, 584
Juniper, 131, 367
Jurassic, 1

Ka, 90, 97, 151, 224
Keel, 145
Key, 469
Kiln, 21
Kilt, 213, 263

King worship, 452
Knives, 13, 16, 18, 22, 60, 67, 96, 145, 200
Kohl, 489, 493

Ladder, 265
Lamentations, 558 f.
Lamp, 18, 83, 99, 147, 234, 314, 565
Lance, 74, 213, 314
Land tenure, 600
Lapis lazuli, 51, 80, 84, 86, 96, 127, 145, 153, 167, 420
Laver, 347, 363
Law codes, 107 ff., 349, 359, 495, 557 f., 583, 627
Lead, 136 f., 145, 406, 533, 566
Lebben, 279
Ledge handles, 18, 46, 60 f., 63
Lemons, 75
Lentils, 290
Leprosy, 499
Levy, 323, 329, 343
Libation, 151, 153
Light well, 156, 268
Lignite, 2
Lily, 347
Limonite, 95
Linen, 139, 142, 147, 273, 290, 310, 362, 367, 409, 519, 533 f.
Lintel, 28, 62, 94, 258
Lion, 56, 119, 122, 150 f., 230, 273, 323
Liver oracle, 308, 522
Lizard, 38
Locusts, 425, 582
Loin cloth, 54
Loom, 274; weights, 60, 63
Loop handles, 18
Lot, 247
Lotus, 69, 96, 99, 151, 153, 156, 229, 234, 240, 408, 419, 456
Lovelock, 54
Lute, 259, 262, 366, 444
Lynx, 13
Lyre, 89, 301, 459

Mace, 60, 364
Machiolations, 258
Magic, 15
Mail, 386, 411
Malachite, 53, 131
Mallow, 55
Manger, 345
Marble, 117
Marginal drafting, 316, 345
Marl, 2 f., 55
Marriage, 39, 273, 327, 499, 558; sacred, 33, 626; cf. mixed marriages.
Marten, 14
Mason's marks, 371
Masts, 137
Mathematics, 123

INDEX OF SUBJECTS

Mauls, 56
Measuring rod, 564
Medallion, 94
Megalithic, 23, 201, 212
Mercenaries, 144, 174, 217, 263, 308, 323 f., 400, 471, 533, 577, 598 ff., 617, 623, 628
Merchants, 31
Mesozoic, 1
Metics, 611
Metope and triglyph, 99
Mice, 295
Microlith, 14
Milk, 38, 87
Millet, 18, 435
Millstone, 288
Miners, 93
Miocene, 3 f.
Mirror, 96, 262, 366, 459
Mixed marriages, 585, 595, 627 f., 635 f.
Moat, 125
Mole, 320
Monotheism, 171 ff.
Months, 360
Moon god, 40
Mortar, 22, 61, 146, 197
Mortice, 64
Mother Earth, 32
Mother of pearl, 81
Mound, 328
Moustache, 142
Mousterian, 9 ff., 13, 37
Mulberries, 72, 254
Mule, 327, 534
Muleherd, 307
Mutton, 95
Myrrh, 55, 145, 187, 238
Myrtle, 564
Mysteries, 625

Nails, 64
Napkins, 456
Nawamis, 52
Necklace, 10, 63, 95, 127
Needle, 10, 14, 63
Negligence, 111
Neolithic, 16 ff., 37
New Moon, 238, 430, 438, 596
New Years, 33, 348, 354
Nomadism, 35

Oak, 12, 106, 127, 200, 205, 211, 230, 287, 301, 327, 533; of Bashan, 442
Oath, 109, 112 f., 593, 601, 603 f., 628
Oats, 62
Obelisk, 138
Obsidian, 20, 95 f.
Ochre, 116, 153
Offerings, 561, 603, 607

Oil, 57, 63, 87 f., 136, 138, 145 f., 168, 185, 189, 209, 346, 373 f.; press, 23; tax, 329
Ointment, 63, 95
Oleander, 211, 214, 254
Oligocene, 3 f.
Olives, 23, 62, 72, 104 f., 329, 496
Omens, 41, 302
Oracle, 32, 64, 246, 299, 311, 313, 392, 563
Oranges, 75
Orientation, 27, 119, 224, 347
Orthostate, 82 f., 119, 285
Ostrich, 38; feathers, 54, 118, 234.
Oven, 63, 152
Ox, 22, 110 f., 347; wild, 8; carts, 321, 480
Oyster, 62

Paint, 22, 63, 98; body, 53; eye, 89; pot, 489
Palace, 82, 261, 268, 285, 306, 320, 346, 363, 409, 411, 420, 472, 617
Palæolithic, 7 ff., 52
Palæozoic, 1
Palette, 22, 64, 69, 98
Palm, 44, 55, 75, 208, 254, 278
Pannier, 89
Panther, 13, 230
Papyri, 91, 291 f.
Paradise, 617
Parapet, 150
Parasol, 291
Parchment, 291
Partridge, 95, 207, 245
Passover, 40, 349, 464, 497, 501, 557
Paste, white, 20
Peace offerings, 238
Peaches, 75
Pearls, 534
Pectoral, 96
Pen, 91, 372, 456
Pendant, 80, 95, 150, 153
Pentecost, 557
Perfumer, 343, 590
Pestilence, 156, 184, 295, 330, 414, 416, 431, 481
Pestle, 62
Physician, 167
Pig, 18 f., 64, 154, 222, 497, 626
Pigtail, 258, 261 f.
Pilgrimage, 34, 41, 300
Pillar, 61, 275, 320, 347, 400, 519, 606, 609
Pine, 2, 70, 72, 211, 299, 367
Pins, 63, 80, 95, 117, 122, 201, 234
Pipe, 365
Pistachio, 62
Place, sacred. 18 f., 33, 77, 83, 94, 106, 149, 201, 238, 298, 343, 482, 582

INDEX OF SUBJECTS

Plaster, 62, 82, 124, 316
Platform, 82
Pledge, 359, 498
Pleistocene, 4, 7
Pliocene, 3 ff.
Plow, 22, 62, 102; share, 296; tip, 306; plowing, 188
Plum, 72, 75
Plumb line, 425
Plummet, 371, 566
Pluvial periods, 6
Poetry, Arab, 37
Points, 10, 13 f., 30, 61
Pole, sacred, 82, 101, 286
Pole star, 76
Polished stone implements, 16
Pomegranate, 62, 75, 234, 347, 496
Pool, 372
Poplar, 276, 333
Porcupine, 38, 62
Porphyry, 1
Portico, 615
Potsherd, 198
Potter's marks, 61, 63
Pottery, 16, 18, 20 ff., 30, 46, 60 f., 63, 70, 99, 122, 126, 145, 147, 201, 233, 255, 258, 263, 268, 297, 306, 315, 419, 465, 619
Precambrian, 1
Priest, 31, 100, 239, 275, 321, 353, 626 ff.
Primates, 4
Prime minister, 329
Prophets, 172, 300 f., 378 ff., sons of, 379, 393
Proselytes, 601, 637
Prostitution, religious, 34, 437, 498, 557
Pulpit, 585
Pulse, 619
Purple, 66, 76, 234, 362, 367, 376, 481, 533 f.
Pylon, 149, 224, 264
Pyramid, 54, 94
Pyramidion, 69

Quartzite, 63
Quay, 362
Quinquiremes, 618
Quit claim, 601, 603
Quiver, 142, 257

Rabbit, 262
Raft, 101, 346
Raisins, 75, 238; cakes, 438
Ram, 376
Ramp, 146
Ransom, 168
Razor, 272
Reed mats, 82
Religion, nomad, 40

Resident, 144, 159 f., 165 f., 176, 189 f., 484
Resident alien, 252, 276, 296, 359, 389, 499, 558, 617, 635
Rhinoceros, 8
Rib, 145
Riddle, 273
Rider, 326
Ring, 26, 63, 94 f., 144 f., 156, 509
Rivet, 80, 117
Road, 578
Roof, 62, 82, 146, 158, 224, 258
Rope, 290
Rose, Jericho, 55
Rosette, 95 f.
Rubbing stone, 23, 56, 60, 152
Rubble, 60, 125, 158, 345
Rudder, 145
Runner, 334

Sabbath, 349, 400, 430, 438, 557, 594, 596, 635
Sackcloth, 312, 443, 478
Sacrifice, 40 f., 149 f., 252; human, 34, 64, 67, 82, 94, 282, 374, 392
Sail, 145
Salt, 3, 6, 287, 584
Sandal, 88, 95, 234, 262, 429
Sarcophagus, 95, 210, 240, 263, 621
Satrap, 559, 599
Satrapies, 577
Saw, 13, 16, 22, 64, 74, 324, 475
Scales, 463
Scaling ladder, 58
Scapegoat, 34
Scarab, 88, 94 f., 98, 122 f., 127, 147, 153, 156, 185, 405
Scarabæus beetle, 99
Scarping, 146, 315, 371
Scepter, 69, 95, 145, 153, 331, 615
School, 235
Scimitar, 122, 153, 224
Scraper, 8, 13 f., 16, 30, 60, 67
Scribe, 233, 329, 495, 583, 629 f.
Scythe, 623
Sea, bronze, 347, 452
Seal, 61, 380, 419, 461, 487, 515, 528, 546, 570; cf. cylinder seal, scarab
Seal bearer, 55
Sebilian, 13 f.
Seer, 41, 300, 408
Seraph, 441
Serpent, 203; bronze, 248, 321; goddess, 124, 153
Serpentine, 3, 224
Sesame, 238, 535, 619
Shaveling priests, 482, 490, 500, 502
Sheep, 22, 38, 41, 44, 49, 57, 62, 64, 111, 135. 168
Sheepfold, 204

INDEX OF SUBJECTS

Shekel, 114, 167, 169, 181, 274 f.
Shells, 17, 52
Shield, 224, 257, 262 f., 310, 323, 346, 365, 410, 509
Ship, 75, 144, 163 f., 205, 263, 280, 340, 390, 442, 483, 533, 618
Shoes, 88, 142, 261 f., 377
Shovel, 348
Show Bread, 307, 596
Sickle, 33, 60, 62, 210
Sign of life, 69, 99, 151, 153, 157, 578
Silver, 94 ff., 238, 533; mines, 47
Silversmith, 275
Sin, 40; sin offerings, 238
Sistrum, 69, 90, 148
Skin clothing, 8, 63
Slave, 110, 132, 136, 143, 173, 232, 349, 499, 525, 593, 603
Sledge, threshing, 62
Sling stones, 306
Slinger, 203, 299
Slip, 16, 21 f., 46, 99
Smelting, 53, 56, 64
Smithy, 231
Snails, 14, 619
Soap, 582
Socket, 62, 258
Soothsaying, 34, 41
Sorceress, 114
Sowing, 62
Spear, 64, 80, 89, 185, 234, 257, 263, 410; butts, 157; head, 10, 201; spearmen, 132
Spelt, 435
Sphinx, 92, 99, 240, 260, 364, 412
Spindle whorls, 20, 60, 63, 80, 185, 306
Spoons, 63, 96
Stable, 343, 345
Staff, 262
Stag, 10, 13, 22, 62, 153, 261
Stairway, 158
Standard, 224, 265
Standing stones, 24, 60 f., 64, 88, 90, 106, 151, 200, 285, 381
Stater, 608
Steatite, 80, 99, 153
Steel makers, 92 f.
Stool, 262
Storm god, 40
Straw, chopped, 62
Street, 62, 345
Stucco, 120
Studding, 261
Sun dial, 464, 482
Sun disk, 419
Sun god, 40
Swastika, 269
Sword, 64, 130, 200, 410; broadsword, 263; curved, 120
Sycamore, 105, 329, 424, 445

Table, 152, 240, 259, 261
Tamarisk, 55, 249, 312
Tambourine, 282, 301, 307, 456
Tank, 149 f.
Tariff of sacrifices, 627
Taskwork, 204
Tattoo, 557
Tax, 136, 329, 372, 465, 576, 587, 592
Temple, 82, 94, 106, 148, 150, 156, 216, 224, 233, 268, 298, 363, 410; Jerusalem, 347, 414 f., 441 f., 495, 501, 519, 527, 556, 560 ff., 572, 577, 633; Elephantine, 603 ff.
Tent, 39, 44, 135, 252; of meeting, 321, 335, 348
Teraphim, 275, 307, 522
Terebinth, 62, 209, 231, 255, 283
Textiles, 18, 60, 63
Theft, 112
Threshing, 62; floor, 209, 308, 330, 497; sledges, 426
Throne, 69, 94, 96, 151, 156, 347, 455
Thyme, 55
Tin, 406, 533
Tithe, 343, 429, 497, 594, 596
Tomb, 23 f., 95, 201, 234, 240, 468
Top, 365
Torque, 80, 95, 115
Tower, 28, 61, 82, 149, 158, 222
Trader, Babylonian, 107
Treaty, 117, 144, 225
Tree of Life, 364, 412
Tree, sacred, 30, 32, 153, 197
Trespass, 111
Triassic, 1
Tribe, 39
Tribute, 142, 158, 177 f., 296
Tripod, 234
Triremes, 618
Truffles, 38
Trumpet, 296
Trumpeter, 590
Tunic, 262
Tunnel, 61, 132
Turban, 364
Turquoise, 1, 44, 52 ff.
Tyrant, 268, 274, 309 f.

Unleavened bread, 33, 349, 557, 605
Uræus, 94 ff., 118, 234, 488, 615, 622
Urim, 303, 420
Ushabit, 263

Vault, false, 27
Veil, 262
Vermilion, 511, 521
Vetch, 62
Vine, 58, 202, 237
Vineyard, 33; royal, 329
Vintage, 287

INDEX OF SUBJECTS

Volcano, 4, 252
Vow, 300
Vulture, 38, 157

Wagon, 115
Waist cloth, 54
Wall, 22, 31, 58 ff., 80, 94, 107, 119 f., 124 f., 134, 137, 146, 149, 152, 197, 258, 261, 272, 285, 299, 315 f., 343, 345, 358, 371, 389 f., 411, 417, 476, 591, 620
Walnuts, 70, 72, 105, 338
Water hole, 49, 246, 392
Water skin, 63, 90
Weaving, 20
Weeks, feast, 349
Weights, 185, 229, 463, 558, 600
Weregeld, 321
Wheat, 18, 22, 33, 62, 87, 207 ff., 346
Wheel, potter's, 63, 80, 99
Whetstone, 306
Whip, 365

Wig, 152, 263, 411, 488
Wine, 63, 75, 87, 105, 136, 145, 185, 237 f., 253, 265, 329, 331, 373, 514, 534; press, 63, 283, 497; vat, 444
Winged disk, 411
Winnowing, 62, 209
Witch, 30, 41
Wolf, 62
Wood offerings, 594
Wool, 375
Writing, Akkadian, 83, 99, 148 ff., 235; Assyrian, 461; Cretan, 157, 264; Cypriote, 126, 147, 153, 157, 617; Egyptian, 69, 86, 90, 92, 153, 233, 240, 269; Hebrew, 330; Hittite, 116; "Hittite," 157, 234, 258, 324, 367; Phœnician, 240; cf. alphabet

Yard, 145
Youths, 222

Zodiacal Signs, 482, 500